Not

The History of ELDRIDGE

In 1854 George Eldridge of Chatham, a celebrated cartographer, published "Eldridge's Pilot for Vineyard Sound and Monomoy Shoals." Its 32 pages were devoted to "Dangers," embellished with his personal observations, and to Compass Courses and Distances, etc. This volume was the precursor of the Tide and Pilot Book, which followed 21 years later. In 1870 George Eldridge published another small book, called the "Compass Test," and asked his son, George W. Eldridge, to go to Vineyard Haven and sell it for him, along with the charts he produced.

Son George W. Eldridge was dynamic, restless, and inventive. He was glad to move to the Vineyard, for Vineyard Haven was at that time an important harbor for large vessels. Frequently as many as 100 schooners would anchor to await a fair current and George W. would go out to them in his catboat to sell his father's publications. He was constantly asked by mariners what time the current turned to run East or West in the Sound, so he began making observations. One day, while in the ship chandlery of Charles Holmes, he made the first draft of a current table. Shortly after, with the help of his father, he worked out the tables for places other than Vineyard Sound, and in 1875 the first Tide Book was published. It did not take long for mariners to realize the value of this information, and it soon became an indispensable book to all who sailed the Atlantic Coast from New York east. Gradually George W. added more important information, such as his explanation of the unusual currents which caused so many vessels to founder in the "Graveyard."

Captain George W. Eldridge based the tables on his own observations. In later years, knowing that the government's scientific calculations are the most accurate obtainable, the publishers have made use of them; some tables are directly taken from government figures and others, which the government does not give in daily schedules, are computed by the publishers from government predictions. Since the Captain's day there have been many changes and additions in the book to keep abreast of modern navigational aids.

In 1910 Captain George W. Eldridge transferred the management of the book to the next generation of his family, as he was interested in developing his chart business and inventing aids to navigation. On his death in 1914, his son-in-law, Wilfrid O. White became Publisher. An expert in marine navigation and President of Wilfrid O. White & Sons Co., compass manufacturers, Wilfrid served as Publisher until his death in 1955. Wilfrid's son Robert (Bob) Eldridge White and Bob's wife Molly then became publishers and expanded the coverage of the book and significantly increased its readership. On Bob's death in 1990, Molly continued as Publisher with valuable assistance from her son Ridge and daughter-in-law Linda. On Molly's passing in 2004 the book moved once again into the hands of the next (fifth) generation. Ridge and Linda continued the book's traditions while modernizing its production. With Linda's passing in 2015, daughter Jenny and her husband Peter joined Ridge as publishers, becoming the sixth generation of family members to hold the title.

Whether new to ELDRIDGE or a longtime reader, we welcome you aboard! Please continue to offer your suggestions and, where necessary, corrections. Your sharp eyes keep us on course. We hope, as did Captain George W. Eldridge, that this book might ensure for you a "Fair Tide" and the safety of your ship.

The Publishers

ELDRIDGE

TIDE AND PILOT BOOK

2021

Our One Hundred Forty-Seventh Year of Continuous Publication

CONTENTS

☛ **NOTE:** The information in this volume has been compiled from U. S. Government sources and others, and carefully checked. The Publishers cannot assume any liability for errors, omissions, or changes.

Printed in U.S.A. ISBN 978-1-883465-27-8

From the Publishers

Dear Readers:

In looking back at the strange times of the past year, getting off the land and onto the water seems more sensible than ever. Taking to a boat—be it a dinghy or a yacht, for work or for pleasure—is a reliable way to refresh your perspective, give yourself a bit of space, and, hopefully, feel renewed when you rejoin folks ashore. These days, those are huge benefits. Go boating, feel better, and pass the word.

Below we highlight a few changes in this, our 147th edition:

- ☛ Sharp-eyed readers will note that the position of The Narrows current station has moved by a few seconds (pp. 122-127)
- ☛ Want to get yourself a bit closer to the sea? Check out "Wild Swimming" by Christopher Borgatti (p.178)
- ☛ In "The Secret Life of Black Sea Bass," Nick King reviews the habits—and remarkable biology—of a fish that is exploring new waters (p. 207)
- ☛ Share in the memory of a boat that will never be forgotten as you read story contest winner Kim Metz Allsup's "*MALABAR III*" (p. 210)
- ☛ Jake Lundberg gives an informal history of Hell Gate and its "Thousand Dizzying Eddies" (p. 239)
- ☛ It's never a bad time to be prepared: review updated hypothermia (p. 244) and emergency first aid guidance (p. 245) and take a moment to complete emergency call scripts for your vessel (p. 262)
- ☛ Lou Tabory challenges anglers to take a new look at favorite spots in "Keeping it Fresh in Salt Water" (p. 250)
- ☛ Daydream along with Liesbet Collaert in "The Lure of a New Sailing Adventure" (p. 252)
- ☛ Jan Adkins offers some ideas on how to get moving again after running "Aground!" (p. 271)
- ☛ Look for illustrations from Erica M. Szuplat (www.wishastudios.com) and Sam O. White (www.samowhite.com) throughout

We remain deeply appreciative of you, our readers, as well as the contributors, advisors, and advertisers that make each edition possible.

Yours for a fair tide,

Jenny White Kuliesis, Peter Kuliesis, and Robert Eldridge White, Jr.

Contact Us

18 Overlook Road
Arlington, MA 02474

pilot@eldridgetide.com

(617) 449-7393

Free Supplement

Available June 1 — Changes and updates through May 15, 2021

Download or sign up to receive a copy via email at http://eldridgetide.com/updates/, or mail a self-addressed, stamped envelope to the address above.

Yours for a fair tide
Geo. W. Eldridge

INLAND NAVIGATION RULES

Good Seamanship Rule (Rule 7): Every vessel shall use all available means appropriate to the prevailing circumstances and conditions to determine if risk of collision exists. If there is any doubt, such risk shall be deemed to exist.

General right-of-way (Rule 18): Vessel categories are listed in decreasing order of having the right-of-way:

- Vessel not under command (most right of way)
- Vessel restricted in ability to maneuver, in a narrow fairway or channel
- Vessel engaged in fishing with nets, lines, or trawls (but not trolling lines)
- Sailing vessel (sails only)
- Power-driven vessel (least right of way)

Vessels Under Power

Overtaking (Rule 13): A vessel overtaking another is the "give-way" vessel and must stay clear of the overtaken or "stand-on" vessel. The overtaking vessel is to sound one short blast if it intends to pass on the other vessel's starboard side, and two short blasts if it intends to pass on the other's port side. The overtaken vessel must respond with the identical sound signal if it agrees, and must maintain course and speed during the passing situation.

Meeting head-on (Rule 14): When two vessels are meeting approximately head-on, neither has right-of-way. Unless it is otherwise agreed, each vessel should turn to starboard and pass port to port.

Memorized for generations by mariners, the verse below tells what to do when power vessels meet at night.

The Rule of the Road

When all three lights I see ahead,
I turn to **Starboard** and show my **Red:**
Green to Green, Red to Red,
Perfect Safety – **Go Ahead.**

But if to **Starboard Red appear,**
It is my duty to keep clear –
To act as judgment says is proper:
To **Port** or **Starboard, Back** or **Stop** her.

And if upon my **Port** is seen
A Steamer's **Starboard** light of **Green,**
I hold my course and watch to see
That **Green** to **Port** keeps Clear of me.

Both in safety and in doubt
Always keep a good look out.
In danger, with no room to turn,
Ease her, **Stop** her, **Go Astern.**

Crossing (Rule 15): When two vessels approaching each other are neither in an overtaking or meeting situation, they are deemed to be crossing. The power vessel which has the other on its starboard side is the give-way vessel and must change course, slow down, or stop. The vessel which is on the right, is in the right.

Vessels Under Sail

Port-Starboard (Rule 12): A vessel on the port tack shall keep clear of one on the starboard tack.

Windward-Leeward (Rule 12): When both vessels are on the same tack, the vessel to windward shall keep clear of a vessel to leeward.

Sail vs. Power (Rule 18): Generally, a sailboat has right of way over a powerboat. However: (1) a sailboat overtaking a powerboat must keep clear; (2) sailboats operating in a narrow channel shall keep clear of a power vessel which can safely navigate only within a narrow channel; (3) sailboats must give way to a vessel which is fishing, a vessel restricted in its ability to maneuver, and a vessel not under command.

FEDERAL SAFETY EQUIPMENT REQUIREMENTS

(These are minimum requirements. Some states require additional equipment.)

Sound Signaling Devices

Under 39.4' or 12 meters:
Must have some means of making an efficient sound signal

Over 39.4' or 12 meters to 65' or 20 meters:
Must have a whistle or horn

Over 65' or 20 meters:
Must have a whistle or horn and a bell

Visual Distress Signals

Under 16' or 5 meters:
Night: 1 electric SOS flashlight or 3 day/night red flares

Over 16' or 5 meters:
Day only: 1 orange flag, 3 floating or hand-held orange smoke signals
Day and night: 3 hand-held, or 3 pistol, or 3 hand-held rocket, or 3 red flares

The following signals indicate distress or need of assistance:

- A gun or other explosive signal fired at intervals of about 1 minute
- A continuous sounding with any fog-signaling apparatus
- Rockets or shells, fired one at a time or at short intervals
- SOS transmitted by any signaling method
- "Mayday" on the radiotelephone (channel 16)
- International Code Signal flags "NC"
- An orange square flag with a black square over a black ball
- Flames on the vessel
- Rocket parachute flare or hand-held flare
- Orange colored smoke
- Slowly and repeatedly raising and lowering outstretched arms
- Signals transmitted by EPIRB
- High intensity white light flashing 50-70 times per minute

Personal Flotation Devices (must be USCG approved)

Under 16' or 5 meters:
1 Type I, II, III, or V per person, USCG approved

Over 16' or 5 meters:
1 Type I, II, III, or V per person, and 1 Type IV per boat, USCG approved

Portable Fire Extinguishers (approved)

Under 26'	1 B-I, if no fixed extinguisher system in machinery space. (Not required on out-boards built so that vapor entrapment cannot occur.)
26-39'	2 B-I or 1 B-II if no fixed exting. system; 1 B-I, with a fixed exting. system.
40-65'	3 B-I or 1 B-II & 1 B-I, if no fixed exting. system; 2 B-I or 1 B-II with a fixed exting. system.

Back-Fire Flame Arrestor

One approved device per carburetor of all inboard gasoline engines.

At least 2 ventilator ducts fitted with cowls or their equivalent to ventilate efficiently the bilges of every engine and fuel tank compartment of boats using gasoline or other fuel with a flashpoint less than 110°F.

NAVIGATION LIGHTS

Definition of Lights

Masthead Light — a white light fixed over the centerline showing an unbroken light over an arc of 225°, from dead ahead to 22.5° abaft the beam on either side.

Sidelights — a green light on the starboard side and a red light on the port side showing an unbroken light over an arc of the horizon of 112.5°, from dead ahead to 22.5° abaft the beam on either side.

Sternlight — a white light placed as nearly as practicable at the stern showing an unbroken light over an arc of the horizon of 135°, 67.5° from dead aft to each side of the vessel.

All-round Light — an unbroken light over an arc of the horizon of 360°.

Towing Light — a yellow light with same characteristics as the sternlight.

Note: R. and Y. Flashing Lights are now authorized for vessels assigned to Traffic Control, Medical Emergencies, Search and Rescue, Fire-Fighting, Salvage, and Disabled Vessels.

When under way, in all weathers from sunset to sunrise, every vessel shall carry and exhibit the following lights

When Under Power Alone or When Under Power and Sail Combined

Under 39.4' or 12 meters:
- **Masthead light** visible 2 miles
- **Sidelights** visible 1 mile
- **Sternlight** visible 2 miles (or in lieu of separate masthead light and sternlight, an all-round white light visible 2 miles)

Over 39.4' or 12 meters to 65' or 20 meters:
- **Masthead light** visible 3 miles
- **Sidelights** visible 2 miles
- **Sternlight** visible 2 miles

Sailing Vessels Under Way (Sail Only)

Under 22' or 7 meters:
Either the lights listed below for sailing vessels under 65'; or a white light to be exhibited (for example, by shining it on the sail) in sufficient time to prevent collision

Under 65' or 20 meters: *may be combined in one tricolor lantern carried near top of mast*
- **Sidelights** visible 2 miles
- **Sternlight** visible 2 miles

At Anchor

Vessels under 50 meters (165') must show an all-round white light visible 2 miles.

Vessels under 7 meters (22') need no light unless they are near a channel, a fairway, an anchorage or area where other vessels navigate.

Fishing

Vessels Trawling shall show, in addition to the appropriate lights above, 2 all-round lights in a vertical line, the upper green and the lower white.

Vessels Fishing (other than trawling) shall show, in addition to the appropriate lights above, 2 all-round lights, the upper red and the lower white.

When Towing or Being Towed

Towing Vessel: 2 masthead lights (if tow is less than 200 meters); 3 masthead lights in a vertical line forward (if tow exceeds 200 meters); sidelights; sternlight; a yellow tow light in vertical line above sternlight; a diamond shape where it can best be seen (if tow exceeds 200 meters).

Vessel Being Towed: sidelights; sternlight; a diamond shape where it can best be seen (if tow exceeds 200 meters).

SOUND SIGNALS FOR FOG

Ask your Chart Dealer for the latest Navigation Rules—Inland/International

Frequently, in fog, small sail or power boats cannot be heard or picked up by other vessels' radar. The Coast Guard strongly recommends that, to avoid collisions, all vessels carry Radar Reflectors mounted as high as possible.

All signals prescribed by this article for vessels under way shall be given:

First: By Power-driven Vessels – On the Whistle or Horn.
Second: By Sailing Vessels or Vessels being Towed – On the Fog Horn.

A prolonged blast shall mean a blast of 4 to 6 seconds' duration.
A short blast shall mean a blast of about one second's duration.

A power-driven vessel making way through the water shall sound at intervals of no more than 2 minutes 1 prolonged blast.

A power-driven vessel under way, but stopped and making no way through the water, shall sound at intervals of no more than 2 minutes 2 prolonged blasts with about 2 seconds between them.

A sailing vessel under way shall sound at intervals of not more than 2 minutes 1 prolonged blast followed by 2 short blasts regardless of tack.

A fishing vessel or a power-driven vessel towing or pushing another vessel shall sound every 2 minutes 1 prolonged blast followed by 2 short blasts. A vessel being towed shall sound 1 prolonged blast followed by 3 short blasts.

A vessel at anchor shall ring a bell rapidly for about 5 seconds at intervals of not more than 1 minute and may in addition sound 3 blasts — 1 short, 1 prolonged, 1 short — to give warning of her position to an approaching vessel. Vessels under 20 meters (65') shall not be required to sound these signals when anchored in a special anchorage area.

A vessel aground shall give the bell signal and shall, in addition, give 3 separate and distinct strokes of the bell both before and after the rapid ringing of the bell.

MANEUVERING AND WARNING SIGNALS

Inland Rules:

1 short blast: I intend to leave you on my port side.
2 short blasts: I intend to leave you on my starboard side.
3 short blasts: I am backing
5 or more short and rapid blasts: danger or doubt

Response: If in agreement, upon hearing the 1 or 2 blast signal, a vessel shall sound the same signal and take the steps necessary to effect a safe passing. If not agreeable, or if in doubt, sound the danger/doubt signal.

International Rules:

1 short blast: I am altering my course to starboard.
2 short blasts: I am altering my course to port.
2 prolonged, 1 short blast: I am overtaking you on your starboard side.
2 prolonged, 2 short blasts: I am overtaking you on your port side.

Response in overtaking: prolonged blast, short blast, prolonged blast, short blast if agreeable. If not agreerable, or if in doubt, sound the danger/doubt signal.
3 short blasts: I am backing
5 or more short and rapid blasts: danger or doubt.

Why Tides and Currents Often Behave Differently

Frequently Asked Questions

We are often asked such questions as, **"Why are the times of high water and current change not the same?"** Shouldn't an ebb current begin right after a high tide? Although tides (vertical height of water) and currents (horizontal movement) are inextricably related, they often behave rather differently.

If the Earth had a uniform seabed and no land masses, it is likely that a high tide at one point would occur simultaneously with a change in the current direction. However, the existence of continents, a sea bottom which is anything but uniform, and the great ocean currents and different prevailing winds around the world, make the picture extremely complex.

As one example of how a time of high tide can differ greatly from the time of a current change, see the Relationship of High Water and Ebb Current, p. 161. Picture a fjord or long indentation into the coastline, with a narrow opening to the ocean. When a flood current is reaching its peak, or the tide is high outside the mouth of this fjord, the fjord is still filling, unable to keep pace with conditions on the outer coast.

Why do the heights of tides differ so much from one place to the next? Turn to Time of High Water at various ports, pp. 12-20, and compare the Rise in Feet of tides for Nova Scotia's outer coast — 2.6 to 4.8 feet — to those for the Bay of Fundy, just below, that range of up to 38.4 feet. Why the difference? The answer is geography, both above and below water. Tidal ranges of points out on the edge of an outer coast (Nantucket, for instance) tend to be moderate, while estuaries and deep bays with narrowing contours often experience a funneling effect which exaggerates the tidal range. Another explanation is proximity to the continental shelf: the closer a port is to the shelf, the more likely it is to experience a lower tidal range; the farther from the shelf, the more likely it is that a harbor is subject to surges, as when a wave crest hits the shallow water at a beach.

There are other anomalies between tides and currents. **Do stronger currents indicate higher tides?** Woods Hole, MA often has very strong currents through its narrow passage, sometimes as fast as 7 knots, but the tidal range is less than 2 feet. Conversely, Boston Harbor has a mean tidal range of about 9.6 feet, but the average currents at the opening, between Deer Island and Hull, do not exceed 2 knots. There is no necessary correlation between current strength and range of tide.

Why did the tidal or current prediction in ELDRIDGE differ from what I saw? Unless there was an error in the Government tables we take our data from, the answer is either (1) weather-related, as when a storm either retards or advances a tidal event, or (2) the discrepancy is small enough to be explained by the approximate nature of tide and current predictions, and figures are sometimes rounded off. We appreciate hearing from readers of any observed discrepancies or errors. Contact us by emailing pilot@eldridgetide.com, or calling 617-449-7393.

HOW TO USE THE TIDE AND CURRENT TABLES AND CURRENT CHARTS

High and Low Water Tide Tables

In addition to presenting tide tables for nine reference ports, from Portland to Miami, we show the approximate time of High Water and the mean (average) height of high at some 350 substations.

- On pp. 12-20, find your harbor, or the nearest one to it, and note the time difference between it and the reference port.
- Apply this time difference to the reference table for that date. On average the Low Water will follow by about 6 hours, 12 minutes.
- When the height of High Water in the reference table is higher or lower than the average, it will be correspondingly higher or lower at your harbor.

Current Tables

There are eight current tables covering from Massachusetts to the Chesapeake. At over 300 other points, on pp. 22-29, we show the approximate time of current change, the directions of ebb and flood, and the average maximum velocities.

- Find the place you are concerned with, or the listed position nearest to it, and note the time difference between it and the reference location.
- Apply this time difference to the reference table for that date. On average, the current will change approximately every 6 hours, 12 minutes.
- When the velocity of the current in the reference table exceeds the average maximum, the current in your area will also exceed the average maximum.

Naming Currents

While it is traditional to name currents as Ebb or Flood, these terms can easily confuse. We recommend using the direction as the name of the current. It is more helpful to refer to an Easterly current, which means it is Eastbound or runs toward the East, than it is to name it as an Ebb or Flood Current, which leaves the listener guessing its direction.

Current Charts and Diagrams

- Find the appropriate current chart and note the table to which it is referenced. For instance, the Long Island Sound charts (pp. 98-103) reference the Race tables.
- Turn to this table, which shows the time of start of Flood and start of Ebb, and find the time of the start of the advantageous current for that day.
- The difference between having a fair current or a head current means hours and dollars to the slower moving vessel such as a trawler or auxiliary sailboat. See Smarter Boating, p. 36.

Effect of the Moon

It is wise to pay particular attention to the phase or position of the Moon. "Astronomical" tides and currents occur around the times of full and new moons, especially when the Moon is at perigee, or closest to the Earth. Tides will be both higher and lower than average, and currents will run stronger than average. See pp. 236-237.

TIME OF HIGH WATER

Time figures shown are the *average* differences throughout the year. Rise in feet is mean range. (Low Water times are given *only* when they vary more than 20 min. from High Water times.)

NOTE: *Asterisk indicates that NOAA has removed these substations from its listing because the data are judged to be of questionable accuracy. We have published NOAA's most recently available figures with this warning: Mariners are cautioned that the starred information is only approximate and not supported by NOAA or the Publishers of Eldridge.

For ***Canadian Ports****, if your watch is set for Atlantic Time, use the time differences listed here; if your watch is set for Eastern Time, subtract one hour from these time differences.*

NOVA SCOTIA, Outer Coast	Hr.	Min.			Rise in feet
Guysborough	*3*	*00*	*before*	*PORTLAND*	*3.8*
Whitehaven Harbour	*3*	*15*	"	"	*3.7*
Liscomb Harbour	*3*	*20*	"	"	*4.2*
Sheet Harbour	*3*	*15*	"	"	*4.2*
Ship Harbour	*3*	*15*	"	"	*4.2*
Jeddore Harbour	*3*	*15*	"	"	*4.3*
Halifax	*3*	*10*	"	"	*4.4*
Sable Island, north side	*3*	*20*	"	"	*2.6*
Sable Island, south side	*3*	*15*	"	"	*3.9*
Chester, Mahone Bay	*3*	*10*	"	"	*4.4*
Mahone Harbour, Mahone Bay	*3*	*10*	"	"	*4.5*
Lunenburg	*3*	*05*	"	"	*4.2*
Riverport, La Have River	*3*	*00*	"	"	*4.5*
Liverpool Bay	*3*	*00*	"	"	*4.3*
Lockeport .... **high 2 45** *before, low*	*3*	*10*	"	"	*4.6*
Shelburne	*2*	*40*	"	"	*4.8*

NOVA SCOTIA & NEW BRUNSWICK, Bay of Fundy	Hr.	Min.			Rise in feet
Lower E. Pubnico	*1*	*15*	*before*	*PORTLAND*	*8.7*
Yarmouth Harbour	*0*	*25*	"	"	*11.5*
Annapolis Royal, Annapolis R.	*0*	*55*	*after*	"	*22.6*
Parrsboro, Minas Basin, Partridge Is.	*1*	*35*	"	"	*34.4*
Burntcoat Head, Minas Basin	*1*	*55*	"	"	*38.4*
Amherst Point, Cumberland Basin	*1*	*25*	"	"	*35.6*
Grindstone Is, Petitcodiac River	*1*	*10*	"	"	*31.1*
Hopewell Cape, Petitcodiac River **high 1 00** *after, low*	*1*	*25*	"	"	*33.2*
Saint John	*0*	*45*	"	"	*20.8*
Indiantown, Saint John River....... **high 2 15** *after, low*	*3*	*10*	"	"	*1.2*
L'Etang Harbor	*0*	*50*	"	"	*18.4*

REVERSING FALLS, SAINT JOHN, N.B.

The most turbulence in the gorge occurs on days when the tides are largest. On largest tides the outward fall is between 15 and 16 1/2 feet and is accompanied by a greater turbulence than the inward fall which is between 11 and 12 1/2 feet. The outward fall is at its greatest between two hours before and one hour after low water at St. John; the inward fall is greater just before the time of high water. For complete tidal information of Canadian ports see Tide Tables of the Atlantic Coast of Canada. (Purchase tables from nautical dealers in Canadian ports or from the Queen's Printer, Department of Public Printing, Ottawa).

PORTLAND Tables, pp. 30-35

TIME OF HIGH WATER

Time figures shown are the *average* differences throughout the year. Rise in feet is mean range. (Low Water times are given *only* when they vary more than 20 min. from High Water times.)

U.S. ATLANTIC COAST, from Maine southward

	Hr. Min.			Rise in feet
MAINE				
Eastport	*0 15*	*before*	*PORTLAND*	*18.4*
Cutler, Little River	*0 30*	"	"	*13.5*
Shoppee Pt., Englishman Bay	*0 25*	"	"	*12.1*
Steele Harbor Island	*0 25*	"	"	*11.6*
**Jonesport*	*0 20*	"	"	*11.5*
Green Island, Petit Manan Bar	*0 25*	"	"	*10.6*
Prospect Harbor	*0 20*	"	"	*10.5*
Winter Harbor, Frenchman Bay	*0 15*	"	"	*10.1*
Bar Harbor, Mt. Desert Island	*0 20*	"	"	*10.6*
Southwest Harbor, Mt. Desert Is. **high 0 20** *before, low*	*0 45*	"	"	*10.2*
Bass Harbor **high 0 15** *before, low*	*0 45*	"	"	*9.9*
Blue Hill Harbor, Blue Hill Bay	*0 10*	"	"	*10.1*
Burnt Coat Harbor, Swans Island	*0 15*	"	"	*9.5*
Penobscot Bay				
Center Harbor, Eggemoggin Reach.	*0 10*	"	"	*10.1*
Little Deer Isle, Eggemoggin Reach	*0 05*	"	"	*10.0*
Isle Au Haut **high 0 20** *before, low*	*0 45*	"	"	*9.3*
Stonington, Deer Isle	*0 15*	"	"	*9.7*
Matinicus Harbor, Wheaton Is. **high 0 15** *before, low*	0 45	"	"	9.0
Vinalhaven	*0 10*	"	"	*9.3*
North Haven	*0 10*	"	"	*9.7*
Pulpit Harbor, North Haven Is.	*0 10*	"	"	*9.9*
Castine	*0 05*	"	"	*10.1*
Bucksport, Penobscott River	*0 15*	"	"	*10.8*
Bangor, Penobscot River **high 0 25** *before, low*	*same as*		"	*13.4*
Belfast	*0 15*	*before*	"	*10.2*
**Camden*	*0 10*	"	"	*9.6*
Rockland	*0 10*	"	"	*9.8*
MAINE, Outer Coast				
Tenants Harbor	*0 10*	*before*	*PORTLAND*	*9.3*
Monhegan Island	*0 10*	"	"	*8.8*
Port Clyde, St. George River	*0 10*	"	"	*8.9*
Thomaston, St. George River	*0 05*	"	"	*9.4*
New Harbor, Muscongus Bay	*0 10*	"	"	*8.8*
Friendship Harbor	*0 15*	"	"	*9.0*
Waldoboro, Medomak River	*0 10*	"	"	*9.5*
East Boothbay, Damariscotta River	*same as*		"	*8.9*
Boothbay Harbor	*0 05*	*before*	"	*8.8*
Wiscasset, Sheepscot River	*0 10*	*after*	"	*9.4*
Robinhood, Sasanoa River	*0 15*	"	"	*8.8*
Phippsburg, Kennebec River	*0 25*	"	"	*8.0*
Bath, Kennebec River	*1 10*	"	"	*6.4*
Casco Bay				
**Small Point Harbor*	*0 10*	*before*	"	*8.8*
Cundy Harbor, New Meadows River	*same as*		"	*8.9*
South Harpswell, Potts Harbor	*same as*		"	*8.9*
South Freeport	*0 10*	*after*	"	*9.0*

PORTLAND Tables, pp. 30-35

When a high tide exceeds avg. ht., the *following* low tide will be lower than avg.
*Times and Hts. are approximate. *Important*: See NOTE, top p. 12.

TIME OF HIGH WATER

Time figures shown are the *average* differences throughout the year. Rise in feet is mean range. (Low Water times are given *only* when they vary more than 20 min. from High Water times.)

	Hr. Min.			Rise in feet
MAINE, Cont.				
Falmouth Foreside	*same as*		*PORTLAND*	*9.2*
Great Chebeague Island	*same as*		"	*9.1*
Portland Head Light	*same as*		"	*8.9*
Cape Porpoise	*0 15*	*after*	"	*8.7*
Kennebunkport	*0 05*	"	"	*8.8*
York Harbor	*0 10*	"	"	*8.6*
NEW HAMPSHIRE				
Portsmouth	*0 20*	*after*	*PORTLAND*	*7.8*
Gosport Harbor, Isles of Shoals	*same as*		"	*8.5*
Hampton Harbor	*0 25*	*after*	"	*8.3*
MASSACHUSETTS, Outer Coast				
Newburyport, Merrimack River .. **high 0 30** *after, low*	*1 10*	*after*	*PORTLAND*	*7.8*
Plum Island Sound, S. End **high 0 10** *after, low*	*0 35*	"	"	*8.6*
Annisquam, Lobster Cove	*0 10*	"	"	*8.8*
Rockport	*0 05*	"	"	*8.7*
Gloucester Harbor	*same as*		*BOSTON*	*8.8*
**Manchester*	*same as*		"	*8.8*
Salem	*0 05*	*before*	"	*8.9*
**Marblehead*	*same as*		"	*9.1*
Lynn, Lynn Harbor	*same as*		"	*9.2*
Neponset, Neponset R.	*same as*		"	*9.5*
Weymouth, Fore River Bridge	*0 10*	*after*	"	*9.5*
Hingham	*0 10*	"	"	*9.5*
Hull	*0 05*	"	"	*9.3*
Cohasset Harbor (White Head)	*same as*		"	*8.8*
Scituate, Scituate Harbor	*same as*		"	*8.9*
Cape Cod Bay				
Duxbury Harbor **high 0 05** *after, low*	*0 35*	*after*	"	*9.9*
Plymouth	*0 10*	"	"	*9.8*
Cape Cod Canal, East Entrance	*same as*		"	*8.7*
Barnstable Harbor, Beach Point	*0 20*	*after*	"	*9.5*
Wellfleet	*0 20*	"	"	*10.0*
Provincetown	*0 15*	"	"	*9.1*
Cape Cod				
Stage Harbor, Chatham **high 0 45** *after, low*	*0 20*	"	"	*4.0*
Chatham Hbr, Aunt Lydias Cove	*1 05*	"	"	*5.8*
Pleasant Bay, Chatham **high 2 30** *after, low*	*3 25*	"	"	*3.2*
Nantucket Sound				
Wychmere Harbor **high 0 50** *after, low*	*0 25*	"	"	*3.7*
Dennisport **high 1 05** *after, low*	*0 40*	"	"	*3.4*
South Yarmouth, Bass River	*1 45*	"	"	*2.8*
Hyannis Port **high 1 00** *after, low*	*0 25*	"	"	*3.2*
Cotuit Highlands **high 1 15** *after, low*	*0 45*	"	"	*2.5*
Falmouth Heights	*0 15*	*before*	"	*1.3*
Nantucket Island				
Great Point	*0 35*	*after*	"	*3.1*
Nantucket	*1 05*	"	"	*3.0*
Muskeget Island, North side	*0 20*	"	"	*2.0*

PORTLAND Tables, pp. 30-35, BOSTON Tables, pp. 38-43

When a high tide exceeds avg. ht., the *following* low tide will be lower than avg.
*Times and Hts. are approximate. *Important*: See NOTE, top p. 12.

TIME OF HIGH WATER

Time figures shown are the *average* differences throughout the year. Rise in feet is mean range. (Low Water times are given *only* when they vary more than 20 min. from High Water times.)

Station	Hr. Min.			Rise in feet
MASSACHUSETTS, Martha's Vineyard				
**Lake Tashmoo (inside)*	2 35	*before*	*BOSTON*	2.0
Vineyard Haven	3 35	*after*	*NEWPORT*	1.6
Oak Bluffs	3 55	"	"	1.7
Edgartown	4 20	"	"	2.1
Wasque Point, Chappaquiddick **high 2 00** *after, low*	3 20	"	"	1.1
Squibnocket Point **high 0 45** *before, low*	*same as*		"	2.9
Nomans Land **high 0 20** *before, low*	0 20	*after*	"	3.0
Gay Head **high 0 05** *before, low*	0 45	"	"	2.9
Cedar Tree Neck **high 0 10** *after, low*	1 30	"	"	2.2
Menemsha Bight* **high *same as, low*	0 35	"	"	2.7
Vineyard Sound				
Little Hbr., Woods Hole **high 0 30** *after, low*	2 20	"	"	1.4
Quick's Hole, N. side	0 10	*before*	"	3.5
Cuttyhunk	1 20	*after*	"	3.4
Buzzards Bay				
**Cuttyhunk Pond Entr.*	*same as*		"	3.4
W. Falmouth Harbor, Chappaquoit Pt.	0 05	*after*	"	3.8
**Pocasset Hbr., Barlows Landing*	0 20	"	"	4.0
Monument Beach	0 25	"	"	4.0
**Wareham River*	0 20	"	"	4.1
Great Hill	0 10	"	"	4.0
Marion, Sippican Harbor	0 10	"	"	4.0
Mattapoisett Harbor	0 15	"	"	3.9
Clarks Point	0 20	"	"	3.6
New Bedford	0 05	"	"	3.7
**South Dartmouth*	0 30	"	"	3.7
Westport Harbor, Westport River. **high 0 10** *after, low*	0 35	"	"	3.0
RHODE ISLAND & MASS, Narragansett Bay				
Sakonnet, Sakonnet River **high 0 10** *before, low*	0 15	*after*	*NEWPORT*	3.2
Beavertail Point, Conanicut Island	*same as*		"	3.3
Conanicut Point, Conanicut Island	*same as*		"	3.8
Prudence Island (south end)	0 05	*after*	"	3.7
Bristol Harbor	0 05	"	"	4.1
Fall River, MA	0 10	"	"	4.4
Bay Spring, Bullock Cove	0 05	"	"	4.3
Providence, State Pier no. 1	0 05	"	"	4.4
Pawtucket, Seekonk River	0 15	"	"	4.6
East Greenwich	0 10	"	"	4.1
Wickford	*same as*		"	3.7
Narragansett Pier **high 0 10** *before, low*	0 10	*after*	"	3.2
RHODE ISLAND, Outer Coast				
Pt. Judith, Harbor of Refuge **high** *same as, low*	0 35	*after*	*NEWPORT*	3.0
Block Island, Old Harbor **high 0 15** *before, low*	0 15	"	"	2.9
Watch Hill Pt. **high 0 40** *after, low*	1 15	"	"	2.6
CONNECTICUT, L.I. Sound				
**Stonington*	2 15	*before*	*BRIDGEPORT*	2.7
**Noank*	2 05	"	"	2.3
New London, Thames River (State Pier)	1 45	"	"	2.6
Norwich, Thames River	1 25	"	"	3.0

BOSTON Tables, pp. 38-43, NEWPORT Tables, pp. 84-89, BRIDGEPORT Tables, pp. 104-109

When a high tide exceeds avg. ht., the *following* low tide will be lower than avg.
*Times and Hts. are approximate. *Important*: See NOTE, top p. 12.

TIME OF HIGH WATER

Time figures shown are the *average* differences throughout the year. Rise in feet is mean range. (Low Water times are given *only* when they vary more than 20 min. from High Water times.)

	Hr. Min.			Rise in feet
CONNECTICUT, L.I. Sound, Cont.				
Saybrook Jetty, Connecticut Riv... **high 0 35** *before, low*	*1 00*	*before*	BRIDGEPORT	*3.5*
Essex, Connecticut River	*0 05*	"	"	*3.0*
Madison	*0 25*	"	"	*4.9*
Branford, Branford River	*0 10*	"	"	*5.9*
New Haven Harbor, New Haven Reach	*0 05*	"	"	*6.2*
Milford Harbor	*same as*		"	*6.3*
Sniffens Point, Housatonic River	*0 10*	*after*	"	*6.4*
South Norwalk	*0 10*	"	"	*7.1*
Stamford	*0 05*	"	"	*7.2*
Cos Cob Harbor	*0 10*	"	"	*7.2*
**Greenwich*	*same as*		"	*7.4*
NEW YORK, Long Island Sound, North Side				
Rye Beach	*0 25*	*before*	*KINGS POINT*	*7.3*
New Rochelle	*0 15*	"	"	*7.3*
Throgs Neck, Fort Schuyler	*same as*		"	*7.1*
Whitestone, East River	*0 10*	*after*	"	*7.1*
College Point, Flushing Bay	*0 15*	"	"	*6.8*
Hunts Point, East River	*0 10*	"	"	*6.9*
North Brother Island, East River	*0 20*	"	"	*6.6*
Port Morris, Stony Pt., East River	*0 10*	"	"	*6.2*
NEW YORK, Long Island, North Shore				
Willets Point	*same as*		*KINGS POINT*	*7.2*
Port Washington, Manhasset Bay	*0 10*	*before*	"	*7.3*
Glen Cove, Hempstead Harbor	*0 25*	"	"	*7.3*
Oyster Bay Harbor, Oyster Bay	*0 10*	*after*	BRIDGEPORT	*7.3*
Cold Spring Harbor, Oyster Bay	*0 05*	*before*	"	*7.3*
Eatons Neck Point	*0 05*	*after*	"	*7.1*
Lloyd Harbor, Huntington Bay	*0 05*	"	"	*7.0*
Northport, Northport Bay	*same as*		"	*7.3*
Port Jefferson Harbor Entrance	*same as*		"	*6.6*
Mattituck Inlet	*0 05*	*after*	"	*5.1*
Shelter Island Sound				
Orient	*1 10*	*before*	"	*2.5*
Greenport **high 0 35** *before, low*	*1 00*	"	"	*2.4*
Southold	*0 05*	"	"	*2.3*
Sag Harbor	*0 50*	"	"	*2.4*
New Suffolk, Peconic Bay	*0 35*	*after*	"	*2.6*
South Jamesport, Peconic Bay	*0 55*	"	"	*2.8*
Threemile Harbor, Entr., Gardiners Bay	*1 15*	*before*	"	*2.5*
Montauk Harbor Entr.	*2 05*	"	"	*1.9*
Long Island, South Shore				
Shinnecock Inlet, Ocean **high 0 15** *before, low*	*1 10*	*before*	*SANDY HOOK*	*3.1*
Moriches Inlet. Coast Guard Sta	*0 45*	*after*	"	*2.2*
Democrat Point, Fire Island Inlet	*0 35*	*before*	"	*2.6*
Patchogue, Great South Bay	*3 25*	*after*	"	*1.1*
Bay Shore, Watchogue Creek Entrance	*2 20*	"	"	*1.0*
Babylon **high 2 10** *after, low*	*2 40*	"	"	*0.6*
Jones Inlet (Point Lookout)	*0 20*	*before*	"	*3.6*
Bellmore Creek, Hempstead Bay **high 1 30** *after, low*	*2 00*	*after*	"	*2.0*

BRIDGEPORT Tables, pp. 104-109, KINGS POINT Tables, pp. 110-115, SANDY HOOK Tables, pp. 140-145

When a high tide exceeds avg. ht., the *following* low tide will be lower than avg.
*Times and Hts. are approximate. *Important*: See NOTE, top p. 12.

TIME OF HIGH WATER

Time figures shown are the *average* differences throughout the year. Rise in feet is mean range. (Low Water times are given *only* when they vary more than 20 min. from High Water times.)

	Hr. Min.			Rise in feet
NEW YORK, Long Island, South Shore, Cont.				
Freeport, Baldwin Bay	*0 45*	*after*	*SANDY HOOK*	*3.0*
E. Rockaway Inlet	*0 15*	*before*	"	*4.4*
Barren Is., Rockaway Inlet, Jamaica Bay	*0 05*	"	"	*5.0*
NEW YORK & NEW JERSEY				
New York Harbor				
Coney Island	*0 10*	*before*	*SANDY HOOK*	*4.7*
Fort Hamilton, The Narrows	*0 05*	*after*	"	*4.7*
Tarrytown, Hudson River	*1 55*	"	*BATTERY*	*3.2*
Poughkeepsie, Hudson River	*4 40*	"	"	*3.1*
Kingston, Hudson River	*5 30*	"	"	*3.7*
NY & NJ, the Kills and Newark Bay				
Constable Hook, Kill Van Kull	*0 15*	*before*	"	*4.6*
Port Elizabeth	*0 05*	*after*	"	*5.1*
Bellville, Passaic River **high 0 10** *after, low*	*0 50*	"	"	*5.6*
Kearny Pt., Hackensack River.	*0 15*	"	"	*5.2*
Hackensack, Hackensack River	*1 05*	"	"	*6.0*
Lower NY Bay, Raritan Bay				
Great Kills Harbor	*same as*		*SANDY HOOK*	*4.9*
South Amboy, Raritan River	*same as*		"	*5.1*
New Brunswick, Raritan River	*0 40*	*after*	"	*5.7*
Keyport	*same as*		"	*5.0*
Atlantic Highlands, Sandy Hook Bay	*0 10*	*before*	"	*4.7*
Highlands, Shrewsbury R., Rte. 36 bridge, Sandy Hook	*0 15*	*after*	"	*4.2*
Red Bank, Navesink River, Sandy Hook Bay **high 1 20** *after, low*	*2 00*	"	"	*3.5*
Sea Bright, Shrewsbury River, Sandy Hook Bay	*1 10*	"	"	*3.2*
NEW JERSEY, Outer Coast				
Shark River Island, Fixed RR. Bridge, Shark River	*0 10*	*before*	"	*4.3*
Manasquan Inlet, USCG Station	*0 20*	"	"	*4.0*
Brielle, Rte. 35 bridge, Manasquan River	*0 15*	"	"	*3.9*
Barnegat Inlet, USCG Station, Barnegat Bay	*0 05*	"	"	*2.2*
Manahawkin Drawbridge **high 2 50** *after, low*	*3 40*	*after*	"	*1.3*
Beach Haven, USCG Station, Little Egg Harbor	*1 20*	"	"	*2.2*
Absecon Creek, Rte. 30 bridge	*1 10*	"	"	*3.9*
Atlantic City, Ocean	*0 25*	*before*	"	*4.0*
Beesleys Pt., Great Egg Hbr. Bay **high 0 30** *after, low*	*1 10*	*after*	"	*3.6*
Townsends Inlet, Ocean Dr. bridge	*same as*		"	*4.0*
Stone Harbor, Great Channel, Hereford Inlet	*0 30*	*after*	"	*4.2*
Cape May Harbor, Cape May Inlet	*same as*		"	*4.5*
NEW JERSEY & DELAWARE BAY				
Delaware Bay, Eastern Shore				
Brandywine Shoal Light **high 0 30** *after, low*	*1 00*	*after*	*BATTERY*	*4.9*
Cape May Point, Sunset Beach **high 0 15** *after, low*	*0 40*	"	"	*4.8*
Dennis Creek, 2.5 mi. above Entr. **high 1 15** *after, low*	*2 00*	"	"	*5.2*
Mauricetown, Maurice R. **high 2 40** *after, low*	*3 15*	"	"	*4.4*
Millville, Maurice R. **high 3 55** *after, low*	*4 20*	"	"	*5.0*

SANDY HOOK Tables, pp. 140-145, BATTERY Tables, pp. 128-133

When a high tide exceeds avg. ht., the *following* low tide will be lower than avg.
*Times and Hts. are approximate. *Important*: See NOTE, top p. 12.

TIME OF HIGH WATER

Time figures shown are the *average* differences throughout the year. Rise in feet is mean range. (Low Water times are given *only* when they vary more than 20 min. from High Water times.)

	Hr. Min.			Rise in feet
NEW JERSEY & DELAWARE BAY, Cont.				
Delaware Bay, Western Shore				
**Cape Henlopen*	0 10	*after*	*BATTERY*	*4.1*
Lewes (Breakwater Harbor) **high 0 20** *after, low*	0 45	"	"	*4.1*
St. Jones River Ent.* **high 1 10 *after, low*	1 55	"	"	*4.8*
Delaware River				
**Liston Point, Delaware*	2 05	"	"	*5.7*
Salem, Salem River, NJ	4 00	"	"	*4.2*
Reedy Point, Delaware	3 15	"	"	*5.3*
C&D Summit Bridge, Delaware	2 35	"	"	*3.5*
Chesapeake City, MD.	2 15	"	"	*2.9*
New Castle, Delaware **high 3 35** *after, low*	4 05	"	"	*5.2*
Wilmington Marine Terminal **high 3 55** *after, low*	4 30	"	"	*5.3*
Philadelphia, PA, USCG Station	5 40	"	"	*6.0*
Burlington, NJ **high 6 25** *after, low*	7 00	"	"	*7.2*
Trenton, NJ **high 6 45** *after, low*	7 45	"	"	*8.2*
DELAWARE, MARYLAND & VIRGINIA				
Indian River Inlet, USCG Station, Delaware **high 0 55** *after, low*	0 25	*after*	*SANDY HOOK*	*2.5*
Ocean City Fishing Pier	0 20	*before*	"	*3.4*
Harbor of Refuge, Chincoteague Bay	0 15	*after*	"	*2.4*
Chincoteague Channel, south end	0 25	"	"	*2.2*
Chincoteague Island, USCG Station	0 45	"	"	*1.6*
Metompkin Inlet	0 30	"	"	*3.6*
Wachapreague, Wachapreague Channel	0 45	"	"	*4.0*
**Quinby Inlet Entrance*	0 05	"	"	*4.0*
Great Machipongo Inlet, inside	0 40	"	"	*3.9*
Chesapeake Bay, Eastern Shore				
Cape Charles Harbor	0 40	*after*	*BATTERY*	*2.3*
Crisfield, Little Annemessex River	4 30	"	"	*1.9*
Salisbury, Wicomico River	7 10	"	"	*3.0*
Middle Hooper Island	4 40	*before*	*BALTIMORE*	*1.5*
Taylors Island, Little Choptank River, Slaughter Creek	3 10	"	"	*1.3*
**Sharps Is. Lt.*	3 50	"	"	*1.3*
Cambridge, Choptank River	2 35	"	"	*1.6*
Dover Bridge, Choptank River	0 30	"	"	*1.7*
Oxford, Tred Avon River	2 50	"	"	*1.4*
Easton Pt., Tred Avon River	2 40	"	"	*1.6*
St. Michaels, Miles River	2 10	"	"	*1.4*
Kent Island Narrows	1 25	"	"	*1.2*
**Bloody Pt. Bar Lt.*	2 40	"	"	*1.1*
Worton Creek Entrance	1 20	*after*	"	*1.3*
Town Point Wharf, Elk River	3 10	"	"	*2.2*
Chesapeake Bay, Western Shore				
Havre de Grace, Susquehanna River	3 20	*after*	"	*1.9*
**Pooles Is.*	0 55	"	"	*1.2*
Annapolis, Severn River (US Naval Academy)	1 35	*before*	"	*1.0*
**Sandy Point*	1 20	"	"	*0.8*
Thomas Pt. Shoal Lt.	2 05	"	"	*0.9*
**Drum Point, Pawtuxent River*	4 50	"	"	*1.2*
Solomons Island, Pawtuxent River	4 40	"	"	*1.2*

BATTERY Tables, pp. 128-133, SANDY HOOK Tables, pp. 140-145, BALTIMORE Tables, pp. 162-165

When a high tide exceeds avg. ht., the *following* low tide will be lower than avg.

*Times and Hts. are approximate. *Important*: See NOTE, top p. 12.

TIME OF HIGH WATER

Time figures shown are the *average* differences throughout the year. Rise in feet is mean range. (Low Water times are given *only* when they vary more than 20 min. from High Water times.)

DELAWARE, MARYLAND & VIRGINIA, Cont.	Hr.	Min.			Rise in feet
Point Lookout	*5*	*30*	*before*	*BALTIMORE*	*1.2*
Sunnybank, Little Wicomico River	*6*	*30*	*after*	*BATTERY*	*0.8*
Glebe Point, Great Wicomico River	*4*	*15*	"	"	*1.2*
Windmill Point, Rappahannock River	*2*	*50*	"	"	*1.2*
**Orchard Point, Rappahannock River*	*3*	*20*	"	"	*1.4*
**New Point Comfort, Mobjack Bay*	*0*	*45*	"	"	*2.3*
Tue Marshes Light, York River	*0*	*50*	"	"	*2.2*
**Perrin River, York River*	*1*	*05*	"	"	*2.3*
Yorktown, Goodwin Neck, York River	*1*	*00*	"	"	*2.2*
Hampton Roads, Sewells Pt.	*0*	*45*	"	"	*2.4*
Norfolk, Elizabeth River	*1*	*05*	"	"	*2.8*
Newport News, James River	*1*	*15*	"	"	*2.6*
**Windmill Pt., James River*	*6*	*20*	"	"	*2.3*
Chesapeake Bay Br. Tunnel	*0*	*15*	*before*	"	*2.6*
NORTH CAROLINA					
Roanoke Sound Channel	*1*	*10*	*after*	*BATTERY*	*0.5*
Oregon Inlet Marina	*0*	*15*	*before*	"	*0.9*
Oregon Inlet, USCG Station	*0*	*50*	"	"	*2.0*
Oregon Inlet Channel	*0*	*35*	"	"	*1.2*
Cape Hatteras Fishing Pier	*1*	*05*	"	"	*3.0*
Hatteras Inlet	*0*	*55*	"	"	*2.0*
Ocracoke Inlet	*0*	*55*	"	"	*1.9*
Beaufort Inlet Channel Range	*0*	*55*	"	"	*3.2*
Morehead City	*0*	*40*	"	"	*3.1*
Bogue Inlet	*0*	*50*	"	"	*2.2*
New River Inlet	*0*	*50*	"	"	*3.0*
New Topsail Inlet* …… **high 0 40 *before, low*	*0*	*10*	"	"	*3.0*
Bald Head, Cape Fear River	*0*	*50*	"	"	*4.5*
Wilmington …… **high 1 20** *after, low*	*1*	*45*	*after*	"	*4.3*
Lockwoods Folly Inlet	*1*	*00*	"	"	*4.2*
SOUTH CAROLINA					
Little River Neck, north end	*1*	*30*	*after*	*BATTERY*	*4.6*
Hog Inlet Pier	*0*	*45*	"	"	*5.0*
Myrtle Beach, Springmaid Pier	*0*	*50*	"	"	*5.0*
Pawleys Island Pier (ocean)	*0*	*55*	"	"	*4.9*
Winyah Bay Entrance, south jetty	*0*	*50*	*before*	"	*4.6*
South Island Plantation, C.G. Station	*0*	*10*	*after*	"	*3.8*
Georgetown, Sampit River …… **high 1 00** *after, low*	*1*	*40*	"	"	*3.7*
North Santee River Inlet	*0*	*30*	*before*	"	*4.5*
Charleston (Custom House Wharf)	*0*	*25*	"	"	*5.2*
Folly River, north, Folly Island … **high** *same as, low*	*0*	*35*	"	"	*5.4*
Rockville, Bohicket Creek, North Edisto River	*0*	*15*	"	"	*5.8*
Edisto Marina, Big Bay Creek entr., South Edisto River	*0*	*25*	"	"	*6.0*
Harbor River Bridge, St. Helena Sound	*0*	*20*	"	"	*6.1*
Hutchinson Island, Ashepoo River, St. Helena Sound	*0*	*20*	*after*	"	*6.0*
Fripps Inlet, Hunting Island Bridge, St. Helena Sound	*0*	*30*	*before*	"	*6.1*
Port Royal Plantation, Hilton Head Is.	*0*	*25*	"	"	*6.1*
Battery Creek, Beaufort River Port Royal Sd, 4 mi. above entr. …… **high 1 00** *after, low*	*0*	*15*	*after*	"	*7.6*

BALTIMORE Tables, pp. 162-165, BATTERY Tables, pp. 128-133

When a high tide exceeds avg. ht., the *following* low tide will be lower than avg.

*Times and Hts. are approximate. *Important*: See NOTE, top p. 12.

TIDE STATIONS

TIME OF HIGH WATER

Time figures shown are the *average* differences throughout the year. Rise in feet is mean range.
(Low Water times are given *only* when they vary more than 20 min. from High Water times.)

	Hr. Min.			Rise in feet
SOUTH CAROLINA, Cont.				
Beaufort, Beaufort River .... **high 0 55** *after, low*	*0 30*	*after*	*BATTERY*	*7.4*
Braddock Point, Hilton Head Island, Calibogue Sd.	*0 15*	*before*	"	*6.7*
GEORGIA				
Savannah River Entrance, Fort Pulaski	*0 15*	*before*	*BATTERY*	*6.9*
Tybee Creek Entrance	*0 20*	"	"	*6.8*
Wilmington River, north entrance	*0 25*	*after*	"	*7.6*
Isle of Hope, Skidaway River ...... **high 0 35** *after, low*	*0 10*	"	"	*7.8*
Egg Islands, Ossabaw Sound	*0 10*	*before*	"	*7.2*
Walburg Creek Entr., St. Catherines Sd.	*same as*		"	*7.1*
Blackbeard Island	*same as*		"	*6.9*
Blackbeard Creek, Blackbeard Island.. .... **high 0 05** *after, low*	*0 30*	*after*	"	*6.5*
Old Tower, Sapelo Island, Doboy Sound	*0 05*	*before*	"	*6.8*
Threemile Cut Entrance, Darien River	*0 30*	*after*	"	*7.1*
St. Simons Sound Bar	*0 20*	*before*	"	*6.5*
Frederica River, St. Simons Sound	*0 35*	*after*	"	*7.2*
Brunswick, East River, Howe St. Pier, St. Simons Sound	*0 20*	"	"	*7.1*
Jekyll Is. Marina, Jekyll Creek, St. Andrew Sound	*0 35*	"	"	*6.8*
Cumberland Wharf, Cumberland River	*0 30*	*after*	"	*6.8*
FLORIDA, East Coast				
St. Marys Entrance, north jetty, Cumberland Sd.	*same as*		*BATTERY*	*5.8*
Fernandina Beach, Amelia R. ...... **high 0 30** *after, low*	*0 05*	*after*	"	*6.0*
Amelia City, South Amelia River	*0 50*	"	"	*5.4*
Nassau River Entrance .... **high 0 10** *after, low*	*0 50*	"	"	*5.2*
Mayport, (Bar Pilot Dock) .... **high 0 15** *after, low*	*0 15*	*before*	"	*4.6*
St. Augustine, City Dock	*0 10*	*after*	"	*4.5*
Ponce Inlet, Halifax River .... **high 0 05** *after, low*	*0 30*	*after*	*MIAMI*	*2.8*
Cape Canaveral .... **high 1 05** *before, low*	*0 45*	*before*	"	*3.5*
Port Canaveral, Trident Pier	*same as*		"	*3.5*
Sebastian Inlet bridge .... **high 0 50** *before, low*	*0 25*	*before*	"	*2.2*
St. Lucie, Indian River .... **high 0 40** *after, low*	*1 45*	*after*	"	*1.1*
Vero Beach, ocean	*0 45*	*before*	"	*3.4*
Fort Pierce Inlet, south jetty	*0 25*	"	"	*2.6*
Stuart, St. Lucie River .... **high 2 15** *after, low*	*3 30*	*after*	"	*0.9*
Jupiter Inlet, south jetty	*0 10*	*before*	"	*2.5*
North Palm Beach, Lake Worth .. **high 0 15** *before, low*	*0 15*	*after*	"	*2.8*
Port of Palm Beach, Lake Worth . **high 0 20** *before, low*	*0 05*	"	"	*2.7*
Lake Worth Pier, ocean .... **high 0 45** *before, low*	*0 20*	*before*	"	*2.7*
Hillsboro Inlet, C.G. Light Station	*0 05*	"	"	*2.5*
Hillsboro Inlet Marina .... **high 0 05** *before, low*	*0 25*	*after*	"	*2.5*
Lauderdale-by-the-Sea, fish pier	*0 25*	*before*	"	*2.6*
Bahia Mar Yacht Club .... **high 0 05** *before, low*	*0 35*	*after*	"	*2.4*
Port Everglades, Turning Basin	*0 20*	*before*	"	*2.5*
North Miami Beach, fishing pier	*0 10*	"	"	*2.5*
Miami, Miamarina, Biscayne Bays **high 0 20** *after, low*	*0 50*	*after*	"	*2.2*
Dinner Key Marina, Biscayne Bay **high 0 55** *after, low*	*1 50*	"	"	*1.9*
Key Biscayne Yt. Club, Biscayne B **high 0 45** *after low*	*1 30*	"	"	*2.0*
Ocean Reef Hbr., Key Largo .... **high 0 10** *before, low*	*0 15*	"	"	*2.3*
Tavernier Harbor, Hawk Ch.	*0 15*	"	"	*2.0*
Key West	*0 50*	*before*	*BOSTON*	*1.3*

BATTERY Tables, pp. 128-133, MIAMI Tables, pp. 166-169, BOSTON Tables, pp. 38-43

When a high tide exceeds avg. ht., the *following* low tide will be lower than avg.

*Times and Hts. are approximate. *Important*: See NOTE, top p. 12.

Piloting in a Cross Current

See also p. 58, Coping with Currents

When we are piloting in a body of water with an active current from ahead or astern, our course is not affected and the arithmetic for speed is easy. (See p. 36.) When the current comes at an angle to the bow or stern, unless our speed is far greater than the current, we need to alter course to compensate.

First, what not to do: When in a cross current it is a major mistake simply to steer toward our destination. The current will carry us more and more off course, with the heading or bearing to our destination changing all the time. We may finally get there, but we will have traveled considerably farther, on what is termed a hooked course, and possibly have entered dangerous water while doing so.

By GPS: With GPS it's all too easy to find the new heading. We enter our destination waypoint and press GoTo. There are several screens to choose from. First, carefully check the Map screen to see if there are any hazards or obstructions between us and our destination. The Highway screen, considered perhaps the most useful display, will show if we are on course by displaying the highway as straight ahead. The screen will also indicate how far to the left or right of our course we are. This is crosstrack error. We steer to that side which brings us back onto the center of the highway, and then continue to steer in such a way that we stay in the middle. We have changed our heading to achieve the desired COG, course over ground. Now the Course and Bearing numbers should be the same, and we have compensated for cross current.

By eye: Without the help of electronics but with good visibility, we know we need to alter course toward the current until a foreground object, let's say a point on the shore, remains steady in relation to an object farther away, perhaps a distant steeple. This alignment is called a range. Once we find the corrected heading, we can use our compass to maintain it, checking those objects periodically in case current or wind conditions change.

By a chart: With compromised visibility and again without electronics, the problem is solved the traditional way with a paper chart. First, consult the proper current table to determine the speed and direction of the current for the hour(s) in question. (Keep in mind that speeds and times are predictions only. They are approximate and can be altered by weather.) Plot the course, let's say 090°, as if there is no current. Then construct a one-hour vector diagram. From the departure point, construct a line in the direction of the current, let's say 180°, whose length is the distance the current would carry an object in one hour. If the predicted current is 2 knots, that's 2 n.m. Now we set our dividers for a distance which represents how far our boat speed will take us through the water in one hour, let's say 8 n.m. We will put one point of the dividers on the far end of the line representing current, and then swing the dividers until the second point intercepts the line of our intended course. The direction of that third line represents what our boat's heading needs to be (the course to steer) to maintain the original course we drew. The intercept point represents about where our boat will be along the intended course line (COG) at the end of one hour. If this leg is longer or shorter than one hour, it doesn't matter. The course to steer is the same as we determined in our one-hour vector plot, until conditions change.

TIME OF CURRENT CHANGE

(See Note at bottom of Boston Tables, pp. 38-43: Rule-of-Thumb for Current Velocities.)

CURRENTS IN THE GULF OF MAINE - In the Gulf of Maine, on the western side, the Flood Current splits at Cape Ann, Mass., and floods north and east along the shore towards the Bay of Fundy. At the same time, on the eastern side of the Gulf, at the southern tip of Nova Scotia, the Flood Current runs to the west and then north and eastwards along the shore into the Bay of Fundy. The Ebb Current is just the reverse. In addition to these large principal currents, along the Maine Coast, at least at the mouths of principal bays, there is a shoreward set during the Flood and an offshore set during the Ebb, although this set is of considerably less velocity.

West of Mount Desert, the average along-shore current is rarely more than a knot but the farther east one goes, the greater are the average velocities to be expected, up to 2 knots or more. When heading west, therefore, start off at the time shown for High Water in your area (see p. 13) and have a fair Ebb current for 6 hours. Headed east, start at the time for Low Water in your area (about 6 ½ hours after High Water) and carry the beneficial Flood current. East of Schoodic Point, the average currents are up to 2 knots and taking advantage of them will save considerable time and fuel.

Off shore, in the Gulf of Maine, unlike the along-shore currents that come to dead slack and reverse, there are so-called rotary currents. These currents constantly change direction in a clockwise flow completing the circle in about 12 ½ hours. The maximum currents are when it is flooding in the northeasterly direction or ebbing in a southwesterly direction; minimum currents occur halfway between. There is no slack water.

Entering the Bay of Fundy through Grand Manan Channel, one finds that the average velocities are from 1-2 ½ knots, although in the narrower channels off the Bay, velocities are higher (Friar Roads at Eastport has average velocities of 3 knots of more). The Current in the Bay Floods to the Northeast and Ebbs to the Southwest.

In using this table, bear in mind that **actual times of Slack or Maximum occasionally differ from the predicted times** by as much as half an hour and in rare instances as much as an hour. Referring the Time of Current Change at the subordinate stations listed below, to the predicted Current Change at the reference station gives the approximate time only. Therefore, to make make sure of getting the full advantage of a favorable current or slack water, the navigator should reach the entrance or strait at least half an hour before the predicted time. (This is essentially the same precautionary note found in the U.S. Tidal Currents Table Book.)

Figures shown below are **average maximum** velocities in knots. To find the Time of Current Change (Start of Flood and Start of Ebb) at a selected point, refer to the table heading that particular section (in bold type) and add or subtract the time listed.

	TIME DIFFERENCES Flood Starts; Ebb Starts Hr. Min.	MAXIMUM FLOOD Dir.(true) in degrees	Avg. Max. in knots	MAXIMUM EBB Dir.(true) in degrees	Avg. Max. in knots
MAINE COAST – based on Portland, pp. 30-35 (Flood starts at Low Water; Ebb starts at High Water)					
Isle Au Haut, 0.8 mi. E of Richs Pt.	-0 10	336	1.4	139	1.5
Damariscotta R., off Cavis Pt.	F+1 15, E+0 05	350	0.6	215	1.0
Sheepscot R., off Barter Is.	F+1 15, E+0 15	005	0.8	200	1.1
Lowe Pt., NE of, Sasanoa R.	F+1 15, E+0 45	327	1.7	152	1.8
Lower Hell Gate, Knubble Bay*	F+1 40, E+0 45	290	3.0	155	3.5

*Velocities up to 9.0 kts. have been observed in the vicinity of the Boilers.

Important: **See NOTE, bottom p. 29.**

TIME OF CURRENT CHANGE

(See Note at bottom of Boston Tables, pp. 38-43: Rule-of-Thumb for Current Velocities.)

	TIME DIFFERENCES Flood Starts; Ebb Starts Hr. Min.	MAXIMUM FLOOD Dir.(true) in degrees	Avg. Max. in knots	MAXIMUM EBB Dir.(true) in degrees	Avg. Max. in knots
KENNEBEC RIVER – based on Portland, pp. 30-35 (Flood starts at Low Water; Ebb starts at High Water)					
Hunniwell Pt., NE of	F+2 10, E+1 35	332	2.4	151	2.9
Bald Head, 0.3 mi. SW of	F+2 30, E+1 25	321	1.6	153	2.3
Bluff Head, W of	F+2 40, E+1 55	014	2.3	184	3.4
Fiddler Ledge, N of	F+2 50, E+1 50	267	1.9	113	2.6
Doubling Pt., S of	F+2 30, E+1 50	300	2.6	127	3.0
Bath Iron Works	F+2 45, E+2 15	004	1.9	178	2.5
CASCO BAY – based on Portland, pp. 30-35 (Flood starts at Low Water; Ebb starts at High Water)					
Broad Sound, W. of Eagle Is.	+0 10	351	1.0	187	1.1
Hussey Sound, Cow Islands	F-0 20, E+0 40	012	1.1	178	0.8
Portland Hbr. entr, 19ft depth	F+0 45, E+0 15	313	0.7	137	1.1
Portland, Fore River Bridge	F+0 50, E+0 05	229	0.5	065	0.4
PORTSMOUTH HARBOR – based on Boston, pp. 38-43 (Flood starts at Low Water; Ebb starts at High Water)					
Portsmouth Hbr. entr.	F+2 05, E+1 30	342	1.2	194	1.5
Fort Point	F+2 30, E+1 30	328	1.6	098	2.0
Clark Is., S of	F+2 40, E+2 00	270	1.6	085	2.3
Henderson Pt., W of	F+2 15, E+1 35	285	2.4	138	2.8
MASSACHUSETTS COAST – based on Boston, pp. 38-43 (Flood starts at Low Water; Ebb starts at High Water)					
Merrimack River entr.	+0 25	285	2.2	105	1.4
Newburyport, Merrimack R.	+0 50	288	1.5	098	1.4
Plum Is. Sound entr.	-0 05	316	1.6	184	1.5
Gloucester Hbr., Blynman Canal entr.	F-0 35, E-1 15	310	3.0	130	3.3
Marblehead Channel	F+0 20, E-0 30	280	0.3	171	0.3
Hypocrite Channel	-0 15	262	0.9	070	1.0
BOSTON HARBOR – based on Boston, pp. 38-43 (Flood starts at Low Water; Ebb starts at High Water)					
Pt. Allerton, 0.4 mi. NW.	-0 40	265	0.7	080	0.8
Deer Island Lt	F-0 20, E-0 55	264	1.3	112	1.2
Nantasket Rds					
Hull Gut	F-045, E-1 10	162	1.9	340	2.5
West Head (W. Gut) 0.2mi. SW	F-0 35, E+0 05	167	1.4	322	1.4
Weir R. entr., Worlds End, N of	-0 15	076	0.7	272	0.8
Bumkin Is., 0.4mi. W. of	-0 40	195	0.5	303	0.3
Weymouth Back R., betw. Grape I. and Lower Neck	-0 45	094	0.7	281	0.9
CAPE COD BAY – based on Boston, pp. 38-43 (Flood starts at Low Water; Ebb starts at High Water)					
Barnstable Harbor	F-0 10, E-0 40	192	1.2	004	1.4
NANTUCKET SOUND – based on Pollock Rip Channel, pp. 66-71					
Pollock Rip Channel, E end	-0 20	053	2.0	212	1.8

CURRENT STATIONS

Important: **See NOTE, bottom p. 29.**

TIME OF CURRENT CHANGE

(See Note at bottom of Boston Tables, pp. 38-43: Rule-of-Thumb for Current Velocities.)

	TIME DIFFERENCES Flood Starts; Ebb Starts Hr. Min.	MAXIMUM FLOOD Dir.(true) in degrees	MAXIMUM FLOOD Avg. Max. in knots	MAXIMUM EBB Dir.(true) in degrees	MAXIMUM EBB Avg. Max. in knots
***POLLOCK RIP CHANNEL at Butler Hole - See table, pp. 66-71**					
Monomoy Point, 0.2 mi. W of	+0 10	170	1.7	346	2.0
Halfmoon Shoal, 3.5 mi. E of	+1 10	088	1.1	295	1.0
Great Point, 0.5 mi. W of	F+0 25, E+1 15	029	1.1	195	1.2
Tuckernuck Shoal, off E end	+1 15	113	0.9	287	0.9
Nantucket Hbr. entr. chan.	F+3 20, E+2 45	171	1.2	350	1.5
Muskeget Is. chan., 1 mi. NE of	F+1 30, E+1 00	108	1.1	295	1.5
Muskeget Rock, 1.3 mi. SW of	+1 05	024	1.3	192	1.0
Muskeget Channel	+1 35	021	3.8	200	3.3
Betw. Long Shoal-Norton Shoal	+1 30	100	1.4	260	1.1
Cape Poge Lt., 1.7 mi. SSE of	+0 55	025	1.6	215	1.3
Cross Rip Channel	+1 50	091	1.3	272	0.9
Cape Poge, 3.2 mi. NE of	+2 35	095	1.6	300	1.2
Betw. Broken Gr.-Horseshoe Sh.	F+1 45, E+1 15	107	1.1	276	0.9
Point Gammon, 1.2 mi. S of	+1 10	105	1.1	260	1.0
Lewis Bay entr. chan.	+2 45	004	0.9	184	1.3
Betw. Wreck Shoal-Eldridge Shoal	+1 45	062	1.7	245	1.4
Hedge Fence Lighted Gong Buoy 22	+2 45	108	1.4	268	1.2
Betw. E. Chop-Squash Meadow	F+2 10, E+1 45	131	1.4	329	1.8
East Chop, 1 mi. N of	F+2 40, E+2 15	116	2.2	297	2.2
West Chop, 0.8 mi. N of	F+2 50, E+2 20	096	3.1	282	3.0
Betw. Hedge Fence and L'hommedieu Shoal	F+2 30, E+2 00	106	2.1	276	2.2
Waquoit Bay entr.	+3 30	348	1.5	203	1.4
L'hommedieu Shoal, N of W end	+2 20	080	2.3	268	2.3
Nobska Point, 1.8 mi. E of	+2 05	063	2.3	240	1.7
VINEYARD SOUND – based on Pollock Rip Channel, pp. 66-71					
West Chop, 0.2 mi. W of	F+1 20, E+1 50	059	2.7	241	1.4
Nobska Point, 1 mi. SE of	+2 30	071	2.6	259	2.4
Norton Point, 0.5 mi. N of	+2 00	050	3.4	240	2.4
Tarpaulin Cove, 1.5 mi. E of	F+2 50, E+2 10	055	1.9	232	2.3
Robinsons Hole, 1.2 mi. SE of	+2 20	060	1.9	240	2.1
Gay Head, 3 mi. N of	+2 05	074	1.1	255	1.2
Gay Head, 1.5 mi. NW of	+1 35	012	2.0	249	2.0
VINEYARD SOUND-BUZZARDS BAY – based on Woods Hole, pp. 52-57					
Robinsons Hole, Naushon Pt.	+0 40	151	3.0	332	2.9
Quicks Hole, S end	F+1 20, E+0 30	140	1.9	300	2.0
Quicks Hole, Middle	F+1 30, E+1 00	157	2.3	327	1.8
Quicks Hole, N end	F+1 40, E+0 55	165	2.0	002	2.6
Canapitsit Channel	F+1 00, E+0 15	131	1.7	312	1.6
BUZZARDS BAY – based on Woods Hole, pp. 52-57					
Westport River entr.	-1 20	290	2.2	108	2.5
Gooseberry Nk., 2 mi. SSE of (41°27'N- 71°01'W) *Rotary current, no slack water. Avg. max. 0.6 kts, approx. dir. 52° true 3:20 hrs. after Flood starts at Pollock Rip. Avg. max. 0.5 kts, approx. dir. 232° true 2:45 hrs. after Ebb starts at Pollock Rip.*					
Betw. Ribbon Reef-Sow &Pigs Rf.	F-1 45, E-3 45	062	0.8	237	1.2
Penikese Is., 0.8 mi. NW of	F-3 00, E-1 55	050	1.2	254	1.1
Betw. Gull Is.-Nashawena Is.	F-3 40, E-3 00	091	0.9	247	1.1
Dumpling Rocks, 0.2 mi. SE of	F-3 10, E-2 30	066	0.8	190	1.1
BUZZARDS BAY – based on Cape Cod Canal, pp. 46-51					
Abiels Ledge	F+0 10, E-0 20	069	1.3	236	1.8
CAPE COD CANAL - table, pp. 46-51		070	4.0	250	4.5

**See Tidal Current Chart Buzzards Bay, Vineyard and Nantucket Sounds, pp. 72-83*

Important: **See NOTE, bottom p. 29.**

TIME OF CURRENT CHANGE

(See Note at bottom of Boston Tables, pp. 38-43: Rule-of-Thumb for Current Velocities.)

	TIME DIFFERENCES Flood Starts; Ebb Starts Hr. Min.	MAXIMUM FLOOD Dir.(true) in degrees	MAXIMUM FLOOD Avg. Max. in knots	MAXIMUM EBB Dir.(true) in degrees	MAXIMUM EBB Avg. Max. in knots
***NARRAGANSETT BAY – based on Pollock Rip Channel, pp. 66-71**					
Tiverton, Stone Bridge, Sakonnet	F-3 00, E-2 25	010	2.7	190	2.7
Tiverton, RR Bridge, Sakonnet R.	F-3 25, E-2 50	000	2.3	180	2.4
Castle Hill, W of East Passage	F-0 05, E-1 05	013	0.7	237	1.2
Bull Point, E of	-1 10	001	1.2	206	1.5
Rose Is., NE of	F-1 55, E-1 15	310	0.8	124	1.0
Rose Is., W of	F-0 40, E-1 20	001	0.7	172	1.0
Dyer Is., W of	-1 00	023	0.8	216	1.0
Mount Hope Bridge	-1 15	047	1.1	230	1.4
Kickamuit R., Mt. Hope Bay	F-2 05, E-1 20	000	1.4	191	1.7
Warren R., Warren	-0 20	358	1.0	171	0.9
Beavertail Point, 0.8 mi NW of	F-0 10, E-1 30	003	0.5	188	1.0
Betw. Dutch Is.-Beaver Head	-1 55	030	1.0	233	1.0
Dutch Is., W of	-1 25	014	1.3	206	1.2
India Pt. RR Bridge, Seekonk R.	-1 40	020	1.0	180	1.4
BLOCK ISLAND SOUND – based on The Race, pp. 92-97					
Pt. Judith Pond entr.	-3 10	351	1.8	186	1.5
Sandy Pt., Block Is. 1.5 mi N of	F-0 25, E-1 05	315	1.9	063	2.1
Lewis Pt., 1.0 mi. SW of	F-1 30, E-0 25	298	1.9	136	1.8
Lewis Pt., 1.5 mi. W of	F-1 35, E-0 50	318	1.4	170	1.7
Southwest Ledge	-0 25	321	1.5	141	2.1
Watch Hill Pt., 2.2 mi. E of	F-0 30, E+0 45	260	1.2	086	0.7
Montauk Pt., 1.2 mi. E of	F-1 20, E-0 40	346	2.8	162	2.8
Montauk Pt., 1 mi. NE of	F-2 05, E-1 15	356	2.4	145	1.9
Betw. Shagwong Reef-Cerberus Shoal	-0 30	241	1.9	056	1.8
Betw. Cerberus Sh.-Fishers Is.	F-1 00, E+0 05	264	1.3	096	1.3
Gardiners Is., 3 mi. NE of	F-0 50, E-0 25	305	0.9	138	1.0
GARDINERS BAY etc. – based on The Race, pp. 92-97					
Goff Point, 0.4 mi. NW of	-1 35	225	1.2	010	1.6
Acabonack Hbr. entr., 0.6 mi. ESE of	F-1 35, E-1 05	345	1.4	140	1.2
Gardiners Pt. Ruins, 1.1 mi. N of	-0 10	270	1.2	066	1.8
Betw. Gardiners Point-Plum Is.	-0 25	288	1.4	100	1.6
Jennings Pt., 0.2 mi. NNW of	+0 35	290	1.6	055	1.5
Cedar Pt., 0.2 mi. W of	F-0 10, E+0 30	195	1.8	005	1.6
North Haven Peninsula, N of	F+0 10, E+0 40	230	2.4	035	2.1
Paradise Pt., 0.4 mi. E of	+0 35	145	1.5	345	1.5
Little Peconic Bay entr.	+0 45	240	1.6	015	1.5
Robins Is., 0.5 mi. S of	F+0 30, E+0 55	245	1.7	065	0.6
FISHERS ISLAND SOUND – based on The Race, pp. 92-97					
Napatree Point, 0.7 mi. SW of	-0 50	284	1.7	113	2.2
Little Narragansett Bay entr.	-2 05	092	1.3	268	1.3
Ram Island Reef, S of	-0 50	255	1.3	088	1.6
LONG ISLAND SOUND – based on The Race, pp. 92-97					
****THE RACE (near Valiant Rock) – See pp. 92-97**		291	3.3	106	4.2
Race Point, 0.4 mi. SW of	-0 25	288	2.6	135	3.5
Little Gull Is., 1.1 mi. ENE of	+0 05	301	4.0	130	4.7
Little Gull Is., 0.8 mi. NNW of	F+0 25, E-2 20	258	1.9	043	2.9
Great Gull Is., SW of	-0 40	320	2.3	147	3.3
New London St. Pier, Thames R.	-1 30	358	0.4	178	0.4
Goshen Pt., 1.9 mi. SSE of	-0 55	285	1.2	062	1.6
Bartlett Reef, 0.2 mi. S of	F-2 05, E-1 05	255	1.4	090	1.3
Twotree Is. Channel	F-1 00, E-0 35	267	1.2	099	1.6

**Floods somewhat unstable. Flood currents differing from predicted should be expected.*
*** See Tidal Current Chart Long Is. and Block Is. Sounds, pp. 98-103*

Important: **See NOTE, bottom p. 29.**

CURRENT STATIONS

TIME OF CURRENT CHANGE

(See Note at bottom of Boston Tables, pp. 38-43: Rule-of-Thumb for Current Velocities.)

	TIME DIFFERENCES Flood Starts; Ebb Starts Hr. Min.	MAXIMUM FLOOD Dir.(true) in degrees	MAXIMUM FLOOD Avg. Max. in knots	MAXIMUM EBB Dir.(true) in degrees	MAXIMUM EBB Avg. Max. in knots
LONG ISLAND SOUND – based on The Race, pp. 92-97 (cont.)					
Black Point, 0.8 mi. S of	F-0 40, E-0 15	260	1.3	073	1.4
Betw. Black Pt.-Plum Is.	+0 35	236	2.1	076	2.4
Plum Is., 0.8 mi. NNW of	F+0 10,E-1 05	247	1.7	065	2.4
Plum Gut	-1 00	306	1.9	116	3.0
Hatchett Pt., 1.1 mi. WSW of	F-2 30, E-0 40	240	1.3	045	1.2
Saybrook Bkwtr., 1.5 mi. SE of	F-1 20, E-0 45	260	1.9	070	2.0
Conn. River I-95 Bridge	F+1 15, E+0 20	356	0.9	166	1.8
Mulford Pt., 3.1 mi. NW of	+0 05	269	1.9	066	2.3
Cornfield Point, 2.8 mi. SE of	F-1 30, E-0 30	249	1.9	085	1.4
Cornfield Point, 1.1 mi. S of	-0 50	293	1.4	108	1.6
Kelsey Point, 1 mi. S of	F-1 35, E-1 05	249	2.0	118	1.5
Six Mile Reef, 2 mi. E of	F-0 30, E+0 05	235	1.6	040	2.1
Sachem Head, 1 mi. SSE of	-0 30	255	1.1	065	1.0
New Haven Harbor entr.	-0 05	277	0.7	122	0.5
Housatonic R., Milford Pt., 0.2 mi. W of	F+0 00, E+0 25	330	1.2	135	1.2
Point No Point, 2.1 mi. S of	F-0 20, E+0 05	251	1.3	074	1.2
Port Jefferson Harbor entr.	-0 10	150	1.6	336	1.0
Crane Neck Point, 0.5 mi. NW of	F-0 45, E-1 40	256	1.3	016	1.5
Eatons Neck Pt., 1.3 mi. N of	+0 20	283	1.4	075	1.4
Lloyd Point, 1.3 mi. NNW of	+1 30	255	1.0	055	0.9
EAST RIVER – based on Hell Gate, pp. 116-121					
Cryders Pt., 0.4 mi. NNW of	-0 30	110	1.3	285	1.1
College Pt. Rf., .25 mi. NW of	-0 30	074	1.5	261	1.4
Rikers Is. Chann. off La Guardia Field	+0 05	088	1.1	261	1.3
Hunts Point, SW of	0 00	108	1.7	280	1.3
S. Brother Is. NW of	- 0 10	054	1.5	252	1.2
Off Winthrop Ave., Astoria	0 00	040	3.4	220	2.5
Mill Rock, NE of	-0 25	103	2.3	288	0.6
Mill Rock, W of	F-0 25, E+0 00	000	1.2	180	1.0
HELL GATE (off Mill Rock) – table, pp. 116-121		050	3.4	230	4.6
Roosevelt Is., W of, off 75th St.	-0 05	037	3.8	215	4.7
Roosevelt Is., E of, off 36th Ave.	-0 10	030	3.5	210	3.4
Roosevelt Is., W of, off 67th St.	+0 10	011	3.6	230	4.0
Pier 67 (Off 19th St.)	-0 10	355	1.8	179	1.9
Williamsburg Br., 0.3 mi. N of	-0 05	020	2.7	220	2.9
Brooklyn Bridge, 0.1 mi. SW of	-0 10	046	2.9	222	3.5
LONG ISLAND, South Coast – based on The Narrows, pp. 122-127					
Shinnecock Inlet	F+0 15, E-0 -35	350	2.5	170	2.3
Fire Is. Inlet, 0.5 mi. S. of Oak Bch.	+0 25	082	2.4	244	2.4
Jones Inlet	-0 50	035	3.1	217	2.6
East Rockaway Inlet	-1 15	042	2.2	227	2.3
JAMAICA BAY – based on The Narrows, pp. 122-127					
Rockaway Inlet entr.	-1 35	085	1.8	244	2.7
Barren Is., E of	F-1 30, E-2 05	004	1.2	192	1.7
Beach Channel (bridge)	F-1 25, E-1 00	062	1.9	225	2.0
Grass Hassock Channel	-1 00	052	1.0	228	1.0
NEW YORK HARBOR ENTRANCE – based on The Narrows, pp. 122-127					
Ambrose Channel	-0 30	303	1.6	123	1.7
Norton Pt., WSW of	+0 15	341	1.0	166	1.2
THE NARROWS – table, pp. 122-127		325	1.3	142	1.6

Important: **See NOTE, bottom p. 29.**

TIME OF CURRENT CHANGE

(See Note at bottom of Boston Tables, pp. 38-43: Rule-of-Thumb for Current Velocities.)

	TIME DIFFERENCES Flood Starts; Ebb Starts Hr. Min.	MAXIMUM FLOOD Dir.(true) in degrees	MAXIMUM FLOOD Avg. Max. in knots	MAXIMUM EBB Dir.(true) in degrees	MAXIMUM EBB Avg. Max. in knots
NEW YORK HARBOR, Upper Bay – based on The Narrows, pp. 122-127					
Bay Ridge, W of	F+0 10, E+0 40	354	1.4	185	1.5
Red Hook Channel	F-0 40, E-0 05	353	1.0	170	0.7
Robbins Reef Light, E of	F+0 40, E+0 00	016	1.3	204	1.6
Red Hook, 1 mi. W of	+0 55	024	1.3	206	2.3
Statue of Liberty, E of	F+1 20, E+0 55	031	1.4	205	1.9
HUDSON RIVER, Midchannel – based on The Narrows, pp. 122-127					
George Washington Bridge	+1 45	010	1.8	203	2.5
Spuyten Duyvil	F+1 30, E+1 55	020	1.6	200	2.1
Riverdale	F+2 30, E+2 00	015	1.4	200	2.0
Dobbs Ferry	F+2 50, E+2 20	010	1.3	190	1.7
Tarrytown	F+3 00, E+2 35	000	1.1	180	1.5
West Point, off Duck Is.	F+3 50, E+3 45	010	1.0	190	1.1
NEW YORK HARBOR, Lower Bay – based on The Narrows, pp. 122-127					
Sandy Hook Channel	F-1 30, E-1 10	286	1.6	094	0.9
Sandy Hook Channel, 0.4 mi. W of N. tip	-1 30	235	2.0	050	1.6
Coney Is. Lt., 1.5 mi. SSE of	-1 00	310	1.1	125	1.3
Rockaway Inlet Jetty, 1 mi. SW of	F-1 55, E-1 30	287	1.2	142	1.4
Coney Is. Channel, W end	F-1 00, E-0 30	293	1.1	102	1.2
SANDY HOOK BAY – based on The Narrows, pp. 122-127					
Highlands Bridge, Shrewsbury R.	+0 35	170	2.6	000	2.5
Seabright Br., Shrewsbury R.	F+1 20, E+0 50	185	1.4	000	1.7
RARITAN RIVER – based on The Narrows, pp. 122-127					
Washington Canal, N entr.	F-0 50, E-1 35	240	1.5	060	1.5
South River entr.	F-1 30, E-0 30	180	1.1	000	1.0
ARTHUR KILL & KILL VAN KULL – based on The Narrows, pp. 122-127					
Tottenville, Arthur Kill River	-0 45	023	1.0	211	1.1
Tufts Pt.-Smoking Pt.	-0 25	109	1.2	267	1.2
Elizabethport	+0 30	090	1.4	262	1.1
Bergen Pt., East Reach	F-1 10, E-1 40	274	1.1	094	1.2
New Brighton	-1 25	262	1.3	072	1.9
NEW JERSEY COAST – based on Del. Bay Entr., pp. 146-151					
Manasquan Inlet	F-1 00, E-1 40	300	1.7	120	1.8
Manasquan R. Hwy. Br. Main Ch.	F-1 00, E-1 40	230	2.2	050	2.1
Pt. Pleasant Canal, north bridge*	F+1 25, E+0 20	170	1.8	350	2.0
Barnegat Inlet	F+0 40, E-0 10	270	2.2	090	2.5
Manahawkin Drawbridge	+2 05	030	1.1	210	0.9
McCrie Shoal	-1 05	280	1.3	100	1.4
Cape May Harbor entr.	-2 00	324	1.6	142	1.7
Cape May Canal, E end	-2 15	310	1.9	130	1.9
DELAWARE BAY & RIVER – based on Del. Bay Entr., pp. 146-151					
Cape May Channel	-1 35	306	1.5	150	2.3
DELAWARE BAY ENTR. – table, pp. 146-151		342	1.8	152	1.7
Cape Henlopen, 0.7 mi. ESE of	F-0 25, E-1 05	331	1.8	139	2.4
Cape Henlopen, 2 mi. NE of	F+0 00, E-0 30	315	2.0	145	2.3
Cape Henlopen, 5 mi. N of	+0 10	344	2.0	173	1.9

**Waters are extremely turbulent. Currents of 6 to 7 knots have been reported near the bridges.*

Important: **See NOTE, bottom p. 29.**

TIME OF CURRENT CHANGE

(See Note at bottom of Boston Tables, pp. 38-43: Rule-of-Thumb for Current Velocities.)

	TIME DIFFERENCES Flood Starts; Ebb Starts Hr. Min.	MAXIMUM FLOOD Dir.(true) in degrees	Avg. Max. in knots	MAXIMUM EBB Dir.(true) in degrees	Avg. Max. in knots
DELAWARE BAY & RIVER – based on Del. Bay Entr., pp. 146-151 (cont.)					
Mispillion River Mouth	F+2 15, E+1 20	025	1.5	190	1.0
Bay Shore chan., City of Town Bank	F-0 50, E-1 10	006	0.9	183	1.0
Fourteen Ft. Bk., Lt., 1.2 mi. E of	-0 05	339	1.3	174	1.5
Maurice River entr.	+0 35	012	1.1	192	1.0
Kelly Island, 1.5 mi. E of	+0 25	348	0.9	164	1.2
Miah Maull rge. at Cross Ledge rge	+1 00	335	1.5	160	1.8
False Egg Is. Pt., 2 mi. off	F+0 05, E-0 15	342	1.1	158	1.3
Ben Davis Pt. Shoal., SW of	F+1 30, E+1 05	321	1.8	147	1.9
Cohansey R., 0.5 mi. above entr.	+1 05	074	1.2	254	1.4
Arnold Point, 2.2 mi. WSW of	+2 00	324	2.1	145	1.9
Smyrna River entr.	+1 30	250	1.2	070	1.5
Stony Point chan., W of	F+2 50, E+1 40	324	1.5	151	1.9
Appoquinimink R. entr.	F+2 00, E+1 20	231	1.0	048	1.2
Reedy Is., off end of pier	F+2 30, E+2 00	027	2.4	194	2.6
Alloway Creek entr., 0.2 mi. above	F+1 50, E+1 20	129	2.1	325	2.1
Reedy Point, 0.85 mi. NE of	F+3 00, E+2 05	341	1.6	163	2.2
Salem River entr.	F+3 10, E+2 40	062	1.5	245	1.6
Bulkhead Sh. chan., off Del. City	F+2 40, E+2 05	308	2.1	138	2.1
Pea Patch Is., chan., E of	F+2 55, E+2 35	319	2.3	148	2.3
New Castle, chan., abreast of	F+3 00, E+2 10	051	1.9	230	2.4
CHESAPEAKE BAY – based on The Race, pp. 92-97 (over 90% correlation within 15 min. throughout year)					
Cape Henry Light, 2.0 nmi. N of	+0 05	289	1.2	110	1.1
Chesapeake Bay entr., Buoy LB2CH	-0 10	297	1.1	112	1.1
Cape Henry Light, 4.6 mi. N of	-0 35	294	1.3	104	1.3
Cape Henry Light, 8.3 mi. NW of.	F+0 10, E-0 15	329	1.0	133	1.1
Tail of the Horseshoe	F+0 00, E-0 40	300	0.9	110	1.0
Chesapeake Channel (Bridge Tunnel)	F+0 00, E-0 25	335	1.8	145	1.5
Fisherman Is., 1.7 nmi. S of	F-0 25, E-1 15	297	1.0	126	1.4
York Spit Channel N buoy "26"	F+1 30, E+0 25	010	0.8	195	1.1
Old Plantation Flats Lt., 0.5 mi. W of	F+1 30, E+0 55	005	1.2	175	1.3
Wolf Trap Lt., 0.5 mi. W of	F+1 40, E+0 35	015	1.0	190	1.2
Stingray Point, 5.5 mi. E of	+2 25	343	1.0	179	0.9
Stingray Point, 12.5 mi. E of	F+2 15, E+1 10	030	1.0	175	0.8
Smith Point Lt., 6.0 mi. N of	F+4 25, E+3 20	350	0.4	135	1.0
Cove Point - See Chesapeake Bay Current Diagram, p. 160					
Pooles Island - See Chesapeake Bay Current Diagram, p. 160					
Worton Point - See Chesapeake Bay Current Diagram, p. 160					
CHESAPEAKE & DELAWARE CANAL - table, pp. 154-159		097	2.0	278	1.9
HAMPTON ROADS – based on The Race, pp. 92-97 (over 90% correlation within 15 min. throughout year)					
Thimble Shoal Channel (West End)	F-0 20, E-1 00	293	0.9	116	1.2
Old Point Comfort, 0.2 mi. S of	F-0 40, E-1 50	240	1.7	075	1.4
Willoughby Spit, 0.8 mi. NW of	F-1 35, E-2 40	260	0.7	040	1.0
Sewells Point, chan., W of	F-0 45, E-2 20	195	0.9	000	1.2
Newport News, chan.,middle	F-0 45, E-1 10	244	1.1	076	1.1

Important: **See NOTE, bottom p. 29.**

TIME OF CURRENT CHANGE

(See Note at bottom of Boston Tables, pp. 38-43: Rule-of-Thumb for Current Velocities.)

	TIME DIFFERENCES Flood Starts; Ebb Starts Hr. Min.	MAXIMUM FLOOD Dir.(true) in degrees	MAXIMUM FLOOD Avg. Max. in knots	MAXIMUM EBB Dir.(true) in degrees	MAXIMUM EBB Avg. Max. in knots
C&D CANAL POINTS – based on C&D Canal, pp. 154-159					
Back Creek, 0.3 nmi. W of Sandy Pt.	-0 10	057	1.2	244	1.4
Reedy Point Radio Tower, S of	F-1 05, E-0 10	078	1.9	263	1.3
VA, NC, SC, GA & FL, outer coast – based on Hell Gate, pp. 116-121 (over 90% correlation within 15 min. throughout year)					
Hatteras Inlet	F+1 00, E+0 40	307	2.1	148	2.0
Ocracoke Inlet chan. entr.	F+1 10, E+0 05	000	1.7	145	2.4
Beaufort Inlet Approach	F+0 25, E-1 05	358	0.3	161	1.4
Cape Fear R. Bald Head Shoal	F+1 00, E-2 05	013	0.6	208	1.7
Winyah Bay entr.	F+0 05, E-0 35	320	1.9	140	2.0
North Santee R. entr.	F-0 40, E-1 35	010	1.5	165	1.8
South Santee R. entr.	-1 15	045	1.5	240	1.6
Charleston Hbr. entr., betw. jetties	-1 40	320	1.8	121	1.8
Charleston Hbr., off Ft. Sumter	-1 40	313	1.7	127	2.0
Charleston Hbr. S. ch. 0.8 mi. ENE of Ft. Johnson	F-0 55, E-1 50	275	0.8	115	2.6
Charleston Hbr., Drum Is., E of (bridge)	-1 20	020	1.2	183	2.0
North Edisto River entr.	-0 35	332	2.9	142	3.7
South Edisto River entr.	F-1 20, E-1 50	350	1.8	146	2.2
Ashepoo R. off Jefford Cr. entr.	F-0 35, E-0 40	016	1.5	197	1.6
Port Royal Sd., SE chan. entr.	F-2 10, E-1 50	310	1.3	150	1.6
Hilton Head	-1 15	324	1.8	146	1.8
Beaufort River entr.	-1 20	010	1.3	195	1.4
Savannah River entr.	-0 55	286	2.0	110	2.0
Vernon R. 1.2 mi. S of Possum Pt.	F-1 25, E-1 00	324	1.1	166	1.7
Raccoon Key & Egg Is. Shoal bet.	F-0 40, E -1 15	254	1.6	129	2.0
St. Catherines Sound entr.	F-1 40, E-0 35	291	1.8	126	1.7
Sapelo Sound entr.	F-1 30, E-0 55	290	1.7	118	2.2
Doboy Sound entr.	-1 25	289	1.6	106	1.8
Altamaha Sd., 1 mi. SE of Onemile Cut	F-0 15, E-2 00	272	1.0	092	1.9
St. Simons Sound Bar Channel	F-1 15, E-0 40	308	0.8	119	1.7
St. Andrews Sound entr.	F-1 20, E-0 50	268	2.1	103	2.2
Cumberland Sd., St. Mary's River, Ft. Clinch, 0.3 nmi. N	F-1 15, E -0 50	275	1.4	087	1.6
Drum Point Is., rge. D chan.	-0 35	350	1.1	170	1.5
Nassau Sd., midsound, 1 mi. N of Sawpit Cr. entr.	-0 20	312	1.7	135	1.7
FLORIDA EAST COAST – based on The Narrows, pp. 122-127 (over 90% correlation within 15 min. throughout year)					
St. Johns R. entr. betw. jetties	+0 30	262	2.0	081	2.0
Mayport	+0 40	211	2.2	026	3.3
St. Johns Bluff	F+1 05, E-0 10	244	1.6	059	2.4
FLORIDA EAST COAST – based on Hell Gate, pp. 116-121 (over 90% correlation within 15 min. throughout year)					
Fort Pierce Inlet entr.	+0 40	258	2.7	080	2.8
Lake Worth Inlet, entr.	-0 55	267	1.6	086	1.3
Miami Hbr., Bakers Haulover Cut	-0 10	270	2.9	090	2.5
Miami Hbr. entr.	-0 15	293	2.3	113	2.4

NOTE: Velocities shown are from U.S. Gov't. figures. It is obvious, however, to local mariners and other observers, that coastal inlets may have far greater velocities than indicated here. Strong winds and opposing tides can cause even more dangerous conditions, and great caution should be used. Separate times for Flood and Ebb are given only when the times are more than 20 minutes apart.

2021 HIGH & LOW WATER
PORTLAND, ME
43°39.4'N, 70°14.8'W

Standard Time

DAY OF MONTH	DAY OF WEEK	JANUARY HIGH a.m.	Ht.	p.m.	Ht.	LOW a.m.	p.m.
1	F	12:19	8.7	**12:17**	10.1	6:04	**6:42**
2	S	12:57	8.8	**12:59**	10.1	6:46	**7:23**
3	S	1:39	8.9	**1:44**	10.0	7:32	**8:08**
4	M	2:24	9.0	**2:34**	9.8	8:22	**8:56**
5	T	3:14	9.2	**3:29**	9.5	9:18	**9:47**
6	W	4:07	9.4	**4:29**	9.2	10:17	**10:42**
7	T	5:03	9.7	**5:33**	9.0	11:20	**11:40**
8	F	6:02	9.9	**6:40**	8.9	...	**12:26**
9	S	7:04	10.2	**7:47**	8.9	12:41	**1:32**
10	S	8:03	10.5	**8:48**	9.1	1:43	**2:33**
11	M	9:00	10.8	**9:45**	9.3	2:42	**3:30**
12	T	9:54	10.9	**10:39**	9.4	3:37	**4:24**
13	W	10:47	11.0	**11:30**	9.4	4:30	**5:15**
14	T	11:37	10.9	...	...	5:21	**6:03**
15	F	12:18	9.4	**12:25**	10.6	6:10	**6:49**
16	S	1:04	9.3	**1:12**	10.2	6:58	**7:34**
17	S	1:50	9.1	**1:59**	9.6	7:47	**8:19**
18	M	2:37	8.9	**2:48**	9.1	8:37	**9:05**
19	T	3:24	8.7	**3:40**	8.5	9:29	**9:51**
20	W	4:12	8.6	**4:34**	8.1	10:23	**10:39**
21	T	5:02	8.5	**5:31**	7.7	11:20	**11:30**
22	F	5:54	8.5	**6:30**	7.5	...	**12:19**
23	S	6:47	8.5	**7:29**	7.6	12:24	**1:18**
24	S	7:40	8.7	**8:22**	7.7	1:20	**2:11**
25	M	8:28	9.0	**9:10**	7.9	2:10	**2:58**
26	T	9:13	9.4	**9:53**	8.2	2:56	**3:40**
27	W	9:55	9.7	**10:34**	8.5	3:38	**4:21**
28	T	10:36	10.1	**11:14**	8.8	4:20	**5:00**
29	F	11:17	10.4	**11:53**	9.1	5:01	**5:39**
30	S	11:58	10.5	...	...	5:44	**6:19**
31	S	12:33	9.4	**12:41**	10.5	6:28	**7:00**

Standard Time

DAY OF MONTH	DAY OF WEEK	FEBRUARY HIGH a.m.	Ht.	p.m.	Ht.	LOW a.m.	p.m.
1	M	1:15	9.7	**1:27**	10.4	7:14	**7:44**
2	T	1:59	9.8	**2:16**	10.0	8:04	**8:31**
3	W	2:47	9.9	**3:11**	9.6	8:59	**9:22**
4	T	3:41	9.9	**4:12**	9.1	9:58	**10:17**
5	F	4:38	9.9	**5:17**	8.7	11:01	**11:18**
6	S	5:40	9.8	**6:28**	8.5	...	**12:10**
7	S	6:47	9.8	**7:38**	8.5	12:24	**1:20**
8	M	7:53	10.0	**8:41**	8.7	1:32	**2:25**
9	T	8:53	10.2	**9:37**	8.9	2:34	**3:23**
10	W	9:47	10.4	**10:28**	9.2	3:30	**4:14**
11	T	10:38	10.5	**11:15**	9.3	4:22	**5:02**
12	F	11:25	10.4	**11:58**	9.4	5:10	**5:46**
13	S	...	...	**12:08**	10.2	5:55	**6:26**
14	S	12:39	9.4	**12:50**	9.9	6:37	**7:04**
15	M	1:17	9.3	**1:31**	9.4	7:19	**7:42**
16	T	1:56	9.1	**2:13**	8.9	8:02	**8:20**
17	W	2:36	8.9	**2:59**	8.4	8:47	**9:01**
18	T	3:19	8.7	**3:48**	8.0	9:35	**9:46**
19	F	4:05	8.5	**4:42**	7.6	10:27	**10:35**
20	S	4:56	8.4	**5:40**	7.3	11:23	**11:29**
21	S	5:52	8.3	**6:43**	7.3	...	**12:25**
22	M	6:52	8.5	**7:42**	7.5	12:29	**1:26**
23	T	7:49	8.8	**8:33**	7.8	1:28	**2:19**
24	W	8:39	9.3	**9:19**	8.3	2:21	**3:06**
25	T	9:25	9.8	**10:02**	8.8	3:08	**3:48**
26	F	10:10	10.2	**10:43**	9.4	3:53	**4:30**
27	S	10:54	10.6	**11:24**	9.9	4:38	**5:11**
28	S	11:38	10.8	...	...	5:23	**5:52**

Dates when Ht. of **Low** Water is below Mean Lower Low with Ht. of lowest given for each period and Date of lowest in ( ):

January:
1st–5th: -0.5' (2nd)
9th–16th: -1.3' (13th)
28th–31st: -1.0' (31st)

February:
1st–3rd: -0.9' (1st)
8th–14th: -0.9' (11th)
25th–28th: -1.2' (28th)

Average Rise and Fall 9.1 ft.

When a high tide exceeds avg. ht., the *following* low tide will be lower than avg.

2021 HIGH & LOW WATER PORTLAND, ME

43°39.4'N, 70°14.8'W

***Daylight Time starts March 14 at 2 a.m.** **Daylight Saving Time**

DAY OF MONTH	DAY OF WEEK	MARCH						DAY OF MONTH	DAY OF WEEK	APRIL					
		HIGH				LOW				HIGH				LOW	
		a.m.	Ht.	**p.m.**	Ht.	a.m.	**p.m.**			a.m.	Ht.	**p.m.**	Ht.	a.m.	**p.m.**
1	**M**	12:06	10.3	**12:23**	10.8	6:09	**6:35**	1	**T**	2:10	11.3	**2:47**	10.1	8:30	**8:46**
2	**T**	12:48	10.6	**1:10**	10.6	6:57	**7:19**	2	**F**	3:01	10.9	**3:44**	9.6	9:26	**9:42**
3	**W**	1:33	10.6	**2:01**	10.1	7:47	**8:07**	3	**S**	3:58	10.5	**4:48**	9.1	10:27	**10:43**
4	**T**	2:22	10.5	**2:57**	9.6	8:42	**9:00**	4	**S**	5:02	10.0	**5:56**	8.6	11:33	**11:50**
5	**F**	3:17	10.3	**3:59**	9.0	9:41	**9:58**	5	**M**	6:11	9.6	**7:06**	8.5	...	**12:43**
6	**S**	4:18	9.9	**5:06**	8.6	10:46	**11:02**	6	**T**	7:23	9.3	**8:14**	8.6	1:03	**1:54**
7	**S**	5:24	9.6	**6:18**	8.3	11:57	...	7	**W**	8:31	9.3	**9:14**	8.8	2:15	**2:58**
8	**M**	6:36	9.5	**7:29**	8.4	12:13	**1:10**	8	**T**	9:30	9.4	**10:05**	9.1	3:17	**3:51**
9	**T**	7:44	9.6	**8:31**	8.6	1:25	**2:15**	9	**F**	10:21	9.6	**10:49**	9.4	4:10	**4:37**
10	**W**	8:45	9.8	**9:25**	8.9	2:28	**3:11**	10	**S**	11:07	9.6	**11:29**	9.6	4:56	**5:17**
11	**T**	9:38	10.0	**10:13**	9.2	3:23	**4:00**	11	**S**	11:49	9.5	...	...	5:38	**5:54**
12	**F**	10:26	10.1	**10:55**	9.4	4:12	**4:43**	12	**M**	12:05	9.7	**12:28**	9.4	6:17	**6:28**
13	**S**	11:09	10.0	**11:34**	9.6	4:56	**5:23**	13	**T**	12:39	9.8	**1:04**	9.2	6:53	**7:00**
14	**S**	...	...	***12:49**	9.8	*6:37	***6:58**	14	**W**	1:11	9.7	**1:40**	8.9	7:27	**7:33**
15	**M**	1:10	9.6	**1:27**	9.6	7:15	**7:32**	15	**T**	1:43	9.6	**2:17**	8.7	8:02	**8:07**
16	**T**	1:44	9.5	**2:04**	9.2	7:53	**8:06**	16	**F**	2:17	9.4	**2:56**	8.4	8:39	**8:45**
17	**W**	2:17	9.4	**2:42**	8.8	8:30	**8:41**	17	**S**	2:55	9.1	**3:38**	8.1	9:20	**9:27**
18	**T**	2:53	9.2	**3:23**	8.4	9:10	**9:19**	18	**S**	3:38	8.9	**4:26**	7.8	10:06	**10:15**
19	**F**	3:31	8.9	**4:09**	8.0	9:53	**10:02**	19	**M**	4:27	8.8	**5:19**	7.7	10:57	**11:07**
20	**S**	4:16	8.7	**4:59**	7.7	10:41	**10:50**	20	**T**	5:22	8.7	**6:15**	7.8	11:52	...
21	**S**	5:06	8.5	**5:55**	7.4	11:34	**11:43**	21	**W**	6:21	8.7	**7:13**	8.1	12:05	**12:50**
22	**M**	6:02	8.4	**6:56**	7.4	...	**12:33**	22	**T**	7:23	9.0	**8:09**	8.6	1:07	**1:48**
23	**T**	7:04	8.5	**7:57**	7.6	12:43	**1:36**	23	**F**	8:23	9.4	**9:00**	9.3	2:08	**2:42**
24	**W**	8:06	8.8	**8:52**	8.1	1:45	**2:34**	24	**S**	9:19	9.8	**9:48**	10.0	3:05	**3:33**
25	**T**	9:02	9.3	**9:41**	8.7	2:44	**3:25**	25	**S**	10:12	10.2	**10:35**	10.8	3:58	**4:20**
26	**F**	9:53	9.8	**10:25**	9.4	3:37	**4:11**	26	**M**	11:03	10.6	**11:21**	11.3	4:49	**5:07**
27	**S**	10:41	10.3	**11:09**	10.1	4:25	**4:55**	27	**T**	11:54	10.7	...	...	5:39	**5:55**
28	**S**	11:28	10.7	**11:52**	10.7	5:13	**5:39**	28	**W**	12:09	11.7	**12:46**	10.7	6:30	**6:45**
29	**M**	...	...	**12:16**	10.9	6:01	**6:23**	29	**T**	12:58	11.8	**1:39**	10.4	7:22	**7:35**
30	**T**	12:36	11.1	**1:04**	10.9	6:49	**7:09**	30	**F**	1:49	11.6	**2:33**	10.0	8:15	**8:28**
31	**W**	1:22	11.3	**1:54**	10.6	7:39	**7:56**								

Dates when Ht. of **Low** Water is below Mean Lower Low with Ht. of lowest given for each period and Date of lowest in ( ):

1st–5th: -1.2' (1st)
10th–13th: -0.4' (12th)
26th–31st: -1.7' (31st)

1st–3rd: -1.5' (1st)
24th–30th: -1.9' (28th, 29th)

Average Rise and Fall 9.1 ft.

When a high tide exceeds avg. ht., the *following* low tide will be lower than avg.

2021 HIGH & LOW WATER
PORTLAND, ME
43°39.4'N, 70°14.8'W

		Daylight Saving Time								Daylight Saving Time					
DAY OF MONTH	DAY OF WEEK	MAY						DAY OF MONTH	DAY OF WEEK	JUNE					
		HIGH				LOW				HIGH				LOW	
		a.m.	Ht.	**p.m.**	Ht.	a.m.	**p.m.**			a.m.	Ht.	**p.m.**	Ht.	a.m.	**p.m.**
1	**S**	2:44	11.1	**3:32**	9.6	9:12	**9:26**	1	**T**	4:29	10.0	**5:19**	9.1	10:56	**11:17**
2	**S**	3:42	10.6	**4:36**	9.2	10:13	**10:29**	2	**W**	5:31	9.5	**6:18**	9.0	11:55	...
3	**M**	4:47	10.0	**5:41**	8.9	11:17	**11:37**	3	**T**	6:33	9.1	**7:15**	9.1	12:22	**12:53**
4	**T**	5:54	9.5	**6:47**	8.8	...	**12:23**	4	**F**	7:34	8.8	**8:09**	9.2	1:26	**1:49**
5	**W**	7:02	9.2	**7:50**	8.9	12:47	**1:29**	5	**S**	8:33	8.6	**8:58**	9.4	2:26	**2:41**
6	**T**	8:07	9.1	**8:47**	9.1	1:55	**2:29**	6	**S**	9:25	8.6	**9:42**	9.5	3:19	**3:27**
7	**F**	9:06	9.1	**9:36**	9.3	2:56	**3:20**	7	**M**	10:13	8.5	**10:23**	9.6	4:06	**4:09**
8	**S**	9:57	9.1	**10:19**	9.6	3:48	**4:05**	8	**T**	10:57	8.5	**11:01**	9.7	4:48	**4:48**
9	**S**	10:43	9.1	**10:57**	9.7	4:34	**4:45**	9	**W**	11:39	8.5	**11:39**	9.8	5:28	**5:25**
10	**M**	11:25	9.0	**11:34**	9.8	5:15	**5:22**	10	**T**	...	...	**12:19**	8.5	6:05	**6:02**
11	**T**	...	...	**12:04**	8.9	5:53	**5:56**	11	**F**	12:15	9.8	**12:57**	8.5	6:42	**6:38**
12	**W**	12:08	9.8	**12:42**	8.8	6:29	**6:30**	12	**S**	12:51	9.8	**1:35**	8.4	7:18	**7:16**
13	**T**	12:41	9.8	**1:19**	8.7	7:04	**7:04**	13	**S**	1:28	9.7	**2:12**	8.4	7:55	**7:55**
14	**F**	1:15	9.7	**1:55**	8.5	7:39	**7:40**	14	**M**	2:06	9.7	**2:52**	8.4	8:34	**8:37**
15	**S**	1:50	9.5	**2:33**	8.3	8:16	**8:18**	15	**T**	2:48	9.6	**3:34**	8.5	9:15	**9:24**
16	**S**	2:27	9.4	**3:14**	8.2	8:55	**9:00**	16	**W**	3:34	9.5	**4:20**	8.7	10:01	**10:15**
17	**M**	3:10	9.2	**3:59**	8.1	9:39	**9:47**	17	**T**	4:25	9.4	**5:09**	9.0	10:48	**11:10**
18	**T**	3:57	9.1	**4:49**	8.1	10:27	**10:39**	18	**F**	5:19	9.4	**6:00**	9.4	11:38	...
19	**W**	4:50	9.1	**5:40**	8.4	11:18	**11:35**	19	**S**	6:17	9.3	**6:53**	9.8	12:08	**12:31**
20	**T**	5:47	9.1	**6:34**	8.7	...	**12:11**	20	**S**	7:19	9.3	**7:49**	10.3	1:09	**1:28**
21	**F**	6:46	9.2	**7:28**	9.2	12:34	**1:06**	21	**M**	8:22	9.4	**8:45**	10.8	2:11	**2:25**
22	**S**	7:48	9.4	**8:22**	9.9	1:36	**2:02**	22	**T**	9:24	9.5	**9:40**	11.2	3:11	**3:22**
23	**S**	8:48	9.7	**9:14**	10.6	2:36	**2:56**	23	**W**	10:22	9.7	**10:34**	11.5	4:08	**4:17**
24	**M**	9:45	10.0	**10:04**	11.2	3:33	**3:48**	24	**T**	11:19	9.8	**11:29**	11.6	5:04	**5:12**
25	**T**	10:40	10.2	**10:54**	11.6	4:27	**4:39**	25	**F**	...	...	**12:16**	9.9	5:59	**6:07**
26	**W**	11:35	10.3	**11:46**	11.9	5:20	**5:31**	26	**S**	12:24	11.6	**1:10**	9.8	6:53	**7:01**
27	**T**	...	...	**12:30**	10.3	6:13	**6:23**	27	**S**	1:18	11.4	**2:04**	9.7	7:46	**7:56**
28	**F**	12:38	11.8	**1:25**	10.1	7:07	**7:17**	28	**M**	2:11	11.0	**2:58**	9.6	8:39	**8:51**
29	**S**	1:32	11.6	**2:20**	9.9	8:01	**8:12**	29	**T**	3:06	10.5	**3:53**	9.4	9:32	**9:49**
30	**S**	2:27	11.1	**3:18**	9.6	8:57	**9:10**	30	**W**	4:03	9.9	**4:47**	9.3	10:26	**10:49**
31	**M**	3:26	10.6	**4:18**	9.3	9:56	**10:12**								

Dates when Ht. of **Low** Water is below Mean Lower Low with Ht. of lowest given for each period and Date of lowest in ( ):

1st–2nd: -1.2' (1st)
24th–31st: -1.9' (27th)

22nd–29th: -1.5' (25th, 26th)

Average Rise and Fall 9.1 ft.

When a high tide exceeds avg. ht., the *following* low tide will be lower than avg.

2021 HIGH & LOW WATER
PORTLAND, ME
43°39.4'N, 70°14.8'W

Daylight Saving Time

DAY OF MONTH	DAY OF WEEK	JULY HIGH a.m.	Ht.	p.m.	Ht.	JULY LOW a.m.	p.m.
1	**T**	5:01	9.3	**5:41**	9.2	11:18	**11:48**
2	**F**	5:57	8.8	**6:33**	9.1	...	**12:10**
3	**S**	6:55	8.4	**7:24**	9.1	12:48	**1:02**
4	**S**	7:53	8.2	**8:15**	9.2	1:47	**1:54**
5	**M**	8:49	8.1	**9:03**	9.3	2:43	**2:45**
6	**T**	9:40	8.1	**9:47**	9.4	3:33	**3:31**
7	**W**	10:27	8.2	**10:30**	9.5	4:18	**4:14**
8	**T**	11:11	8.3	**11:10**	9.7	5:00	**4:55**
9	**F**	11:53	8.4	**11:50**	9.8	5:39	**5:34**
10	**S**	...	...	**12:32**	8.5	6:17	**6:13**
11	**S**	12:29	9.9	**1:10**	8.6	6:54	**6:53**
12	**M**	1:07	10.0	**1:48**	8.7	7:31	**7:33**
13	**T**	1:46	10.0	**2:26**	8.9	8:10	**8:16**
14	**W**	2:27	10.0	**3:07**	9.1	8:50	**9:02**
15	**T**	3:13	9.9	**3:51**	9.4	9:34	**9:53**
16	**F**	4:03	9.7	**4:39**	9.6	10:20	**10:48**
17	**S**	4:57	9.4	**5:30**	9.9	11:10	**11:45**
18	**S**	5:56	9.2	**6:25**	10.1	...	**12:03**
19	**M**	6:58	9.0	**7:23**	10.4	12:47	**1:01**
20	**T**	8:05	9.0	**8:24**	10.6	1:51	**2:02**
21	**W**	9:09	9.1	**9:24**	10.9	2:55	**3:04**
22	**T**	10:10	9.3	**10:21**	11.1	3:56	**4:02**
23	**F**	11:07	9.4	**11:17**	11.2	4:52	**4:59**
24	**S**	...	...	**12:02**	9.6	5:47	**5:54**
25	**S**	12:11	11.2	**12:54**	9.7	6:39	**6:47**
26	**M**	1:03	11.1	**1:44**	9.7	7:28	**7:38**
27	**T**	1:53	10.7	**2:32**	9.6	8:15	**8:29**
28	**W**	2:42	10.2	**3:20**	9.5	9:02	**9:21**
29	**T**	3:33	9.6	**4:08**	9.3	9:48	**10:14**
30	**F**	4:25	9.1	**4:56**	9.2	10:35	**11:08**
31	**S**	5:18	8.6	**5:45**	9.0	11:23	...

Daylight Saving Time

DAY OF MONTH	DAY OF WEEK	AUGUST HIGH a.m.	Ht.	p.m.	Ht.	AUGUST LOW a.m.	p.m.
1	**S**	6:14	8.1	**6:35**	8.9	12:03	**12:12**
2	**M**	7:10	7.8	**7:28**	8.9	1:01	**1:05**
3	**T**	8:09	7.7	**8:21**	8.9	2:00	**2:00**
4	**W**	9:04	7.8	**9:12**	9.1	2:55	**2:53**
5	**T**	9:54	8.0	**9:58**	9.4	3:44	**3:41**
6	**F**	10:39	8.2	**10:42**	9.6	4:28	**4:24**
7	**S**	11:22	8.4	**11:23**	9.9	5:09	**5:06**
8	**S**	...	...	**12:02**	8.7	5:48	**5:47**
9	**M**	12:03	10.1	**12:40**	9.0	6:25	**6:28**
10	**T**	12:43	10.3	**1:18**	9.3	7:03	**7:10**
11	**W**	1:24	10.4	**1:56**	9.6	7:42	**7:54**
12	**T**	2:07	10.3	**2:37**	9.9	8:22	**8:41**
13	**F**	2:53	10.1	**3:22**	10.0	9:06	**9:32**
14	**S**	3:44	9.8	**4:11**	10.2	9:54	**10:28**
15	**S**	4:40	9.4	**5:05**	10.2	10:46	**11:27**
16	**M**	5:40	9.1	**6:03**	10.2	11:42	...
17	**T**	6:46	8.8	**7:06**	10.2	12:30	**12:43**
18	**W**	7:55	8.7	**8:12**	10.3	1:38	**1:49**
19	**T**	9:01	8.8	**9:16**	10.5	2:46	**2:55**
20	**F**	10:01	9.1	**10:14**	10.7	3:47	**3:55**
21	**S**	10:56	9.3	**11:08**	10.8	4:42	**4:50**
22	**S**	11:47	9.6	**11:59**	10.8	5:33	**5:42**
23	**M**	...	...	**12:34**	9.7	6:21	**6:32**
24	**T**	12:47	10.6	**1:18**	9.8	7:05	**7:18**
25	**W**	1:32	10.3	**2:00**	9.7	7:46	**8:03**
26	**T**	2:16	9.8	**2:41**	9.6	8:27	**8:49**
27	**F**	3:01	9.3	**3:23**	9.3	9:07	**9:35**
28	**S**	3:48	8.8	**4:07**	9.1	9:50	**10:25**
29	**S**	4:38	8.3	**4:55**	8.9	10:35	**11:17**
30	**M**	5:31	7.9	**5:45**	8.7	11:24	...
31	**T**	6:28	7.7	**6:40**	8.6	12:12	**12:17**

Dates when Ht. of **Low** Water is below Mean Lower Low with Ht. of lowest given for each period and Date of lowest in ( ):

21st–28th: -1.1' (24th, 25th)

10th–13th: -0.5' (12th)
20th–25th: -0.7' (22nd, 23rd)

Average Rise and Fall 9.1 ft.

When a high tide exceeds avg. ht., the *following* low tide will be lower than avg.

2021 HIGH & LOW WATER
PORTLAND, ME
43°39.4'N, 70°14.8'W

DAY OF MONTH	DAY OF WEEK	SEPTEMBER (Daylight Saving Time)						DAY OF MONTH	DAY OF WEEK	OCTOBER (Daylight Saving Time)					
		HIGH				LOW				HIGH				LOW	
		a.m.	Ht.	**p.m.**	Ht.	a.m.	**p.m.**			a.m.	Ht.	**p.m.**	Ht.	a.m.	**p.m.**
1	**W**	7:28	7.6	**7:38**	8.7	1:12	**1:15**	1	**F**	7:45	7.7	**7:52**	8.8	1:24	**1:32**
2	**T**	8:26	7.7	**8:34**	8.9	2:12	**2:13**	2	**S**	8:37	8.1	**8:46**	9.2	2:20	**2:29**
3	**F**	9:18	7.9	**9:24**	9.3	3:05	**3:06**	3	**S**	9:24	8.6	**9:35**	9.7	3:09	**3:19**
4	**S**	10:03	8.3	**10:10**	9.7	3:51	**3:53**	4	**M**	10:06	9.2	**10:21**	10.1	3:52	**4:06**
5	**S**	10:45	8.7	**10:53**	10.1	4:33	**4:36**	5	**T**	10:47	9.9	**11:06**	10.4	4:34	**4:51**
6	**M**	11:25	9.2	**11:35**	10.4	5:12	**5:19**	6	**W**	11:28	10.5	**11:51**	10.6	5:15	**5:37**
7	**T**	...	...	**12:04**	9.7	5:51	**6:02**	7	**T**	...	...	**12:11**	10.9	5:58	**6:24**
8	**W**	12:17	10.6	**12:44**	10.1	6:31	**6:47**	8	**F**	12:38	10.7	**12:54**	11.2	6:42	**7:12**
9	**T**	1:01	10.6	**1:24**	10.4	7:11	**7:33**	9	**S**	1:26	10.5	**1:41**	11.3	7:28	**8:02**
10	**F**	1:46	10.5	**2:07**	10.6	7:54	**8:21**	10	**S**	2:17	10.2	**2:31**	11.1	8:17	**8:56**
11	**S**	2:34	10.2	**2:54**	10.6	8:40	**9:13**	11	**M**	3:13	9.7	**3:26**	10.7	9:11	**9:55**
12	**S**	3:27	9.8	**3:47**	10.5	9:31	**10:10**	12	**T**	4:15	9.3	**4:29**	10.3	10:11	**11:00**
13	**M**	4:26	9.3	**4:45**	10.3	10:26	**11:12**	13	**W**	5:22	8.9	**5:37**	9.9	11:16	...
14	**T**	5:30	8.9	**5:48**	10.1	11:27	...	14	**T**	6:31	8.8	**6:47**	9.7	12:08	**12:26**
15	**W**	6:39	8.7	**6:57**	9.9	12:19	**12:34**	15	**F**	7:39	8.8	**7:56**	9.7	1:18	**1:38**
16	**T**	7:49	8.7	**8:06**	10.0	1:29	**1:44**	16	**S**	8:41	9.1	**8:59**	9.8	2:23	**2:44**
17	**F**	8:54	8.9	**9:10**	10.1	2:37	**2:51**	17	**S**	9:35	9.4	**9:53**	9.8	3:20	**3:40**
18	**S**	9:51	9.2	**10:06**	10.3	3:37	**3:50**	18	**M**	10:22	9.7	**10:42**	9.8	4:09	**4:30**
19	**S**	10:42	9.5	**10:57**	10.4	4:29	**4:42**	19	**T**	11:04	9.9	**11:26**	9.7	4:52	**5:15**
20	**M**	11:28	9.7	**11:44**	10.3	5:15	**5:30**	20	**W**	11:43	10.0	...	...	5:31	**5:56**
21	**T**	...	...	**12:10**	9.9	5:58	**6:15**	21	**T**	12:08	9.6	**12:19**	9.9	6:08	**6:35**
22	**W**	12:28	10.1	**12:49**	9.9	6:37	**6:57**	22	**F**	12:47	9.3	**12:54**	9.8	6:43	**7:11**
23	**T**	1:09	9.8	**1:26**	9.8	7:14	**7:37**	23	**S**	1:25	9.0	**1:28**	9.6	7:17	**7:48**
24	**F**	1:49	9.4	**2:02**	9.6	7:50	**8:17**	24	**S**	2:03	8.7	**2:03**	9.4	7:53	**8:26**
25	**S**	2:30	9.0	**2:40**	9.4	8:27	**8:58**	25	**M**	2:43	8.4	**2:42**	9.1	8:31	**9:08**
26	**S**	3:12	8.6	**3:20**	9.1	9:07	**9:43**	26	**T**	3:26	8.1	**3:26**	8.9	9:14	**9:55**
27	**M**	4:00	8.1	**4:06**	8.8	9:51	**10:32**	27	**W**	4:16	7.8	**4:16**	8.7	10:02	**10:46**
28	**T**	4:51	7.8	**4:58**	8.6	10:40	**11:26**	28	**T**	5:09	7.7	**5:11**	8.6	10:55	**11:40**
29	**W**	5:47	7.6	**5:54**	8.5	11:34	...	29	**F**	6:04	7.7	**6:09**	8.6	11:52	...
30	**T**	6:45	7.6	**6:53**	8.6	12:24	**12:32**	30	**S**	6:59	8.0	**7:08**	8.8	12:36	**12:51**
								31	**S**	7:52	8.4	**8:05**	9.1	1:31	**1:50**

Dates when Ht. of **Low** Water is below Mean Lower Low with Ht. of lowest given for each period and Date of lowest in ( ):

7th–12th: -0.7' (9th, 10th)
19th–21st: -0.3' (19th, 20th)

5th–12th: -1.3' (8th, 9th)

Average Rise and Fall 9.1 ft.

When a high tide exceeds avg. ht., the *following* low tide will be lower than avg.

2021 HIGH & LOW WATER
PORTLAND, ME
43°39.4'N, 70°14.8'W

***Standard Time starts Nov. 7 at 2 a.m.** **Standard Time**

DAY OF MONTH	DAY OF WEEK	NOVEMBER						DAY OF MONTH	DAY OF WEEK	DECEMBER					
		HIGH				LOW				HIGH				LOW	
		a.m.	Ht.	**p.m.**	Ht.	a.m.	**p.m.**			a.m.	Ht.	**p.m.**	Ht.	a.m.	**p.m.**
1	**M**	8:42	9.1	**8:59**	9.5	2:23	**2:45**	1	**W**	7:50	10.2	**8:20**	9.6	1:31	**2:08**
2	**T**	9:27	9.8	**9:49**	9.9	3:11	**3:36**	2	**T**	8:38	10.8	**9:13**	9.9	2:22	**3:00**
3	**W**	10:11	10.5	**10:38**	10.3	3:56	**4:24**	3	**F**	9:27	11.4	**10:06**	10.1	3:12	**3:52**
4	**T**	10:55	11.1	**11:27**	10.5	4:41	**5:13**	4	**S**	10:18	11.7	**11:00**	10.2	4:03	**4:44**
5	**F**	11:41	11.5	**...**	...	5:28	**6:02**	5	**S**	11:09	11.8	**11:54**	10.1	4:54	**5:37**
6	**S**	12:17	10.5	**12:29**	11.7	6:16	**6:53**	6	**M**	...	...	**12:02**	11.7	5:47	**6:31**
7	**S**	1:09	10.4	***12:19**	11.6	*6:05	***6:45**	7	**T**	12:48	10.0	**12:57**	11.4	6:41	**7:26**
8	**M**	1:02	10.1	**1:12**	11.3	6:58	**7:40**	8	**W**	1:44	9.7	**1:55**	10.9	7:38	**8:23**
9	**T**	1:59	9.7	**2:10**	10.8	7:54	**8:40**	9	**T**	2:44	9.4	**2:56**	10.3	8:39	**9:24**
10	**W**	3:02	9.3	**3:14**	10.3	8:56	**9:45**	10	**F**	3:46	9.2	**4:01**	9.7	9:44	**10:25**
11	**T**	4:08	9.0	**4:22**	9.8	10:03	**10:51**	11	**S**	4:48	9.1	**5:05**	9.2	10:51	**11:25**
12	**F**	5:15	8.9	**5:31**	9.5	11:13	**11:57**	12	**S**	5:48	9.1	**6:10**	8.8	11:58	**...**
13	**S**	6:19	9.0	**6:38**	9.3	...	**12:23**	13	**M**	6:45	9.1	**7:12**	8.6	12:24	**1:02**
14	**S**	7:18	9.2	**7:39**	9.2	12:59	**1:28**	14	**T**	7:38	9.3	**8:08**	8.5	1:20	**2:00**
15	**M**	8:10	9.5	**8:34**	9.2	1:54	**2:24**	15	**W**	8:25	9.4	**8:58**	8.5	2:10	**2:49**
16	**T**	8:56	9.7	**9:22**	9.2	2:42	**3:12**	16	**T**	9:08	9.6	**9:43**	8.5	2:55	**3:34**
17	**W**	9:37	9.8	**10:06**	9.1	3:25	**3:56**	17	**F**	9:48	9.6	**10:25**	8.5	3:36	**4:15**
18	**T**	10:15	9.9	**10:47**	9.0	4:03	**4:36**	18	**S**	10:26	9.7	**11:05**	8.5	4:14	**4:53**
19	**F**	10:51	9.9	**11:26**	8.9	4:40	**5:13**	19	**S**	11:03	9.7	**11:43**	8.5	4:51	**5:29**
20	**S**	11:26	9.8	**...**	...	5:15	**5:49**	20	**M**	11:39	9.6	**...**	...	5:27	**6:05**
21	**S**	12:03	8.7	**12:01**	9.6	5:50	**6:25**	21	**T**	12:20	8.4	**12:15**	9.6	6:03	**6:40**
22	**M**	12:40	8.5	**12:36**	9.5	6:25	**7:01**	22	**W**	12:56	8.3	**12:52**	9.5	6:40	**7:17**
23	**T**	1:18	8.3	**1:14**	9.3	7:03	**7:41**	23	**T**	1:33	8.3	**1:30**	9.4	7:19	**7:56**
24	**W**	1:59	8.1	**1:55**	9.1	7:44	**8:24**	24	**F**	2:13	8.3	**2:13**	9.2	8:03	**8:38**
25	**T**	2:44	7.9	**2:42**	8.9	8:30	**9:11**	25	**S**	2:56	8.4	**3:01**	9.1	8:51	**9:23**
26	**F**	3:32	7.9	**3:33**	8.8	9:21	**10:00**	26	**S**	3:43	8.6	**3:53**	8.9	9:43	**10:12**
27	**S**	4:23	8.1	**4:28**	8.8	10:16	**10:51**	27	**M**	4:32	8.9	**4:50**	8.8	10:40	**11:03**
28	**S**	5:14	8.4	**5:26**	8.8	11:13	**11:44**	28	**T**	5:24	9.3	**5:50**	8.8	11:39	**11:58**
29	**M**	6:06	8.9	**6:25**	9.0	...	**12:13**	29	**W**	6:19	9.7	**6:54**	8.9	...	**12:41**
30	**T**	6:58	9.5	**7:24**	9.3	12:38	**1:12**	30	**T**	7:16	10.3	**7:56**	9.1	12:56	**1:43**
								31	**F**	8:12	10.8	**8:54**	9.2	1:54	**2:41**

Dates when Ht. of **Low** Water is below Mean Lower Low with Ht. of lowest given for each period and Date of lowest in ( ):

3rd–10th: -1.8' (6th)

1st–9th: -2.0' (5th)
30th–31st: -1.0' (31st)

Average Rise and Fall 9.1 ft.

When a high tide exceeds avg. ht., the *following* low tide will be lower than avg.

Smarter Boating in Currents

If your vessel is a sailboat or a displacement powerboat your normal cruising speed is probably under 10 knots. In this range, current can become a significant factor. (See the Current Tables for the Cape Cod Canal and the Race, and the Current Diagrams for Vineyard Sound, showing some currents of 4 to 5 knots.) You can save a remarkable amount of time and, if under power, a great deal of fuel expense by using the current for maximum efficiency.

SAIL: Slow vs. Flow

The arithmetic is simple. If your 35' sailboat has a boat speed (BS) through the water of 5 knots under power or sail, then a 2-knot current directly against you means your speed made good (SMG) is 3 knots, and the same current going with you boosts that to 7 knots. Tacking into or with a current changes the simple arithmetic shown here (see Coping With Currents, p. 58.) The time difference can be great: a destination 10 miles away is 3 hours 20 minutes against the current, but only 1 hour 26 minutes with the current. Leaving earlier or later to go with the current leaves more time (almost 2 hours) to relax either at your departure point or destination. Of course if you're just out for a sail on a beautiful day, the arithmetic may not matter! If your sailboat is under power, keep reading.

POWER: Ego vs. Eco

As long as speed thrills, as we know it does, some boaters will demand it. But the trend is headed the other way. Today it is more about being economical, not egomaniacal. By far the most dramatic saving in fuel cost, or nautical miles per gallon (NMPG), comes from cutting back on the throttle; however, there are further savings from using the current to your advantage, especially with slower vessels.

Consider a trawler that burns 10 gallons of fuel per hour at a speed of 8 knots. If the cost of fuel is, say, $4 per gallon, that's $40 per hour. For a destination 24 nautical miles away, going directly against a current of 2 knots, her SMG is only 6 knots, requiring 4 hours for the trip, and costing her owner $160. If the skipper had gone with a current of 2 knots, then her SMG would be 10 knots, her transit time 2 hours 24 minutes, with a fuel expense of only $96. The time saved, 1 hour 36 minutes, allows more time for relaxation (TFR) either before departure or after arrival, and the $64 saved could buy a nice meal ashore. That's smarter boating!

Consult the table below for SMG and time/fuel consequences in currents.

SMG *WITH* CURRENT, and Time/Fuel GAINS

Current Speed Kts *With* +		**+1 kt**	**+2 kts**	**+3 kts**	**+4 kts**
Boat Speed: **4 kts**	SMG =	**5 kts**	**6 kts**	**7 kts**	**8 kts**
Time/Fuel **Gain**		**20%**	**33%**	**43%**	**50%**
Boat Speed: **6 kts**	SMG =	**7 kts**	**8 kts**	**9 kts**	**10 kts**
Time/Fuel **Gain**		**14%**	**25%**	**33%**	**40%**
Boat Speed: **8 kts**	SMG =	**9 kts**	**10 kts**	**11 kts**	**12 kts**
Time/Fuel **Gain**		**11%**	**20%**	**28%**	**33%**
Boat Speed: **10 kts**	SMG =	**11 kts**	**12 kts**	**13 kts**	**14 kts**
Time/Fuel **Gain**		**9%**	**17%**	**24%**	**29%**

SMG *AGAINST* CURRENT, and Time/Fuel LOSSES

Current Speed Kts *Against* -		**-1 kt**	**-2 kts**	**-3 kts**	**-4 kts**
Boat Speed: **4 kts**	SMG =	**3 kts**	**2 kts**	**1 kts**	**0 kts**
Time/Fuel **Loss**		**33%**	**100%**	**300%**	**---**
Boat Speed: **6 kts**	SMG =	**5 kts**	**4 kts**	**3 kts**	**2 kts**
Time/Fuel **Loss**		**20%**	**50%**	**100%**	**200%**
Boat Speed: **8 kts**	SMG =	**7 kts**	**6 kts**	**5 kts**	**4 kts**
Time/Fuel **Loss**		**14%**	**33%**	**60%**	**100%**
Boat Speed: **10 kts**	SMG =	**9 kts**	**8 kts**	**7 kts**	**6 kts**
Time/Fuel **Loss**		**11%**	**25%**	**43%**	**67%**

Boston Harbor Currents

This diagram shows the direction of the Flood Currents in Boston Harbor at the Maximum* Flood velocity, generally 3.5 hours after Low Water at Boston. The Ebb Currents flow in precisely the opposite direction (note one exception, shown by dotted arrow east of Winthrop), and reach these maximum velocities about 4 hours after High Water at Boston. The velocities of the Ebb Currents are about the same as those of the Flood Currents. Where the Ebb Current differs by .2 kts., the velocity of the Ebb is shown in parentheses.

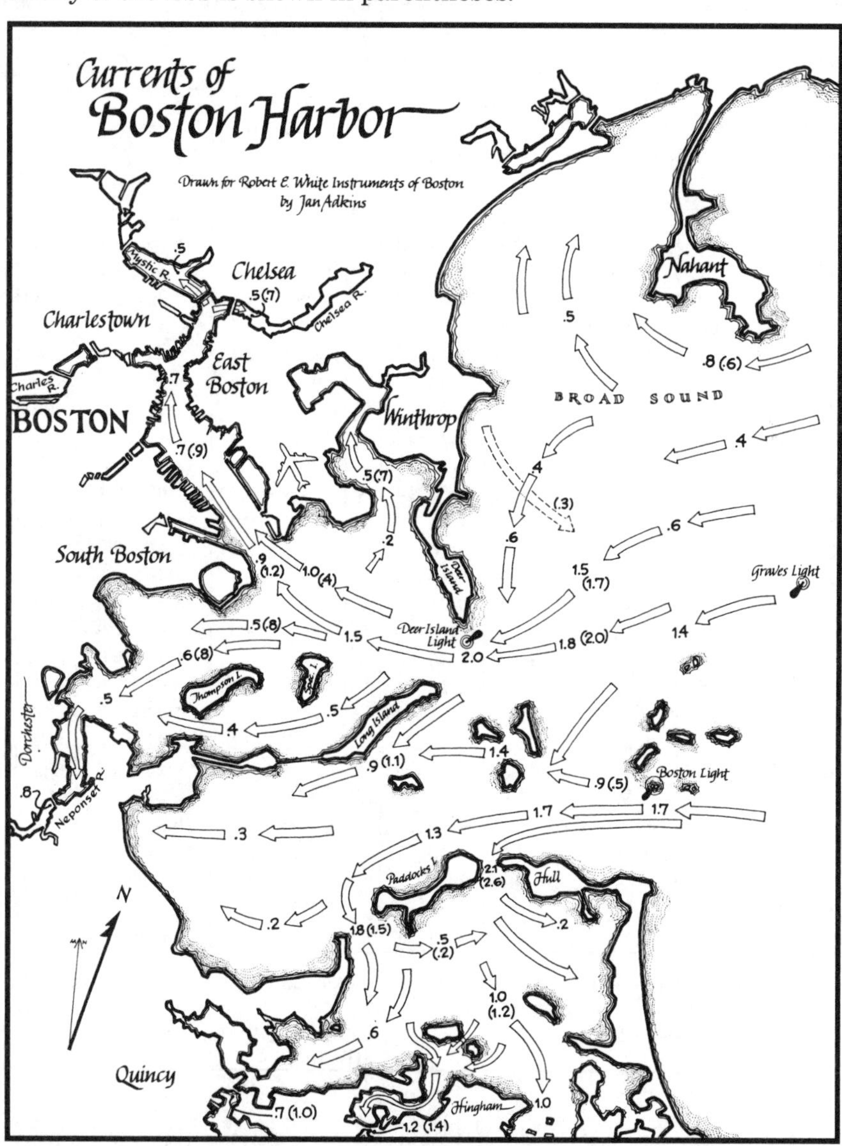

*The Velocities shown on this Current Diagram are the **maximums** normally encountered each month at Full Moon and at New Moon. At other times the velocities will be lower. As a rule of thumb, the velocities shown are those found on days when High Water at Boston is 11.0' to 11.5' (see Boston High Water Tables pp. 38-43). When the height of High Water is 10.5', subtract 10% from the velocities shown; at 10.0', subtract 20%; at 9.0', 30%; at 8.0', 40%; below 7.5', 50%.

2021 HIGH & LOW WATER
BOSTON, MA
42°21.3'N, 71°03'W

Standard Time

DAY OF MONTH	DAY OF WEEK	JANUARY					
		HIGH				LOW	
		a.m.	Ht.	**p.m.**	Ht.	a.m.	**p.m.**
1	**F**	12:30	8.9	**12:31**	10.4	6:22	**6:58**
2	**S**	1:11	9.0	**1:15**	10.4	7:05	**7:41**
3	**S**	1:53	9.1	**2:00**	10.3	7:52	**8:26**
4	**M**	2:39	9.3	**2:50**	10.1	8:42	**9:14**
5	**T**	3:28	9.5	**3:44**	9.8	9:37	**10:06**
6	**W**	4:20	9.7	**4:42**	9.5	10:35	**11:00**
7	**T**	5:16	9.9	**5:44**	9.3	11:36	**11:57**
8	**F**	6:13	10.2	**6:47**	9.1	...	**12:38**
9	**S**	7:12	10.5	**7:52**	9.1	12:55	**1:40**
10	**S**	8:11	10.7	**8:54**	9.2	1:54	**2:41**
11	**M**	9:08	11.0	**9:52**	9.4	2:52	**3:38**
12	**T**	10:02	11.1	**10:46**	9.5	3:47	**4:31**
13	**W**	10:54	11.1	**11:38**	9.5	4:40	**5:22**
14	**T**	11:45	11.0	...	...	5:31	**6:11**
15	**F**	12:27	9.5	**12:35**	10.8	6:20	**6:58**
16	**S**	1:14	9.4	**1:23**	10.4	7:09	**7:43**
17	**S**	2:00	9.3	**2:10**	9.9	7:57	**8:28**
18	**M**	2:45	9.1	**2:58**	9.3	8:46	**9:14**
19	**T**	3:32	8.9	**3:49**	8.8	9:38	**10:01**
20	**W**	4:20	8.8	**4:42**	8.4	10:31	**10:50**
21	**T**	5:09	8.7	**5:37**	8.0	11:26	**11:40**
22	**F**	6:00	8.7	**6:33**	7.8	...	**12:22**
23	**S**	6:52	8.8	**7:31**	7.8	12:32	**1:18**
24	**S**	7:45	9.0	**8:25**	7.9	1:24	**2:12**
25	**M**	8:34	9.3	**9:14**	8.1	2:15	**3:01**
26	**T**	9:20	9.6	**9:59**	8.4	3:03	**3:46**
27	**W**	10:03	10.0	**10:41**	8.7	3:49	**4:29**
28	**T**	10:45	10.3	**11:22**	9.0	4:32	**5:10**
29	**F**	11:27	10.6	...	...	5:16	**5:52**
30	**S**	12:03	9.3	**12:11**	10.7	6:00	**6:34**
31	**S**	12:45	9.6	**12:55**	10.8	6:45	**7:17**

Standard Time

DAY OF MONTH	DAY OF WEEK	FEBRUARY					
		HIGH				LOW	
		a.m.	Ht.	**p.m.**	Ht.	a.m.	**p.m.**
1	**M**	1:29	9.9	**1:42**	10.6	7:32	**8:01**
2	**T**	2:13	10.1	**2:31**	10.3	8:22	**8:49**
3	**W**	3:01	10.2	**3:25**	9.8	9:16	**9:40**
4	**T**	3:53	10.2	**4:23**	9.4	10:14	**10:35**
5	**F**	4:50	10.1	**5:26**	8.9	11:16	**11:34**
6	**S**	5:50	10.1	**6:33**	8.7	...	**12:20**
7	**S**	6:54	10.1	**7:41**	8.6	12:35	**1:25**
8	**M**	7:58	10.2	**8:47**	8.8	1:38	**2:29**
9	**T**	8:59	10.4	**9:44**	9.0	2:40	**3:28**
10	**W**	9:55	10.6	**10:36**	9.2	3:36	**4:20**
11	**T**	10:45	10.6	**11:23**	9.4	4:28	**5:08**
12	**F**	11:33	10.6	...	...	5:17	**5:52**
13	**S**	12:07	9.5	**12:17**	10.4	6:03	**6:34**
14	**S**	12:48	9.5	**1:00**	10.1	6:47	**7:14**
15	**M**	1:28	9.4	**1:42**	9.7	7:30	**7:54**
16	**T**	2:07	9.3	**2:25**	9.2	8:14	**8:34**
17	**W**	2:47	9.1	**3:10**	8.8	9:00	**9:17**
18	**T**	3:31	8.9	**3:59**	8.3	9:48	**10:04**
19	**F**	4:18	8.8	**4:52**	7.9	10:41	**10:54**
20	**S**	5:09	8.6	**5:48**	7.6	11:36	**11:46**
21	**S**	6:03	8.6	**6:47**	7.6	...	**12:32**
22	**M**	7:00	8.8	**7:45**	7.7	12:41	**1:30**
23	**T**	7:55	9.1	**8:38**	8.0	1:37	**2:24**
24	**W**	8:47	9.5	**9:26**	8.5	2:30	**3:13**
25	**T**	9:34	10.0	**10:09**	9.0	3:19	**3:58**
26	**F**	10:19	10.5	**10:51**	9.5	4:06	**4:41**
27	**S**	11:03	10.9	**11:34**	10.1	4:52	**5:24**
28	**S**	11:49	11.0	...	...	5:38	**6:07**

Dates when Ht. of **Low** Water is below Mean Lower Low with Ht. of lowest given for each period and Date of lowest in ( ):

1st–4th: -0.4' (1st–3rd)
9th–16th: -1.2' (13th)
28th–31st: -1.0' (31st)

1st–3rd: -0.9' (1st)
8th–14th: -0.7' (10th–12th)
26th–28th: -1.2' (28th)

Average Rise and Fall 9.5 ft.

When a high tide exceeds avg. ht., the *following* low tide will be lower than avg. Since there is a high degree of correlation between the height of High Water and the velocities of the Flood and Ebb Currents for that same day, we offer a rough rule of thumb for estimating the current velocities, for ALL the Current Charts and Diagrams in this book. **Rule of Thumb:** Refer to Boston High Water. If the height of High Water is 11.0' or over, use the Current Chart velocities as shown. When the height is 10.5', subtract 10%; at 10.0', subtract 20%; at 9.0', 30%; at 8.0', 40%; below 7.5', 50%.

2021 HIGH & LOW WATER
BOSTON, MA
42°21.3'N, 71°03'W

***Daylight Time starts March 14 at 2 a.m.** | **Daylight Saving Time**

DAY OF MONTH	DAY OF WEEK	MARCH HIGH a.m.	Ht.	**p.m.**	Ht.	LOW a.m.	**p.m.**	DAY OF MONTH	DAY OF WEEK	APRIL HIGH a.m.	Ht.	**p.m.**	Ht.	LOW a.m.	**p.m.**
1	M	12:18	10.5	**12:36**	11.0	6:25	**6:51**	1	T	2:24	11.6	**2:58**	10.4	8:45	**9:03**
2	T	1:01	10.8	**1:24**	10.8	7:13	**7:36**	2	F	3:14	11.3	**3:54**	9.9	9:40	**9:57**
3	W	1:47	10.9	**2:14**	10.4	8:03	**8:25**	3	S	4:09	10.8	**4:55**	9.3	10:38	**10:56**
4	T	2:36	10.8	**3:08**	9.9	8:57	**9:17**	4	S	5:11	10.3	**6:02**	8.9	11:42	...
5	F	3:30	10.6	**4:08**	9.3	9:56	**10:14**	5	M	6:18	9.8	**7:11**	8.7	12:01	**12:48**
6	S	4:29	10.2	**5:13**	8.8	10:58	**11:15**	6	T	7:28	9.6	**8:20**	8.7	1:06	**1:55**
7	S	5:33	9.9	**6:22**	8.5	...	**12:04**	7	W	8:37	9.5	**9:23**	9.0	2:14	**3:00**
8	M	6:41	9.8	**7:33**	8.5	12:20	**1:12**	8	T	9:39	9.6	**10:15**	9.3	3:18	**3:55**
9	T	7:49	9.8	**8:39**	8.7	1:26	**2:18**	9	F	10:31	9.8	**10:58**	9.6	4:13	**4:42**
10	W	8:52	9.9	**9:34**	9.1	2:30	**3:16**	10	S	11:15	9.8	**11:36**	9.8	5:00	**5:22**
11	T	9:46	10.1	**10:21**	9.3	3:27	**4:05**	11	S	11:56	9.8	...	...	5:42	**5:59**
12	F	10:33	10.2	**11:03**	9.6	4:16	**4:48**	12	M	12:12	9.9	**12:34**	9.7	6:21	**6:35**
13	S	11:17	10.2	**11:42**	9.7	5:01	**5:28**	13	T	12:46	10.0	**1:12**	9.5	6:59	**7:11**
14	S	...	...	***12:57**	10.0	*6:43	***7:06**	14	W	1:21	9.9	**1:50**	9.3	7:37	**7:48**
15	M	1:18	9.7	**1:36**	9.8	7:23	**7:43**	15	T	1:56	9.8	**2:29**	9.0	8:16	**8:26**
16	T	1:54	9.7	**2:15**	9.5	8:03	**8:20**	16	F	2:34	9.7	**3:09**	8.7	8:56	**9:05**
17	W	2:30	9.6	**2:55**	9.1	8:43	**8:58**	17	S	3:14	9.5	**3:53**	8.4	9:39	**9:49**
18	T	3:08	9.4	**3:37**	8.7	9:25	**9:38**	18	S	3:57	9.2	**4:41**	8.2	10:26	**10:37**
19	F	3:48	9.2	**4:22**	8.3	10:10	**10:23**	19	M	4:47	9.1	**5:33**	8.0	11:18	**11:31**
20	S	4:34	9.0	**5:13**	8.0	11:00	**11:12**	20	T	5:41	9.0	**6:28**	8.1	...	**12:12**
21	S	5:24	8.8	**6:08**	7.7	11:54	...	21	W	6:38	9.1	**7:24**	8.4	12:27	**1:08**
22	M	6:19	8.7	**7:05**	7.7	12:06	**12:50**	22	T	7:36	9.3	**8:18**	8.9	1:25	**2:03**
23	T	7:17	8.8	**8:03**	7.9	1:02	**1:47**	23	F	8:34	9.7	**9:10**	9.6	2:23	**2:56**
24	W	8:15	9.1	**8:59**	8.3	1:59	**2:43**	24	S	9:30	10.2	**9:58**	10.3	3:19	**3:47**
25	T	9:11	9.6	**9:49**	8.9	2:56	**3:35**	25	S	10:22	10.6	**10:45**	11.1	4:12	**4:36**
26	F	10:02	10.1	**10:34**	9.6	3:49	**4:23**	26	M	11:13	10.9	**11:32**	11.6	5:03	**5:23**
27	S	10:51	10.6	**11:18**	10.3	4:39	**5:09**	27	T	...	...	**12:04**	11.0	5:53	**6:11**
28	S	11:38	11.0	...	...	5:27	**5:53**	28	W	12:20	12.0	**12:56**	11.0	6:44	**7:00**
29	M	12:02	10.9	**12:26**	11.2	6:15	**6:39**	29	T	1:10	12.1	**1:49**	10.7	7:35	**7:51**
30	T	12:48	11.4	**1:15**	11.1	7:04	**7:25**	30	F	2:01	11.9	**2:44**	10.3	8:28	**8:43**
31	W	1:34	11.6	**2:06**	10.9	7:54	**8:13**								

Dates when Ht. of **Low** Water is below Mean Lower Low with Ht. of lowest given for each period and Date of lowest in ( ):

March:
1st–5th: -1.2' (1st)
12th: -0.2'
27th–31st: -1.7' (31st)

April:
1st–3rd: -1.5' (1st)
25th–30th: -1.8' (28th, 29th)

Average Rise and Fall 9.5 ft.

When a high tide exceeds avg. ht., the *following* low tide will be lower than avg. Since there is a high degree of correlation between the height of High Water and the velocities of the Flood and Ebb Currents for that same day, we offer a rough rule of thumb for estimating the current velocities, for ALL the Current Charts and Diagrams in this book. **Rule of Thumb:** Refer to Boston High Water. If the height of High Water is 11.0' or over, use the Current Chart velocities as shown. When the height is 10.5', subtract 10%; at 10.0', subtract 20%; at 9.0', 30%; at 8.0', 40%; below 7.5', 50%.

2021 HIGH & LOW WATER BOSTON, MA

42°21.3'N, 71°03'W

Daylight Saving Time

DAY OF MONTH	DAY OF WEEK	MAY HIGH a.m.	Ht.	**p.m.**	Ht.	LOW a.m.	**p.m.**
1	S	2:56	11.5	**3:41**	9.9	9:23	**9:39**
2	S	3:52	10.9	**4:42**	9.4	10:22	**10:39**
3	M	4:55	10.3	**5:48**	9.1	11:24	**11:43**
4	T	6:01	9.8	**6:53**	9.0	...	**12:28**
5	W	7:09	9.5	**7:57**	9.1	12:49	**1:30**
6	T	8:14	9.3	**8:54**	9.3	1:55	**2:30**
7	F	9:14	9.3	**9:44**	9.5	2:57	**3:24**
8	S	10:06	9.3	**10:26**	9.7	3:51	**4:09**
9	S	10:50	9.4	**11:04**	9.9	4:37	**4:50**
10	M	11:31	9.3	**11:39**	10.0	5:18	**5:27**
11	T	...	...	**12:09**	9.3	5:57	**6:04**
12	W	12:14	10.1	**12:48**	9.2	6:34	**6:41**
13	T	12:50	10.1	**1:26**	9.1	7:12	**7:19**
14	F	1:27	10.0	**2:05**	8.9	7:51	**7:57**
15	S	2:06	9.9	**2:46**	8.7	8:31	**8:38**
16	S	2:46	9.7	**3:28**	8.6	9:13	**9:21**
17	M	3:29	9.6	**4:14**	8.5	9:58	**10:09**
18	T	4:17	9.5	**5:03**	8.5	10:47	**11:01**
19	W	5:09	9.4	**5:55**	8.7	11:39	**11:57**
20	T	6:05	9.4	**6:47**	9.1	...	**12:32**
21	F	7:02	9.6	**7:40**	9.6	12:54	**1:25**
22	S	8:01	9.8	**8:33**	10.2	1:52	**2:19**
23	S	8:59	10.1	**9:25**	10.9	2:50	**3:12**
24	M	9:56	10.3	**10:15**	11.5	3:46	**4:04**
25	T	10:50	10.6	**11:05**	12.0	4:40	**4:56**
26	W	11:44	10.6	**11:56**	12.2	5:33	**5:47**
27	T	...	...	**12:38**	10.6	6:25	**6:38**
28	F	12:49	12.1	**1:34**	10.4	7:18	**7:31**
29	S	1:43	11.9	**2:29**	10.2	8:12	**8:25**
30	S	2:38	11.4	**3:26**	9.9	9:06	**9:21**
31	M	3:36	10.9	**4:25**	9.6	10:03	**10:20**

Daylight Saving Time

DAY OF MONTH	DAY OF WEEK	JUNE HIGH a.m.	Ht.	**p.m.**	Ht.	LOW a.m.	**p.m.**
1	T	4:37	10.3	**5:25**	9.4	11:01	**11:22**
2	W	5:38	9.8	**6:25**	9.3	...	**12:01**
3	T	6:40	9.4	**7:21**	9.3	12:25	**12:56**
4	F	7:41	9.1	**8:15**	9.4	1:26	**1:51**
5	S	8:39	8.9	**9:04**	9.5	2:26	**2:42**
6	S	9:33	8.9	**9:49**	9.7	3:20	**3:30**
7	M	10:20	8.9	**10:29**	9.9	4:08	**4:13**
8	T	11:02	8.9	**11:07**	10.0	4:50	**4:53**
9	W	11:43	8.9	**11:45**	10.1	5:30	**5:33**
10	T	...	...	**12:23**	8.9	6:10	**6:12**
11	F	12:23	10.1	**1:03**	8.9	6:49	**6:52**
12	S	1:02	10.1	**1:43**	8.8	7:28	**7:32**
13	S	1:42	10.1	**2:24**	8.8	8:08	**8:14**
14	M	2:23	10.0	**3:05**	8.8	8:50	**8:58**
15	T	3:06	9.9	**3:48**	8.9	9:33	**9:44**
16	W	3:52	9.9	**4:34**	9.1	10:19	**10:36**
17	T	4:42	9.8	**5:23**	9.3	11:08	**11:30**
18	F	5:37	9.7	**6:14**	9.7	11:59	...
19	S	6:34	9.6	**7:06**	10.2	12:27	**12:52**
20	S	7:33	9.7	**8:00**	10.7	1:25	**1:46**
21	M	8:33	9.7	**8:55**	11.1	2:25	**2:42**
22	T	9:33	9.9	**9:50**	11.6	3:24	**3:38**
23	W	10:31	10.0	**10:44**	11.9	4:20	**4:33**
24	T	11:27	10.1	**11:38**	12.0	5:15	**5:26**
25	F	...	...	**12:23**	10.2	6:09	**6:20**
26	S	12:33	11.9	**1:19**	10.1	7:03	**7:14**
27	S	1:28	11.6	**2:13**	10.0	7:55	**8:08**
28	M	2:22	11.2	**3:07**	9.9	8:47	**9:02**
29	T	3:16	10.7	**4:00**	9.7	9:39	**9:57**
30	W	4:11	10.2	**4:54**	9.5	10:31	**10:54**

Dates when Ht. of **Low** Water is below Mean Lower Low with Ht. of lowest given for each period and Date of lowest in ( ):

1st–2nd: -1.0' (1st)
24th–31st: -1.7' (27th, 28th)

22nd–29th: -1.4' (25th)

Average Rise and Fall 9.5 ft.

When a high tide exceeds avg. ht., the *following* low tide will be lower than avg. Since there is a high degree of correlation between the height of High Water and the velocities of the Flood and Ebb Currents for that same day, we offer a rough rule of thumb for estimating the current velocities, for ALL the Current Charts and Diagrams in this book. **Rule of Thumb:** Refer to Boston High Water. If the height of High Water is 11.0' or over, use the Current Chart velocities as shown. When the height is 10.5', subtract 10%; at 10.0', subtract 20%; at 9.0', 30%; at 8.0', 40%; below 7.5', 50%.

2021 HIGH & LOW WATER BOSTON, MA

42°21.3'N, 71°03'W

		Daylight Saving Time								**Daylight Saving Time**					
DAY OF MONTH	DAY OF WEEK	**JULY**						DAY OF MONTH	DAY OF WEEK	**AUGUST**					
		HIGH				LOW				HIGH				LOW	
		a.m.	Ht.	**p.m.**	Ht.	a.m.	**p.m.**			a.m.	Ht.	**p.m.**	Ht.	a.m.	**p.m.**
1	**T**	5:09	9.6	**5:47**	9.4	11:24	**11:53**	1	**S**	6:21	8.5	**6:41**	9.2	12:09	**12:22**
2	**F**	6:05	9.1	**6:38**	9.4	...	**12:16**	2	**M**	7:16	8.2	**7:33**	9.2	1:04	**1:13**
3	**S**	7:02	8.8	**7:29**	9.4	12:50	**1:07**	3	**T**	8:12	8.1	**8:25**	9.3	1:59	**2:05**
4	**S**	7:58	8.5	**8:19**	9.4	1:46	**1:57**	4	**W**	9:08	8.1	**9:17**	9.4	2:54	**2:57**
5	**M**	8:53	8.4	**9:07**	9.5	2:41	**2:47**	5	**T**	9:59	8.3	**10:04**	9.7	3:45	**3:47**
6	**T**	9:45	8.4	**9:53**	9.7	3:33	**3:35**	6	**F**	10:45	8.5	**10:48**	10.0	4:31	**4:33**
7	**W**	10:32	8.5	**10:36**	9.9	4:20	**4:20**	7	**S**	11:27	8.8	**11:31**	10.2	5:14	**5:17**
8	**T**	11:15	8.6	**11:17**	10.0	5:02	**5:03**	8	**S**	...	...	**12:08**	9.1	5:55	**6:00**
9	**F**	11:57	8.7	**11:57**	10.1	5:43	**5:45**	9	**M**	12:12	10.4	**12:48**	9.4	6:35	**6:43**
10	**S**	...	...	**12:38**	8.8	6:24	**6:26**	10	**T**	12:54	10.6	**1:28**	9.7	7:16	**7:27**
11	**S**	12:38	10.2	**1:18**	8.9	7:04	**7:08**	11	**W**	1:37	10.6	**2:09**	10.0	7:57	**8:12**
12	**M**	1:19	10.3	**1:58**	9.1	7:44	**7:51**	12	**T**	2:22	10.6	**2:51**	10.2	8:39	**9:00**
13	**T**	2:00	10.3	**2:39**	9.3	8:24	**8:35**	13	**F**	3:08	10.4	**3:36**	10.4	9:24	**9:50**
14	**W**	2:44	10.3	**3:20**	9.5	9:07	**9:22**	14	**S**	3:58	10.1	**4:24**	10.5	10:12	**10:45**
15	**T**	3:29	10.2	**4:05**	9.7	9:51	**10:12**	15	**S**	4:53	9.7	**5:18**	10.6	11:04	**11:44**
16	**F**	4:19	10.0	**4:53**	10.0	10:39	**11:07**	16	**M**	5:53	9.4	**6:15**	10.6	...	**12:01**
17	**S**	5:13	9.8	**5:44**	10.3	11:30	...	17	**T**	6:55	9.1	**7:16**	10.6	12:45	**1:00**
18	**S**	6:10	9.6	**6:38**	10.5	12:04	**12:24**	18	**W**	8:01	9.0	**8:19**	10.6	1:48	**2:02**
19	**M**	7:11	9.4	**7:34**	10.8	1:03	**1:20**	19	**T**	9:07	9.1	**9:22**	10.8	2:51	**3:04**
20	**T**	8:13	9.4	**8:33**	11.0	2:04	**2:18**	20	**F**	10:08	9.4	**10:21**	10.9	3:53	**4:04**
21	**W**	9:17	9.4	**9:33**	11.2	3:05	**3:18**	21	**S**	11:04	9.6	**11:15**	11.0	4:48	**4:59**
22	**T**	10:17	9.6	**10:30**	11.4	4:05	**4:15**	22	**S**	11:55	9.9	...	...	5:39	**5:51**
23	**F**	11:14	9.8	**11:25**	11.5	5:01	**5:11**	23	**M**	12:06	11.0	**12:42**	10.0	6:27	**6:40**
24	**S**	...	...	**12:09**	9.9	5:55	**6:05**	24	**T**	12:55	10.8	**1:27**	10.0	7:12	**7:28**
25	**S**	12:19	11.5	**1:02**	10.0	6:46	**6:57**	25	**W**	1:42	10.5	**2:09**	10.0	7:55	**8:13**
26	**M**	1:12	11.3	**1:53**	10.0	7:35	**7:49**	26	**T**	2:27	10.1	**2:51**	9.9	8:36	**8:59**
27	**T**	2:03	10.9	**2:41**	9.9	8:23	**8:39**	27	**F**	3:11	9.7	**3:32**	9.7	9:19	**9:46**
28	**W**	2:53	10.5	**3:28**	9.8	9:10	**9:29**	28	**S**	3:58	9.2	**4:16**	9.5	10:02	**10:35**
29	**T**	3:43	9.9	**4:14**	9.6	9:56	**10:21**	29	**S**	4:47	8.7	**5:04**	9.2	10:49	**11:27**
30	**F**	4:33	9.4	**5:02**	9.4	10:44	**11:15**	30	**M**	5:40	8.3	**5:55**	9.1	11:39	...
31	**S**	5:26	8.9	**5:51**	9.3	11:32	...	31	**T**	6:35	8.0	**6:48**	9.0	12:21	**12:31**

Dates when Ht. of **Low** Water is below Mean Lower Low with Ht. of lowest given for each period and Date of lowest in ( ):

21st–27th: -1.0' (24th)

10th–13th: -0.3' (11th, 12th)
20th–24th: -0.5' (22nd, 23rd)

Average Rise and Fall 9.5 ft.

When a high tide exceeds avg. ht., the *following* low tide will be lower than avg. Since there is a high degree of correlation between the height of High Water and the velocities of the Flood and Ebb Currents for that same day, we offer a rough rule of thumb for estimating the current velocities, for ALL the Current Charts and Diagrams in this book. **Rule of Thumb:** Refer to Boston High Water. If the height of High Water is 11.0' or over, use the Current Chart velocities as shown. When the height is 10.5', subtract 10%; at 10.0', subtract 20%; at 9.0', 30%; at 8.0', 40%; below 7.5', 50%.

2021 HIGH & LOW WATER BOSTON, MA

42°21.3'N, 71°03'W

Daylight Saving Time

DAY OF MONTH	DAY OF WEEK	SEPTEMBER HIGH a.m.	Ht.	p.m.	Ht.	LOW a.m.	p.m.
1	W	7:33	7.9	**7:44**	9.1	1:17	**1:25**
2	T	8:29	8.0	**8:39**	9.3	2:13	**2:20**
3	F	9:23	8.3	**9:31**	9.6	3:07	**3:13**
4	S	10:10	8.7	**10:17**	10.0	3:56	**4:03**
5	S	10:53	9.1	**11:01**	10.4	4:40	**4:49**
6	M	11:33	9.6	**11:44**	10.7	5:22	**5:33**
7	T	...	...	**12:13**	10.1	6:03	**6:18**
8	W	12:28	10.9	**12:55**	10.5	6:45	**7:03**
9	T	1:13	10.9	**1:37**	10.8	7:27	**7:50**
10	F	2:00	10.8	**2:21**	11.0	8:11	**8:38**
11	S	2:48	10.5	**3:08**	11.1	8:58	**9:30**
12	S	3:40	10.1	**4:00**	10.9	9:48	**10:26**
13	M	4:37	9.6	**4:56**	10.7	10:43	**11:26**
14	T	5:40	9.2	**5:58**	10.5	11:43	...
15	W	6:46	9.0	**7:03**	10.3	12:30	**12:46**
16	T	7:54	8.9	**8:10**	10.3	1:35	**1:50**
17	F	9:00	9.1	**9:15**	10.4	2:40	**2:55**
18	S	9:59	9.4	**10:13**	10.5	3:40	**3:55**
19	S	10:50	9.8	**11:05**	10.6	4:33	**4:48**
20	M	11:36	10.0	**11:51**	10.5	5:20	**5:36**
21	T	...	...	**12:17**	10.1	6:03	**6:22**
22	W	12:36	10.4	**12:57**	10.2	6:44	**7:05**
23	T	1:18	10.1	**1:35**	10.1	7:23	**7:47**
24	F	1:59	9.8	**2:13**	10.0	8:02	**8:29**
25	S	2:41	9.4	**2:52**	9.8	8:42	**9:12**
26	S	3:24	8.9	**3:34**	9.5	9:24	**9:57**
27	M	4:11	8.5	**4:20**	9.2	10:09	**10:47**
28	T	5:02	8.2	**5:11**	9.0	10:59	**11:41**
29	W	5:57	8.0	**6:06**	8.9	11:52	...
30	T	6:54	7.9	**7:03**	9.0	12:37	**12:48**

Daylight Saving Time

DAY OF MONTH	DAY OF WEEK	OCTOBER HIGH a.m.	Ht.	p.m.	Ht.	LOW a.m.	p.m.
1	F	7:51	8.1	**7:59**	9.2	1:32	**1:44**
2	S	8:43	8.5	**8:54**	9.6	2:26	**2:39**
3	S	9:31	9.0	**9:44**	10.0	3:16	**3:31**
4	M	10:15	9.6	**10:30**	10.4	4:03	**4:19**
5	T	10:57	10.3	**11:16**	10.8	4:47	**5:06**
6	W	11:39	10.9	...	...	5:30	**5:52**
7	T	12:02	10.9	**12:22**	11.3	6:13	**6:39**
8	F	12:49	11.0	**1:07**	11.6	6:58	**7:28**
9	S	1:39	10.8	**1:54**	11.7	7:45	**8:18**
10	S	2:30	10.5	**2:45**	11.5	8:34	**9:11**
11	M	3:24	10.0	**3:39**	11.2	9:27	**10:08**
12	T	4:24	9.6	**4:39**	10.7	10:25	**11:10**
13	W	5:29	9.2	**5:44**	10.3	11:28	...
14	T	6:37	9.0	**6:52**	10.0	12:15	**12:34**
15	F	7:45	9.1	**8:01**	9.9	1:20	**1:40**
16	S	8:48	9.3	**9:05**	9.9	2:24	**2:45**
17	S	9:44	9.6	**10:01**	10.0	3:23	**3:44**
18	M	10:31	9.9	**10:50**	10.0	4:13	**4:35**
19	T	11:12	10.1	**11:33**	10.0	4:57	**5:20**
20	W	11:50	10.2	...	...	5:37	**6:01**
21	T	12:14	9.8	**12:26**	10.2	6:15	**6:41**
22	F	12:54	9.6	**1:02**	10.2	6:52	**7:21**
23	S	1:33	9.3	**1:39**	10.0	7:30	**8:01**
24	S	2:14	9.0	**2:18**	9.8	8:09	**8:42**
25	M	2:55	8.7	**2:59**	9.6	8:50	**9:25**
26	T	3:40	8.4	**3:43**	9.3	9:34	**10:13**
27	W	4:29	8.2	**4:33**	9.1	10:23	**11:04**
28	T	5:21	8.0	**5:27**	9.0	11:16	**11:58**
29	F	6:16	8.1	**6:23**	9.0	...	**12:12**
30	S	7:09	8.4	**7:19**	9.2	12:51	**1:08**
31	S	8:01	8.8	**8:15**	9.5	1:44	**2:03**

Dates when Ht. of **Low** Water is below Mean Lower Low with Ht. of lowest given for each period and Date of lowest in ( ):

7th–12th: -0.6' (9th, 10th)

6th–11th: -1.3' (8th)

Average Rise and Fall 9.5 ft.

When a high tide exceeds avg. ht., the *following* low tide will be lower than avg. Since there is a high degree of correlation between the height of High Water and the velocities of the Flood and Ebb Currents for that same day, we offer a rough rule of thumb for estimating the current velocities, for ALL the Current Charts and Diagrams in this book. **Rule of Thumb:** Refer to Boston High Water. If the height of High Water is 11.0' or over, use the Current Chart velocities as shown. When the height is 10.5', subtract 10%; at 10.0', subtract 20%; at 9.0', 30%; at 8.0', 40%; below 7.5', 50%.

2021 HIGH & LOW WATER
BOSTON, MA
42°21.3'N, 71°03'W

***Standard Time starts Nov. 7 at 2 a.m.** **Standard Time**

DAY OF MONTH	DAY OF WEEK	NOVEMBER HIGH a.m.	Ht.	p.m.	Ht.	LOW a.m.	p.m.
1	**M**	8:51	9.4	**9:08**	9.9	2:35	**2:58**
2	**T**	9:37	10.1	**9:59**	10.3	3:24	**3:50**
3	**W**	10:22	10.9	**10:48**	10.6	4:11	**4:39**
4	**T**	11:07	11.5	**11:37**	10.8	4:58	**5:28**
5	**F**	11:53	11.9	...	...	5:44	**6:18**
6	**S**	12:27	10.8	**12:41**	12.1	6:32	**7:08**
7	**S**	1:20	10.6	***12:32**	12.0	*6:22	***7:00**
8	**M**	1:14	10.3	**1:25**	11.7	7:14	**7:54**
9	**T**	2:10	9.9	**2:21**	11.2	8:09	**8:52**
10	**W**	3:10	9.6	**3:23**	10.6	9:08	**9:53**
11	**T**	4:15	9.3	**4:29**	10.1	10:12	**10:56**
12	**F**	5:21	9.2	**5:37**	9.8	11:18	**11:59**
13	**S**	6:26	9.2	**6:43**	9.5	...	**12:24**
14	**S**	7:26	9.4	**7:46**	9.4	1:00	**1:28**
15	**M**	8:19	9.7	**8:42**	9.4	1:56	**2:27**
16	**T**	9:05	9.9	**9:30**	9.4	2:45	**3:17**
17	**W**	9:45	10.1	**10:12**	9.3	3:29	**4:00**
18	**T**	10:22	10.1	**10:52**	9.2	4:08	**4:40**
19	**F**	10:57	10.1	**11:31**	9.1	4:46	**5:19**
20	**S**	11:34	10.1	...	...	5:24	**5:57**
21	**S**	12:10	8.9	**12:11**	10.0	6:02	**6:36**
22	**M**	12:50	8.8	**12:50**	9.8	6:41	**7:16**
23	**T**	1:31	8.6	**1:30**	9.6	7:22	**7:58**
24	**W**	2:13	8.4	**2:13**	9.4	8:05	**8:42**
25	**T**	2:58	8.3	**3:00**	9.2	8:51	**9:30**
26	**F**	3:47	8.2	**3:51**	9.1	9:42	**10:20**
27	**S**	4:37	8.4	**4:45**	9.1	10:37	**11:11**
28	**S**	5:28	8.7	**5:41**	9.1	11:33	...
29	**M**	6:19	9.2	**6:38**	9.3	12:02	**12:29**
30	**T**	7:10	9.8	**7:34**	9.6	12:54	**1:26**

DAY OF MONTH	DAY OF WEEK	DECEMBER HIGH a.m.	Ht.	p.m.	Ht.	LOW a.m.	p.m.
1	**W**	8:01	10.5	**8:30**	9.9	1:47	**2:21**
2	**T**	8:50	11.2	**9:23**	10.2	2:38	**3:15**
3	**F**	9:39	11.7	**10:16**	10.4	3:29	**4:07**
4	**S**	10:29	12.1	**11:09**	10.4	4:19	**4:58**
5	**S**	11:20	12.2	...	...	5:10	**5:51**
6	**M**	12:03	10.3	**12:14**	12.0	6:02	**6:44**
7	**T**	12:59	10.1	**1:09**	11.7	6:56	**7:38**
8	**W**	1:55	9.9	**2:05**	11.1	7:51	**8:33**
9	**T**	2:53	9.6	**3:05**	10.5	8:50	**9:31**
10	**F**	3:54	9.4	**4:08**	9.9	9:51	**10:30**
11	**S**	4:55	9.3	**5:12**	9.4	10:56	**11:29**
12	**S**	5:55	9.3	**6:15**	9.0	...	**12:01**
13	**M**	6:51	9.3	**7:17**	8.8	12:26	**1:02**
14	**T**	7:45	9.4	**8:14**	8.7	1:20	**2:01**
15	**W**	8:32	9.6	**9:05**	8.7	2:11	**2:52**
16	**T**	9:15	9.7	**9:49**	8.7	2:57	**3:37**
17	**F**	9:54	9.9	**10:30**	8.7	3:39	**4:18**
18	**S**	10:32	9.9	**11:10**	8.7	4:19	**4:57**
19	**S**	11:10	9.9	**11:49**	8.6	4:58	**5:35**
20	**M**	11:48	9.9	...	...	5:37	**6:14**
21	**T**	12:28	8.6	**12:27**	9.9	6:17	**6:53**
22	**W**	1:08	8.6	**1:07**	9.8	6:57	**7:33**
23	**T**	1:47	8.5	**1:48**	9.6	7:39	**8:14**
24	**F**	2:28	8.6	**2:32**	9.5	8:24	**8:57**
25	**S**	3:12	8.6	**3:19**	9.3	9:12	**9:44**
26	**S**	3:59	8.8	**4:11**	9.2	10:05	**10:33**
27	**M**	4:48	9.1	**5:06**	9.1	11:00	**11:25**
28	**T**	5:39	9.6	**6:04**	9.1	11:58	...
29	**W**	6:33	10.0	**7:04**	9.2	12:18	**12:57**
30	**T**	7:28	10.6	**8:05**	9.4	1:13	**1:56**
31	**F**	8:23	11.1	**9:02**	9.4	2:10	**2:53**

Dates when Ht. of **Low** Water is below Mean Lower Low with Ht. of lowest given for each period and Date of lowest in ( ):

November: 3rd–10th: -1.7' (6th)

December: 1st–9th: -1.9' (5th)
30th–31st: -0.9' (31st)

Average Rise and Fall 9.5 ft.

When a high tide exceeds avg. ht., the *following* low tide will be lower than avg. Since there is a high degree of correlation between the height of High Water and the velocities of the Flood and Ebb Currents for that same day, we offer a rough rule of thumb for estimating the current velocities, for ALL the Current Charts and Diagrams in this book. **Rule of Thumb:** Refer to Boston High Water. If the height of High Water is 11.0' or over, use the Current Chart velocities as shown. When the height is 10.5', subtract 10%; at 10.0', subtract 20%; at 9.0', 30%; at 8.0', 40%; below 7.5', 50%.

Cape Cod Canal

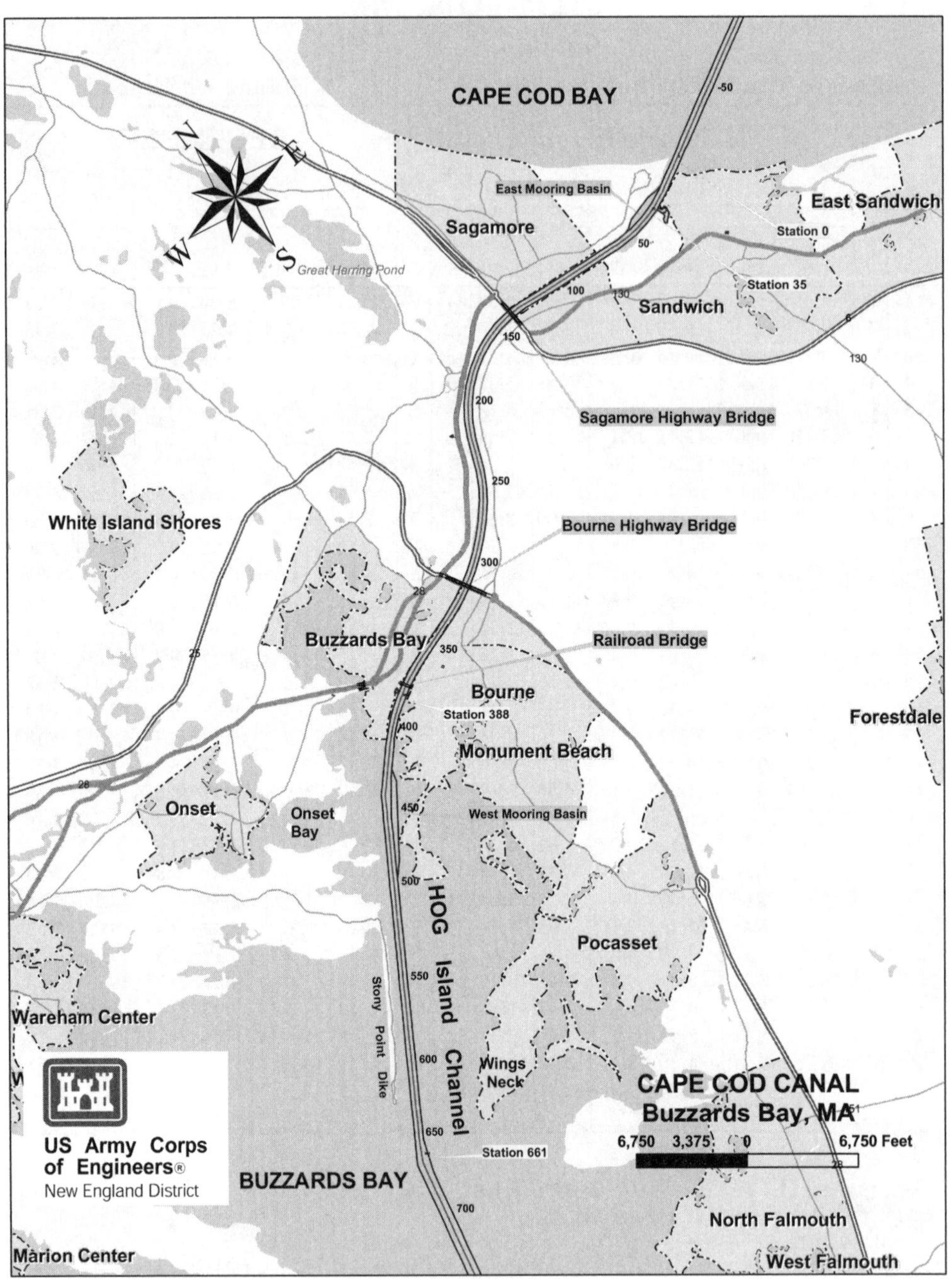

SMALL BOAT BASINS ON EITHER END OF THE CANAL: On E. end, 13-ft. mean low water, on S. side of Sandwich, available for mooring small boat traffic; On W. end, channel 13-ft. at mean low water, 100 ft. wide leads from NE side of Hog Is. Ch. abreast of Hog Is. to harbor in Onset Bay. Fuel, supplies and phone services at both locations.

See Cape Cod Canal Currents pp. 46-51.

Cape Cod Canal Regulations

For complete regulations see 33 CFR, Part 207 and 36 CFR, Part 327

Call on **Channel 13** to establish contact

No excessive wake - Speed Limit 10 m.p.h. (8.7 kts.)

Vessels going *with* the current have right of way over those going *against* it.

Clearance under all bridges: 135 feet at mean high water. Available clearance can be reduced by construction work on the bridges so mariners are advised to contact the Marine Traffic Controller for current clearance dimensions prior to transit. Buzzards Bay Railroad Bridge is maintained in up, or open position, except when lowered for trains or maintenance.

Obtaining Clearance

Vessels 65 feet and over shall not enter the Canal until clearance has been given by radio from the Marine Traffic Controller. These vessels shall request clearance at least 15 minutes prior to entering the Canal at any point.

Vessels of any kind unable to make a through transit of the Canal against a head current of 6 kts. within a time limit of 2-1/2 hrs. are required to obtain helper tug assistance or wait for a fair current prior to receiving clearance from the Controller.

Two-way traffic through the Canal for all vessels is allowed when Controller on duty considers conditions suitable.

Communications

Direct communications are available at all hours by VHF radio or by phoning 978-318-8500. Call on Channel 13 to establish contact. Transmissions may then be switched to Channel 14 as the working channel. Channel 16 is also available but should be limited to emergency situations. Vessels shall maintain a radio guard on Channel 13 during the entire passage.

Traffic Lights

Traffic Lights are at Eastern End at Sandwich (Cape Cod Bay entrance) and at Western End near Wings Neck (Buzzards Bay entrance). When traffic lights are extinguished: all vessels over 65 feet are cautioned not to enter Canal until clearance given, as above.

Entering From EASTERN END: (Lights on South side of entrance to Canal.)

RED LIGHT: Any type of vessel 65 feet in length and over must stop clear of the Cape Cod Bay entrance channel.

YELLOW LIGHT: Vessels 65 feet in length and over and drawing less than 25 feet may proceed as far as the East Mooring Basin where they must stop.

GREEN LIGHT: Vessels may proceed westward through the Canal.

Entering From WESTERN END: (Lights near Wings Neck at West Entrance to Hog Is. Channel)

RED LIGHT: Vessels 65 feet and over in length and drawing less than 25 feet must keep southerly of Hog Island Channel Entrance Buoys Nos. 1 and 2 and utilize the general anchorage areas adjacent to the improved channel. Vessel traffic drawing 25 feet and over are directed not to enter the Canal channel at the Cleveland Ledge Light entrance and shall lay to or anchor in Buzzards Bay until clearance is granted by the Marine Traffic Controller or a green traffic light at Wings Neck is displayed.

YELLOW LIGHT: Vessels may proceed through Hog Island Channel as far as the West Mooring Basin where they must stop.

GREEN LIGHT: Vessels may proceed eastward through the Canal.

Prohibited Activities

Jet skis, sea planes, paddle-driven craft and sailing vessels not under power are prohibited from transiting the Canal.

Fishing from a vessel within the channel limits of the Canal is prohibited.

Anchoring within the channel limits of the Canal, except in emergencies with notice given to the Traffic Controller, is prohibited.

2021 CURRENT TABLE
CAPE COD CANAL

41°44.56'N, 70°36.85'W at R.R. Bridge

Standard Time

JANUARY

DAY OF MONTH	DAY OF WEEK	CURRENT TURNS TO					
		EAST Flood Starts			WEST Ebb Starts		
		a.m.	**p.m.**	Kts.	a.m.	**p.m.**	Kts.
1	**F**	4:49	**5:12**	p4.9	10:54	**11:42**	a5.5
2	**S**	5:30	**5:54**	5.0	11:42	...	5.8
3	**S**	6:18	**6:42**	5.1	12:30	**12:30**	p6.0
4	**M**	7:06	**7:30**	5.1	1:18	**1:24**	p6.0
5	**T**	8:00	**8:30**	5.0	2:06	**2:18**	p5.8
6	**W**	9:00	**9:24**	p4.9	3:00	**3:18**	p5.6
7	**T**	10:00	**10:24**	p4.8	3:54	**4:18**	a5.4
8	**F**	11:00	**11:24**	p4.6	4:48	**5:24**	a5.3
9	**S**	...	**12:01**	4.4	5:48	**6:30**	a5.3
10	**S**	12:24	**1:00**	a4.4	6:42	**7:30**	a5.3
11	**M**	1:18	**1:54**	p4.5	7:36	**8:24**	a5.4
12	**T**	2:18	**2:48**	p4.6	8:36	**9:24**	a5.4
13	**W**	3:12	**3:42**	p4.7	9:24	**10:12**	a5.4
14	**T**	4:00	**4:30**	p4.7	10:18	**11:06**	a5.3
15	**F**	4:54	**5:18**	p4.5	11:12	**11:54**	a5.2
16	**S**	5:42	**6:12**	p4.3	...	**12:01**	5.0
17	**S**	6:36	**7:00**	p4.1	12:42	**12:54**	p4.8
18	**M**	7:30	**7:48**	p3.9	1:30	**1:42**	p4.5
19	**T**	8:18	**8:42**	p3.6	2:18	**2:36**	4.1
20	**W**	9:12	**9:30**	p3.4	3:12	**3:24**	a3.8
21	**T**	10:12	**10:24**	3.2	4:00	**4:18**	a3.5
22	**F**	11:00	**11:12**	p3.2	4:48	**5:12**	a3.4
23	**S**	11:54	...	3.1	5:30	**6:06**	a3.3
24	**S**	12:01	**12:36**	3.2	6:18	**6:54**	a3.4
25	**M**	12:48	**1:18**	p3.4	7:00	**7:42**	a3.7
26	**T**	1:30	**2:00**	p3.7	7:42	**8:24**	a4.1
27	**W**	2:12	**2:42**	p4.2	8:24	**9:06**	a4.6
28	**T**	2:54	**3:24**	p4.6	9:06	**9:48**	a5.1
29	**F**	3:36	**4:00**	p5.0	9:48	**10:30**	a5.6
30	**S**	4:18	**4:42**	p5.3	10:30	**11:12**	a6.1
31	**S**	5:06	**5:30**	5.5	11:18	...	6.3

Standard Time

FEBRUARY

DAY OF MONTH	DAY OF WEEK	CURRENT TURNS TO					
		EAST Flood Starts			WEST Ebb Starts		
		a.m.	**p.m.**	Kts.	a.m.	**p.m.**	Kts.
1	**M**	5:49	**6:18**	5.5	12:01	**12:12**	p6.4
2	**T**	6:42	**7:06**	5.4	12:48	**1:06**	p6.3
3	**W**	7:36	**8:00**	5.1	1:36	**2:00**	a6.0
4	**T**	8:30	**9:00**	4.7	2:30	**3:00**	a5.7
5	**F**	9:36	**10:00**	4.4	3:24	**4:00**	a5.4
6	**S**	10:36	**11:00**	4.1	4:24	**5:06**	a5.1
7	**S**	11:42	...	3.9	5:24	**6:12**	a4.9
8	**M**	12:06	**12:42**	p4.2	6:24	**7:12**	a4.8
9	**T**	1:06	**1:36**	p4.5	7:24	**8:12**	a4.8
10	**W**	2:00	**2:30**	p4.7	8:18	**9:06**	a5.0
11	**T**	2:54	**3:24**	p4.8	9:12	**9:54**	a5.1
12	**F**	3:42	**4:12**	p4.8	10:00	**10:42**	a5.2
13	**S**	4:36	**5:00**	p4.6	10:48	**11:30**	a5.2
14	**S**	5:24	**5:42**	p4.4	11:36	...	5.1
15	**M**	6:12	**6:30**	a4.1	12:12	**12:30**	p4.8
16	**T**	7:00	**7:18**	3.8	1:00	**1:18**	4.5
17	**W**	7:48	**8:06**	p3.6	1:48	**2:06**	a4.2
18	**T**	8:42	**8:54**	p3.3	2:30	**2:54**	a3.8
19	**F**	9:30	**9:42**	p3.1	3:18	**3:48**	a3.5
20	**S**	10:24	**10:36**	p3.1	4:00	**4:36**	a3.3
21	**S**	11:12	**11:24**	p3.1	4:48	**5:30**	a3.3
22	**M**	...	**12:01**	3.1	5:36	**6:18**	a3.4
23	**T**	12:12	**12:42**	3.4	6:18	**7:06**	a3.7
24	**W**	1:00	**1:24**	p3.9	7:06	**7:48**	4.2
25	**T**	1:42	**2:12**	p4.4	7:54	**8:36**	4.8
26	**F**	2:24	**2:54**	p5.0	8:36	**9:18**	a5.5
27	**S**	3:12	**3:36**	p5.4	9:24	**10:00**	a6.1
28	**S**	3:54	**4:18**	p5.7	10:12	**10:48**	a6.4

The Kts. (knots) columns show the **maximum** predicted velocities of the stronger one of the Flood Currents and the stronger one of the Ebb Currents for each day.
The letter "a" means the velocity shown should occur **after** the **a.m.** Current Change. The letter "p" means the velocity shown should occur **after** the **p.m.** Current Change (even if next morning). No "a" or "p" means a.m. and p.m. velocities are the same for that day.
Avg. Max. Velocity: Flood 4.0 Kts., Ebb 4.5 Kts.
Max. Flood 3 hrs. after Flood Starts, ±20 min.
Max. Ebb 3 hrs. after Ebb Starts, ±20 min.
Average rise and fall: canal east end, 8.7 ft. (time of high water same as Boston); west end, at Monument Beach, 4.0 ft. (time of high water 15 min. after Newport).

See pp. 22-29 for Current Change at other points.

2021 CURRENT TABLE
CAPE COD CANAL

41°44.56'N, 70°36.85'W at R.R. Bridge

***Daylight Time starts Mar. 14 at 2 a.m.** **Daylight Saving Time**

MARCH

DAY OF MONTH	DAY OF WEEK	CURRENT TURNS TO EAST Flood Starts a.m.	**p.m.**	Kts.	CURRENT TURNS TO WEST Ebb Starts a.m.	**p.m.**	Kts.
1	**M**	4:43	**5:06**	5.8	11:00	**11:30**	a6.6
2	**T**	5:30	**5:54**	5.7	11:54	...	6.5
3	**W**	6:18	**6:42**	a5.5	12:18	**12:48**	a6.3
4	**T**	7:12	**7:36**	a5.0	1:12	**1:42**	a6.1
5	**F**	8:12	**8:36**	a4.5	2:06	**2:42**	a5.8
6	**S**	9:12	**9:42**	a4.1	3:00	**3:48**	a5.3
7	**S**	10:18	**10:48**	a3.8	4:00	**4:54**	a4.8
8	**M**	11:24	**11:48**	a3.9	5:00	**5:54**	a4.5
9	**T**	...	**12:24**	4.2	6:06	**6:54**	a4.3
10	**W**	12:48	**1:24**	p4.5	7:06	**7:54**	4.5
11	**T**	1:42	**2:12**	p4.8	8:00	**8:42**	4.8
12	**F**	2:36	**3:00**	p4.8	8:54	**9:30**	5.0
13	**S**	3:24	**3:48**	p4.8	9:42	**10:18**	a5.2
14	**S**	*5:12	***5:30**	p4.6	*11:30	...	5.1
15	**M**	6:00	**6:18**	4.3	12:01	**12:12**	5.0
16	**T**	6:42	**7:00**	4.1	12:42	**1:00**	a4.8
17	**W**	7:30	**7:42**	a3.9	1:24	**1:48**	a4.5
18	**T**	8:12	**8:30**	3.6	2:06	**2:36**	a4.2
19	**F**	9:00	**9:18**	3.3	2:48	**3:24**	a3.9
20	**S**	9:48	**10:06**	3.1	3:30	**4:12**	a3.7
21	**S**	10:36	**10:54**	p3.1	4:18	**5:00**	a3.5
22	**M**	11:30	**11:48**	p3.3	5:00	**5:48**	a3.5
23	**T**	...	**12:18**	3.4	5:54	**6:42**	a3.6
24	**W**	12:36	**1:06**	p3.7	6:42	**7:30**	4.0
25	**T**	1:24	**1:54**	p4.2	7:36	**8:18**	p4.6
26	**F**	2:12	**2:36**	p4.8	8:24	**9:00**	5.2
27	**S**	3:00	**3:24**	p5.3	9:12	**9:48**	5.8
28	**S**	3:42	**4:12**	p5.7	10:00	**10:36**	a6.3
29	**M**	4:30	**4:54**	5.8	10:54	**11:18**	6.5
30	**T**	5:18	**5:42**	5.8	11:42	...	6.5
31	**W**	6:06	**6:30**	a5.7	12:06	**12:36**	a6.6

APRIL

DAY OF MONTH	DAY OF WEEK	CURRENT TURNS TO EAST Flood Starts a.m.	**p.m.**	Kts.	CURRENT TURNS TO WEST Ebb Starts a.m.	**p.m.**	Kts.
1	**T**	7:01	**7:24**	a5.3	12:54	**1:30**	a6.4
2	**F**	7:54	**8:18**	a4.8	1:48	**2:30**	a6.1
3	**S**	8:48	**9:18**	a4.3	2:42	**3:30**	a5.6
4	**S**	9:54	**10:24**	a3.8	3:36	**4:30**	a5.0
5	**M**	11:00	**11:30**	a3.7	4:42	**5:36**	a4.5
6	**T**	...	**12:06**	3.9	5:42	**6:36**	a4.1
7	**W**	12:30	**1:06**	p4.2	6:48	**7:36**	p4.2
8	**T**	1:30	**2:00**	p4.5	7:48	**8:30**	p4.6
9	**F**	2:24	**2:48**	p4.7	8:42	**9:18**	p4.9
10	**S**	3:12	**3:36**	p4.7	9:30	**10:00**	p5.1
11	**S**	4:00	**4:24**	4.6	10:18	**10:48**	5.0
12	**M**	4:48	**5:06**	a4.5	11:06	**11:30**	4.9
13	**T**	5:30	**5:48**	a4.3	11:48	...	4.7
14	**W**	6:12	**6:30**	a4.1	12:06	**12:36**	a4.7
15	**T**	7:00	**7:12**	a3.9	12:48	**1:18**	a4.5
16	**F**	7:42	**7:54**	a3.7	1:30	**2:06**	a4.3
17	**S**	8:24	**8:36**	a3.5	2:06	**2:48**	a4.1
18	**S**	9:06	**9:24**	a3.4	2:48	**3:36**	a4.0
19	**M**	9:54	**10:18**	3.4	3:36	**4:24**	a3.9
20	**T**	10:42	**11:12**	p3.6	4:24	**5:12**	a3.9
21	**W**	11:36	...	3.8	5:18	**6:00**	a4.1
22	**T**	12:01	**12:30**	p4.2	6:12	**6:54**	a4.5
23	**F**	12:54	**1:18**	p4.6	7:06	**7:42**	p5.0
24	**S**	1:42	**2:06**	p5.1	8:00	**8:30**	p5.6
25	**S**	2:30	**2:54**	p5.4	8:48	**9:18**	p6.1
26	**M**	3:18	**3:42**	p5.7	9:42	**10:06**	p6.4
27	**T**	4:12	**4:30**	5.7	10:36	**10:54**	p6.6
28	**W**	5:00	**5:18**	a5.7	11:30	**11:42**	p6.5
29	**T**	5:48	**6:12**	a5.4	...	**12:24**	5.8
30	**F**	6:42	**7:06**	a5.0	12:30	**1:18**	a6.3

The Kts. (knots) columns show the **maximum** predicted velocities of the stronger one of the Flood Currents and the stronger one of the Ebb Currents for each day.
The letter "a" means the velocity shown should occur **after** the **a.m.** Current Change. The letter "p" means the velocity shown should occur **after** the **p.m.** Current Change (even if next morning). No "a" or "p" means a.m. and p.m. velocities are the same for that day.

Avg. Max. Velocity: Flood 4.0 Kts., Ebb 4.5 Kts.

Max. Flood 3 hrs. after Flood Starts, ±20 min.

Max. Ebb 3 hrs. after Ebb Starts, ±20 min.

Average rise and fall: canal east end, 8.7 ft. (time of high water same as Boston); west end, at Monument Beach, 4.0 ft. (time of high water 15 min. after Newport).

See pp. 22-29 for Current Change at other points.

2021 CURRENT TABLE
CAPE COD CANAL
41°44.56'N, 70°36.85'W at R.R. Bridge

Daylight Saving Time

MAY

DAY OF MONTH	DAY OF WEEK	CURRENT TURNS TO					
		EAST Flood Starts			WEST Ebb Starts		
		a.m.	**p.m.**	Kts.	a.m.	**p.m.**	Kts.
1	S	7:37	**8:00**	a4.5	1:24	**2:18**	a5.8
2	S	8:30	**9:00**	a4.0	2:24	**3:12**	a5.3
3	M	9:36	**10:06**	a3.8	3:24	**4:12**	a4.7
4	T	10:36	**11:12**	a3.8	4:24	**5:12**	a4.3
5	W	11:42	...	4.0	5:24	**6:12**	a4.0
6	T	12:12	**12:36**	p4.2	6:24	**7:06**	p4.2
7	F	1:06	**1:30**	p4.4	7:24	**8:00**	p4.6
8	S	2:00	**2:18**	p4.5	8:18	**8:48**	p4.8
9	S	2:48	**3:06**	4.4	9:06	**9:30**	p4.9
10	M	3:36	**3:54**	a4.4	9:54	**10:12**	p4.8
11	T	4:24	**4:36**	a4.3	10:42	**10:54**	p4.7
12	W	5:06	**5:18**	a4.1	11:24	**11:36**	p4.6
13	T	5:48	**5:54**	a4.0	...	**12:06**	4.2
14	F	6:24	**6:36**	3.9	12:12	**12:48**	a4.5
15	S	7:06	**7:18**	3.8	12:48	**1:30**	a4.4
16	S	7:42	**8:06**	3.8	1:30	**2:18**	a4.4
17	M	8:24	**8:48**	3.8	2:12	**3:00**	a4.4
18	T	9:12	**9:42**	3.9	3:00	**3:48**	a4.5
19	W	10:06	**10:30**	p4.1	3:48	**4:36**	a4.6
20	T	11:00	**11:30**	p4.4	4:42	**5:24**	a4.8
21	F	11:54	...	4.6	5:36	**6:18**	a5.0
22	S	12:24	**12:48**	p4.9	6:36	**7:12**	p5.3
23	S	1:18	**1:36**	p5.2	7:30	**8:00**	p5.7
24	M	2:06	**2:30**	p5.3	8:30	**8:54**	p6.1
25	T	3:00	**3:24**	p5.4	9:24	**9:42**	p6.3
26	W	3:48	**4:12**	a5.4	10:18	**10:30**	p6.4
27	T	4:42	**5:06**	a5.3	11:12	**11:24**	p6.2
28	F	5:36	**5:54**	a5.0	...	**12:06**	5.3
29	S	6:24	**6:48**	a4.7	12:12	**1:06**	a5.9
30	S	7:18	**7:48**	a4.3	1:06	**2:00**	a5.5
31	M	8:18	**8:48**	a4.0	2:06	**2:54**	a5.1

Daylight Saving Time

JUNE

DAY OF MONTH	DAY OF WEEK	CURRENT TURNS TO					
		EAST Flood Starts			WEST Ebb Starts		
		a.m.	**p.m.**	Kts.	a.m.	**p.m.**	Kts.
1	T	9:13	**9:48**	a3.9	3:06	**3:54**	a4.7
2	W	10:12	**10:48**	a3.9	4:00	**4:48**	a4.3
3	T	11:12	**11:48**	a4.0	5:00	**5:42**	a4.0
4	F	...	**12:06**	4.0	6:00	**6:36**	p4.1
5	S	12:42	**1:00**	p4.0	6:54	**7:30**	p4.4
6	S	1:36	**1:48**	p4.0	7:48	**8:18**	p4.5
7	M	2:24	**2:36**	a4.1	8:42	**9:00**	p4.5
8	T	3:12	**3:24**	a4.1	9:30	**9:42**	p4.5
9	W	3:54	**4:06**	a4.0	10:12	**10:24**	p4.4
10	T	4:36	**4:48**	3.9	10:54	**11:00**	p4.4
11	F	5:12	**5:24**	p4.0	11:36	**11:36**	p4.5
12	S	5:54	**6:06**	p4.1	...	**12:18**	4.2
13	S	6:30	**6:48**	p4.2	12:12	**1:00**	a4.7
14	M	7:12	**7:30**	4.3	12:54	**1:42**	a4.9
15	T	7:54	**8:12**	4.4	1:42	**2:24**	a5.1
16	W	8:36	**9:06**	4.5	2:24	**3:12**	a5.2
17	T	9:30	**10:00**	4.6	3:18	**4:00**	a5.3
18	F	10:24	**10:54**	4.7	4:12	**4:54**	a5.3
19	S	11:18	**11:54**	a4.9	5:12	**5:48**	5.3
20	S	...	**12:18**	5.0	6:12	**6:42**	p5.5
21	M	12:48	**1:12**	p5.0	7:12	**7:36**	p5.7
22	T	1:48	**2:06**	p5.0	8:12	**8:30**	p5.9
23	W	2:42	**3:00**	4.9	9:12	**9:24**	p6.0
24	T	3:36	**3:54**	a4.9	10:06	**10:12**	p6.0
25	F	4:30	**4:48**	a4.8	11:00	**11:06**	p5.8
26	S	5:18	**5:42**	a4.7	11:54	...	5.0
27	S	6:12	**6:36**	a4.5	12:01	**12:48**	a5.6
28	M	7:06	**7:30**	a4.3	12:54	**1:42**	a5.3
29	T	7:54	**8:24**	a4.1	1:48	**2:36**	a5.0
30	W	8:54	**9:24**	a4.0	2:42	**3:24**	a4.7

The Kts. (knots) columns show the **maximum** predicted velocities of the stronger one of the Flood Currents and the stronger one of the Ebb Currents for each day.
The letter "a" means the velocity shown should occur **after** the **a.m.** Current Change. The letter "p" means the velocity shown should occur **after** the **p.m.** Current Change (even if next morning). No "a" or "p" means a.m. and p.m. velocities are the same for that day.
Avg. Max. Velocity: Flood 4.0 Kts., Ebb 4.5 Kts.
Max. Flood 3 hrs. after Flood Starts, ±20 min.
Max. Ebb 3 hrs. after Ebb Starts, ±20 min.
Average rise and fall: canal east end, 8.7 ft. (time of high water same as Boston); west end, at Monument Beach, 4.0 ft. (time of high water 15 min. after Newport).

See pp. 22-29 for Current Change at other points.

2021 CURRENT TABLE
CAPE COD CANAL

41°44.56'N, 70°36.85'W at R.R. Bridge

		JULY — Daylight Saving Time								AUGUST — Daylight Saving Time					
DAY OF MONTH	DAY OF WEEK	CURRENT TURNS TO EAST Flood Starts			CURRENT TURNS TO WEST Ebb Starts			DAY OF MONTH	DAY OF WEEK	CURRENT TURNS TO EAST Flood Starts			CURRENT TURNS TO WEST Ebb Starts		
		a.m.	**p.m.**	Kts.	a.m.	**p.m.**	Kts.			a.m.	**p.m.**	Kts.	a.m.	**p.m.**	Kts.
1	**T**	9:49	**10:18**	a3.9	3:36	**4:18**	a4.3	1	**S**	11:01	**11:42**	a3.3	5:00	**5:24**	3.5
2	**F**	10:42	**11:18**	a3.8	4:36	**5:12**	a4.0	2	**M**	11:54	...	3.1	5:54	**6:12**	p3.4
3	**S**	11:36	...	3.7	5:30	**6:00**	p3.9	3	**T**	12:36	**12:48**	a3.2	6:48	**7:00**	p3.4
4	**S**	12:12	**12:30**	p3.6	6:24	**6:54**	p4.0	4	**W**	1:24	**1:36**	a3.3	7:42	**7:48**	p3.5
5	**M**	1:06	**1:18**	a3.6	7:18	**7:42**	p4.0	5	**T**	2:12	**2:18**	a3.4	8:30	**8:30**	p3.7
6	**T**	1:54	**2:06**	a3.7	8:12	**8:24**	p4.0	6	**F**	2:54	**3:06**	p3.6	9:12	**9:12**	p4.1
7	**W**	2:42	**2:54**	a3.7	9:00	**9:06**	p4.0	7	**S**	3:30	**3:48**	p4.1	9:54	**9:54**	p4.6
8	**T**	3:24	**3:36**	a3.7	9:48	**9:48**	p4.2	8	**S**	4:12	**4:24**	p4.5	10:36	**10:36**	p5.2
9	**F**	4:06	**4:18**	p3.9	10:30	**10:24**	p4.5	9	**M**	4:48	**5:06**	p4.9	11:12	**11:18**	p5.7
10	**S**	4:42	**4:54**	p4.2	11:06	**11:06**	p4.8	10	**T**	5:30	**5:48**	p5.3	11:54	...	5.4
11	**S**	5:18	**5:36**	p4.4	11:48	**11:42**	p5.1	11	**W**	6:12	**6:30**	p5.4	12:01	**12:36**	a6.1
12	**M**	6:00	**6:18**	p4.7	...	**12:24**	4.8	12	**T**	6:54	**7:12**	a5.5	12:48	**1:24**	a6.3
13	**T**	6:36	**6:54**	p4.9	12:24	**1:06**	a5.5	13	**F**	7:42	**8:06**	a5.5	1:36	**2:12**	a6.3
14	**W**	7:24	**7:42**	5.0	1:12	**1:54**	a5.8	14	**S**	8:30	**9:00**	a5.3	2:30	**3:00**	a6.1
15	**T**	8:06	**8:30**	a5.1	2:00	**2:42**	a5.9	15	**S**	9:24	**10:00**	a5.0	3:30	**3:54**	p5.7
16	**F**	9:00	**9:24**	a5.1	2:54	**3:30**	a5.9	16	**M**	10:24	**11:00**	a4.6	4:30	**4:48**	p5.4
17	**S**	9:54	**10:24**	a5.0	3:48	**4:24**	a5.7	17	**T**	11:30	...	4.3	5:36	**5:48**	p5.1
18	**S**	10:48	**11:24**	a4.9	4:48	**5:18**	5.4	18	**W**	12:06	**12:36**	4.1	6:42	**6:48**	p4.9
19	**M**	11:48	...	4.7	5:48	**6:12**	p5.4	19	**T**	1:12	**1:36**	a4.0	7:42	**7:54**	p4.9
20	**T**	12:30	**12:48**	p4.6	6:54	**7:12**	p5.4	20	**F**	2:06	**2:30**	a4.4	8:42	**8:48**	p5.0
21	**W**	1:24	**1:48**	4.4	8:00	**8:06**	p5.4	21	**S**	3:06	**3:30**	a4.6	9:36	**9:42**	p5.2
22	**T**	2:24	**2:48**	a4.5	8:54	**9:06**	p5.5	22	**S**	4:00	**4:18**	a4.8	10:30	**10:36**	p5.3
23	**F**	3:18	**3:42**	a4.6	9:54	**10:00**	p5.5	23	**M**	4:48	**5:06**	a4.8	11:18	**11:24**	p5.4
24	**S**	4:12	**4:36**	a4.7	10:48	**10:54**	p5.5	24	**T**	5:36	**6:00**	a4.7	...	**12:06**	5.1
25	**S**	5:06	**5:30**	a4.7	11:36	**11:42**	p5.4	25	**W**	6:18	**6:48**	a4.5	12:18	**12:48**	a5.3
26	**M**	5:54	**6:18**	a4.6	...	**12:30**	4.9	26	**T**	7:06	**7:36**	a4.2	1:06	**1:36**	a5.0
27	**T**	6:42	**7:06**	a4.4	12:36	**1:18**	a5.3	27	**F**	7:54	**8:24**	a4.0	1:54	**2:24**	a4.7
28	**W**	7:36	**8:00**	a4.2	1:30	**2:06**	a5.1	28	**S**	8:42	**9:18**	a3.7	2:42	**3:12**	a4.3
29	**T**	8:24	**8:54**	a4.0	2:18	**2:54**	a4.8	29	**S**	9:30	**10:12**	a3.4	3:36	**3:54**	a3.8
30	**F**	9:12	**9:48**	a3.7	3:12	**3:42**	a4.4	30	**M**	10:24	**11:06**	a3.1	4:30	**4:42**	p3.4
31	**S**	10:06	**10:48**	a3.5	4:06	**4:36**	a3.9	31	**T**	11:18	...	2.9	5:24	**5:36**	p3.2

The Kts. (knots) columns show the **maximum** predicted velocities of the stronger one of the Flood Currents and the stronger one of the Ebb Currents for each day.
The letter "a" means the velocity shown should occur **after** the **a.m.** Current Change. The letter "p" means the velocity shown should occur **after** the **p.m.** Current Change (even if next morning). No "a" or "p" means a.m. and p.m. velocities are the same for that day.
Avg. Max. Velocity: Flood 4.0 Kts., Ebb 4.5 Kts.
Max. Flood 3 hrs. after Flood Starts, ±20 min.
Max. Ebb 3 hrs. after Ebb Starts, ±20 min.
Average rise and fall: canal east end, 8.7 ft. (time of high water same as Boston); west end, at Monument Beach, 4.0 ft. (time of high water 15 min. after Newport).

See pp. 22-29 for Current Change at other points.

2021 CURRENT TABLE
CAPE COD CANAL

41°44.56'N, 70°36.85'W at R.R. Bridge

SEPTEMBER (Daylight Saving Time)								OCTOBER (Daylight Saving Time)							
DAY OF MONTH	DAY OF WEEK	CURRENT TURNS TO						DAY OF MONTH	DAY OF WEEK	CURRENT TURNS TO					
		EAST Flood Starts			WEST Ebb Starts					EAST Flood Starts			WEST Ebb Starts		
		a.m.	**p.m.**	Kts.	a.m.	**p.m.**	Kts.			a.m.	**p.m.**	Kts.	a.m.	**p.m.**	Kts.
1	**W**	12:02	**12:12**	2.9	6:18	**6:24**	p3.1	1	**F**	12:07	**12:24**	p3.2	6:30	**6:30**	p3.5
2	**T**	12:48	**1:00**	3.0	7:06	**7:12**	p3.3	2	**S**	12:54	**1:12**	p3.6	7:12	**7:18**	p4.0
3	**F**	1:36	**1:48**	p3.4	7:54	**7:54**	p3.7	3	**S**	1:36	**1:54**	p4.2	8:00	**8:06**	p4.7
4	**S**	2:18	**2:30**	p3.8	8:36	**8:42**	p4.3	4	**M**	2:24	**2:42**	p4.7	8:42	**8:54**	p5.3
5	**S**	3:00	**3:12**	p4.4	9:18	**9:24**	p5.0	5	**T**	3:06	**3:24**	p5.3	9:24	**9:42**	p5.9
6	**M**	3:36	**3:54**	p4.9	10:00	**10:06**	p5.6	6	**W**	3:48	**4:06**	p5.6	10:12	**10:24**	p6.3
7	**T**	4:18	**4:36**	p5.4	10:42	**10:48**	p6.1	7	**T**	4:30	**4:54**	5.8	10:54	**11:18**	p6.5
8	**W**	5:00	**5:18**	p5.7	11:24	**11:36**	p6.4	8	**F**	5:18	**5:42**	a5.9	11:36	...	6.6
9	**T**	5:42	**6:00**	p5.8	...	**12:06**	6.3	9	**S**	6:00	**6:30**	a5.7	12:06	**12:24**	p6.6
10	**F**	6:24	**6:48**	a5.8	12:24	**12:54**	a6.5	10	**S**	6:54	**7:18**	a5.4	1:00	**1:18**	p6.4
11	**S**	7:12	**7:42**	a5.6	1:18	**1:42**	p6.4	11	**M**	7:48	**8:18**	a4.9	2:00	**2:12**	p6.0
12	**S**	8:06	**8:36**	a5.2	2:12	**2:30**	p6.1	12	**T**	8:48	**9:18**	a4.3	3:00	**3:06**	p5.4
13	**M**	9:00	**9:36**	a4.7	3:12	**3:24**	p5.6	13	**W**	9:48	**10:24**	3.8	4:00	**4:06**	p4.9
14	**T**	10:06	**10:42**	a4.2	4:12	**4:24**	p5.2	14	**T**	10:54	**11:30**	p3.8	5:00	**5:12**	p4.4
15	**W**	11:12	**11:48**	3.8	5:18	**5:30**	p4.7	15	**F**	...	**12:01**	3.5	6:06	**6:18**	p4.2
16	**T**	...	**12:18**	3.6	6:24	**6:36**	p4.5	16	**S**	12:30	**1:00**	a4.1	7:06	**7:18**	p4.3
17	**F**	12:54	**1:18**	a4.1	7:24	**7:36**	p4.5	17	**S**	1:30	**2:00**	a4.4	8:00	**8:12**	p4.6
18	**S**	1:54	**2:18**	a4.4	8:24	**8:36**	p4.8	18	**M**	2:24	**2:48**	a4.6	8:48	**9:06**	p4.9
19	**S**	2:48	**3:12**	a4.7	9:18	**9:30**	p5.1	19	**T**	3:12	**3:36**	a4.7	9:36	**9:54**	a5.1
20	**M**	3:36	**4:00**	a4.8	10:06	**10:18**	p5.2	20	**W**	4:00	**4:24**	4.6	10:24	**10:42**	a5.2
21	**T**	4:24	**4:48**	a4.8	10:54	**11:06**	5.2	21	**T**	4:42	**5:12**	4.4	11:06	**11:30**	a5.1
22	**W**	5:12	**5:36**	a4.7	11:36	**11:54**	a5.2	22	**F**	5:24	**5:54**	4.2	11:48	...	4.9
23	**T**	5:54	**6:24**	a4.4	...	**12:18**	5.0	23	**S**	6:12	**6:42**	a4.1	12:18	**12:30**	p4.6
24	**F**	6:36	**7:06**	a4.2	12:42	**1:06**	a4.9	24	**S**	6:54	**7:24**	a3.8	1:06	**1:12**	p4.4
25	**S**	7:24	**7:54**	a3.9	1:30	**1:48**	a4.5	25	**M**	7:42	**8:12**	a3.5	1:54	**1:54**	p4.1
26	**S**	8:12	**8:42**	a3.6	2:18	**2:36**	4.1	26	**T**	8:30	**8:54**	a3.3	2:36	**2:42**	p3.8
27	**M**	9:00	**9:36**	a3.3	3:06	**3:18**	p3.7	27	**W**	9:18	**9:42**	3.2	3:24	**3:24**	p3.7
28	**T**	9:54	**10:24**	a3.0	4:00	**4:06**	p3.4	28	**T**	10:06	**10:36**	p3.2	4:12	**4:12**	p3.6
29	**W**	10:42	**11:18**	2.9	4:48	**4:54**	p3.2	29	**F**	10:54	**11:24**	p3.5	5:00	**5:00**	p3.8
30	**T**	11:36	...	3.0	5:42	**5:42**	p3.3	30	**S**	11:48	...	3.6	5:48	**5:54**	p4.1
								31	**S**	12:12	**12:36**	p4.0	6:36	**6:42**	p4.5

The Kts. (knots) columns show the **maximum** predicted velocities of the stronger one of the Flood Currents and the stronger one of the Ebb Currents for each day.
The letter "a" means the velocity shown should occur **after** the **a.m.** Current Change. The letter "p" means the velocity shown should occur **after** the **p.m.** Current Change (even if next morning). No "a" or "p" means a.m. and p.m. velocities are the same for that day.
Avg. Max. Velocity: Flood 4.0 Kts., Ebb 4.5 Kts.
Max. Flood 3 hrs. after Flood Starts, ±20 min.
Max. Ebb 3 hrs. after Ebb Starts, ±20 min.
Average rise and fall: canal east end, 8.7 ft. (time of high water same as Boston); west end, at Monument Beach, 4.0 ft. (time of high water 15 min. after Newport).

See pp. 22-29 for Current Change at other points.

2021 CURRENT TABLE
CAPE COD CANAL

41°44.56'N, 70°36.85'W at R.R. Bridge

***Standard Time starts Nov. 7 at 2 a.m.** — **Standard Time**

NOVEMBER								DECEMBER							
		CURRENT TURNS TO								CURRENT TURNS TO					
		EAST Flood Starts			WEST Ebb Starts					EAST Flood Starts			WEST Ebb Starts		
DAY OF MONTH	DAY OF WEEK	a.m.	**p.m.**	Kts.	a.m.	**p.m.**	Kts.	DAY OF MONTH	DAY OF WEEK	a.m.	**p.m.**	Kts.	a.m.	**p.m.**	Kts.
1	**M**	1:01	**1:24**	p4.5	7:18	**7:36**	p5.0	1	**W**	12:13	**12:42**	5.0	6:36	**7:00**	5.5
2	**T**	1:48	**2:12**	p5.0	8:06	**8:24**	p5.6	2	**T**	1:00	**1:30**	a5.3	7:24	**7:54**	a5.9
3	**W**	2:30	**2:54**	p5.4	8:54	**9:18**	p6.0	3	**F**	1:54	**2:24**	5.4	8:12	**8:54**	a6.3
4	**T**	3:18	**3:42**	5.6	9:42	**10:06**	a6.3	4	**S**	2:42	**3:12**	5.4	9:06	**9:48**	a6.4
5	**F**	4:06	**4:30**	5.7	10:24	**11:00**	a6.6	5	**S**	3:36	**4:06**	5.3	9:54	**10:42**	a6.4
6	**S**	4:54	**5:24**	a5.7	11:12	**11:54**	a6.6	6	**M**	4:30	**5:00**	5.0	10:48	**11:36**	a6.2
7	**S**	*4:42	***5:12**	a5.4	*11:06	***11:48**	a6.5	7	**T**	5:24	**5:48**	a4.7	11:42	...	5.9
8	**M**	5:36	**6:06**	a5.0	11:54	...	6.2	8	**W**	6:18	**6:48**	4.3	12:30	**12:36**	p5.5
9	**T**	6:30	**7:00**	a4.5	12:48	**12:54**	p5.7	9	**T**	7:18	**7:42**	a4.0	1:24	**1:36**	p5.1
10	**W**	7:30	**8:00**	4.0	1:42	**1:48**	p5.2	10	**F**	8:12	**8:42**	p3.9	2:24	**2:30**	p4.6
11	**T**	8:36	**9:06**	p3.8	2:42	**2:48**	p4.7	11	**S**	9:18	**9:42**	p3.9	3:18	**3:30**	p4.3
12	**F**	9:36	**10:06**	p3.9	3:42	**3:54**	p4.3	12	**S**	10:18	**10:36**	p3.9	4:12	**4:30**	4.0
13	**S**	10:42	**11:06**	p4.1	4:42	**4:54**	p4.1	13	**M**	11:12	**11:36**	p4.0	5:06	**5:30**	a4.1
14	**S**	11:42	...	3.8	5:36	**5:54**	p4.2	14	**T**	...	**12:12**	3.9	6:00	**6:24**	a4.3
15	**M**	12:06	**12:36**	a4.2	6:30	**6:48**	a4.5	15	**W**	12:24	**1:00**	p4.1	6:54	**7:18**	a4.5
16	**T**	12:54	**1:24**	a4.4	7:24	**7:42**	a4.8	16	**T**	1:12	**1:48**	p4.2	7:36	**8:12**	a4.6
17	**W**	1:42	**2:18**	4.4	8:12	**8:36**	a4.9	17	**F**	2:00	**2:36**	p4.2	8:24	**9:00**	a4.6
18	**T**	2:30	**3:00**	p4.4	8:54	**9:24**	a5.0	18	**S**	2:48	**3:24**	p4.1	9:06	**9:42**	a4.5
19	**F**	3:12	**3:48**	p4.3	9:36	**10:06**	a4.9	19	**S**	3:36	**4:06**	p4.0	9:48	**10:30**	a4.4
20	**S**	4:00	**4:30**	p4.1	10:18	**10:54**	a4.7	20	**M**	4:18	**4:42**	p3.9	10:30	**11:12**	a4.4
21	**S**	4:42	**5:12**	3.9	11:00	**11:36**	a4.5	21	**T**	5:00	**5:24**	p3.9	11:06	**11:48**	a4.4
22	**M**	5:24	**5:54**	3.7	11:42	...	4.3	22	**W**	5:36	**6:00**	p4.0	11:48	...	4.6
23	**T**	6:12	**6:36**	3.6	12:24	**12:18**	p4.2	23	**T**	6:18	**6:42**	p4.1	12:30	**12:30**	p4.7
24	**W**	6:54	**7:18**	3.6	1:06	**1:00**	p4.2	24	**F**	7:00	**7:24**	4.2	1:12	**1:12**	p4.9
25	**T**	7:36	**8:00**	3.6	1:48	**1:48**	p4.2	25	**S**	7:48	**8:06**	p4.4	1:54	**2:00**	p5.1
26	**F**	8:24	**8:48**	p3.8	2:30	**2:30**	p4.3	26	**S**	8:36	**9:00**	p4.6	2:36	**2:48**	p5.1
27	**S**	9:12	**9:42**	p4.0	3:18	**3:24**	p4.5	27	**M**	9:30	**9:54**	p4.8	3:24	**3:42**	p5.2
28	**S**	10:06	**10:30**	p4.3	4:06	**4:12**	p4.7	28	**T**	10:24	**10:48**	p4.9	4:18	**4:42**	p5.2
29	**M**	11:00	**11:24**	p4.7	4:54	**5:12**	p4.9	29	**W**	11:18	**11:42**	p5.0	5:12	**5:42**	a5.3
30	**T**	11:48	...	4.7	5:42	**6:06**	p5.2	30	**T**	...	**12:18**	4.8	6:06	**6:42**	a5.6
								31	**F**	12:36	**1:12**	a5.0	7:00	**7:42**	a5.8

The Kts. (knots) columns show the **maximum** predicted velocities of the stronger one of the Flood Currents and the stronger one of the Ebb Currents for each day.
The letter "a" means the velocity shown should occur **after** the **a.m.** Current Change. The letter "p" means the velocity shown should occur **after** the **p.m.** Current Change (even if next morning). No "a" or "p" means a.m. and p.m. velocities are the same for that day.

Avg. Max. Velocity: Flood 4.0 Kts., Ebb 4.5 Kts.

Max. Flood 3 hrs. after Flood Starts, ±20 min.

Max. Ebb 3 hrs. after Ebb Starts, ±20 min.

Average rise and fall: canal east end, 8.7 ft. (time of high water same as Boston); west end, at Monument Beach, 4.0 ft. (time of high water 15 min. after Newport).

See pp. 22-29 for Current Change at other points.

2021 CURRENT TABLE
WOODS HOLE, MA, The Strait

41°31.16'N, 70°40.97'W

Standard Time

JANUARY

DAY OF MONTH	DAY OF WEEK	CURRENT TURNS TO SOUTHEAST Flood Starts			CURRENT TURNS TO NORTHWEST Ebb Starts		
		a.m.	**p.m.**	Kts.	a.m.	**p.m.**	Kts.
1	**F**	5:25	**6:06**	p3.8	11:54	...	4.1
2	**S**	6:12	**6:48**	p3.9	12:36	**12:36**	p4.3
3	**S**	7:00	**7:36**	p3.9	1:18	**1:24**	p4.4
4	**M**	7:54	**8:24**	p3.9	2:06	**2:18**	p4.3
5	**T**	8:48	**9:24**	p3.9	3:00	**3:12**	p4.2
6	**W**	9:54	**10:18**	p3.9	3:48	**4:12**	3.9
7	**T**	10:54	**11:18**	p3.8	4:42	**5:12**	a3.7
8	**F**	...	**12:01**	3.4	5:42	**6:12**	a3.6
9	**S**	12:12	**1:00**	a3.6	6:42	**7:18**	a3.6
10	**S**	1:12	**2:00**	3.5	7:42	**8:18**	a3.7
11	**M**	2:06	**2:54**	p3.8	8:36	**9:12**	a3.8
12	**T**	3:06	**3:48**	p4.0	9:30	**10:06**	a3.7
13	**W**	4:00	**4:42**	p4.1	10:24	**11:00**	a3.7
14	**T**	4:54	**5:36**	p4.0	11:12	**11:54**	a3.6
15	**F**	5:42	**6:24**	p3.9	...	**12:06**	3.5
16	**S**	6:36	**7:12**	p3.7	12:42	**12:54**	p3.4
17	**S**	7:24	**7:54**	p3.5	1:30	**1:42**	p3.2
18	**M**	8:18	**8:42**	p3.2	2:18	**2:30**	p3.0
19	**T**	9:12	**9:30**	p2.9	3:06	**3:24**	p2.8
20	**W**	10:06	**10:18**	p2.7	3:54	**4:12**	2.5
21	**T**	10:54	**11:06**	p2.5	4:42	**5:06**	2.3
22	**F**	11:48	**11:48**	p2.5	5:30	**5:54**	a2.3
23	**S**	...	**12:36**	2.4	6:18	**6:48**	a2.4
24	**S**	12:36	**1:18**	a2.6	7:06	**7:36**	a2.5
25	**M**	1:18	**2:06**	a2.8	7:54	**8:24**	a2.8
26	**T**	2:06	**2:48**	a3.0	8:36	**9:12**	a3.1
27	**W**	2:48	**3:30**	3.2	9:18	**9:54**	a3.5
28	**T**	3:30	**4:12**	p3.6	10:00	**10:36**	a3.8
29	**F**	4:18	**4:54**	p3.9	10:42	**11:18**	a4.1
30	**S**	5:00	**5:42**	4.0	11:24	...	4.4
31	**S**	5:48	**6:24**	4.1	12:06	**12:12**	p4.6

Standard Time

FEBRUARY

DAY OF MONTH	DAY OF WEEK	CURRENT TURNS TO SOUTHEAST Flood Starts			CURRENT TURNS TO NORTHWEST Ebb Starts		
		a.m.	**p.m.**	Kts.	a.m.	**p.m.**	Kts.
1	**M**	6:37	**7:12**	4.1	12:54	**1:06**	p4.6
2	**T**	7:30	**8:00**	p4.1	1:42	**1:54**	p4.5
3	**W**	8:30	**8:54**	p4.0	2:30	**2:54**	4.2
4	**T**	9:30	**9:54**	p3.8	3:24	**3:48**	a4.0
5	**F**	10:36	**10:54**	p3.5	4:18	**4:54**	a3.8
6	**S**	11:42	**11:54**	p3.3	5:18	**5:54**	a3.5
7	**S**	...	**12:42**	3.3	6:18	**7:00**	a3.3
8	**M**	12:54	**1:42**	p3.5	7:18	**8:00**	a3.3
9	**T**	1:54	**2:42**	p3.8	8:18	**9:00**	a3.4
10	**W**	2:48	**3:36**	p4.0	9:12	**9:48**	a3.4
11	**T**	3:42	**4:24**	p4.1	10:06	**10:42**	a3.5
12	**F**	4:36	**5:12**	p4.0	10:54	**11:30**	a3.5
13	**S**	5:24	**6:00**	p3.8	11:42	...	3.4
14	**S**	6:12	**6:42**	p3.6	12:18	**12:30**	p3.4
15	**M**	7:00	**7:24**	p3.3	1:06	**1:18**	p3.2
16	**T**	7:42	**8:06**	3.0	1:48	**2:00**	p3.1
17	**W**	8:36	**8:48**	2.7	2:36	**2:48**	2.8
18	**T**	9:24	**9:36**	p2.6	3:18	**3:36**	2.6
19	**F**	10:18	**10:24**	p2.6	4:06	**4:30**	a2.5
20	**S**	11:12	**11:12**	p2.6	4:48	**5:18**	a2.4
21	**S**	...	**12:01**	2.4	5:36	**6:12**	a2.3
22	**M**	12:01	**12:48**	a2.7	6:24	**7:00**	a2.5
23	**T**	12:48	**1:30**	a2.9	7:12	**7:54**	a2.8
24	**W**	1:30	**2:18**	3.1	8:00	**8:36**	a3.2
25	**T**	2:18	**3:00**	3.4	8:48	**9:24**	a3.6
26	**F**	3:06	**3:42**	p3.8	9:30	**10:06**	a4.0
27	**S**	3:54	**4:30**	p4.1	10:18	**10:54**	a4.4
28	**S**	4:42	**5:12**	p4.3	11:06	**11:36**	a4.6

See the Woods Hole Current Diagram on pp. 60-65.

Mariners should exercise great caution when transiting Woods Hole Passage as velocities have been reported to exceed NOAA's predictions.

To hold longest fair current from Buzzards Bay headed East through Vineyard and Nantucket Sounds go through Woods Hole 2 1/2 hrs. after flood starts SE in Woods Hole. (Any earlier means adverse currents in the Sounds.)

2021 CURRENT TABLE

WOODS HOLE, MA, The Strait

41°31.16'N, 70°40.97'W

***Daylight Time starts Mar. 14 at 2 a.m.** | **Daylight Saving Time**

MARCH

DAY OF MONTH	DAY OF WEEK	CURRENT TURNS TO SOUTHEAST Flood Starts			CURRENT TURNS TO NORTHWEST Ebb Starts		
		a.m.	**p.m.**	Kts.	a.m.	**p.m.**	Kts.
1	**M**	5:31	**6:00**	4.3	11:54	...	4.7
2	**T**	6:18	**6:42**	4.2	12:24	**12:42**	p4.7
3	**W**	7:12	**7:30**	4.0	1:12	**1:36**	4.5
4	**T**	8:06	**8:30**	p3.8	2:06	**2:36**	a4.3
5	**F**	9:12	**9:30**	3.5	3:00	**3:30**	a4.0
6	**S**	10:18	**10:36**	3.2	3:54	**4:36**	a3.7
7	**S**	11:24	**11:36**	a3.2	5:00	**5:36**	a3.2
8	**M**	...	**12:24**	3.3	6:00	**6:42**	a3.0
9	**T**	12:42	**1:24**	p3.6	7:00	**7:42**	a2.9
10	**W**	1:36	**2:24**	p3.8	8:00	**8:36**	a3.1
11	**T**	2:36	**3:12**	p4.0	8:54	**9:30**	a3.2
12	**F**	3:24	**4:00**	p4.0	9:42	**10:18**	a3.3
13	**S**	4:12	**4:48**	p3.9	10:30	**11:06**	a3.4
14	**S**	*6:00	***6:24**	p3.7	...	***12:18**	3.4
15	**M**	6:42	**7:06**	a3.4	12:48	**1:06**	p3.3
16	**T**	7:30	**7:48**	a3.2	1:30	**1:48**	3.2
17	**W**	8:12	**8:24**	a2.9	2:12	**2:36**	3.1
18	**T**	9:00	**9:06**	2.7	2:54	**3:18**	a3.0
19	**F**	9:48	**9:54**	p2.7	3:36	**4:06**	a2.8
20	**S**	10:42	**10:42**	p2.7	4:24	**4:54**	a2.7
21	**S**	11:30	**11:36**	p2.7	5:06	**5:42**	a2.6
22	**M**	...	**12:18**	2.7	5:54	**6:36**	a2.5
23	**T**	12:24	**1:06**	a2.9	6:48	**7:24**	2.6
24	**W**	1:12	**1:54**	3.0	7:36	**8:18**	2.9
25	**T**	2:06	**2:42**	3.3	8:30	**9:06**	3.3
26	**F**	2:54	**3:30**	3.6	9:18	**9:54**	a3.8
27	**S**	3:42	**4:12**	3.9	10:06	**10:36**	a4.2
28	**S**	4:30	**5:00**	p4.2	10:54	**11:24**	4.4
29	**M**	5:18	**5:48**	4.3	11:42	...	4.6
30	**T**	6:12	**6:30**	4.3	12:12	**12:36**	4.6
31	**W**	7:00	**7:18**	a4.2	1:00	**1:30**	a4.7

APRIL

DAY OF MONTH	DAY OF WEEK	CURRENT TURNS TO SOUTHEAST Flood Starts			CURRENT TURNS TO NORTHWEST Ebb Starts		
		a.m.	**p.m.**	Kts.	a.m.	**p.m.**	Kts.
1	**T**	7:55	**8:12**	a3.9	1:54	**2:24**	a4.6
2	**F**	8:54	**9:06**	a3.6	2:42	**3:18**	a4.3
3	**S**	9:54	**10:12**	a3.4	3:36	**4:18**	a3.9
4	**S**	11:00	**11:18**	a3.2	4:36	**5:18**	a3.5
5	**M**	...	**12:06**	3.3	5:36	**6:18**	a3.0
6	**T**	12:24	**1:06**	p3.4	6:42	**7:24**	a2.7
7	**W**	1:24	**2:06**	p3.6	7:42	**8:24**	2.8
8	**T**	2:18	**3:00**	p3.7	8:42	**9:18**	3.0
9	**F**	3:12	**3:48**	p3.8	9:36	**10:06**	p3.2
10	**S**	4:00	**4:30**	p3.8	10:24	**10:48**	3.2
11	**S**	4:48	**5:12**	3.7	11:06	**11:36**	p3.3
12	**M**	5:36	**5:54**	a3.6	11:54	...	3.2
13	**T**	6:18	**6:30**	a3.3	12:18	**12:36**	3.2
14	**W**	7:00	**7:12**	a3.1	1:00	**1:18**	a3.2
15	**T**	7:42	**7:48**	2.9	1:36	**2:06**	a3.2
16	**F**	8:24	**8:30**	a2.9	2:18	**2:48**	a3.1
17	**S**	9:12	**9:12**	2.8	3:00	**3:36**	a3.1
18	**S**	10:00	**10:06**	p2.9	3:42	**4:18**	a3.0
19	**M**	10:48	**11:00**	2.9	4:24	**5:06**	a2.9
20	**T**	11:42	**11:54**	p3.1	5:12	**6:00**	a2.9
21	**W**	...	**12:30**	3.1	6:06	**6:48**	a3.0
22	**T**	12:42	**1:18**	3.3	7:00	**7:42**	3.2
23	**F**	1:36	**2:12**	p3.6	7:54	**8:36**	p3.6
24	**S**	2:30	**3:00**	p3.8	8:48	**9:24**	p4.0
25	**S**	3:18	**3:42**	p4.0	9:42	**10:12**	p4.3
26	**M**	4:12	**4:30**	p4.2	10:36	**11:00**	p4.5
27	**T**	5:00	**5:18**	4.2	11:24	**11:48**	p4.6
28	**W**	5:54	**6:12**	a4.2	...	**12:18**	4.3
29	**T**	6:48	**7:00**	a4.0	12:36	**1:12**	a4.6
30	**F**	7:42	**7:54**	a3.8	1:30	**2:06**	a4.4

See the Woods Hole Current Diagram on pp. 60-65.

Mariners should exercise great caution when transiting Woods Hole Passage as velocities have been reported to exceed NOAA's predictions.

CAUTION: Going *from* Buzzards Bay *into* Vineyard Sound, whether through Woods Hole, Robinsons Hole, or Quicks Hole, *Red* Buoys must be kept on the LEFT or PORT hand, *Green* Buoys kept on the RIGHT or STARBOARD hand. You are considered to be proceeding seaward and should thus follow the rules for LEAVING a harbor.

See pp. 22-29 for Current Change at other points.

2021 CURRENT TABLE
WOODS HOLE, MA, The Strait

41°31.16'N, 70°40.97'W

MAY — Daylight Saving Time								JUNE — Daylight Saving Time							
DAY OF MONTH	DAY OF WEEK	CURRENT TURNS TO						DAY OF MONTH	DAY OF WEEK	CURRENT TURNS TO					
		SOUTHEAST Flood Starts			NORTHWEST Ebb Starts					SOUTHEAST Flood Starts			NORTHWEST Ebb Starts		
		a.m.	**p.m.**	Kts.	a.m.	**p.m.**	Kts.			a.m.	**p.m.**	Kts.	a.m.	**p.m.**	Kts.
1	**S**	8:37	**8:54**	a3.6	2:24	**3:06**	a4.1	1	**T**	10:19	**10:42**	a3.5	4:00	**4:42**	a3.2
2	**S**	9:42	**10:00**	a3.5	3:18	**4:00**	a3.7	2	**W**	11:18	**11:42**	a3.4	4:54	**5:36**	a2.8
3	**M**	10:42	**11:06**	a3.4	4:18	**5:00**	a3.3	3	**T**	...	**12:12**	3.3	5:54	**6:30**	2.5
4	**T**	11:48	...	3.4	5:18	**6:00**	a2.8	4	**F**	12:36	**1:00**	p3.3	6:48	**7:24**	p2.8
5	**W**	12:06	**12:42**	p3.4	6:18	**7:00**	p2.6	5	**S**	1:30	**1:48**	p3.2	7:48	**8:18**	p2.9
6	**T**	1:06	**1:36**	p3.5	7:18	**7:54**	p2.8	6	**S**	2:24	**2:36**	p3.2	8:36	**9:06**	p3.0
7	**F**	2:00	**2:24**	p3.5	8:18	**8:48**	p3.0	7	**M**	3:12	**3:18**	a3.2	9:30	**9:48**	p3.0
8	**S**	2:48	**3:12**	p3.6	9:06	**9:36**	p3.1	8	**T**	3:54	**4:00**	a3.2	10:12	**10:30**	p3.1
9	**S**	3:36	**3:54**	3.5	9:54	**10:18**	p3.2	9	**W**	4:36	**4:42**	a3.2	11:00	**11:12**	p3.2
10	**M**	4:24	**4:36**	a3.5	10:42	**11:00**	p3.2	10	**T**	5:24	**5:18**	a3.1	11:42	**11:48**	p3.3
11	**T**	5:06	**5:18**	a3.4	11:24	**11:42**	p3.2	11	**F**	6:00	**6:00**	3.1	...	**12:24**	3.0
12	**W**	5:48	**5:54**	a3.2	...	**12:12**	3.0	12	**S**	6:42	**6:42**	3.2	12:30	**1:06**	a3.4
13	**T**	6:30	**6:36**	a3.1	12:24	**12:54**	a3.3	13	**S**	7:24	**7:24**	3.3	1:06	**1:48**	a3.6
14	**F**	7:12	**7:12**	a3.1	1:00	**1:36**	a3.3	14	**M**	8:06	**8:06**	3.4	1:48	**2:30**	a3.7
15	**S**	7:54	**7:54**	3.0	1:42	**2:18**	a3.3	15	**T**	8:48	**8:54**	a3.5	2:30	**3:18**	a3.8
16	**S**	8:36	**8:42**	a3.1	2:24	**3:00**	a3.4	16	**W**	9:36	**9:48**	a3.6	3:18	**4:00**	a3.9
17	**M**	9:24	**9:30**	3.1	3:06	**3:48**	a3.4	17	**T**	10:24	**10:48**	a3.7	4:12	**4:54**	a3.9
18	**T**	10:12	**10:24**	3.2	3:48	**4:36**	a3.4	18	**F**	11:18	**11:48**	a3.8	5:06	**5:42**	a3.8
19	**W**	11:00	**11:18**	3.3	4:42	**5:24**	a3.4	19	**S**	...	**12:12**	3.8	6:00	**6:36**	a3.7
20	**T**	11:54	...	3.5	5:36	**6:18**	a3.4	20	**S**	12:48	**1:06**	p3.9	7:00	**7:36**	p3.8
21	**F**	12:18	**12:48**	p3.6	6:30	**7:12**	a3.5	21	**M**	1:42	**2:00**	p3.9	8:06	**8:30**	p4.0
22	**S**	1:12	**1:36**	p3.8	7:30	**8:00**	p3.7	22	**T**	2:42	**2:54**	p3.8	9:06	**9:24**	p4.2
23	**S**	2:06	**2:24**	p3.9	8:24	**8:54**	p4.1	23	**W**	3:36	**3:48**	p3.8	10:00	**10:18**	p4.2
24	**M**	3:00	**3:18**	p4.0	9:24	**9:48**	p4.3	24	**T**	4:36	**4:42**	a3.9	10:54	**11:12**	p4.2
25	**T**	3:54	**4:06**	p4.0	10:18	**10:36**	p4.5	25	**F**	5:30	**5:36**	a4.0	11:48	...	3.6
26	**W**	4:48	**5:00**	4.0	11:12	**11:24**	p4.5	26	**S**	6:24	**6:36**	a4.0	12:01	**12:42**	a4.1
27	**T**	5:42	**5:54**	a4.0	...	**12:06**	4.0	27	**S**	7:18	**7:30**	a3.9	12:54	**1:36**	a3.9
28	**F**	6:36	**6:48**	a3.9	12:18	**1:00**	a4.4	28	**M**	8:06	**8:24**	a3.8	1:48	**2:30**	a3.7
29	**S**	7:30	**7:42**	a3.8	1:12	**1:54**	a4.2	29	**T**	9:00	**9:18**	a3.7	2:42	**3:24**	a3.4
30	**S**	8:24	**8:42**	a3.7	2:06	**2:48**	a3.9	30	**W**	9:54	**10:18**	a3.5	3:36	**4:12**	a3.2
31	**M**	9:24	**9:42**	a3.6	3:00	**3:42**	a3.5								

See the Woods Hole Current Diagram on pp. 60-65.

Mariners should exercise great caution when transiting Woods Hole Passage as velocities have been reported to exceed NOAA's predictions.

To hold longest fair current from Buzzards Bay headed East through Vineyard and Nantucket Sounds go through Woods Hole 2 1/2 hrs. after flood starts SE in Woods Hole. (Any earlier means adverse currents in the Sounds.)

2021 CURRENT TABLE
WOODS HOLE, MA, The Strait

41°31.16'N, 70°40.97'W

		Daylight Saving Time										**Daylight Saving Time**				
JULY								**AUGUST**								
DAY OF MONTH	DAY OF WEEK	CURRENT TURNS TO						DAY OF MONTH	DAY OF WEEK	CURRENT TURNS TO						
		SOUTHEAST Flood Starts			NORTHWEST Ebb Starts					SOUTHEAST Flood Starts			NORTHWEST Ebb Starts			
		a.m.	**p.m.**	Kts.	a.m.	**p.m.**	Kts.			a.m.	**p.m.**	Kts.	a.m.	**p.m.**	Kts.	
1	**T**	10:49	**11:12**	a3.3	4:30	**5:06**	a2.9	1	**S**	11:49	...	2.6	5:42	**6:12**	2.3	
2	**F**	11:36	...	3.1	5:24	**6:00**	a2.6	2	**M**	12:30	**12:30**	a2.5	6:36	**7:06**	p2.4	
3	**S**	12:06	**12:24**	p3.0	6:18	**6:48**	p2.6	3	**T**	1:18	**1:18**	a2.5	7:30	**7:54**	p2.5	
4	**S**	1:00	**1:12**	2.8	7:12	**7:42**	p2.7	4	**W**	2:06	**2:06**	2.5	8:24	**8:42**	p2.6	
5	**M**	1:54	**1:54**	a2.8	8:06	**8:30**	p2.8	5	**T**	2:54	**2:54**	p2.7	9:12	**9:24**	p2.8	
6	**T**	2:42	**2:42**	a2.8	9:00	**9:12**	p2.8	6	**F**	3:36	**3:36**	p2.9	9:54	**10:06**	p3.1	
7	**W**	3:24	**3:24**	a2.9	9:42	**9:54**	p2.9	7	**S**	4:18	**4:18**	p3.2	10:36	**10:42**	p3.5	
8	**T**	4:12	**4:06**	a3.0	10:30	**10:36**	p3.1	8	**S**	5:00	**5:00**	p3.5	11:18	**11:24**	p3.8	
9	**F**	4:54	**4:48**	p3.1	11:12	**11:18**	p3.3	9	**M**	5:42	**5:48**	p3.8	...	**12:01**	3.6	
10	**S**	5:30	**5:30**	p3.3	11:54	**11:54**	p3.6	10	**T**	6:24	**6:30**	p4.0	12:06	**12:48**	a4.2	
11	**S**	6:12	**6:12**	p3.5	...	**12:36**	3.3	11	**W**	7:00	**7:12**	4.1	12:54	**1:30**	a4.4	
12	**M**	6:54	**6:54**	p3.7	12:36	**1:18**	a3.9	12	**T**	7:42	**8:06**	a4.1	1:42	**2:18**	a4.6	
13	**T**	7:30	**7:42**	p3.8	1:18	**2:00**	a4.1	13	**F**	8:30	**8:54**	a4.1	2:30	**3:00**	a4.6	
14	**W**	8:12	**8:30**	3.8	2:06	**2:48**	a4.3	14	**S**	9:18	**9:54**	a4.0	3:24	**3:54**	a4.4	
15	**T**	9:00	**9:24**	a3.9	2:54	**3:30**	a4.3	15	**S**	10:18	**11:00**	a3.9	4:18	**4:48**	a4.1	
16	**F**	9:48	**10:18**	a4.0	3:42	**4:24**	a4.2	16	**M**	11:18	...	3.7	5:18	**5:42**	3.7	
17	**S**	10:48	**11:24**	a3.9	4:36	**5:12**	a4.0	17	**T**	12:06	**12:18**	p3.5	6:24	**6:48**	p3.5	
18	**S**	11:42	...	3.9	5:36	**6:12**	3.8	18	**W**	1:12	**1:18**	p3.3	7:24	**7:48**	p3.4	
19	**M**	12:24	**12:36**	p3.7	6:42	**7:06**	p3.7	19	**T**	2:12	**2:24**	a3.4	8:30	**8:48**	p3.4	
20	**T**	1:24	**1:36**	p3.6	7:42	**8:06**	p3.8	20	**F**	3:12	**3:18**	a3.7	9:30	**9:42**	p3.5	
21	**W**	2:24	**2:36**	p3.5	8:48	**9:06**	p3.8	21	**S**	4:06	**4:18**	a4.0	10:24	**10:36**	p3.6	
22	**T**	3:24	**3:30**	a3.6	9:42	**10:00**	p3.9	22	**S**	5:00	**5:12**	a4.1	11:12	**11:30**	p3.6	
23	**F**	4:24	**4:30**	a3.9	10:42	**10:54**	p3.8	23	**M**	5:48	**6:00**	a4.1	...	**12:06**	3.3	
24	**S**	5:18	**5:24**	a4.1	11:36	**11:48**	p3.8	24	**T**	6:36	**6:48**	a4.0	12:18	**12:54**	a3.6	
25	**S**	6:06	**6:18**	a4.1	...	**12:24**	3.4	25	**W**	7:18	**7:36**	a3.7	1:06	**1:42**	a3.5	
26	**M**	7:00	**7:12**	a4.0	12:36	**1:18**	a3.7	26	**T**	8:00	**8:24**	a3.4	1:54	**2:30**	a3.4	
27	**T**	7:48	**8:00**	a3.8	1:30	**2:06**	a3.6	27	**F**	8:42	**9:12**	a3.1	2:42	**3:12**	a3.2	
28	**W**	8:30	**8:54**	a3.6	2:18	**2:54**	a3.4	28	**S**	9:30	**10:06**	a2.8	3:30	**4:00**	a2.9	
29	**T**	9:18	**9:48**	a3.4	3:12	**3:48**	a3.2	29	**S**	10:18	**11:00**	2.5	4:24	**4:48**	a2.6	
30	**F**	10:06	**10:42**	a3.1	4:00	**4:36**	a2.9	30	**M**	11:06	**11:54**	a2.5	5:12	**5:36**	2.3	
31	**S**	11:00	**11:36**	a2.8	4:54	**5:24**	a2.6	31	**T**	11:54	...	2.4	6:06	**6:24**	p2.2	

See the Woods Hole Current Diagram on pp. 60-65.

Mariners should exercise great caution when transiting Woods Hole Passage as velocities have been reported to exceed NOAA's predictions.

CAUTION: Going *from* Buzzards Bay *into* Vineyard Sound, whether through Woods Hole, Robinsons Hole, or Quicks Hole, *Red* Buoys must be kept on the LEFT or PORT hand, *Green* Buoys kept on the RIGHT or STARBOARD hand. You are considered to be proceeding seaward and should thus follow the rules for LEAVING a harbor.

See pp. 22-29 for Current Change at other points.

2021 CURRENT TABLE
WOODS HOLE, MA, The Strait

41°31.16'N, 70°40.97'W

Daylight Saving Time

SEPTEMBER

DAY OF MONTH	DAY OF WEEK	CURRENT TURNS TO SOUTHEAST Flood Starts a.m.	**p.m.**	Kts.	NORTHWEST Ebb Starts a.m.	**p.m.**	Kts.
1	W	12:42	**12:48**	p2.5	7:00	**7:12**	p2.2
2	T	1:30	**1:30**	p2.6	7:48	**8:00**	p2.5
3	F	2:18	**2:18**	p2.8	8:36	**8:48**	p2.8
4	S	3:00	**3:06**	p3.1	9:24	**9:30**	p3.2
5	S	3:48	**3:48**	p3.4	10:06	**10:12**	p3.7
6	M	4:30	**4:36**	p3.8	10:48	**11:00**	p4.1
7	T	5:06	**5:18**	p4.1	11:30	**11:42**	p4.4
8	W	5:48	**6:06**	p4.2	...	**12:12**	4.3
9	T	6:30	**6:54**	a4.3	12:30	**1:00**	a4.6
10	F	7:18	**7:42**	a4.3	1:18	**1:48**	a4.7
11	S	8:00	**8:36**	a4.2	2:12	**2:36**	a4.6
12	S	8:54	**9:36**	a3.9	3:06	**3:30**	4.3
13	M	9:54	**10:42**	a3.7	4:00	**4:24**	p4.0
14	T	11:00	**11:48**	a3.4	5:00	**5:24**	p3.6
15	W	...	**12:06**	3.2	6:06	**6:24**	p3.2
16	T	12:54	**1:06**	a3.2	7:12	**7:30**	p3.0
17	F	1:54	**2:06**	a3.5	8:12	**8:30**	p3.1
18	S	2:54	**3:06**	a3.7	9:12	**9:30**	p3.2
19	S	3:48	**4:00**	a4.0	10:00	**10:18**	p3.3
20	M	4:36	**4:48**	a4.1	10:54	**11:12**	p3.4
21	T	5:24	**5:42**	a4.0	11:42	...	3.4
22	W	6:06	**6:24**	a3.8	12:01	**12:24**	a3.4
23	T	6:48	**7:12**	a3.5	12:42	**1:12**	a3.4
24	F	7:30	**8:00**	a3.2	1:30	**1:54**	a3.3
25	S	8:12	**8:42**	p2.9	2:18	**2:42**	a3.1
26	S	8:54	**9:30**	2.6	3:06	**3:24**	a2.9
27	M	9:36	**10:24**	2.5	3:54	**4:06**	p2.7
28	T	10:30	**11:18**	2.5	4:42	**4:54**	p2.5
29	W	11:18	...	2.5	5:30	**5:42**	p2.4
30	T	12:06	**12:12**	p2.6	6:18	**6:30**	p2.4

Daylight Saving Time

OCTOBER

DAY OF MONTH	DAY OF WEEK	CURRENT TURNS TO SOUTHEAST Flood Starts a.m.	**p.m.**	Kts.	NORTHWEST Ebb Starts a.m.	**p.m.**	Kts.
1	F	12:55	**1:00**	p2.8	7:12	**7:24**	p2.6
2	S	1:42	**1:48**	p3.0	8:00	**8:12**	p3.0
3	S	2:24	**2:36**	p3.3	8:48	**9:00**	p3.4
4	M	3:12	**3:24**	p3.6	9:30	**9:48**	p3.9
5	T	3:54	**4:06**	p3.9	10:18	**10:30**	p4.2
6	W	4:36	**4:54**	p4.2	11:00	**11:18**	p4.5
7	T	5:18	**5:42**	4.3	11:48	...	4.5
8	F	6:06	**6:36**	a4.4	12:06	**12:30**	p4.7
9	S	6:54	**7:24**	a4.3	1:00	**1:24**	p4.7
10	S	7:42	**8:18**	a4.0	1:54	**2:12**	p4.5
11	M	8:36	**9:18**	a3.7	2:48	**3:06**	p4.2
12	T	9:36	**10:24**	a3.4	3:48	**4:06**	p3.8
13	W	10:42	**11:30**	p3.3	4:48	**5:06**	p3.4
14	T	11:48	...	3.0	5:48	**6:06**	p3.0
15	F	12:36	**12:54**	a3.3	6:48	**7:12**	p2.8
16	S	1:36	**1:54**	a3.5	7:48	**8:12**	p2.9
17	S	2:30	**2:48**	a3.7	8:48	**9:06**	p3.1
18	M	3:18	**3:42**	a3.8	9:42	**10:00**	3.2
19	T	4:06	**4:30**	a3.9	10:30	**10:48**	a3.3
20	W	4:54	**5:18**	a3.8	11:12	**11:36**	a3.3
21	T	5:36	**6:00**	3.6	11:54	...	3.3
22	F	6:12	**6:48**	p3.3	12:18	**12:42**	p3.3
23	S	6:54	**7:30**	p3.1	1:06	**1:24**	p3.2
24	S	7:36	**8:12**	2.8	1:48	**2:06**	p3.1
25	M	8:18	**9:00**	2.7	2:36	**2:48**	p3.0
26	T	9:00	**9:48**	p2.7	3:24	**3:30**	p2.9
27	W	9:54	**10:36**	2.7	4:06	**4:12**	p2.8
28	T	10:42	**11:24**	p2.8	4:54	**5:00**	p2.7
29	F	11:36	...	2.9	5:42	**5:48**	p2.8
30	S	12:12	**12:30**	3.0	6:30	**6:42**	p2.9
31	S	1:00	**1:18**	3.2	7:24	**7:36**	p3.2

See the Woods Hole Current Diagram on pp. 60-65.

Mariners should exercise great caution when transiting Woods Hole Passage as velocities have been reported to exceed NOAA's predictions.

To hold longest fair current from Buzzards Bay headed East through Vineyard and Nantucket Sounds go through Woods Hole 2 1/2 hrs. after flood starts SE in Woods Hole. (Any earlier means adverse currents in the Sounds.)

2021 CURRENT TABLE
WOODS HOLE, MA, The Strait
41°31.16'N, 70°40.97'W

***Standard Time starts Nov. 7 at 2 a.m.** — **Standard Time**

NOVEMBER

DAY OF MONTH	DAY OF WEEK	CURRENT TURNS TO SOUTHEAST Flood Starts a.m.	p.m.	Kts.	CURRENT TURNS TO NORTHWEST Ebb Starts a.m.	p.m.	Kts.
1	M	1:49	2:06	p3.5	8:12	8:30	p3.6
2	T	2:36	2:54	3.7	9:00	9:18	p3.9
3	W	3:18	3:48	3.9	9:48	10:06	p4.2
4	T	4:06	4:36	4.1	10:30	11:00	a4.5
5	F	4:54	5:24	a4.3	11:18	11:54	a4.7
6	S	5:42	6:18	a4.3	...	12:12	4.7
7	S	*5:30	*6:12	a4.1	12:48	*12:01	p4.6
8	M	6:24	7:06	a3.8	12:42	12:54	p4.4
9	T	7:18	8:06	3.5	1:36	1:48	p4.1
10	W	8:24	9:06	p3.4	2:30	2:48	p3.6
11	T	9:30	10:12	p3.4	3:30	3:48	p3.2
12	F	10:36	11:12	p3.4	4:30	4:48	2.8
13	S	11:36	...	3.1	5:30	5:48	2.6
14	S	12:06	12:30	a3.5	6:24	6:48	2.8
15	M	1:00	1:24	a3.5	7:24	7:42	a3.0
16	T	1:48	2:18	a3.6	8:12	8:36	a3.2
17	W	2:36	3:06	3.6	9:00	9:24	a3.2
18	T	3:18	3:48	p3.6	9:42	10:06	a3.3
19	F	4:00	4:36	p3.4	10:24	10:54	a3.2
20	S	4:42	5:18	p3.2	11:06	11:36	a3.2
21	S	5:24	6:00	p3.0	11:48	...	3.2
22	M	6:00	6:42	2.9	12:24	12:30	p3.2
23	T	6:42	7:24	2.9	1:06	1:12	p3.2
24	W	7:30	8:06	p3.0	1:48	1:54	p3.2
25	T	8:18	8:54	p3.0	2:36	2:36	p3.2
26	F	9:06	9:42	p3.2	3:18	3:24	p3.2
27	S	10:00	10:36	p3.3	4:06	4:12	p3.2
28	S	10:54	11:24	p3.5	4:54	5:06	p3.3
29	M	11:48	...	3.4	5:42	6:00	p3.4
30	T	12:12	12:42	a3.7	6:36	7:00	p3.7

DECEMBER

DAY OF MONTH	DAY OF WEEK	CURRENT TURNS TO SOUTHEAST Flood Starts a.m.	p.m.	Kts.	CURRENT TURNS TO NORTHWEST Ebb Starts a.m.	p.m.	Kts.
1	W	1:01	1:30	a3.9	7:30	7:54	3.9
2	T	1:48	2:24	a4.0	8:18	8:48	a4.2
3	F	2:36	3:18	a4.1	9:06	9:42	a4.5
4	S	3:30	4:12	a4.1	10:00	10:36	a4.6
5	S	4:24	5:06	4.0	10:48	11:30	a4.6
6	M	5:18	6:00	3.9	11:42	...	4.4
7	T	6:12	6:54	p3.7	12:24	12:36	p4.2
8	W	7:06	7:48	p3.7	1:18	1:30	p3.9
9	T	8:06	8:48	p3.6	2:12	2:30	p3.5
10	F	9:12	9:48	p3.5	3:12	3:24	p3.2
11	S	10:12	10:42	p3.4	4:06	4:24	2.8
12	S	11:12	11:36	p3.3	5:00	5:18	2.5
13	M	...	12:06	3.1	6:00	6:18	a2.7
14	T	12:24	1:00	a3.3	6:54	7:18	a2.9
15	W	1:12	1:48	3.2	7:42	8:06	a3.0
16	T	2:00	2:36	p3.3	8:30	9:00	a3.1
17	F	2:42	3:24	p3.3	9:12	9:42	a3.1
18	S	3:24	4:06	p3.3	9:54	10:30	a3.1
19	S	4:06	4:48	p3.2	10:36	11:12	a3.2
20	M	4:48	5:30	p3.1	11:18	11:54	a3.2
21	T	5:30	6:12	p3.1	...	12:01	3.4
22	W	6:12	6:54	p3.2	12:36	12:36	p3.5
23	T	6:54	7:30	p3.3	1:18	1:18	p3.6
24	F	7:42	8:18	p3.4	2:00	2:00	p3.7
25	S	8:30	9:00	p3.6	2:42	2:48	p3.7
26	S	9:24	9:54	p3.7	3:30	3:36	p3.7
27	M	10:24	10:42	p3.8	4:18	4:36	p3.6
28	T	11:18	11:36	p3.9	5:12	5:30	3.6
29	W	...	12:18	3.6	6:06	6:30	a3.7
30	T	12:30	1:12	a3.9	7:00	7:30	a3.9
31	F	1:24	2:06	a3.9	7:54	8:30	a4.1

See the Woods Hole Current Diagram on pp. 60-65.

Mariners should exercise great caution when transiting Woods Hole Passage as velocities have been reported to exceed NOAA's predictions.

CAUTION: Going *from* Buzzards Bay *into* Vineyard Sound, whether through Woods Hole, Robinsons Hole, or Quicks Hole, *Red* Buoys must be kept on the LEFT or PORT hand, *Green* Buoys kept on the RIGHT or STARBOARD hand. You are considered to be proceeding seaward and should thus follow the rules for LEAVING a harbor.

See pp. 22-29 for Current Change at other points.

Coping with Currents

See also p. 21, Piloting in a Cross Current

When going directly with or against a current, our piloting problems are simple. (See Smarter Boating, p. 36.) There is no change in course, and our speed over the bottom is easily figured. However, we tend to guess a bit when the current is at some other angle. Where these currents are strong, as between New York and Nantucket, it will be vital to figure the factors carefully, especially in haze or fog.

The Table below tells 1) how many degrees to change your course; 2) by what percent your speed is decreased, with the current off the Bow; 3) or by what percent it is increased, with the current off the Stern.

First: Estimate your boat's speed through the water. Then refer to the appropriate TIDAL CURRENT CHART (see pp. 72-83 or pp. 98-103) and estimate the current's speed. Put these two in the form of a ratio, for example: boat speed is 8 kts, current 2 kts; ratio is 4 to 1.

Second: Using the same CURRENT CHART, estimate the relative direction of the current to the nearest 15°. Example: your desired course is 60°, the current is from the East, or a relative angle of 30° on your starboard bow.

Third: Enter the Tables under Ratio of 4.0; drop down to the 30° block of numbers (indicated in the left margin). The top figure in the block shows you must change your course 7°, always toward the current, and in this example, to 67°. The middle figure, 22%, is the amount by which your speed over the bottom will be decreased if the current is off your bow, i.e. from 8 kts down to 6.25 kts. Had the figure been 30% off your stern, instead of your bow, you would apply the third figure, 21%, adding it to your 8 kts, making your true speed about 9.7 kts.

RATIOS OF BOAT SPEED TO CURRENT SPEED

Relative Angle of Current		2	2½	3	3½	4	5	6	7	8	10	12	15	20
0° from	°	0	0	0	0	0	0	0	0	0	0	0	0	0
Bow	−%	**50**	**40**	**33**	**29**	**25**	**20**	**17**	**14**	**12**	**10**	**8.3**	**6.7**	**5.0**
Stern	+%	50	40	33	29	25	20	17	14	12	10	8.3	6.7	5.0
15° from	°	7.0	6.0	5.0	4.0	3.5	3.0	2.5	2.0	1.5	1.5	1.0	1.0	0.5
Bow	−%	**49**	**39**	**33**	**28**	**24**	**20**	**16**	**14**	**12**	**10**	**8.0**	**6.4**	**4.8**
Stern	+%	48	38	32	27	24	19	16	14	12	10	8.0	6.4	4.8
30° from	°	14	11	9.5	8.0	7.0	5.5	4.5	4.0	3.0	2.5	2.0	2.0	1.0
Bow	−%	**46**	**36**	**30**	**26**	**22**	**18**	**15**	**13**	**11**	**8.8**	**7.3**	**5.9**	**4.3**
Stern	+%	40	33	28	24	21	17	14	12	11	8.6	7.1	5.7	4.3
45° from	°	20	16	13	11	10	8.0	7.0	5.5	5.0	4.0	3.0	2.5	1.5
Bow	−%	**42**	**32**	**26**	**22**	**19**	**15**	**12**	**11**	**9.2**	**7.4**	**6.1**	**4.9**	**3.6**
Stern	+%	29	24	21	18	16	13	11	10	8.4	6.8	5.7	4.5	3.4
60° from	°	25	20	16	14	12	9.5	8.0	7.0	6.0	4.5	3.5	3.0	2.0
Bow	−%	**34**	**26**	**21**	**18**	**15**	**11**	**9.3**	**7.8**	**6.7**	**5.4**	**4.4**	**3.5**	**2.6**
Stern	+%	16	14	13	11	10	8.6	7.3	6.4	5.7	4.6	3.8	3.1	2.4
75° from	°	29	23	18	16	14	10	9.0	7.5	6.5	5.0	4.0	3.5	2.5
Bow	−%	**25**	**18**	**14**	**11**	**9.1**	**6.8**	**5.5**	**4.5**	**3.8**	**3.0**	**2.5**	**1.9**	**1.4**
Stern	+%	0.8	2.5	3.7	3.8	3.6	3.6	3.1	2.9	2.6	2.2	1.9	1.5	1.2
90°	°	30	24	19	17	14	11	9.5	8.0	7.0	5.5	4.5	3.5	2.5
Abeam	−%	**13**	**8.6**	**5.4**	**4.1**	**3.0**	**1.8**	**1.4**	**1.0**	**0.7**	**0.4**	**0.3**	**0.2**	**0.1**

Note: In general, while rounding a headland where head current is strong, hug the shore as far as safety will permit or go well out. (Current is usually apt to be strongest between these two points.)

Woods Hole and Surrounds

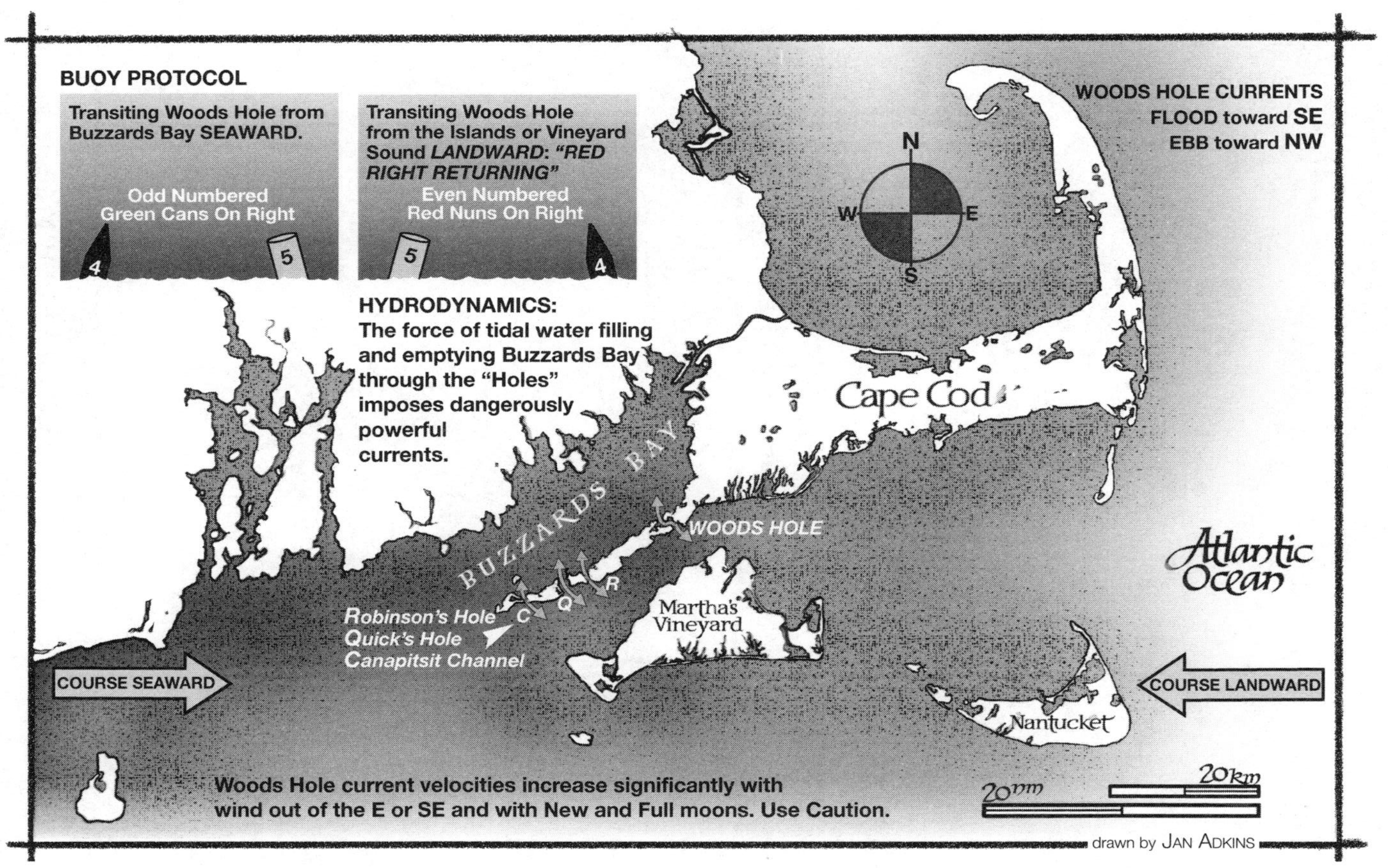

BUOY PROTOCOL
Transiting Woods Hole from Buzzards Bay SEAWARD.
Odd Numbered Green Cans On Right
4
5
Transiting Woods Hole from the Islands or Vineyard Sound *LANDWARD: "RED RIGHT RETURNING"*
Even Numbered Red Nuns On Right
5
4
HYDRODYNAMICS:
The force of tidal water filling and emptying Buzzards Bay through the "Holes" imposes dangerously powerful currents.
WOODS HOLE CURRENTS
FLOOD toward SE
EBB toward NW
N
W
E
S
Cape Cod
BUZZARDS BAY
WOODS HOLE
Atlantic Ocean
R
Q
C
Martha's Vineyard
Robinson's Hole
Quick's Hole
Canapitsit Channel
COURSE SEAWARD
COURSE LANDWARD
Nantucket
Woods Hole current velocities increase significantly with wind out of the E or SE and with New and Full moons. Use Caution.
20nm
20km
drawn by JAN ADKINS

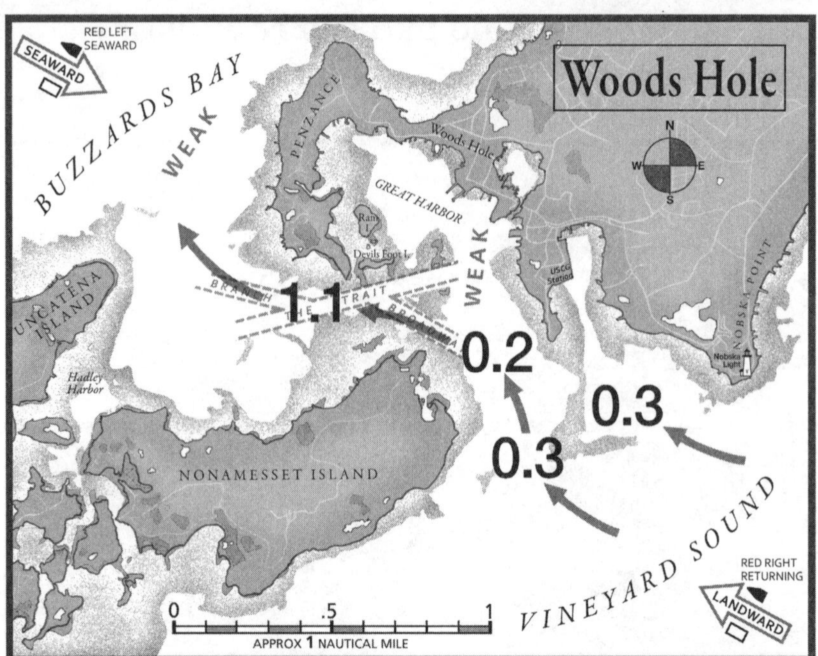

FLOOD STARTS at Pollock Rip Channel

4 hours **AFTER HIGH WATER** at Boston

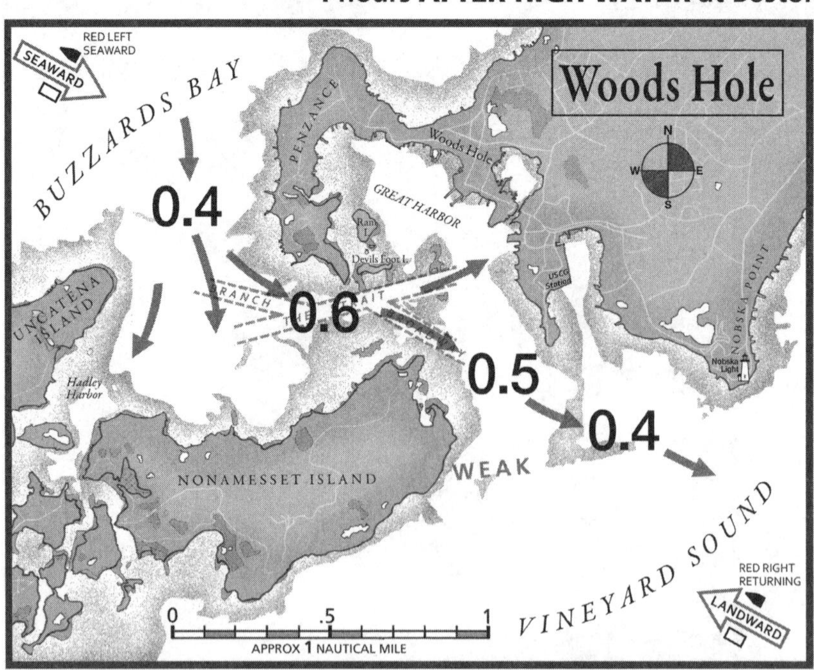

1 HOUR AFTER FLOOD STARTS at Pollock Rip Channel

5 hours **AFTER HIGH WATER** at Boston

Woods Hole velocities increase significantly with wind out of the E or SE and with New and Full Moons. Use Caution. Velocities shown are at Spring Tides. See note at bottom of Boston Tables: Rule-of-Thumb for Current Velocities.

Adapted from Buzzards Bay, Vineyard, and Nantucket Sounds chart on pp. 72–83.

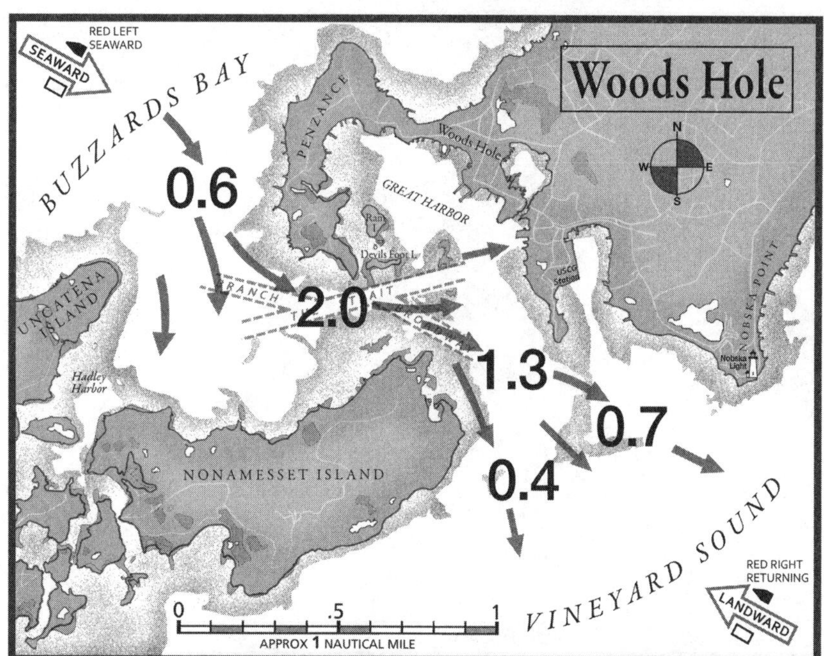

2 HOURS AFTER FLOOD STARTS at Pollock Rip Channel
LOW WATER at Boston

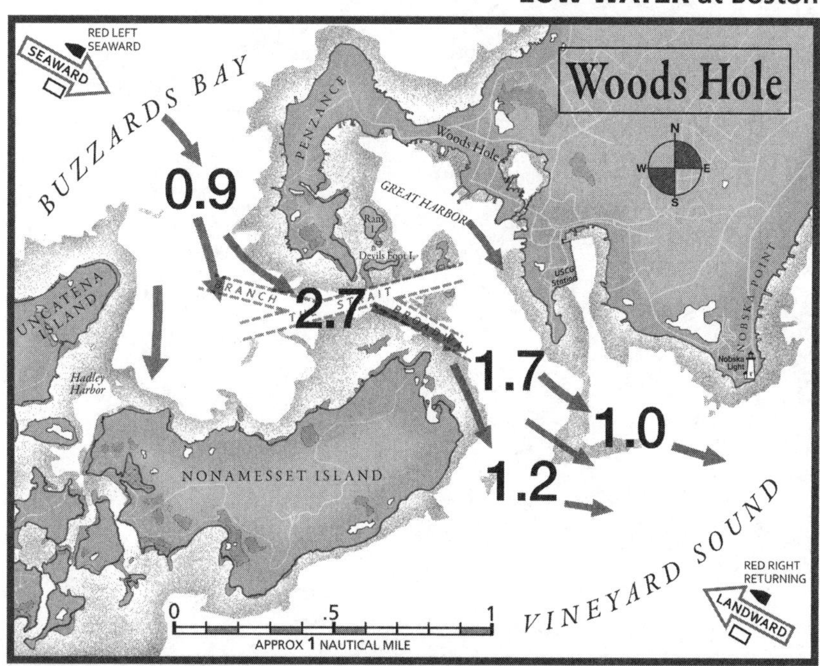

3 HOURS AFTER FLOOD STARTS at Pollock Rip Channel
1 HOUR AFTER LOW WATER at Boston

Woods Hole velocities increase significantly with wind out of the E or SE and with New and Full Moons. Use Caution. Velocities shown are at Spring Tides. See note at bottom of Boston Tables: Rule-of-Thumb for Current Velocities.

Adapted from Buzzards Bay, Vineyard, and Nantucket Sounds chart on pp. 72–83.

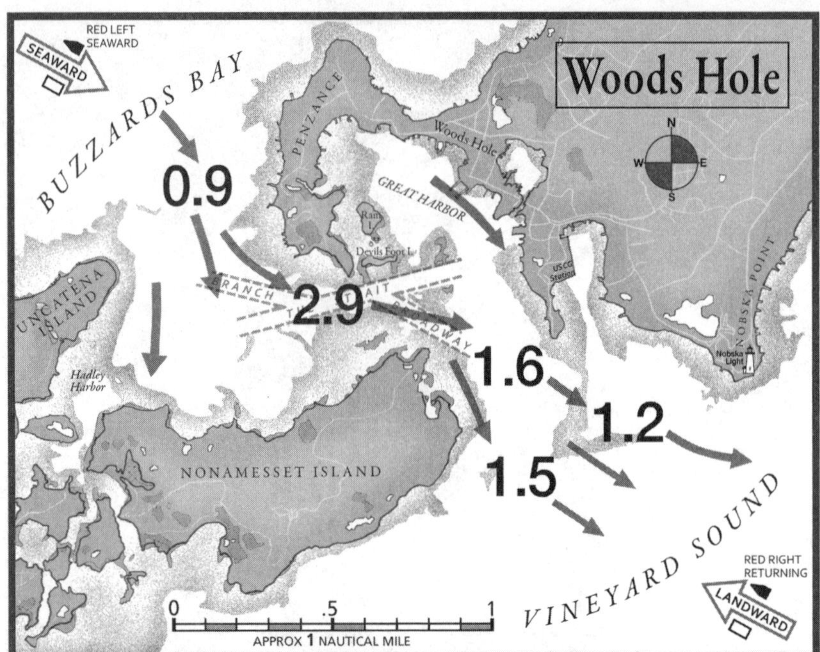

4 HOURS AFTER FLOOD STARTS at Pollock Rip Channel
2 HOURS AFTER LOW WATER at Boston

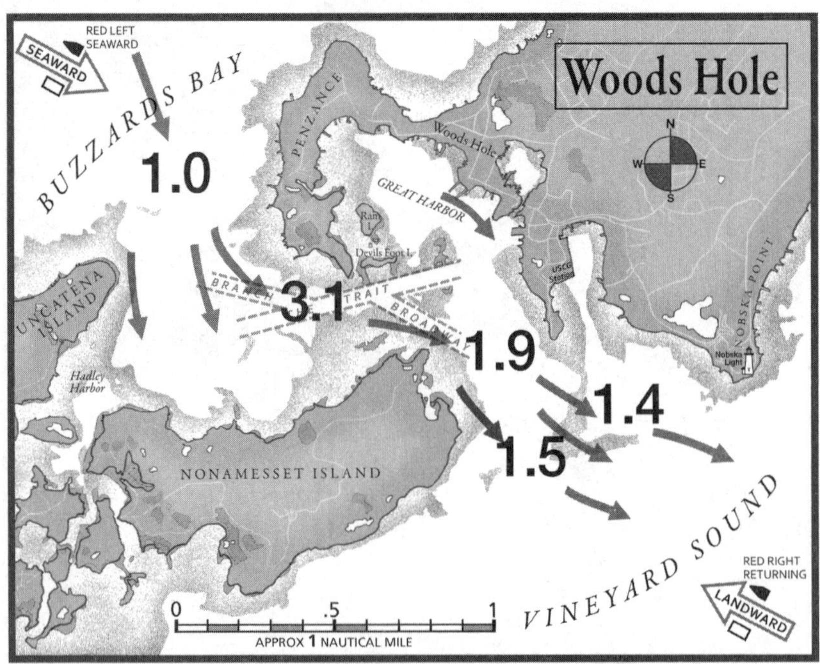

5 hours AFTER FLOOD STARTS at Pollock Rip Channel
3 hours AFTER LOW WATER at Boston

Woods Hole velocities increase significantly with wind out of the E or SE and with New and Full Moons. Use Caution. Velocities shown are at Spring Tides. See note at bottom of Boston Tables: Rule-of-Thumb for Current Velocities.

Adapted from Buzzards Bay, Vineyard, and Nantucket Sounds chart on pp. 72–83.

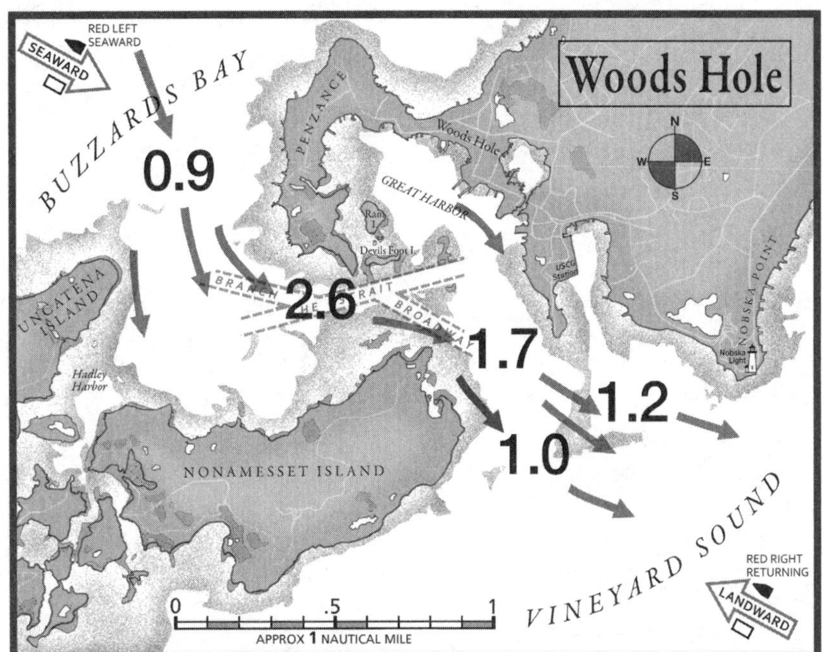

EBB STARTS at Pollock Rip Channel

4 hours **AFTER LOW WATER** at Boston

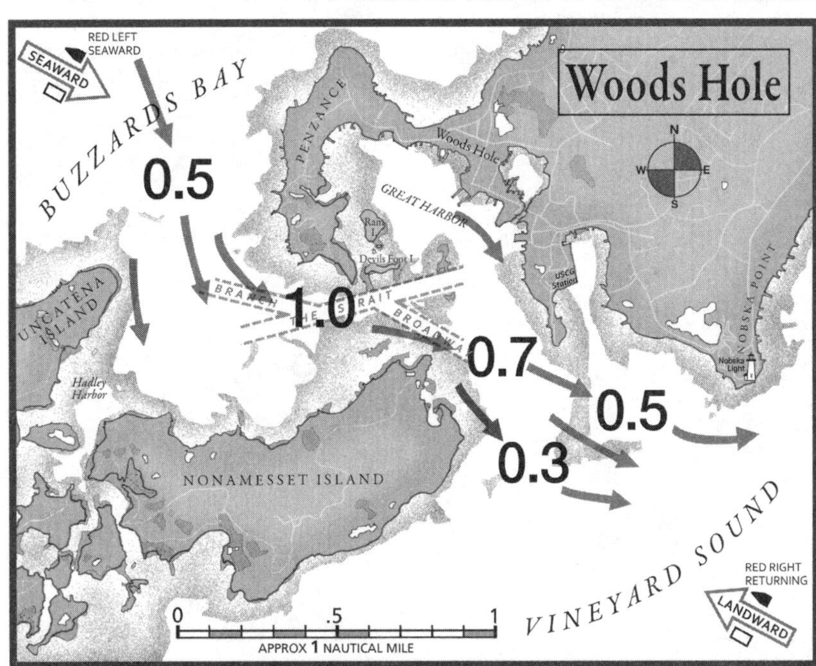

1 HOUR AFTER EBB STARTS at Pollock Rip Channel

5 hours **AFTER LOW WATER** at Boston

Woods Hole velocities increase significantly with wind out of the E or SE and with New and Full Moons. Use Caution. Velocities shown are at Spring Tides. See note at bottom of Boston Tables: Rule-of-Thumb for Current Velocities.

Adapted from Buzzards Bay, Vineyard, and Nantucket Sounds chart on pp. 72–83.

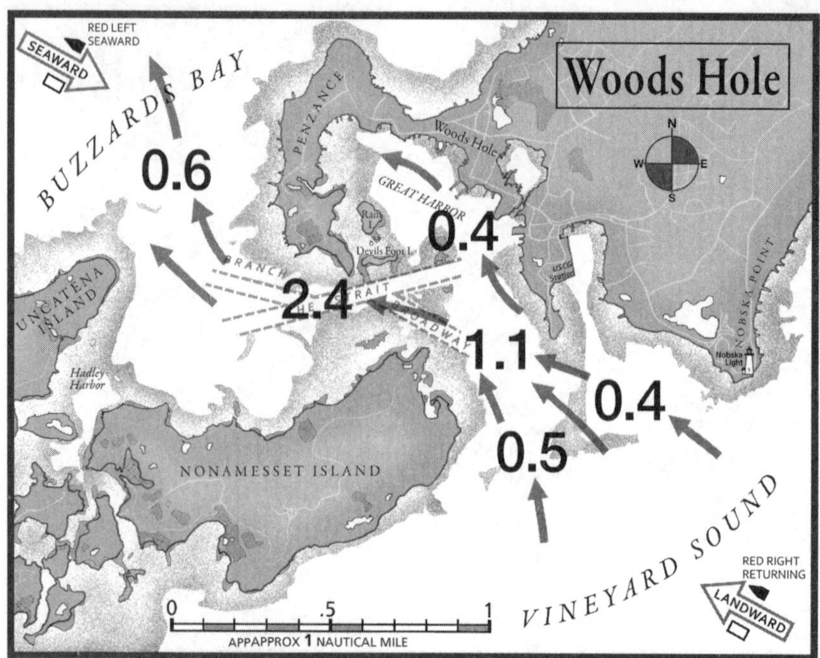

2 HOURS AFTER EBB STARTS at Pollock Rip Channel

HIGH WATER at Boston

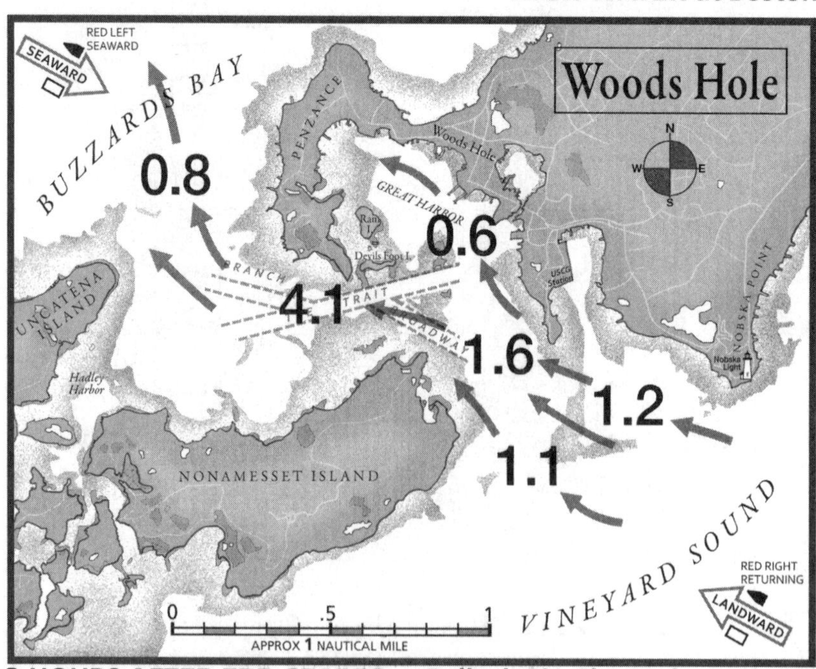

3 HOURS AFTER EBB STARTS at Pollock Rip Channel

1 HOUR AFTER HIGH WATER at Boston

Woods Hole velocities increase significantly with wind out of the E or SE and with New and Full Moons. Use Caution. Velocities shown are at Spring Tides. See note at bottom of Boston Tables: Rule-of-Thumb for Current Velocities.

Adapted from Buzzards Bay, Vineyard, and Nantucket Sounds chart on pp. 72–83.

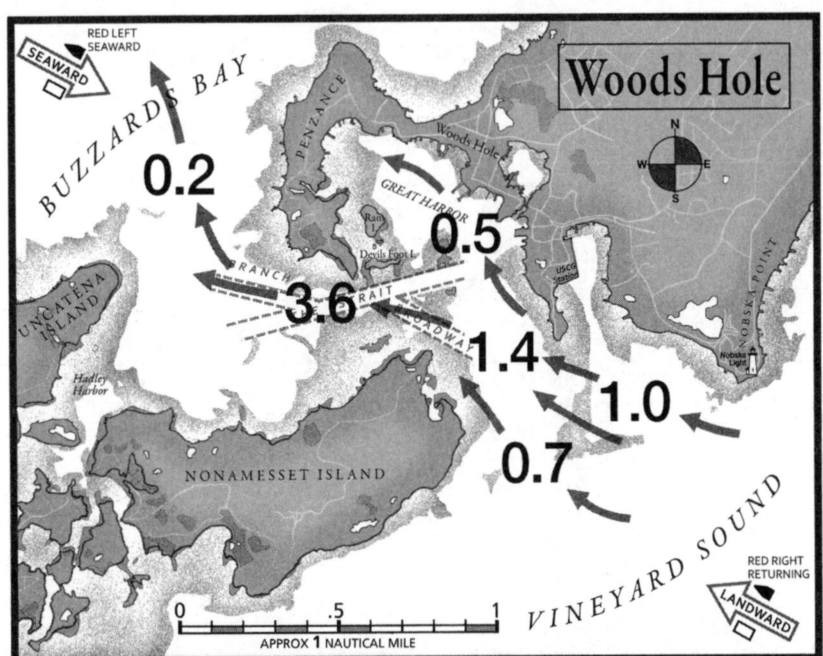

4 HOURS AFTER EBB STARTS at Pollock Rip Channel
2 HOURS AFTER HIGH WATER at Boston

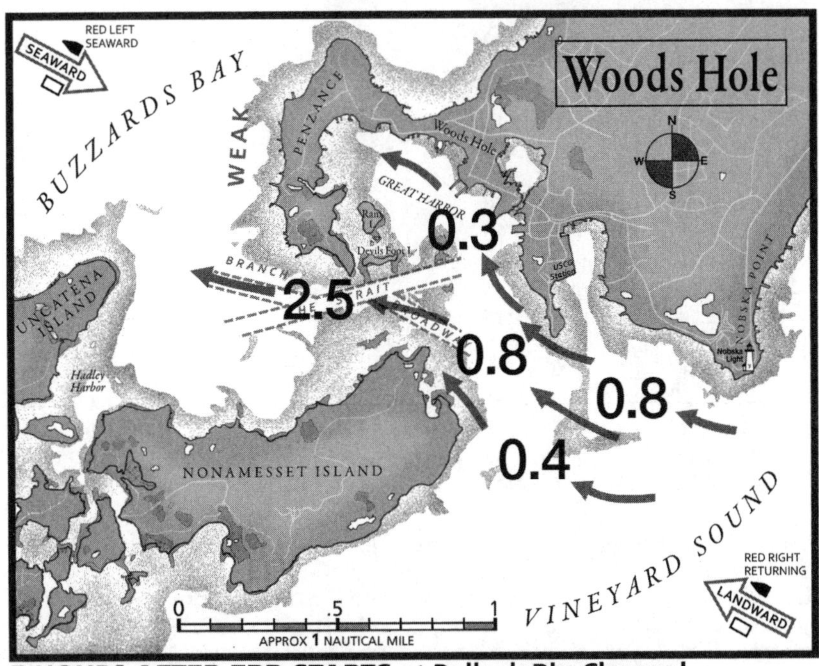

5 HOURS AFTER EBB STARTS at Pollock Rip Channel
3 HOURS AFTER HIGH WATER at Boston

Woods Hole velocities increase significantly with wind out of the E or SE and with New and Full Moons. Use Caution. Velocities shown are at Spring Tides. See note at bottom of Boston Tables: Rule-of-Thumb for Current Velocities.

Adapted from Buzzards Bay, Vineyard, and Nantucket Sounds chart on pp. 72–83.

2021 CURRENT TABLE
POLLOCK RIP CHANNEL, MA
41°33'N, 69°59'W SE of Monomoy Pt. at Butler Hole

Standard Time

JANUARY

DAY OF MONTH	DAY OF WEEK	CURRENT TURNS TO					
		NORTHEAST Flood Starts			SOUTHWEST Ebb Starts		
		a.m.	**p.m.**	Kts.	a.m.	**p.m.**	Kts.
1	**F**	4:31	**4:36**	p2.2	10:48	**11:30**	a1.9
2	**S**	5:12	**5:18**	p2.2	11:30	...	1.9
3	**S**	5:54	**6:06**	p2.2	12:12	**12:12**	p1.9
4	**M**	6:42	**6:54**	p2.2	12:54	**1:06**	p1.9
5	**T**	7:30	**7:48**	p2.1	1:42	**2:00**	1.8
6	**W**	8:24	**8:42**	p2.0	2:36	**3:00**	1.8
7	**T**	9:24	**9:48**	p1.9	3:30	**4:00**	a1.8
8	**F**	10:24	**10:48**	a1.9	4:30	**5:06**	a1.7
9	**S**	11:24	**11:54**	a1.9	5:24	**6:06**	a1.7
10	**S**	...	**12:24**	2.0	6:24	**7:06**	a1.7
11	**M**	1:00	**1:18**	p2.1	7:18	**8:06**	a1.8
12	**T**	2:00	**2:18**	p2.2	8:18	**9:00**	a1.8
13	**W**	2:54	**3:06**	p2.3	9:06	**9:54**	a1.8
14	**T**	3:42	**3:54**	p2.3	10:00	**10:42**	a1.8
15	**F**	4:36	**4:42**	p2.2	10:48	**11:30**	a1.8
16	**S**	5:18	**5:30**	p2.1	11:36	...	1.7
17	**S**	6:06	**6:18**	p2.0	12:18	**12:24**	p1.7
18	**M**	6:54	**7:06**	p1.9	1:06	**1:18**	1.6
19	**T**	7:42	**8:00**	p1.8	1:48	**2:12**	1.5
20	**W**	8:36	**8:48**	p1.8	2:42	**3:06**	a1.5
21	**T**	9:30	**9:48**	1.7	3:30	**4:00**	a1.5
22	**F**	10:18	**10:42**	1.7	4:24	**5:00**	a1.5
23	**S**	11:12	**11:36**	a1.8	5:12	**5:54**	a1.5
24	**S**	...	**12:06**	1.9	6:06	**6:48**	a1.5
25	**M**	12:30	**12:54**	p2.0	6:54	**7:36**	a1.6
26	**T**	1:18	**1:36**	p2.1	7:42	**8:18**	a1.7
27	**W**	2:06	**2:18**	p2.1	8:24	**9:00**	a1.8
28	**T**	2:48	**2:54**	p2.2	9:00	**9:42**	a1.9
29	**F**	3:24	**3:36**	p2.3	9:42	**10:18**	a2.0
30	**S**	4:06	**4:18**	p2.4	10:24	**11:00**	a2.1
31	**S**	4:42	**4:54**	p2.4	11:06	**11:42**	a2.1

Standard Time

FEBRUARY

DAY OF MONTH	DAY OF WEEK	CURRENT TURNS TO					
		NORTHEAST Flood Starts			SOUTHWEST Ebb Starts		
		a.m.	**p.m.**	Kts.	a.m.	**p.m.**	Kts.
1	**M**	5:25	**5:42**	p2.4	11:48	...	2.1
2	**T**	6:12	**6:30**	p2.3	12:24	**12:42**	p2.1
3	**W**	7:00	**7:24**	p2.1	1:12	**1:30**	a2.0
4	**T**	7:54	**8:18**	a2.0	2:06	**2:30**	a1.9
5	**F**	8:54	**9:24**	a1.9	3:00	**3:36**	a1.8
6	**S**	9:54	**10:36**	a1.8	4:00	**4:48**	a1.6
7	**S**	11:06	**11:42**	a1.9	5:06	**5:54**	a1.6
8	**M**	...	**12:12**	2.0	6:12	**7:00**	a1.6
9	**T**	12:54	**1:12**	p2.1	7:12	**8:00**	a1.6
10	**W**	1:54	**2:06**	p2.2	8:06	**8:54**	a1.7
11	**T**	2:48	**3:00**	p2.3	9:00	**9:42**	a1.8
12	**F**	3:36	**3:48**	p2.3	9:48	**10:24**	a1.8
13	**S**	4:18	**4:30**	p2.2	10:30	**11:06**	a1.8
14	**S**	5:00	**5:12**	p2.1	11:18	**11:48**	a1.8
15	**M**	5:36	**5:48**	p2.0	...	**12:01**	1.7
16	**T**	6:18	**6:30**	p1.9	12:30	**12:42**	a1.7
17	**W**	7:00	**7:18**	1.8	1:12	**1:30**	a1.6
18	**T**	7:48	**8:06**	1.7	1:54	**2:24**	a1.6
19	**F**	8:36	**9:00**	a1.7	2:48	**3:18**	a1.5
20	**S**	9:30	**10:00**	a1.7	3:36	**4:18**	a1.4
21	**S**	10:30	**11:00**	a1.7	4:36	**5:12**	a1.4
22	**M**	11:24	...	1.8	5:30	**6:12**	a1.4
23	**T**	12:01	**12:18**	p1.9	6:18	**7:00**	1.5
24	**W**	12:48	**1:00**	p2.0	7:06	**7:48**	1.6
25	**T**	1:36	**1:48**	p2.2	7:54	**8:30**	a1.8
26	**F**	2:18	**2:30**	p2.3	8:36	**9:12**	1.9
27	**S**	3:00	**3:12**	p2.4	9:18	**9:48**	a2.1
28	**S**	3:36	**3:54**	p2.4	10:00	**10:30**	a2.2

The Kts. (knots) columns show the **maximum** predicted velocities of the stronger one of the Flood Currents and the stronger one of the Ebb Currents for each day.
The letter "a" means the velocity shown should occur **after** the **a.m.** Current Change. The letter "p" means the velocity shown should occur **after** the **p.m.** Current Change (even if next morning). No "a" or "p" means a.m. and p.m. velocities are the same for that day.
Avg. Max. Velocity: Flood 2.0 Kts., Ebb 1.8 Kts.
Max. Flood 3 hrs. 20 min. after Flood Starts, ±15 min.
Max. Ebb 2 hrs. 45 min. after Ebb Starts, ±15 min.
Gay Head (1 1/2 mi. NW of): avg. max velocity, Flood 2.0 kts., Ebb 2.0 kts. Time of Flood and Ebb 1 hr. 35 min. after Pollock Rip. Cross Rip: avg. max. velocity, Flood 1.3 kts., Ebb 0.9 kts. Time of Flood and Ebb 1 hr. 50 min. after Pollock Rip. Use POLLOCK RIP tables with current charts on pp. 72-83. See pp. 22-29 for Current Change at other points.

2021 CURRENT TABLE
POLLOCK RIP CHANNEL, MA

41°33'N, 69°59'W SE of Monomoy Pt. at Butler Hole

***Daylight Time starts March 14 at 2 a.m.** | **Daylight Saving Time**

MARCH								APRIL							
DAY OF MONTH	DAY OF WEEK	CURRENT TURNS TO NORTHEAST Flood Starts			SOUTHWEST Ebb Starts			DAY OF MONTH	DAY OF WEEK	CURRENT TURNS TO NORTHEAST Flood Starts			SOUTHWEST Ebb Starts		
		a.m.	**p.m.**	Kts.	a.m.	**p.m.**	Kts.			a.m.	**p.m.**	Kts.	a.m.	**p.m.**	Kts.
1	**M**	4:19	**4:36**	p2.4	10:42	**11:12**	2.2	1	**T**	6:19	**6:48**	a2.4	12:30	**1:00**	a2.2
2	**T**	5:00	**5:18**	p2.4	11:30	**11:54**	a2.2	2	**F**	7:12	**7:42**	a2.2	1:18	**1:54**	a2.0
3	**W**	5:42	**6:06**	a2.3	...	**12:18**	2.1	3	**S**	8:06	**8:48**	a2.0	2:12	**3:00**	a1.8
4	**T**	6:30	**7:00**	a2.2	12:42	**1:12**	2.0	4	**S**	9:12	**10:00**	a1.9	3:18	**4:06**	a1.6
5	**F**	7:24	**8:00**	a2.0	1:36	**2:12**	a1.9	5	**M**	10:24	**11:12**	a1.8	4:24	**5:18**	1.4
6	**S**	8:30	**9:06**	a1.9	2:36	**3:18**	a1.7	6	**T**	11:36	...	1.9	5:36	**6:30**	1.4
7	**S**	9:36	**10:24**	a1.8	3:42	**4:30**	a1.5	7	**W**	12:24	**12:42**	p2.0	6:42	**7:30**	1.5
8	**M**	10:48	**11:36**	a1.9	4:48	**5:42**	1.4	8	**T**	1:30	**1:48**	p2.1	7:48	**8:24**	1.6
9	**T**	...	**12:01**	2.0	6:00	**6:48**	a1.5	9	**F**	2:24	**2:36**	p2.2	8:42	**9:12**	1.7
10	**W**	12:48	**1:06**	p2.1	7:00	**7:48**	1.6	10	**S**	3:12	**3:24**	p2.2	9:30	**9:54**	p1.8
11	**T**	1:42	**2:00**	p2.2	7:54	**8:36**	1.7	11	**S**	3:48	**4:06**	2.1	10:12	**10:30**	1.8
12	**F**	2:30	**2:48**	p2.3	8:48	**9:18**	a1.8	12	**M**	4:24	**4:42**	2.1	10:48	**11:06**	p1.8
13	**S**	3:18	**3:30**	p2.2	9:30	**10:00**	a1.8	13	**T**	5:00	**5:18**	a2.1	11:30	**11:42**	1.7
14	**S**	*4:54	***5:06**	p2.2	*11:12	***11:36**	a1.8	14	**W**	5:30	**5:54**	a2.0	...	**12:06**	1.7
15	**M**	5:30	**5:42**	p2.1	11:54	...	1.8	15	**T**	6:06	**6:30**	a2.0	12:18	**12:48**	a1.7
16	**T**	6:06	**6:24**	2.0	12:18	**12:30**	1.7	16	**F**	6:48	**7:12**	a1.9	1:00	**1:30**	a1.7
17	**W**	6:42	**7:00**	a1.9	12:54	**1:12**	1.7	17	**S**	7:30	**8:00**	a1.9	1:42	**2:18**	a1.6
18	**T**	7:18	**7:42**	a1.9	1:30	**2:00**	a1.7	18	**S**	8:12	**8:54**	a1.8	2:30	**3:06**	a1.5
19	**F**	8:06	**8:30**	a1.8	2:18	**2:48**	a1.6	19	**M**	9:06	**9:48**	a1.8	3:18	**4:06**	a1.5
20	**S**	8:54	**9:24**	a1.7	3:06	**3:42**	a1.5	20	**T**	10:00	**10:48**	a1.8	4:18	**5:00**	1.4
21	**S**	9:48	**10:24**	a1.7	4:00	**4:36**	a1.4	21	**W**	11:00	**11:42**	a1.8	5:12	**5:54**	p1.5
22	**M**	10:42	**11:24**	a1.7	4:54	**5:36**	a1.4	22	**T**	11:54	...	1.9	6:06	**6:48**	p1.6
23	**T**	11:42	...	1.8	5:48	**6:30**	1.4	23	**F**	12:36	**12:48**	p2.0	7:00	**7:36**	1.7
24	**W**	12:24	**12:36**	p1.9	6:48	**7:24**	1.5	24	**S**	1:24	**1:42**	p2.2	7:54	**8:18**	p1.9
25	**T**	1:12	**1:30**	p2.0	7:36	**8:12**	p1.7	25	**S**	2:12	**2:30**	p2.2	8:36	**9:06**	2.0
26	**F**	2:00	**2:12**	p2.2	8:24	**8:54**	1.8	26	**M**	2:54	**3:18**	p2.3	9:24	**9:48**	2.1
27	**S**	2:48	**3:00**	p2.3	9:06	**9:36**	2.0	27	**T**	3:36	**4:00**	a2.4	10:12	**10:30**	2.2
28	**S**	3:24	**3:42**	p2.4	9:48	**10:18**	2.1	28	**W**	4:24	**4:48**	a2.4	11:00	**11:18**	2.2
29	**M**	4:06	**4:24**	p2.4	10:36	**11:00**	2.2	29	**T**	5:06	**5:42**	a2.4	11:48	...	2.1
30	**T**	4:48	**5:12**	2.4	11:18	**11:42**	a2.3	30	**F**	6:00	**6:36**	a2.4	12:06	**12:42**	a2.1
31	**W**	5:30	**6:00**	a2.4	...	**12:06**	2.2								

The Kts. (knots) columns show the **maximum** predicted velocities of the stronger one of the Flood Currents and the stronger one of the Ebb Currents for each day.
The letter "a" means the velocity shown should occur **after** the **a.m.** Current Change. The letter "p" means the velocity shown should occur **after** the **p.m.** Current Change (even if next morning). No "a" or "p" means a.m. and p.m. velocities are the same for that day.
Avg. Max. Velocity: Flood 2.0 Kts., Ebb 1.8 Kts.
Max. Flood 3 hrs. 20 min. after Flood Starts, ±15 min.
Max. Ebb 2 hrs. 45 min. after Ebb Starts, ±15 min.
Gay Head (1 1/2 mi. NW of): avg. max velocity, Flood 2.0 kts., Ebb 2.0 kts. Time of Flood and Ebb 1 hr. 35 min. after Pollock Rip. Cross Rip: avg. max. velocity, Flood 1.3 kts., Ebb 0.9 kts. Time of Flood and Ebb 1 hr. 50 min. after Pollock Rip. Use POLLOCK RIP tables with current charts on pp. 72-83. See pp. 22-29 for Current Change at other points.

2021 CURRENT TABLE
POLLOCK RIP CHANNEL, MA

41°33'N, 69°59'W SE of Monomoy Pt. at Butler Hole

Daylight Saving Time

MAY

DAY OF MONTH	DAY OF WEEK	CURRENT TURNS TO NORTHEAST Flood Starts a.m.	**p.m.**	Kts.	CURRENT TURNS TO SOUTHWEST Ebb Starts a.m.	**p.m.**	Kts.
1	**S**	6:49	**7:30**	a2.2	1:00	**1:42**	a2.0
2	**S**	7:48	**8:36**	a2.1	1:54	**2:48**	a1.8
3	**M**	8:54	**9:48**	a1.9	3:00	**3:54**	a1.6
4	**T**	10:06	**11:00**	a1.9	4:06	**5:00**	1.4
5	**W**	11:12	...	2.0	5:18	**6:00**	p1.5
6	**T**	12:06	**12:18**	p2.0	6:24	**7:00**	p1.6
7	**F**	1:06	**1:18**	p2.1	7:24	**7:54**	p1.7
8	**S**	1:54	**2:12**	p2.1	8:18	**8:36**	p1.7
9	**S**	2:42	**2:54**	2.1	9:00	**9:18**	1.7
10	**M**	3:18	**3:36**	a2.1	9:48	**10:00**	1.7
11	**T**	3:54	**4:18**	a2.1	10:24	**10:36**	1.7
12	**W**	4:30	**4:54**	a2.1	11:06	**11:12**	p1.7
13	**T**	5:06	**5:30**	a2.0	11:42	**11:48**	p1.7
14	**F**	5:36	**6:06**	a2.0	...	**12:24**	1.6
15	**S**	6:18	**6:48**	a2.0	12:30	**1:06**	a1.7
16	**S**	6:54	**7:36**	a1.9	1:12	**1:48**	a1.7
17	**M**	7:42	**8:24**	a1.9	1:54	**2:36**	a1.6
18	**T**	8:30	**9:18**	a1.9	2:48	**3:30**	a1.6
19	**W**	9:24	**10:12**	a1.9	3:42	**4:24**	a1.6
20	**T**	10:24	**11:06**	a1.9	4:36	**5:12**	1.6
21	**F**	11:18	...	2.0	5:30	**6:06**	p1.7
22	**S**	12:01	**12:12**	p2.0	6:24	**6:54**	p1.8
23	**S**	12:48	**1:06**	p2.1	7:18	**7:42**	p1.9
24	**M**	1:36	**2:00**	2.1	8:12	**8:30**	p2.0
25	**T**	2:24	**2:54**	a2.3	9:00	**9:18**	p2.1
26	**W**	3:12	**3:42**	a2.3	9:54	**10:06**	p2.1
27	**T**	4:00	**4:36**	a2.4	10:42	**10:54**	p2.1
28	**F**	4:48	**5:30**	a2.4	11:36	**11:48**	p2.0
29	**S**	5:42	**6:24**	a2.3	...	**12:36**	1.8
30	**S**	6:36	**7:24**	a2.2	12:42	**1:30**	a1.9
31	**M**	7:36	**8:24**	a2.1	1:42	**2:30**	a1.7

Daylight Saving Time

JUNE

DAY OF MONTH	DAY OF WEEK	CURRENT TURNS TO NORTHEAST Flood Starts a.m.	**p.m.**	Kts.	CURRENT TURNS TO SOUTHWEST Ebb Starts a.m.	**p.m.**	Kts.
1	**T**	8:37	**9:30**	a2.0	2:42	**3:30**	a1.6
2	**W**	9:42	**10:30**	a2.0	3:48	**4:30**	1.5
3	**T**	10:48	**11:30**	a2.0	4:54	**5:30**	p1.5
4	**F**	11:48	...	2.0	5:54	**6:24**	p1.6
5	**S**	12:30	**12:42**	p2.0	6:54	**7:18**	p1.6
6	**S**	1:18	**1:36**	2.0	7:42	**8:00**	p1.7
7	**M**	2:06	**2:24**	a2.0	8:36	**8:48**	p1.7
8	**T**	2:48	**3:06**	a2.1	9:18	**9:24**	p1.7
9	**W**	3:24	**3:48**	a2.1	10:00	**10:06**	p1.7
10	**T**	4:00	**4:24**	a2.1	10:42	**10:42**	p1.7
11	**F**	4:36	**5:06**	a2.1	11:18	**11:24**	p1.7
12	**S**	5:12	**5:42**	a2.1	...	**12:01**	1.6
13	**S**	5:48	**6:24**	a2.1	12:01	**12:42**	a1.7
14	**M**	6:30	**7:06**	a2.1	12:42	**1:24**	a1.7
15	**T**	7:12	**7:54**	a2.1	1:30	**2:06**	1.7
16	**W**	8:00	**8:42**	a2.0	2:18	**2:54**	1.7
17	**T**	8:54	**9:36**	a2.0	3:06	**3:48**	1.7
18	**F**	9:48	**10:24**	a2.0	4:00	**4:36**	1.7
19	**S**	10:42	**11:18**	a2.0	5:00	**5:30**	p1.8
20	**S**	11:42	...	2.0	5:54	**6:24**	p1.8
21	**M**	12:12	**12:42**	2.0	6:54	**7:12**	p1.9
22	**T**	1:06	**1:36**	a2.1	7:48	**8:06**	p1.9
23	**W**	2:00	**2:36**	a2.2	8:48	**9:00**	p2.0
24	**T**	2:54	**3:30**	a2.3	9:42	**9:48**	p2.0
25	**F**	3:48	**4:24**	a2.3	10:36	**10:42**	p1.9
26	**S**	4:36	**5:18**	a2.3	11:30	**11:36**	p1.9
27	**S**	5:30	**6:12**	a2.3	...	**12:24**	1.7
28	**M**	6:24	**7:06**	a2.2	12:30	**1:12**	a1.8
29	**T**	7:18	**8:00**	a2.1	1:24	**2:06**	a1.7
30	**W**	8:12	**9:00**	a2.0	2:18	**3:06**	1.6

The Kts. (knots) columns show the **maximum** predicted velocities of the stronger one of the Flood Currents and the stronger one of the Ebb Currents for each day.
The letter "a" means the velocity shown should occur **after** the **a.m.** Current Change. The letter "p" means the velocity shown should occur **after** the **p.m.** Current Change (even if next morning). No "a" or "p" means a.m. and p.m. velocities are the same for that day.
Avg. Max. Velocity: Flood 2.0 Kts., Ebb 1.8 Kts.
Max. Flood 3 hrs. 20 min. after Flood Starts, ±15 min.
Max. Ebb 2 hrs. 45 min. after Ebb Starts, ±15 min.
Gay Head (1 1/2 mi. NW of): avg. max velocity, Flood 2.0 kts., Ebb 2.0 kts. Time of Flood and Ebb 1 hr. 35 min. after Pollock Rip. Cross Rip: avg. max. velocity, Flood 1.3 kts., Ebb 0.9 kts. Time of Flood and Ebb 1 hr. 50 min. after Pollock Rip. Use POLLOCK RIP tables with current charts on pp. 72-83. See pp. 22-29 for Current Change at other points.

2021 CURRENT TABLE
POLLOCK RIP CHANNEL, MA
41°33'N, 69°59'W SE of Monomoy Pt. at Butler Hole

Daylight Saving Time — Daylight Saving Time

JULY								AUGUST							
DAY OF MONTH	DAY OF WEEK	CURRENT TURNS TO						DAY OF MONTH	DAY OF WEEK	CURRENT TURNS TO					
		NORTHEAST Flood Starts			SOUTHWEST Ebb Starts					NORTHEAST Flood Starts			SOUTHWEST Ebb Starts		
		a.m.	**p.m.**	Kts.	a.m.	**p.m.**	Kts.			a.m.	**p.m.**	Kts.	a.m.	**p.m.**	Kts.
1	T	9:13	**9:54**	a2.0	3:18	**4:00**	1.5	1	S	10:31	**11:00**	1.7	4:42	**5:00**	p1.5
2	F	10:12	**10:54**	a1.9	4:18	**4:54**	1.5	2	M	11:24	**11:54**	p1.8	5:36	**5:54**	p1.5
3	S	11:06	**11:48**	1.8	5:18	**5:42**	p1.5	3	T	...	**12:24**	1.6	6:36	**6:48**	p1.5
4	S	...	**12:06**	1.8	6:18	**6:36**	p1.6	4	W	12:48	**1:18**	a1.9	7:30	**7:36**	p1.5
5	M	12:36	**1:00**	a1.9	7:12	**7:24**	p1.6	5	T	1:36	**2:06**	a2.0	8:18	**8:24**	p1.6
6	T	1:24	**1:48**	a2.0	8:00	**8:12**	p1.6	6	F	2:24	**2:54**	a2.0	9:06	**9:12**	p1.7
7	W	2:12	**2:36**	a2.0	8:48	**8:54**	p1.6	7	S	3:06	**3:36**	a2.1	9:48	**9:48**	p1.8
8	T	2:54	**3:18**	a2.1	9:36	**9:36**	p1.7	8	S	3:42	**4:12**	a2.2	10:30	**10:30**	p1.9
9	F	3:36	**4:00**	a2.1	10:18	**10:18**	p1.7	9	M	4:24	**4:54**	a2.2	11:06	**11:06**	p2.0
10	S	4:12	**4:42**	a2.1	10:54	**10:54**	p1.8	10	T	5:00	**5:30**	a2.3	11:42	**11:48**	p2.0
11	S	4:48	**5:18**	a2.1	11:36	**11:36**	p1.8	11	W	5:42	**6:06**	a2.3	...	**12:24**	2.0
12	M	5:24	**6:00**	a2.2	...	**12:12**	1.7	12	T	6:24	**6:48**	a2.3	12:30	**1:06**	a2.1
13	T	6:06	**6:36**	a2.2	12:18	**12:54**	a1.9	13	F	7:06	**7:36**	a2.3	1:18	**1:48**	a2.1
14	W	6:48	**7:24**	a2.2	1:00	**1:36**	a1.9	14	S	7:54	**8:24**	a2.1	2:06	**2:36**	a2.0
15	T	7:36	**8:06**	a2.2	1:48	**2:24**	a1.9	15	S	8:48	**9:18**	a2.0	3:00	**3:30**	1.8
16	F	8:24	**9:00**	a2.1	2:36	**3:12**	a1.9	16	M	9:48	**10:18**	p1.9	4:06	**4:30**	1.7
17	S	9:18	**9:48**	a2.0	3:30	**4:00**	1.8	17	T	10:54	**11:24**	p1.9	5:12	**5:30**	1.6
18	S	10:12	**10:48**	1.9	4:30	**4:54**	p1.8	18	W	...	**12:06**	1.6	6:18	**6:36**	p1.6
19	M	11:12	**11:48**	p1.9	5:30	**5:54**	p1.8	19	T	12:30	**1:12**	a1.9	7:24	**7:36**	p1.6
20	T	...	**12:18**	1.8	6:30	**6:48**	p1.7	20	F	1:36	**2:18**	a2.1	8:24	**8:36**	p1.7
21	W	12:48	**1:18**	a2.0	7:36	**7:48**	p1.8	21	S	2:36	**3:12**	a2.2	9:24	**9:30**	p1.8
22	T	1:48	**2:24**	a2.1	8:36	**8:42**	p1.8	22	S	3:30	**4:06**	a2.3	10:12	**10:18**	p1.8
23	F	2:42	**3:18**	a2.2	9:30	**9:36**	p1.8	23	M	4:18	**4:54**	a2.3	11:00	**11:06**	p1.8
24	S	3:36	**4:18**	a2.2	10:24	**10:30**	p1.9	24	T	5:06	**5:36**	a2.2	11:42	**11:54**	p1.8
25	S	4:30	**5:06**	a2.3	11:18	**11:24**	p1.9	25	W	5:48	**6:18**	a2.2	...	**12:24**	1.7
26	M	5:18	**5:54**	a2.3	...	**12:06**	1.7	26	T	6:30	**7:00**	a2.0	12:36	**1:06**	1.7
27	T	6:12	**6:42**	a2.2	12:12	**12:54**	a1.8	27	F	7:18	**7:42**	a1.9	1:24	**1:54**	a1.7
28	W	7:00	**7:30**	a2.1	1:00	**1:42**	a1.8	28	S	8:00	**8:30**	a1.8	2:12	**2:36**	1.5
29	T	7:48	**8:24**	a2.0	1:54	**2:30**	a1.7	29	S	8:54	**9:18**	p1.7	3:06	**3:30**	p1.5
30	F	8:36	**9:12**	a1.9	2:48	**3:18**	a1.6	30	M	9:48	**10:12**	p1.7	4:00	**4:18**	p1.4
31	S	9:30	**10:06**	a1.8	3:42	**4:12**	p1.5	31	T	10:48	**11:12**	p1.7	5:00	**5:18**	p1.4

The Kts. (knots) columns show the **maximum** predicted velocities of the stronger one of the Flood Currents and the stronger one of the Ebb Currents for each day.
The letter "a" means the velocity shown should occur **after** the **a.m.** Current Change. The letter "p" means the velocity shown should occur **after** the **p.m.** Current Change (even if next morning). No "a" or "p" means a.m. and p.m. velocities are the same for that day.
Avg. Max. Velocity: Flood 2.0 Kts., Ebb 1.8 Kts.
Max. Flood 3 hrs. 20 min. after Flood Starts, ±15 min.
Max. Ebb 2 hrs. 45 min. after Ebb Starts, ±15 min.
Gay Head (1 1/2 mi. NW of): avg. max velocity, Flood 2.0 kts., Ebb 2.0 kts. Time of Flood and Ebb 1 hr. 35 min. after Pollock Rip. Cross Rip: avg. max. velocity, Flood 1.3 kts., Ebb 0.9 kts. Time of Flood and Ebb 1 hr. 50 min. after Pollock Rip. Use POLLOCK RIP tables with current charts on pp. 72-83. See pp. 22-29 for Current Change at other points.

2021 CURRENT TABLE
POLLOCK RIP CHANNEL, MA

41°33'N, 69°59'W SE of Monomoy Pt. at Butler Hole

Daylight Saving Time

SEPTEMBER

DAY OF MONTH	DAY OF WEEK	CURRENT TURNS TO NORTHEAST Flood Starts			CURRENT TURNS TO SOUTHWEST Ebb Starts		
		a.m.	**p.m.**	Kts.	a.m.	**p.m.**	Kts.
1	**W**	11:49	...	1.5	6:00	**6:12**	p1.4
2	**T**	12:06	**12:42**	a1.8	6:54	**7:06**	p1.5
3	**F**	1:00	**1:36**	a1.9	7:48	**7:54**	p1.6
4	**S**	1:48	**2:24**	a2.0	8:30	**8:42**	p1.7
5	**S**	2:36	**3:06**	a2.1	9:12	**9:24**	p1.8
6	**M**	3:12	**3:42**	a2.2	9:54	**10:00**	p2.0
7	**T**	3:54	**4:18**	a2.3	10:30	**10:42**	p2.1
8	**W**	4:30	**4:54**	a2.4	11:12	**11:24**	p2.2
9	**T**	5:12	**5:36**	a2.4	11:48	...	2.1
10	**F**	5:54	**6:18**	2.3	12:06	**12:30**	a2.2
11	**S**	6:42	**7:06**	2.2	12:54	**1:18**	2.1
12	**S**	7:30	**7:54**	2.1	1:42	**2:06**	a2.0
13	**M**	8:30	**8:54**	p2.0	2:42	**3:00**	1.8
14	**T**	9:30	**10:00**	p1.9	3:48	**4:06**	1.6
15	**W**	10:42	**11:12**	p1.9	4:54	**5:12**	p1.5
16	**T**	...	**12:01**	1.6	6:06	**6:24**	p1.5
17	**F**	12:24	**1:06**	a2.0	7:12	**7:30**	p1.6
18	**S**	1:30	**2:12**	a2.1	8:12	**8:24**	p1.7
19	**S**	2:24	**3:00**	a2.2	9:06	**9:18**	p1.8
20	**M**	3:18	**3:48**	a2.3	9:54	**10:06**	1.8
21	**T**	4:06	**4:30**	a2.2	10:36	**10:48**	1.8
22	**W**	4:48	**5:06**	a2.2	11:18	**11:30**	1.8
23	**T**	5:24	**5:48**	a2.1	11:54	...	1.7
24	**F**	6:06	**6:24**	1.9	12:12	**12:36**	1.7
25	**S**	6:42	**7:00**	1.8	1:00	**1:12**	1.6
26	**S**	7:30	**7:48**	p1.8	1:42	**2:00**	1.5
27	**M**	8:18	**8:36**	p1.7	2:30	**2:48**	p1.5
28	**T**	9:12	**9:30**	p1.7	3:24	**3:42**	p1.4
29	**W**	10:12	**10:30**	p1.7	4:24	**4:36**	1.3
30	**T**	11:12	**11:24**	p1.8	5:24	**5:36**	p1.4

Daylight Saving Time

OCTOBER

DAY OF MONTH	DAY OF WEEK	CURRENT TURNS TO NORTHEAST Flood Starts			CURRENT TURNS TO SOUTHWEST Ebb Starts		
		a.m.	**p.m.**	Kts.	a.m.	**p.m.**	Kts.
1	**F**	...	**12:06**	1.5	6:18	**6:30**	1.4
2	**S**	12:24	**1:00**	a1.9	7:06	**7:24**	p1.6
3	**S**	1:12	**1:48**	a2.0	7:54	**8:06**	p1.7
4	**M**	2:00	**2:30**	a2.1	8:36	**8:48**	p1.9
5	**T**	2:42	**3:06**	a2.2	9:18	**9:30**	p2.0
6	**W**	3:24	**3:48**	2.3	10:00	**10:12**	p2.2
7	**T**	4:06	**4:24**	2.4	10:36	**10:54**	2.2
8	**F**	4:48	**5:06**	2.4	11:18	**11:42**	2.2
9	**S**	5:30	**5:48**	p2.4	...	**12:01**	2.2
10	**S**	6:18	**6:36**	p2.3	12:30	**12:48**	2.1
11	**M**	7:12	**7:30**	p2.1	1:24	**1:42**	1.9
12	**T**	8:12	**8:36**	p2.0	2:24	**2:42**	1.7
13	**W**	9:24	**9:42**	p1.9	3:30	**3:48**	1.5
14	**T**	10:36	**10:54**	p1.9	4:42	**5:00**	1.4
15	**F**	11:48	...	1.6	5:54	**6:12**	p1.5
16	**S**	12:06	**12:54**	a2.0	6:54	**7:12**	p1.6
17	**S**	1:12	**1:54**	a2.1	7:54	**8:12**	p1.7
18	**M**	2:12	**2:42**	a2.2	8:42	**9:00**	p1.8
19	**T**	3:00	**3:24**	a2.2	9:30	**9:48**	1.8
20	**W**	3:42	**4:06**	a2.2	10:12	**10:30**	a1.8
21	**T**	4:24	**4:42**	2.1	10:48	**11:12**	a1.8
22	**F**	5:00	**5:18**	p2.0	11:24	**11:48**	a1.7
23	**S**	5:36	**5:54**	p2.0	...	**12:01**	1.7
24	**S**	6:18	**6:30**	p1.9	12:30	**12:42**	1.6
25	**M**	7:00	**7:12**	p1.8	1:18	**1:24**	p1.6
26	**T**	7:42	**8:00**	p1.8	2:00	**2:12**	p1.5
27	**W**	8:36	**8:48**	p1.7	2:54	**3:06**	1.4
28	**T**	9:36	**9:48**	p1.7	3:48	**4:00**	1.4
29	**F**	10:30	**10:42**	p1.8	4:42	**5:00**	1.4
30	**S**	11:30	**11:42**	p1.9	5:36	**5:54**	p1.5
31	**S**	...	**12:18**	1.7	6:30	**6:42**	1.6

The Kts. (knots) columns show the **maximum** predicted velocities of the stronger one of the Flood Currents and the stronger one of the Ebb Currents for each day.
The letter "a" means the velocity shown should occur **after** the **a.m.** Current Change. The letter "p" means the velocity shown should occur **after** the **p.m.** Current Change (even if next morning). No "a" or "p" means a.m. and p.m. velocities are the same for that day.
Avg. Max. Velocity: Flood 2.0 Kts., Ebb 1.8 Kts.
Max. Flood 3 hrs. 20 min. after Flood Starts, ±15 min.
Max. Ebb 2 hrs. 45 min. after Ebb Starts, ±15 min.
Gay Head (1 1/2 mi. NW of): avg. max velocity, Flood 2.0 kts., Ebb 2.0 kts. Time of Flood and Ebb 1 hr. 35 min. after Pollock Rip. Cross Rip: avg. max. velocity, Flood 1.3 kts., Ebb 0.9 kts. Time of Flood and Ebb 1 hr. 50 min. after Pollock Rip. Use POLLOCK RIP tables with current charts on pp. 72-83. See pp. 22-29 for Current Change at other points.

2021 CURRENT TABLE
POLLOCK RIP CHANNEL, MA
41°33'N, 69°59'W SE of Monomoy Pt. at Butler Hole

***Standard Time starts Nov. 7 at 2 a.m.** **Standard Time**

NOVEMBER

DAY OF MONTH	DAY OF WEEK	CURRENT TURNS TO NORTHEAST Flood Starts a.m.	**p.m.**	Kts.	CURRENT TURNS TO SOUTHWEST Ebb Starts a.m.	**p.m.**	Kts.
1	**M**	12:31	**1:06**	a2.0	7:18	**7:36**	p1.8
2	**T**	1:24	**1:54**	a2.1	8:00	**8:18**	1.9
3	**W**	2:06	**2:36**	2.2	8:42	**9:06**	2.0
4	**T**	2:54	**3:18**	2.3	9:24	**9:48**	2.1
5	**F**	3:36	**4:00**	p2.4	10:06	**10:36**	2.2
6	**S**	4:24	**4:42**	p2.5	10:48	**11:24**	a2.2
7	**S**	*4:12	***4:30**	p2.4	*10:36	***11:18**	a2.2
8	**M**	5:06	**5:18**	p2.3	11:24	...	2.0
9	**T**	6:00	**6:18**	p2.1	12:12	**12:24**	1.9
10	**W**	7:00	**7:18**	p2.0	1:12	**1:24**	1.7
11	**T**	8:12	**8:30**	p1.9	2:18	**2:30**	1.5
12	**F**	9:24	**9:36**	p1.9	3:24	**3:42**	a1.5
13	**S**	10:30	**10:48**	p2.0	4:30	**4:54**	1.5
14	**S**	11:36	**11:48**	p2.1	5:30	**5:54**	a1.6
15	**M**	...	**12:30**	2.0	6:24	**6:48**	a1.7
16	**T**	12:48	**1:18**	2.1	7:18	**7:42**	1.7
17	**W**	1:36	**2:00**	2.1	8:00	**8:30**	a1.8
18	**T**	2:18	**2:36**	p2.1	8:42	**9:12**	a1.8
19	**F**	3:00	**3:12**	p2.1	9:18	**9:48**	a1.7
20	**S**	3:36	**3:48**	p2.1	9:54	**10:30**	a1.7
21	**S**	4:12	**4:24**	p2.0	10:30	**11:12**	a1.7
22	**M**	4:54	**5:00**	p2.0	11:12	**11:54**	a1.7
23	**T**	5:36	**5:42**	p1.9	11:54	...	1.6
24	**W**	6:18	**6:24**	p1.9	12:36	**12:42**	p1.6
25	**T**	7:06	**7:12**	p1.9	1:24	**1:30**	1.5
26	**F**	8:00	**8:06**	p1.9	2:12	**2:24**	1.5
27	**S**	8:54	**9:00**	p1.9	3:06	**3:18**	1.5
28	**S**	9:48	**9:54**	p1.9	3:54	**4:12**	1.6
29	**M**	10:36	**10:54**	p2.0	4:48	**5:06**	1.6
30	**T**	11:30	**11:42**	p2.0	5:36	**6:00**	a1.8

DECEMBER

DAY OF MONTH	DAY OF WEEK	CURRENT TURNS TO NORTHEAST Flood Starts a.m.	**p.m.**	Kts.	CURRENT TURNS TO SOUTHWEST Ebb Starts a.m.	**p.m.**	Kts.
1	**W**	...	**12:18**	2.1	6:24	**6:48**	a1.9
2	**T**	12:36	**1:00**	p2.2	7:06	**7:42**	a2.0
3	**F**	1:24	**1:48**	p2.3	7:54	**8:30**	a2.1
4	**S**	2:18	**2:36**	p2.4	8:42	**9:18**	a2.1
5	**S**	3:06	**3:24**	p2.4	9:30	**10:12**	a2.1
6	**M**	4:00	**4:12**	p2.4	10:18	**11:06**	a2.1
7	**T**	4:54	**5:06**	p2.3	11:12	...	2.0
8	**W**	5:48	**6:06**	p2.2	12:01	**12:06**	p1.9
9	**T**	6:48	**7:06**	p2.1	1:00	**1:06**	1.7
10	**F**	7:54	**8:06**	p2.0	2:00	**2:12**	1.6
11	**S**	9:00	**9:12**	p2.0	3:00	**3:18**	1.5
12	**S**	10:00	**10:18**	p1.9	4:00	**4:24**	1.5
13	**M**	11:00	**11:18**	p1.9	5:00	**5:24**	a1.6
14	**T**	11:54	...	2.0	5:54	**6:24**	a1.6
15	**W**	12:18	**12:48**	p2.0	6:42	**7:18**	a1.6
16	**T**	1:06	**1:30**	p2.1	7:30	**8:06**	a1.7
17	**F**	1:54	**2:12**	p2.1	8:12	**8:48**	a1.7
18	**S**	2:36	**2:48**	p2.1	8:54	**9:30**	a1.7
19	**S**	3:18	**3:24**	p2.1	9:30	**10:06**	a1.7
20	**M**	3:54	**4:00**	p2.1	10:06	**10:48**	a1.7
21	**T**	4:30	**4:36**	p2.1	10:48	**11:30**	a1.7
22	**W**	5:12	**5:18**	p2.1	11:30	...	1.7
23	**T**	5:54	**6:00**	p2.1	12:06	**12:12**	p1.7
24	**F**	6:36	**6:42**	p2.0	12:48	**12:54**	1.7
25	**S**	7:24	**7:30**	p2.0	1:36	**1:48**	1.7
26	**S**	8:12	**8:24**	p2.0	2:24	**2:36**	1.7
27	**M**	9:00	**9:18**	p1.9	3:12	**3:30**	1.7
28	**T**	9:54	**10:12**	p1.9	4:06	**4:30**	1.7
29	**W**	10:48	**11:12**	1.9	4:54	**5:24**	a1.8
30	**T**	11:42	...	2.0	5:48	**6:24**	a1.8
31	**F**	12:06	**12:36**	p2.1	6:42	**7:18**	a1.9

The Kts. (knots) columns show the **maximum** predicted velocities of the stronger one of the Flood Currents and the stronger one of the Ebb Currents for each day.
The letter "a" means the velocity shown should occur **after** the **a.m.** Current Change. The letter "p" means the velocity shown should occur **after** the **p.m.** Current Change (even if next morning). No "a" or "p" means a.m. and p.m. velocities are the same for that day.

Avg. Max. Velocity: Flood 2.0 Kts., Ebb 1.8 Kts.

Max. Flood 3 hrs. 20 min. after Flood Starts, ±15 min.

Max. Ebb 2 hrs. 45 min. after Ebb Starts, ±15 min.

Gay Head (1 1/2 mi. NW of): avg. max velocity, Flood 2.0 kts., Ebb 2.0 kts. Time of Flood and Ebb 1 hr. 35 min. after Pollock Rip. Cross Rip: avg. max. velocity, Flood 1.3 kts., Ebb 0.9 kts. Time of Flood and Ebb 1 hr. 50 min. after Pollock Rip. Use POLLOCK RIP tables with current charts on pp. 72-83. See pp. 22-29 for Current Change at other points.

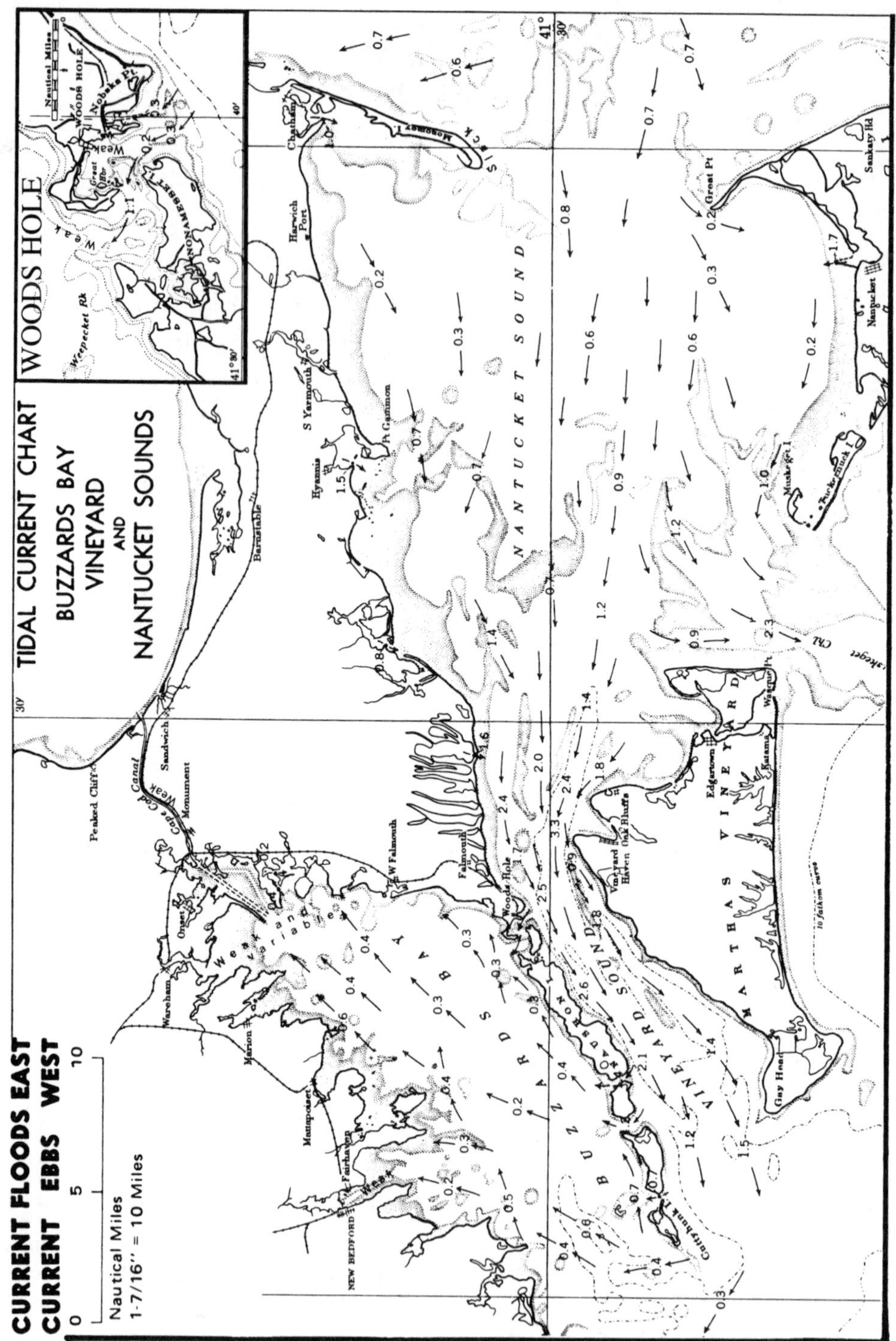

FLOOD STARTS AT POLLOCK RIP CHANNEL
OR: 4 HOURS **AFTER** HIGH WATER AT BOSTON

Velocities shown are at Spring Tides. See note at bottom of Boston Tables: Rule-of-Thumb for Current Velocities. See pp. 60–65 for an enlarged version of Woods Hole inset. Pollock Rip Ch. is SE of Monomoy Pt.

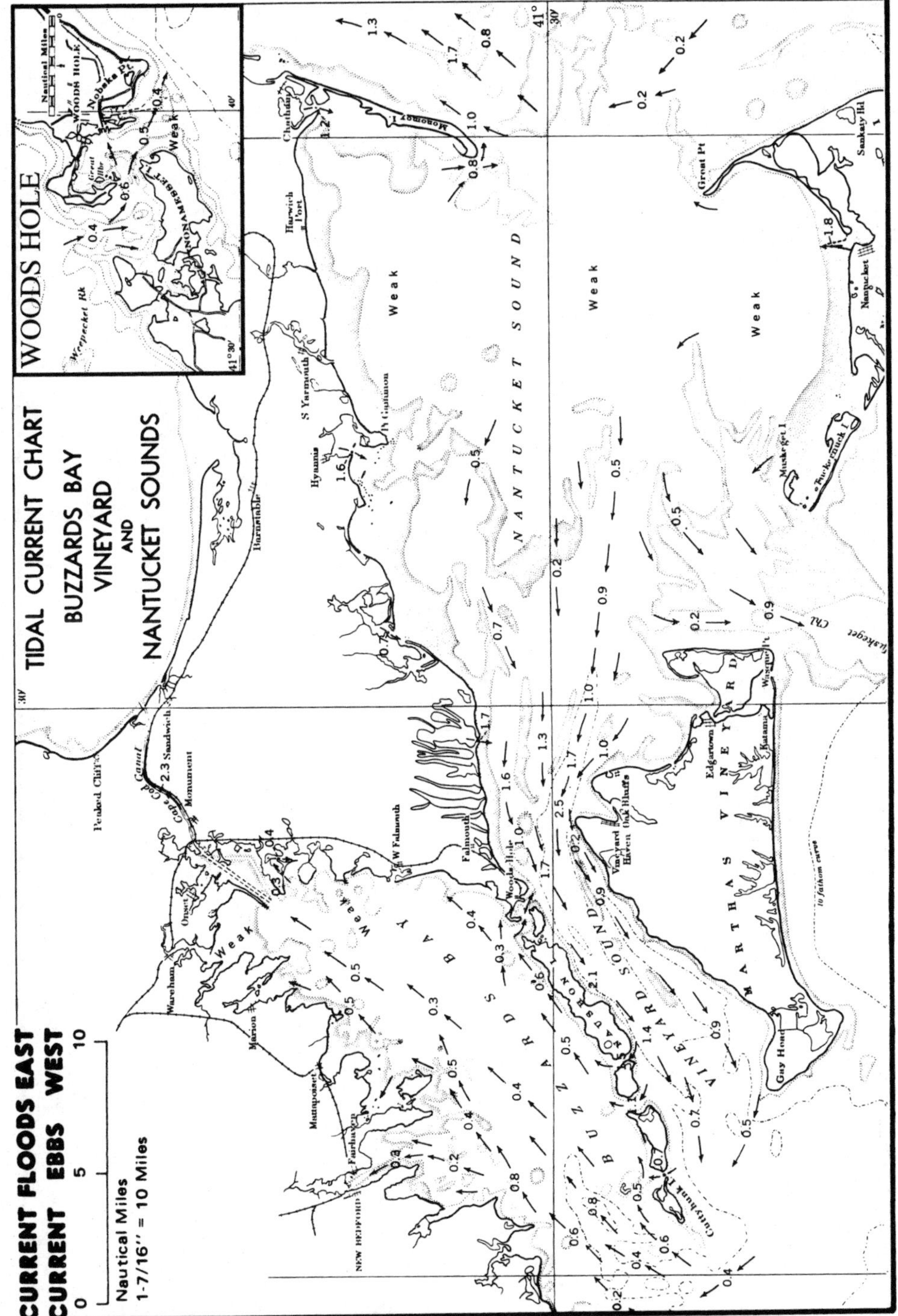

1 HOUR **AFTER** FLOOD STARTS AT POLLOCK RIP CHANNEL
OR: 5 HOURS **AFTER** HIGH WATER AT BOSTON

Velocities shown are at Spring Tides. See note at bottom of Boston Tables: Rule-of-Thumb for Current Velocities. See pp. 60–65 for an enlarged version of Woods Hole inset.
Pollock Rip Ch. is SE of Monomoy Pt.

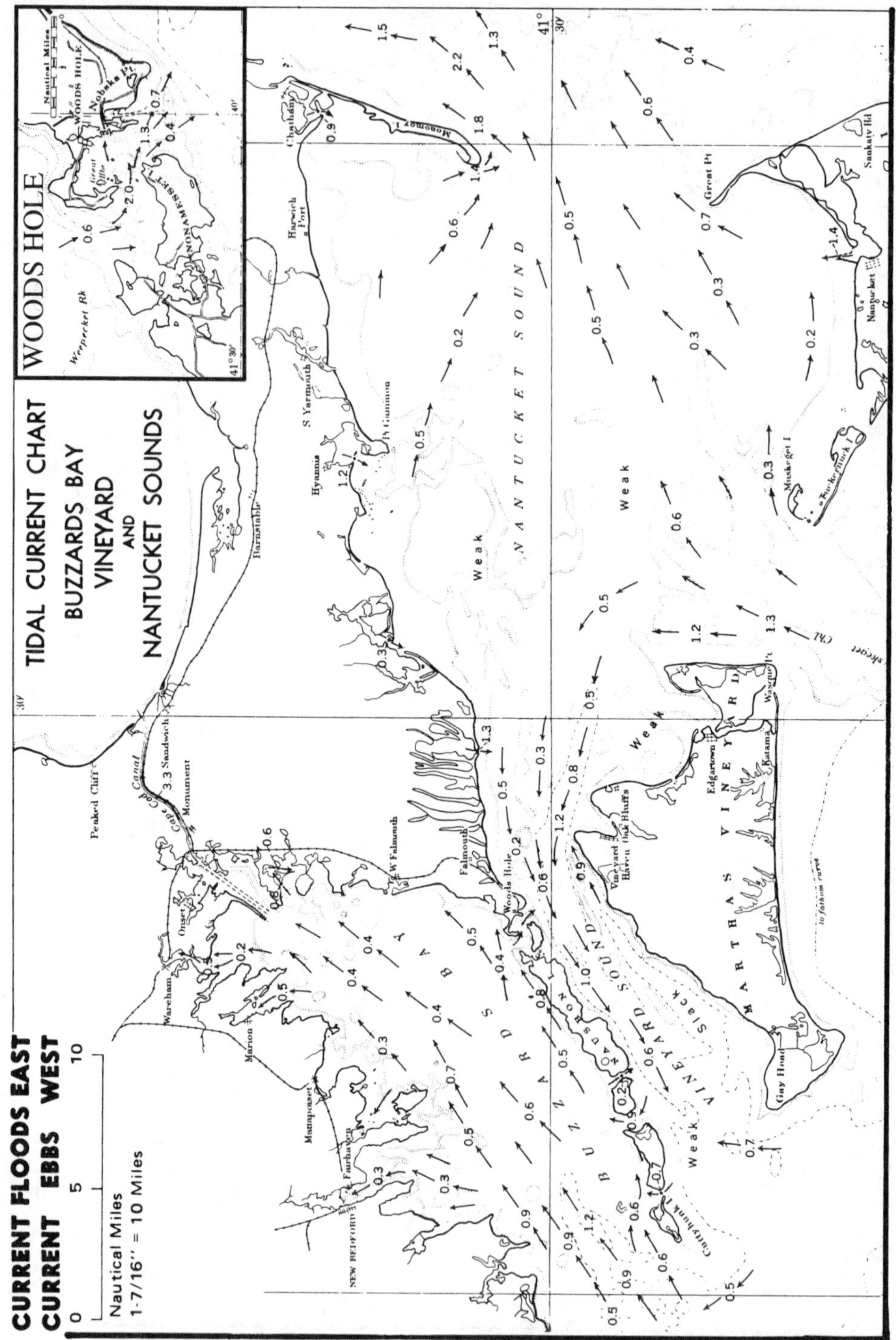

2 HOURS **AFTER** FLOOD STARTS AT POLLOCK RIP CHANNEL
OR: LOW WATER AT BOSTON

Velocities shown are at Spring Tides. See note at bottom of Boston Tables: Rule-of-Thumb for Current Velocities. See pp. 60–65 for an enlarged version of Woods Hole inset. Pollock Rip Ch. is SE of Monomoy Pt.

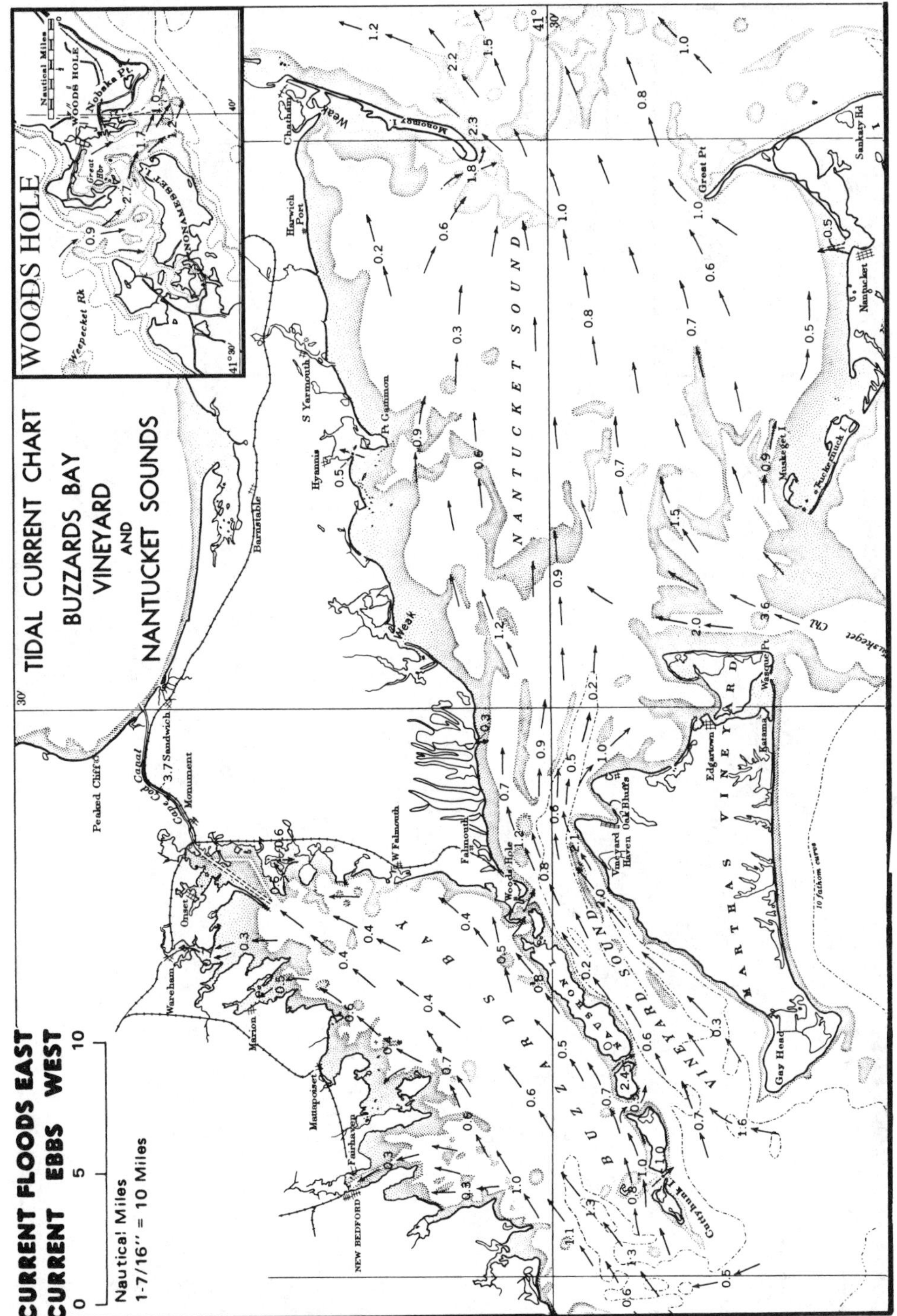

3 HOURS **AFTER** FLOOD STARTS AT POLLOCK RIP CHANNEL

OR: 1 HOUR **AFTER** LOW WATER AT BOSTON

Velocities shown are at Spring Tides. See note at bottom of Boston Tables: Rule-of-Thumb for Current Velocities. See pp. 60–65 for an enlarged version of Woods Hole inset. Pollock Rip Ch. is SE of Monomoy Pt.

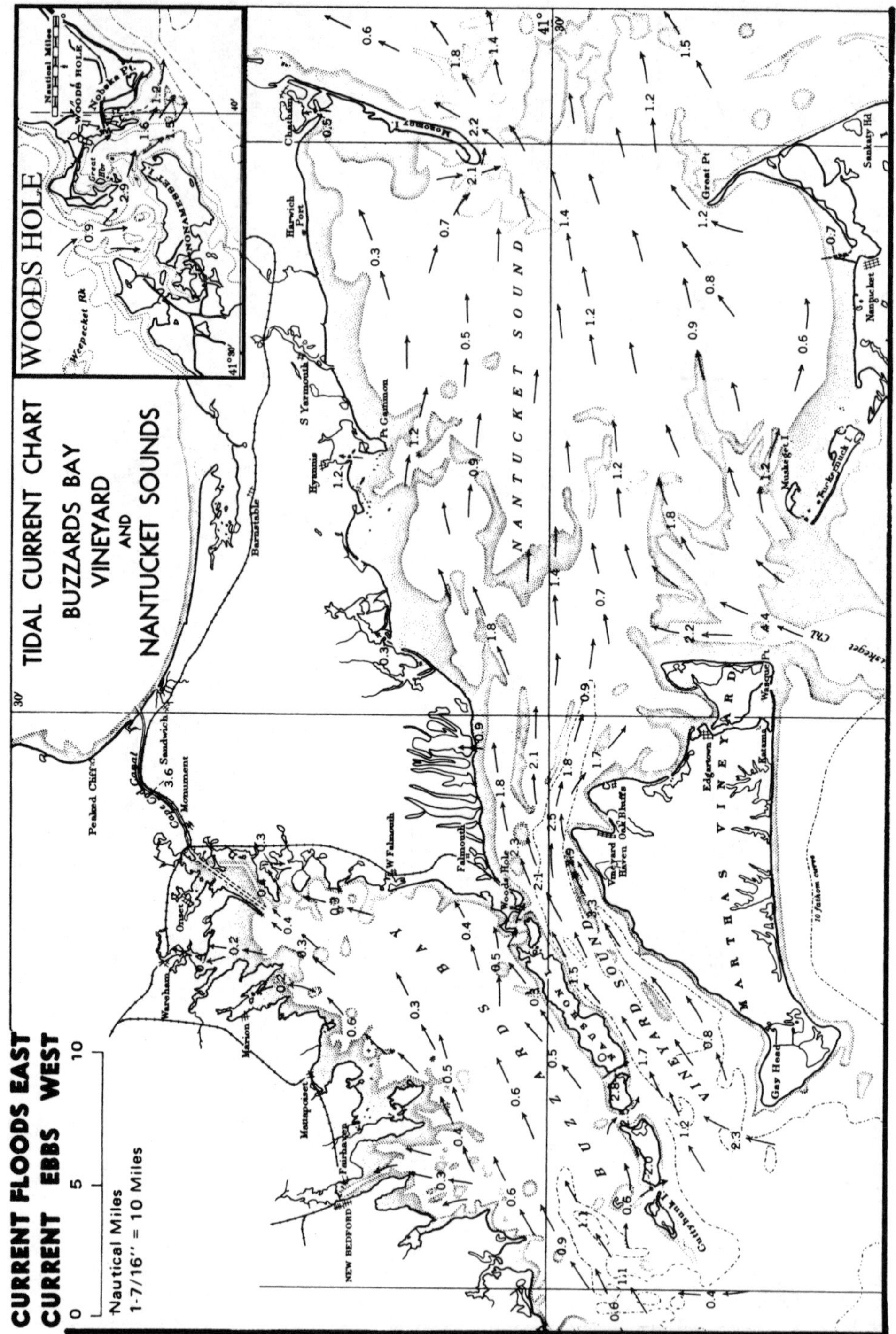

4 HOURS **AFTER** FLOOD STARTS AT POLLOCK RIP CHANNEL

OR: 2 HOURS **AFTER** LOW WATER AT BOSTON

Velocities shown are at Spring Tides. See note at bottom of Boston Tables: Rule-of-Thumb for Current Velocities. See pp. 60–65 for an enlarged version of Woods Hole inset. Pollock Rip Ch. is SE of Monomoy Pt.

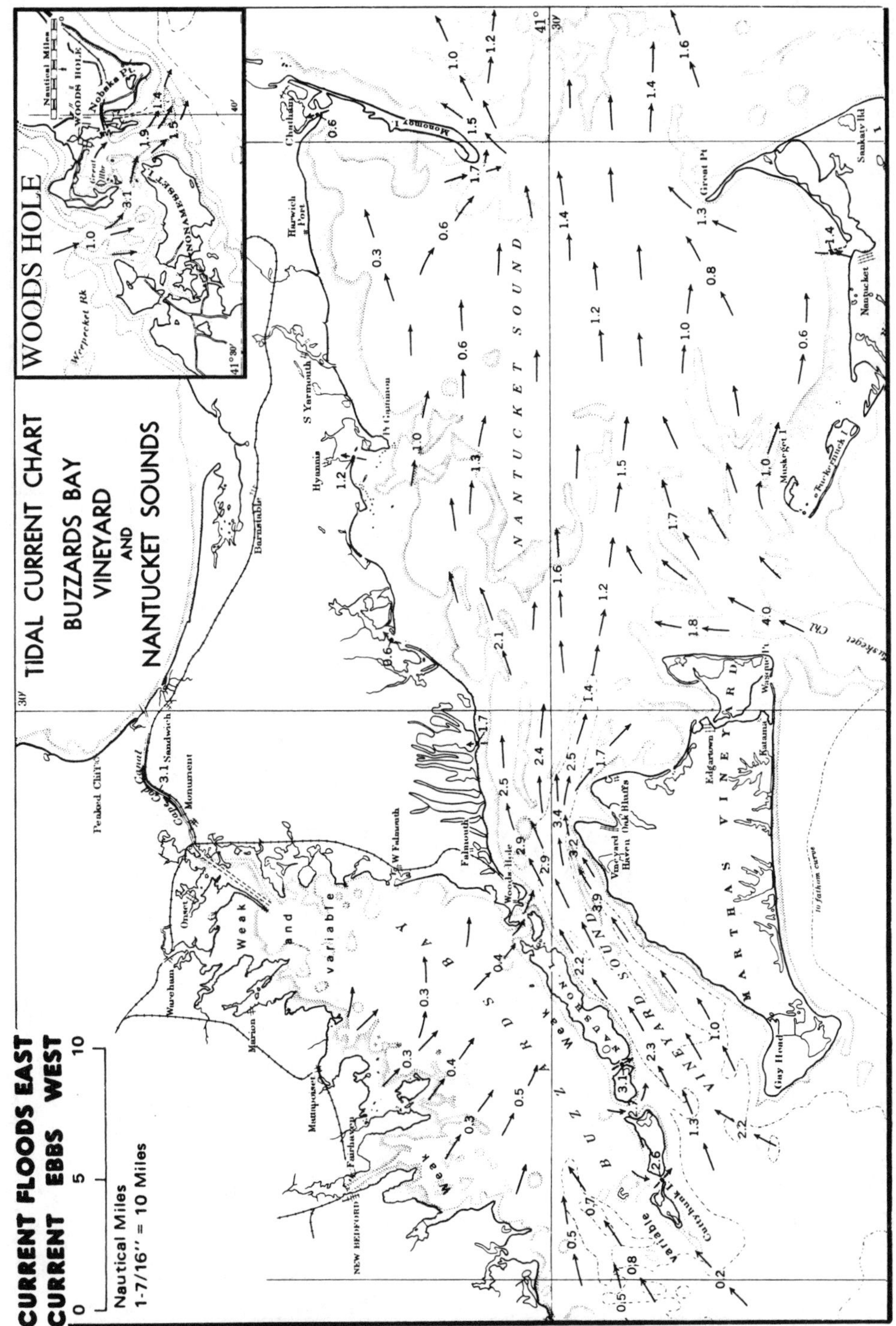

5 HOURS **AFTER** FLOOD STARTS AT POLLOCK RIP CHANNEL
OR: 3 HOURS **AFTER** LOW WATER AT BOSTON

Velocities shown are at Spring Tides. See note at bottom of Boston Tables: Rule-of-Thumb for Current Velocities. See pp. 60–65 for an enlarged version of Woods Hole inset.
Pollock Rip Ch. is SE of Monomoy Pt.

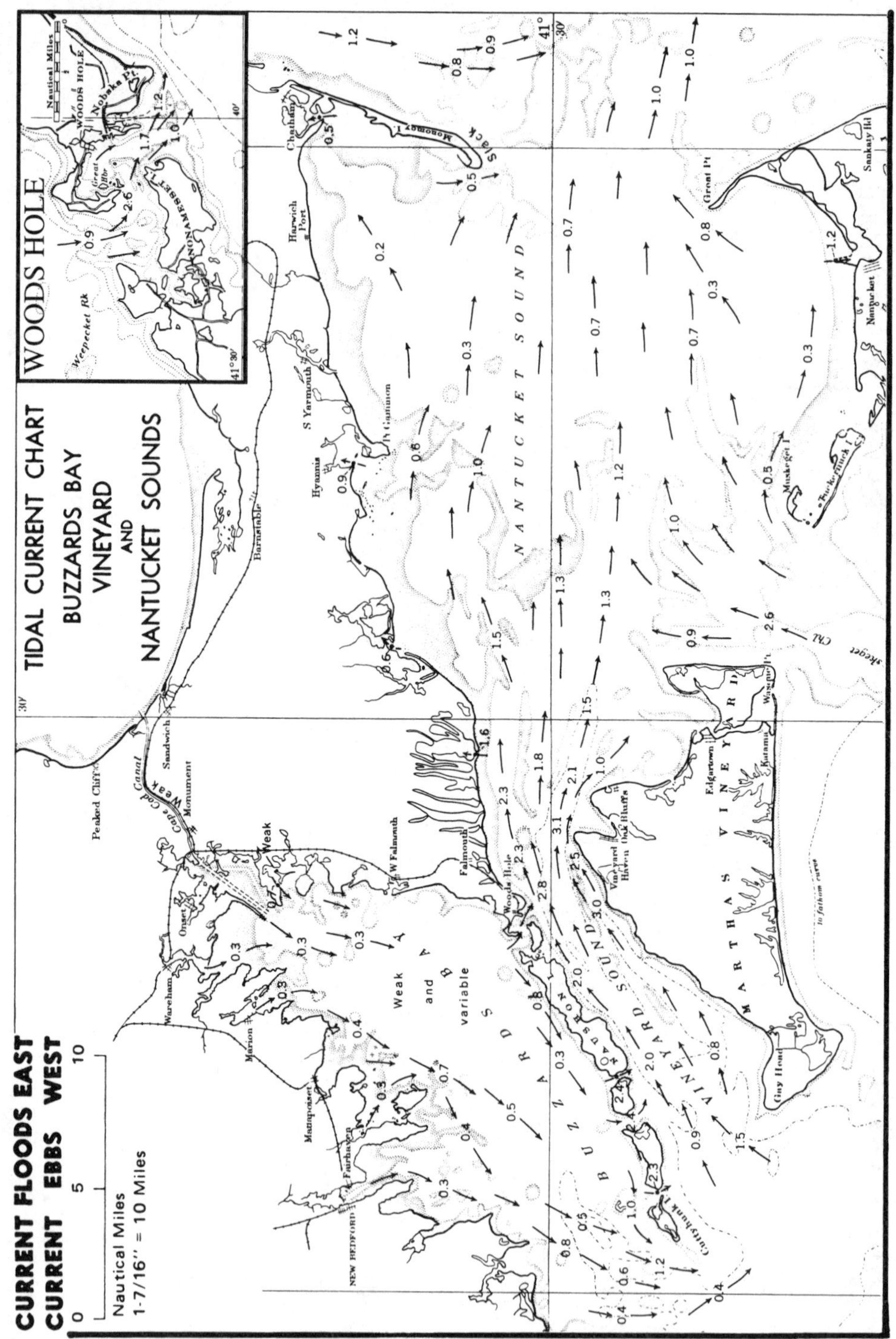

EBB STARTS AT POLLOCK RIP CHANNEL

OR: 4 HOURS **AFTER** LOW WATER AT BOSTON

Velocities shown are at Spring Tides. See note at bottom of Boston Tables: Rule-of-Thumb for Current Velocities. See pp. 60–65 for an enlarged version of Woods Hole inset. Pollock Rip Ch. is SE of Monomoy Pt.

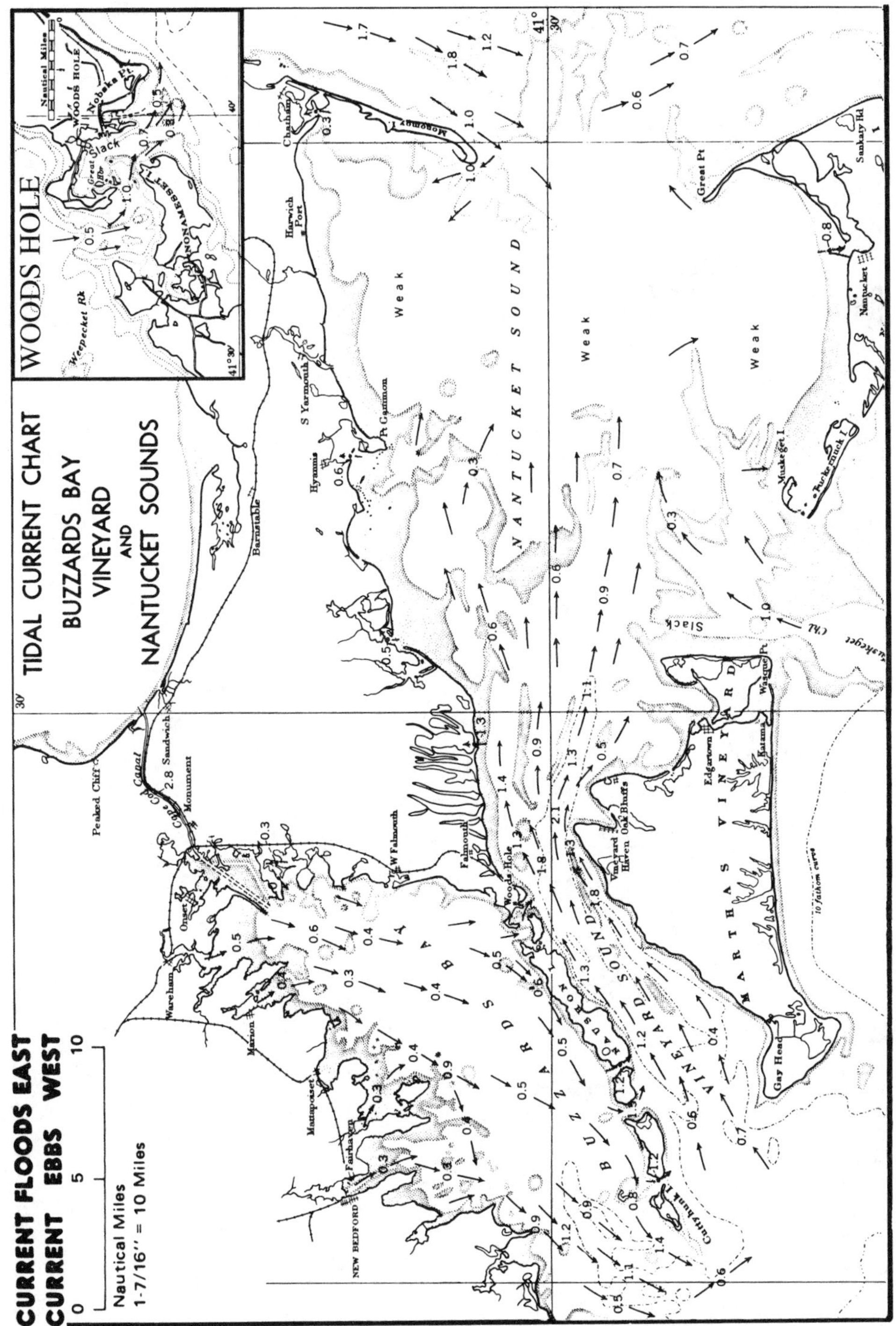

1 HOUR **AFTER** EBB STARTS AT POLLOCK RIP CHANNEL
OR: 5 HOURS **AFTER** LOW WATER AT BOSTON

Velocities shown are at Spring Tides. See note at bottom of Boston Tables: Rule-of-Thumb for Current Velocities. See pp. 60–65 for an enlarged version of Woods Hole inset. Pollock Rip Ch. is SE of Monomoy Pt.

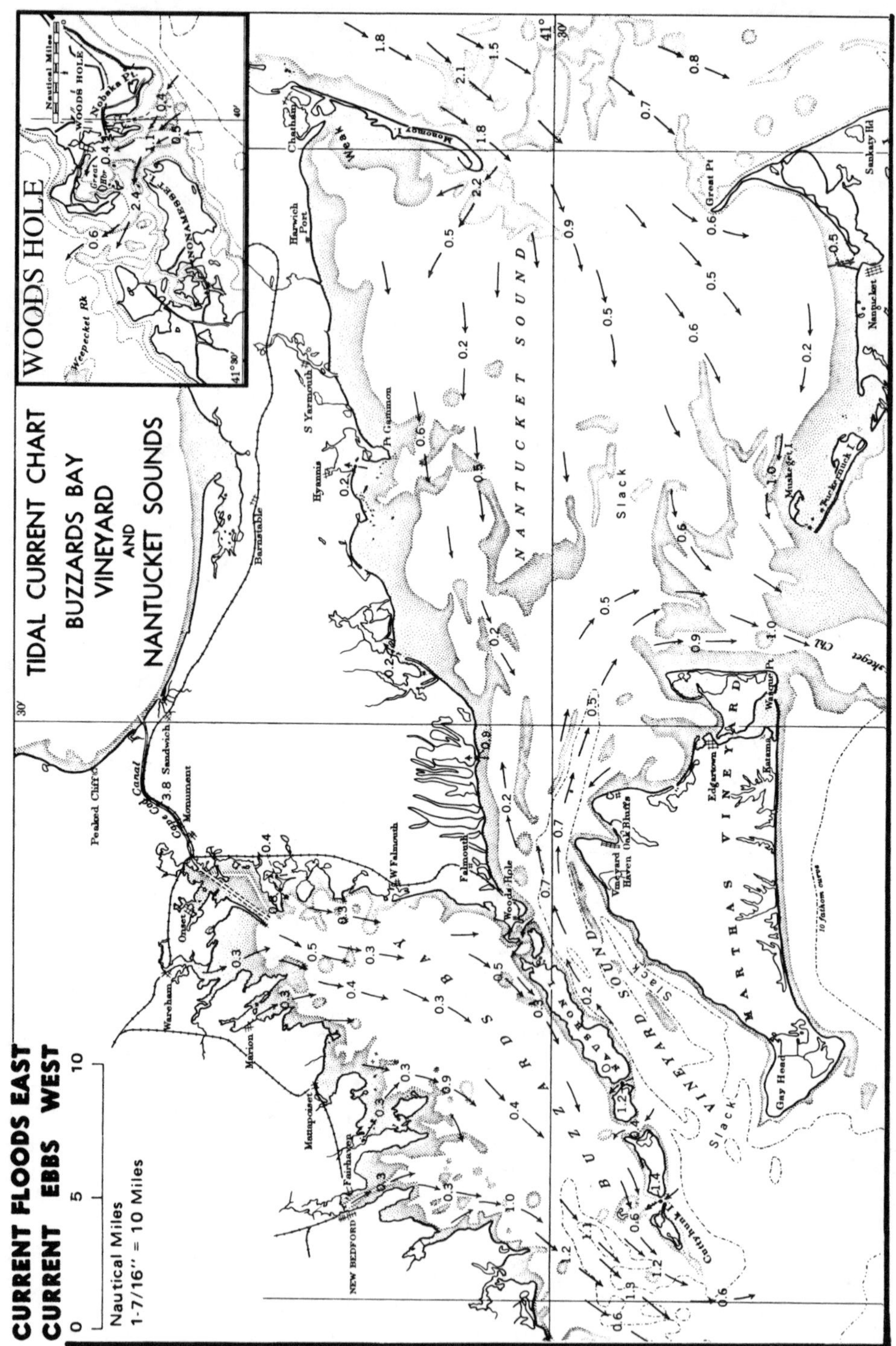

2 HOURS **AFTER** EBB STARTS AT POLLOCK RIP CHANNEL
OR: HIGH WATER AT BOSTON

Velocities shown are at Spring Tides. See note at bottom of Boston Tables: Rule-of-Thumb for Current Velocities. See pp. 60–65 for an enlarged version of Woods Hole inset.
Pollock Rip Ch. is SE of Monomoy Pt.

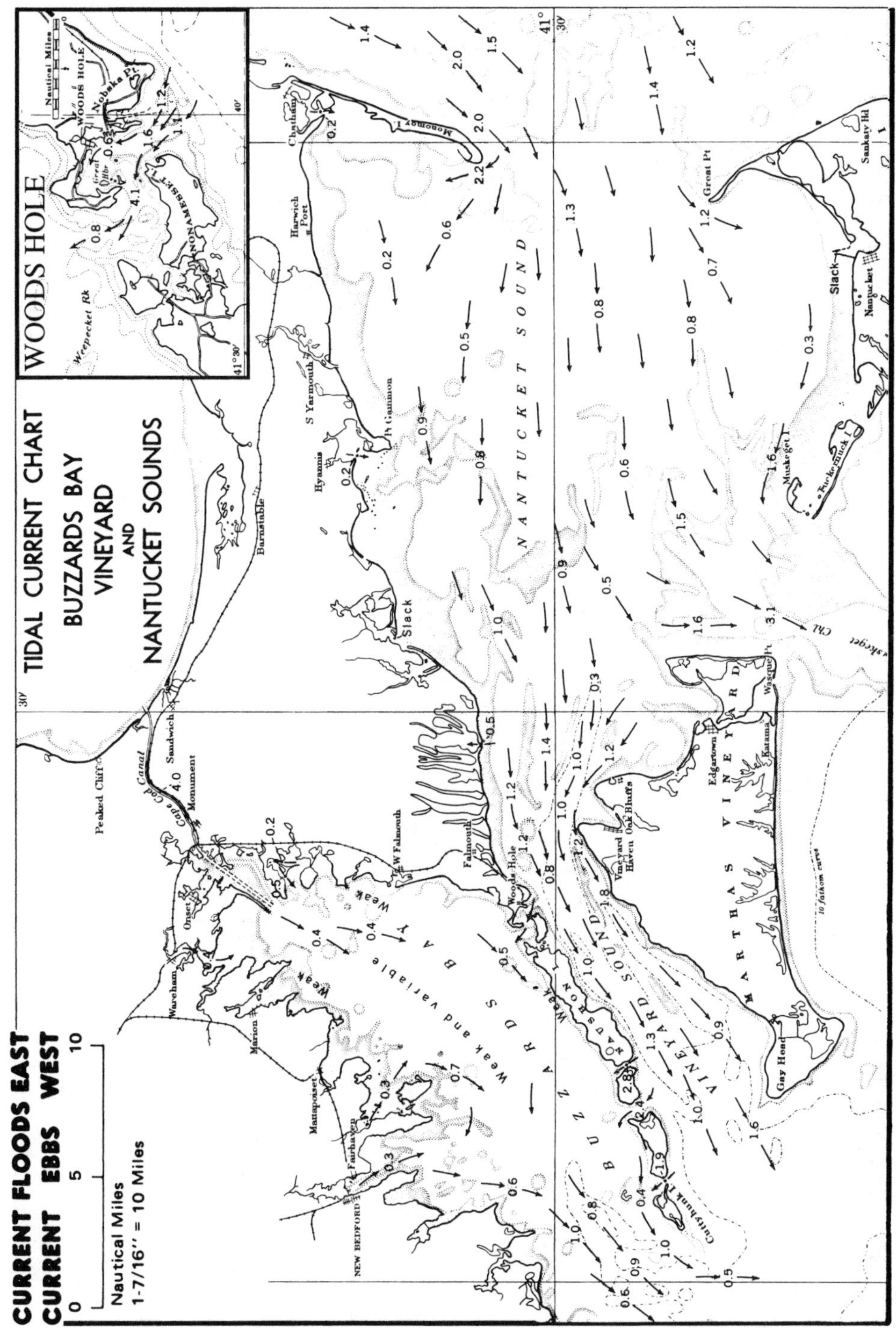

3 HOURS **AFTER** EBB STARTS AT POLLOCK RIP CHANNEL
OR: 1 HOUR **AFTER** HIGH WATER AT BOSTON

Velocities shown are at Spring Tides. See note at bottom of Boston Tables: Rule-of-Thumb for Current Velocities. See pp. 60–65 for an enlarged version of Woods Hole inset.

Pollock Rip Ch. is SE of Monomoy Pt.

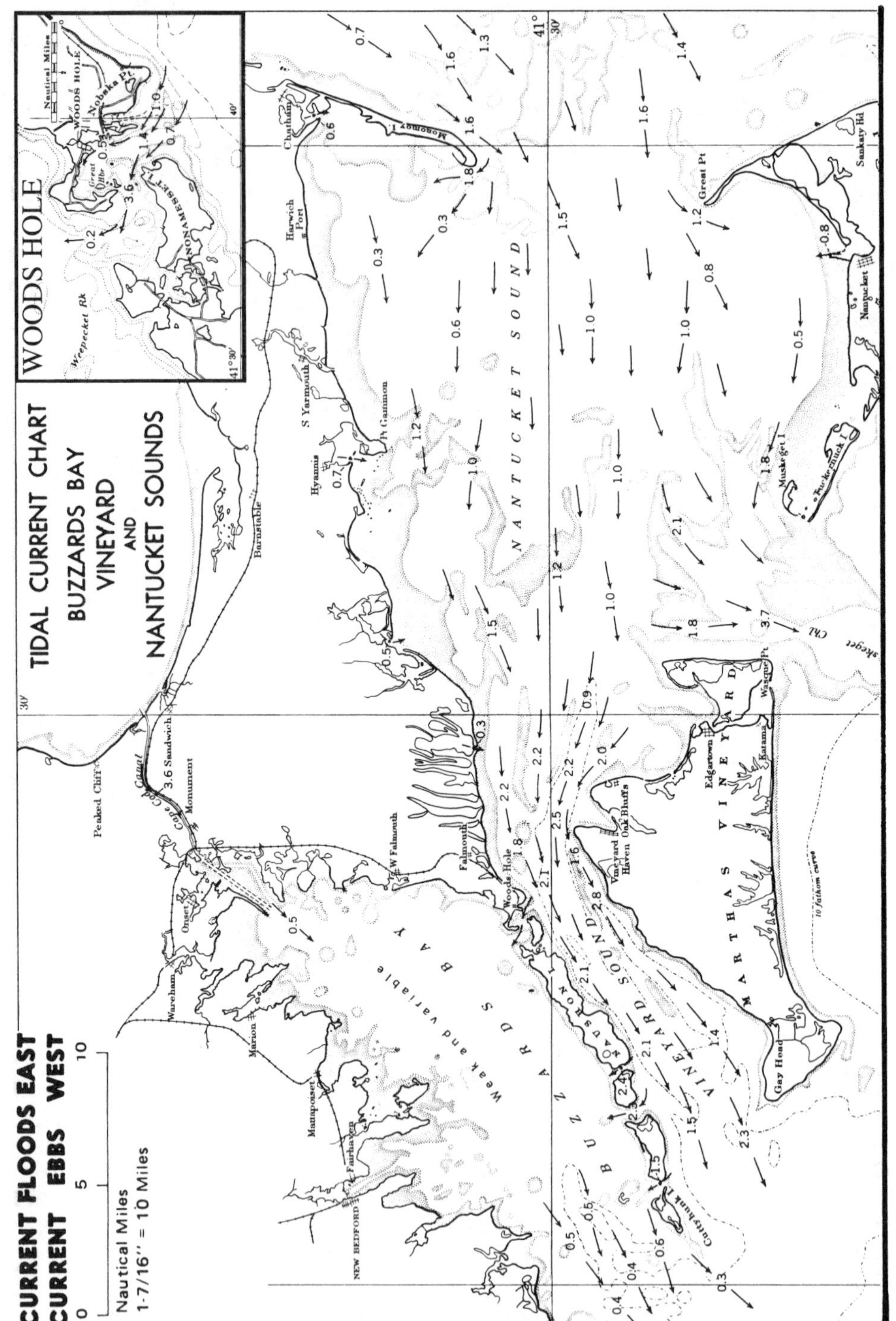

4 HOURS **AFTER** EBB STARTS AT POLLOCK RIP CHANNEL
OR: 2 HOURS **AFTER** HIGH WATER AT BOSTON

Velocities shown are at Spring Tides. See note at bottom of Boston Tables: Rule-of-Thumb for Current Velocities. See pp. 60–65 for an enlarged version of Woods Hole inset. Pollock Rip Ch. is SE of Monomoy Pt.

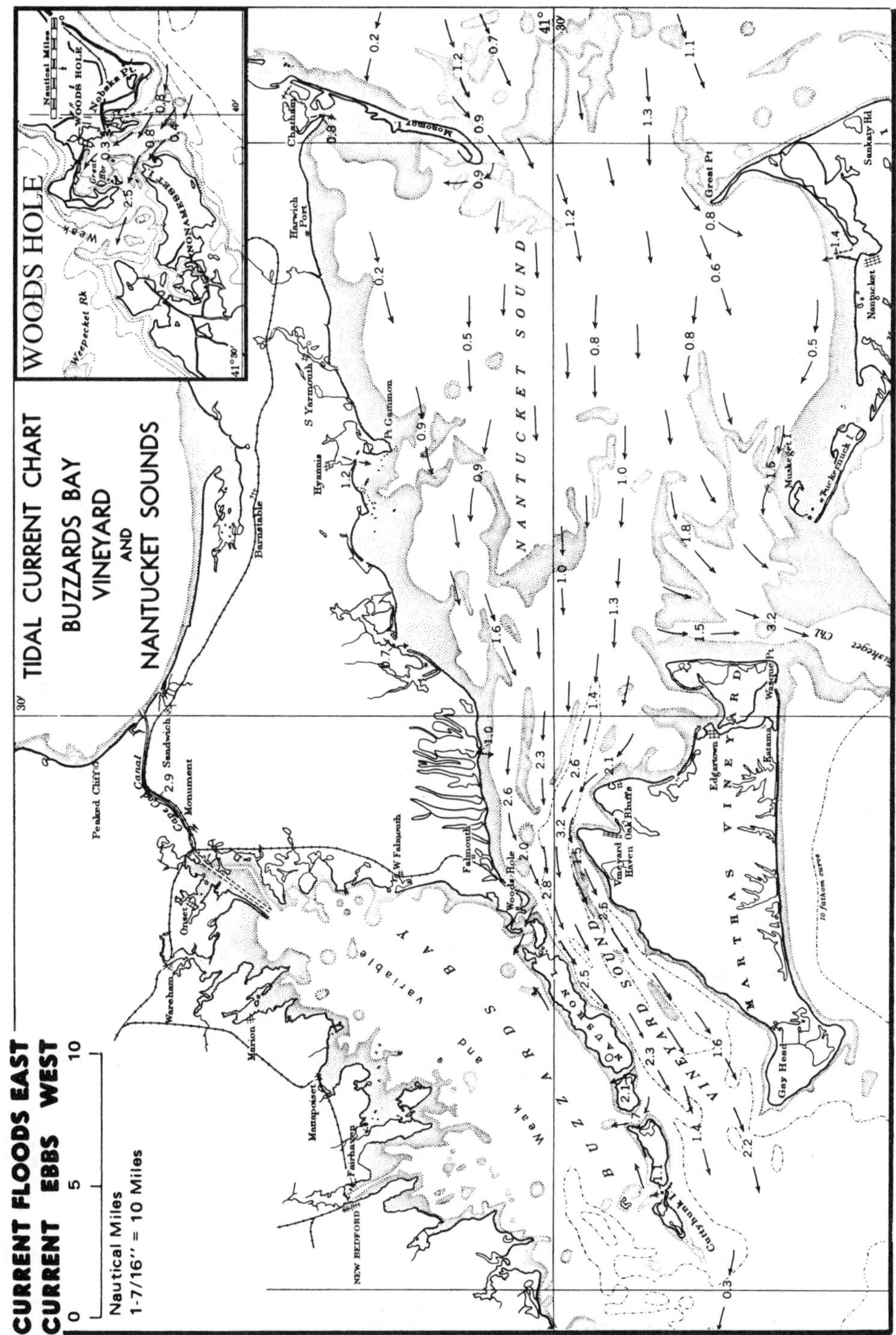

5 HOURS **AFTER** EBB STARTS AT POLLOCK RIP CHANNEL

OR: 3 HOURS **AFTER** HIGH WATER AT BOSTON

Velocities shown are at Spring Tides. See note at bottom of Boston Tables: Rule-of-Thumb for Current Velocities. See pp. 60–65 for an enlarged version of Woods Hole inset. Pollock Rip Ch. is SE of Monomoy Pt.

2021 HIGH & LOW WATER NEWPORT, RI

41°30.3'N, 71°19.6'W

Standard Time

DAY OF MONTH	DAY OF WEEK	JANUARY					
		HIGH				LOW	
		a.m.	Ht.	**p.m.**	Ht.	a.m.	**p.m.**
1	**F**	8:58	3.7	**9:28**	3.2	2:04	**3:00**
2	**S**	9:42	3.7	**10:16**	3.2	2:46	**3:34**
3	**S**	10:31	3.6	**11:07**	3.3	3:30	**4:11**
4	**M**	11:24	3.5	...	...	4:18	**4:54**
5	**T**	12:01	3.4	**12:19**	3.3	5:15	**5:45**
6	**W**	12:56	3.5	**1:15**	3.2	6:26	**6:46**
7	**T**	1:53	3.6	**2:15**	3.1	7:58	**7:52**
8	**F**	2:55	3.8	**3:21**	3.1	9:26	**8:56**
9	**S**	4:00	3.9	**4:27**	3.2	10:32	**9:56**
10	**S**	5:03	4.1	**5:28**	3.3	11:27	**10:51**
11	**M**	5:59	4.3	**6:23**	3.5	-A-	**11:43**
12	**T**	6:52	4.4	**7:14**	3.7	...	**1:09**
13	**W**	7:41	4.4	**8:03**	3.7	12:34	**1:55**
14	**T**	8:29	4.2	**8:51**	3.7	1:26	**2:33**
15	**F**	9:16	4.0	**9:38**	3.6	2:14	**3:06**
16	**S**	10:02	3.7	**10:26**	3.4	2:58	**3:38**
17	**S**	10:48	3.4	**11:15**	3.2	3:41	**4:10**
18	**M**	11:34	3.1	...	...	4:25	**4:47**
19	**T**	12:03	3.1	**12:20**	2.8	5:15	**5:29**
20	**W**	12:50	2.9	**1:05**	2.5	6:18	**6:18**
21	**T**	1:35	2.8	**1:51**	2.4	7:40	**7:14**
22	**F**	2:24	2.8	**2:44**	2.3	8:57	**8:14**
23	**S**	3:20	2.8	**3:44**	2.3	9:55	**9:11**
24	**S**	4:19	2.8	**4:41**	2.4	10:42	**10:04**
25	**M**	5:09	3.0	**5:30**	2.6	11:25	**10:51**
26	**T**	5:53	3.2	**6:14**	2.9	-B-	**11:37**
27	**W**	6:33	3.5	**6:56**	3.1	...	**12:48**
28	**T**	7:14	3.7	**7:38**	3.3	12:21	**1:28**
29	**F**	7:55	3.8	**8:21**	3.5	1:06	**2:04**
30	**S**	8:39	3.9	**9:07**	3.6	1:51	**2:38**
31	**S**	9:24	3.8	**9:54**	3.7	2:36	**3:12**

Standard Time

DAY OF MONTH	DAY OF WEEK	FEBRUARY					
		HIGH				LOW	
		a.m.	Ht.	**p.m.**	Ht.	a.m.	**p.m.**
1	**M**	10:13	3.7	**10:45**	3.7	3:21	**3:47**
2	**T**	11:04	3.5	**11:38**	3.7	4:08	**4:27**
3	**W**	11:59	3.3	...	...	5:02	**5:14**
4	**T**	12:34	3.7	**12:56**	3.1	6:09	**6:10**
5	**F**	1:32	3.7	**1:57**	3.0	7:51	**7:19**
6	**S**	2:35	3.6	**3:04**	2.9	9:33	**8:36**
7	**S**	3:45	3.7	**4:13**	3.0	10:38	**9:50**
8	**M**	4:51	3.8	**5:16**	3.2	11:31	**10:51**
9	**T**	5:49	3.9	**6:10**	3.4	-C-	**11:43**
10	**W**	6:40	4.1	**6:59**	3.6	...	**1:00**
11	**T**	7:27	4.1	**7:45**	3.7	12:32	**1:35**
12	**F**	8:10	4.0	**8:29**	3.7	1:18	**2:04**
13	**S**	8:52	3.8	**9:12**	3.6	2:00	**2:31**
14	**S**	9:33	3.6	**9:54**	3.5	2:40	**3:00**
15	**M**	10:13	3.3	**10:35**	3.3	3:18	**3:31**
16	**T**	10:54	3.0	**11:17**	3.1	3:57	**4:04**
17	**W**	11:36	2.7	**11:58**	2.9	4:38	**4:41**
18	**T**	...	...	**12:19**	2.5	5:26	**5:24**
19	**F**	12:40	2.8	**1:03**	2.3	6:28	**6:16**
20	**S**	1:24	2.7	**1:53**	2.2	7:55	**7:19**
21	**S**	2:17	2.6	**2:52**	2.2	9:17	**8:28**
22	**M**	3:22	2.7	**3:58**	2.4	10:14	**9:33**
23	**T**	4:28	2.9	**4:55**	2.7	10:59	**10:28**
24	**W**	5:21	3.2	**5:44**	3.0	11:40	**11:17**
25	**T**	6:07	3.5	**6:30**	3.3	...	**12:18**
26	**F**	6:50	3.8	**7:14**	3.7	12:04	**12:55**
27	**S**	7:34	4.0	**7:58**	3.9	12:51	**1:32**
28	**S**	8:18	4.1	**8:44**	4.1	1:38	**2:08**

A also at 12:19 p.m. **B** also at 12:07 p.m. **C** also at 12:18 p.m.

Dates when Ht. of **Low** Water is below Mean Lower Low with Ht. of lowest given for each period and Date of lowest in ( ):

January:

1st–3rd: -0.3' (1st)
9th–16th: -0.4' (11th, 13th, 14th)
26th: -0.2'
28th–31st: -0.5' (29th–31st)

February:

1st–3rd: -0.5' (1st)
9th–15th: -0.3' (11th–14th)
24th–28th: -0.7' (28th)

Average Rise and Fall 3.5 ft.

When a high tide exceeds avg. ht., the *following* low tide will be lower than avg.

2021 HIGH & LOW WATER NEWPORT, RI

41°30.3'N, 71°19.6'W

***Daylight Time starts March 14 at 2 a.m.** **Daylight Saving Time**

DAY OF MONTH	DAY OF WEEK	MARCH						DAY OF MONTH	DAY OF WEEK	APRIL					
		HIGH				LOW				HIGH				LOW	
		a.m.	Ht.	**p.m.**	Ht.	a.m.	**p.m.**			a.m.	Ht.	**p.m.**	Ht.	a.m.	**p.m.**
1	**M**	9:06	4.0	**9:32**	4.2	2:25	**2:45**	1	**T**	11:31	3.7	**11:58**	4.3	4:49	**4:42**
2	**T**	9:54	3.8	**10:23**	4.2	3:11	**3:22**	2	**F**	...	...	**12:27**	3.5	5:42	**5:30**
3	**W**	10:46	3.6	**11:17**	4.0	3:58	**4:03**	3	**S**	12:57	4.0	**1:27**	3.3	6:53	**6:28**
4	**T**	11:42	3.3	...	...	4:50	**4:49**	4	**S**	1:59	3.7	**2:29**	3.2	9:02	**7:52**
5	**F**	12:14	3.9	**12:41**	3.1	5:57	**5:45**	5	**M**	3:03	3.5	**3:34**	3.1	10:20	**10:16**
6	**S**	1:14	3.7	**1:42**	3.0	8:03	**6:58**	6	**T**	4:12	3.4	**4:41**	3.2	11:16	**11:21**
7	**S**	2:19	3.5	**2:49**	2.9	9:34	**8:42**	7	**W**	5:19	3.4	**5:43**	3.4	11:58	...
8	**M**	3:30	3.5	**3:59**	3.0	10:35	**10:12**	8	**T**	6:14	3.5	**6:35**	3.6	12:07	**12:29**
9	**T**	4:39	3.5	**5:02**	3.2	11:23	**11:06**	9	**F**	7:01	3.6	**7:20**	3.8	12:42	**12:51**
10	**W**	5:36	3.7	**5:55**	3.5	-A-	**11:50**	10	**S**	7:42	3.6	**8:00**	3.9	1:13	**1:12**
11	**T**	6:24	3.8	**6:42**	3.7	...	**12:34**	11	**S**	8:21	3.6	**8:38**	3.9	1:46	**1:39**
12	**F**	7:07	3.8	**7:25**	3.8	12:28	**12:59**	12	**M**	8:57	3.5	**9:13**	3.9	2:21	**2:11**
13	**S**	7:47	3.8	**8:05**	3.8	1:05	**1:23**	13	**T**	9:33	3.4	**9:46**	3.7	2:57	**2:46**
14	**S**	*9:26	3.7	***9:43**	3.8	1:42	***2:51**	14	**W**	10:09	3.2	**10:19**	3.6	3:33	**3:21**
15	**M**	10:03	3.5	**10:20**	3.6	3:19	**3:22**	15	**T**	10:46	3.0	**10:53**	3.4	4:08	**3:57**
16	**T**	10:40	3.2	**10:55**	3.4	3:55	**3:55**	16	**F**	11:26	2.8	**11:30**	3.2	4:43	**4:33**
17	**W**	11:17	3.0	**11:31**	3.2	4:31	**4:28**	17	**S**	...	...	**12:09**	2.7	5:19	**5:11**
18	**T**	11:57	2.7	...	...	5:08	**5:04**	18	**S**	12:14	3.0	**12:57**	2.6	6:01	**5:56**
19	**F**	12:09	3.0	**12:40**	2.5	5:48	**5:43**	19	**M**	1:04	2.9	**1:47**	2.6	6:57	**6:54**
20	**S**	12:50	2.8	**1:26**	2.4	6:36	**6:30**	20	**T**	1:58	2.9	**2:41**	2.7	8:21	**8:08**
21	**S**	1:37	2.7	**2:16**	2.4	7:46	**7:31**	21	**W**	2:56	3.0	**3:40**	2.9	9:41	**9:27**
22	**M**	2:30	2.7	**3:12**	2.4	9:28	**8:46**	22	**T**	4:00	3.1	**4:42**	3.2	10:33	**10:36**
23	**T**	3:33	2.7	**4:15**	2.5	10:37	**10:01**	23	**F**	5:05	3.3	**5:40**	3.6	11:14	**11:33**
24	**W**	4:42	2.9	**5:18**	2.9	11:23	**11:03**	24	**S**	6:04	3.6	**6:33**	4.1	11:54	...
25	**T**	5:44	3.2	**6:13**	3.3	-B-	**11:55**	25	**S**	6:56	3.9	**7:23**	4.5	12:25	**12:35**
26	**F**	6:36	3.6	**7:02**	3.7	...	**12:38**	26	**M**	7:46	4.1	**8:12**	4.8	1:16	**1:18**
27	**S**	7:23	3.9	**7:48**	4.1	12:45	**1:15**	27	**T**	8:36	4.1	**9:01**	5.0	2:08	**2:03**
28	**S**	8:10	4.1	**8:35**	4.4	1:34	**1:54**	28	**W**	9:27	4.1	**9:52**	4.9	3:01	**2:50**
29	**M**	8:57	4.2	**9:22**	4.6	2:24	**2:35**	29	**T**	10:19	4.0	**10:45**	4.7	3:52	**3:37**
30	**T**	9:45	4.1	**10:11**	4.7	3:13	**3:16**	30	**F**	11:14	3.8	**11:41**	4.4	4:42	**4:25**
31	**W**	10:36	3.9	**11:02**	4.5	4:01	**3:58**								

A also at 12:03 p.m. **B** also at 12:01 p.m.

Dates when Ht. of **Low** Water is below Mean Lower Low with Ht. of lowest given for each period and Date of lowest in ( ):

1st–4th: -0.7' (1st)
13th–15th: -0.2'
25th–31st: -0.8' (29th, 30th)

1st: -0.4'
24th–30th: -0.6' (26th–28th)

Average Rise and Fall 3.5 ft.

When a high tide exceeds avg. ht., the *following* low tide will be lower than avg.

2021 HIGH & LOW WATER
NEWPORT, RI
41°30.3'N, 71°19.6'W

Daylight Saving Time — Daylight Saving Time

DAY OF MONTH	DAY OF WEEK	MAY						DAY OF MONTH	DAY OF WEEK	JUNE					
		HIGH				LOW				HIGH				LOW	
		a.m.	Ht.	p.m.	Ht.	a.m.	p.m.			a.m.	Ht.	p.m.	Ht.	a.m.	p.m.
1	S	...	...	12:12	3.6	5:36	5:17	1	T	1:21	3.8	1:51	3.6	7:48	7:48
2	S	12:41	4.1	1:12	3.5	6:52	6:18	2	W	2:16	3.5	2:48	3.5	8:54	9:32
3	M	1:42	3.8	2:13	3.4	8:39	8:10	3	T	3:11	3.3	3:45	3.5	9:39	10:30
4	T	2:43	3.5	3:14	3.3	9:49	10:07	4	F	4:07	3.1	4:42	3.5	10:10	11:12
5	W	3:45	3.3	4:17	3.4	10:40	11:04	5	S	5:04	3.0	5:36	3.6	10:38	11:47
6	T	4:48	3.3	5:17	3.5	11:15	11:46	6	S	5:55	3.0	6:22	3.7	11:10	...
7	F	5:44	3.3	6:09	3.7	11:39	...	7	M	6:41	3.1	7:03	3.8	12:20	-C-
8	S	6:31	3.3	6:53	3.8	12:19	-A-	8	T	7:21	3.1	7:39	3.8	12:56	12:24
9	S	7:13	3.3	7:33	3.9	12:49	12:26	9	W	8:00	3.2	8:14	3.8	1:35	1:04
10	M	7:52	3.3	8:09	3.9	1:21	12:58	10	T	8:38	3.2	8:49	3.8	2:16	1:45
11	T	8:29	3.3	8:43	3.9	1:57	1:35	11	F	9:16	3.2	9:24	3.7	2:57	2:27
12	W	9:05	3.3	9:15	3.8	2:36	2:13	12	S	9:55	3.2	10:02	3.7	3:35	3:09
13	T	9:42	3.2	9:49	3.6	3:14	2:52	13	S	10:37	3.1	10:43	3.6	4:10	3:49
14	F	10:20	3.0	10:24	3.5	3:50	3:30	14	M	11:22	3.1	11:29	3.5	4:43	4:30
15	S	11:00	2.9	11:04	3.3	4:25	4:08	15	T	...	...	12:09	3.1	5:18	5:15
16	S	11:45	2.8	11:49	3.2	4:59	4:48	16	W	12:18	3.5	12:59	3.2	5:59	6:07
17	M	...	...	12:33	2.8	5:38	5:32	17	T	1:10	3.4	1:50	3.4	6:48	7:12
18	T	12:40	3.2	1:23	2.9	6:25	6:27	18	F	2:03	3.4	2:43	3.6	7:45	8:29
19	W	1:33	3.2	2:15	3.0	7:27	7:37	19	S	3:00	3.4	3:40	3.9	8:45	9:47
20	T	2:28	3.2	3:10	3.3	8:36	8:56	20	S	4:02	3.4	4:41	4.2	9:43	10:54
21	F	3:27	3.3	4:09	3.6	9:35	10:09	21	M	5:07	3.5	5:43	4.5	10:38	11:53
22	S	4:30	3.4	5:09	4.0	10:25	11:11	22	T	6:10	3.6	6:40	4.8	11:31	...
23	S	5:33	3.6	6:06	4.4	11:13	...	23	W	7:07	3.8	7:35	4.9	12:48	12:23
24	M	6:31	3.8	6:59	4.8	12:06	-B-	24	T	8:01	4.0	8:28	5.0	1:45	1:17
25	T	7:25	3.9	7:51	5.0	1:00	12:47	25	F	8:54	4.1	9:21	4.9	2:42	2:12
26	W	8:18	4.1	8:43	5.1	1:54	1:36	26	S	9:47	4.1	10:13	4.7	3:35	3:08
27	T	9:10	4.1	9:35	5.0	2:50	2:28	27	S	10:40	4.0	11:06	4.4	4:22	4:02
28	F	10:03	4.0	10:29	4.8	3:44	3:21	28	M	11:34	3.9	11:59	4.1	5:04	4:53
29	S	10:58	3.9	11:25	4.4	4:35	4:13	29	T	...	...	12:29	3.8	5:46	5:47
30	S	11:55	3.8	...	...	5:27	5:06	30	W	12:51	3.7	1:23	3.7	6:29	6:53
31	M	12:22	4.1	12:53	3.7	6:29	6:08								

A also at 11:59 a.m. **B** also at 11:59 a.m. **C** also at 11:46 a.m.

Dates when Ht. of **Low** Water is below Mean Lower Low with Ht. of lowest given for each period and Date of lowest in ( ):

23rd–28th: -0.5' (25th, 26th)

22nd–25th: -0.3' (23rd, 24th)

Average Rise and Fall 3.5 ft.

When a high tide exceeds avg. ht., the *following* low tide will be lower than avg.

2021 HIGH & LOW WATER NEWPORT, RI

41°30.3'N, 71°19.6'W

DAY OF MONTH	DAY OF WEEK	JULY (Daylight Saving Time) HIGH a.m.	Ht.	**p.m.**	Ht.	LOW a.m.	**p.m.**	DAY OF MONTH	DAY OF WEEK	AUGUST (Daylight Saving Time) HIGH a.m.	Ht.	**p.m.**	Ht.	LOW a.m.	**p.m.**
1	**T**	1:43	3.4	**2:15**	3.6	7:16	**8:26**	1	**S**	2:39	2.8	**3:11**	3.3	7:51	**9:42**
2	**F**	2:32	3.2	**3:06**	3.5	8:05	**9:38**	2	**M**	3:29	2.7	**4:04**	3.2	8:48	**10:39**
3	**S**	3:22	3.0	**3:59**	3.4	8:53	**10:30**	3	**T**	4:27	2.7	**5:02**	3.2	9:47	**11:26**
4	**S**	4:17	2.8	**4:54**	3.4	9:40	**11:12**	4	**W**	5:26	2.7	**5:56**	3.3	10:42	...
5	**M**	5:13	2.8	**5:46**	3.5	10:26	**11:52**	5	**T**	6:17	2.9	**6:40**	3.5	12:09	**-B-**
6	**T**	6:05	2.8	**6:31**	3.5	11:11	...	6	**F**	7:01	3.1	**7:20**	3.7	12:50	**12:19**
7	**W**	6:50	3.0	**7:10**	3.6	12:32	**-A-**	7	**S**	7:42	3.3	**7:58**	3.9	1:31	**1:04**
8	**T**	7:31	3.1	**7:47**	3.7	1:13	**12:39**	8	**S**	8:23	3.5	**8:37**	4.0	2:11	**1:49**
9	**F**	8:11	3.2	**8:24**	3.8	1:56	**1:23**	9	**M**	9:04	3.7	**9:18**	4.1	2:47	**2:33**
10	**S**	8:50	3.3	**9:02**	3.8	2:39	**2:07**	10	**T**	9:47	3.8	**10:01**	4.1	3:20	**3:18**
11	**S**	9:30	3.4	**9:41**	3.8	3:17	**2:51**	11	**W**	10:32	3.9	**10:47**	4.0	3:52	**4:01**
12	**M**	10:13	3.4	**10:23**	3.8	3:51	**3:33**	12	**T**	11:19	4.0	**11:36**	3.8	4:25	**4:46**
13	**T**	10:57	3.5	**11:08**	3.8	4:22	**4:15**	13	**F**	...	...	**12:10**	4.1	5:02	**5:35**
14	**W**	11:45	3.5	**11:57**	3.7	4:54	**5:00**	14	**S**	12:29	3.7	**1:04**	4.1	5:44	**6:34**
15	**T**	...	...	**12:35**	3.7	5:31	**5:50**	15	**S**	1:25	3.5	**1:59**	4.1	6:35	**7:54**
16	**F**	12:49	3.6	**1:26**	3.8	6:14	**6:51**	16	**M**	2:23	3.4	**2:59**	4.1	7:37	**9:41**
17	**S**	1:42	3.5	**2:20**	3.9	7:06	**8:08**	17	**T**	3:26	3.3	**4:04**	4.1	8:49	**10:58**
18	**S**	2:39	3.4	**3:17**	4.1	8:06	**9:34**	18	**W**	4:34	3.3	**5:13**	4.2	10:05	**11:55**
19	**M**	3:40	3.3	**4:19**	4.2	9:10	**10:49**	19	**T**	5:40	3.5	**6:15**	4.3	11:13	...
20	**T**	4:47	3.3	**5:25**	4.4	10:13	**11:50**	20	**F**	6:40	3.8	**7:10**	4.5	12:45	**12:11**
21	**W**	5:53	3.5	**6:26**	4.6	11:14	...	21	**S**	7:32	4.0	**8:00**	4.6	1:29	**1:04**
22	**T**	6:52	3.7	**7:22**	4.7	12:45	**12:11**	22	**S**	8:21	4.2	**8:46**	4.5	2:10	**1:55**
23	**F**	7:47	4.0	**8:15**	4.8	1:39	**1:06**	23	**M**	9:08	4.3	**9:31**	4.4	2:44	**2:43**
24	**S**	8:38	4.1	**9:05**	4.7	2:31	**2:02**	24	**T**	9:53	4.2	**10:14**	4.1	3:14	**3:26**
25	**S**	9:29	4.2	**9:54**	4.6	3:17	**2:57**	25	**W**	10:38	4.1	**10:57**	3.8	3:44	**4:07**
26	**M**	10:18	4.1	**10:42**	4.3	3:55	**3:47**	26	**T**	11:22	3.9	**11:41**	3.5	4:16	**4:47**
27	**T**	11:08	4.0	**11:30**	4.0	4:27	**4:33**	27	**F**	...	...	**12:07**	3.7	4:49	**5:28**
28	**W**	11:58	3.9	...	...	4:59	**5:18**	28	**S**	12:26	3.2	**12:51**	3.5	5:26	**6:17**
29	**T**	12:17	3.6	**12:48**	3.7	5:34	**6:07**	29	**S**	1:11	3.0	**1:35**	3.3	6:08	**7:20**
30	**F**	1:05	3.3	**1:36**	3.5	6:13	**7:09**	30	**M**	1:57	2.8	**2:20**	3.1	6:59	**8:49**
31	**S**	1:51	3.0	**2:23**	3.4	6:58	**8:28**	31	**T**	2:46	2.7	**3:10**	3.0	8:02	**10:06**

A also at 11:55 a.m. **B** also at 11:32 a.m.

Dates when Ht. of **Low** Water is below Mean Lower Low with Ht. of lowest given for each period and Date of lowest in ( ):

Average Rise and Fall 3.5 ft.

When a high tide exceeds avg. ht., the *following* low tide will be lower than avg.

2021 HIGH & LOW WATER
NEWPORT, RI
41°30.3'N, 71°19.6'W

Daylight Saving Time | **Daylight Saving Time**

DAY OF MONTH	DAY OF WEEK	SEPTEMBER						DAY OF MONTH	DAY OF WEEK	OCTOBER					
		HIGH				LOW				HIGH				LOW	
		a.m.	Ht.	p.m.	Ht.	a.m.	p.m.			a.m.	Ht.	p.m.	Ht.	a.m.	p.m.
1	W	3:42	2.6	4:10	3.1	9:11	11:00	1	F	4:01	2.8	4:23	3.1	9:47	11:10
2	T	4:43	2.7	5:13	3.2	10:16	11:43	2	S	5:00	3.1	5:22	3.4	10:48	11:45
3	F	5:40	3.0	6:04	3.4	11:11	...	3	S	5:53	3.4	6:12	3.7	11:37	...
4	S	6:28	3.2	6:48	3.7	12:22	-A-	4	M	6:40	3.8	6:58	4.0	12:17	12:23
5	S	7:12	3.6	7:29	4.0	12:58	12:44	5	T	7:25	4.2	7:43	4.2	12:51	1:09
6	M	7:54	3.9	8:10	4.1	1:33	1:29	6	W	8:09	4.6	8:29	4.3	1:27	1:56
7	T	8:36	4.1	8:53	4.2	2:07	2:15	7	T	8:55	4.8	9:16	4.2	2:05	2:44
8	W	9:20	4.3	9:38	4.2	2:42	3:01	8	F	9:42	4.8	10:06	4.1	2:46	3:33
9	T	10:06	4.4	10:25	4.1	3:18	3:47	9	S	10:33	4.8	10:59	3.9	3:29	4:21
10	F	10:55	4.5	11:17	3.9	3:56	4:33	10	S	11:27	4.6	11:56	3.7	4:13	5:12
11	S	11:47	4.4	...	...	4:36	5:22	11	M	...	...	12:26	4.3	5:01	6:14
12	S	12:12	3.7	12:43	4.3	5:20	6:21	12	T	12:57	3.5	1:28	4.1	5:56	8:21
13	M	1:10	3.5	1:43	4.2	6:12	8:01	13	W	1:59	3.4	2:32	3.9	7:09	9:49
14	T	2:11	3.4	2:45	4.0	7:18	9:56	14	T	3:02	3.4	3:37	3.8	9:29	10:48
15	W	3:14	3.3	3:52	4.0	8:46	11:01	15	F	4:08	3.5	4:44	3.8	10:50	11:34
16	T	4:22	3.4	5:01	4.0	10:26	11:52	16	S	5:12	3.7	5:43	3.8	11:41	...
17	F	5:28	3.6	6:03	4.1	11:32	...	17	S	6:08	3.9	6:34	3.9	12:08	12:22
18	S	6:26	3.9	6:55	4.2	12:33	12:21	18	M	6:56	4.1	7:18	3.9	12:32	12:56
19	S	7:16	4.1	7:41	4.3	1:07	1:04	19	T	7:39	4.2	7:59	3.9	12:52	1:28
20	M	8:01	4.3	8:24	4.2	1:34	1:44	20	W	8:19	4.2	8:38	3.8	1:18	2:02
21	T	8:44	4.3	9:05	4.1	2:00	2:23	21	T	8:57	4.2	9:16	3.6	1:49	2:38
22	W	9:25	4.3	9:45	3.9	2:30	3:02	22	F	9:33	4.0	9:54	3.4	2:24	3:15
23	T	10:05	4.1	10:24	3.6	3:02	3:40	23	S	10:08	3.8	10:32	3.2	3:01	3:52
24	F	10:44	3.9	11:05	3.4	3:36	4:17	24	S	10:43	3.6	11:13	3.0	3:39	4:29
25	S	11:23	3.7	11:47	3.1	4:11	4:55	25	M	11:22	3.3	11:57	2.8	4:17	5:07
26	S	...	...	12:04	3.4	4:48	5:37	26	T	...	...	12:05	3.1	4:57	5:51
27	M	12:32	2.9	12:47	3.2	5:29	6:28	27	W	12:46	2.7	12:54	3.0	5:42	6:50
28	T	1:20	2.7	1:34	3.0	6:16	7:47	28	T	1:36	2.7	1:46	3.0	6:38	8:25
29	W	2:09	2.7	2:24	3.0	7:17	9:29	29	F	2:27	2.7	2:40	3.0	7:51	9:37
30	T	3:02	2.7	3:21	3.0	8:33	10:28	30	S	3:22	2.9	3:38	3.1	9:11	10:21
								31	S	4:20	3.2	4:38	3.3	10:19	10:57

A also at 11:59 a.m.

Dates when Ht. of **Low** Water is below Mean Lower Low with Ht. of lowest given for each period and Date of lowest in ( ):

8th–10th: -0.2'

5th–10th: -0.4' (7th, 8th)

Average Rise and Fall 3.5 ft.

When a high tide exceeds avg. ht., the *following* low tide will be lower than avg.

2021 HIGH & LOW WATER
NEWPORT, RI
41°30.3'N, 71°19.6'W

***Standard Time starts Nov. 7 at 2 a.m.** **Standard Time**

DAY OF MONTH	DAY OF WEEK	NOVEMBER						DAY OF MONTH	DAY OF WEEK	DECEMBER					
		HIGH				LOW				HIGH				LOW	
		a.m.	Ht.	**p.m.**	Ht.	a.m.	**p.m.**			a.m.	Ht.	**p.m.**	Ht.	a.m.	**p.m.**
1	**M**	5:17	3.6	**5:36**	3.5	11:13	**11:33**	1	**W**	4:39	4.1	**5:01**	3.5	10:42	**10:35**
2	**T**	6:08	4.0	**6:28**	3.8	...	**12:02**	2	**T**	5:32	4.4	**5:56**	3.7	11:33	**11:21**
3	**W**	6:57	4.4	**7:18**	4.0	12:11	**12:49**	3	**F**	6:24	4.8	**6:48**	3.9	...	**12:24**
4	**T**	7:45	4.8	**8:07**	4.1	12:51	**1:39**	4	**S**	7:15	4.9	**7:40**	4.0	12:09	**1:18**
5	**F**	8:33	5.0	**8:57**	4.1	1:34	**2:29**	5	**S**	8:07	4.9	**8:33**	4.0	1:00	**2:12**
6	**S**	9:23	5.0	**9:49**	4.1	2:20	**3:21**	6	**M**	9:00	4.8	**9:27**	3.9	1:53	**3:04**
7	**S**	*9:15	4.8	***9:43**	3.9	*2:08	***3:12**	7	**T**	9:55	4.5	**10:24**	3.8	2:46	**3:56**
8	**M**	10:11	4.6	**10:40**	3.7	2:57	**4:04**	8	**W**	10:53	4.2	**11:22**	3.6	3:39	**4:51**
9	**T**	11:10	4.3	**11:41**	3.6	3:48	**5:10**	9	**T**	11:51	3.8	...	...	4:36	**6:06**
10	**W**	...	...	**12:12**	4.0	4:46	**7:03**	10	**F**	12:22	3.5	**12:48**	3.5	5:53	**7:28**
11	**T**	12:43	3.5	**1:14**	3.8	6:08	**8:22**	11	**S**	1:20	3.5	**1:45**	3.3	8:04	**8:26**
12	**F**	1:45	3.5	**2:15**	3.6	8:34	**9:19**	12	**S**	2:19	3.4	**2:42**	3.1	9:15	**9:06**
13	**S**	2:48	3.5	**3:17**	3.5	9:42	**10:01**	13	**M**	3:19	3.4	**3:41**	3.0	10:06	**9:34**
14	**S**	3:50	3.6	**4:16**	3.4	10:30	**10:29**	14	**T**	4:16	3.5	**4:36**	2.9	10:44	**10:02**
15	**M**	4:45	3.8	**5:07**	3.4	11:08	**10:49**	15	**W**	5:07	3.5	**5:25**	2.9	11:17	**10:35**
16	**T**	5:33	3.9	**5:52**	3.4	11:39	**11:12**	16	**T**	5:51	3.6	**6:08**	3.0	11:48	**11:11**
17	**W**	6:15	4.0	**6:33**	3.4	-A-	**11:41**	17	**F**	6:30	3.6	**6:47**	3.0	-B-	**11:50**
18	**T**	6:54	4.0	**7:12**	3.4	...	**12:41**	18	**S**	7:06	3.6	**7:25**	3.1	...	**1:01**
19	**F**	7:30	4.0	**7:49**	3.3	12:16	**1:17**	19	**S**	7:41	3.6	**8:02**	3.0	12:31	**1:40**
20	**S**	8:04	3.8	**8:27**	3.2	12:54	**1:55**	20	**M**	8:15	3.5	**8:40**	3.0	1:13	**2:19**
21	**S**	8:38	3.7	**9:05**	3.1	1:34	**2:33**	21	**T**	8:50	3.4	**9:19**	2.9	1:55	**2:54**
22	**M**	9:13	3.5	**9:44**	2.9	2:14	**3:09**	22	**W**	9:27	3.3	**10:00**	2.9	2:35	**3:27**
23	**T**	9:51	3.3	**10:27**	2.8	2:53	**3:46**	23	**T**	10:08	3.2	**10:45**	2.8	3:14	**3:59**
24	**W**	10:34	3.2	**11:14**	2.7	3:33	**4:24**	24	**F**	10:54	3.1	**11:33**	2.9	3:55	**4:35**
25	**T**	11:21	3.0	...	...	4:15	**5:08**	25	**S**	11:43	3.1	...	...	4:40	**5:17**
26	**F**	12:04	2.7	**12:12**	3.0	5:05	**6:05**	26	**S**	12:23	3.0	**12:35**	3.0	5:37	**6:09**
27	**S**	12:54	2.8	**1:05**	3.0	6:10	**7:13**	27	**M**	1:14	3.2	**1:29**	3.0	6:49	**7:09**
28	**S**	1:46	3.0	**2:00**	3.1	7:29	**8:12**	28	**T**	2:09	3.4	**2:28**	3.0	8:10	**8:11**
29	**M**	2:42	3.3	**3:00**	3.2	8:45	**9:03**	29	**W**	3:09	3.6	**3:34**	3.0	9:24	**9:10**
30	**T**	3:41	3.7	**4:02**	3.3	9:48	**9:49**	30	**T**	4:12	4.0	**4:39**	3.2	10:26	**10:06**
								31	**F**	5:12	4.3	**5:38**	3.5	11:22	**10:59**

A also at 12:09 p.m. **B** also at 12:23 p.m.

Dates when Ht. of **Low** Water is below Mean Lower Low with Ht. of lowest given for each period and Date of lowest in ( ):

3rd–8th: -0.6' (5th, 6th)

1st–7th: -0.7' (4th, 5th)
29th–31st: -0.5' (31st)

Average Rise and Fall 3.5 ft.

When a high tide exceeds avg. ht., the *following* low tide will be lower than avg.

Narragansett Bay Currents

This current diagram shows current **directions** and **average maximum velocities** when the tides have a normal (3.5 ft.) range at Newport. (pp. 84-89).

Average maximum Ebb currents occur about 3 hours *after* High Water at Newport and are shown by light arrows.

Average maximum Flood currents occur about 2 1/2 hours *before* High Water at Newport and are shown by black arrows.

When height of High Water at Newport is 3.0 ft., subtract 30% from velocities shown. When height is 4.0 ft., add 20%; when 4.5 ft., add 40%; when 5.0 ft., add 60%.

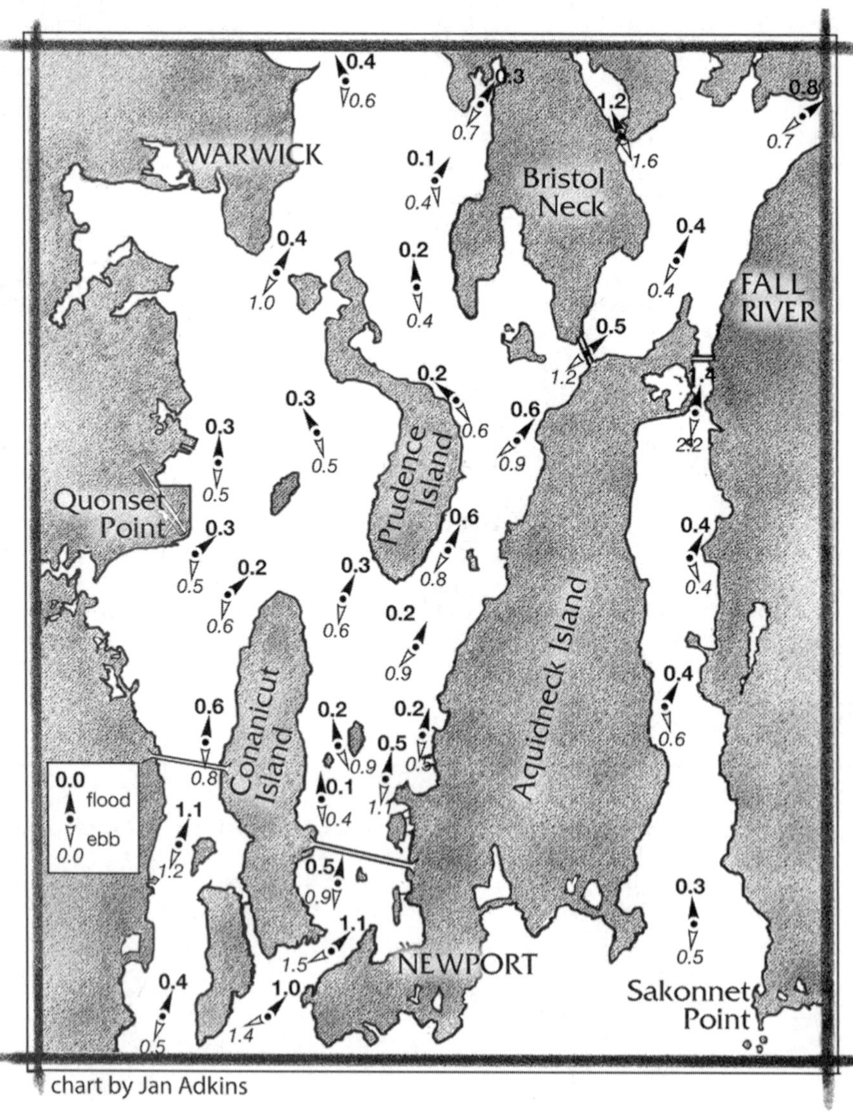

chart by Jan Adkins

Holding a Fair Current Between Eastern Long Island and Nantucket

There is a curious phenomenon which can be used to advantage by every vessel, and particularly the slower cruiser or auxiliary, in making the passage *either* way between eastern Long Island Sound, on the west, and Buzzards Bay, Vineyard and Nantucket Sounds on the east.

Note in the very simplified diagram below, that in Long Island Sound, the Ebb Current flows to the *east*, and in Buzzards Bay, Vineyard and Nantucket Sounds the Ebb Current flows to the *west*. (Off Newport, these opposed Ebb Currents merge and flow *south*.) The reverse is also true: the Flood Current flows *west* through Long Island Sound and *east* through Buzzards Bay, Vineyard and Nantucket Sounds. (Half arrow indicates Ebb Current, whole arrow indicates Flood Current.)

In making a *complete* passage through the area of the diagram, simply ride the favoring Ebb Current toward Newport from either direction and, pick up the favoring Flood Current in leaving the Newport area.

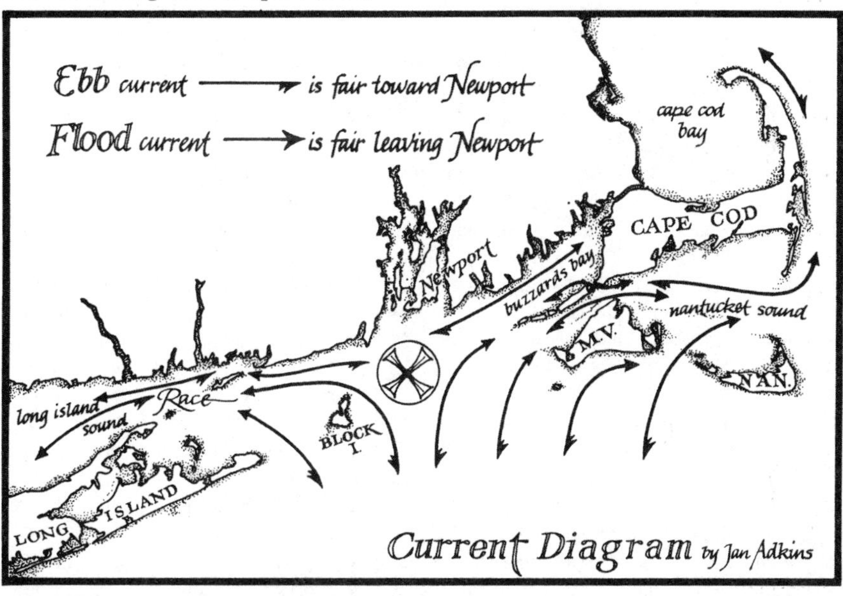

Arrive at "X" at the times shown for "Current Turns to Northwest at The Race," tables pp. 92-97.

The E-W currents between Pt. Judith and Cuttyhunk are only 1/2 to 1 kt., while those to the West of Pt. Judith and to the East of Cuttyhunk are much greater. Bearing this in mind, those making *only a partial trip* through the area may find it better even to buck a slight head current in the Pt. Judith-Cuttyhunk area so as to pick up the maximum hours of strong favoring currents beyond those points.

For example, if headed for the Cape Cod Canal, refer to the Tidal Current Chart Buzzards Bay, Vineyard & Nantucket Sound, pp. 72-83 and arrive just N. of Cuttyhunk as Flood Starts at Pollock Rip, pp. 66-71 to ensure the most favorable currents. If headed for Nantucket, refer to the same Charts and arrive just S. of Cuttyhunk at 3 hours after Flood Starts at Pollock Rip, pp. 66-71. If headed into Long Island Sound, refer to the Tidal Current Chart Long Island Sound and Block Island Sound, pp. 98-103 and arrive at Pt. Judith when Flood Current turns West at The Race, p. 101.

2021 CURRENT TABLE
THE RACE, LONG ISLAND SOUND
41°13.69'N, 72°03.75'W 0.2 nm E.N.E. of Valiant Rock

JANUARY (Standard Time)								FEBRUARY (Standard Time)							
DAY OF MONTH	DAY OF WEEK	CURRENT TURNS TO						DAY OF MONTH	DAY OF WEEK	CURRENT TURNS TO					
		NORTHWEST Flood Starts			SOUTHEAST Ebb Starts					NORTHWEST Flood Starts			SOUTHEAST Ebb Starts		
		a.m.	**p.m.**	Kts.	a.m.	**p.m.**	Kts.			a.m.	**p.m.**	Kts.	a.m.	**p.m.**	Kts.
1	F	7:01	**7:36**	3.6	12:42	**12:48**	p4.7	1	M	8:19	**8:36**	p3.9	1:48	**2:06**	a4.9
2	S	7:48	**8:18**	p3.6	1:24	**1:36**	p4.7	2	T	9:12	**9:24**	p3.8	2:36	**3:00**	a4.8
3	S	8:36	**9:00**	p3.6	2:12	**2:24**	p4.5	3	W	10:06	**10:18**	p3.6	3:30	**3:54**	a4.7
4	M	9:30	**9:48**	p3.6	3:00	**3:18**	4.4	4	T	11:12	**11:18**	p3.4	4:24	**4:54**	a4.5
5	T	10:30	**10:42**	p3.5	3:54	**4:12**	a4.4	5	F	...	**12:18**	2.8	5:24	**6:00**	a4.4
6	W	11:30	**11:42**	p3.5	4:48	**5:12**	a4.4	6	S	12:24	**1:24**	a3.3	6:30	**7:12**	a4.3
7	T	...	**12:30**	2.9	5:42	**6:18**	a4.5	7	S	1:30	**2:24**	a3.2	7:30	**8:18**	a4.4
8	F	12:42	**1:36**	a3.5	6:42	**7:24**	a4.5	8	M	2:30	**3:24**	a3.3	8:36	**9:18**	a4.5
9	S	1:42	**2:36**	a3.5	7:48	**8:24**	a4.7	9	T	3:30	**4:18**	a3.5	9:30	**10:12**	a4.6
10	S	2:42	**3:36**	a3.6	8:42	**9:24**	a4.9	10	W	4:30	**5:06**	3.6	10:24	**11:00**	a4.7
11	M	3:36	**4:30**	a3.7	9:42	**10:24**	a5.0	11	T	5:18	**5:54**	3.7	11:12	**11:48**	a4.7
12	T	4:36	**5:24**	a3.8	10:36	**11:12**	a5.0	12	F	6:06	**6:36**	p3.7	...	**12:01**	4.6
13	W	5:30	**6:12**	3.8	11:24	...	5.0	13	S	6:54	**7:18**	p3.6	12:30	**12:42**	a4.5
14	T	6:24	**7:00**	3.7	12:06	**12:18**	p4.8	14	S	7:42	**8:00**	p3.4	1:12	**1:24**	a4.4
15	F	7:12	**7:42**	p3.6	12:54	**1:06**	p4.6	15	M	8:30	**8:36**	p3.1	1:54	**2:06**	a4.2
16	S	8:06	**8:30**	p3.4	1:42	**1:54**	4.2	16	T	9:12	**9:18**	p2.9	2:30	**2:48**	a4.0
17	S	8:54	**9:18**	p3.1	2:24	**2:36**	a4.1	17	W	10:00	**10:06**	p2.6	3:12	**3:36**	a3.7
18	M	9:48	**10:00**	p2.9	3:12	**3:24**	a3.8	18	T	10:48	**10:54**	p2.4	3:54	**4:18**	a3.5
19	T	10:42	**10:48**	p2.6	4:00	**4:18**	a3.6	19	F	11:42	**11:42**	p2.3	4:36	**5:12**	a3.3
20	W	11:36	**11:42**	p2.5	4:42	**5:06**	a3.4	20	S	...	**12:36**	2.0	5:30	**6:06**	a3.2
21	T	...	**12:30**	2.0	5:30	**6:00**	a3.3	21	S	12:36	**1:24**	a2.3	6:18	**7:00**	a3.3
22	F	12:30	**1:24**	a2.4	6:18	**6:54**	a3.3	22	M	1:30	**2:18**	2.4	7:12	**7:54**	a3.5
23	S	1:24	**2:12**	a2.4	7:06	**7:48**	a3.4	23	T	2:24	**3:00**	2.7	8:06	**8:48**	a3.8
24	S	2:12	**3:00**	a2.5	8:00	**8:36**	a3.6	24	W	3:12	**3:48**	p3.1	9:00	**9:36**	a4.2
25	M	3:00	**3:42**	2.7	8:48	**9:24**	a3.9	25	T	3:54	**4:30**	p3.5	9:48	**10:18**	a4.6
26	T	3:42	**4:24**	3.0	9:30	**10:06**	a4.2	26	F	4:42	**5:12**	p3.9	10:36	**11:06**	a4.9
27	W	4:24	**5:06**	3.3	10:18	**10:54**	a4.5	27	S	5:30	**5:54**	p4.2	11:24	**11:48**	5.1
28	T	5:12	**5:42**	3.6	11:00	**11:36**	a4.7	28	S	6:18	**6:36**	p4.3	...	**12:06**	5.1
29	F	5:54	**6:24**	3.8	11:42	...	4.9								
30	S	6:36	**7:06**	p4.0	12:18	**12:30**	p5.0								
31	S	7:24	**7:48**	p4.0	1:00	**1:18**	p4.9								

The Kts. (knots) columns show the **maximum** predicted velocities of the stronger one of the Flood Currents and the stronger one of the Ebb Currents for each day.
The letter "a" means the velocity shown should occur **after** the **a.m.** Current Change. The letter "p" means the velocity shown should occur **after** the **p.m.** Current Change (even if next morning). No "a" or "p" means a.m. and p.m. velocities are the same for that day.
Avg. Max. Velocity: Flood 3.3 Kts., Ebb 4.2 Kts.
Max. Flood 2 hrs. 45 min. after Flood Starts, ±15 min.
Max. Ebb 3 hrs. 25 min. after Ebb Starts, ±15 min.
Use THE RACE tables with current charts pp. 98-103

See pp. 22-29 for Current Change at other points.

2021 CURRENT TABLE
THE RACE, LONG ISLAND SOUND

41°13.69'N, 72°03.75'W 0.2 nm E.N.E. of Valiant Rock

***Daylight Time starts March 14 at 2 a.m.** **Daylight Saving Time**

MARCH

DAY OF MONTH	DAY OF WEEK	CURRENT TURNS TO NORTHWEST Flood Starts a.m.	**p.m.**	Kts.	CURRENT TURNS TO SOUTHEAST Ebb Starts a.m.	**p.m.**	Kts.
1	**M**	7:07	**7:24**	p4.3	12:36	**12:54**	a5.3
2	**T**	7:54	**8:12**	p4.1	1:24	**1:48**	a5.3
3	**W**	8:48	**9:00**	p3.9	2:12	**2:42**	a5.1
4	**T**	9:48	**10:00**	p3.5	3:06	**3:36**	a4.8
5	**F**	10:54	**11:06**	p3.2	4:06	**4:42**	a4.5
6	**S**	...	**12:01**	2.7	5:06	**5:48**	a4.2
7	**S**	12:12	**1:12**	a3.0	6:12	**7:00**	a4.1
8	**M**	1:24	**2:12**	a3.0	7:24	**8:06**	a4.1
9	**T**	2:24	**3:12**	3.2	8:24	**9:00**	a4.2
10	**W**	3:24	**4:06**	p3.4	9:24	**9:54**	a4.4
11	**T**	4:18	**4:48**	p3.6	10:12	**10:42**	4.4
12	**F**	5:06	**5:30**	p3.7	11:00	**11:24**	p4.5
13	**S**	5:54	**6:12**	p3.6	11:42	...	4.3
14	**S**	*7:36	***7:48**	p3.5	12:01	***1:24**	a4.5
15	**M**	8:18	**8:24**	p3.3	1:36	**2:00**	a4.4
16	**T**	8:54	**9:00**	p3.1	2:12	**2:36**	a4.3
17	**W**	9:36	**9:42**	p2.9	2:48	**3:18**	a4.0
18	**T**	10:18	**10:24**	p2.6	3:30	**3:54**	a3.8
19	**F**	11:06	**11:12**	p2.4	4:06	**4:42**	a3.6
20	**S**	11:54	...	2.2	4:54	**5:30**	a3.4
21	**S**	12:01	**12:48**	a2.3	5:42	**6:24**	a3.3
22	**M**	1:00	**1:42**	a2.4	6:36	**7:18**	a3.3
23	**T**	1:54	**2:30**	2.5	7:36	**8:12**	a3.5
24	**W**	2:48	**3:24**	p2.9	8:30	**9:06**	3.8
25	**T**	3:36	**4:06**	p3.3	9:30	**10:00**	p4.4
26	**F**	4:30	**4:54**	p3.7	10:18	**10:48**	p4.8
27	**S**	5:18	**5:36**	p4.1	11:12	**11:36**	p5.3
28	**S**	6:06	**6:24**	p4.4	...	**12:01**	5.1
29	**M**	6:54	**7:12**	p4.5	12:24	**12:48**	a5.5
30	**T**	7:42	**8:00**	p4.4	1:06	**1:36**	a5.6
31	**W**	8:36	**8:48**	p4.2	2:00	**2:30**	a5.5

APRIL

DAY OF MONTH	DAY OF WEEK	CURRENT TURNS TO NORTHWEST Flood Starts a.m.	**p.m.**	Kts.	CURRENT TURNS TO SOUTHEAST Ebb Starts a.m.	**p.m.**	Kts.
1	**T**	9:31	**9:42**	p3.8	2:48	**3:24**	a5.3
2	**F**	10:30	**10:48**	p3.4	3:42	**4:24**	a4.9
3	**S**	11:36	**11:54**	p3.1	4:42	**5:30**	a4.4
4	**S**	...	**12:48**	2.8	5:48	**6:36**	a4.1
5	**M**	1:06	**1:54**	a2.9	7:00	**7:42**	a3.9
6	**T**	2:12	**2:54**	p3.0	8:06	**8:48**	a3.9
7	**W**	3:18	**3:48**	p3.2	9:12	**9:42**	p4.1
8	**T**	4:12	**4:42**	p3.4	10:06	**10:30**	p4.3
9	**F**	5:06	**5:24**	p3.5	10:54	**11:18**	p4.5
10	**S**	5:48	**6:06**	p3.5	11:42	**11:54**	p4.5
11	**S**	6:30	**6:42**	p3.5	...	**12:18**	3.9
12	**M**	7:12	**7:18**	p3.4	12:30	**1:00**	a4.5
13	**T**	7:48	**7:54**	p3.2	1:06	**1:36**	a4.4
14	**W**	8:30	**8:30**	3.0	1:42	**2:12**	a4.3
15	**T**	9:06	**9:06**	p2.9	2:12	**2:48**	a4.1
16	**F**	9:42	**9:48**	2.7	2:54	**3:24**	a3.9
17	**S**	10:24	**10:36**	2.6	3:30	**4:06**	a3.8
18	**S**	11:12	**11:24**	2.5	4:18	**4:54**	a3.6
19	**M**	...	**12:06**	2.5	5:06	**5:48**	a3.5
20	**T**	12:24	**12:54**	p2.6	6:00	**6:42**	a3.5
21	**W**	1:18	**1:48**	p2.8	7:00	**7:36**	p3.7
22	**T**	2:12	**2:42**	p3.1	8:00	**8:36**	p4.2
23	**F**	3:06	**3:30**	p3.5	8:54	**9:24**	p4.7
24	**S**	4:00	**4:18**	p3.9	9:54	**10:18**	p5.1
25	**S**	4:54	**5:06**	p4.2	10:48	**11:06**	p5.5
26	**M**	5:42	**5:54**	p4.5	11:36	**11:54**	p5.7
27	**T**	6:36	**6:42**	p4.5	...	**12:30**	5.0
28	**W**	7:24	**7:36**	p4.4	12:48	**1:18**	a5.7
29	**T**	8:18	**8:30**	p4.1	1:36	**2:12**	a5.6
30	**F**	9:12	**9:30**	3.7	2:30	**3:12**	a5.3

The Kts. (knots) columns show the **maximum** predicted velocities of the stronger one of the Flood Currents and the stronger one of the Ebb Currents for each day.
The letter "a" means the velocity shown should occur **after** the **a.m.** Current Change. The letter "p" means the velocity shown should occur **after** the **p.m.** Current Change (even if next morning). No "a" or "p" means a.m. and p.m. velocities are the same for that day.
Avg. Max. Velocity: Flood 3.3 Kts., Ebb 4.2 Kts.
Max. Flood 2 hrs. 45 min. after Flood Starts, ±15 min.
Max. Ebb 3 hrs. 25 min. after Ebb Starts, ±15 min.
Use THE RACE tables with current charts pp. 98-103

See pp. 22-29 for Current Change at other points.

2021 CURRENT TABLE
THE RACE, LONG ISLAND SOUND
41°13.69'N, 72°03.75'W 0.2 nm E.N.E. of Valiant Rock

Daylight Saving Time

MAY

DAY OF MONTH	DAY OF WEEK	CURRENT TURNS TO NORTHWEST Flood Starts a.m.	p.m.	Kts.	CURRENT TURNS TO SOUTHEAST Ebb Starts a.m.	p.m.	Kts.
1	S	10:13	**10:30**	a3.4	3:24	**4:12**	a4.8
2	S	11:18	**11:36**	a3.1	4:24	**5:12**	a4.4
3	M	...	**12:24**	2.9	5:30	**6:18**	a4.0
4	T	12:48	**1:30**	p2.9	6:36	**7:24**	3.7
5	W	1:54	**2:30**	p3.0	7:48	**8:24**	p3.8
6	T	3:00	**3:18**	p3.1	8:48	**9:12**	p4.1
7	F	3:54	**4:12**	p3.2	9:42	**10:00**	p4.3
8	S	4:42	**4:54**	p3.3	10:30	**10:42**	p4.4
9	S	5:30	**5:36**	p3.3	11:18	**11:24**	p4.4
10	M	6:06	**6:12**	p3.2	11:54	...	3.6
11	T	6:48	**6:48**	p3.2	12:01	**12:30**	a4.4
12	W	7:24	**7:24**	3.1	12:36	**1:06**	a4.4
13	T	8:00	**8:00**	3.0	1:06	**1:42**	a4.3
14	F	8:36	**8:42**	3.0	1:42	**2:18**	a4.2
15	S	9:12	**9:18**	2.9	2:24	**3:00**	a4.1
16	S	9:54	**10:06**	2.8	3:00	**3:42**	a4.0
17	M	10:36	**10:54**	a2.8	3:48	**4:24**	a3.9
18	T	11:24	**11:48**	a2.8	4:36	**5:18**	a3.8
19	W	...	**12:18**	3.0	5:30	**6:12**	3.8
20	T	12:48	**1:06**	p3.1	6:30	**7:06**	p4.0
21	F	1:42	**2:00**	p3.4	7:30	**8:00**	p4.4
22	S	2:42	**2:54**	p3.7	8:30	**8:54**	p4.8
23	S	3:36	**3:48**	p4.0	9:24	**9:48**	p5.2
24	M	4:30	**4:36**	p4.2	10:24	**10:42**	p5.5
25	T	5:24	**5:30**	p4.3	11:18	**11:36**	p5.6
26	W	6:18	**6:24**	p4.4	...	**12:12**	4.8
27	T	7:12	**7:18**	p4.3	12:24	**1:06**	a5.6
28	F	8:06	**8:12**	4.0	1:18	**2:00**	a5.5
29	S	9:00	**9:12**	a3.7	2:12	**2:54**	a5.2
30	S	9:54	**10:12**	a3.5	3:06	**3:54**	a4.8
31	M	10:54	**11:18**	a3.2	4:06	**4:54**	a4.3

Daylight Saving Time

JUNE

DAY OF MONTH	DAY OF WEEK	CURRENT TURNS TO NORTHWEST Flood Starts a.m.	p.m.	Kts.	CURRENT TURNS TO SOUTHEAST Ebb Starts a.m.	p.m.	Kts.
1	T	11:55	...	3.1	5:06	**5:54**	a3.9
2	W	12:24	**12:54**	p3.0	6:12	**6:48**	p3.7
3	T	1:30	**1:48**	p2.9	7:12	**7:48**	p3.8
4	F	2:30	**2:42**	p2.9	8:18	**8:36**	p3.9
5	S	3:30	**3:30**	p2.9	9:12	**9:24**	p4.0
6	S	4:18	**4:18**	p2.9	10:00	**10:06**	p4.1
7	M	5:00	**5:00**	p3.0	10:48	**10:48**	p4.2
8	T	5:42	**5:42**	p3.0	11:24	**11:24**	p4.2
9	W	6:18	**6:18**	p3.1	...	**12:06**	3.4
10	T	6:54	**6:54**	3.1	12:01	**12:42**	a4.3
11	F	7:30	**7:36**	3.1	12:42	**1:18**	a4.3
12	S	8:06	**8:12**	p3.2	1:18	**1:54**	a4.3
13	S	8:48	**8:54**	a3.2	1:54	**2:36**	a4.3
14	M	9:24	**9:42**	a3.2	2:36	**3:18**	a4.3
15	T	10:06	**10:30**	a3.2	3:24	**4:00**	a4.2
16	W	10:54	**11:24**	a3.2	4:12	**4:48**	a4.1
17	T	11:42	...	3.3	5:06	**5:42**	p4.1
18	F	12:18	**12:36**	p3.4	6:00	**6:36**	p4.3
19	S	1:18	**1:30**	p3.5	7:00	**7:30**	p4.5
20	S	2:18	**2:24**	p3.7	8:00	**8:30**	p4.8
21	M	3:18	**3:24**	p3.8	9:06	**9:24**	p5.1
22	T	4:12	**4:18**	p4.0	10:06	**10:24**	p5.3
23	W	5:12	**5:12**	p4.1	11:00	**11:18**	p5.4
24	T	6:06	**6:12**	p4.2	...	**12:01**	4.6
25	F	6:54	**7:06**	p4.1	12:12	**12:54**	a5.4
26	S	7:48	**8:00**	3.9	1:06	**1:42**	a5.3
27	S	8:42	**9:00**	a3.8	1:54	**2:36**	a5.0
28	M	9:30	**9:54**	a3.6	2:48	**3:30**	a4.7
29	T	10:24	**10:54**	a3.4	3:42	**4:24**	a4.2
30	W	11:18	...	3.1	4:42	**5:18**	3.8

The Kts. (knots) columns show the **maximum** predicted velocities of the stronger one of the Flood Currents and the stronger one of the Ebb Currents for each day.
The letter "a" means the velocity shown should occur **after** the **a.m.** Current Change. The letter "p" means the velocity shown should occur **after** the **p.m.** Current Change (even if next morning). No "a" or "p" means a.m. and p.m. velocities are the same for that day.
Avg. Max. Velocity: Flood 3.3 Kts., Ebb 4.2 Kts.
Max. Flood 2 hrs. 45 min. after Flood Starts, ±15 min.
Max. Ebb 3 hrs. 25 min. after Ebb Starts, ±15 min.
Use THE RACE tables with current charts pp. 98-103

See pp. 22-29 for Current Change at other points.

2021 CURRENT TABLE
THE RACE, LONG ISLAND SOUND

41°13.69'N, 72°03.75'W 0.2 nm E.N.E. of Valiant Rock

Daylight Saving Time

JULY

DAY OF MONTH	DAY OF WEEK	CURRENT TURNS TO NORTHWEST Flood Starts a.m.	**p.m.**	Kts.	CURRENT TURNS TO SOUTHEAST Ebb Starts a.m.	**p.m.**	Kts.
1	**T**	12:02	**12:12**	p2.9	5:36	**6:12**	p3.7
2	**F**	1:00	**1:06**	p2.7	6:36	**7:06**	p3.6
3	**S**	2:00	**2:00**	p2.6	7:36	**7:54**	p3.6
4	**S**	2:54	**2:54**	p2.6	8:30	**8:42**	p3.7
5	**M**	3:42	**3:42**	p2.6	9:24	**9:30**	p3.8
6	**T**	4:30	**4:24**	p2.7	10:12	**10:12**	p3.9
7	**W**	5:12	**5:06**	p2.8	10:54	**10:54**	p4.1
8	**T**	5:48	**5:48**	p3.0	11:30	**11:36**	p4.2
9	**F**	6:24	**6:30**	p3.2	...	**12:12**	3.6
10	**S**	7:06	**7:06**	p3.3	12:12	**12:48**	a4.4
11	**S**	7:42	**7:48**	3.4	12:54	**1:30**	a4.5
12	**M**	8:18	**8:30**	3.5	1:36	**2:06**	a4.6
13	**T**	8:54	**9:18**	a3.6	2:18	**2:48**	a4.6
14	**W**	9:36	**10:06**	a3.6	3:00	**3:36**	a4.5
15	**T**	10:24	**11:00**	a3.6	3:48	**4:24**	p4.5
16	**F**	11:12	**11:54**	a3.6	4:42	**5:12**	p4.4
17	**S**	...	**12:06**	3.5	5:36	**6:06**	p4.4
18	**S**	1:00	**1:06**	p3.5	6:36	**7:06**	p4.5
19	**M**	2:00	**2:06**	p3.5	7:42	**8:06**	p4.6
20	**T**	3:00	**3:06**	p3.6	8:48	**9:12**	p4.8
21	**W**	4:00	**4:06**	p3.7	9:54	**10:12**	p4.9
22	**T**	5:00	**5:06**	p3.9	10:48	**11:06**	p5.1
23	**F**	5:54	**6:00**	p4.0	11:42	...	4.5
24	**S**	6:42	**6:54**	3.9	12:01	**12:36**	a5.1
25	**S**	7:30	**7:48**	a3.9	12:48	**1:24**	a5.0
26	**M**	8:18	**8:42**	a3.8	1:42	**2:18**	a4.8
27	**T**	9:06	**9:30**	a3.6	2:30	**3:06**	a4.5
28	**W**	9:54	**10:24**	a3.4	3:18	**3:48**	4.1
29	**T**	10:42	**11:24**	a3.1	4:06	**4:36**	p3.9
30	**F**	11:30	...	2.8	5:00	**5:24**	p3.6
31	**S**	12:18	**12:24**	p2.5	5:54	**6:12**	p3.4

Daylight Saving Time

AUGUST

DAY OF MONTH	DAY OF WEEK	CURRENT TURNS TO NORTHWEST Flood Starts a.m.	**p.m.**	Kts.	CURRENT TURNS TO SOUTHEAST Ebb Starts a.m.	**p.m.**	Kts.
1	**S**	1:19	**1:18**	p2.3	6:48	**7:06**	p3.3
2	**M**	2:12	**2:12**	p2.3	7:42	**7:54**	p3.3
3	**T**	3:00	**3:00**	p2.3	8:36	**8:48**	p3.5
4	**W**	3:48	**3:48**	p2.5	9:30	**9:36**	p3.7
5	**T**	4:30	**4:36**	p2.8	10:12	**10:18**	p3.9
6	**F**	5:12	**5:18**	p3.1	11:00	**11:06**	p4.2
7	**S**	5:54	**6:00**	p3.3	11:36	**11:48**	p4.5
8	**S**	6:30	**6:42**	p3.6	...	**12:18**	4.2
9	**M**	7:06	**7:24**	3.7	12:30	**1:00**	a4.7
10	**T**	7:48	**8:06**	a3.9	1:12	**1:42**	a4.8
11	**W**	8:24	**8:54**	a4.0	1:54	**2:24**	p4.9
12	**T**	9:06	**9:42**	a4.0	2:42	**3:06**	p4.9
13	**F**	9:54	**10:36**	a3.8	3:30	**3:54**	p4.8
14	**S**	10:48	**11:36**	a3.7	4:24	**4:48**	p4.6
15	**S**	11:42	...	3.5	5:18	**5:48**	p4.4
16	**M**	12:36	**12:48**	p3.3	6:24	**6:48**	p4.3
17	**T**	1:42	**1:54**	p3.3	7:30	**7:54**	p4.3
18	**W**	2:48	**2:54**	p3.3	8:36	**9:00**	p4.4
19	**T**	3:48	**4:00**	p3.5	9:42	**10:00**	p4.6
20	**F**	4:48	**4:54**	p3.7	10:36	**10:54**	p4.8
21	**S**	5:36	**5:54**	p3.8	11:30	**11:48**	p4.8
22	**S**	6:24	**6:42**	3.8	...	**12:18**	4.6
23	**M**	7:12	**7:30**	a3.9	12:36	**1:06**	a4.8
24	**T**	7:54	**8:18**	a3.8	1:24	**1:48**	4.6
25	**W**	8:36	**9:06**	a3.6	2:06	**2:30**	p4.5
26	**T**	9:18	**9:54**	a3.3	2:54	**3:12**	p4.2
27	**F**	10:06	**10:42**	a3.0	3:36	**3:54**	p3.9
28	**S**	10:48	**11:36**	a2.7	4:18	**4:36**	p3.6
29	**S**	11:42	...	2.4	5:06	**5:24**	p3.3
30	**M**	12:30	**12:36**	p2.2	6:00	**6:12**	p3.1
31	**T**	1:24	**1:30**	p2.1	6:54	**7:06**	p3.1

The Kts. (knots) columns show the **maximum** predicted velocities of the stronger one of the Flood Currents and the stronger one of the Ebb Currents for each day.
The letter "a" means the velocity shown should occur **after** the **a.m.** Current Change. The letter "p" means the velocity shown should occur **after** the **p.m.** Current Change (even if next morning). No "a" or "p" means a.m. and p.m. velocities are the same for that day.
Avg. Max. Velocity: Flood 3.3 Kts., Ebb 4.2 Kts.
Max. Flood 2 hrs. 45 min. after Flood Starts, ±15 min.
Max. Ebb 3 hrs. 25 min. after Ebb Starts, ±15 min.
Use THE RACE tables with current charts pp. 98-103

See pp. 22-29 for Current Change at other points.

2021 CURRENT TABLE
THE RACE, LONG ISLAND SOUND
41°13.69'N, 72°03.75'W 0.2 nm E.N.E. of Valiant Rock

Daylight Saving Time								Daylight Saving Time							
SEPTEMBER								**OCTOBER**							
DAY OF MONTH	DAY OF WEEK	CURRENT TURNS TO						DAY OF MONTH	DAY OF WEEK	CURRENT TURNS TO					
		NORTHWEST Flood Starts			SOUTHEAST Ebb Starts					NORTHWEST Flood Starts			SOUTHEAST Ebb Starts		
		a.m.	**p.m.**	Kts.	a.m.	**p.m.**	Kts.			a.m.	**p.m.**	Kts.	a.m.	**p.m.**	Kts.
1	**W**	2:13	**2:24**	p2.2	7:48	**8:00**	p3.3	1	**F**	2:19	**2:36**	p2.5	8:00	**8:12**	p3.5
2	**T**	3:06	**3:12**	p2.5	8:42	**8:54**	p3.5	2	**S**	3:06	**3:24**	p2.8	8:48	**9:06**	p3.9
3	**F**	3:48	**4:00**	p2.8	9:30	**9:48**	p3.9	3	**S**	3:48	**4:12**	p3.2	9:42	**10:00**	p4.2
4	**S**	4:36	**4:42**	p3.1	10:18	**10:30**	p4.2	4	**M**	4:36	**5:00**	p3.6	10:24	**10:48**	4.6
5	**S**	5:12	**5:30**	p3.5	11:00	**11:18**	p4.6	5	**T**	5:18	**5:42**	3.9	11:12	**11:36**	a5.1
6	**M**	5:54	**6:12**	p3.8	11:48	...	4.7	6	**W**	6:00	**6:30**	a4.2	...	**12:01**	5.4
7	**T**	6:36	**6:54**	4.0	12:01	**12:30**	p5.0	7	**T**	6:42	**7:18**	a4.4	12:24	**12:42**	p5.6
8	**W**	7:18	**7:42**	a4.2	12:48	**1:12**	p5.2	8	**F**	7:30	**8:06**	a4.4	1:12	**1:30**	p5.6
9	**T**	8:00	**8:30**	a4.2	1:36	**1:54**	p5.3	9	**S**	8:18	**9:00**	a4.2	2:00	**2:18**	p5.4
10	**F**	8:42	**9:18**	a4.2	2:18	**2:42**	p5.2	10	**S**	9:12	**10:00**	a4.0	2:54	**3:12**	p5.1
11	**S**	9:30	**10:18**	a4.0	3:12	**3:36**	p5.0	11	**M**	10:12	**11:00**	a3.6	3:54	**4:12**	p4.7
12	**S**	10:24	**11:18**	a3.7	4:06	**4:30**	p4.7	12	**T**	11:18	...	3.2	4:54	**5:12**	p4.3
13	**M**	11:30	...	3.4	5:06	**5:30**	p4.3	13	**W**	12:06	**12:24**	p3.0	6:00	**6:18**	p4.0
14	**T**	12:24	**12:36**	p3.1	6:12	**6:36**	p4.1	14	**T**	1:12	**1:36**	2.9	7:06	**7:30**	p3.9
15	**W**	1:30	**1:42**	p3.0	7:18	**7:42**	p4.1	15	**F**	2:18	**2:42**	3.0	8:12	**8:36**	p4.0
16	**T**	2:36	**2:48**	p3.1	8:24	**8:48**	p4.2	16	**S**	3:18	**3:42**	3.2	9:12	**9:36**	4.1
17	**F**	3:36	**3:54**	p3.3	9:30	**9:54**	p4.3	17	**S**	4:12	**4:36**	a3.4	10:06	**10:30**	a4.4
18	**S**	4:30	**4:48**	p3.5	10:24	**10:48**	p4.5	18	**M**	5:00	**5:30**	a3.5	10:54	**11:18**	a4.6
19	**S**	5:24	**5:42**	3.6	11:12	**11:36**	a4.6	19	**T**	5:42	**6:12**	a3.6	11:36	...	4.7
20	**M**	6:06	**6:30**	a3.8	...	**12:01**	4.7	20	**W**	6:24	**6:54**	a3.6	12:06	**12:12**	p4.7
21	**T**	6:48	**7:18**	a3.8	12:24	**12:42**	p4.7	21	**T**	7:00	**7:36**	a3.4	12:42	**12:48**	p4.5
22	**W**	7:30	**8:00**	a3.7	1:06	**1:18**	p4.6	22	**F**	7:42	**8:12**	a3.3	1:24	**1:24**	p4.4
23	**T**	8:06	**8:42**	a3.5	1:48	**2:00**	p4.4	23	**S**	8:18	**8:54**	a3.1	2:00	**2:00**	p4.2
24	**F**	8:48	**9:24**	a3.2	2:24	**2:36**	p4.2	24	**S**	9:00	**9:30**	a2.9	2:36	**2:42**	p3.9
25	**S**	9:30	**10:06**	a2.9	3:06	**3:12**	p3.9	25	**M**	9:42	**10:12**	a2.7	3:12	**3:18**	p3.7
26	**S**	10:12	**10:54**	a2.6	3:48	**3:54**	p3.6	26	**T**	10:24	**11:00**	a2.5	3:54	**4:00**	p3.5
27	**M**	11:00	**11:42**	a2.4	4:30	**4:42**	p3.3	27	**W**	11:12	**11:48**	2.4	4:42	**4:48**	p3.4
28	**T**	11:54	...	2.2	5:18	**5:30**	p3.2	28	**T**	...	**12:06**	2.3	5:30	**5:42**	p3.3
29	**W**	12:30	**12:48**	p2.2	6:06	**6:24**	p3.1	29	**F**	12:36	**1:00**	a2.5	6:24	**6:36**	p3.4
30	**T**	1:24	**1:42**	p2.3	7:06	**7:18**	p3.3	30	**S**	1:30	**1:54**	a2.7	7:18	**7:36**	p3.6
								31	**S**	2:18	**2:48**	a3.0	8:12	**8:30**	3.9

The Kts. (knots) columns show the **maximum** predicted velocities of the stronger one of the Flood Currents and the stronger one of the Ebb Currents for each day.
The letter "a" means the velocity shown should occur **after** the **a.m.** Current Change. The letter "p" means the velocity shown should occur **after** the **p.m.** Current Change (even if next morning). No "a" or "p" means a.m. and p.m. velocities are the same for that day.
Avg. Max. Velocity: Flood 3.3 Kts., Ebb 4.2 Kts.
Max. Flood 2 hrs. 45 min. after Flood Starts, ±15 min.
Max. Ebb 3 hrs. 25 min. after Ebb Starts, ±15 min.
Use THE RACE tables with current charts pp. 98-103

See pp. 22-29 for Current Change at other points.

2021 CURRENT TABLE
THE RACE, LONG ISLAND SOUND

41°13.69'N, 72°03.75'W 0.2 nm E.N.E. of Valiant Rock

***Standard Time starts Nov. 7 at 2 a.m.** **Standard Time**

NOVEMBER

DAY OF MONTH	DAY OF WEEK	CURRENT TURNS TO NORTHWEST Flood Starts			CURRENT TURNS TO SOUTHEAST Ebb Starts		
		a.m.	**p.m.**	Kts.	a.m.	**p.m.**	Kts.
1	**M**	3:07	**3:42**	3.3	9:00	**9:30**	a4.4
2	**T**	3:54	**4:30**	a3.7	9:54	**10:18**	a4.9
3	**W**	4:42	**5:18**	a4.0	10:42	**11:12**	a5.3
4	**T**	5:30	**6:06**	a4.3	11:30	...	5.6
5	**F**	6:18	**7:00**	a4.4	12:01	**12:18**	p5.7
6	**S**	7:06	**7:48**	a4.4	12:54	**1:06**	p5.6
7	**S**	*7:00	***7:42**	a4.2	*1:00	***1:00**	p5.4
8	**M**	7:54	**8:42**	a3.9	1:42	**1:54**	p5.1
9	**T**	9:00	**9:42**	a3.6	2:36	**2:54**	p4.6
10	**W**	10:00	**10:48**	a3.2	3:42	**3:54**	p4.2
11	**T**	11:12	**11:54**	p3.0	4:42	**5:06**	p3.9
12	**F**	...	**12:24**	2.8	5:48	**6:12**	a3.8
13	**S**	12:54	**1:30**	a3.1	6:48	**7:18**	a3.9
14	**S**	1:48	**2:24**	a3.2	7:48	**8:18**	a4.1
15	**M**	2:42	**3:18**	a3.3	8:36	**9:12**	a4.3
16	**T**	3:30	**4:12**	a3.3	9:24	**10:00**	a4.5
17	**W**	4:12	**4:54**	a3.3	10:06	**10:42**	a4.5
18	**T**	4:54	**5:36**	a3.3	10:42	**11:18**	a4.5
19	**F**	5:36	**6:12**	a3.2	11:24	...	4.4
20	**S**	6:12	**6:48**	a3.1	12:01	**12:01**	p4.3
21	**S**	6:54	**7:24**	a3.0	12:36	**12:30**	p4.1
22	**M**	7:30	**8:00**	2.9	1:12	**1:12**	p4.0
23	**T**	8:12	**8:42**	2.8	1:48	**1:48**	p3.9
24	**W**	8:54	**9:24**	p2.8	2:30	**2:30**	p3.8
25	**T**	9:42	**10:06**	p2.8	3:12	**3:18**	p3.7
26	**F**	10:30	**10:54**	p2.9	4:00	**4:06**	p3.6
27	**S**	11:24	**11:42**	p3.0	4:48	**5:00**	a3.7
28	**S**	...	**12:24**	2.8	5:42	**6:00**	a3.9
29	**M**	12:36	**1:18**	a3.2	6:36	**7:00**	a4.2
30	**T**	1:24	**2:12**	a3.5	7:24	**7:54**	a4.6

DECEMBER

DAY OF MONTH	DAY OF WEEK	CURRENT TURNS TO NORTHWEST Flood Starts			CURRENT TURNS TO SOUTHEAST Ebb Starts		
		a.m.	**p.m.**	Kts.	a.m.	**p.m.**	Kts.
1	**W**	2:19	**3:06**	a3.8	8:18	**8:54**	a5.0
2	**T**	3:12	**3:54**	a4.0	9:12	**9:48**	a5.3
3	**F**	4:00	**4:48**	a4.2	10:06	**10:42**	a5.6
4	**S**	4:54	**5:42**	a4.4	11:00	**11:36**	a5.6
5	**S**	5:48	**6:36**	a4.3	11:48	...	5.6
6	**M**	6:48	**7:30**	a4.2	12:30	**12:42**	p5.4
7	**T**	7:42	**8:24**	a3.9	1:24	**1:42**	p5.0
8	**W**	8:42	**9:24**	a3.6	2:24	**2:36**	p4.6
9	**T**	9:48	**10:24**	p3.3	3:18	**3:36**	4.2
10	**F**	10:54	**11:24**	p3.1	4:18	**4:42**	a4.0
11	**S**	...	**12:01**	2.7	5:18	**5:42**	a3.9
12	**S**	12:18	**1:06**	a3.0	6:18	**6:48**	a3.9
13	**M**	1:18	**2:06**	a3.0	7:12	**7:48**	a4.0
14	**T**	2:12	**3:00**	a3.0	8:06	**8:42**	a4.1
15	**W**	3:00	**3:48**	a3.0	8:54	**9:30**	a4.2
16	**T**	3:48	**4:30**	a3.0	9:36	**10:18**	a4.2
17	**F**	4:30	**5:06**	3.0	10:18	**10:54**	a4.2
18	**S**	5:06	**5:48**	3.0	10:54	**11:30**	a4.2
19	**S**	5:48	**6:24**	3.0	11:30	...	4.2
20	**M**	6:24	**7:00**	p3.1	12:06	**12:06**	p4.2
21	**T**	7:06	**7:36**	3.1	12:42	**12:42**	p4.2
22	**W**	7:42	**8:12**	p3.1	1:18	**1:24**	p4.1
23	**T**	8:24	**8:48**	p3.2	2:00	**2:06**	p4.1
24	**F**	9:12	**9:30**	p3.2	2:42	**2:48**	p4.0
25	**S**	10:00	**10:18**	p3.3	3:24	**3:36**	a4.0
26	**S**	10:54	**11:06**	p3.3	4:12	**4:30**	a4.1
27	**M**	11:48	...	2.9	5:06	**5:30**	a4.2
28	**T**	12:01	**12:48**	a3.4	6:00	**6:30**	a4.4
29	**W**	12:54	**1:48**	a3.5	6:54	**7:30**	a4.6
30	**T**	1:48	**2:42**	a3.7	7:54	**8:30**	a4.9
31	**F**	2:48	**3:42**	a3.9	8:54	**9:30**	a5.2

The Kts. (knots) columns show the **maximum** predicted velocities of the stronger one of the Flood Currents and the stronger one of the Ebb Currents for each day.
The letter "a" means the velocity shown should occur **after** the **a.m.** Current Change. The letter "p" means the velocity shown should occur **after** the **p.m.** Current Change (even if next morning). No "a" or "p" means a.m. and p.m. velocities are the same for that day.
Avg. Max. Velocity: Flood 3.3 Kts., Ebb 4.2 Kts.
Max. Flood 2 hrs. 45 min. after Flood Starts, ±15 min.
Max. Ebb 3 hrs. 25 min. after Ebb Starts, ±15 min.
Use THE RACE tables with current charts pp. 98-103

See pp. 22-29 for Current Change at other points.

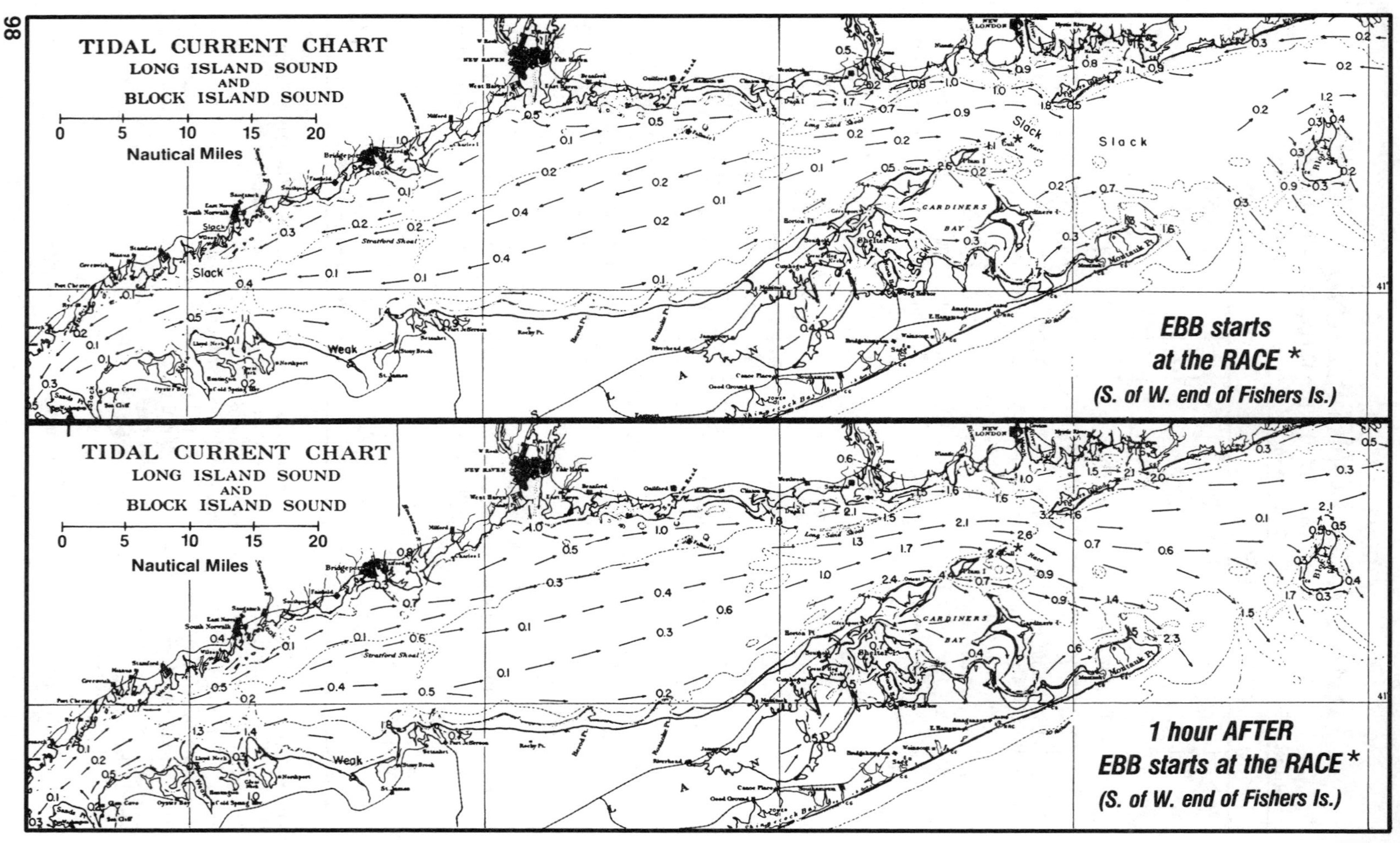
TIDAL CURRENT CHART
LONG ISLAND SOUND
AND
BLOCK ISLAND SOUND
0 5 10 15 20
Nautical Miles
EBB starts
at the RACE *
(S. of W. end of Fishers Is.)
TIDAL CURRENT CHART
LONG ISLAND SOUND
AND
BLOCK ISLAND SOUND
0 5 10 15 20
Nautical Miles
1 hour AFTER
EBB starts at the RACE *
(S. of W. end of Fishers Is.)

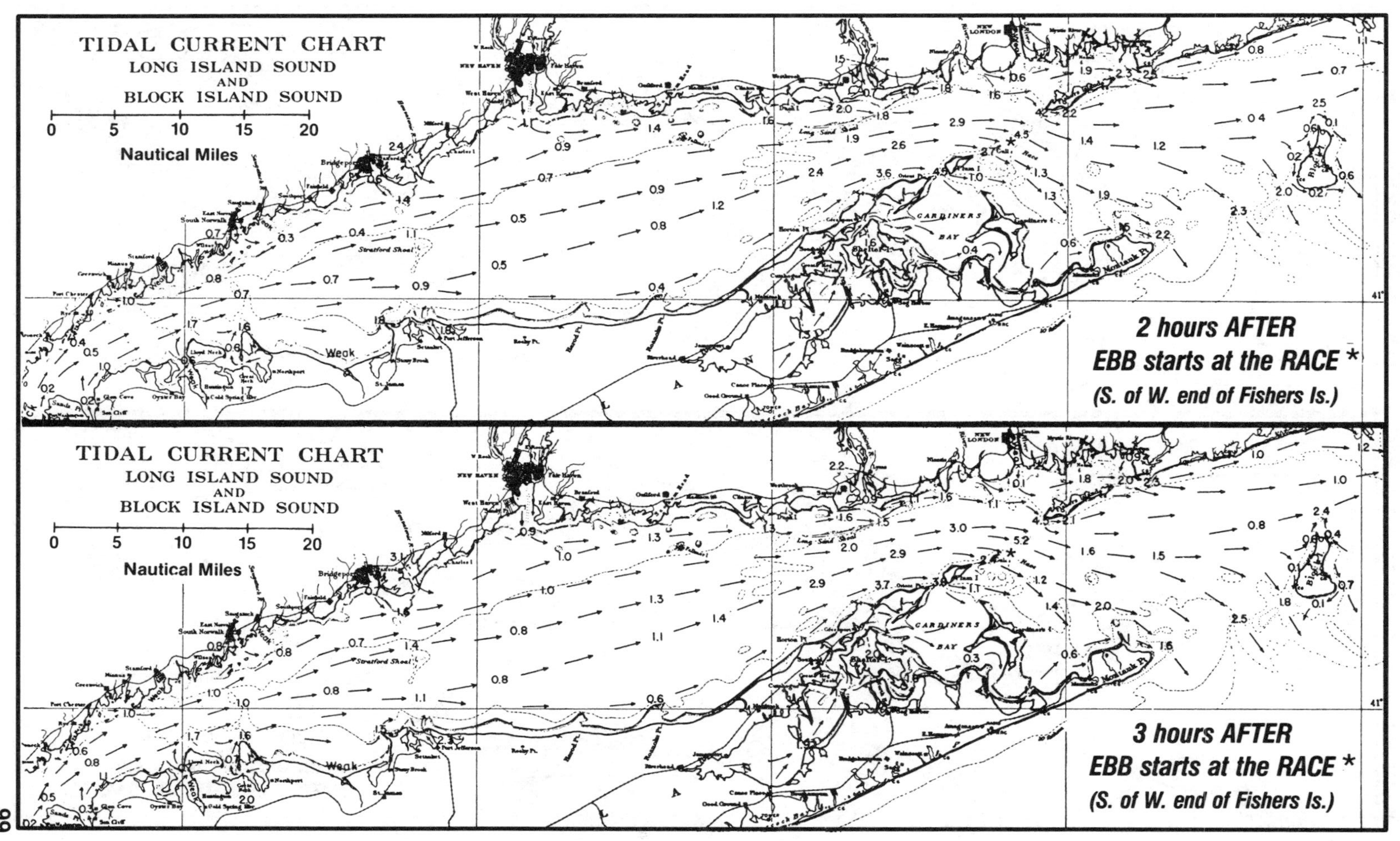
TIDAL CURRENT CHART
LONG ISLAND SOUND
AND
BLOCK ISLAND SOUND
0 5 10 15 20
Nautical Miles
2 hours AFTER
EBB starts at the RACE *
(S. of W. end of Fishers Is.)
TIDAL CURRENT CHART
LONG ISLAND SOUND
AND
BLOCK ISLAND SOUND
0 5 10 15 20
Nautical Miles
3 hours AFTER
EBB starts at the RACE *
(S. of W. end of Fishers Is.)

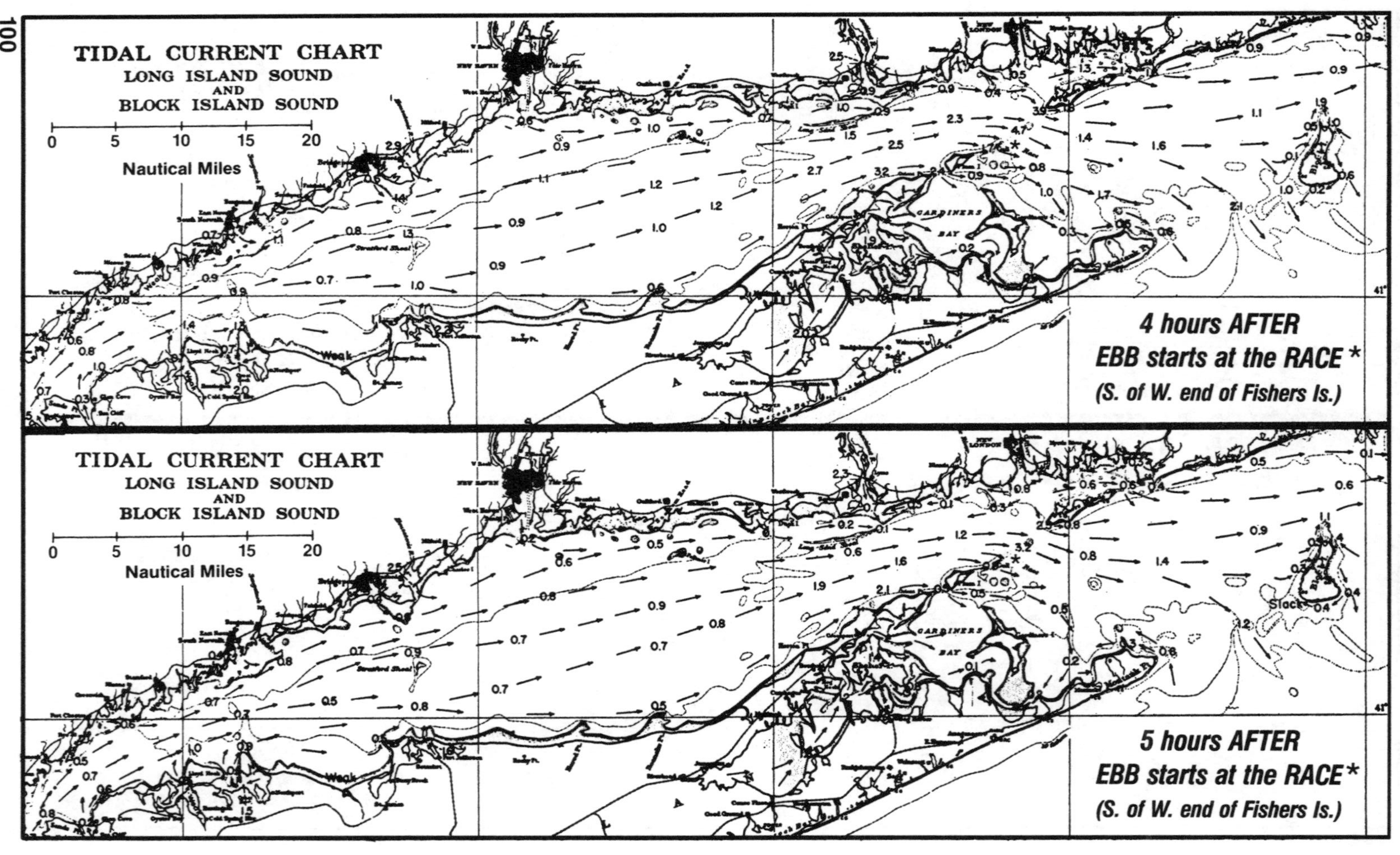

TIDAL CURRENT CHART
LONG ISLAND SOUND
AND
BLOCK ISLAND SOUND
0 5 10 15 20
Nautical Miles
GARDINERS BAY
4 hours AFTER
EBB starts at the RACE *
(S. of W. end of Fishers Is.)
TIDAL CURRENT CHART
LONG ISLAND SOUND
AND
BLOCK ISLAND SOUND
0 5 10 15 20
Nautical Miles
GARDINERS BAY
Slack
5 hours AFTER
EBB starts at the RACE *
(S. of W. end of Fishers Is.)

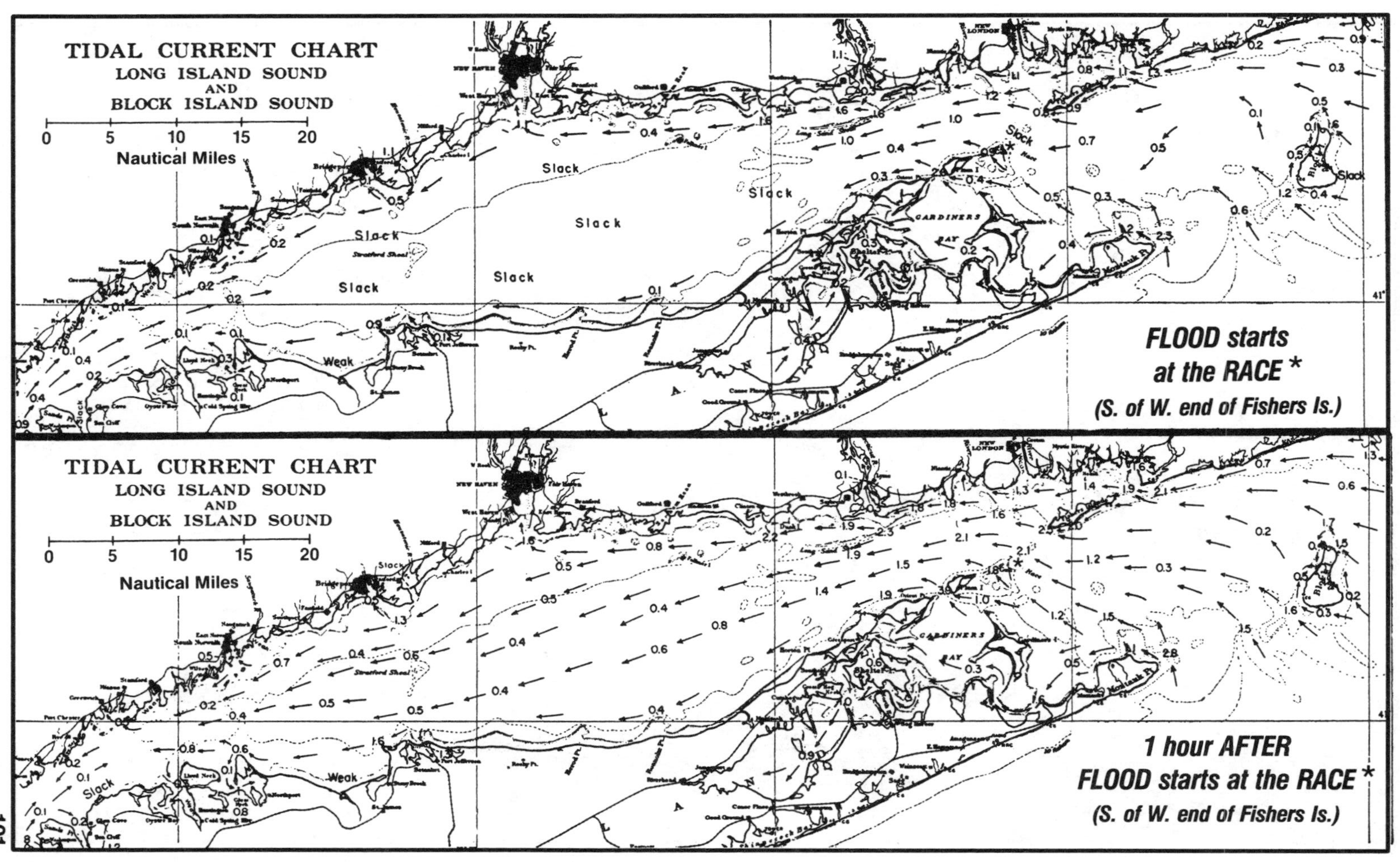
TIDAL CURRENT CHART
LONG ISLAND SOUND
AND
BLOCK ISLAND SOUND
0 5 10 15 20
Nautical Miles
FLOOD starts
at the RACE *
(S. of W. end of Fishers Is.)
TIDAL CURRENT CHART
LONG ISLAND SOUND
AND
BLOCK ISLAND SOUND
0 5 10 15 20
Nautical Miles
1 hour AFTER
FLOOD starts at the RACE *
(S. of W. end of Fishers Is.)

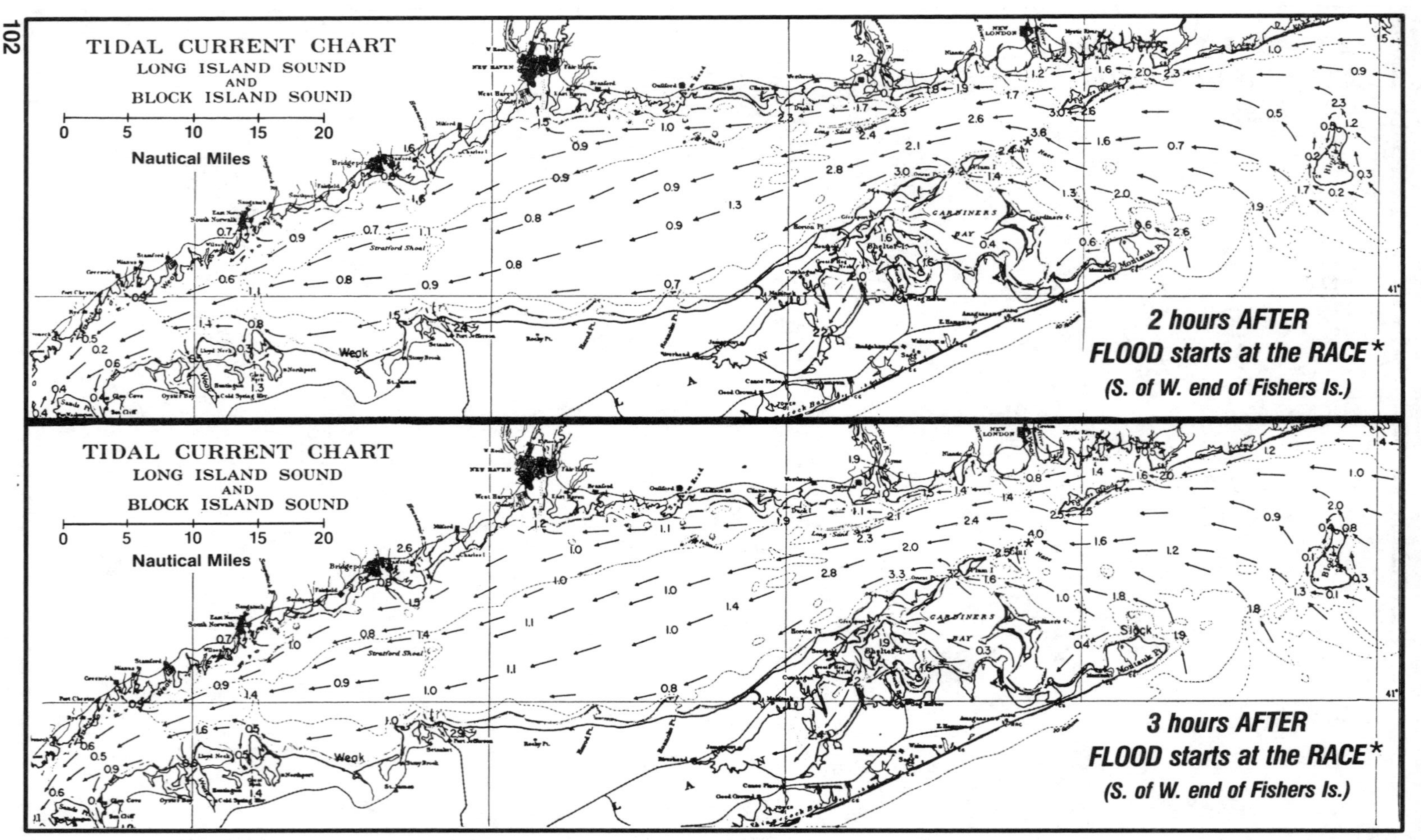

TIDAL CURRENT CHART
LONG ISLAND SOUND
AND
BLOCK ISLAND SOUND
0 5 10 15 20
Nautical Miles
2 hours AFTER
FLOOD starts at the RACE*
(S. of W. end of Fishers Is.)
TIDAL CURRENT CHART
LONG ISLAND SOUND
AND
BLOCK ISLAND SOUND
0 5 10 15 20
Nautical Miles
3 hours AFTER
FLOOD starts at the RACE*
(S. of W. end of Fishers Is.)

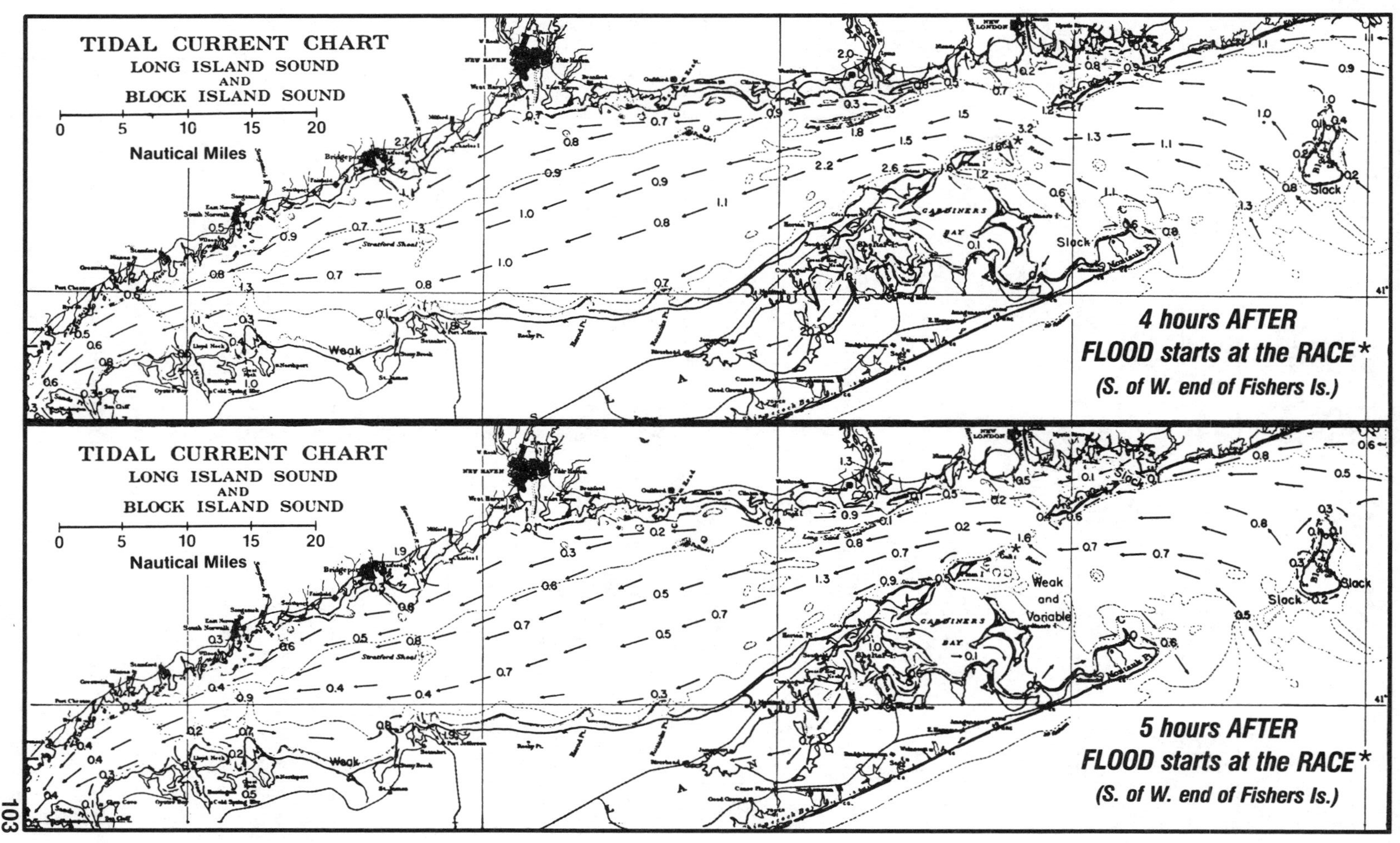
TIDAL CURRENT CHART
LONG ISLAND SOUND
AND
BLOCK ISLAND SOUND
0 5 10 15 20
Nautical Miles
NEW HAVEN
NEW LONDON
Bridgeport
GARDINERS BAY
Stratford Shoal
Weak
Slack
4 hours AFTER
FLOOD starts at the RACE*
(S. of W. end of Fishers Is.)
TIDAL CURRENT CHART
LONG ISLAND SOUND
AND
BLOCK ISLAND SOUND
0 5 10 15 20
Nautical Miles
Weak and Variable
Slack
5 hours AFTER
FLOOD starts at the RACE*
(S. of W. end of Fishers Is.)

2021 HIGH & LOW WATER
BRIDGEPORT, CT
41°10.4'N, 73°10.9'W

Day of Month	Day of Week	JANUARY (Standard Time)						Day of Month	Day of Week	FEBRUARY (Standard Time)					
		HIGH				LOW				HIGH				LOW	
		a.m.	Ht.	p.m.	Ht.	a.m.	p.m.			a.m.	Ht.	p.m.	Ht.	a.m.	p.m.
1	F	12:24	6.3	12:31	7.1	6:25	7:01	1	M	1:27	6.9	1:45	7.1	7:40	8:06
2	S	1:06	6.4	1:16	7.0	7:10	7:45	2	T	2:14	7.0	2:36	6.8	8:33	8:55
3	S	1:51	6.4	2:03	6.9	7:58	8:31	3	W	3:05	7.1	3:30	6.5	9:29	9:49
4	M	2:39	6.6	2:55	6.7	8:51	9:21	4	T	4:00	7.0	4:30	6.2	10:31	10:47
5	T	3:30	6.7	3:50	6.5	9:49	10:14	5	F	5:00	6.9	5:35	6.0	11:36	11:50
6	W	4:25	6.8	4:50	6.3	10:51	11:11	6	S	6:04	6.9	6:42	5.9	...	12:41
7	T	5:24	6.9	5:53	6.2	11:55	...	7	S	7:09	6.9	7:47	6.0	12:54	1:45
8	F	6:24	7.1	6:58	6.1	12:10	12:58	8	M	8:11	7.0	8:47	6.2	1:57	2:45
9	S	7:25	7.3	7:59	6.2	1:10	1:59	9	T	9:09	7.2	9:41	6.4	2:56	3:39
10	S	8:23	7.5	8:57	6.4	2:08	2:57	10	W	10:01	7.2	10:30	6.6	3:51	4:29
11	M	9:18	7.6	9:52	6.5	3:05	3:52	11	T	10:48	7.2	11:16	6.7	4:41	5:14
12	T	10:10	7.6	10:43	6.6	4:00	4:43	12	F	11:34	7.2	11:59	6.7	5:28	5:57
13	W	11:00	7.6	11:33	6.6	4:52	5:32	13	S	...	...	12:17	7.0	6:12	6:37
14	T	11:50	7.4	...	...	5:42	6:19	14	S	12:41	6.7	1:00	6.8	6:55	7:16
15	F	12:21	6.6	12:38	7.1	6:31	7:04	15	M	1:23	6.6	1:43	6.5	7:38	7:55
16	S	1:09	6.5	1:26	6.8	7:20	7:49	16	T	2:04	6.5	2:27	6.2	8:22	8:36
17	S	1:56	6.4	2:13	6.5	8:09	8:34	17	W	2:47	6.4	3:13	5.9	9:09	9:19
18	M	2:43	6.3	3:02	6.2	8:59	9:19	18	T	3:31	6.2	4:02	5.6	9:58	10:07
19	T	3:31	6.2	3:53	5.8	9:51	10:07	19	F	4:20	6.0	4:56	5.4	10:51	11:00
20	W	4:20	6.1	4:46	5.6	10:46	10:56	20	S	5:13	5.9	5:53	5.3	11:48	11:56
21	T	5:12	6.1	5:42	5.4	11:41	11:48	21	S	6:11	5.9	6:51	5.4	...	12:45
22	F	6:05	6.1	6:39	5.4	...	12:36	22	M	7:08	6.1	7:46	5.6	12:53	1:40
23	S	6:58	6.1	7:34	5.4	12:41	1:29	23	T	8:03	6.3	8:36	5.9	1:48	2:31
24	S	7:50	6.3	8:25	5.6	1:33	2:20	24	W	8:52	6.7	9:22	6.2	2:40	3:19
25	M	8:38	6.5	9:11	5.8	2:23	3:07	25	T	9:38	7.0	10:05	6.6	3:28	4:04
26	T	9:22	6.7	9:54	6.0	3:10	3:51	26	F	10:22	7.3	10:48	6.9	4:14	4:46
27	W	10:05	6.9	10:35	6.2	3:55	4:34	27	S	11:06	7.5	11:31	7.2	5:00	5:29
28	T	10:47	7.1	11:16	6.4	4:39	5:15	28	S	11:51	7.5	...	...	5:45	6:11
29	F	11:29	7.2	11:58	6.6	5:22	5:56								
30	S	...	...	12:12	7.3	6:06	6:38								
31	S	12:41	6.8	12:57	7.2	6:51	7:21								

Dates when Ht. of **Low** Water is below Mean Lower Low with Ht. of lowest given for each period and Date of lowest in ( ):

January	February
1st–4th: -0.3' (1st–3rd)	1st–3rd: -0.6' (1st)
8th–16th: -0.8' (12th, 13th)	8th–13th: -0.5' (10th–12th)
27th–31st: -0.7' (30th, 31st)	25th–28th: -0.8' (28th)

Average Rise and Fall 6.8 ft.

When a high tide exceeds avg. ht., the *following* low tide will be lower than avg.

2021 HIGH & LOW WATER
BRIDGEPORT, CT
41°10.4'N, 73°10.9'W

***Daylight Time starts March 14 at 2 a.m.** **Daylight Saving Time**

DAY OF MONTH	DAY OF WEEK	MARCH						DAY OF MONTH	DAY OF WEEK	APRIL					
		HIGH				LOW				HIGH				LOW	
		a.m.	Ht.	**p.m.**	Ht.	a.m.	**p.m.**			a.m.	Ht.	**p.m.**	Ht.	a.m.	**p.m.**
1	**M**	12:16	7.5	**12:37**	7.5	6:33	**6:55**	1	**T**	2:28	8.0	**3:01**	7.1	8:57	**9:12**
2	**T**	1:01	7.6	**1:26**	7.2	7:22	**7:41**	2	**F**	3:21	7.7	**3:58**	6.7	9:54	**10:10**
3	**W**	1:50	7.6	**2:18**	6.9	8:15	**8:32**	3	**S**	4:20	7.3	**4:59**	6.4	10:56	**11:14**
4	**T**	2:42	7.5	**3:13**	6.6	9:11	**9:27**	4	**S**	5:24	7.0	**6:06**	6.2	...	**12:01**
5	**F**	3:38	7.2	**4:14**	6.2	10:13	**10:29**	5	**M**	6:33	6.7	**7:14**	6.2	12:22	**1:07**
6	**S**	4:41	6.9	**5:20**	6.0	11:18	**11:35**	6	**T**	7:43	6.6	**8:19**	6.4	1:31	**2:11**
7	**S**	5:48	6.7	**6:29**	5.9	...	**12:26**	7	**W**	8:46	6.7	**9:17**	6.6	2:35	**3:09**
8	**M**	6:57	6.7	**7:35**	6.1	12:43	**1:31**	8	**T**	9:42	6.8	**10:06**	6.9	3:33	**3:59**
9	**T**	8:02	6.8	**8:35**	6.3	1:48	**2:30**	9	**F**	10:30	6.9	**10:49**	7.1	4:23	**4:44**
10	**W**	8:59	6.9	**9:27**	6.6	2:47	**3:23**	10	**S**	11:12	6.9	**11:29**	7.2	5:08	**5:23**
11	**T**	9:48	7.0	**10:13**	6.8	3:40	**4:10**	11	**S**	11:52	6.9	...	...	5:49	**6:00**
12	**F**	10:33	7.1	**10:55**	6.9	4:27	**4:52**	12	**M**	12:05	7.2	**12:30**	6.8	6:27	**6:36**
13	**S**	11:14	7.0	**11:34**	7.0	5:10	**5:30**	13	**T**	12:41	7.2	**1:08**	6.7	7:04	**7:11**
14	**S**	...	...	***12:54**	6.9	*6:51	***7:07**	14	**W**	1:16	7.1	**1:47**	6.6	7:41	**7:47**
15	**M**	1:11	7.0	**1:34**	6.7	7:30	**7:43**	15	**T**	1:52	7.0	**2:27**	6.4	8:19	**8:25**
16	**T**	1:49	6.9	**2:14**	6.5	8:09	**8:19**	16	**F**	2:30	6.8	**3:08**	6.3	8:58	**9:05**
17	**W**	2:26	6.8	**2:55**	6.3	8:48	**8:57**	17	**S**	3:11	6.6	**3:52**	6.1	9:41	**9:51**
18	**T**	3:05	6.6	**3:38**	6.1	9:30	**9:38**	18	**S**	3:57	6.4	**4:40**	6.0	10:29	**10:42**
19	**F**	3:47	6.4	**4:24**	5.8	10:16	**10:24**	19	**M**	4:48	6.3	**5:33**	5.9	11:23	**11:39**
20	**S**	4:34	6.2	**5:14**	5.7	11:06	**11:17**	20	**T**	5:45	6.2	**6:29**	6.0	...	**12:20**
21	**S**	5:26	6.0	**6:10**	5.6	...	**12:02**	21	**W**	6:46	6.3	**7:26**	6.3	12:40	**1:17**
22	**M**	6:25	6.0	**7:08**	5.6	12:15	**1:00**	22	**T**	7:47	6.6	**8:20**	6.7	1:39	**2:12**
23	**T**	7:26	6.1	**8:06**	5.8	1:15	**1:58**	23	**F**	8:44	6.8	**9:12**	7.2	2:37	**3:04**
24	**W**	8:25	6.4	**8:59**	6.2	2:13	**2:53**	24	**S**	9:37	7.2	**10:00**	7.7	3:31	**3:54**
25	**T**	9:19	6.8	**9:47**	6.6	3:08	**3:43**	25	**S**	10:28	7.4	**10:48**	8.1	4:23	**4:42**
26	**F**	10:08	7.1	**10:33**	7.1	3:59	**4:30**	26	**M**	11:17	7.6	**11:35**	8.4	5:14	**5:29**
27	**S**	10:55	7.4	**11:18**	7.6	4:49	**5:14**	27	**T**	...	...	**12:07**	7.6	6:04	**6:17**
28	**S**	11:42	7.6	...	...	5:37	**5:59**	28	**W**	12:24	8.5	**12:58**	7.6	6:55	**7:07**
29	**M**	12:03	7.9	**12:29**	7.7	6:25	**6:43**	29	**T**	1:14	8.4	**1:51**	7.4	7:46	**7:59**
30	**T**	12:49	8.1	**1:17**	7.6	7:13	**7:30**	30	**F**	2:07	8.2	**2:46**	7.1	8:40	**8:55**
31	**W**	1:37	8.1	**2:08**	7.4	8:04	**8:19**								

Dates when Ht. of **Low** Water is below Mean Lower Low with Ht. of lowest given for each period and Date of lowest in ( ):

1st–4th: -0.9' (1st)
11th–14th: -0.2'
27th–31st: -1.1' (30th)

1st–2nd: -0.7' (1st)
25th–30th: -1.1' (28th)

Average Rise and Fall 6.8 ft.

When a high tide exceeds avg. ht., the *following* low tide will be lower than avg.

2021 HIGH & LOW WATER
BRIDGEPORT, CT
41°10.4'N, 73°10.9'W

DAY OF MONTH	DAY OF WEEK	MAY HIGH a.m.	Ht.	p.m.	Ht.	LOW a.m.	p.m.	DAY OF MONTH	DAY OF WEEK	JUNE HIGH a.m.	Ht.	p.m.	Ht.	LOW a.m.	p.m.
		Daylight Saving Time								Daylight Saving Time					
1	**S**	3:04	7.8	**3:43**	6.9	9:37	**9:55**	1	**T**	4:46	7.0	**5:24**	6.8	11:13	**11:43**
2	**S**	4:03	7.4	**4:44**	6.7	10:38	**10:59**	2	**W**	5:46	6.6	**6:23**	6.8	...	**12:10**
3	**M**	5:07	7.0	**5:48**	6.5	11:40	...	3	**T**	6:47	6.4	**7:20**	6.8	12:45	**1:06**
4	**T**	6:13	6.7	**6:53**	6.5	12:06	**12:43**	4	**F**	7:47	6.3	**8:13**	6.9	1:44	**1:58**
5	**W**	7:19	6.5	**7:54**	6.7	1:12	**1:43**	5	**S**	8:42	6.3	**9:02**	7.1	2:39	**2:47**
6	**T**	8:21	6.5	**8:49**	6.9	2:14	**2:37**	6	**S**	9:32	6.3	**9:46**	7.2	3:29	**3:33**
7	**F**	9:16	6.6	**9:38**	7.1	3:10	**3:26**	7	**M**	10:17	6.4	**10:27**	7.3	4:14	**4:16**
8	**S**	10:04	6.6	**10:20**	7.2	4:00	**4:10**	8	**T**	10:59	6.5	**11:05**	7.3	4:56	**4:57**
9	**S**	10:47	6.7	**10:59**	7.3	4:44	**4:51**	9	**W**	11:40	6.5	**11:43**	7.2	5:36	**5:37**
10	**M**	11:27	6.7	**11:35**	7.3	5:24	**5:29**	10	**T**	...	...	**12:19**	6.6	6:14	**6:16**
11	**T**	...	...	**12:05**	6.7	6:02	**6:05**	11	**F**	12:21	7.2	**12:58**	6.6	6:52	**6:56**
12	**W**	12:11	7.3	**12:44**	6.6	6:39	**6:42**	12	**S**	1:00	7.1	**1:38**	6.6	7:30	**7:36**
13	**T**	12:47	7.2	**1:22**	6.6	7:16	**7:20**	13	**S**	1:40	7.1	**2:19**	6.6	8:10	**8:18**
14	**F**	1:24	7.1	**2:02**	6.5	7:53	**7:58**	14	**M**	2:21	7.0	**3:01**	6.6	8:51	**9:03**
15	**S**	2:02	6.9	**2:43**	6.4	8:32	**8:40**	15	**T**	3:06	7.0	**3:45**	6.7	9:35	**9:51**
16	**S**	2:44	6.8	**3:26**	6.3	9:14	**9:25**	16	**W**	3:54	6.9	**4:32**	6.8	10:21	**10:45**
17	**M**	3:29	6.7	**4:11**	6.3	10:00	**10:15**	17	**T**	4:46	6.8	**5:22**	7.0	11:11	**11:42**
18	**T**	4:18	6.6	**5:01**	6.3	10:50	**11:10**	18	**F**	5:42	6.7	**6:16**	7.2	...	**12:04**
19	**W**	5:13	6.6	**5:54**	6.5	11:44	...	19	**S**	6:41	6.7	**7:12**	7.5	12:42	**12:59**
20	**T**	6:11	6.6	**6:49**	6.8	12:09	**12:38**	20	**S**	7:42	6.7	**8:09**	7.8	1:42	**1:55**
21	**F**	7:12	6.7	**7:44**	7.1	1:08	**1:33**	21	**M**	8:43	6.8	**9:04**	8.1	2:41	**2:51**
22	**S**	8:11	6.8	**8:38**	7.6	2:07	**2:27**	22	**T**	9:41	7.0	**9:59**	8.3	3:39	**3:47**
23	**S**	9:08	7.1	**9:30**	8.0	3:04	**3:20**	23	**W**	10:36	7.1	**10:53**	8.4	4:35	**4:43**
24	**M**	10:02	7.2	**10:21**	8.4	3:59	**4:11**	24	**T**	11:30	7.2	**11:46**	8.4	5:29	**5:38**
25	**T**	10:55	7.4	**11:11**	8.6	4:53	**5:03**	25	**F**	...	...	**12:24**	7.2	6:22	**6:32**
26	**W**	11:47	7.4	...	...	5:45	**5:55**	26	**S**	12:40	8.2	**1:18**	7.2	7:14	**7:27**
27	**T**	12:03	8.6	**12:40**	7.4	6:37	**6:48**	27	**S**	1:34	8.0	**2:11**	7.2	8:05	**8:22**
28	**F**	12:56	8.4	**1:34**	7.3	7:30	**7:42**	28	**M**	2:28	7.7	**3:05**	7.1	8:57	**9:17**
29	**S**	1:50	8.1	**2:30**	7.2	8:24	**8:39**	29	**T**	3:22	7.3	**3:58**	7.0	9:48	**10:14**
30	**S**	2:47	7.8	**3:26**	7.0	9:19	**9:38**	30	**W**	4:17	6.9	**4:51**	7.0	10:40	**11:12**
31	**M**	3:45	7.4	**4:24**	6.9	10:16	**10:40**								

Dates when Ht. of **Low** Water is below Mean Lower Low with Ht. of lowest given for each period and Date of lowest in ( ):

1st: -0.2'
24th–30th: -0.9' (26th, 27th)

22nd–27th: -0.6' (24th, 25th)

Average Rise and Fall 6.8 ft.

When a high tide exceeds avg. ht., the *following* low tide will be lower than avg.

2021 HIGH & LOW WATER
BRIDGEPORT, CT
41°10.4'N, 73°10.9'W

Day of Month	Day of Week	JULY (Daylight Saving Time)						Day of Month	Day of Week	AUGUST (Daylight Saving Time)					
		HIGH				LOW				HIGH				LOW	
		a.m.	Ht.	**p.m.**	Ht.	a.m.	**p.m.**			a.m.	Ht.	**p.m.**	Ht.	a.m.	**p.m.**
1	**T**	5:13	6.6	**5:44**	6.9	11:31	...	1	**S**	6:24	6.0	**6:44**	6.7	12:23	**12:28**
2	**F**	6:09	6.3	**6:38**	6.9	12:10	**12:22**	2	**M**	7:21	5.9	**7:38**	6.7	1:18	**1:22**
3	**S**	7:06	6.1	**7:30**	6.9	1:06	**1:14**	3	**T**	8:17	5.9	**8:31**	6.8	2:12	**2:15**
4	**S**	8:02	6.0	**8:21**	6.9	2:01	**2:04**	4	**W**	9:10	6.1	**9:21**	6.9	3:03	**3:07**
5	**M**	8:56	6.1	**9:09**	7.0	2:52	**2:54**	5	**T**	9:58	6.3	**10:08**	7.0	3:52	**3:56**
6	**T**	9:45	6.2	**9:54**	7.1	3:40	**3:41**	6	**F**	10:42	6.5	**10:51**	7.2	4:37	**4:42**
7	**W**	10:30	6.3	**10:37**	7.1	4:25	**4:26**	7	**S**	11:23	6.7	**11:32**	7.4	5:19	**5:26**
8	**T**	11:12	6.4	**11:17**	7.2	5:07	**5:10**	8	**S**	...	...	**12:03**	6.9	5:59	**6:08**
9	**F**	11:53	6.6	**11:57**	7.2	5:48	**5:52**	9	**M**	12:13	7.5	**12:43**	7.1	6:39	**6:50**
10	**S**	...	...	**12:33**	6.6	6:27	**6:33**	10	**T**	12:54	7.6	**1:24**	7.3	7:18	**7:34**
11	**S**	12:37	7.3	**1:12**	6.7	7:06	**7:14**	11	**W**	1:37	7.6	**2:06**	7.5	7:59	**8:19**
12	**M**	1:18	7.3	**1:53**	6.8	7:46	**7:56**	12	**T**	2:22	7.5	**2:50**	7.6	8:41	**9:08**
13	**T**	2:00	7.3	**2:34**	7.0	8:26	**8:41**	13	**F**	3:10	7.3	**3:37**	7.7	9:26	**10:01**
14	**W**	2:44	7.2	**3:18**	7.1	9:08	**9:29**	14	**S**	4:01	7.1	**4:28**	7.7	10:16	**10:58**
15	**T**	3:31	7.1	**4:04**	7.3	9:53	**10:22**	15	**S**	4:57	6.8	**5:24**	7.7	11:11	...
16	**F**	4:22	7.0	**4:54**	7.4	10:42	**11:19**	16	**M**	5:59	6.6	**6:25**	7.6	12:01	**12:11**
17	**S**	5:17	6.8	**5:48**	7.5	11:34	...	17	**T**	7:04	6.5	**7:30**	7.6	1:04	**1:15**
18	**S**	6:17	6.6	**6:46**	7.6	12:19	**12:31**	18	**W**	8:10	6.5	**8:34**	7.7	2:09	**2:20**
19	**M**	7:20	6.6	**7:46**	7.8	1:21	**1:31**	19	**T**	9:13	6.7	**9:35**	7.8	3:10	**3:22**
20	**T**	8:23	6.6	**8:46**	7.9	2:23	**2:31**	20	**F**	10:11	7.0	**10:30**	7.9	4:08	**4:21**
21	**W**	9:24	6.8	**9:44**	8.1	3:23	**3:31**	21	**S**	11:03	7.2	**11:22**	7.9	5:00	**5:15**
22	**T**	10:22	6.9	**10:40**	8.1	4:21	**4:30**	22	**S**	11:52	7.4	...	...	5:49	**6:05**
23	**F**	11:16	7.1	**11:34**	8.1	5:15	**5:25**	23	**M**	12:10	7.8	**12:38**	7.5	6:34	**6:52**
24	**S**	...	...	**12:09**	7.2	6:06	**6:19**	24	**T**	12:56	7.7	**1:22**	7.5	7:16	**7:38**
25	**S**	12:26	8.0	**12:59**	7.3	6:56	**7:10**	25	**W**	1:41	7.4	**2:05**	7.4	7:57	**8:23**
26	**M**	1:16	7.8	**1:49**	7.3	7:43	**8:01**	26	**T**	2:26	7.1	**2:48**	7.3	8:38	**9:09**
27	**T**	2:06	7.5	**2:37**	7.3	8:29	**8:52**	27	**F**	3:11	6.8	**3:31**	7.1	9:19	**9:56**
28	**W**	2:55	7.2	**3:25**	7.2	9:15	**9:43**	28	**S**	3:58	6.5	**4:16**	6.9	10:03	**10:45**
29	**T**	3:45	6.8	**4:13**	7.1	10:00	**10:35**	29	**S**	4:48	6.2	**5:04**	6.7	10:51	**11:38**
30	**F**	4:35	6.5	**5:01**	6.9	10:48	**11:29**	30	**M**	5:42	6.0	**5:57**	6.6	11:44	...
31	**S**	5:28	6.2	**5:51**	6.8	11:37	...	31	**T**	6:39	5.9	**6:54**	6.5	12:34	**12:40**

Dates when Ht. of **Low** Water is below Mean Lower Low with Ht. of lowest given for each period and Date of lowest in ( ):

22nd–26th: -0.4' (24th)

Average Rise and Fall 6.8 ft.

When a high tide exceeds avg. ht., the *following* low tide will be lower than avg.

2021 HIGH & LOW WATER BRIDGEPORT, CT

41°10.4'N, 73°10.9'W

SEPTEMBER — Daylight Saving Time

Day of Month	Day of Week	High a.m.	Ht.	High p.m.	Ht.	Low a.m.	Low p.m.
1	W	7:38	5.9	7:52	6.6	1:30	1:38
2	T	8:33	6.1	8:47	6.7	2:24	2:33
3	F	9:23	6.4	9:36	7.0	3:15	3:25
4	S	10:08	6.7	10:22	7.3	4:02	4:13
5	S	10:50	7.0	11:04	7.5	4:46	4:58
6	M	11:31	7.4	11:46	7.7	5:27	5:42
7	T	...	...	12:11	7.7	6:07	6:26
8	W	12:29	7.8	12:53	7.9	6:47	7:11
9	T	1:13	7.8	1:36	8.1	7:29	7:58
10	F	2:00	7.6	2:22	8.1	8:13	8:48
11	S	2:49	7.4	3:12	8.1	9:01	9:42
12	S	3:43	7.1	4:06	7.9	9:54	10:41
13	M	4:41	6.8	5:05	7.6	10:53	11:44
14	T	5:45	6.5	6:11	7.4	11:58	...
15	W	6:53	6.5	7:19	7.3	12:51	1:06
16	T	8:01	6.6	8:26	7.4	1:56	2:13
17	F	9:03	6.8	9:26	7.5	2:57	3:15
18	S	9:58	7.1	10:19	7.6	3:53	4:11
19	S	10:47	7.4	11:07	7.6	4:42	5:02
20	M	11:32	7.6	11:51	7.6	5:27	5:48
21	T	...	...	12:13	7.6	6:08	6:32
22	W	12:33	7.4	12:52	7.6	6:46	7:13
23	T	1:14	7.2	1:31	7.5	7:24	7:54
24	F	1:56	6.9	2:10	7.3	8:01	8:35
25	S	2:39	6.7	2:50	7.1	8:40	9:18
26	S	3:23	6.4	3:33	6.9	9:23	10:04
27	M	4:11	6.2	4:21	6.6	10:10	10:55
28	T	5:03	6.0	5:13	6.4	11:03	11:50
29	W	5:58	5.9	6:11	6.4	...	12:01
30	T	6:56	6.0	7:12	6.4	12:47	1:01

OCTOBER — Daylight Saving Time

Day of Month	Day of Week	High a.m.	Ht.	High p.m.	Ht.	Low a.m.	Low p.m.
1	F	7:54	6.2	8:09	6.6	1:44	1:58
2	S	8:45	6.5	9:01	6.9	2:36	2:52
3	S	9:32	6.9	9:49	7.3	3:24	3:42
4	M	10:15	7.4	10:34	7.6	4:09	4:29
5	T	10:57	7.8	11:18	7.7	4:52	5:15
6	W	11:39	8.2	...	...	5:34	6:01
7	T	12:03	7.8	12:23	8.4	6:16	6:48
8	F	12:50	7.7	1:09	8.5	7:01	7:37
9	S	1:39	7.6	1:58	8.4	7:48	8:28
10	S	2:31	7.3	2:50	8.2	8:39	9:24
11	M	3:27	7.0	3:48	7.8	9:36	10:25
12	T	4:27	6.7	4:50	7.5	10:39	11:29
13	W	5:33	6.5	5:58	7.2	11:48	...
14	T	6:42	6.5	7:08	7.0	12:36	12:57
15	F	7:49	6.7	8:14	7.1	1:40	2:04
16	S	8:49	6.9	9:12	7.1	2:39	3:04
17	S	9:41	7.2	10:03	7.2	3:32	3:58
18	M	10:27	7.5	10:48	7.2	4:18	4:46
19	T	11:08	7.6	11:30	7.2	5:00	5:29
20	W	11:46	7.6	...	...	5:39	6:09
21	T	12:10	7.1	12:22	7.6	6:16	6:48
22	F	12:49	6.9	12:59	7.4	6:52	7:26
23	S	1:29	6.7	1:36	7.2	7:29	8:04
24	S	2:10	6.5	2:15	7.0	8:07	8:45
25	M	2:53	6.3	2:57	6.8	8:49	9:28
26	T	3:38	6.1	3:43	6.6	9:35	10:17
27	W	4:27	6.0	4:34	6.4	10:27	11:10
28	T	5:20	5.9	5:31	6.3	11:24	...
29	F	6:15	6.0	6:30	6.3	12:06	12:24
30	S	7:11	6.2	7:28	6.5	1:01	1:22
31	S	8:04	6.6	8:24	6.8	1:54	2:18

Dates when Ht. of **Low** Water is below Mean Lower Low with Ht. of lowest given for each period and Date of lowest in ( ):

9th: -0.2'

6th–9th: -0.6' (7th)

Average Rise and Fall 6.8 ft.

When a high tide exceeds avg. ht., the *following* low tide will be lower than avg.

2021 HIGH & LOW WATER
BRIDGEPORT, CT
41°10.4'N, 73°10.9'W

***Standard Time starts Nov. 7 at 2 a.m.** **Standard Time**

DAY OF MONTH	DAY OF WEEK	NOVEMBER HIGH a.m.	Ht.	**p.m.**	Ht.	LOW a.m.	**p.m.**
1	M	8:54	7.1	**9:15**	7.1	2:43	**3:10**
2	T	9:40	7.6	**10:04**	7.3	3:31	**4:01**
3	W	10:25	8.1	**10:51**	7.5	4:16	**4:50**
4	T	11:10	8.4	**11:39**	7.6	5:02	**5:38**
5	F	11:57	8.6	...	...	5:48	**6:27**
6	S	12:28	7.5	**12:45**	8.6	6:36	**7:18**
7	S	1:20	7.3	***12:37**	8.4	*6:27	***7:11**
8	M	1:14	7.1	**1:32**	8.1	7:22	**8:07**
9	T	2:12	6.9	**2:32**	7.6	8:21	**9:08**
10	W	3:13	6.7	**3:35**	7.2	9:26	**10:11**
11	T	4:17	6.5	**4:41**	6.9	10:34	**11:14**
12	F	5:24	6.6	**5:48**	6.7	11:42	...
13	S	6:28	6.7	**6:52**	6.6	12:16	**12:47**
14	S	7:26	6.9	**7:50**	6.6	1:12	**1:46**
15	M	8:17	7.2	**8:40**	6.7	2:03	**2:38**
16	T	9:01	7.3	**9:26**	6.7	2:49	**3:25**
17	W	9:41	7.4	**10:07**	6.7	3:31	**4:07**
18	T	10:19	7.4	**10:47**	6.6	4:10	**4:46**
19	F	10:55	7.3	**11:25**	6.5	4:48	**5:24**
20	S	11:31	7.2	...	...	5:25	**6:01**
21	S	12:04	6.4	**12:08**	7.0	6:02	**6:38**
22	M	12:44	6.3	**12:47**	6.8	6:41	**7:18**
23	T	1:26	6.2	**1:29**	6.7	7:22	**7:59**
24	W	2:09	6.1	**2:13**	6.5	8:06	**8:44**
25	T	2:55	6.0	**3:01**	6.4	8:56	**9:33**
26	F	3:44	6.0	**3:54**	6.3	9:50	**10:25**
27	S	4:35	6.1	**4:50**	6.3	10:47	**11:18**
28	S	5:29	6.4	**5:48**	6.3	11:46	...
29	M	6:23	6.7	**6:46**	6.5	12:11	**12:44**
30	T	7:16	7.2	**7:42**	6.7	1:03	**1:40**

DAY OF MONTH	DAY OF WEEK	DECEMBER HIGH a.m.	Ht.	**p.m.**	Ht.	LOW a.m.	**p.m.**
1	W	8:07	7.7	**8:36**	6.9	1:54	**2:34**
2	T	8:56	8.1	**9:27**	7.1	2:45	**3:26**
3	F	9:45	8.4	**10:18**	7.2	3:35	**4:18**
4	S	10:35	8.5	**11:10**	7.2	4:26	**5:09**
5	S	11:27	8.4	...	...	5:17	**6:02**
6	M	12:03	7.1	**12:21**	8.2	6:11	**6:55**
7	T	12:58	6.9	**1:17**	7.8	7:07	**7:50**
8	W	1:55	6.8	**2:15**	7.4	8:06	**8:47**
9	T	2:54	6.6	**3:15**	7.0	9:08	**9:46**
10	F	3:54	6.5	**4:17**	6.6	10:13	**10:45**
11	S	4:56	6.5	**5:20**	6.3	11:17	**11:42**
12	S	5:56	6.6	**6:22**	6.1	...	**12:20**
13	M	6:53	6.7	**7:20**	6.1	12:37	**1:18**
14	T	7:45	6.8	**8:12**	6.1	1:28	**2:11**
15	W	8:31	6.9	**9:00**	6.1	2:16	**2:59**
16	T	9:13	7.0	**9:43**	6.2	3:01	**3:42**
17	F	9:53	7.0	**10:24**	6.2	3:43	**4:22**
18	S	10:31	7.0	**11:03**	6.2	4:23	**5:00**
19	S	11:09	6.9	**11:42**	6.2	5:02	**5:38**
20	M	11:47	6.8	...	...	5:40	**6:16**
21	T	12:21	6.2	**12:25**	6.7	6:19	**6:54**
22	W	1:00	6.1	**1:05**	6.6	6:59	**7:34**
23	T	1:41	6.1	**1:48**	6.6	7:42	**8:15**
24	F	2:24	6.1	**2:33**	6.4	8:28	**8:59**
25	S	3:09	6.2	**3:21**	6.3	9:19	**9:47**
26	S	3:58	6.3	**4:15**	6.2	10:14	**10:38**
27	M	4:50	6.5	**5:12**	6.2	11:13	**11:32**
28	T	5:45	6.8	**6:13**	6.2	...	**12:13**
29	W	6:41	7.1	**7:13**	6.3	12:27	**1:13**
30	T	7:38	7.5	**8:12**	6.4	1:23	**2:11**
31	F	8:33	7.8	**9:07**	6.5	2:19	**3:07**

Dates when Ht. of **Low** Water is below Mean Lower Low with Ht. of lowest given for each period and Date of lowest in ( ):

November: 3rd–8th: -0.9' (5th)

December: 1st–8th: -1.1' (4th)
30th–31st: -0.8' (31st)

Average Rise and Fall 6.8 ft.

When a high tide exceeds avg. ht., the *following* low tide will be lower than avg.

2021 HIGH & LOW WATER
KINGS POINT, NY
40°48.7'N, 73°45.9'W

Standard Time

DAY OF MONTH	DAY OF WEEK	JANUARY					
		HIGH				LOW	
		a.m.	Ht.	**p.m.**	Ht.	a.m.	**p.m.**
1	F	12:08	7.0	**12:10**	7.9	6:15	**6:56**
2	S	12:47	7.1	**12:55**	7.9	6:58	**7:36**
3	S	1:31	7.2	**1:43**	7.8	7:46	**8:21**
4	M	2:19	7.4	**2:35**	7.6	8:38	**9:10**
5	T	3:11	7.5	**3:31**	7.3	9:37	**10:03**
6	W	4:07	7.6	**4:32**	7.0	10:45	**11:03**
7	T	5:09	7.7	**5:43**	6.8	...	**12:12**
8	F	6:18	7.8	**7:07**	6.7	12:11	**1:36**
9	S	7:31	8.0	**8:21**	6.9	1:31	**2:42**
10	S	8:37	8.2	**9:22**	7.1	2:44	**3:41**
11	M	9:35	8.4	**10:17**	7.3	3:46	**4:35**
12	T	10:29	8.4	**11:08**	7.4	4:42	**5:26**
13	W	11:20	8.4	**11:58**	7.4	5:34	**6:14**
14	T	...	...	**12:09**	8.2	6:23	**7:01**
15	F	12:46	7.4	**12:57**	7.9	7:11	**7:45**
16	S	1:34	7.3	**1:44**	7.5	7:59	**8:29**
17	S	2:21	7.1	**2:31**	7.1	8:48	**9:11**
18	M	3:07	7.0	**3:20**	6.7	9:40	**9:50**
19	T	3:54	6.8	**4:14**	6.3	10:37	**10:27**
20	W	4:44	6.7	**5:15**	6.0	11:35	**11:05**
21	T	5:40	6.6	**6:19**	5.9	...	**12:32**
22	F	6:39	6.6	**7:19**	5.9	12:06	**1:27**
23	S	7:34	6.6	**8:13**	6.1	1:12	**2:19**
24	S	8:24	6.8	**9:01**	6.3	2:08	**3:07**
25	M	9:06	7.0	**9:42**	6.5	2:55	**3:52**
26	T	9:40	7.2	**10:17**	6.7	3:35	**4:32**
27	W	10:07	7.5	**10:46**	6.9	4:09	**5:07**
28	T	10:38	7.8	**11:13**	7.2	4:43	**5:37**
29	F	11:14	8.0	**11:47**	7.4	5:21	**6:06**
30	S	11:56	8.1	...	...	6:02	**6:39**
31	S	12:27	7.7	**12:40**	8.1	6:46	**7:16**

Standard Time

DAY OF MONTH	DAY OF WEEK	FEBRUARY					
		HIGH				LOW	
		a.m.	Ht.	**p.m.**	Ht.	a.m.	**p.m.**
1	M	1:12	7.8	**1:28**	7.9	7:33	**7:59**
2	T	1:58	8.0	**2:19**	7.7	8:24	**8:46**
3	W	2:48	8.0	**3:14**	7.2	9:22	**9:38**
4	T	3:44	7.8	**4:16**	6.8	10:35	**10:40**
5	F	4:46	7.7	**5:34**	6.5	...	**12:11**
6	S	6:04	7.5	**7:08**	6.5	12:05	**1:28**
7	S	7:31	7.6	**8:21**	6.7	1:37	**2:33**
8	M	8:40	7.8	**9:20**	7.0	2:45	**3:31**
9	T	9:38	8.0	**10:12**	7.3	3:44	**4:24**
10	W	10:29	8.1	**11:00**	7.5	4:37	**5:12**
11	T	11:16	8.1	**11:45**	7.6	5:26	**5:57**
12	F	11:59	8.0	...	...	6:12	**6:39**
13	S	12:27	7.6	**12:41**	7.8	6:54	**7:17**
14	S	1:06	7.5	**1:19**	7.4	7:34	**7:48**
15	M	1:41	7.4	**1:55**	7.1	8:10	**8:02**
16	T	2:11	7.2	**2:30**	6.7	8:38	**8:19**
17	W	2:40	7.0	**3:08**	6.4	9:03	**8:54**
18	T	3:13	6.8	**3:51**	6.1	9:42	**9:38**
19	F	3:54	6.6	**4:47**	5.9	10:36	**10:29**
20	S	4:45	6.4	**6:13**	5.8	-A-	**11:28**
21	S	5:48	6.3	**7:26**	5.9	...	**1:30**
22	M	7:18	6.4	**8:21**	6.1	12:35	**2:27**
23	T	8:21	6.8	**9:05**	6.4	1:52	**3:15**
24	W	9:04	7.2	**9:41**	6.8	2:56	**3:58**
25	T	9:41	7.6	**10:12**	7.2	3:43	**4:35**
26	F	10:17	8.0	**10:45**	7.7	4:25	**5:08**
27	S	10:57	8.2	**11:23**	8.1	5:06	**5:40**
28	S	11:40	8.4	...	...	5:49	**6:15**

A also at 12:21 p.m.

Dates when Ht. of **Low** Water is below Mean Lower Low with Ht. of lowest given for each period and Date of lowest in ( ):

1st–4th: -0.4' (1st–3rd)
8th–16th: -1.2' (12th)
27th–31st: -0.8' (30th, 31st)

1st–3rd: -0.7' (1st)
7th–13th: -1.0' (10th)
25th–28th: -1.0' (28th)

Average Rise and Fall 7.1 ft.

When a high tide exceeds avg. ht., the *following* low tide will be lower than avg.

2021 HIGH & LOW WATER KINGS POINT, NY

40°48.7'N, 73°45.9'W

***Daylight Time starts March 14 at 2 a.m.** **Daylight Saving Time**

DAY OF MONTH	DAY OF WEEK	MARCH						DAY OF MONTH	DAY OF WEEK	APRIL					
		HIGH				LOW				HIGH				LOW	
		a.m.	Ht.	**p.m.**	Ht.	a.m.	**p.m.**			a.m.	Ht.	**p.m.**	Ht.	a.m.	**p.m.**
1	M	12:05	8.4	12:25	8.3	6:33	6:54	1	T	2:16	8.9	2:53	7.8	9:05	9:08
2	T	12:48	8.6	1:13	8.1	7:21	7:36	2	F	3:09	8.5	3:55	7.3	10:12	10:10
3	W	1:36	8.6	2:05	7.7	8:13	8:24	3	S	4:10	8.0	5:11	6.9	11:34	11:47
4	T	2:27	8.4	3:01	7.3	9:13	9:19	4	S	5:29	7.5	6:39	6.8	...	12:50
5	F	3:23	8.0	4:08	6.8	10:36	10:31	5	M	7:05	7.2	7:54	6.9	1:13	1:57
6	S	4:31	7.6	5:40	6.5	...	12:04	6	T	8:20	7.3	8:57	7.2	2:21	2:58
7	S	6:06	7.3	7:06	6.6	12:17	1:16	7	W	9:22	7.5	9:51	7.5	3:22	3:52
8	M	7:31	7.4	8:13	6.8	1:34	2:18	8	T	10:14	7.7	10:39	7.8	4:17	4:42
9	T	8:37	7.6	9:10	7.2	2:38	3:15	9	F	11:01	7.8	11:21	8.0	5:06	5:27
10	W	9:31	7.8	9:59	7.5	3:34	4:06	10	S	11:43	7.8	11:59	8.1	5:51	6:07
11	T	10:19	7.9	10:44	7.8	4:25	4:53	11	S	...	...	12:22	7.7	6:33	6:43
12	F	11:03	8.0	11:25	7.9	5:11	5:35	12	M	12:33	8.1	12:57	7.5	7:10	7:11
13	S	11:43	7.9	...	...	5:54	6:13	13	T	1:00	7.9	1:29	7.3	7:42	7:19
14	S	12:02	7.9	*1:20	7.7	*7:33	*7:44	14	W	1:17	7.8	1:54	7.1	8:02	7:33
15	M	1:34	7.8	1:53	7.4	8:08	8:02	15	T	1:37	7.7	2:17	7.0	8:11	8:05
16	T	1:58	7.6	2:22	7.1	8:33	8:08	16	F	2:07	7.5	2:48	6.8	8:39	8:44
17	W	2:18	7.5	2:49	6.9	8:44	8:36	17	S	2:46	7.4	3:27	6.7	9:18	9:28
18	T	2:46	7.3	3:21	6.6	9:11	9:14	18	S	3:30	7.2	4:12	6.5	10:04	10:18
19	F	3:22	7.1	4:01	6.4	9:50	9:58	19	M	4:19	7.0	5:03	6.4	10:57	11:14
20	S	4:04	6.9	4:47	6.2	10:38	10:49	20	T	5:14	6.9	6:02	6.5	11:58	...
21	S	4:53	6.7	5:42	6.0	11:34	11:46	21	W	6:16	6.9	7:07	6.7	12:16	1:05
22	M	5:50	6.5	6:51	6.0	...	12:42	22	T	7:24	7.1	8:13	7.2	1:23	2:14
23	T	6:56	6.6	8:15	6.2	12:49	2:22	23	F	8:33	7.4	9:09	7.8	2:35	3:15
24	W	8:12	6.8	9:13	6.7	2:00	3:26	24	S	9:33	7.8	9:58	8.4	3:42	4:06
25	T	9:18	7.3	9:56	7.2	3:12	4:13	25	S	10:26	8.1	10:44	8.9	4:40	4:53
26	F	10:08	7.7	10:35	7.8	4:12	4:54	26	M	11:15	8.3	11:30	9.3	5:32	5:38
27	S	10:52	8.1	11:15	8.4	5:03	5:31	27	T	...	...	12:04	8.4	6:22	6:24
28	S	11:36	8.4	11:56	8.8	5:49	6:09	28	W	12:17	9.5	12:55	8.3	7:12	7:11
29	M	...	...	12:22	8.5	6:35	6:49	29	T	1:06	9.4	1:48	8.1	8:04	8:02
30	T	12:40	9.1	1:09	8.4	7:22	7:31	30	F	1:59	9.0	2:47	7.8	9:03	9:00
31	W	1:26	9.1	1:59	8.1	8:11	8:16								

Dates when Ht. of **Low** Water is below Mean Lower Low with Ht. of lowest given for each period and Date of lowest in ( ):

March	April
1st–4th: -1.0' (1st, 2nd)	1st–2nd: -0.8' (1st)
9th–15th: -0.7' (11th)	8th–13th: -0.4' (10th, 11th)
26th–31st: -1.3' (30th)	25th–30th: -1.3' (28th)

Average Rise and Fall 7.1 ft.

When a high tide exceeds avg. ht., the *following* low tide will be lower than avg.

2021 HIGH & LOW WATER
KINGS POINT, NY
40°48.7'N, 73°45.9'W

DAY OF MONTH	DAY OF WEEK	MAY HIGH a.m.	Ht.	p.m.	Ht.	MAY LOW a.m.	p.m.	DAY OF MONTH	DAY OF WEEK	JUNE HIGH a.m.	Ht.	p.m.	Ht.	JUNE LOW a.m.	p.m.
		Daylight Saving Time								Daylight Saving Time					
1	S	2:58	8.5	**3:54**	7.4	10:10	**10:18**	1	T	5:12	7.5	**5:58**	7.4	...	**12:02**
2	S	4:05	8.0	**5:09**	7.2	11:22	**11:44**	2	W	6:21	7.2	**7:00**	7.4	12:32	**1:00**
3	M	5:28	7.5	**6:24**	7.1	...	**12:30**	3	T	7:25	7.1	**7:58**	7.5	1:33	**1:55**
4	T	6:49	7.3	**7:32**	7.2	12:56	**1:32**	4	F	8:24	7.0	**8:50**	7.7	2:30	**2:47**
5	W	7:58	7.2	**8:32**	7.4	2:01	**2:30**	5	S	9:17	7.0	**9:38**	7.9	3:23	**3:36**
6	T	8:57	7.3	**9:24**	7.7	2:59	**3:23**	6	S	10:06	7.1	**10:21**	7.9	4:12	**4:21**
7	F	9:49	7.4	**10:11**	8.0	3:53	**4:11**	7	M	10:50	7.1	**11:00**	7.9	4:58	**5:03**
8	S	10:35	7.5	**10:53**	8.1	4:42	**4:56**	8	T	11:31	7.2	**11:34**	7.9	5:41	**5:40**
9	S	11:18	7.5	**11:31**	8.1	5:27	**5:36**	9	W	...	...	**12:10**	7.2	6:19	**6:10**
10	M	11:57	7.4	...	...	6:08	**6:12**	10	T	12:01	7.8	**12:43**	7.1	6:54	**6:24**
11	T	12:03	8.1	**12:34**	7.3	6:45	**6:39**	11	F	12:18	7.7	**1:10**	7.1	7:21	**6:47**
12	W	12:29	7.9	**1:06**	7.2	7:18	**6:47**	12	S	12:42	7.7	**1:30**	7.1	7:36	**7:21**
13	T	12:43	7.8	**1:31**	7.1	7:39	**7:06**	13	S	1:16	7.7	**1:59**	7.1	8:01	**8:01**
14	F	1:05	7.7	**1:51**	7.0	7:49	**7:40**	14	M	1:57	7.7	**2:37**	7.2	8:37	**8:45**
15	S	1:38	7.6	**2:21**	6.9	8:17	**8:20**	15	T	2:42	7.7	**3:21**	7.3	9:19	**9:34**
16	S	2:18	7.6	**3:00**	6.9	8:55	**9:05**	16	W	3:31	7.7	**4:09**	7.4	10:06	**10:27**
17	M	3:03	7.5	**3:44**	6.9	9:40	**9:54**	17	T	4:23	7.6	**5:01**	7.6	10:57	**11:26**
18	T	3:53	7.4	**4:34**	6.9	10:30	**10:49**	18	F	5:20	7.4	**5:57**	7.8	11:51	...
19	W	4:46	7.3	**5:29**	7.0	11:26	**11:49**	19	S	6:21	7.3	**6:56**	8.1	12:30	**12:48**
20	T	5:45	7.2	**6:28**	7.3	...	**12:24**	20	S	7:29	7.3	**7:58**	8.4	1:42	**1:49**
21	F	6:49	7.3	**7:30**	7.7	12:54	**1:25**	21	M	8:39	7.4	**8:59**	8.8	3:00	**2:52**
22	S	7:57	7.4	**8:30**	8.2	2:05	**2:25**	22	T	9:45	7.6	**9:58**	9.0	4:10	**3:59**
23	S	9:02	7.7	**9:25**	8.8	3:16	**3:23**	23	W	10:45	7.8	**10:54**	9.2	5:10	**5:04**
24	M	10:02	7.9	**10:17**	9.2	4:21	**4:19**	24	T	11:42	7.9	**11:50**	9.1	6:06	**6:04**
25	T	10:57	8.1	**11:07**	9.4	5:18	**5:14**	25	F	...	...	**12:38**	7.9	6:59	**7:02**
26	W	11:50	8.2	**11:59**	9.4	6:12	**6:07**	26	S	12:46	9.0	**1:34**	7.9	7:52	**7:59**
27	T	...	...	**12:44**	8.1	7:06	**7:01**	27	S	1:43	8.7	**2:32**	7.8	8:44	**8:57**
28	F	12:52	9.2	**1:41**	8.0	8:00	**7:59**	28	M	2:42	8.3	**3:29**	7.7	9:37	**9:58**
29	S	1:48	8.9	**2:42**	7.8	8:57	**9:03**	29	T	3:42	7.9	**4:26**	7.6	10:32	**10:59**
30	S	2:50	8.4	**3:47**	7.6	9:58	**10:15**	30	W	4:43	7.5	**5:23**	7.5	11:26	...
31	M	3:59	7.9	**4:53**	7.4	11:01	**11:26**								

Dates when Ht. of **Low** Water is below Mean Lower Low with Ht. of lowest given for each period and Date of lowest in ( ):

1st: -0.3'
9th–11th: -0.3' (10th)
24th–30th: -1.2' (27th)

22nd–28th: -1.0' (25th)

Average Rise and Fall 7.1 ft.

When a high tide exceeds avg. ht., the *following* low tide will be lower than avg.

2021 HIGH & LOW WATER
KINGS POINT, NY
40°48.7'N, 73°45.9'W

Daylight Saving Time — Daylight Saving Time

DAY OF MONTH	DAY OF WEEK	JULY HIGH a.m.	Ht.	p.m.	Ht.	LOW a.m.	p.m.	DAY OF MONTH	DAY OF WEEK	AUGUST HIGH a.m.	Ht.	p.m.	Ht.	LOW a.m.	p.m.
1	**T**	5:45	7.1	**6:20**	7.4	12:01	**12:20**	1	**S**	7:02	6.4	**7:19**	7.1	1:14	**1:07**
2	**F**	6:46	6.8	**7:16**	7.4	12:59	**1:13**	2	**M**	8:02	6.4	**8:17**	7.1	2:09	**2:06**
3	**S**	7:45	6.7	**8:09**	7.5	1:55	**2:05**	3	**T**	8:57	6.5	**9:10**	7.2	3:02	**3:01**
4	**S**	8:41	6.7	**9:00**	7.5	2:49	**2:55**	4	**W**	9:48	6.7	**9:57**	7.3	3:52	**3:51**
5	**M**	9:33	6.7	**9:47**	7.6	3:39	**3:43**	5	**T**	10:33	6.9	**10:38**	7.5	4:39	**4:36**
6	**T**	10:20	6.8	**10:29**	7.6	4:27	**4:28**	6	**F**	11:12	7.1	**11:10**	7.6	5:21	**5:13**
7	**W**	11:04	7.0	**11:07**	7.6	5:11	**5:09**	7	**S**	11:46	7.2	**11:35**	7.8	5:58	**5:43**
8	**T**	11:43	7.1	**11:37**	7.7	5:52	**5:43**	8	**S**	...	...	**12:11**	7.4	6:30	**6:13**
9	**F**	-A-		**11:58**	7.7	6:28	**6:06**	9	**M**	12:03	8.0	**12:36**	7.7	6:54	**6:48**
10	**S**	...	...	**12:44**	7.2	6:59	**6:31**	10	**T**	12:38	8.2	**1:09**	7.9	7:20	**7:28**
11	**S**	12:23	7.8	**1:06**	7.2	7:21	**7:05**	11	**W**	1:19	8.3	**1:48**	8.2	7:54	**8:11**
12	**M**	12:58	7.9	**1:36**	7.4	7:45	**7:44**	12	**T**	2:04	8.2	**2:32**	8.4	8:33	**8:59**
13	**T**	1:38	8.0	**2:14**	7.6	8:18	**8:28**	13	**F**	2:52	8.0	**3:19**	8.5	9:16	**9:51**
14	**W**	2:23	8.0	**2:57**	7.8	8:58	**9:16**	14	**S**	3:44	7.8	**4:10**	8.5	10:05	**10:50**
15	**T**	3:11	7.9	**3:44**	8.0	9:42	**10:08**	15	**S**	4:40	7.4	**5:06**	8.3	10:59	...
16	**F**	4:02	7.7	**4:34**	8.1	10:30	**11:06**	16	**M**	5:45	7.1	**6:10**	8.1	12:06	**12:03**
17	**S**	4:58	7.5	**5:29**	8.2	11:23	...	17	**T**	7:07	6.9	**7:29**	8.1	1:40	**1:29**
18	**S**	5:59	7.2	**6:29**	8.3	12:12	**12:21**	18	**W**	8:35	7.0	**8:53**	8.1	2:54	**3:01**
19	**M**	7:10	7.1	**7:36**	8.4	1:33	**1:26**	19	**T**	9:43	7.3	**10:00**	8.4	3:57	**4:09**
20	**T**	8:29	7.1	**8:46**	8.5	2:57	**2:43**	20	**F**	10:40	7.7	**10:56**	8.5	4:53	**5:07**
21	**W**	9:42	7.3	**9:53**	8.7	4:04	**4:03**	21	**S**	11:31	8.0	**11:47**	8.6	5:44	**6:00**
22	**T**	10:43	7.6	**10:54**	8.8	5:03	**5:09**	22	**S**	...	...	**12:19**	8.1	6:31	**6:48**
23	**F**	11:38	7.8	**11:50**	8.8	5:58	**6:06**	23	**M**	12:34	8.5	**1:03**	8.2	7:16	**7:35**
24	**S**	...	...	**12:31**	7.9	6:48	**6:59**	24	**T**	1:19	8.3	**1:46**	8.2	7:57	**8:19**
25	**S**	12:43	8.7	**1:22**	8.0	7:37	**7:50**	25	**W**	2:02	8.0	**2:25**	8.0	8:34	**9:02**
26	**M**	1:35	8.5	**2:12**	8.0	8:23	**8:41**	26	**T**	2:44	7.6	**3:02**	7.8	9:03	**9:45**
27	**T**	2:26	8.2	**3:01**	7.9	9:09	**9:32**	27	**F**	3:26	7.2	**3:36**	7.6	9:17	**10:30**
28	**W**	3:16	7.8	**3:49**	7.8	9:54	**10:26**	28	**S**	4:10	6.9	**4:10**	7.3	9:45	**11:21**
29	**T**	4:07	7.3	**4:37**	7.6	10:38	**11:21**	29	**S**	5:01	6.5	**4:51**	7.1	10:26	...
30	**F**	5:01	6.9	**5:27**	7.4	11:23	...	30	**M**	6:04	6.3	**5:43**	6.8	12:21	**-B-**
31	**S**	5:59	6.6	**6:21**	7.2	12:18	**12:12**	31	**T**	7:15	6.2	**7:07**	6.7	1:22	**12:17**

A also at 12:18 p.m. (7.1) **B** also at 11:16 a.m.

Dates when Ht. of **Low** Water is below Mean Lower Low with Ht. of lowest given for each period and Date of lowest in ( ):

21st–27th: -0.8' (24th)

10th–12th: -0.2'
20th–24th: -0.6' (22nd)

Average Rise and Fall 7.1 ft.

When a high tide exceeds avg. ht., the *following* low tide will be lower than avg.

2021 HIGH & LOW WATER KINGS POINT, NY

40°48.7'N, 73°45.9'W

DAY OF MONTH	DAY OF WEEK	SEPTEMBER (Daylight Saving Time)						DAY OF MONTH	DAY OF WEEK	OCTOBER (Daylight Saving Time)					
		HIGH				LOW				HIGH				LOW	
		a.m.	Ht.	**p.m.**	Ht.	a.m.	**p.m.**			a.m.	Ht.	**p.m.**	Ht.	a.m.	**p.m.**
1	W	8:19	6.3	**8:26**	6.8	2:20	**1:41**	1	F	8:25	6.6	**8:17**	6.9	2:23	**1:55**
2	T	9:11	6.6	**9:20**	7.1	3:13	**3:06**	2	S	9:11	6.9	**9:11**	7.3	3:13	**3:06**
3	F	9:57	6.9	**10:02**	7.4	4:01	**3:56**	3	S	9:48	7.4	**9:52**	7.7	3:55	**3:58**
4	S	10:35	7.2	**10:35**	7.7	4:44	**4:37**	4	M	10:20	7.9	**10:31**	8.1	4:31	**4:42**
5	S	11:06	7.5	**11:05**	8.0	5:20	**5:14**	5	T	10:53	8.5	**11:11**	8.4	5:04	**5:25**
6	M	11:32	7.9	**11:38**	8.3	5:50	**5:50**	6	W	11:30	8.9	**11:54**	8.5	5:39	**6:08**
7	T	...	...	**12:03**	8.3	6:18	**6:29**	7	T	...	...	**12:11**	9.2	6:17	**6:52**
8	W	12:16	8.4	**12:40**	8.6	6:49	**7:10**	8	F	12:39	8.4	**12:55**	9.4	6:59	**7:39**
9	T	12:59	8.4	**1:21**	8.9	7:26	**7:54**	9	S	1:27	8.2	**1:43**	9.2	7:44	**8:30**
10	F	1:45	8.3	**2:06**	8.9	8:07	**8:43**	10	S	2:19	7.9	**2:35**	8.9	8:33	**9:30**
11	S	2:34	8.0	**2:55**	8.8	8:53	**9:37**	11	M	3:17	7.6	**3:33**	8.5	9:30	**10:51**
12	S	3:28	7.7	**3:49**	8.6	9:44	**10:44**	12	T	4:26	7.2	**4:42**	8.0	10:47	...
13	M	4:28	7.3	**4:49**	8.2	10:44	...	13	W	5:56	7.0	**6:17**	7.6	12:15	**12:33**
14	T	5:44	7.0	**6:06**	7.9	12:18	**12:12**	14	T	7:19	7.1	**7:43**	7.6	1:25	**1:48**
15	W	7:21	6.9	**7:43**	7.8	1:38	**1:52**	15	F	8:26	7.4	**8:49**	7.7	2:27	**2:51**
16	T	8:37	7.2	**8:58**	7.9	2:44	**3:03**	16	S	9:22	7.8	**9:45**	7.9	3:23	**3:48**
17	F	9:37	7.6	**9:58**	8.2	3:43	**4:03**	17	S	10:12	8.1	**10:33**	8.0	4:14	**4:40**
18	S	10:30	7.9	**10:49**	8.3	4:36	**4:57**	18	M	10:56	8.4	**11:18**	8.0	5:01	**5:28**
19	S	11:17	8.2	**11:36**	8.4	5:25	**5:46**	19	T	11:37	8.5	**11:59**	7.9	5:43	**6:12**
20	M	...	...	**12:01**	8.4	6:09	**6:32**	20	W	...	...	**12:13**	8.4	6:22	**6:53**
21	T	12:18	8.2	**12:39**	8.4	6:50	**7:15**	21	T	12:37	7.7	**12:43**	8.2	6:55	**7:30**
22	W	12:59	8.0	**1:15**	8.3	7:26	**7:55**	22	F	1:12	7.4	**1:07**	8.0	7:13	**8:01**
23	T	1:36	7.7	**1:45**	8.1	7:53	**8:30**	23	S	1:44	7.2	**1:26**	7.8	7:20	**8:15**
24	F	2:12	7.4	**2:10**	7.9	8:02	**8:57**	24	S	2:11	7.0	**1:55**	7.6	7:48	**8:31**
25	S	2:46	7.1	**2:36**	7.6	8:23	**9:13**	25	M	2:40	6.8	**2:32**	7.3	8:26	**9:06**
26	S	3:20	6.8	**3:11**	7.4	8:59	**9:45**	26	T	3:18	6.6	**3:15**	7.1	9:11	**9:51**
27	M	4:00	6.6	**3:53**	7.1	9:43	**10:31**	27	W	4:02	6.4	**4:04**	6.9	10:01	**10:44**
28	T	4:48	6.3	**4:42**	6.8	10:34	**11:30**	28	T	4:54	6.4	**4:58**	6.8	10:57	**11:45**
29	W	5:53	6.2	**5:39**	6.7	11:32	...	29	F	5:54	6.4	**5:59**	6.8	11:59	...
30	T	7:22	6.3	**6:51**	6.7	1:18	**12:38**	30	S	7:02	6.6	**7:06**	6.9	12:52	**1:07**
								31	S	8:04	7.1	**8:13**	7.2	1:57	**2:16**

Dates when Ht. of **Low** Water is below Mean Lower Low with Ht. of lowest given for each period and Date of lowest in ( ):

7th–10th: -0.4' (8th, 9th)
18th–21st: -0.4' (19th, 20th)

5th–10th: -0.8' (7th, 8th)
17th–20th: -0.4' (19th)

Average Rise and Fall 7.1 ft.

When a high tide exceeds avg. ht., the *following* low tide will be lower than avg.

2021 HIGH & LOW WATER KINGS POINT, NY

40°48.7'N, 73°45.9'W

***Standard Time starts Nov. 7 at 2 a.m.** **Standard Time**

DAY OF MONTH	DAY OF WEEK	NOVEMBER						DAY OF MONTH	DAY OF WEEK	DECEMBER					
		HIGH				LOW				HIGH				LOW	
		a.m.	Ht.	**p.m.**	Ht.	a.m.	**p.m.**			a.m.	Ht.	**p.m.**	Ht.	a.m.	**p.m.**
1	**M**	8:53	7.7	**9:09**	7.6	2:50	**3:19**	1	**W**	7:58	8.4	**8:30**	7.6	1:50	**2:47**
2	**T**	9:35	8.3	**9:59**	7.9	3:36	**4:12**	2	**T**	8:48	8.9	**9:24**	7.8	2:44	**3:45**
3	**W**	10:18	8.8	**10:46**	8.2	4:20	**5:02**	3	**F**	9:38	9.2	**10:16**	7.9	3:38	**4:39**
4	**T**	11:01	9.3	**11:32**	8.3	5:04	**5:50**	4	**S**	10:28	9.3	**11:08**	7.9	4:30	**5:32**
5	**F**	11:46	9.5	...	...	5:50	**6:39**	5	**S**	11:19	9.2	...	...	5:24	**6:26**
6	**S**	12:21	8.2	**12:34**	9.5	6:36	**7:29**	6	**M**	12:03	7.8	**12:14**	8.9	6:19	**7:23**
7	**S**	1:12	8.1	***12:25**	9.2	*6:26	***7:25**	7	**T**	1:02	7.6	**1:14**	8.5	7:20	**8:24**
8	**M**	1:08	7.8	**1:21**	8.8	7:21	**8:31**	8	**W**	2:07	7.4	**2:20**	8.0	8:32	**9:28**
9	**T**	2:12	7.4	**2:25**	8.2	8:28	**9:46**	9	**T**	3:17	7.2	**3:34**	7.6	9:50	**10:32**
10	**W**	3:29	7.2	**3:44**	7.7	10:02	**10:58**	10	**F**	4:26	7.2	**4:48**	7.2	11:01	**11:33**
11	**T**	4:49	7.1	**5:11**	7.4	11:23	...	11	**S**	5:32	7.2	**5:56**	7.0	...	**12:06**
12	**F**	6:01	7.2	**6:25**	7.3	12:03	**12:31**	12	**S**	6:33	7.4	**6:59**	6.8	12:30	**1:06**
13	**S**	7:04	7.5	**7:28**	7.4	1:02	**1:32**	13	**M**	7:28	7.5	**7:55**	6.8	1:24	**2:01**
14	**S**	7:59	7.8	**8:23**	7.4	1:56	**2:28**	14	**T**	8:19	7.7	**8:46**	6.9	2:15	**2:53**
15	**M**	8:48	8.1	**9:12**	7.5	2:47	**3:19**	15	**W**	9:04	7.8	**9:32**	6.9	3:03	**3:41**
16	**T**	9:32	8.2	**9:56**	7.5	3:33	**4:06**	16	**T**	9:46	7.8	**10:15**	7.0	3:48	**4:25**
17	**W**	10:11	8.3	**10:37**	7.4	4:16	**4:49**	17	**F**	10:24	7.7	**10:55**	6.9	4:28	**5:06**
18	**T**	10:47	8.2	**11:16**	7.3	4:54	**5:30**	18	**S**	10:57	7.6	**11:31**	6.9	5:04	**5:44**
19	**F**	11:17	8.0	**11:51**	7.1	5:27	**6:06**	19	**S**	11:22	7.5	...	...	5:29	**6:16**
20	**S**	11:38	7.8	...	...	5:44	**6:37**	20	**M**	12:03	6.8	**-B-**		5:40	**6:38**
21	**S**	12:22	6.9	**-A-**		5:54	**6:51**	21	**T**	12:26	6.7	**12:06**	7.4	6:07	**6:52**
22	**M**	12:45	6.8	**12:25**	7.4	6:23	**7:06**	22	**W**	12:48	6.7	**12:42**	7.3	6:43	**7:21**
23	**T**	1:11	6.7	**1:03**	7.3	7:02	**7:40**	23	**T**	1:20	6.7	**1:23**	7.3	7:25	**7:59**
24	**W**	1:47	6.6	**1:46**	7.2	7:45	**8:23**	24	**F**	2:00	6.8	**2:09**	7.2	8:10	**8:43**
25	**T**	2:29	6.5	**2:34**	7.1	8:34	**9:12**	25	**S**	2:45	6.9	**2:58**	7.1	9:01	**9:31**
26	**F**	3:17	6.6	**3:26**	7.0	9:27	**10:05**	26	**S**	3:34	7.1	**3:52**	7.0	9:56	**10:22**
27	**S**	4:10	6.7	**4:22**	6.9	10:26	**11:01**	27	**M**	4:27	7.3	**4:50**	6.9	10:57	**11:17**
28	**S**	5:06	6.9	**5:24**	6.9	11:29	**11:59**	28	**T**	5:24	7.6	**5:54**	6.8	...	**12:03**
29	**M**	6:05	7.3	**6:28**	7.1	...	**12:37**	29	**W**	6:25	7.9	**7:02**	6.9	12:15	**1:17**
30	**T**	7:03	7.8	**7:32**	7.3	12:55	**1:44**	30	**T**	7:26	8.2	**8:09**	7.1	1:16	**2:32**
								31	**F**	8:26	8.6	**9:12**	7.2	2:20	**3:37**

A also at 11:56 a.m. (7.6) **B** also at 11:39 a.m. (7.4)

Dates when Ht. of **Low** Water is below Mean Lower Low with Ht. of lowest given for each period and Date of lowest in ( ):

2nd–8th: -1.2' (5th)
15th–19th: -0.4' (16th–18th)

1st–9th: -1.3' (4th)
14th–18th: -0.4' (16th)
30th–31st: -0.9' (31st)

Average Rise and Fall 7.1 ft.

When a high tide exceeds avg. ht., the *following* low tide will be lower than avg.

2021 CURRENT TABLE
HELL GATE, NY (EAST RIVER)
40°46.7'N, 73°56.3'W Off Mill Rock

		JANUARY (Standard Time)								FEBRUARY (Standard Time)					
		CURRENT TURNS TO								CURRENT TURNS TO					
		NORTHEAST Flood Starts			SOUTHWEST Ebb Starts					NORTHEAST Flood Starts			SOUTHWEST Ebb Starts		
DAY OF MONTH	DAY OF WEEK	a.m.	**p.m.**	Kts.	a.m.	**p.m.**	Kts.	DAY OF MONTH	DAY OF WEEK	a.m.	**p.m.**	Kts.	a.m.	**p.m.**	Kts.
1	F	5:13	**5:48**	a3.5	11:12	**11:36**	a5.0	1	M	6:25	**6:48**	a3.7	12:01	**12:24**	5.0
2	S	5:54	**6:30**	a3.5	11:54	...	5.0	2	T	7:12	**7:36**	a3.6	12:48	**1:18**	a5.0
3	S	6:42	**7:12**	a3.5	12:18	**12:42**	p4.9	3	W	8:06	**8:30**	a3.5	1:36	**2:12**	a4.9
4	M	7:30	**8:06**	a3.4	1:06	**1:36**	4.8	4	T	9:12	**9:36**	3.3	2:36	**3:12**	a4.8
5	T	8:30	**9:00**	a3.3	2:00	**2:30**	a4.8	5	F	10:18	**10:42**	p3.2	3:36	**4:12**	a4.6
6	W	9:30	**10:00**	3.2	2:54	**3:30**	a4.7	6	S	11:24	**11:48**	p3.2	4:42	**5:24**	a4.5
7	T	10:36	**11:00**	3.2	4:00	**4:30**	a4.7	7	S	...	**12:36**	3.1	5:48	**6:24**	a4.5
8	F	11:42	...	3.2	5:00	**5:36**	a4.7	8	M	12:54	**1:36**	3.3	6:54	**7:30**	a4.6
9	S	12:06	**12:48**	3.3	6:06	**6:42**	a4.8	9	T	1:54	**2:30**	a3.5	7:54	**8:24**	a4.7
10	S	1:06	**1:48**	a3.5	7:06	**7:36**	a4.9	10	W	2:48	**3:24**	a3.6	8:48	**9:12**	a4.8
11	M	2:06	**2:48**	a3.6	8:06	**8:36**	a5.0	11	T	3:36	**4:12**	a3.7	9:36	**10:00**	4.8
12	T	3:00	**3:36**	a3.7	9:00	**9:24**	a5.0	12	F	4:24	**4:54**	a3.7	10:24	**10:48**	a4.9
13	W	3:54	**4:30**	a3.7	9:48	**10:18**	a5.0	13	S	5:12	**5:36**	a3.7	11:12	**11:30**	a4.8
14	T	4:42	**5:18**	a3.7	10:42	**11:06**	a5.0	14	S	5:54	**6:18**	a3.6	11:54	...	4.7
15	F	5:36	**6:06**	a3.6	11:30	**11:54**	a4.9	15	M	6:36	**7:00**	a3.4	12:12	**12:36**	a4.7
16	S	6:24	**6:54**	a3.5	...	**12:18**	4.7	16	T	7:18	**7:42**	a3.3	12:54	**1:18**	a4.5
17	S	7:12	**7:42**	a3.3	12:42	**1:06**	a4.6	17	W	8:00	**8:24**	a3.1	1:36	**2:00**	a4.4
18	M	8:00	**8:30**	a3.1	1:24	**1:54**	4.4	18	T	8:48	**9:06**	a2.9	2:18	**2:48**	a4.2
19	T	8:48	**9:18**	a2.9	2:12	**2:42**	a4.3	19	F	9:36	**10:00**	a2.8	3:06	**3:36**	a4.1
20	W	9:42	**10:06**	a2.8	3:00	**3:30**	4.1	20	S	10:30	**10:54**	2.7	4:00	**4:30**	a4.0
21	T	10:36	**10:54**	2.7	3:54	**4:18**	a4.1	21	S	11:30	**11:48**	p2.8	4:54	**5:24**	a4.0
22	F	11:24	**11:48**	2.7	4:42	**5:12**	a4.1	22	M	...	**12:24**	2.8	5:48	**6:18**	a4.1
23	S	...	**12:18**	2.8	5:36	**6:06**	4.1	23	T	12:42	**1:12**	3.0	6:42	**7:12**	a4.3
24	S	12:36	**1:06**	p2.9	6:24	**6:54**	a4.3	24	W	1:30	**2:00**	3.2	7:30	**8:00**	4.5
25	M	1:18	**1:54**	3.0	7:12	**7:42**	4.4	25	T	2:12	**2:48**	3.5	8:18	**8:42**	4.7
26	T	2:06	**2:36**	3.2	8:00	**8:24**	a4.6	26	F	3:00	**3:30**	3.7	9:06	**9:30**	p5.0
27	W	2:48	**3:18**	3.4	8:42	**9:06**	a4.8	27	S	3:42	**4:12**	a3.9	9:54	**10:12**	5.1
28	T	3:30	**4:00**	a3.6	9:30	**9:48**	4.9	28	S	4:30	**4:54**	a4.0	10:36	**10:54**	p5.2
29	F	4:06	**4:42**	a3.7	10:12	**10:30**	5.0								
30	S	4:54	**5:24**	a3.8	10:54	**11:18**	a5.1								
31	S	5:36	**6:06**	a3.8	11:42	...	5.1								

The Kts. (knots) columns show the **maximum** predicted velocities of the stronger one of the Flood Currents and the stronger one of the Ebb Currents for each day.
The letter "a" means the velocity shown should occur **after** the **a.m.** Current Change. The letter "p" means the velocity shown should occur **after** the **p.m.** Current Change (even if next morning). No "a" or "p" means a.m. and p.m. velocities are the same for that day.
Avg. Max. Velocity: Flood 3.4 Kts., Ebb 4.6 Kts.
Max. Flood 3 hrs. after Flood Starts, ±10 min.
Max. Ebb 3 hrs. after Ebb Starts, ±10 min.

At **City Island** the Current turns 2 hours before Hell Gate. At **Throg's Neck** the Current turns 1 hour before Hell Gate. At **Whitestone Pt.** the Current turns 25 min. before Hell Gate. At **College Pt.** the Current turns 30 min. before Hell Gate.

2021 CURRENT TABLE

HELL GATE, NY (EAST RIVER)

40°46.7'N, 73°56.3'W Off Mill Rock

***Daylight Time starts March 14 at 2 a.m.** **Daylight Saving Time**

MARCH

DAY OF MONTH	DAY OF WEEK	CURRENT TURNS TO NORTHEAST Flood Starts			CURRENT TURNS TO SOUTHWEST Ebb Starts		
		a.m.	**p.m.**	Kts.	a.m.	**p.m.**	Kts.
1	**M**	5:13	**5:36**	a4.0	11:24	**11:42**	p5.2
2	**T**	6:00	**6:24**	a3.9	...	**12:12**	5.0
3	**W**	6:54	**7:12**	a3.8	12:30	**1:00**	a5.1
4	**T**	7:48	**8:06**	3.5	1:24	**1:54**	a4.9
5	**F**	8:48	**9:12**	a3.3	2:18	**2:54**	a4.7
6	**S**	10:00	**10:18**	3.1	3:24	**4:00**	a4.4
7	**S**	11:12	**11:30**	p3.1	4:30	**5:12**	a4.3
8	**M**	...	**12:18**	3.1	5:42	**6:18**	a4.2
9	**T**	12:42	**1:18**	3.2	6:48	**7:18**	4.3
10	**W**	1:42	**2:12**	3.4	7:48	**8:12**	4.5
11	**T**	2:30	**3:00**	a3.6	8:36	**9:00**	4.6
12	**F**	3:18	**3:42**	a3.7	9:24	**9:42**	4.7
13	**S**	4:00	**4:24**	a3.7	10:06	**10:24**	p4.8
14	**S**	*5:42	***6:00**	a3.7	*11:48	...	4.7
15	**M**	6:18	**6:42**	a3.7	12:01	**12:24**	a4.8
16	**T**	7:00	**7:18**	a3.6	12:36	**1:06**	a4.7
17	**W**	7:36	**7:54**	a3.4	1:18	**1:42**	a4.6
18	**T**	8:18	**8:30**	a3.2	1:54	**2:24**	a4.5
19	**F**	9:00	**9:18**	a3.0	2:36	**3:06**	a4.3
20	**S**	9:48	**10:06**	a2.9	3:24	**3:54**	a4.2
21	**S**	10:42	**11:00**	p2.8	4:18	**4:48**	a4.1
22	**M**	11:42	...	2.7	5:12	**5:48**	a4.0
23	**T**	12:01	**12:42**	2.8	6:12	**6:42**	a4.1
24	**W**	1:00	**1:36**	p3.1	7:12	**7:36**	4.2
25	**T**	1:54	**2:24**	3.3	8:06	**8:30**	4.5
26	**F**	2:42	**3:12**	3.6	8:54	**9:18**	p4.8
27	**S**	3:30	**4:00**	3.8	9:42	**10:00**	p5.1
28	**S**	4:18	**4:42**	4.0	10:30	**10:48**	p5.2
29	**M**	5:06	**5:30**	a4.1	11:18	**11:36**	p5.3
30	**T**	5:54	**6:12**	a4.1	...	**12:06**	5.1
31	**W**	6:42	**7:00**	a4.0	12:24	**12:54**	a5.3

APRIL

DAY OF MONTH	DAY OF WEEK	CURRENT TURNS TO NORTHEAST Flood Starts			CURRENT TURNS TO SOUTHWEST Ebb Starts		
		a.m.	**p.m.**	Kts.	a.m.	**p.m.**	Kts.
1	**T**	7:37	**7:54**	a3.8	1:12	**1:48**	a5.1
2	**F**	8:36	**8:54**	3.5	2:06	**2:42**	a4.9
3	**S**	9:36	**10:00**	a3.3	3:06	**3:42**	a4.6
4	**S**	10:42	**11:12**	p3.1	4:12	**4:48**	a4.3
5	**M**	11:54	...	3.0	5:18	**6:00**	a4.1
6	**T**	12:18	**1:00**	a3.1	6:30	**7:06**	4.1
7	**W**	1:24	**2:00**	3.2	7:30	**8:00**	4.2
8	**T**	2:24	**2:54**	3.4	8:30	**8:48**	4.4
9	**F**	3:12	**3:36**	3.5	9:18	**9:36**	p4.6
10	**S**	3:54	**4:18**	3.6	10:00	**10:12**	p4.7
11	**S**	4:36	**4:54**	a3.7	10:36	**10:54**	p4.7
12	**M**	5:12	**5:30**	a3.7	11:18	**11:30**	p4.8
13	**T**	5:48	**6:06**	a3.6	11:54	...	4.6
14	**W**	6:24	**6:42**	3.5	12:06	**12:30**	a4.7
15	**T**	7:06	**7:18**	a3.4	12:42	**1:12**	a4.7
16	**F**	7:42	**7:54**	a3.3	1:24	**1:48**	a4.6
17	**S**	8:24	**8:36**	a3.1	2:00	**2:30**	a4.5
18	**S**	9:12	**9:24**	2.9	2:48	**3:18**	a4.3
19	**M**	10:00	**10:18**	p2.9	3:36	**4:12**	a4.2
20	**T**	11:00	**11:18**	p2.9	4:36	**5:06**	a4.1
21	**W**	...	**12:01**	2.9	5:36	**6:06**	4.2
22	**T**	12:24	**1:00**	3.1	6:36	**7:00**	p4.4
23	**F**	1:18	**1:48**	p3.4	7:30	**7:54**	p4.7
24	**S**	2:12	**2:42**	p3.7	8:24	**8:42**	p5.0
25	**S**	3:06	**3:30**	p3.9	9:18	**9:36**	p5.2
26	**M**	4:00	**4:18**	4.0	10:06	**10:24**	p5.3
27	**T**	4:48	**5:06**	4.1	10:54	**11:12**	p5.3
28	**W**	5:36	**5:54**	4.0	11:42	...	5.1
29	**T**	6:30	**6:48**	3.9	12:01	**12:36**	a5.3
30	**F**	7:24	**7:42**	3.7	12:54	**1:30**	a5.1

The Kts. (knots) columns show the **maximum** predicted velocities of the stronger one of the Flood Currents and the stronger one of the Ebb Currents for each day.
The letter "a" means the velocity shown should occur **after** the **a.m.** Current Change. The letter "p" means the velocity shown should occur **after** the **p.m.** Current Change (even if next morning). No "a" or "p" means a.m. and p.m. velocities are the same for that day.
Avg. Max. Velocity: Flood 3.4 Kts., Ebb 4.6 Kts.
Max. Flood 3 hrs. after Flood Starts, ±10 min.
Max. Ebb 3 hrs. after Ebb Starts, ±10 min.

See pp. 22-29 for Current Change at other points.

2021 CURRENT TABLE
HELL GATE, NY (EAST RIVER)
40°46.7'N, 73°56.3'W Off Mill Rock

Daylight Saving Time — **Daylight Saving Time**

MAY

DAY OF MONTH	DAY OF WEEK	CURRENT TURNS TO NORTHEAST Flood Starts			CURRENT TURNS TO SOUTHWEST Ebb Starts		
		a.m.	**p.m.**	Kts.	a.m.	**p.m.**	Kts.
1	**S**	8:25	**8:42**	a3.5	1:54	**2:24**	a4.8
2	**S**	9:24	**9:48**	3.2	2:54	**3:30**	a4.6
3	**M**	10:30	**11:00**	3.0	3:54	**4:30**	a4.3
4	**T**	11:42	...	3.0	5:00	**5:36**	a4.1
5	**W**	12:06	**12:42**	3.0	6:06	**6:36**	4.1
6	**T**	1:06	**1:36**	3.1	7:06	**7:30**	p4.3
7	**F**	2:00	**2:24**	3.2	8:00	**8:18**	p4.4
8	**S**	2:48	**3:06**	p3.4	8:42	**9:00**	p4.5
9	**S**	3:30	**3:48**	3.4	9:24	**9:42**	p4.6
10	**M**	4:06	**4:24**	3.5	10:06	**10:18**	p4.7
11	**T**	4:48	**5:00**	3.5	10:42	**10:54**	p4.8
12	**W**	5:24	**5:36**	3.5	11:18	**11:30**	p4.8
13	**T**	6:00	**6:12**	a3.5	...	**12:01**	4.6
14	**F**	6:36	**6:48**	a3.4	12:12	**12:36**	a4.7
15	**S**	7:18	**7:24**	a3.3	12:48	**1:18**	a4.7
16	**S**	8:00	**8:06**	3.1	1:30	**2:00**	a4.6
17	**M**	8:42	**8:54**	3.0	2:12	**2:42**	a4.5
18	**T**	9:36	**9:48**	p3.0	3:06	**3:36**	a4.4
19	**W**	10:30	**10:48**	3.0	4:00	**4:30**	a4.4
20	**T**	11:24	**11:48**	p3.2	5:00	**5:30**	4.4
21	**F**	...	**12:24**	3.2	6:00	**6:24**	p4.6
22	**S**	12:54	**1:18**	3.4	6:54	**7:18**	p4.8
23	**S**	1:48	**2:12**	p3.7	7:54	**8:12**	p5.0
24	**M**	2:42	**3:06**	p3.8	8:48	**9:06**	p5.2
25	**T**	3:36	**3:54**	3.9	9:42	**10:00**	p5.3
26	**W**	4:30	**4:48**	p4.0	10:30	**10:54**	p5.3
27	**T**	5:24	**5:42**	3.9	11:24	**11:48**	p5.2
28	**F**	6:18	**6:36**	3.8	...	**12:18**	4.9
29	**S**	7:18	**7:30**	3.6	12:42	**1:12**	a5.0
30	**S**	8:12	**8:30**	3.4	1:36	**2:12**	a4.8
31	**M**	9:12	**9:36**	3.2	2:36	**3:06**	a4.6

JUNE

DAY OF MONTH	DAY OF WEEK	CURRENT TURNS TO NORTHEAST Flood Starts			CURRENT TURNS TO SOUTHWEST Ebb Starts		
		a.m.	**p.m.**	Kts.	a.m.	**p.m.**	Kts.
1	**T**	10:13	**10:36**	3.0	3:36	**4:06**	a4.3
2	**W**	11:12	**11:42**	3.0	4:36	**5:06**	a4.2
3	**T**	...	**12:12**	3.0	5:36	**6:00**	4.1
4	**F**	12:36	**1:06**	3.0	6:30	**6:54**	p4.2
5	**S**	1:30	**1:48**	3.1	7:24	**7:42**	p4.3
6	**S**	2:18	**2:36**	p3.2	8:06	**8:24**	p4.4
7	**M**	3:00	**3:12**	p3.3	8:48	**9:06**	p4.5
8	**T**	3:36	**3:54**	3.3	9:30	**9:48**	p4.6
9	**W**	4:18	**4:30**	p3.4	10:12	**10:24**	p4.7
10	**T**	4:54	**5:06**	3.4	10:48	**11:06**	p4.8
11	**F**	5:36	**5:42**	3.4	11:30	**11:42**	p4.8
12	**S**	6:12	**6:24**	p3.4	...	**12:06**	4.6
13	**S**	6:54	**7:00**	3.3	12:24	**12:48**	a4.8
14	**M**	7:36	**7:42**	p3.3	1:06	**1:30**	a4.7
15	**T**	8:18	**8:30**	3.2	1:48	**2:12**	a4.7
16	**W**	9:06	**9:24**	p3.2	2:36	**3:06**	a4.6
17	**T**	9:54	**10:18**	p3.2	3:30	**3:54**	a4.6
18	**F**	10:54	**11:24**	p3.3	4:24	**4:54**	4.6
19	**S**	11:48	...	3.3	5:24	**5:54**	p4.7
20	**S**	12:24	**12:48**	p3.4	6:24	**6:54**	p4.8
21	**M**	1:24	**1:48**	p3.6	7:24	**7:48**	p5.0
22	**T**	2:24	**2:42**	p3.7	8:24	**8:48**	p5.1
23	**W**	3:24	**3:36**	p3.8	9:18	**9:42**	p5.2
24	**T**	4:18	**4:30**	p3.9	10:12	**10:36**	p5.2
25	**F**	5:12	**5:30**	p3.8	11:06	**11:30**	p5.1
26	**S**	6:06	**6:24**	p3.8	...	**12:01**	4.9
27	**S**	7:00	**7:18**	3.6	12:24	**12:54**	a5.0
28	**M**	7:54	**8:12**	3.4	1:18	**1:48**	a4.8
29	**T**	8:48	**9:12**	a3.3	2:12	**2:42**	a4.6
30	**W**	9:42	**10:06**	3.1	3:12	**3:36**	a4.4

The Kts. (knots) columns show the **maximum** predicted velocities of the stronger one of the Flood Currents and the stronger one of the Ebb Currents for each day.
The letter "a" means the velocity shown should occur **after** the **a.m.** Current Change. The letter "p" means the velocity shown should occur **after** the **p.m.** Current Change (even if next morning). No "a" or "p" means a.m. and p.m. velocities are the same for that day.
Avg. Max. Velocity: Flood 3.4 Kts., Ebb 4.6 Kts.
Max. Flood 3 hrs. after Flood Starts, ±10 min.
Max. Ebb 3 hrs. after Ebb Starts, ±10 min.

At **City Island** the Current turns 2 hours before Hell Gate. At **Throg's Neck** the Current turns 1 hour before Hell Gate. At **Whitestone Pt.** the Current turns 25 min. before Hell Gate. At **College Pt.** the Current turns 30 min. before Hell Gate.

2021 CURRENT TABLE
HELL GATE, NY (EAST RIVER)
40°46.7'N, 73°56.3'W Off Mill Rock

Daylight Saving Time | **Daylight Saving Time**

JULY

DAY OF MONTH	DAY OF WEEK	NORTHEAST Flood Starts a.m.	**p.m.**	Kts.	SOUTHWEST Ebb Starts a.m.	**p.m.**	Kts.
1	**T**	10:37	**11:06**	3.0	4:06	**4:30**	a4.2
2	**F**	11:30	...	2.9	5:00	**5:24**	4.1
3	**S**	12:01	**12:24**	2.9	5:54	**6:12**	p4.1
4	**S**	12:48	**1:12**	2.9	6:42	**7:00**	p4.1
5	**M**	1:36	**1:54**	3.0	7:30	**7:48**	p4.3
6	**T**	2:24	**2:36**	p3.1	8:18	**8:36**	p4.4
7	**W**	3:06	**3:18**	p3.2	9:00	**9:18**	p4.5
8	**T**	3:48	**4:00**	p3.3	9:42	**10:00**	p4.6
9	**F**	4:30	**4:36**	p3.4	10:24	**10:42**	p4.7
10	**S**	5:06	**5:18**	p3.5	11:06	**11:18**	p4.8
11	**S**	5:48	**5:54**	p3.5	11:42	...	4.7
12	**M**	6:30	**6:36**	p3.5	12:01	**12:24**	a4.8
13	**T**	7:06	**7:18**	p3.5	12:42	**1:06**	a4.8
14	**W**	7:48	**8:06**	p3.5	1:30	**1:48**	a4.8
15	**T**	8:36	**8:54**	3.4	2:18	**2:36**	4.7
16	**F**	9:24	**9:54**	3.4	3:06	**3:30**	4.7
17	**S**	10:18	**10:54**	3.3	4:00	**4:30**	p4.7
18	**S**	11:18	...	3.4	5:00	**5:30**	p4.7
19	**M**	12:01	**12:18**	p3.4	6:06	**6:30**	p4.7
20	**T**	1:06	**1:24**	p3.5	7:06	**7:36**	p4.8
21	**W**	2:06	**2:24**	p3.6	8:06	**8:36**	p4.8
22	**T**	3:06	**3:24**	p3.7	9:06	**9:30**	p4.9
23	**F**	4:06	**4:18**	p3.8	10:00	**10:30**	p5.0
24	**S**	5:00	**5:12**	p3.8	10:54	**11:18**	p4.9
25	**S**	5:48	**6:06**	p3.8	11:48	...	4.8
26	**M**	6:36	**6:54**	p3.7	12:12	**12:36**	a4.9
27	**T**	7:24	**7:48**	3.5	1:00	**1:24**	a4.7
28	**W**	8:12	**8:36**	3.4	1:54	**2:12**	a4.6
29	**T**	9:00	**9:24**	3.2	2:42	**3:00**	a4.4
30	**F**	9:54	**10:18**	3.0	3:30	**3:54**	a4.2
31	**S**	10:42	**11:06**	2.9	4:18	**4:42**	4.0

AUGUST

DAY OF MONTH	DAY OF WEEK	NORTHEAST Flood Starts a.m.	**p.m.**	Kts.	SOUTHWEST Ebb Starts a.m.	**p.m.**	Kts.
1	**S**	11:31	...	2.8	5:12	**5:36**	3.9
2	**M**	12:01	**12:24**	2.8	6:06	**6:24**	p3.9
3	**T**	12:54	**1:12**	p2.9	6:54	**7:18**	p4.0
4	**W**	1:42	**2:00**	p3.1	7:42	**8:06**	p4.2
5	**T**	2:30	**2:42**	p3.2	8:30	**8:48**	p4.4
6	**F**	3:18	**3:24**	p3.4	9:18	**9:36**	p4.5
7	**S**	4:00	**4:06**	p3.5	10:00	**10:18**	p4.7
8	**S**	4:36	**4:48**	p3.7	10:42	**11:00**	p4.8
9	**M**	5:18	**5:30**	p3.8	11:18	**11:42**	p4.9
10	**T**	5:54	**6:12**	p3.8	...	**12:01**	4.9
11	**W**	6:36	**6:54**	p3.8	12:24	**12:42**	4.9
12	**T**	7:18	**7:42**	3.7	1:12	**1:30**	4.9
13	**F**	8:06	**8:30**	3.6	1:54	**2:18**	4.8
14	**S**	8:54	**9:24**	3.5	2:48	**3:06**	4.7
15	**S**	9:48	**10:30**	a3.4	3:42	**4:06**	p4.6
16	**M**	10:48	**11:36**	a3.4	4:42	**5:12**	p4.5
17	**T**	...	**12:01**	3.3	5:48	**6:18**	p4.4
18	**W**	12:48	**1:06**	p3.4	6:54	**7:24**	p4.5
19	**T**	1:54	**2:12**	p3.6	8:00	**8:30**	p4.6
20	**F**	2:54	**3:12**	p3.7	9:00	**9:24**	p4.7
21	**S**	3:48	**4:06**	p3.8	9:54	**10:18**	p4.8
22	**S**	4:36	**4:54**	p3.9	10:42	**11:06**	p4.8
23	**M**	5:24	**5:42**	p3.9	11:30	**11:54**	4.8
24	**T**	6:12	**6:30**	p3.8	...	**12:12**	4.7
25	**W**	6:54	**7:12**	3.6	12:42	**1:00**	a4.7
26	**T**	7:36	**7:54**	3.5	1:24	**1:42**	4.5
27	**F**	8:18	**8:42**	3.3	2:06	**2:24**	4.3
28	**S**	9:00	**9:24**	3.1	2:54	**3:12**	4.1
29	**S**	9:48	**10:18**	2.9	3:42	**4:00**	3.9
30	**M**	10:36	**11:12**	2.8	4:30	**4:54**	3.8
31	**T**	11:30	...	2.8	5:24	**5:48**	p3.8

The Kts. (knots) columns show the **maximum** predicted velocities of the stronger one of the Flood Currents and the stronger one of the Ebb Currents for each day.
The letter "a" means the velocity shown should occur **after** the **a.m.** Current Change. The letter "p" means the velocity shown should occur **after** the **p.m.** Current Change (even if next morning). No "a" or "p" means a.m. and p.m. velocities are the same for that day.
Avg. Max. Velocity: Flood 3.4 Kts., Ebb 4.6 Kts.
Max. Flood 3 hrs. after Flood Starts, ±10 min.
Max. Ebb 3 hrs. after Ebb Starts, ±10 min.

See pp. 22-29 for Current Change at other points.

2021 CURRENT TABLE
HELL GATE, NY (EAST RIVER)
40°46.7'N, 73°56.3'W Off Mill Rock

Daylight Saving Time

SEPTEMBER

DAY OF MONTH	DAY OF WEEK	CURRENT TURNS TO NORTHEAST Flood Starts			CURRENT TURNS TO SOUTHWEST Ebb Starts		
		a.m.	**p.m.**	Kts.	a.m.	**p.m.**	Kts.
1	**W**	12:07	**12:24**	p2.9	6:18	**6:42**	p3.9
2	**T**	1:00	**1:18**	p3.0	7:12	**7:36**	p4.0
3	**F**	1:54	**2:06**	p3.2	8:00	**8:24**	p4.3
4	**S**	2:42	**2:54**	p3.5	8:48	**9:12**	p4.5
5	**S**	3:24	**3:36**	p3.7	9:30	**9:54**	p4.7
6	**M**	4:06	**4:18**	p3.9	10:12	**10:36**	p4.9
7	**T**	4:48	**5:00**	p4.0	10:54	**11:18**	p5.0
8	**W**	5:24	**5:42**	p4.0	11:36	...	5.0
9	**T**	6:06	**6:30**	p4.0	12:06	**12:18**	p5.1
10	**F**	6:48	**7:18**	3.9	12:48	**1:06**	p5.0
11	**S**	7:36	**8:12**	a3.8	1:36	**1:54**	p4.9
12	**S**	8:30	**9:06**	a3.6	2:30	**2:54**	p4.7
13	**M**	9:24	**10:12**	a3.4	3:30	**3:54**	p4.5
14	**T**	10:36	**11:24**	a3.3	4:30	**5:00**	p4.3
15	**W**	11:48	...	3.2	5:42	**6:12**	p4.2
16	**T**	12:36	**1:00**	p3.3	6:48	**7:18**	p4.2
17	**F**	1:42	**2:00**	p3.5	7:48	**8:18**	p4.4
18	**S**	2:36	**3:00**	p3.7	8:48	**9:12**	p4.5
19	**S**	3:30	**3:48**	p3.8	9:36	**10:00**	4.6
20	**M**	4:18	**4:36**	p3.9	10:24	**10:48**	4.7
21	**T**	5:00	**5:18**	p3.9	11:06	**11:30**	4.7
22	**W**	5:36	**6:00**	3.8	11:48	...	4.7
23	**T**	6:18	**6:36**	3.7	12:12	**12:24**	p4.7
24	**F**	6:54	**7:18**	3.5	12:54	**1:06**	4.5
25	**S**	7:36	**8:00**	a3.4	1:30	**1:48**	p4.4
26	**S**	8:12	**8:42**	a3.2	2:18	**2:30**	p4.2
27	**M**	9:00	**9:30**	a3.0	3:00	**3:18**	4.0
28	**T**	9:48	**10:24**	2.8	3:54	**4:12**	p3.9
29	**W**	10:42	**11:24**	2.8	4:48	**5:06**	p3.8
30	**T**	11:42	...	2.8	5:42	**6:06**	p3.9

Daylight Saving Time

OCTOBER

DAY OF MONTH	DAY OF WEEK	CURRENT TURNS TO NORTHEAST Flood Starts			CURRENT TURNS TO SOUTHWEST Ebb Starts		
		a.m.	**p.m.**	Kts.	a.m.	**p.m.**	Kts.
1	**F**	12:19	**12:42**	p3.0	6:36	**7:00**	p4.0
2	**S**	1:12	**1:30**	p3.3	7:30	**7:54**	p4.3
3	**S**	2:06	**2:24**	p3.5	8:12	**8:42**	p4.5
4	**M**	2:48	**3:06**	p3.8	9:00	**9:24**	p4.8
5	**T**	3:30	**3:54**	p4.0	9:42	**10:12**	4.9
6	**W**	4:18	**4:36**	p4.1	10:24	**10:54**	a5.1
7	**T**	5:00	**5:24**	4.1	11:12	**11:42**	a5.2
8	**F**	5:42	**6:12**	a4.1	11:54	...	5.2
9	**S**	6:30	**7:00**	a4.0	12:30	**12:42**	p5.1
10	**S**	7:18	**7:54**	a3.8	1:18	**1:36**	p4.9
11	**M**	8:12	**8:54**	a3.6	2:12	**2:36**	p4.7
12	**T**	9:18	**10:06**	a3.4	3:12	**3:36**	p4.4
13	**W**	10:24	**11:18**	a3.2	4:18	**4:48**	p4.2
14	**T**	11:42	...	3.1	5:30	**6:00**	p4.1
15	**F**	12:24	**12:48**	p3.3	6:36	**7:06**	p4.2
16	**S**	1:30	**1:54**	p3.4	7:36	**8:06**	p4.3
17	**S**	2:24	**2:42**	p3.6	8:24	**8:54**	p4.5
18	**M**	3:12	**3:30**	p3.7	9:12	**9:42**	4.6
19	**T**	3:54	**4:12**	3.7	9:54	**10:18**	a4.7
20	**W**	4:30	**4:54**	3.7	10:36	**11:00**	a4.7
21	**T**	5:12	**5:30**	3.7	11:12	**11:36**	a4.7
22	**F**	5:48	**6:12**	3.6	11:54	...	4.7
23	**S**	6:24	**6:48**	a3.5	12:18	**12:30**	p4.6
24	**S**	7:00	**7:24**	a3.4	12:54	**1:06**	p4.5
25	**M**	7:36	**8:06**	a3.2	1:36	**1:48**	p4.4
26	**T**	8:24	**8:54**	a3.0	2:18	**2:36**	p4.2
27	**W**	9:12	**9:48**	a2.9	3:06	**3:24**	p4.1
28	**T**	10:06	**10:48**	2.8	4:00	**4:24**	p4.0
29	**F**	11:06	**11:42**	p2.9	4:54	**5:18**	p4.0
30	**S**	...	**12:06**	3.0	5:54	**6:18**	p4.2
31	**S**	12:36	**1:00**	p3.2	6:42	**7:12**	p4.4

The Kts. (knots) columns show the **maximum** predicted velocities of the stronger one of the Flood Currents and the stronger one of the Ebb Currents for each day.
The letter "a" means the velocity shown should occur **after** the **a.m.** Current Change. The letter "p" means the velocity shown should occur **after** the **p.m.** Current Change (even if next morning). No "a" or "p" means a.m. and p.m. velocities are the same for that day.
Avg. Max. Velocity: Flood 3.4 Kts., Ebb 4.6 Kts.
Max. Flood 3 hrs. after Flood Starts, ±10 min.
Max. Ebb 3 hrs. after Ebb Starts, ±10 min.

At **City Island** the Current turns 2 hours before Hell Gate. At **Throg's Neck** the Current turns 1 hour before Hell Gate. At **Whitestone Pt.** the Current turns 25 min. before Hell Gate. At **College Pt.** the Current turns 30 min. before Hell Gate.

2021 CURRENT TABLE
HELL GATE, NY (EAST RIVER)
40°46.7'N, 73°56.3'W Off Mill Rock

***Standard Time starts Nov. 7 at 2 a.m.** — **Standard Time**

NOVEMBER								DECEMBER							
DAY OF MONTH	DAY OF WEEK	CURRENT TURNS TO						DAY OF MONTH	DAY OF WEEK	CURRENT TURNS TO					
		NORTHEAST Flood Starts			SOUTHWEST Ebb Starts					NORTHEAST Flood Starts			SOUTHWEST Ebb Starts		
		a.m.	**p.m.**	Kts.	a.m.	**p.m.**	Kts.			a.m.	**p.m.**	Kts.	a.m.	**p.m.**	Kts.
1	**M**	1:31	**1:54**	p3.5	7:36	**8:00**	p4.6	1	**W**	12:49	**1:18**	p3.6	6:48	**7:18**	a5.0
2	**T**	2:18	**2:42**	p3.7	8:24	**8:54**	p4.9	2	**T**	1:36	**2:12**	p3.8	7:42	**8:12**	a5.2
3	**W**	3:06	**3:30**	p3.9	9:12	**9:42**	a5.1	3	**F**	2:30	**3:06**	3.9	8:30	**9:00**	a5.3
4	**T**	3:48	**4:18**	4.0	9:54	**10:30**	a5.3	4	**S**	3:18	**4:00**	a4.0	9:24	**9:54**	a5.4
5	**F**	4:36	**5:06**	a4.1	10:42	**11:18**	a5.3	5	**S**	4:12	**4:48**	a4.0	10:18	**10:48**	a5.3
6	**S**	5:24	**6:00**	a4.1	11:36	...	5.3	6	**M**	5:06	**5:48**	a3.9	11:06	**11:42**	a5.2
7	**S**	*5:12	***5:54**	a4.0	12:06	**-A-**	5.0	7	**T**	6:00	**6:42**	a3.7	...	**12:06**	5.0
8	**M**	6:06	**6:48**	a3.8	12:01	**12:18**	p5.0	8	**W**	7:00	**7:42**	a3.5	12:36	**1:00**	p4.8
9	**T**	7:06	**7:48**	a3.5	12:54	**1:18**	p4.7	9	**T**	8:00	**8:42**	a3.3	1:36	**2:00**	4.5
10	**W**	8:12	**9:00**	a3.3	1:54	**2:24**	4.4	10	**F**	9:06	**9:48**	a3.1	2:36	**3:06**	4.3
11	**T**	9:24	**10:06**	a3.1	3:00	**3:30**	p4.2	11	**S**	10:12	**10:48**	a3.0	3:36	**4:06**	4.2
12	**F**	10:30	**11:12**	a3.1	4:06	**4:36**	4.1	12	**S**	11:18	**11:42**	3.0	4:36	**5:06**	4.2
13	**S**	11:36	...	3.1	5:12	**5:42**	p4.2	13	**M**	...	**12:12**	3.0	5:30	**6:00**	a4.3
14	**S**	12:12	**12:36**	p3.3	6:06	**6:36**	4.3	14	**T**	12:36	**1:00**	p3.1	6:18	**6:48**	4.3
15	**M**	1:00	**1:30**	p3.4	6:54	**7:24**	4.4	15	**W**	1:18	**1:48**	p3.2	7:06	**7:36**	4.4
16	**T**	1:48	**2:12**	3.4	7:42	**8:06**	a4.6	16	**T**	2:00	**2:30**	3.2	7:48	**8:18**	a4.5
17	**W**	2:30	**2:54**	3.5	8:24	**8:48**	a4.7	17	**F**	2:42	**3:06**	3.3	8:30	**8:54**	a4.6
18	**T**	3:06	**3:30**	3.5	9:00	**9:30**	a4.7	18	**S**	3:18	**3:48**	3.3	9:12	**9:36**	a4.7
19	**F**	3:42	**4:12**	3.5	9:42	**10:06**	a4.8	19	**S**	4:00	**4:24**	a3.4	9:48	**10:12**	a4.8
20	**S**	4:18	**4:48**	a3.5	10:18	**10:42**	a4.8	20	**M**	4:36	**5:06**	a3.4	10:30	**10:54**	a4.8
21	**S**	5:00	**5:24**	3.4	10:54	**11:24**	a4.7	21	**T**	5:12	**5:42**	a3.4	11:06	**11:30**	a4.8
22	**M**	5:36	**6:06**	a3.3	11:36	...	4.7	22	**W**	5:48	**6:24**	a3.3	11:48	...	4.8
23	**T**	6:12	**6:48**	a3.2	12:01	**12:18**	p4.6	23	**T**	6:30	**7:06**	a3.2	12:12	**12:30**	p4.7
24	**W**	6:54	**7:30**	a3.1	12:42	**1:00**	p4.5	24	**F**	7:12	**7:48**	a3.2	12:54	**1:12**	p4.6
25	**T**	7:42	**8:18**	a3.0	1:30	**1:48**	p4.4	25	**S**	8:00	**8:36**	a3.1	1:36	**2:00**	p4.6
26	**F**	8:30	**9:12**	a2.9	2:18	**2:36**	p4.3	26	**S**	8:54	**9:24**	a3.1	2:24	**2:54**	4.5
27	**S**	9:30	**10:06**	2.9	3:06	**3:36**	p4.3	27	**M**	9:54	**10:24**	3.1	3:18	**3:54**	a4.6
28	**S**	10:30	**11:00**	p3.1	4:00	**4:30**	p4.4	28	**T**	10:54	**11:18**	p3.3	4:18	**4:54**	a4.7
29	**M**	11:30	**11:54**	p3.3	5:00	**5:30**	4.5	29	**W**	...	**12:01**	3.3	5:18	**5:54**	a4.8
30	**T**	...	**12:24**	3.4	5:54	**6:24**	4.7	30	**T**	12:18	**1:00**	3.4	6:18	**6:48**	a4.9
								31	**F**	1:12	**1:54**	3.6	7:12	**7:48**	a5.1

A also at *11:24 a.m. 5.2

The Kts. (knots) columns show the **maximum** predicted velocities of the stronger one of the Flood Currents and the stronger one of the Ebb Currents for each day.
The letter "a" means the velocity shown should occur **after** the **a.m.** Current Change. The letter "p" means the velocity shown should occur **after** the **p.m.** Current Change (even if next morning). No "a" or "p" means a.m. and p.m. velocities are the same for that day.
Avg. Max. Velocity: Flood 3.4 Kts., Ebb 4.6 Kts.
Max. Flood 3 hrs. after Flood Starts, ±10 min.
Max. Ebb 3 hrs. after Ebb Starts, ±10 min.

See pp. 22-29 for Current Change at other points.

2021 CURRENT TABLE
THE NARROWS

40°36.36'N, 74°02.29'W

Standard Time

JANUARY

DAY OF MONTH	DAY OF WEEK	CURRENT TURNS TO NORTH Flood Starts a.m.	p.m.	Kts.	CURRENT TURNS TO SOUTH Ebb Starts a.m.	p.m.	Kts.
1	F	5:25	**6:24**	a1.7	11:00	**11:24**	1.9
2	S	6:12	**7:06**	a1.8	11:48	...	2.0
3	S	7:00	**7:48**	a1.7	12:12	**12:36**	2.0
4	M	8:00	**8:42**	a1.6	1:06	**1:24**	p2.1
5	T	9:00	**9:36**	a1.4	2:00	**2:18**	2.0
6	W	10:06	**10:36**	p1.3	2:54	**3:12**	2.0
7	T	11:18	**11:30**	p1.3	4:00	**4:12**	p2.0
8	F	...	**12:24**	0.9	5:00	**5:18**	2.0
9	S	12:30	**1:24**	a1.3	6:06	**6:18**	p2.1
10	S	1:18	**2:18**	a1.4	7:00	**7:18**	2.1
11	M	2:12	**3:12**	a1.5	7:54	**8:12**	2.1
12	T	3:00	**4:06**	a1.6	8:42	**9:06**	2.0
13	W	3:48	**4:48**	a1.6	9:30	**9:54**	1.9
14	T	4:42	**5:36**	a1.5	10:18	**10:48**	a1.9
15	F	5:30	**6:24**	a1.5	11:06	**11:36**	a1.9
16	S	6:18	**7:12**	a1.4	...	**12:01**	1.9
17	S	7:12	**8:00**	a1.3	12:30	**12:48**	p2.0
18	M	8:06	**8:48**	a1.1	1:18	**1:36**	p2.0
19	T	9:06	**9:42**	0.9	2:06	**2:24**	p2.0
20	W	10:12	**10:42**	0.8	2:54	**3:12**	p1.9
21	T	11:24	**11:36**	p0.8	3:48	**4:00**	p2.0
22	F	...	**12:36**	0.6	4:42	**5:00**	p2.0
23	S	12:24	**1:30**	a0.8	5:36	**5:54**	2.0
24	S	1:06	**2:18**	a0.9	6:30	**6:42**	2.0
25	M	1:42	**2:54**	a1.0	7:18	**7:30**	a2.0
26	T	2:18	**3:30**	a1.1	8:00	**8:12**	1.9
27	W	2:54	**4:00**	a1.3	8:42	**8:54**	1.8
28	T	3:30	**4:30**	a1.5	9:18	**9:36**	p1.8
29	F	4:12	**5:06**	a1.7	10:00	**10:24**	p1.8
30	S	5:00	**5:48**	a1.8	10:48	**11:06**	p1.9
31	S	5:48	**6:30**	a1.8	11:30	...	1.9

Standard Time

FEBRUARY

DAY OF MONTH	DAY OF WEEK	CURRENT TURNS TO NORTH Flood Starts a.m.	p.m.	Kts.	CURRENT TURNS TO SOUTH Ebb Starts a.m.	p.m.	Kts.
1	M	6:43	**7:12**	a1.7	12:01	**12:18**	a2.0
2	T	7:36	**8:06**	a1.6	12:48	**1:06**	2.0
3	W	8:36	**9:00**	p1.4	1:42	**1:54**	2.0
4	T	9:48	**10:00**	p1.3	2:36	**2:48**	1.9
5	F	11:00	**11:06**	p1.2	3:36	**3:48**	p1.9
6	S	...	**12:12**	0.8	4:36	**5:00**	p1.9
7	S	12:06	**1:18**	a1.2	5:42	**6:06**	p2.0
8	M	1:06	**2:12**	a1.3	6:48	**7:12**	p2.1
9	T	2:00	**3:00**	a1.5	7:42	**8:06**	p2.1
10	W	2:48	**3:48**	a1.6	8:36	**9:00**	2.0
11	T	3:36	**4:30**	a1.6	9:24	**9:48**	1.9
12	F	4:24	**5:06**	a1.7	10:06	**10:36**	1.9
13	S	5:06	**5:48**	a1.6	10:54	**11:18**	a1.9
14	S	5:54	**6:30**	a1.5	11:36	...	1.9
15	M	6:42	**7:12**	a1.4	12:06	**12:24**	p2.0
16	T	7:36	**8:00**	a1.2	12:48	**1:06**	p2.0
17	W	8:30	**8:48**	p1.0	1:30	**1:48**	p2.0
18	T	9:30	**9:42**	p0.9	2:12	**2:24**	p1.9
19	F	10:36	**10:36**	p0.8	2:54	**3:12**	1.8
20	S	11:42	**11:30**	p0.8	3:42	**4:06**	1.8
21	S	...	**12:42**	0.4	4:36	**5:06**	1.8
22	M	12:18	**1:30**	a0.9	5:36	**6:06**	1.8
23	T	1:00	**2:12**	a1.0	6:36	**7:00**	1.8
24	W	1:42	**2:42**	a1.2	7:24	**7:48**	1.8
25	T	2:24	**3:18**	a1.4	8:12	**8:36**	1.8
26	F	3:06	**3:54**	a1.6	9:00	**9:18**	p1.8
27	S	3:48	**4:30**	a1.7	9:42	**10:06**	p1.9
28	S	4:36	**5:12**	a1.8	10:30	**10:54**	p1.9

The Kts. (knots) columns show the **maximum** predicted velocities of the stronger one of the Flood Currents and the stronger one of the Ebb Currents for each day.
The letter "a" means the velocity shown should occur **after** the **a.m.** Current Change. The letter "p" means the velocity shown should occur **after** the **p.m.** Current Change (even if next morning). No "a" or "p" means a.m. and p.m. velocities are the same for that day.
Avg. Max. Velocity: Flood 1.4 Kts., Ebb 1.9 Kts.
Max. Flood 2 hrs. 45 min. after Flood Starts, ±30 min.
Max. Ebb 3 hrs. 25 min. after Ebb Starts, ±25 min.

At **The Battery, Desbrosses St., & Chelsea Dock** Current turns 1 1/2 hrs. after the Narrows. At **42nd St.** and the **George Washington Bridge**, the Current turns 1 3/4 hrs. after the Narrows. See pp. 22-29 for Current Change at other points.

2021 CURRENT TABLE
THE NARROWS

40°36.36'N, 74°02.29'W

***Daylight Time starts March 14 at 2 a.m.** **Daylight Saving Time**

MARCH

DAY OF MONTH	DAY OF WEEK	CURRENT TURNS TO NORTH Flood Starts a.m.	**p.m.**	Kts.	CURRENT TURNS TO SOUTH Ebb Starts a.m.	**p.m.**	Kts.
1	**M**	5:31	**5:54**	a1.8	11:12	**11:36**	p1.9
2	**T**	6:24	**6:42**	p1.7	...	**12:01**	1.9
3	**W**	7:24	**7:36**	p1.6	12:30	**12:42**	a2.0
4	**T**	8:24	**8:30**	p1.4	1:18	**1:36**	a2.0
5	**F**	9:36	**9:36**	p1.2	2:12	**2:30**	1.8
6	**S**	10:48	**10:48**	p1.1	3:06	**3:30**	p1.8
7	**S**	-A-	**12:06**	0.7	4:12	**4:42**	p1.8
8	**M**	...	**1:12**	0.9	5:24	**5:54**	p2.0
9	**T**	1:00	**2:06**	1.2	6:30	**7:00**	p2.1
10	**W**	1:54	**2:48**	1.4	7:30	**8:00**	2.1
11	**T**	2:42	**3:30**	1.6	8:18	**8:48**	2.1
12	**F**	3:30	**4:06**	a1.7	9:06	**9:36**	2.0
13	**S**	4:12	**4:42**	a1.7	9:48	**10:18**	2.0
14	**S**	*5:54	***6:18**	a1.6	*11:30	***11:54**	a2.0
15	**M**	6:36	**7:00**	1.4	...	**12:12**	2.0
16	**T**	7:24	**7:36**	1.3	12:36	**12:48**	p2.0
17	**W**	8:12	**8:18**	p1.2	1:12	**1:24**	p2.0
18	**T**	9:00	**9:06**	p1.2	1:48	**2:00**	p2.0
19	**F**	9:54	**9:54**	p1.1	2:24	**2:42**	p2.0
20	**S**	10:54	**10:48**	p1.0	3:00	**3:24**	p1.9
21	**S**	11:59	**11:42**	p1.0	3:48	**4:12**	1.8
22	**M**	...	**12:54**	0.5	4:42	**5:18**	p1.8
23	**T**	12:36	**1:42**	a1.0	5:42	**6:24**	1.8
24	**W**	1:24	**2:24**	a1.1	6:48	**7:24**	1.8
25	**T**	2:12	**3:06**	a1.2	7:48	**8:24**	1.9
26	**F**	3:00	**3:42**	a1.4	8:42	**9:12**	p2.0
27	**S**	3:42	**4:18**	1.5	9:30	**9:54**	p2.0
28	**S**	4:36	**5:00**	1.6	10:18	**10:42**	p2.0
29	**M**	5:24	**5:42**	p1.8	11:00	**11:24**	p2.0
30	**T**	6:18	**6:30**	p1.8	11:48	...	1.9
31	**W**	7:12	**7:18**	p1.7	12:12	**12:30**	a2.0

APRIL

DAY OF MONTH	DAY OF WEEK	CURRENT TURNS TO NORTH Flood Starts a.m.	**p.m.**	Kts.	CURRENT TURNS TO SOUTH Ebb Starts a.m.	**p.m.**	Kts.
1	**T**	8:13	**8:12**	p1.5	1:00	**1:18**	a2.0
2	**F**	9:12	**9:12**	p1.3	1:54	**2:12**	a2.0
3	**S**	10:24	**10:18**	p1.1	2:48	**3:06**	a1.9
4	**S**	11:42	**11:36**	p0.9	3:42	**4:12**	1.7
5	**M**	...	**1:00**	0.8	4:48	**5:24**	1.8
6	**T**	12:48	**2:00**	1.0	6:00	**6:36**	p2.0
7	**W**	1:54	**2:48**	p1.2	7:06	**7:42**	p2.2
8	**T**	2:48	**3:36**	p1.5	8:06	**8:42**	p2.3
9	**F**	3:36	**4:12**	p1.6	9:00	**9:30**	2.2
10	**S**	4:24	**4:48**	p1.6	9:42	**10:12**	2.2
11	**S**	5:06	**5:18**	p1.6	10:24	**10:48**	2.1
12	**M**	5:48	**5:54**	1.4	11:00	**11:24**	2.0
13	**T**	6:24	**6:30**	p1.3	11:36	...	2.0
14	**W**	7:06	**7:06**	p1.3	12:01	**12:12**	2.0
15	**T**	7:54	**7:48**	p1.3	12:30	**12:42**	p2.1
16	**F**	8:36	**8:30**	p1.3	1:06	**1:18**	p2.1
17	**S**	9:24	**9:12**	p1.3	1:36	**2:00**	2.0
18	**S**	10:18	**10:06**	p1.2	2:18	**2:42**	2.0
19	**M**	11:12	**11:00**	p1.1	3:00	**3:36**	a2.0
20	**T**	...	**12:12**	0.6	3:54	**4:36**	a1.9
21	**W**	12:01	**1:00**	a1.1	5:00	**5:48**	1.9
22	**T**	12:54	**1:42**	a1.2	6:06	**6:54**	1.9
23	**F**	1:48	**2:24**	a1.2	7:12	**7:48**	2.0
24	**S**	2:36	**3:06**	p1.4	8:06	**8:42**	p2.1
25	**S**	3:30	**3:48**	p1.6	9:00	**9:30**	p2.1
26	**M**	4:24	**4:30**	p1.7	9:48	**10:18**	p2.1
27	**T**	5:18	**5:18**	p1.7	10:30	**11:00**	p2.1
28	**W**	6:12	**6:06**	p1.7	11:18	**11:48**	p2.0
29	**T**	7:06	**7:00**	p1.6	...	**12:06**	1.9
30	**F**	8:06	**7:54**	p1.4	12:36	**12:54**	a2.0

A also at 11:54 p.m. 1.1

The Kts. (knots) columns show the **maximum** predicted velocities of the stronger one of the Flood Currents and the stronger one of the Ebb Currents for each day.
The letter "a" means the velocity shown should occur **after** the **a.m.** Current Change. The letter "p" means the velocity shown should occur **after** the **p.m.** Current Change (even if next morning). No "a" or "p" means a.m. and p.m. velocities are the same for that day.
Avg. Max. Velocity: Flood 1.4 Kts., Ebb 1.9 Kts.
Max. Flood 2 hrs. 45 min. after Flood Starts, ±30 min.
Max. Ebb 3 hrs. 25 min. after Ebb Starts, ±25 min.

See pp. 22-29 for Current Change at other points.

2021 CURRENT TABLE
THE NARROWS

40°36.36'N, 74°02.29'W

MAY

Daylight Saving Time

DAY OF MONTH	DAY OF WEEK	CURRENT TURNS TO NORTH Flood Starts a.m.	**p.m.**	Kts.	CURRENT TURNS TO SOUTH Ebb Starts a.m.	**p.m.**	Kts.
1	**S**	9:07	**8:54**	p1.2	1:30	**1:54**	a1.9
2	**S**	10:12	**10:06**	p1.0	2:24	**2:54**	a1.9
3	**M**	11:30	**11:18**	p0.9	3:18	**4:00**	1.8
4	**T**	...	**12:42**	0.9	4:24	**5:06**	1.9
5	**W**	12:30	**1:36**	p1.0	5:30	**6:18**	p2.1
6	**T**	1:42	**2:24**	p1.2	6:36	**7:24**	p2.3
7	**F**	2:36	**3:06**	p1.4	7:36	**8:18**	p2.4
8	**S**	3:30	**3:42**	p1.5	8:30	**9:00**	2.4
9	**S**	4:12	**4:18**	p1.5	9:12	**9:42**	2.3
10	**M**	4:54	**4:48**	p1.4	9:54	**10:18**	2.2
11	**T**	5:36	**5:24**	p1.3	10:30	**10:54**	a2.1
12	**W**	6:18	**5:54**	p1.3	11:00	**11:24**	2.0
13	**T**	6:54	**6:30**	p1.3	11:36	**11:54**	a2.0
14	**F**	7:30	**7:12**	p1.4	...	**12:06**	2.0
15	**S**	8:12	**7:54**	p1.4	12:30	**12:48**	2.0
16	**S**	8:54	**8:42**	p1.4	1:06	**1:30**	2.0
17	**M**	9:42	**9:30**	p1.4	1:48	**2:18**	a2.1
18	**T**	10:30	**10:24**	p1.3	2:36	**3:12**	a2.1
19	**W**	11:24	**11:24**	p1.3	3:30	**4:12**	a2.0
20	**T**	...	**12:18**	1.0	4:30	**5:18**	a2.0
21	**F**	12:24	**1:06**	1.2	5:36	**6:24**	2.0
22	**S**	1:24	**1:48**	p1.3	6:36	**7:24**	2.1
23	**S**	2:18	**2:30**	p1.5	7:36	**8:18**	p2.2
24	**M**	3:12	**3:18**	p1.7	8:30	**9:06**	p2.2
25	**T**	4:06	**4:00**	p1.7	9:18	**9:54**	2.1
26	**W**	5:00	**4:48**	p1.7	10:06	**10:36**	2.0
27	**T**	5:54	**5:42**	p1.6	10:54	**11:24**	1.9
28	**F**	6:48	**6:36**	p1.5	11:42	...	1.8
29	**S**	7:48	**7:36**	p1.4	12:18	**12:42**	a1.8
30	**S**	8:48	**8:36**	p1.2	1:12	**1:42**	a1.8
31	**M**	9:48	**9:42**	p1.0	2:06	**2:42**	a1.8

JUNE

Daylight Saving Time

DAY OF MONTH	DAY OF WEEK	CURRENT TURNS TO NORTH Flood Starts a.m.	**p.m.**	Kts.	CURRENT TURNS TO SOUTH Ebb Starts a.m.	**p.m.**	Kts.
1	**T**	10:55	**10:48**	p1.0	3:06	**3:48**	a1.8
2	**W**	...	**12:01**	1.0	4:06	**4:48**	1.9
3	**T**	12:06	**12:54**	p1.1	5:06	**5:54**	a2.1
4	**F**	1:12	**1:42**	p1.3	6:12	**6:54**	2.2
5	**S**	2:12	**2:24**	p1.4	7:06	**7:48**	2.3
6	**S**	3:06	**3:06**	p1.4	8:00	**8:36**	2.3
7	**M**	3:54	**3:42**	p1.4	8:42	**9:18**	2.2
8	**T**	4:42	**4:12**	p1.4	9:24	**9:54**	2.1
9	**W**	5:18	**4:48**	p1.3	10:00	**10:24**	a2.0
10	**T**	5:54	**5:18**	p1.3	10:30	**10:54**	1.8
11	**F**	6:24	**5:54**	p1.4	11:06	**11:30**	a1.8
12	**S**	7:00	**6:36**	p1.5	11:48	...	1.7
13	**S**	7:36	**7:18**	p1.6	12:06	**12:30**	1.8
14	**M**	8:18	**8:06**	p1.7	12:48	**1:18**	a1.9
15	**T**	9:00	**8:54**	p1.6	1:36	**2:12**	a2.0
16	**W**	9:48	**9:54**	p1.5	2:24	**3:06**	a2.0
17	**T**	10:42	**10:54**	p1.4	3:18	**4:00**	a2.0
18	**F**	11:36	...	1.4	4:12	**5:00**	a2.0
19	**S**	12:01	**12:24**	p1.5	5:12	**6:00**	2.0
20	**S**	1:00	**1:12**	p1.6	6:12	**7:00**	2.1
21	**M**	1:54	**2:00**	p1.7	7:12	**7:54**	2.1
22	**T**	2:48	**2:48**	p1.7	8:06	**8:48**	2.1
23	**W**	3:42	**3:30**	p1.8	9:00	**9:36**	2.0
24	**T**	4:36	**4:24**	p1.7	9:54	**10:24**	1.9
25	**F**	5:30	**5:12**	p1.7	10:42	**11:12**	a1.8
26	**S**	6:24	**6:12**	p1.6	11:36	...	1.6
27	**S**	7:18	**7:06**	p1.5	12:06	**12:36**	a1.6
28	**M**	8:12	**8:06**	p1.3	1:00	**1:36**	a1.6
29	**T**	9:06	**9:06**	p1.2	2:00	**2:36**	a1.7
30	**W**	10:06	**10:12**	1.2	2:54	**3:36**	a1.8

The Kts. (knots) columns show the **maximum** predicted velocities of the stronger one of the Flood Currents and the stronger one of the Ebb Currents for each day.
The letter "a" means the velocity shown should occur **after** the **a.m.** Current Change. The letter "p" means the velocity shown should occur **after** the **p.m.** Current Change (even if next morning). No "a" or "p" means a.m. and p.m. velocities are the same for that day.
Avg. Max. Velocity: Flood 1.4 Kts., Ebb 1.9 Kts.
Max. Flood 2 hrs. 45 min. after Flood Starts, ±30 min.
Max. Ebb 3 hrs. 25 min. after Ebb Starts, ±25 min.

At **The Battery, Desbrosses St., & Chelsea Dock** Current turns 1 1/2 hrs. after the Narrows. At **42nd St.** and the **George Washington Bridge**, the Current turns 1 3/4 hrs. after the Narrows. See pp. 22-29 for Current Change at other points.

2021 CURRENT TABLE
THE NARROWS

40°36.36'N, 74°02.29'W

Daylight Saving Time

JULY

DAY OF MONTH	DAY OF WEEK	CURRENT TURNS TO NORTH Flood Starts a.m.	**p.m.**	Kts.	CURRENT TURNS TO SOUTH Ebb Starts a.m.	**p.m.**	Kts.
1	**T**	11:01	**11:24**	a1.2	3:48	**4:30**	a1.9
2	**F**	...	**12:01**	1.3	4:42	**5:30**	1.9
3	**S**	12:30	**12:48**	p1.3	5:42	**6:24**	2.0
4	**S**	1:36	**1:36**	p1.3	6:36	**7:18**	2.1
5	**M**	2:30	**2:18**	p1.4	7:30	**8:06**	2.1
6	**T**	3:18	**2:54**	p1.4	8:12	**8:48**	a2.1
7	**W**	4:00	**3:24**	p1.4	8:54	**9:24**	a1.9
8	**T**	4:36	**4:00**	p1.4	9:36	**10:00**	a1.8
9	**F**	5:12	**4:36**	p1.5	10:12	**10:36**	a1.6
10	**S**	5:42	**5:12**	p1.6	10:54	**11:12**	1.5
11	**S**	6:18	**5:54**	p1.7	11:36	**11:54**	1.5
12	**M**	6:54	**6:36**	p1.8	...	**12:18**	1.5
13	**T**	7:36	**7:30**	p1.9	12:42	**1:12**	1.6
14	**W**	8:18	**8:24**	p1.8	1:30	**2:00**	1.7
15	**T**	9:06	**9:18**	p1.7	2:18	**2:54**	a1.8
16	**F**	9:54	**10:24**	a1.6	3:06	**3:48**	a1.9
17	**S**	10:54	**11:30**	a1.7	4:00	**4:42**	a1.9
18	**S**	11:48	...	1.7	4:54	**5:42**	a1.9
19	**M**	12:36	**12:42**	p1.8	6:00	**6:42**	1.9
20	**T**	1:30	**1:30**	p1.8	7:00	**7:42**	1.9
21	**W**	2:24	**2:18**	p1.8	7:54	**8:36**	1.9
22	**T**	3:18	**3:06**	p1.8	8:54	**9:24**	a1.9
23	**F**	4:12	**4:00**	p1.8	9:48	**10:18**	a1.7
24	**S**	5:00	**4:48**	p1.8	10:42	**11:06**	a1.6
25	**S**	5:48	**5:42**	p1.7	11:36	...	1.4
26	**M**	6:42	**6:36**	p1.6	12:01	**12:30**	1.4
27	**T**	7:30	**7:30**	p1.5	12:54	**1:30**	a1.5
28	**W**	8:24	**8:30**	1.4	1:48	**2:24**	a1.6
29	**T**	9:12	**9:30**	a1.4	2:36	**3:18**	a1.7
30	**F**	10:06	**10:36**	a1.3	3:30	**4:06**	a1.7
31	**S**	11:00	**11:42**	a1.3	4:18	**5:00**	a1.8

Daylight Saving Time

AUGUST

DAY OF MONTH	DAY OF WEEK	CURRENT TURNS TO NORTH Flood Starts a.m.	**p.m.**	Kts.	CURRENT TURNS TO SOUTH Ebb Starts a.m.	**p.m.**	Kts.
1	**S**	11:55	...	1.3	5:12	**5:48**	1.8
2	**M**	12:48	**12:42**	p1.3	6:06	**6:42**	p1.9
3	**T**	1:42	**1:24**	p1.3	6:54	**7:36**	1.9
4	**W**	2:30	**2:06**	p1.3	7:48	**8:18**	1.8
5	**T**	3:12	**2:42**	p1.4	8:30	**9:00**	a1.7
6	**F**	3:48	**3:18**	p1.5	9:12	**9:42**	a1.6
7	**S**	4:18	**3:54**	p1.7	9:54	**10:18**	a1.5
8	**S**	4:54	**4:30**	p1.8	10:36	**11:00**	a1.4
9	**M**	5:30	**5:18**	p1.9	11:18	**11:42**	p1.4
10	**T**	6:06	**6:06**	p2.0	...	**12:06**	1.4
11	**W**	6:48	**7:00**	p1.9	12:24	**12:54**	1.4
12	**T**	7:36	**7:54**	1.8	1:12	**1:48**	1.5
13	**F**	8:24	**8:54**	a1.9	2:06	**2:42**	a1.7
14	**S**	9:18	**10:00**	a1.9	2:54	**3:30**	a1.7
15	**S**	10:18	**11:06**	a1.8	3:48	**4:30**	a1.7
16	**M**	11:18	...	1.8	4:42	**5:24**	a1.7
17	**T**	12:12	**12:12**	p1.7	5:42	**6:30**	1.7
18	**W**	1:12	**1:12**	p1.7	6:48	**7:30**	a1.8
19	**T**	2:06	**2:00**	p1.8	7:48	**8:24**	a1.8
20	**F**	2:54	**2:54**	p1.9	8:48	**9:18**	a1.8
21	**S**	3:42	**3:42**	p1.9	9:42	**10:06**	a1.7
22	**S**	4:30	**4:30**	p1.9	10:36	**10:54**	1.5
23	**M**	5:18	**5:18**	p1.8	11:24	**11:42**	1.4
24	**T**	6:06	**6:12**	1.7	...	**12:18**	1.3
25	**W**	6:54	**7:06**	1.6	12:36	**1:06**	a1.5
26	**T**	7:42	**8:00**	1.5	1:24	**1:54**	a1.5
27	**F**	8:30	**9:00**	a1.4	2:12	**2:42**	a1.6
28	**S**	9:18	**10:00**	a1.3	2:54	**3:30**	a1.7
29	**S**	10:12	**11:06**	a1.3	3:42	**4:12**	a1.7
30	**M**	11:06	...	1.2	4:30	**5:06**	a1.7
31	**T**	12:06	**-A-**	0.9	5:24	**5:54**	1.7

A also at 11:54 a.m. 1.2

The Kts. (knots) columns show the **maximum** predicted velocities of the stronger one of the Flood Currents and the stronger one of the Ebb Currents for each day.
The letter "a" means the velocity shown should occur **after** the **a.m.** Current Change. The letter "p" means the velocity shown should occur **after** the **p.m.** Current Change (even if next morning). No "a" or "p" means a.m. and p.m. velocities are the same for that day.
Avg. Max. Velocity: Flood 1.4 Kts., Ebb 1.9 Kts.
Max. Flood 2 hrs. 45 min. after Flood Starts, ±30 min.
Max. Ebb 3 hrs. 25 min. after Ebb Starts, ±25 min.

See pp. 22-29 for Current Change at other points.

2021 CURRENT TABLE
THE NARROWS

40°36.36'N, 74°02.29'W

SEPTEMBER

Daylight Saving Time

DAY OF MONTH	DAY OF WEEK	NORTH Flood Starts a.m.	NORTH Flood Starts **p.m.**	NORTH Flood Starts Kts.	SOUTH Ebb Starts a.m.	SOUTH Ebb Starts **p.m.**	SOUTH Ebb Starts Kts.
1	W	1:01	12:42	p1.2	6:18	6:48	1.7
2	T	1:48	1:24	p1.3	7:12	7:42	1.7
3	F	2:24	2:06	p1.5	8:00	8:24	1.6
4	S	3:00	2:42	p1.6	8:48	9:12	a1.6
5	S	3:36	3:24	p1.8	9:30	9:54	a1.5
6	M	4:12	4:06	p1.9	10:12	10:36	1.4
7	T	4:48	4:54	p1.9	11:00	11:18	1.4
8	W	5:30	5:48	p1.9	11:42	...	1.4
9	T	6:12	6:42	a1.9	12:01	12:30	p1.5
10	F	7:00	7:42	a1.9	12:48	1:24	1.5
11	S	7:54	8:42	a1.9	1:36	2:12	1.6
12	S	8:54	9:48	a1.8	2:30	3:06	1.6
13	M	9:54	10:54	a1.7	3:24	4:06	a1.6
14	T	10:54	...	1.6	4:24	5:06	a1.6
15	W	12:01	12:01	p1.6	5:24	6:06	1.6
16	T	1:00	1:00	p1.6	6:36	7:12	1.7
17	F	1:54	1:54	p1.7	7:36	8:06	1.8
18	S	2:42	2:48	p1.8	8:36	9:00	1.8
19	S	3:30	3:36	p1.8	9:30	9:48	a1.8
20	M	4:12	4:24	1.8	10:18	10:36	a1.7
21	T	5:00	5:12	1.8	11:06	11:18	1.6
22	W	5:42	6:00	a1.7	11:48	...	1.5
23	T	6:24	6:54	a1.6	12:06	12:30	a1.6
24	F	7:06	7:42	a1.5	12:48	1:18	1.6
25	S	7:54	8:36	a1.4	1:30	2:00	a1.7
26	S	8:42	9:30	a1.3	2:12	2:42	a1.7
27	M	9:30	10:30	a1.3	3:00	3:24	a1.7
28	T	10:24	11:30	a1.2	3:42	4:06	a1.7
29	W	11:12	...	1.2	4:30	5:00	a1.7
30	T	12:24	12:06	p1.3	5:30	5:54	p1.7

OCTOBER

Daylight Saving Time

DAY OF MONTH	DAY OF WEEK	NORTH Flood Starts a.m.	NORTH Flood Starts **p.m.**	NORTH Flood Starts Kts.	SOUTH Ebb Starts a.m.	SOUTH Ebb Starts **p.m.**	SOUTH Ebb Starts Kts.
1	F	1:07	12:54	p1.3	6:24	6:48	p1.7
2	S	1:48	1:36	p1.5	7:18	7:42	1.7
3	S	2:30	2:18	p1.6	8:12	8:30	1.7
4	M	3:06	3:06	p1.7	8:54	9:18	1.7
5	T	3:42	3:54	p1.7	9:42	10:00	a1.7
6	W	4:18	4:42	1.7	10:24	10:42	a1.7
7	T	5:00	5:36	a1.8	11:12	11:30	a1.7
8	F	5:48	6:36	a1.9	...	12:01	1.6
9	S	6:42	7:36	a1.9	12:18	12:48	p1.7
10	S	7:36	8:36	a1.8	1:06	1:42	p1.7
11	M	8:36	9:42	a1.6	2:00	2:36	a1.7
12	T	9:36	10:48	a1.4	2:54	3:36	a1.7
13	W	10:48	11:54	a1.3	4:00	4:36	1.6
14	T	11:54	...	1.3	5:06	5:42	1.7
15	F	1:00	1:00	p1.4	6:12	6:42	p1.9
16	S	1:54	1:54	p1.5	7:18	7:42	2.0
17	S	2:36	2:48	1.6	8:18	8:36	2.0
18	M	3:24	3:36	1.7	9:06	9:24	2.0
19	T	4:00	4:24	a1.7	9:54	10:06	a2.0
20	W	4:42	5:12	a1.7	10:36	10:48	p1.9
21	T	5:24	6:00	a1.6	11:12	11:24	1.8
22	F	6:00	6:42	a1.5	11:54	...	1.7
23	S	6:42	7:30	a1.4	12:06	12:30	a1.8
24	S	7:24	8:18	a1.3	12:42	1:06	a1.8
25	M	8:12	9:06	a1.3	1:24	1:48	1.8
26	T	8:54	10:00	a1.3	2:06	2:30	1.8
27	W	9:48	10:54	a1.3	2:54	3:12	1.8
28	T	10:36	11:42	a1.2	3:42	4:00	1.8
29	F	11:30	...	1.3	4:36	5:00	p1.8
30	S	12:30	12:24	p1.3	5:36	5:54	1.8
31	S	1:18	1:18	p1.4	6:36	6:54	p1.9

The Kts. (knots) columns show the **maximum** predicted velocities of the stronger one of the Flood Currents and the stronger one of the Ebb Currents for each day.
The letter "a" means the velocity shown should occur **after** the **a.m.** Current Change. The letter "p" means the velocity shown should occur **after** the **p.m.** Current Change (even if next morning). No "a" or "p" means a.m. and p.m. velocities are the same for that day.
Avg. Max. Velocity: Flood 1.4 Kts., Ebb 1.9 Kts.
Max. Flood 2 hrs. 45 min. after Flood Starts, ±30 min.
Max. Ebb 3 hrs. 25 min. after Ebb Starts, ±25 min.

At **The Battery, Desbrosses St., & Chelsea Dock** Current turns 1 1/2 hrs. after the Narrows. At **42nd St.** and the **George Washington Bridge**, the Current turns 1 3/4 hrs. after the Narrows. See pp. 22-29 for Current Change at other points.

2021 CURRENT TABLE
THE NARROWS

40°36.36'N, 74°02.29'W

***Standard Time starts Nov. 7 at 2 a.m.** | **Standard Time**

NOVEMBER								DECEMBER							
DAY OF MONTH	DAY OF WEEK	CURRENT TURNS TO						DAY OF MONTH	DAY OF WEEK	CURRENT TURNS TO					
		NORTH Flood Starts			SOUTH Ebb Starts					NORTH Flood Starts			SOUTH Ebb Starts		
		a.m.	**p.m.**	Kts.	a.m.	**p.m.**	Kts.			a.m.	**p.m.**	Kts.	a.m.	**p.m.**	Kts.
1	M	2:01	**2:06**	p1.4	7:30	**7:48**	1.9	1	W	1:13	**1:42**	a1.4	6:48	**7:00**	2.2
2	T	2:36	**2:54**	1.4	8:18	**8:36**	2.0	2	T	1:54	**2:36**	a1.6	7:36	**7:54**	a2.2
3	W	3:18	**3:48**	a1.6	9:06	**9:24**	a2.0	3	F	2:36	**3:30**	a1.7	8:24	**8:42**	a2.2
4	T	4:00	**4:36**	a1.7	9:54	**10:06**	a2.0	4	S	3:24	**4:30**	a1.7	9:12	**9:30**	a2.1
5	F	4:42	**5:36**	a1.8	10:36	**10:54**	a1.9	5	S	4:18	**5:24**	a1.7	10:00	**10:18**	1.9
6	S	5:30	**6:30**	a1.8	11:24	**11:42**	1.8	6	M	5:12	**6:18**	a1.6	10:54	**11:12**	1.8
7	S	*5:24	***6:30**	a1.7	*11:18	***11:30**	a1.8	7	T	6:06	**7:12**	a1.5	11:42	...	1.8
8	M	6:18	**7:30**	a1.6	...	**12:12**	1.7	8	W	7:06	**8:12**	a1.3	12:12	**12:42**	1.8
9	T	7:24	**8:30**	a1.4	12:30	**1:06**	1.7	9	T	8:06	**9:12**	a1.1	1:12	**1:36**	1.8
10	W	8:24	**9:42**	a1.2	1:30	**2:06**	1.7	10	F	9:18	**10:18**	1.0	2:12	**2:36**	1.8
11	T	9:36	**10:48**	a1.1	2:36	**3:06**	1.7	11	S	10:30	**11:24**	1.0	3:12	**3:36**	p1.9
12	F	10:48	**11:48**	1.1	3:42	**4:06**	p1.9	12	S	11:42	...	1.0	4:18	**4:36**	p2.1
13	S	11:54	...	1.2	4:48	**5:12**	p2.0	13	M	12:18	**12:48**	1.1	5:24	**5:36**	p2.3
14	S	12:42	**12:54**	1.3	5:54	**6:12**	p2.2	14	T	1:06	**1:48**	a1.3	6:18	**6:36**	2.3
15	M	1:30	**1:48**	1.4	6:48	**7:06**	p2.3	15	W	1:54	**2:42**	a1.4	7:12	**7:24**	2.4
16	T	2:12	**2:42**	a1.6	7:42	**7:54**	2.3	16	T	2:30	**3:30**	a1.4	7:54	**8:06**	2.3
17	W	2:48	**3:30**	a1.6	8:24	**8:36**	2.2	17	F	3:06	**4:12**	a1.4	8:36	**8:48**	2.2
18	T	3:30	**4:12**	a1.5	9:06	**9:12**	2.1	18	S	3:42	**4:48**	a1.3	9:12	**9:24**	2.0
19	F	4:06	**4:54**	a1.4	9:42	**9:48**	2.0	19	S	4:18	**5:24**	a1.2	9:48	**10:00**	1.9
20	S	4:42	**5:36**	a1.3	10:12	**10:24**	1.9	20	M	4:54	**5:54**	a1.3	10:18	**10:36**	p1.9
21	S	5:18	**6:18**	a1.3	10:48	**11:00**	p1.9	21	T	5:30	**6:30**	a1.4	10:54	**11:12**	p1.9
22	M	6:00	**7:00**	a1.3	11:24	**11:42**	p1.9	22	W	6:06	**7:06**	a1.5	11:30	**11:54**	1.9
23	T	6:42	**7:42**	a1.4	...	**12:01**	1.9	23	T	6:48	**7:42**	a1.5	...	**12:12**	2.0
24	W	7:24	**8:24**	a1.4	12:24	**12:42**	1.9	24	F	7:36	**8:30**	a1.5	12:42	**1:00**	p2.1
25	T	8:12	**9:12**	a1.4	1:06	**1:30**	p2.0	25	S	8:30	**9:18**	a1.5	1:30	**1:48**	p2.1
26	F	9:06	**10:06**	a1.3	2:00	**2:18**	p2.0	26	S	9:30	**10:12**	a1.3	2:24	**2:36**	p2.1
27	S	10:00	**10:54**	a1.3	2:54	**3:12**	p2.0	27	M	10:30	**11:00**	p1.3	3:18	**3:36**	p2.1
28	S	11:00	**11:42**	a1.3	3:48	**4:12**	p2.0	28	T	11:36	**11:54**	p1.4	4:18	**4:36**	p2.1
29	M	11:54	...	1.2	4:54	**5:12**	p2.1	29	W	...	**12:36**	1.0	5:18	**5:36**	2.1
30	T	12:24	**12:48**	a1.3	5:54	**6:06**	2.1	30	T	12:42	**1:30**	a1.4	6:18	**6:36**	p2.2
								31	F	1:30	**2:30**	a1.5	7:12	**7:30**	2.2

The Kts. (knots) columns show the **maximum** predicted velocities of the stronger one of the Flood Currents and the stronger one of the Ebb Currents for each day.
The letter "a" means the velocity shown should occur **after** the **a.m.** Current Change. The letter "p" means the velocity shown should occur **after** the **p.m.** Current Change (even if next morning). No "a" or "p" means a.m. and p.m. velocities are the same for that day.
Avg. Max. Velocity: Flood 1.4 Kts., Ebb 1.9 Kts.
Max. Flood 2 hrs. 45 min. after Flood Starts, ±30 min.
Max. Ebb 3 hrs. 25 min. after Ebb Starts, ±25 min.

See pp. 22-29 for Current Change at other points.

2021 HIGH & LOW WATER THE BATTERY, NY HARBOR

40°42'N, 74°00.8'W

Standard Time

DAY OF MONTH	DAY OF WEEK	JANUARY HIGH a.m.	Ht.	**p.m.**	Ht.	LOW a.m.	**p.m.**
1	**F**	9:09	5.0	**9:58**	4.0	3:19	**4:11**
2	**S**	9:51	4.9	**10:47**	4.0	3:59	**4:51**
3	**S**	10:41	4.8	**11:39**	4.1	4:43	**5:35**
4	**M**	11:36	4.7	...	...	5:33	**6:25**
5	**T**	12:31	4.2	**12:32**	4.5	6:39	**7:24**
6	**W**	1:25	4.4	**1:31**	4.3	7:55	**8:26**
7	**T**	2:23	4.6	**2:34**	4.1	9:06	**9:26**
8	**F**	3:24	4.8	**3:44**	4.0	10:10	**10:22**
9	**S**	4:28	5.0	**4:55**	4.1	11:08	**11:17**
10	**S**	5:29	5.2	**5:58**	4.2	...	**12:05**
11	**M**	6:24	5.4	**6:54**	4.3	12:11	**12:59**
12	**T**	7:16	5.5	**7:45**	4.4	1:05	**1:51**
13	**W**	8:05	5.5	**8:35**	4.4	1:57	**2:40**
14	**T**	8:53	5.4	**9:26**	4.4	2:46	**3:26**
15	**F**	9:42	5.2	**10:17**	4.3	3:34	**4:11**
16	**S**	10:31	4.9	**11:08**	4.2	4:19	**4:54**
17	**S**	11:20	4.6	**11:56**	4.1	5:05	**5:37**
18	**M**	...	...	**12:07**	4.3	5:54	**6:22**
19	**T**	12:43	4.0	**12:54**	4.0	6:49	**7:10**
20	**W**	1:28	4.0	**1:41**	3.7	7:50	**8:02**
21	**T**	2:14	3.9	**2:32**	3.5	8:52	**8:54**
22	**F**	3:04	3.9	**3:29**	3.4	9:48	**9:44**
23	**S**	3:57	4.0	**4:29**	3.4	10:39	**10:32**
24	**S**	4:50	4.2	**5:25**	3.5	11:27	**11:19**
25	**M**	5:39	4.4	**6:13**	3.7	...	**12:14**
26	**T**	6:22	4.6	**6:56**	3.8	12:05	**1:00**
27	**W**	7:01	4.8	**7:35**	4.0	12:51	**1:44**
28	**T**	7:38	5.0	**8:13**	4.2	1:37	**2:26**
29	**F**	8:16	5.1	**8:53**	4.3	2:21	**3:07**
30	**S**	8:55	5.2	**9:36**	4.4	3:05	**3:47**
31	**S**	9:39	5.1	**10:23**	4.5	3:48	**4:27**

Standard Time

DAY OF MONTH	DAY OF WEEK	FEBRUARY HIGH a.m.	Ht.	**p.m.**	Ht.	LOW a.m.	**p.m.**
1	**M**	10:29	4.9	**11:14**	4.6	4:34	**5:09**
2	**T**	11:22	4.7	...	...	5:24	**5:56**
3	**W**	12:07	4.7	**12:18**	4.4	6:25	**6:51**
4	**T**	1:01	4.7	**1:17**	4.2	7:36	**7:56**
5	**F**	1:59	4.7	**2:21**	4.0	8:48	**9:03**
6	**S**	3:03	4.7	**3:33**	3.8	9:54	**10:05**
7	**S**	4:11	4.8	**4:46**	3.9	10:54	**11:03**
8	**M**	5:17	4.9	**5:50**	4.1	11:50	**11:59**
9	**T**	6:15	5.1	**6:45**	4.3	...	**12:43**
10	**W**	7:06	5.2	**7:34**	4.5	12:52	**1:33**
11	**T**	7:52	5.3	**8:19**	4.6	1:42	**2:19**
12	**F**	8:36	5.2	**9:04**	4.6	2:30	**3:02**
13	**S**	9:19	5.1	**9:48**	4.5	3:14	**3:43**
14	**S**	10:03	4.8	**10:31**	4.4	3:56	**4:20**
15	**M**	10:46	4.5	**11:14**	4.3	4:38	**4:57**
16	**T**	11:30	4.2	**11:55**	4.2	5:19	**5:32**
17	**W**	...	...	**12:14**	4.0	6:05	**6:08**
18	**T**	12:35	4.1	**1:00**	3.7	6:59	**6:51**
19	**F**	1:16	4.0	**1:48**	3.5	8:03	**7:50**
20	**S**	2:00	3.9	**2:44**	3.3	9:06	**8:56**
21	**S**	2:52	3.9	**3:46**	3.3	10:03	**9:54**
22	**M**	3:56	4.0	**4:49**	3.5	10:54	**10:47**
23	**T**	4:59	4.2	**5:42**	3.7	11:42	**11:37**
24	**W**	5:51	4.6	**6:27**	4.0	...	**12:29**
25	**T**	6:35	4.9	**7:08**	4.3	12:26	**1:14**
26	**F**	7:16	5.1	**7:47**	4.7	1:15	**1:57**
27	**S**	7:56	5.3	**8:27**	4.9	2:02	**2:39**
28	**S**	8:38	5.3	**9:11**	5.1	2:48	**3:21**

Dates when Ht. of **Low** Water is below Mean Lower Low with Ht. of lowest given for each period and Date of lowest in ( ):

January:

1st–3rd: -0.3' (1st)
7th–17th: -0.9' (13th)
27th–31st: -0.6' (29th–31st)

February:

1st–3rd: -0.5' (1st)
8th–14th: -0.7' (11th, 12th)
25th–28th: -0.8' (28th)

Average Rise and Fall 4.6 ft.

When a high tide exceeds avg. ht., the *following* low tide will be lower than avg.

2021 HIGH & LOW WATER
THE BATTERY, NY HARBOR
40°42'N, 74°00.8'W

***Daylight Time starts March 14 at 2 a.m.** **Daylight Saving Time**

DAY OF MONTH	DAY OF WEEK	MARCH						DAY OF MONTH	DAY OF WEEK	APRIL					
		HIGH				LOW				HIGH				LOW	
		a.m.	Ht.	**p.m.**	Ht.	a.m.	**p.m.**			a.m.	Ht.	**p.m.**	Ht.	a.m.	**p.m.**
1	**M**	9:25	5.3	**9:58**	5.2	3:35	**4:02**	1	**T**	11:59	4.8	...	...	6:01	**6:10**
2	**T**	10:14	5.0	**10:49**	5.2	4:22	**4:44**	2	**F**	12:23	5.5	**1:00**	4.5	6:58	**7:07**
3	**W**	11:09	4.8	**11:43**	5.2	5:13	**5:30**	3	**S**	1:23	5.2	**2:03**	4.3	8:03	**8:16**
4	**T**	...	...	**12:07**	4.5	6:11	**6:26**	4	**S**	2:25	5.0	**3:08**	4.2	9:12	**9:29**
5	**F**	12:40	5.0	**1:09**	4.2	7:19	**7:33**	5	**M**	3:31	4.8	**4:15**	4.1	10:18	**10:36**
6	**S**	1:40	4.9	**2:14**	4.0	8:31	**8:45**	6	**T**	4:39	4.7	**5:22**	4.3	11:17	**11:35**
7	**S**	2:46	4.7	**3:26**	3.9	9:38	**9:51**	7	**W**	5:45	4.7	**6:21**	4.5	...	**12:09**
8	**M**	3:57	4.7	**4:37**	4.0	10:38	**10:50**	8	**T**	6:41	4.8	**7:11**	4.7	12:29	**12:56**
9	**T**	5:05	4.8	**5:40**	4.2	11:32	**11:46**	9	**F**	7:28	4.9	**7:53**	4.9	1:18	**1:41**
10	**W**	6:02	4.9	**6:32**	4.5	...	**12:23**	10	**S**	8:10	4.9	**8:32**	5.1	2:05	**2:22**
11	**T**	6:51	5.1	**7:17**	4.7	12:37	**1:10**	11	**S**	8:49	4.9	**9:07**	5.2	2:48	**3:01**
12	**F**	7:34	5.1	**7:58**	4.8	1:25	**1:53**	12	**M**	9:27	4.8	**9:41**	5.2	3:30	**3:37**
13	**S**	8:14	5.1	**8:37**	4.9	2:11	**2:34**	13	**T**	10:05	4.6	**10:14**	5.1	4:09	**4:11**
14	**S**	*9:54	5.0	***10:15**	4.9	*3:53	***4:11**	14	**W**	10:45	4.4	**10:44**	4.9	4:47	**4:43**
15	**M**	10:33	4.8	**10:52**	4.8	4:33	**4:46**	15	**T**	11:27	4.2	**11:14**	4.8	5:24	**5:11**
16	**T**	11:14	4.5	**11:28**	4.7	5:11	**5:18**	16	**F**	-A-		**11:45**	4.6	6:01	**5:38**
17	**W**	11:56	4.2	...	...	5:49	**5:47**	17	**S**	...	...	**12:55**	3.8	6:40	**6:08**
18	**T**	12:03	4.5	**12:39**	4.0	6:28	**6:14**	18	**S**	12:24	4.5	**1:41**	3.7	7:29	**6:49**
19	**F**	12:38	4.3	**1:24**	3.7	7:12	**6:42**	19	**M**	1:12	4.4	**2:30**	3.7	8:36	**7:58**
20	**S**	1:14	4.2	**2:11**	3.6	8:11	**7:26**	20	**T**	2:08	4.3	**3:23**	3.8	9:43	**9:36**
21	**S**	1:57	4.1	**3:03**	3.5	9:21	**8:55**	21	**W**	3:10	4.4	**4:22**	4.0	10:39	**10:44**
22	**M**	2:50	4.1	**4:02**	3.5	10:24	**10:15**	22	**T**	4:19	4.5	**5:22**	4.3	11:30	**11:42**
23	**T**	3:55	4.1	**5:06**	3.7	11:18	**11:15**	23	**F**	5:27	4.7	**6:16**	4.8	...	**12:17**
24	**W**	5:08	4.3	**6:04**	4.0	...	**12:07**	24	**S**	6:27	5.0	**7:04**	5.3	12:36	**1:04**
25	**T**	6:11	4.6	**6:53**	4.4	12:09	**12:54**	25	**S**	7:20	5.2	**7:50**	5.8	1:29	**1:51**
26	**F**	7:03	5.0	**7:37**	4.8	1:01	**1:40**	26	**M**	8:09	5.3	**8:35**	6.1	2:21	**2:38**
27	**S**	7:49	5.2	**8:19**	5.2	1:52	**2:25**	27	**T**	8:58	5.3	**9:22**	6.2	3:13	**3:26**
28	**S**	8:33	5.4	**9:01**	5.6	2:42	**3:09**	28	**W**	9:50	5.2	**10:12**	6.2	4:04	**4:13**
29	**M**	9:18	5.4	**9:45**	5.8	3:31	**3:52**	29	**T**	10:47	5.0	**11:07**	5.9	4:55	**5:02**
30	**T**	10:06	5.3	**10:33**	5.8	4:20	**4:36**	30	**F**	11:49	4.8	...	...	5:47	**5:53**
31	**W**	11:00	5.1	**11:26**	5.7	5:09	**5:21**								

A also at 12:11 p.m. (4.0)

Dates when Ht. of **Low** Water is below Mean Lower Low with Ht. of lowest given for each period and Date of lowest in ( ):

1st–3rd: -0.8' (1st)
10th–14th: -0.4' (12th, 13th)
27th–31st: -0.8' (29th, 30th)

1st–2nd: -0.5' (1st)
25th–30th: -0.8' (28th, 29th)

Average Rise and Fall 4.6 ft.

When a high tide exceeds avg. ht., the *following* low tide will be lower than avg.

2021 HIGH & LOW WATER THE BATTERY, NY HARBOR

40°42'N, 74°00.8'W

DAY OF MONTH	DAY OF WEEK	MAY (Daylight Saving Time)						DAY OF MONTH	DAY OF WEEK	JUNE (Daylight Saving Time)					
		HIGH				LOW				HIGH				LOW	
		a.m.	Ht.	p.m.	Ht.	a.m.	p.m.			a.m.	Ht.	p.m.	Ht.	a.m.	p.m.
1	S	12:08	5.7	12:52	4.6	6:43	6:51	1	T	1:51	5.1	2:33	4.6	8:21	8:43
2	S	1:09	5.3	1:54	4.5	7:44	7:58	2	W	2:45	4.8	3:28	4.6	9:20	9:48
3	M	2:10	5.1	2:55	4.4	8:50	9:09	3	T	3:40	4.5	4:23	4.6	10:14	10:46
4	T	3:11	4.8	3:56	4.4	9:53	10:15	4	F	4:36	4.4	5:16	4.7	11:02	11:38
5	W	4:13	4.6	4:57	4.5	10:49	11:14	5	S	5:31	4.3	6:06	4.9	11:46	...
6	T	5:14	4.6	5:53	4.7	11:39	...	6	S	6:23	4.2	6:50	5.0	12:26	12:28
7	F	6:09	4.6	6:42	4.9	12:06	12:24	7	M	7:11	4.3	7:30	5.2	1:12	1:09
8	S	6:58	4.6	7:24	5.1	12:54	1:06	8	T	7:54	4.3	8:06	5.2	1:57	1:50
9	S	7:41	4.6	8:02	5.2	1:40	1:46	9	W	8:36	4.3	8:39	5.2	2:40	2:30
10	M	8:22	4.6	8:36	5.3	2:24	2:25	10	T	9:17	4.3	9:11	5.2	3:22	3:10
11	T	9:01	4.5	9:09	5.3	3:06	3:03	11	F	9:57	4.2	9:42	5.1	4:02	3:49
12	W	9:40	4.4	9:39	5.2	3:46	3:39	12	S	10:39	4.1	10:13	5.1	4:41	4:25
13	T	10:20	4.3	10:08	5.1	4:25	4:13	13	S	11:22	4.1	10:50	5.0	5:20	5:01
14	F	11:03	4.1	10:36	4.9	5:02	4:45	14	M	-B-		11:35	4.9	5:58	5:38
15	S	11:47	4.0	11:10	4.8	5:40	5:16	15	T	...	...	12:50	4.1	6:39	6:22
16	S	-A-		11:53	4.7	6:18	5:49	16	W	12:25	4.8	1:35	4.3	7:25	7:20
17	M	...	...	1:16	3.9	7:02	6:32	17	T	1:19	4.8	2:22	4.5	8:20	8:37
18	T	12:45	4.6	2:02	3.9	7:58	7:34	18	F	2:14	4.7	3:13	4.7	9:19	9:50
19	W	1:40	4.6	2:51	4.1	9:01	9:02	19	S	3:13	4.6	4:09	5.0	10:15	10:54
20	T	2:39	4.6	3:45	4.4	9:59	10:15	20	S	4:18	4.6	5:08	5.4	11:09	11:53
21	F	3:41	4.6	4:42	4.7	10:51	11:16	21	M	5:27	4.6	6:07	5.7	...	12:01
22	S	4:48	4.7	5:39	5.2	11:41	...	22	T	6:33	4.7	7:03	6.0	12:50	12:55
23	S	5:53	4.8	6:33	5.6	12:13	12:30	23	W	7:33	4.8	7:56	6.2	1:46	1:50
24	M	6:53	4.9	7:24	6.0	1:08	1:20	24	T	8:29	4.9	8:48	6.2	2:40	2:44
25	T	7:48	5.1	8:13	6.2	2:03	2:11	25	F	9:24	4.9	9:41	6.1	3:33	3:38
26	W	8:42	5.1	9:02	6.3	2:56	3:02	26	S	10:21	4.8	10:37	5.9	4:24	4:30
27	T	9:37	5.0	9:55	6.2	3:49	3:54	27	S	11:20	4.8	11:34	5.6	5:13	5:21
28	F	10:35	4.9	10:52	6.0	4:40	4:45	28	M	...	...	12:18	4.8	6:02	6:14
29	S	11:37	4.8	11:52	5.7	5:32	5:38	29	T	12:30	5.3	1:13	4.7	6:53	7:10
30	S	...	...	12:39	4.7	6:25	6:34	30	W	1:22	5.0	2:04	4.7	7:45	8:11
31	M	12:52	5.3	1:37	4.6	7:21	7:37								

A also at 12:31 p.m. (3.9) **B** also at 12:06 p.m. (4.1)

Dates when Ht. of **Low** Water is below Mean Lower Low with Ht. of lowest given for each period and Date of lowest in ( ):

1st: -0.2'
24th–30th: -0.8' (27th)

23rd–28th: -0.7' (25th)

Average Rise and Fall 4.6 ft.

When a high tide exceeds avg. ht., the *following* low tide will be lower than avg.

2021 HIGH & LOW WATER
THE BATTERY, NY HARBOR
40°42'N, 74°00.8'W

DAY OF MONTH	DAY OF WEEK	JULY (Daylight Saving Time)						DAY OF MONTH	DAY OF WEEK	AUGUST (Daylight Saving Time)					
		HIGH				LOW				HIGH				LOW	
		a.m.	Ht.	**p.m.**	Ht.	a.m.	**p.m.**			a.m.	Ht.	**p.m.**	Ht.	a.m.	**p.m.**
1	**T**	2:14	4.7	**2:54**	4.6	8:39	**9:14**	1	**S**	3:17	4.0	**3:46**	4.6	9:33	**10:32**
2	**F**	3:03	4.4	**3:43**	4.6	9:31	**10:13**	2	**M**	4:11	3.8	**4:37**	4.6	10:25	**11:24**
3	**S**	3:55	4.2	**4:33**	4.7	10:20	**11:07**	3	**T**	5:11	3.8	**5:31**	4.7	11:14	...
4	**S**	4:50	4.0	**5:24**	4.7	11:06	**11:56**	4	**W**	6:08	3.9	**6:22**	4.8	12:12	**12:01**
5	**M**	5:47	4.0	**6:12**	4.8	11:50	...	5	**T**	7:00	4.0	**7:08**	5.0	12:58	**12:48**
6	**T**	6:40	4.0	**6:56**	5.0	12:43	**12:34**	6	**F**	7:44	4.2	**7:48**	5.2	1:44	**1:34**
7	**W**	7:28	4.1	**7:37**	5.1	1:28	**1:17**	7	**S**	8:25	4.4	**8:24**	5.3	2:27	**2:20**
8	**T**	8:11	4.2	**8:13**	5.2	2:13	**2:01**	8	**S**	9:03	4.5	**8:59**	5.4	3:09	**3:04**
9	**F**	8:52	4.2	**8:48**	5.2	2:56	**2:45**	9	**M**	9:40	4.7	**9:35**	5.4	3:49	**3:47**
10	**S**	9:32	4.3	**9:21**	5.2	3:38	**3:27**	10	**T**	10:19	4.8	**10:14**	5.4	4:28	**4:30**
11	**S**	10:11	4.3	**9:56**	5.2	4:18	**4:07**	11	**W**	11:02	4.9	**10:59**	5.3	5:06	**5:13**
12	**M**	10:52	4.3	**10:34**	5.2	4:56	**4:46**	12	**T**	11:48	5.0	**11:49**	5.1	5:44	**6:00**
13	**T**	11:35	4.4	**11:18**	5.1	5:34	**5:27**	13	**F**	...	...	**12:38**	5.1	6:25	**6:54**
14	**W**	...	...	**12:20**	4.5	6:12	**6:12**	14	**S**	12:44	4.8	**1:30**	5.2	7:13	**8:01**
15	**T**	12:07	5.0	**1:07**	4.7	6:54	**7:07**	15	**S**	1:42	4.6	**2:24**	5.3	8:13	**9:13**
16	**F**	1:00	4.8	**1:55**	4.9	7:43	**8:17**	16	**M**	2:43	4.4	**3:23**	5.3	9:22	**10:21**
17	**S**	1:55	4.7	**2:46**	5.1	8:42	**9:30**	17	**T**	3:52	4.3	**4:29**	5.4	10:28	**11:23**
18	**S**	2:54	4.5	**3:42**	5.2	9:44	**10:36**	18	**W**	5:05	4.3	**5:38**	5.5	11:29	...
19	**M**	3:59	4.4	**4:44**	5.4	10:44	**11:37**	19	**T**	6:15	4.5	**6:40**	5.6	12:20	**12:27**
20	**T**	5:11	4.4	**5:48**	5.6	11:42	...	20	**F**	7:15	4.7	**7:35**	5.8	1:14	**1:22**
21	**W**	6:21	4.5	**6:49**	5.8	12:34	**12:38**	21	**S**	8:07	4.9	**8:25**	5.8	2:06	**2:16**
22	**T**	7:23	4.6	**7:45**	6.0	1:30	**1:35**	22	**S**	8:55	5.1	**9:11**	5.8	2:54	**3:06**
23	**F**	8:19	4.8	**8:37**	6.0	2:24	**2:30**	23	**M**	9:41	5.2	**9:56**	5.6	3:40	**3:54**
24	**S**	9:11	4.9	**9:28**	5.9	3:15	**3:23**	24	**T**	10:27	5.1	**10:41**	5.4	4:22	**4:39**
25	**S**	10:04	4.9	**10:19**	5.8	4:04	**4:13**	25	**W**	11:13	5.1	**11:27**	5.1	5:02	**5:23**
26	**M**	10:57	4.9	**11:10**	5.5	4:50	**5:02**	26	**T**	11:59	5.0	...	...	5:41	**6:08**
27	**T**	11:49	4.9	...	...	5:35	**5:50**	27	**F**	12:14	4.7	**12:44**	4.8	6:18	**6:56**
28	**W**	12:01	5.2	**12:40**	4.8	6:19	**6:40**	28	**S**	1:02	4.4	**1:27**	4.7	6:57	**7:50**
29	**T**	12:50	4.9	**1:27**	4.8	7:03	**7:34**	29	**S**	1:50	4.1	**2:10**	4.6	7:41	**8:52**
30	**F**	1:38	4.6	**2:13**	4.7	7:50	**8:34**	30	**M**	2:41	3.9	**2:56**	4.5	8:37	**9:54**
31	**S**	2:26	4.3	**2:59**	4.6	8:41	**9:35**	31	**T**	3:35	3.8	**3:47**	4.4	9:41	**10:50**

Dates when Ht. of **Low** Water is below Mean Lower Low with Ht. of lowest given for each period and Date of lowest in ( ):

22nd–27th: -0.5' (24th, 25th)

21st–24th: -0.4' (23rd)

Average Rise and Fall 4.6 ft.

When a high tide exceeds avg. ht., the *following* low tide will be lower than avg.

2021 HIGH & LOW WATER
THE BATTERY, NY HARBOR
40°42'N, 74°00.8'W

		Daylight Saving Time								Daylight Saving Time					
DAY OF MONTH	DAY OF WEEK	SEPTEMBER						DAY OF MONTH	DAY OF WEEK	OCTOBER					
		HIGH				LOW				HIGH				LOW	
		a.m.	Ht.	**p.m.**	Ht.	a.m.	**p.m.**			a.m.	Ht.	**p.m.**	Ht.	a.m.	**p.m.**
1	**W**	4:36	3.8	**4:45**	4.5	10:39	**11:40**	1	**F**	4:59	3.9	**4:57**	4.6	11:00	**11:52**
2	**T**	5:35	3.9	**5:44**	4.7	11:31	...	2	**S**	5:51	4.2	**5:54**	4.8	11:51	...
3	**F**	6:28	4.1	**6:35**	4.9	12:27	**12:20**	3	**S**	6:38	4.5	**6:42**	5.1	12:36	**12:40**
4	**S**	7:14	4.3	**7:18**	5.2	1:11	**1:07**	4	**M**	7:19	4.9	**7:25**	5.3	1:18	**1:28**
5	**S**	7:53	4.6	**7:56**	5.4	1:54	**1:54**	5	**T**	7:58	5.3	**8:06**	5.5	2:01	**2:17**
6	**M**	8:31	4.9	**8:33**	5.5	2:36	**2:40**	6	**W**	8:36	5.7	**8:48**	5.5	2:43	**3:05**
7	**T**	9:08	5.2	**9:11**	5.6	3:17	**3:26**	7	**T**	9:17	5.9	**9:32**	5.4	3:25	**3:53**
8	**W**	9:47	5.4	**9:53**	5.5	3:57	**4:11**	8	**F**	10:02	6.0	**10:22**	5.2	4:07	**4:42**
9	**T**	10:29	5.5	**10:39**	5.3	4:36	**4:58**	9	**S**	10:52	5.9	**11:20**	4.9	4:51	**5:33**
10	**F**	11:18	5.6	**11:33**	5.1	5:16	**5:46**	10	**S**	11:49	5.8	...	...	5:38	**6:28**
11	**S**	...	...	**12:11**	5.6	5:59	**6:41**	11	**M**	12:24	4.6	**12:51**	5.5	6:32	**7:31**
12	**S**	12:32	4.8	**1:08**	5.5	6:49	**7:46**	12	**T**	1:31	4.4	**1:55**	5.3	7:38	**8:41**
13	**M**	1:35	4.5	**2:07**	5.4	7:53	**8:58**	13	**W**	2:37	4.3	**3:01**	5.1	8:53	**9:49**
14	**T**	2:41	4.3	**3:11**	5.3	9:07	**10:07**	14	**T**	3:44	4.3	**4:07**	5.0	10:04	**10:50**
15	**W**	3:50	4.3	**4:20**	5.2	10:17	**11:08**	15	**F**	4:51	4.4	**5:13**	5.0	11:07	**11:43**
16	**T**	5:02	4.3	**5:29**	5.3	11:19	...	16	**S**	5:53	4.7	**6:11**	5.1	...	**12:02**
17	**F**	6:08	4.6	**6:30**	5.4	12:04	**12:16**	17	**S**	6:46	4.9	**7:01**	5.1	12:32	**12:53**
18	**S**	7:03	4.8	**7:22**	5.5	12:55	**1:09**	18	**M**	7:31	5.2	**7:45**	5.2	1:17	**1:41**
19	**S**	7:51	5.1	**8:07**	5.6	1:44	**2:00**	19	**T**	8:11	5.3	**8:25**	5.1	1:59	**2:27**
20	**M**	8:35	5.3	**8:49**	5.5	2:29	**2:48**	20	**W**	8:48	5.4	**9:04**	5.0	2:39	**3:11**
21	**T**	9:16	5.3	**9:30**	5.4	3:11	**3:33**	21	**T**	9:23	5.4	**9:43**	4.8	3:17	**3:52**
22	**W**	9:55	5.3	**10:11**	5.1	3:51	**4:16**	22	**F**	9:57	5.2	**10:24**	4.5	3:53	**4:32**
23	**T**	10:34	5.2	**10:54**	4.8	4:28	**4:57**	23	**S**	10:31	5.1	**11:08**	4.2	4:27	**5:11**
24	**F**	11:14	5.1	**11:39**	4.5	5:02	**5:38**	24	**S**	11:05	4.9	**11:56**	4.0	4:59	**5:51**
25	**S**	11:54	4.9	...	...	5:35	**6:20**	25	**M**	11:41	4.7	...	...	5:28	**6:33**
26	**S**	12:27	4.2	**12:35**	4.7	6:06	**7:08**	26	**T**	12:46	3.8	**12:23**	4.5	5:57	**7:24**
27	**M**	1:17	4.0	**1:17**	4.5	6:37	**8:07**	27	**W**	1:37	3.7	**1:12**	4.4	6:36	**8:27**
28	**T**	2:08	3.8	**2:03**	4.4	7:23	**9:12**	28	**T**	2:28	3.6	**2:06**	4.3	7:43	**9:31**
29	**W**	3:02	3.7	**2:55**	4.4	8:48	**10:13**	29	**F**	3:20	3.7	**3:04**	4.3	9:19	**10:25**
30	**T**	3:59	3.7	**3:55**	4.4	10:02	**11:05**	30	**S**	4:14	3.9	**4:05**	4.4	10:26	**11:13**
								31	**S**	5:07	4.2	**5:06**	4.6	11:21	**11:57**

Dates when Ht. of **Low** Water is below Mean Lower Low with Ht. of lowest given for each period and Date of lowest in ( ):

8th–10th: -0.3' (8th, 9th)
20th–21st: -0.2'

6th–9th: -0.4' (7th, 8th)

Average Rise and Fall 4.6 ft.

When a high tide exceeds avg. ht., the *following* low tide will be lower than avg.

2021 HIGH & LOW WATER
THE BATTERY, NY HARBOR
40°42'N, 74°00.8'W

***Standard Time starts Nov. 7 at 2 a.m.** | **Standard Time**

DAY OF MONTH	DAY OF WEEK	NOVEMBER						DAY OF MONTH	DAY OF WEEK	DECEMBER					
		HIGH				LOW				HIGH				LOW	
		a.m.	Ht.	**p.m.**	Ht.	a.m.	**p.m.**			a.m.	Ht.	**p.m.**	Ht.	a.m.	**p.m.**
1	**M**	5:58	4.6	**6:02**	4.8	...	**12:13**	1	**W**	5:09	5.2	**5:23**	4.6	11:41	**11:53**
2	**T**	6:43	5.1	**6:52**	5.1	12:41	**1:04**	2	**T**	5:58	5.6	**6:18**	4.8	...	**12:35**
3	**W**	7:26	5.6	**7:40**	5.2	1:25	**1:55**	3	**F**	6:46	5.9	**7:10**	4.8	12:43	**1:28**
4	**T**	8:09	5.9	**8:27**	5.2	2:10	**2:46**	4	**S**	7:34	6.1	**8:03**	4.8	1:33	**2:21**
5	**F**	8:53	6.1	**9:15**	5.1	2:56	**3:36**	5	**S**	8:25	6.0	**8:58**	4.7	2:25	**3:13**
6	**S**	9:40	6.1	**10:09**	4.9	3:43	**4:27**	6	**M**	9:20	5.9	**9:59**	4.6	3:17	**4:04**
7	**S**	*9:33	6.0	***10:09**	4.7	*3:32	***4:19**	7	**T**	10:20	5.6	**11:03**	4.4	4:09	**4:57**
8	**M**	10:33	5.7	**11:16**	4.5	4:22	**5:14**	8	**W**	11:22	5.3	...	...	5:04	**5:53**
9	**T**	11:37	5.4	...	...	5:18	**6:14**	9	**T**	12:06	4.3	**12:22**	5.0	6:04	**6:52**
10	**W**	12:22	4.4	**12:42**	5.2	6:23	**7:20**	10	**F**	1:05	4.3	**1:20**	4.7	7:11	**7:53**
11	**T**	1:26	4.3	**1:44**	4.9	7:36	**8:25**	11	**S**	2:02	4.3	**2:16**	4.4	8:20	**8:51**
12	**F**	2:28	4.3	**2:46**	4.8	8:46	**9:25**	12	**S**	2:59	4.3	**3:13**	4.2	9:22	**9:43**
13	**S**	3:30	4.4	**3:47**	4.6	9:48	**10:17**	13	**M**	3:55	4.4	**4:10**	4.1	10:18	**10:29**
14	**S**	4:29	4.6	**4:44**	4.6	10:43	**11:03**	14	**T**	4:48	4.5	**5:04**	4.0	11:08	**11:13**
15	**M**	5:20	4.8	**5:35**	4.6	11:33	**11:46**	15	**W**	5:35	4.7	**5:53**	4.0	11:55	**11:55**
16	**T**	6:05	5.0	**6:20**	4.6	...	**12:20**	16	**T**	6:17	4.8	**6:38**	4.0	...	**12:41**
17	**W**	6:45	5.2	**7:01**	4.6	12:27	**1:05**	17	**F**	6:55	4.9	**7:20**	4.1	12:36	**1:24**
18	**T**	7:21	5.2	**7:41**	4.5	1:07	**1:48**	18	**S**	7:30	4.9	**8:00**	4.0	1:17	**2:06**
19	**F**	7:54	5.2	**8:20**	4.3	1:46	**2:29**	19	**S**	8:04	4.9	**8:40**	4.0	1:57	**2:47**
20	**S**	8:27	5.1	**9:01**	4.2	2:23	**3:09**	20	**M**	8:37	4.8	**9:21**	3.8	2:36	**3:26**
21	**S**	8:58	4.9	**9:43**	4.0	2:59	**3:48**	21	**T**	9:09	4.7	**10:02**	3.7	3:13	**4:04**
22	**M**	9:29	4.8	**10:28**	3.8	3:32	**4:26**	22	**W**	9:42	4.6	**10:44**	3.7	3:47	**4:41**
23	**T**	10:03	4.6	**11:16**	3.7	4:04	**5:06**	23	**T**	10:19	4.5	**11:27**	3.7	4:21	**5:19**
24	**W**	10:44	4.4	...	...	4:35	**5:49**	24	**F**	11:04	4.4	...	...	4:58	**6:00**
25	**T**	12:04	3.6	**-A-**		5:13	**6:41**	25	**S**	12:10	3.7	**-B-**		5:45	**6:49**
26	**F**	12:50	3.6	**12:25**	4.3	6:06	**7:41**	26	**S**	12:55	3.9	**12:45**	4.2	6:52	**7:47**
27	**S**	1:37	3.7	**1:20**	4.3	7:31	**8:39**	27	**M**	1:43	4.1	**1:41**	4.2	8:14	**8:46**
28	**S**	2:27	3.9	**2:18**	4.3	8:49	**9:31**	28	**T**	2:37	4.4	**2:43**	4.1	9:24	**9:41**
29	**M**	3:20	4.3	**3:20**	4.4	9:52	**10:18**	29	**W**	3:36	4.7	**3:51**	4.1	10:25	**10:35**
30	**T**	4:15	4.7	**4:23**	4.5	10:47	**11:05**	30	**T**	4:36	5.1	**5:00**	4.2	11:22	**11:28**
								31	**F**	5:35	5.4	**6:02**	4.3	...	**12:18**

A also at 11:32 a.m. (4.3) **B** also at 11:53 a.m. (4.3)

Dates when Ht. of **Low** Water is below Mean Lower Low with Ht. of lowest given for each period and Date of lowest in ( ):

3rd–8th: -0.7' (5th, 6th)
30th: -0.2'

1st–8th: -1.0' (5th)
29th–31st: -0.6' (31st)

Average Rise and Fall 4.6 ft.

When a high tide exceeds avg. ht., the *following* low tide will be lower than avg.

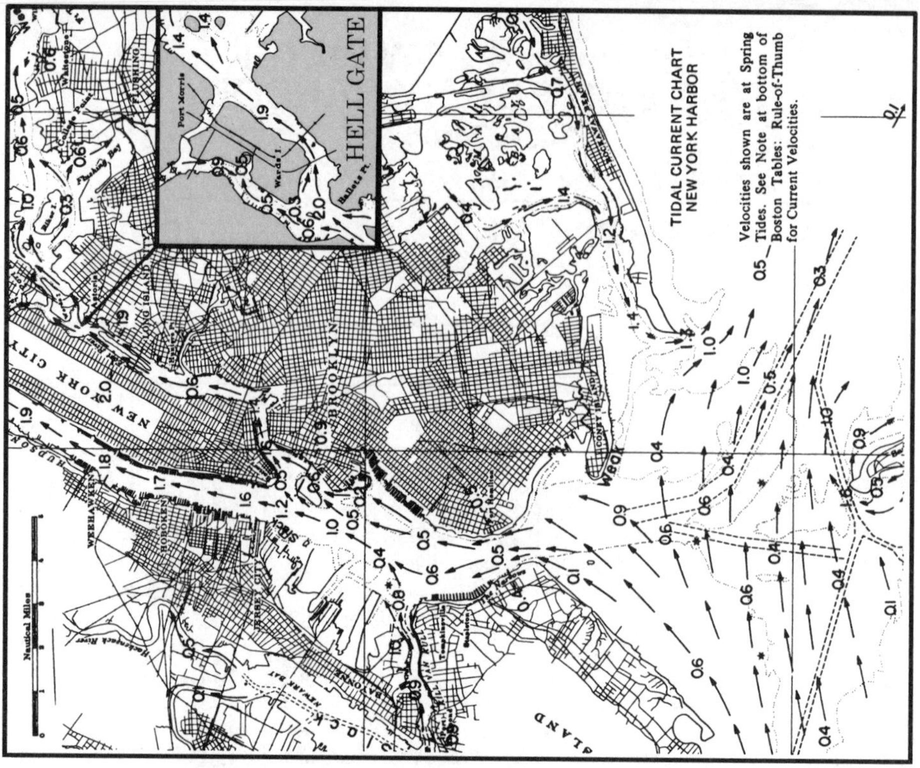
TIDAL CURRENT CHART
NEW YORK HARBOR
Velocities shown are at Spring Tides. See Note at bottom of Boston Tables: Rule-of-Thumb for Current Velocities.
HELL GATE
NEW YORK CITY
BROOKLYN
Nautical Miles

1 HOUR AFTER HIGH WATER AT THE BATTERY

NEW YORK BAY CURRENTS

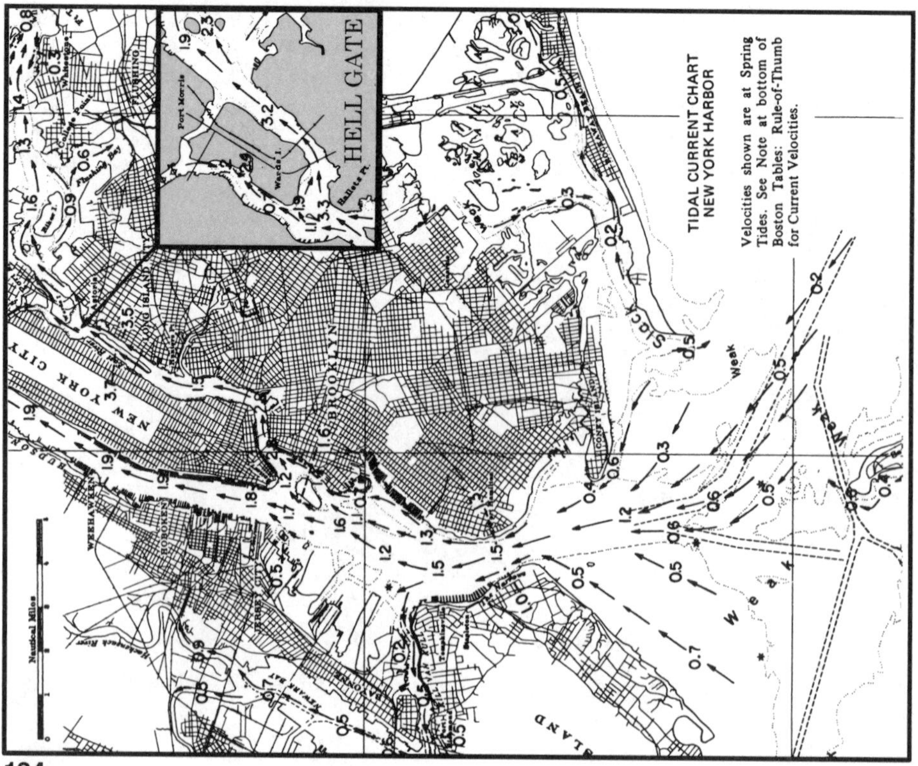
TIDAL CURRENT CHART
NEW YORK HARBOR
Velocities shown are at Spring Tides. See Note at bottom of Boston Tables: Rule-of-Thumb for Current Velocities.
HELL GATE
NEW YORK CITY
BROOKLYN
Nautical Miles

HIGH WATER AT THE BATTERY

3 HOURS AFTER HIGH WATER AT THE BATTERY

TIDAL CURRENT CHART
NEW YORK HARBOR

Velocities shown are at Spring Tides. See Note at bottom of Boston Tables: Rule-of-Thumb for Current Velocities.

NEW YORK BAY CURRENTS

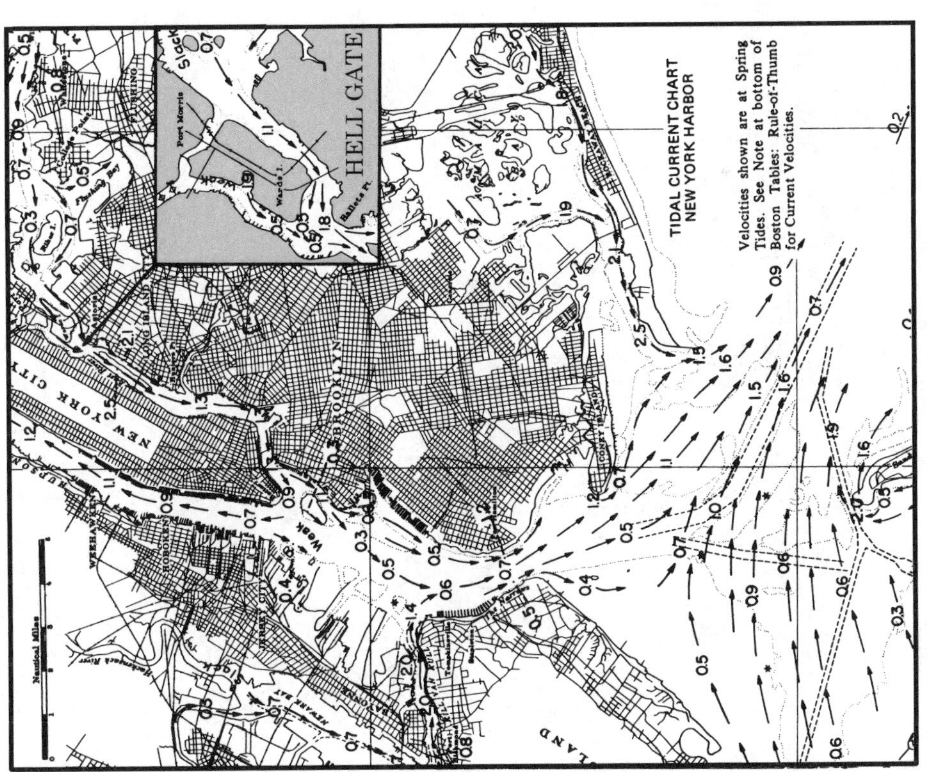

2 HOURS AFTER HIGH WATER AT THE BATTERY

TIDAL CURRENT CHART
NEW YORK HARBOR

Velocities shown are at Spring Tides. See Note at bottom of Boston Tables: Rule-of-Thumb for Current Velocities.

HELL GATE

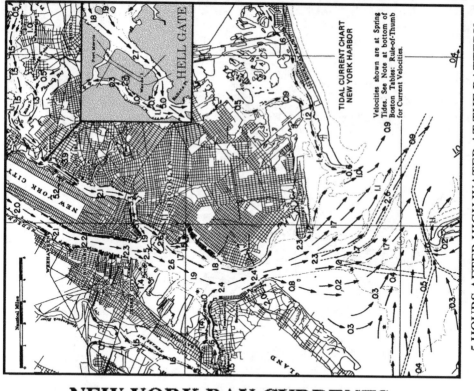

5 HOURS AFTER HIGH WATER AT THE BATTERY

NEW YORK BAY CURRENTS

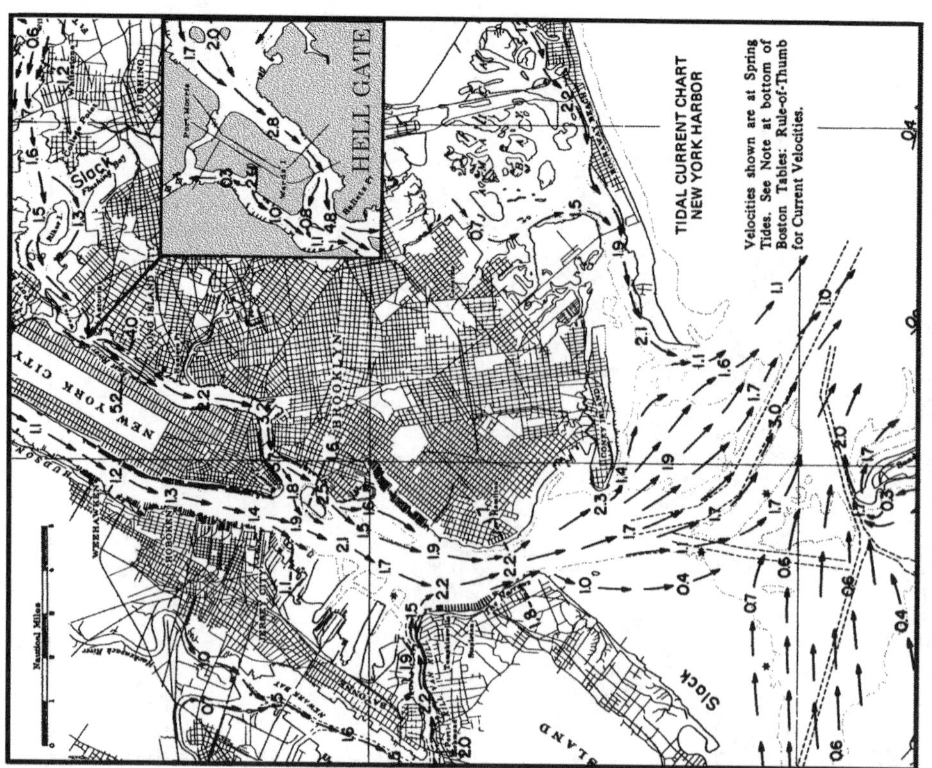

4 HOURS AFTER HIGH WATER AT THE BATTERY

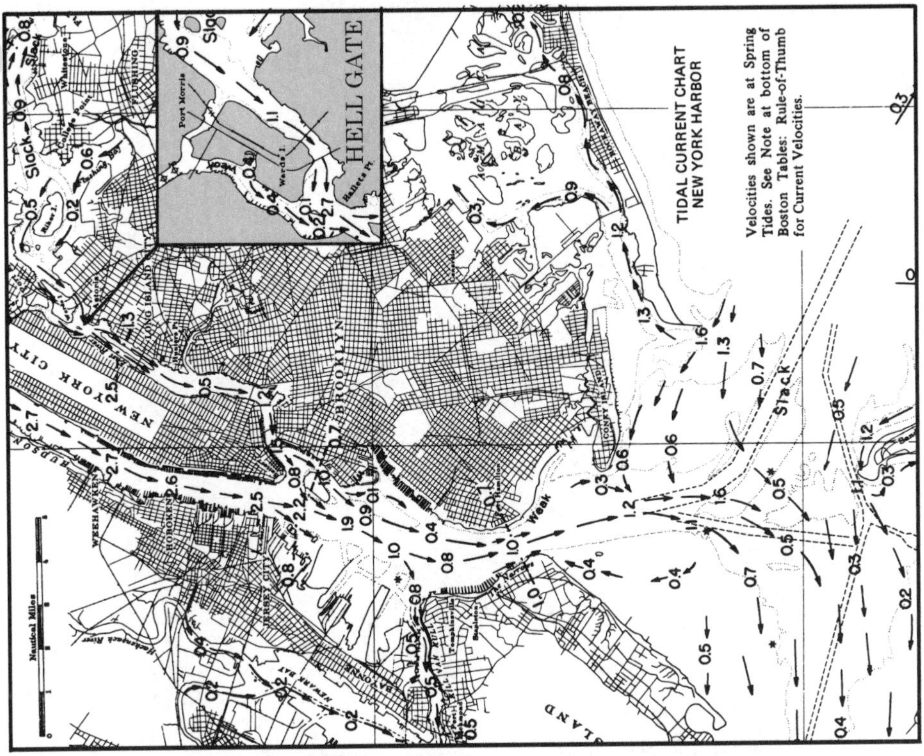

1 HOUR AFTER LOW WATER AT THE BATTERY

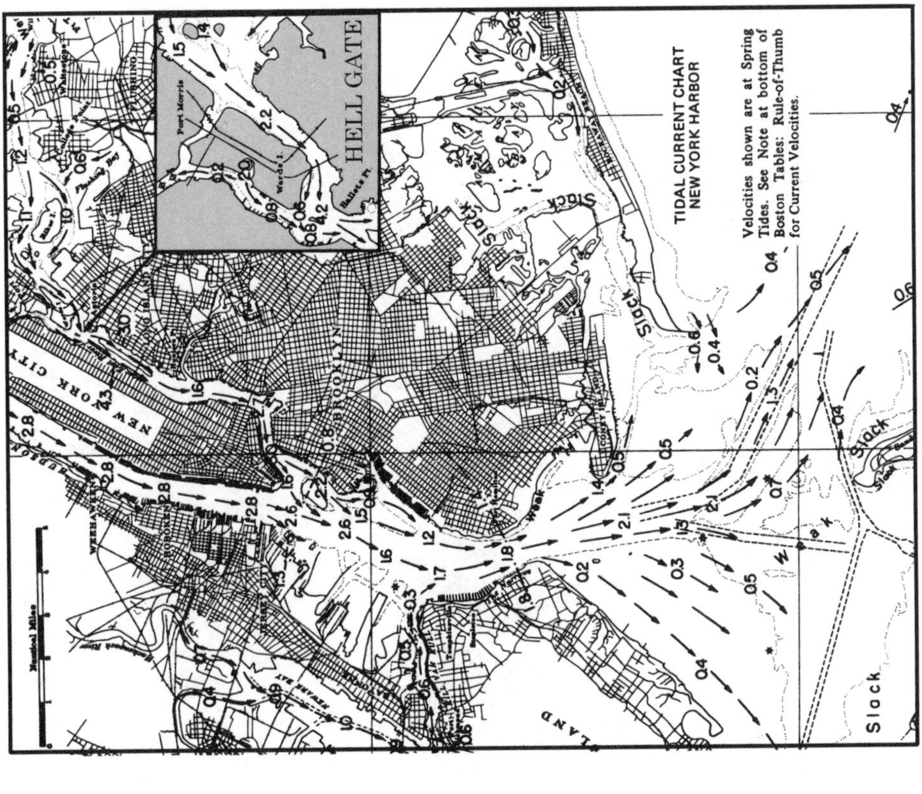

TIDAL CURRENT CHART
NEW YORK HARBOR

Velocities shown are at Spring Tides. See Note at bottom of Boston Tables: Rule-of-Thumb for Current Velocities.

HELL GATE

NEW YORK BAY CURRENTS

LOW WATER AT THE BATTERY

TIDAL CURRENT CHART
NEW YORK HARBOR

Velocities shown are at Spring Tides. See Note at bottom of Boston Tables: Rule-of-Thumb for Current Velocities.

HELL GATE

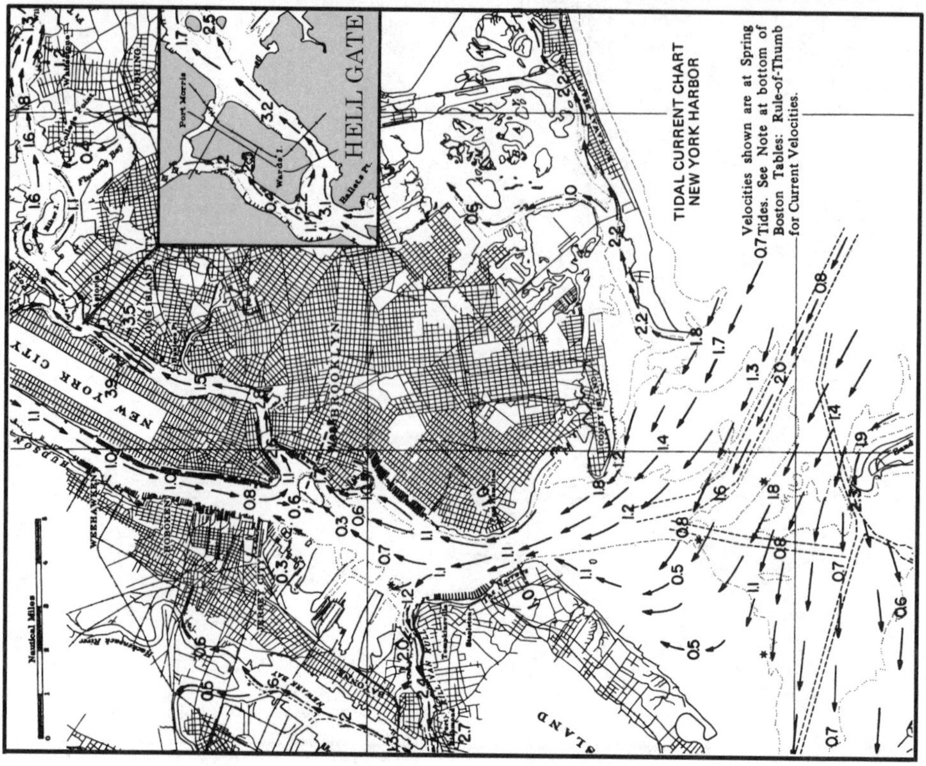

TIDAL CURRENT CHART
NEW YORK HARBOR

Velocities shown are at Spring Tides. See Note at bottom of Boston Tables: Rule-of-Thumb for Current Velocities.

3 HOURS AFTER LOW WATER AT THE BATTERY

NEW YORK BAY CURRENTS

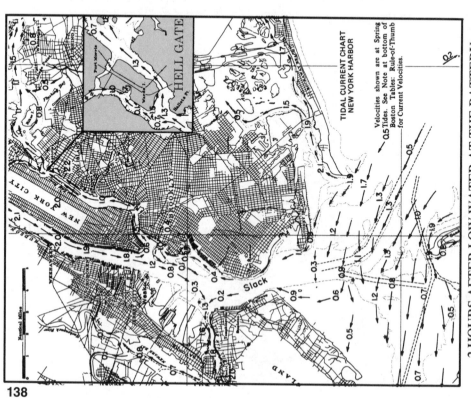

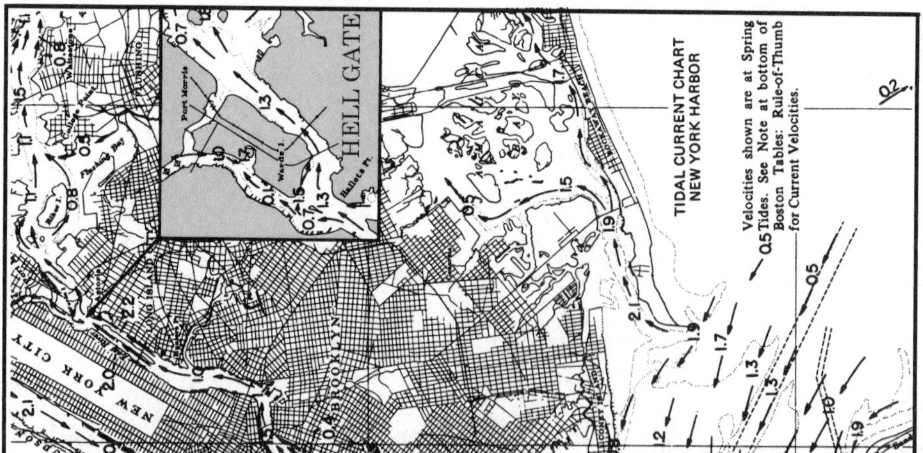

TIDAL CURRENT CHART
NEW YORK HARBOR

Velocities shown are at Spring Tides. See Note at bottom of Boston Tables: Rule-of-Thumb for Current Velocities.

2 HOURS AFTER LOW WATER AT THE BATTERY

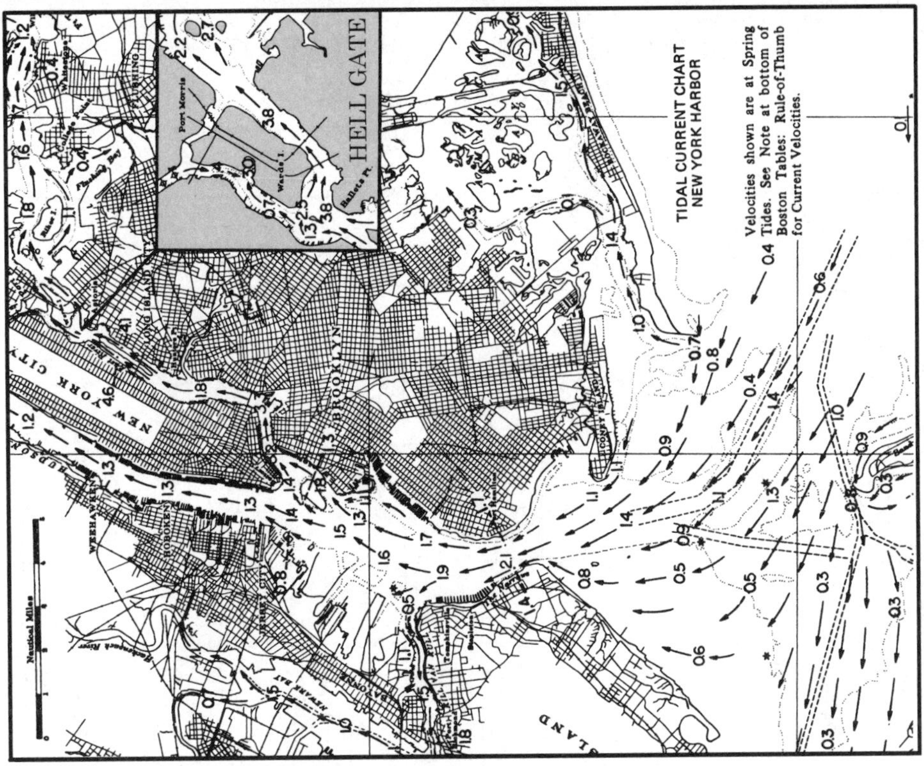
TIDAL CURRENT CHART
NEW YORK HARBOR
Velocities shown are at Spring Tides. See Note at bottom of Boston Tables: Rule-of-Thumb for Current Velocities.
HELL GATE
BROOKLYN
NEW YORK CITY
HOBOKEN

5 HOURS AFTER LOW WATER AT THE BATTERY

NEW YORK BAY CURRENTS

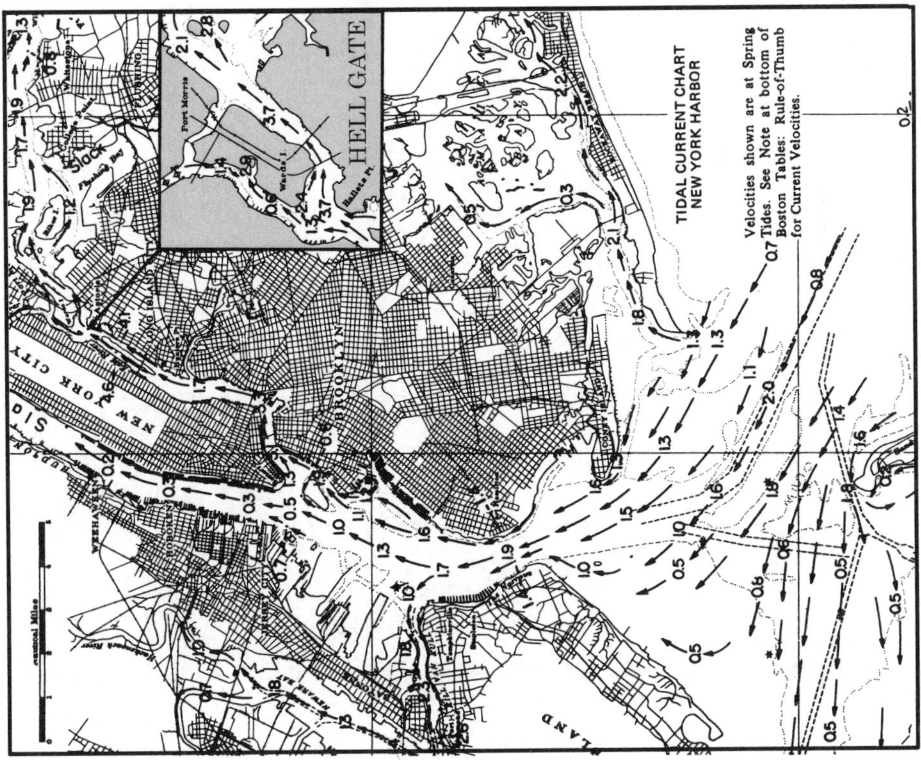
TIDAL CURRENT CHART
NEW YORK HARBOR
Velocities shown are at Spring Tides. See Note at bottom of Boston Tables: Rule-of-Thumb for Current Velocities.
HELL GATE
BROOKLYN
NEW YORK CITY
HOBOKEN

4 HOURS AFTER LOW WATER AT THE BATTERY

2021 HIGH & LOW WATER SANDY HOOK, NJ

40°28.1'N, 74°00.6'W

		Standard Time								Standard Time					
DAY OF MONTH	DAY OF WEEK	JANUARY						DAY OF MONTH	DAY OF WEEK	FEBRUARY					
		HIGH				LOW				HIGH				LOW	
		a.m.	Ht.	**p.m.**	Ht.	a.m.	**p.m.**			a.m.	Ht.	**p.m.**	Ht.	a.m.	**p.m.**
1	**F**	8:51	5.2	**9:32**	4.1	2:51	**3:41**	1	**M**	10:09	5.1	**10:50**	4.8	4:06	**4:39**
2	**S**	9:34	5.1	**10:21**	4.1	3:33	**4:21**	2	**T**	11:00	4.9	**11:43**	4.8	4:55	**5:23**
3	**S**	10:23	5.0	**11:13**	4.2	4:16	**5:03**	3	**W**	11:56	4.6	...	...	5:51	**6:14**
4	**M**	11:17	4.8	...	...	5:05	**5:50**	4	**T**	12:38	4.9	**12:53**	4.3	6:59	**7:17**
5	**T**	12:07	4.3	**12:13**	4.7	6:05	**6:45**	5	**F**	1:35	4.9	**1:55**	4.1	8:14	**8:26**
6	**W**	1:01	4.5	**1:10**	4.5	7:17	**7:48**	6	**S**	2:36	4.9	**3:01**	4.0	9:23	**9:32**
7	**T**	1:58	4.7	**2:11**	4.3	8:31	**8:50**	7	**S**	3:40	5.0	**4:11**	4.0	10:26	**10:32**
8	**F**	2:57	4.9	**3:16**	4.2	9:38	**9:49**	8	**M**	4:45	5.1	**5:16**	4.2	11:23	**11:29**
9	**S**	3:59	5.2	**4:23**	4.2	10:39	**10:45**	9	**T**	5:44	5.3	**6:12**	4.4	...	**12:16**
10	**S**	5:00	5.4	**5:26**	4.3	11:36	**11:40**	10	**W**	6:35	5.4	**7:02**	4.6	12:22	**1:05**
11	**M**	5:56	5.6	**6:23**	4.5	...	**12:30**	11	**T**	7:22	5.5	**7:48**	4.7	1:13	**1:51**
12	**T**	6:48	5.7	**7:15**	4.6	12:34	**1:23**	12	**F**	8:06	5.4	**8:32**	4.7	2:00	**2:34**
13	**W**	7:37	5.7	**8:05**	4.6	1:27	**2:12**	13	**S**	8:49	5.3	**9:15**	4.7	2:44	**3:13**
14	**T**	8:25	5.6	**8:54**	4.6	2:17	**2:58**	14	**S**	9:31	5.0	**9:58**	4.6	3:26	**3:49**
15	**F**	9:13	5.4	**9:44**	4.4	3:04	**3:42**	15	**M**	10:13	4.7	**10:40**	4.5	4:05	**4:23**
16	**S**	10:00	5.1	**10:33**	4.3	3:49	**4:23**	16	**T**	10:57	4.4	**11:21**	4.4	4:45	**4:57**
17	**S**	10:48	4.8	**11:22**	4.2	4:33	**5:03**	17	**W**	11:40	4.1	...	...	5:26	**5:31**
18	**M**	11:35	4.5	...	...	5:18	**5:44**	18	**T**	12:03	4.3	**12:26**	3.8	6:15	**6:11**
19	**T**	12:08	4.1	**12:21**	4.2	6:08	**6:28**	19	**F**	12:45	4.2	**1:14**	3.6	7:16	**7:04**
20	**W**	12:54	4.1	**1:07**	3.9	7:07	**7:17**	20	**S**	1:30	4.1	**2:06**	3.5	8:25	**8:11**
21	**T**	1:39	4.1	**1:56**	3.7	8:11	**8:11**	21	**S**	2:22	4.1	**3:05**	3.4	9:27	**9:16**
22	**F**	2:26	4.1	**2:50**	3.5	9:12	**9:05**	22	**M**	3:21	4.2	**4:07**	3.6	10:21	**10:13**
23	**S**	3:17	4.2	**3:47**	3.5	10:06	**9:56**	23	**T**	4:22	4.4	**5:04**	3.8	11:11	**11:05**
24	**S**	4:10	4.3	**4:44**	3.6	10:55	**10:45**	24	**W**	5:17	4.7	**5:54**	4.2	11:58	**11:56**
25	**M**	5:02	4.5	**5:36**	3.8	11:43	**11:32**	25	**T**	6:06	5.1	**6:39**	4.5	...	**12:44**
26	**T**	5:49	4.8	**6:22**	4.0	...	**12:29**	26	**F**	6:50	5.4	**7:21**	4.8	12:45	**1:28**
27	**W**	6:32	5.0	**7:05**	4.2	12:20	**1:14**	27	**S**	7:33	5.6	**8:04**	5.1	1:33	**2:10**
28	**T**	7:13	5.2	**7:46**	4.3	1:06	**1:57**	28	**S**	8:16	5.6	**8:48**	5.3	2:20	**2:52**
29	**F**	7:53	5.3	**8:27**	4.5	1:52	**2:38**								
30	**S**	8:35	5.4	**9:11**	4.6	2:36	**3:18**								
31	**S**	9:19	5.3	**9:59**	4.7	3:21	**3:58**								

Dates when Ht. of **Low** Water is below Mean Lower Low with Ht. of lowest given for each period and Date of lowest in ( ):

1st–3rd: -0.3' (1st)
8th–17th: -0.8' (12th–14th)
27th–31st: -0.6' (30th, 31st)

1st–3rd: -0.6' (1st)
8th–15th: -0.6' (10th–13th)
25th–28th: -0.8' (28th)

Average Rise and Fall 4.6 ft.

When a high tide exceeds avg. ht., the *following* low tide will be lower than avg.

2021 HIGH & LOW WATER SANDY HOOK, NJ

40°28.1'N, 74°00.6'W

***Daylight Time starts March 14 at 2 a.m.** **Daylight Saving Time**

DAY OF MONTH	DAY OF WEEK	MARCH						DAY OF MONTH	DAY OF WEEK	APRIL					
		HIGH				LOW				HIGH				LOW	
		a.m.	Ht.	**p.m.**	Ht.	a.m.	**p.m.**			a.m.	Ht.	**p.m.**	Ht.	a.m.	**p.m.**
1	**M**	9:03	5.5	**9:35**	5.4	3:06	**3:33**	1	**T**	11:32	5.0	**11:59**	5.7	5:31	**5:38**
2	**T**	9:51	5.3	**10:26**	5.4	3:53	**4:14**	2	**F**	...	...	**12:31**	4.7	6:26	**6:32**
3	**W**	10:45	5.0	**11:20**	5.3	4:43	**4:59**	3	**S**	12:58	5.4	**1:32**	4.4	7:29	**7:37**
4	**T**	11:42	4.6	...	...	5:38	**5:50**	4	**S**	1:58	5.2	**2:34**	4.2	8:40	**8:54**
5	**F**	12:16	5.2	**12:41**	4.3	6:44	**6:54**	5	**M**	3:00	4.9	**3:39**	4.2	9:50	**10:06**
6	**S**	1:15	5.1	**1:44**	4.1	7:57	**8:08**	6	**T**	4:05	4.8	**4:44**	4.3	10:51	**11:08**
7	**S**	2:17	4.9	**2:51**	4.0	9:08	**9:19**	7	**W**	5:08	4.8	**5:45**	4.5	11:43	...
8	**M**	3:24	4.9	**4:00**	4.1	10:11	**10:22**	8	**T**	6:05	4.9	**6:37**	4.8	12:01	**12:29**
9	**T**	4:30	4.9	**5:04**	4.3	11:06	**11:18**	9	**F**	6:54	5.0	**7:21**	5.1	12:50	**1:12**
10	**W**	5:28	5.1	**5:58**	4.6	11:56	...	10	**S**	7:37	5.1	**8:00**	5.2	1:35	**1:51**
11	**T**	6:19	5.2	**6:45**	4.8	12:09	**12:42**	11	**S**	8:17	5.1	**8:36**	5.3	2:18	**2:29**
12	**F**	7:03	5.3	**7:27**	5.0	12:57	**1:25**	12	**M**	8:55	5.0	**9:11**	5.3	2:59	**3:04**
13	**S**	7:43	5.3	**8:06**	5.1	1:41	**2:04**	13	**T**	9:33	4.8	**9:44**	5.2	3:38	**3:38**
14	**S**	*9:22	5.2	***9:44**	5.0	*3:23	***3:40**	14	**W**	10:11	4.6	**10:16**	5.1	4:15	**4:10**
15	**M**	10:01	4.9	**10:20**	4.9	4:02	**4:13**	15	**T**	10:51	4.3	**10:49**	4.9	4:51	**4:41**
16	**T**	10:40	4.7	**10:57**	4.8	4:39	**4:45**	16	**F**	11:33	4.1	**11:23**	4.8	5:27	**5:12**
17	**W**	11:21	4.4	**11:33**	4.7	5:16	**5:15**	17	**S**	...	...	**12:18**	3.9	6:04	**5:46**
18	**T**	...	...	**12:04**	4.1	5:53	**5:46**	18	**S**	12:05	4.6	**1:06**	3.8	6:48	**6:28**
19	**F**	12:10	4.5	**12:49**	3.8	6:33	**6:19**	19	**M**	12:55	4.5	**1:58**	3.8	7:48	**7:31**
20	**S**	12:50	4.4	**1:36**	3.7	7:24	**7:04**	20	**T**	1:52	4.5	**2:53**	3.9	9:00	**8:57**
21	**S**	1:37	4.3	**2:29**	3.6	8:34	**8:15**	21	**W**	2:53	4.5	**3:51**	4.1	10:04	**10:10**
22	**M**	2:31	4.3	**3:26**	3.6	9:45	**9:36**	22	**T**	3:57	4.7	**4:51**	4.5	10:58	**11:10**
23	**T**	3:33	4.3	**4:28**	3.8	10:44	**10:41**	23	**F**	5:02	4.9	**5:47**	4.9	11:46	...
24	**W**	4:39	4.5	**5:28**	4.1	11:36	**11:38**	24	**S**	6:01	5.2	**6:38**	5.5	12:05	**12:33**
25	**T**	5:41	4.8	**6:21**	4.5	...	**12:24**	25	**S**	6:55	5.4	**7:27**	5.9	12:59	**1:20**
26	**F**	6:35	5.2	**7:09**	5.0	12:30	**1:10**	26	**M**	7:45	5.5	**8:14**	6.3	1:51	**2:08**
27	**S**	7:23	5.5	**7:54**	5.4	1:22	**1:55**	27	**T**	8:35	5.6	**9:01**	6.4	2:44	**2:55**
28	**S**	8:09	5.7	**8:38**	5.8	2:12	**2:39**	28	**W**	9:26	5.4	**9:50**	6.4	3:35	**3:43**
29	**M**	8:55	5.7	**9:24**	6.0	3:02	**3:23**	29	**T**	10:20	5.2	**10:44**	6.2	4:26	**4:32**
30	**T**	9:43	5.5	**10:12**	6.0	3:51	**4:07**	30	**F**	11:18	4.9	**11:41**	5.9	5:18	**5:22**
31	**W**	10:35	5.3	**11:03**	5.9	4:40	**4:51**								

Dates when Ht. of **Low** Water is below Mean Lower Low with Ht. of lowest given for each period and Date of lowest in ( ):

1st–3rd: -0.8' (1st)
10th–15th: -0.4' (12th, 13th)
26th–31st: -0.8' (29th–31st)

1st–2nd: -0.5' (1st)
24th–30th: -0.8' (27th–29th)

Average Rise and Fall 4.6 ft.

When a high tide exceeds avg. ht., the *following* low tide will be lower than avg.

2021 HIGH & LOW WATER
SANDY HOOK, NJ
40°28.1'N, 74°00.6'W

Daylight Saving Time

DAY OF MONTH	DAY OF WEEK	MAY					
		HIGH				LOW	
		a.m.	Ht.	**p.m.**	Ht.	a.m.	**p.m.**
1	S	...	...	**12:19**	4.7	6:12	**6:17**
2	S	12:41	5.5	**1:21**	4.5	7:12	**7:22**
3	M	1:41	5.2	**2:21**	4.4	8:18	**8:35**
4	T	2:40	5.0	**3:20**	4.4	9:24	**9:46**
5	W	3:39	4.8	**4:20**	4.5	10:22	**10:46**
6	T	4:37	4.7	**5:16**	4.7	11:11	**11:38**
7	F	5:32	4.7	**6:07**	4.9	11:55	...
8	S	6:22	4.7	**6:50**	5.2	12:25	**12:35**
9	S	7:07	4.8	**7:29**	5.3	1:10	**1:14**
10	M	7:48	4.8	**8:05**	5.4	1:53	**1:52**
11	T	8:28	4.7	**8:39**	5.4	2:34	**2:29**
12	W	9:07	4.6	**9:12**	5.4	3:14	**3:05**
13	T	9:45	4.4	**9:44**	5.2	3:53	**3:41**
14	F	10:26	4.2	**10:16**	5.1	4:30	**4:16**
15	S	11:08	4.1	**10:52**	4.9	5:07	**4:50**
16	S	11:53	4.0	**11:36**	4.8	5:44	**5:26**
17	M	...	...	**12:42**	3.9	6:25	**6:09**
18	T	12:28	4.8	**1:32**	4.0	7:16	**7:07**
19	W	1:24	4.7	**2:24**	4.2	8:18	**8:24**
20	T	2:22	4.8	**3:18**	4.5	9:21	**9:39**
21	F	3:22	4.8	**4:16**	4.8	10:18	**10:44**
22	S	4:26	4.9	**5:13**	5.3	11:09	**11:41**
23	S	5:29	5.0	**6:09**	5.8	11:59	...
24	M	6:28	5.2	**7:01**	6.2	12:37	**12:49**
25	T	7:23	5.2	**7:51**	6.5	1:32	**1:40**
26	W	8:17	5.3	**8:41**	6.6	2:27	**2:31**
27	T	9:10	5.2	**9:33**	6.5	3:20	**3:24**
28	F	10:06	5.1	**10:27**	6.2	4:12	**4:15**
29	S	11:04	4.9	**11:24**	5.9	5:03	**5:07**
30	S	...	...	**12:05**	4.8	5:55	**6:02**
31	M	12:22	5.5	**1:03**	4.7	6:50	**7:02**

Daylight Saving Time

DAY OF MONTH	DAY OF WEEK	JUNE					
		HIGH				LOW	
		a.m.	Ht.	**p.m.**	Ht.	a.m.	**p.m.**
1	T	1:20	5.2	**1:59**	4.6	7:48	**8:09**
2	W	2:13	4.9	**2:54**	4.6	8:48	**9:16**
3	T	3:06	4.7	**3:47**	4.7	9:43	**10:16**
4	F	3:59	4.5	**4:39**	4.8	10:31	**11:09**
5	S	4:53	4.4	**5:29**	4.9	11:14	**11:56**
6	S	5:45	4.4	**6:14**	5.1	11:55	...
7	M	6:34	4.4	**6:56**	5.3	12:41	**12:35**
8	T	7:19	4.4	**7:34**	5.4	1:25	**1:15**
9	W	8:02	4.4	**8:10**	5.4	2:09	**1:56**
10	T	8:42	4.4	**8:45**	5.4	2:51	**2:37**
11	F	9:22	4.3	**9:19**	5.3	3:31	**3:17**
12	S	10:03	4.2	**9:54**	5.2	4:10	**3:56**
13	S	10:45	4.2	**10:32**	5.1	4:48	**4:34**
14	M	11:30	4.1	**11:17**	5.0	5:26	**5:13**
15	T	...	...	**12:18**	4.2	6:05	**5:57**
16	W	12:07	5.0	**1:07**	4.3	6:48	**6:50**
17	T	1:01	4.9	**1:57**	4.6	7:41	**7:58**
18	F	1:56	4.9	**2:49**	4.8	8:40	**9:13**
19	S	2:54	4.8	**3:45**	5.2	9:39	**10:21**
20	S	3:56	4.8	**4:43**	5.5	10:35	**11:21**
21	M	5:02	4.8	**5:42**	5.9	11:29	...
22	T	6:06	4.8	**6:39**	6.2	12:19	**12:23**
23	W	7:06	4.9	**7:33**	6.4	1:16	**1:18**
24	T	8:02	5.0	**8:25**	6.4	2:11	**2:13**
25	F	8:56	5.1	**9:17**	6.3	3:05	**3:08**
26	S	9:51	5.0	**10:10**	6.1	3:56	**4:00**
27	S	10:47	4.9	**11:04**	5.8	4:45	**4:51**
28	M	11:43	4.8	**11:58**	5.5	5:33	**5:42**
29	T	...	...	**12:38**	4.8	6:21	**6:36**
30	W	12:51	5.2	**1:30**	4.7	7:11	**7:34**

Dates when Ht. of **Low** Water is below Mean Lower Low with Ht. of lowest given for each period and Date of lowest in ( ):

1st: -0.2'
23rd–30th: -0.8' (27th)

22nd–28th: -0.6' (25th, 26th)

Average Rise and Fall 4.6 ft.

When a high tide exceeds avg. ht., the *following* low tide will be lower than avg.

2021 HIGH & LOW WATER SANDY HOOK, NJ

40°28.1'N, 74°00.6'W

		Daylight Saving Time								Daylight Saving Time					
DAY OF MONTH	DAY OF WEEK	JULY						DAY OF MONTH	DAY OF WEEK	AUGUST					
		HIGH				LOW				HIGH				LOW	
		a.m.	Ht.	**p.m.**	Ht.	a.m.	**p.m.**			a.m.	Ht.	**p.m.**	Ht.	a.m.	**p.m.**
1	**T**	1:42	4.8	**2:19**	4.7	8:02	**8:37**	1	**S**	2:42	4.2	**3:09**	4.7	8:50	**9:56**
2	**F**	2:30	4.6	**3:07**	4.7	8:54	**9:39**	2	**M**	3:33	4.0	**3:59**	4.7	9:44	**10:50**
3	**S**	3:20	4.3	**3:56**	4.7	9:44	**10:34**	3	**T**	4:29	3.9	**4:51**	4.8	10:37	**11:40**
4	**S**	4:12	4.1	**4:45**	4.8	10:31	**11:24**	4	**W**	5:27	4.0	**5:44**	4.9	11:26	...
5	**M**	5:07	4.1	**5:34**	4.9	11:15	...	5	**T**	6:21	4.1	**6:33**	5.1	12:27	**12:15**
6	**T**	6:01	4.1	**6:21**	5.1	12:11	**-A-**	6	**F**	7:09	4.3	**7:17**	5.3	1:13	**1:02**
7	**W**	6:51	4.2	**7:04**	5.2	12:57	**12:43**	7	**S**	7:52	4.5	**7:58**	5.5	1:57	**1:49**
8	**T**	7:36	4.3	**7:44**	5.3	1:42	**1:28**	8	**S**	8:32	4.7	**8:36**	5.6	2:39	**2:34**
9	**F**	8:18	4.3	**8:22**	5.4	2:25	**2:12**	9	**M**	9:12	4.8	**9:15**	5.6	3:20	**3:18**
10	**S**	8:59	4.4	**8:58**	5.4	3:08	**2:56**	10	**T**	9:52	4.9	**9:55**	5.6	3:59	**4:01**
11	**S**	9:39	4.4	**9:36**	5.4	3:48	**3:38**	11	**W**	10:36	5.1	**10:40**	5.5	4:36	**4:45**
12	**M**	10:20	4.4	**10:15**	5.4	4:26	**4:19**	12	**T**	11:23	5.2	**11:29**	5.3	5:14	**5:31**
13	**T**	11:04	4.5	**10:59**	5.3	5:03	**5:00**	13	**F**	...	...	**12:13**	5.3	5:54	**6:22**
14	**W**	11:51	4.6	**11:48**	5.2	5:41	**5:44**	14	**S**	12:23	5.0	**1:06**	5.4	6:39	**7:23**
15	**T**	...	...	**12:40**	4.8	6:21	**6:35**	15	**S**	1:20	4.8	**2:01**	5.4	7:34	**8:35**
16	**F**	12:41	5.0	**1:31**	5.0	7:07	**7:39**	16	**M**	2:20	4.6	**2:59**	5.5	8:42	**9:48**
17	**S**	1:35	4.9	**2:23**	5.2	8:03	**8:52**	17	**T**	3:24	4.4	**4:02**	5.5	9:53	**10:53**
18	**S**	2:33	4.7	**3:19**	5.4	9:06	**10:02**	18	**W**	4:33	4.4	**5:08**	5.6	10:57	**11:52**
19	**M**	3:36	4.6	**4:19**	5.6	10:09	**11:06**	19	**T**	5:41	4.6	**6:10**	5.8	11:57	...
20	**T**	4:43	4.5	**5:22**	5.8	11:09	...	20	**F**	6:42	4.8	**7:06**	5.9	12:47	**12:53**
21	**W**	5:51	4.6	**6:23**	6.0	12:05	**12:07**	21	**S**	7:36	5.1	**7:56**	6.0	1:38	**1:47**
22	**T**	6:53	4.8	**7:19**	6.2	1:01	**1:04**	22	**S**	8:25	5.2	**8:43**	6.0	2:27	**2:37**
23	**F**	7:49	5.0	**8:11**	6.2	1:56	**1:59**	23	**M**	9:11	5.3	**9:27**	5.8	3:12	**3:25**
24	**S**	8:42	5.1	**9:01**	6.2	2:48	**2:53**	24	**T**	9:56	5.3	**10:11**	5.6	3:53	**4:09**
25	**S**	9:33	5.1	**9:51**	6.0	3:37	**3:44**	25	**W**	10:40	5.2	**10:55**	5.2	4:32	**4:52**
26	**M**	10:24	5.1	**10:40**	5.7	4:22	**4:32**	26	**T**	11:25	5.1	**11:41**	4.9	5:08	**5:34**
27	**T**	11:15	5.0	**11:29**	5.4	5:05	**5:18**	27	**F**	...	...	**12:09**	5.0	5:43	**6:17**
28	**W**	...	...	**12:05**	4.9	5:47	**6:05**	28	**S**	12:28	4.6	**12:52**	4.8	6:19	**7:07**
29	**T**	12:17	5.1	**12:53**	4.8	6:28	**6:56**	29	**S**	1:15	4.2	**1:36**	4.7	6:59	**8:06**
30	**F**	1:05	4.7	**1:38**	4.8	7:11	**7:52**	30	**M**	2:04	4.0	**2:22**	4.6	7:50	**9:12**
31	**S**	1:52	4.4	**2:23**	4.7	7:58	**8:55**	31	**T**	2:57	3.9	**3:12**	4.6	8:55	**10:14**

A also at 11:59 a.m.

Dates when Ht. of **Low** Water is below Mean Lower Low with Ht. of lowest given for each period and Date of lowest in ( ):

22nd–27th: -0.5' (24th, 25th)

21st–24th: -0.3'

Average Rise and Fall 4.6 ft.

When a high tide exceeds avg. ht., the *following* low tide will be lower than avg.

2021 HIGH & LOW WATER SANDY HOOK, NJ

40°28.1'N, 74°00.6'W

Daylight Saving Time

DAY OF MONTH	DAY OF WEEK	SEPTEMBER HIGH a.m.	Ht.	**p.m.**	Ht.	LOW a.m.	**p.m.**
1	**W**	3:54	3.8	**4:07**	4.6	9:59	**11:07**
2	**T**	4:53	3.9	**5:05**	4.8	10:56	**11:55**
3	**F**	5:49	4.2	**6:00**	5.0	11:48	...
4	**S**	6:38	4.5	**6:47**	5.3	12:40	**12:36**
5	**S**	7:22	4.8	**7:30**	5.6	1:24	**1:24**
6	**M**	8:03	5.1	**8:11**	5.7	2:06	**2:11**
7	**T**	8:43	5.4	**8:51**	5.8	2:47	**2:57**
8	**W**	9:24	5.6	**9:34**	5.7	3:27	**3:43**
9	**T**	10:08	5.7	**10:20**	5.5	4:07	**4:29**
10	**F**	10:55	5.7	**11:11**	5.2	4:47	**5:17**
11	**S**	11:48	5.7	...	...	5:29	**6:09**
12	**S**	12:08	4.9	**12:44**	5.6	6:16	**7:10**
13	**M**	1:09	4.7	**1:43**	5.5	7:14	**8:22**
14	**T**	2:12	4.5	**2:45**	5.4	8:28	**9:35**
15	**W**	3:18	4.4	**3:49**	5.4	9:43	**10:41**
16	**T**	4:25	4.4	**4:55**	5.4	10:50	**11:38**
17	**F**	5:31	4.7	**5:56**	5.5	11:48	...
18	**S**	6:29	4.9	**6:50**	5.7	12:29	**12:41**
19	**S**	7:20	5.2	**7:37**	5.7	1:16	**1:31**
20	**M**	8:04	5.4	**8:20**	5.7	2:00	**2:19**
21	**T**	8:45	5.5	**9:01**	5.6	2:42	**3:03**
22	**W**	9:25	5.5	**9:41**	5.3	3:20	**3:45**
23	**T**	10:03	5.4	**10:22**	5.0	3:56	**4:25**
24	**F**	10:42	5.2	**11:05**	4.7	4:29	**5:04**
25	**S**	11:21	5.0	**11:51**	4.3	5:02	**5:44**
26	**S**	...	...	**12:02**	4.8	5:34	**6:26**
27	**M**	12:40	4.1	**12:46**	4.7	6:10	**7:19**
28	**T**	1:30	3.9	**1:34**	4.6	6:55	**8:25**
29	**W**	2:23	3.8	**2:26**	4.5	8:03	**9:33**
30	**T**	3:18	3.8	**3:23**	4.5	9:21	**10:31**

Daylight Saving Time

DAY OF MONTH	DAY OF WEEK	OCTOBER HIGH a.m.	Ht.	**p.m.**	Ht.	LOW a.m.	**p.m.**
1	**F**	4:17	4.0	**4:23**	4.7	10:25	**11:20**
2	**S**	5:12	4.2	**5:20**	4.9	11:19	...
3	**S**	6:03	4.6	**6:12**	5.2	12:05	**12:10**
4	**M**	6:49	5.1	**6:59**	5.5	12:48	**12:58**
5	**T**	7:32	5.5	**7:43**	5.7	1:30	**1:47**
6	**W**	8:14	5.8	**8:27**	5.7	2:13	**2:36**
7	**T**	8:57	6.1	**9:13**	5.6	2:55	**3:24**
8	**F**	9:42	6.2	**10:02**	5.4	3:38	**4:13**
9	**S**	10:31	6.1	**10:56**	5.1	4:22	**5:03**
10	**S**	11:26	5.9	**11:57**	4.8	5:08	**5:57**
11	**M**	...	...	**12:26**	5.7	5:59	**6:57**
12	**T**	1:01	4.5	**1:28**	5.5	7:01	**8:07**
13	**W**	2:05	4.4	**2:31**	5.3	8:17	**9:19**
14	**T**	3:09	4.4	**3:34**	5.2	9:33	**10:23**
15	**F**	4:14	4.5	**4:37**	5.1	10:39	**11:17**
16	**S**	5:16	4.7	**5:36**	5.2	11:35	...
17	**S**	6:11	5.0	**6:28**	5.3	12:05	**12:26**
18	**M**	6:58	5.2	**7:13**	5.3	12:49	**1:13**
19	**T**	7:40	5.4	**7:55**	5.2	1:29	**1:58**
20	**W**	8:18	5.5	**8:34**	5.1	2:08	**2:40**
21	**T**	8:54	5.5	**9:13**	4.9	2:45	**3:21**
22	**F**	9:28	5.4	**9:53**	4.7	3:20	**4:00**
23	**S**	10:03	5.2	**10:34**	4.4	3:54	**4:38**
24	**S**	10:37	5.0	**11:19**	4.1	4:27	**5:16**
25	**M**	11:15	4.8	...	...	5:00	**5:55**
26	**T**	12:07	3.9	**-A-**		5:35	**6:40**
27	**W**	12:58	3.7	**12:49**	4.5	6:17	**7:39**
28	**T**	1:50	3.7	**1:43**	4.4	7:16	**8:47**
29	**F**	2:43	3.8	**2:40**	4.5	8:38	**9:48**
30	**S**	3:37	4.0	**3:39**	4.6	9:50	**10:39**
31	**S**	4:32	4.3	**4:38**	4.8	10:49	**11:25**

A also at 11:58 a.m. (4.6)

Dates when Ht. of **Low** Water is below Mean Lower Low with Ht. of lowest given for each period and Date of lowest in ( ):

September: 8th–10th: -0.3' (8th, 9th)
20th–21st: -0.2'

October: 6th–9th: -0.5' (7th, 8th)

Average Rise and Fall 4.6 ft.

When a high tide exceeds avg. ht., the *following* low tide will be lower than avg.

2021 HIGH & LOW WATER
SANDY HOOK, NJ
40°28.1'N, 74°00.6'W

***Standard Time starts Nov. 7 at 2 a.m.** **Standard Time**

DAY OF MONTH	DAY OF WEEK	NOVEMBER						DAY OF MONTH	DAY OF WEEK	DECEMBER					
		HIGH				LOW				HIGH				LOW	
		a.m.	Ht.	**p.m.**	Ht.	a.m.	**p.m.**			a.m.	Ht.	**p.m.**	Ht.	a.m.	**p.m.**
1	**M**	5:26	4.8	**5:35**	5.0	11:42	...	1	**W**	4:42	5.3	**4:58**	4.8	11:10	**11:21**
2	**T**	6:15	5.3	**6:27**	5.2	12:10	**12:33**	2	**T**	5:34	5.8	**5:54**	4.9	...	**12:04**
3	**W**	7:02	5.8	**7:17**	5.4	12:54	**1:25**	3	**F**	6:24	6.1	**6:47**	5.0	12:11	**12:58**
4	**T**	7:47	6.1	**8:05**	5.4	1:39	**2:16**	4	**S**	7:14	6.3	**7:39**	5.0	1:02	**1:52**
5	**F**	8:33	6.3	**8:54**	5.3	2:26	**3:07**	5	**S**	8:04	6.3	**8:33**	4.9	1:55	**2:44**
6	**S**	9:20	6.4	**9:46**	5.1	3:13	**3:58**	6	**M**	8:57	6.1	**9:31**	4.7	2:47	**3:36**
7	**S**	*9:12	6.2	***9:43**	4.9	*3:02	***3:50**	7	**T**	9:54	5.8	**10:31**	4.6	3:39	**4:28**
8	**M**	10:09	5.9	**10:46**	4.6	3:52	**4:44**	8	**W**	10:54	5.5	**11:33**	4.4	4:34	**5:22**
9	**T**	11:11	5.6	**11:50**	4.5	4:47	**5:42**	9	**T**	11:52	5.2	...	...	5:32	**6:20**
10	**W**	...	...	**12:13**	5.3	5:49	**6:47**	10	**F**	12:32	4.4	**12:49**	4.9	6:37	**7:21**
11	**T**	12:52	4.4	**1:13**	5.1	7:01	**7:55**	11	**S**	1:28	4.4	**1:43**	4.6	7:47	**8:20**
12	**F**	1:53	4.4	**2:13**	4.9	8:15	**8:57**	12	**S**	2:23	4.4	**2:37**	4.3	8:53	**9:12**
13	**S**	2:54	4.5	**3:11**	4.8	9:20	**9:49**	13	**M**	3:18	4.5	**3:32**	4.2	9:50	**9:58**
14	**S**	3:52	4.7	**4:07**	4.7	10:16	**10:35**	14	**T**	4:10	4.6	**4:26**	4.1	10:40	**10:41**
15	**M**	4:45	4.9	**4:59**	4.7	11:05	**11:16**	15	**W**	4:58	4.8	**5:17**	4.1	11:26	**11:21**
16	**T**	5:31	5.1	**5:46**	4.7	11:51	**11:55**	16	**T**	5:42	4.9	**6:03**	4.1	...	**12:10**
17	**W**	6:12	5.3	**6:29**	4.7	...	**12:35**	17	**F**	6:22	5.0	**6:47**	4.2	12:02	**12:53**
18	**T**	6:49	5.4	**7:09**	4.6	12:34	**1:17**	18	**S**	6:59	5.1	**7:27**	4.1	12:43	**1:35**
19	**F**	7:25	5.4	**7:49**	4.5	1:12	**1:58**	19	**S**	7:35	5.1	**8:07**	4.1	1:23	**2:16**
20	**S**	7:58	5.3	**8:28**	4.3	1:49	**2:37**	20	**M**	8:10	5.0	**8:47**	4.0	2:03	**2:55**
21	**S**	8:32	5.1	**9:09**	4.1	2:26	**3:16**	21	**T**	8:44	4.9	**9:27**	3.9	2:42	**3:33**
22	**M**	9:06	4.9	**9:52**	3.9	3:01	**3:53**	22	**W**	9:20	4.8	**10:10**	3.8	3:20	**4:09**
23	**T**	9:42	4.8	**10:38**	3.7	3:37	**4:31**	23	**T**	10:00	4.7	**10:54**	3.8	3:57	**4:46**
24	**W**	10:23	4.6	**11:26**	3.7	4:13	**5:11**	24	**F**	10:44	4.6	**11:41**	3.8	4:35	**5:24**
25	**T**	11:12	4.5	...	...	4:53	**5:58**	25	**S**	11:34	4.5	...	...	5:21	**6:10**
26	**F**	12:16	3.7	**12:06**	4.4	5:44	**6:56**	26	**S**	12:29	4.0	**12:27**	4.4	6:21	**7:05**
27	**S**	1:06	3.8	**1:01**	4.4	6:54	**7:58**	27	**M**	1:20	4.2	**1:23**	4.3	7:35	**8:06**
28	**S**	1:58	4.1	**1:57**	4.5	8:12	**8:54**	28	**T**	2:14	4.5	**2:23**	4.3	8:48	**9:05**
29	**M**	2:51	4.4	**2:57**	4.5	9:18	**9:45**	29	**W**	3:12	4.9	**3:28**	4.3	9:52	**10:01**
30	**T**	3:47	4.8	**3:58**	4.7	10:16	**10:33**	30	**T**	4:12	5.2	**4:34**	4.4	10:51	**10:56**
								31	**F**	5:10	5.6	**5:36**	4.5	11:47	**11:50**

Dates when Ht. of **Low** Water is below Mean Lower Low with Ht. of lowest given for each period and Date of lowest in ( ):

3rd–8th: -0.7' (5th, 6th)
30th: -0.2'

1st–8th: -1.0' (5th)
29th–31st: -0.6' (31st)

Average Rise and Fall 4.6 ft.

When a high tide exceeds avg. ht., the *following* low tide will be lower than avg.

2021 CURRENT TABLE
DELAWARE BAY ENTRANCE
38°46.85'N, 75°02.58'W

Standard Time								**Standard Time**							
JANUARY								**FEBRUARY**							
DAY OF MONTH	DAY OF WEEK	CURRENT TURNS TO						DAY OF MONTH	DAY OF WEEK	CURRENT TURNS TO					
		NORTHWEST Flood Starts			SOUTHEAST Ebb Starts					NORTHWEST Flood Starts			SOUTHEAST Ebb Starts		
		a.m.	**p.m.**	Kts.	a.m.	**p.m.**	Kts.			a.m.	**p.m.**	Kts.	a.m.	**p.m.**	Kts.
1	**F**	4:55	**6:06**	a1.5	11:30	...	1.5	1	**M**	6:25	**7:06**	1.7	12:24	**12:36**	p1.6
2	**S**	5:42	**6:48**	a1.5	12:01	**12:12**	p1.5	2	**T**	7:18	**7:48**	p1.7	1:12	**1:24**	p1.6
3	**S**	6:36	**7:30**	a1.5	12:42	**12:54**	p1.5	3	**W**	8:18	**8:36**	p1.7	2:00	**2:18**	1.5
4	**M**	7:30	**8:18**	1.5	1:30	**1:48**	p1.5	4	**T**	9:24	**9:30**	p1.8	2:54	**3:12**	a1.5
5	**T**	8:30	**9:06**	p1.6	2:24	**2:36**	p1.5	5	**F**	10:30	**10:24**	p1.7	3:54	**4:12**	a1.5
6	**W**	9:36	**10:00**	p1.7	3:24	**3:36**	p1.5	6	**S**	11:30	**11:24**	p1.7	4:54	**5:12**	a1.5
7	**T**	10:42	**10:54**	p1.8	4:18	**4:36**	a1.5	7	**S**	...	**12:36**	1.3	5:54	**6:18**	a1.6
8	**F**	11:48	**11:48**	p1.9	5:18	**5:36**	a1.6	8	**M**	12:24	**1:36**	a1.8	6:54	**7:18**	a1.6
9	**S**	...	**12:48**	1.5	6:12	**6:36**	a1.7	9	**T**	1:18	**2:30**	a1.8	7:48	**8:12**	a1.7
10	**S**	12:42	**1:48**	a1.9	7:06	**7:30**	a1.8	10	**W**	2:18	**3:24**	a1.8	8:42	**9:06**	a1.7
11	**M**	1:36	**2:48**	a2.0	8:00	**8:30**	a1.8	11	**T**	3:06	**4:12**	a1.8	9:30	**9:48**	a1.6
12	**T**	2:30	**3:36**	a2.0	8:54	**9:18**	a1.8	12	**F**	3:54	**4:54**	a1.7	10:18	**10:36**	a1.6
13	**W**	3:24	**4:30**	a1.9	9:48	**10:12**	a1.8	13	**S**	4:36	**5:30**	a1.6	10:54	**11:18**	a1.5
14	**T**	4:12	**5:18**	a1.9	10:36	**10:54**	a1.7	14	**S**	5:18	**6:06**	a1.5	11:36	**11:54**	a1.4
15	**F**	4:54	**6:06**	a1.7	11:18	**11:42**	a1.6	15	**M**	6:00	**6:36**	a1.3	...	**12:12**	1.2
16	**S**	5:42	**6:48**	a1.6	...	**12:06**	1.4	16	**T**	6:42	**7:06**	1.1	12:36	**12:48**	p1.1
17	**S**	6:24	**7:24**	a1.4	12:24	**12:48**	p1.2	17	**W**	7:30	**7:36**	1.0	1:18	**1:30**	0.9
18	**M**	7:12	**8:00**	a1.2	1:12	**1:30**	p1.1	18	**T**	8:18	**8:12**	p1.0	2:00	**2:12**	a0.9
19	**T**	8:00	**8:36**	a1.0	1:54	**2:12**	p0.9	19	**F**	9:24	**8:54**	p1.0	2:48	**3:06**	a0.8
20	**W**	9:00	**9:12**	p0.9	2:48	**3:00**	0.8	20	**S**	10:36	**9:48**	p1.0	3:42	**4:06**	a0.8
21	**T**	10:06	**9:54**	p0.9	3:42	**3:54**	0.8	21	**S**	11:42	**10:48**	p1.0	4:42	**5:12**	a0.9
22	**F**	11:18	**10:42**	p1.0	4:36	**4:48**	a0.8	22	**M**	-B-	**12:42**	0.7	5:48	**6:12**	a1.0
23	**S**	-A-	**12:24**	0.7	5:30	**5:48**	a0.9	23	**T**	...	**1:36**	0.8	6:48	**7:12**	a1.1
24	**S**	...	**1:24**	0.7	6:24	**6:48**	a1.0	24	**W**	12:54	**2:24**	a1.3	7:42	**8:06**	a1.3
25	**M**	12:24	**2:12**	a1.2	7:18	**7:48**	a1.2	25	**T**	1:54	**3:06**	a1.5	8:30	**8:54**	a1.5
26	**T**	1:18	**3:00**	a1.3	8:12	**8:36**	a1.3	26	**F**	2:48	**3:48**	a1.6	9:18	**9:42**	a1.6
27	**W**	2:12	**3:42**	a1.4	9:00	**9:24**	a1.4	27	**S**	3:36	**4:30**	a1.8	10:06	**10:24**	a1.7
28	**T**	3:06	**4:24**	a1.5	9:42	**10:06**	a1.5	28	**S**	4:30	**5:06**	1.8	10:48	**11:12**	a1.8
29	**F**	3:54	**5:00**	a1.6	10:30	**10:54**	a1.6								
30	**S**	4:42	**5:42**	a1.7	11:12	**11:36**	a1.7								
31	**S**	5:36	**6:18**	a1.7	11:54	...	1.7								

A also at 11:30 p.m. 1.1

B also at 11:54 p.m. 1.1

The Kts. (knots) columns show the **maximum** predicted velocities of the stronger one of the Flood Currents and the stronger one of the Ebb Currents for each day.
The letter "a" means the velocity shown should occur **after** the **a.m.** Current Change. The letter "p" means the velocity shown should occur **after** the **p.m.** Current Change (even if next morning). No "a" or "p" means a.m. and p.m. velocities are the same for that day.
Avg. Max. Velocity: Flood 1.8 Kts., Ebb 1.9 Kts.
Max. Flood 3 hrs. 5 min. after Flood Starts, ±15 min.
Max. Ebb 3 hrs. 5 min. after Ebb Starts, ±15 min.

See pp. 22-29 for Current Change at other points.

2021 CURRENT TABLE
DELAWARE BAY ENTRANCE

38°46.85'N, 75°02.58'W

***Daylight Time starts March 14 at 2 a.m.** **Daylight Saving Time**

MARCH

DAY OF MONTH	DAY OF WEEK	CURRENT TURNS TO NORTHWEST Flood Starts			CURRENT TURNS TO SOUTHEAST Ebb Starts		
		a.m.	**p.m.**	Kts.	a.m.	**p.m.**	Kts.
1	**M**	5:19	**5:48**	1.9	11:30	...	1.8
2	**T**	6:12	**6:36**	p1.9	12:01	**12:18**	a1.8
3	**W**	7:06	**7:18**	p1.9	12:48	**1:06**	a1.7
4	**T**	8:06	**8:12**	p1.8	1:36	**1:54**	a1.7
5	**F**	9:06	**9:06**	p1.7	2:30	**2:54**	a1.6
6	**S**	10:12	**10:06**	p1.6	3:30	**3:54**	a1.5
7	**S**	11:18	**11:06**	p1.6	4:36	**5:00**	a1.4
8	**M**	...	**12:24**	1.2	5:36	**6:00**	a1.4
9	**T**	12:12	**1:24**	a1.6	6:36	**7:00**	a1.5
10	**W**	1:12	**2:18**	a1.6	7:36	**7:54**	a1.5
11	**T**	2:06	**3:06**	a1.6	8:24	**8:48**	a1.5
12	**F**	2:54	**3:48**	a1.6	9:12	**9:30**	a1.5
13	**S**	3:42	**4:24**	a1.6	9:54	**10:12**	a1.4
14	**S**	*5:24	***5:54**	a1.5	*11:30	***11:48**	a1.4
15	**M**	6:00	**6:24**	a1.4	...	**12:06**	1.3
16	**T**	6:42	**6:48**	a1.3	12:24	**12:42**	1.2
17	**W**	7:18	**7:18**	p1.2	1:00	**1:18**	a1.1
18	**T**	8:06	**7:48**	p1.1	1:36	**2:00**	a1.0
19	**F**	8:48	**8:30**	p1.0	2:18	**2:42**	a0.9
20	**S**	9:48	**9:12**	p1.0	3:00	**3:30**	a0.9
21	**S**	10:54	**10:12**	p1.0	4:00	**4:30**	a0.8
22	**M**	11:59	**11:18**	p1.0	5:00	**5:36**	a0.9
23	**T**	...	**1:00**	0.8	6:06	**6:42**	a1.0
24	**W**	12:24	**1:54**	a1.1	7:12	**7:36**	a1.2
25	**T**	1:30	**2:42**	a1.3	8:06	**8:30**	a1.4
26	**F**	2:30	**3:24**	a1.5	9:00	**9:24**	1.5
27	**S**	3:30	**4:12**	1.7	9:48	**10:12**	1.7
28	**S**	4:24	**4:54**	1.9	10:36	**11:00**	p1.9
29	**M**	5:12	**5:36**	p2.0	11:24	**11:42**	p2.0
30	**T**	6:06	**6:18**	p2.1	...	**12:06**	1.8
31	**W**	7:00	**7:06**	p2.1	12:30	**12:54**	a2.0

APRIL

DAY OF MONTH	DAY OF WEEK	CURRENT TURNS TO NORTHWEST Flood Starts			CURRENT TURNS TO SOUTHEAST Ebb Starts		
		a.m.	**p.m.**	Kts.	a.m.	**p.m.**	Kts.
1	**T**	7:55	**7:54**	p2.0	1:24	**1:48**	a1.9
2	**F**	8:48	**8:42**	p1.8	2:12	**2:36**	a1.7
3	**S**	9:48	**9:42**	p1.6	3:06	**3:36**	a1.6
4	**S**	10:54	**10:48**	p1.5	4:12	**4:36**	a1.4
5	**M**	11:59	**11:54**	p1.4	5:12	**5:42**	a1.3
6	**T**	...	**1:06**	1.1	6:18	**6:48**	a1.3
7	**W**	12:54	**2:00**	a1.4	7:18	**7:42**	a1.3
8	**T**	1:54	**2:48**	a1.4	8:18	**8:36**	a1.3
9	**F**	2:48	**3:36**	a1.4	9:06	**9:24**	a1.3
10	**S**	3:42	**4:12**	a1.4	9:48	**10:06**	a1.3
11	**S**	4:24	**4:42**	a1.4	10:24	**10:42**	1.3
12	**M**	5:06	**5:12**	1.3	11:00	**11:18**	p1.3
13	**T**	5:48	**5:42**	1.3	11:36	**11:54**	1.2
14	**W**	6:24	**6:06**	p1.3	...	**12:18**	1.1
15	**T**	7:06	**6:36**	p1.2	12:30	**12:54**	a1.2
16	**F**	7:42	**7:12**	p1.1	1:06	**1:36**	a1.1
17	**S**	8:30	**7:54**	p1.1	1:42	**2:18**	a1.0
18	**S**	9:18	**8:42**	p1.0	2:30	**3:06**	a1.0
19	**M**	10:18	**9:42**	p1.0	3:24	**4:06**	a0.9
20	**T**	11:18	**10:54**	p1.1	4:24	**5:06**	a1.0
21	**W**	...	**12:18**	0.9	5:30	**6:12**	a1.1
22	**T**	12:01	**1:12**	a1.2	6:36	**7:06**	1.2
23	**F**	1:06	**2:00**	1.4	7:30	**8:00**	1.4
24	**S**	2:12	**2:48**	p1.7	8:24	**8:54**	p1.7
25	**S**	3:06	**3:30**	p1.9	9:18	**9:42**	p1.9
26	**M**	4:06	**4:18**	p2.1	10:06	**10:30**	p2.1
27	**T**	5:00	**5:00**	p2.2	10:54	**11:18**	p2.1
28	**W**	5:48	**5:48**	p2.2	11:48	...	1.8
29	**T**	6:42	**6:36**	p2.1	12:06	**12:36**	a2.1
30	**F**	7:36	**7:30**	p2.0	1:00	**1:24**	a1.9

The Kts. (knots) columns show the **maximum** predicted velocities of the stronger one of the Flood Currents and the stronger one of the Ebb Currents for each day.
The letter "a" means the velocity shown should occur **after** the **a.m.** Current Change. The letter "p" means the velocity shown should occur **after** the **p.m.** Current Change (even if next morning). No "a" or "p" means a.m. and p.m. velocities are the same for that day.
Avg. Max. Velocity: Flood 1.8 Kts., Ebb 1.9 Kts.
Max. Flood 3 hrs. 5 min. after Flood Starts, ±15 min.
Max. Ebb 3 hrs. 5 min. after Ebb Starts, ±15 min.

See pp. 22-29 for Current Change at other points.

2021 CURRENT TABLE
DELAWARE BAY ENTRANCE

38°46.85'N, 75°02.58'W

MAY

Daylight Saving Time

DAY OF MONTH	DAY OF WEEK	CURRENT TURNS TO					
		NORTHWEST Flood Starts			SOUTHEAST Ebb Starts		
		a.m.	**p.m.**	Kts.	a.m.	**p.m.**	Kts.
1	**S**	8:37	**8:24**	p1.7	1:54	**2:18**	a1.8
2	**S**	9:36	**9:18**	p1.5	2:48	**3:18**	a1.6
3	**M**	10:36	**10:24**	p1.4	3:48	**4:18**	a1.4
4	**T**	11:42	**11:30**	p1.3	4:48	**5:24**	a1.2
5	**W**	...	**12:36**	1.0	5:54	**6:24**	a1.2
6	**T**	12:36	**1:30**	a1.2	6:54	**7:24**	a1.1
7	**F**	1:36	**2:18**	a1.2	7:42	**8:12**	1.1
8	**S**	2:30	**2:54**	1.2	8:30	**9:00**	p1.2
9	**S**	3:24	**3:30**	p1.3	9:12	**9:36**	p1.2
10	**M**	4:06	**4:00**	p1.3	9:54	**10:18**	p1.3
11	**T**	4:48	**4:30**	p1.3	10:36	**10:54**	p1.3
12	**W**	5:30	**5:00**	p1.3	11:12	**11:30**	p1.3
13	**T**	6:12	**5:36**	p1.3	11:54	...	1.0
14	**F**	6:48	**6:12**	p1.3	12:06	**12:36**	a1.2
15	**S**	7:30	**6:48**	p1.2	12:42	**1:18**	a1.2
16	**S**	8:12	**7:36**	p1.1	1:24	**2:00**	a1.1
17	**M**	9:00	**8:24**	p1.1	2:06	**2:48**	a1.1
18	**T**	9:48	**9:24**	p1.1	3:00	**3:42**	a1.1
19	**W**	10:42	**10:30**	p1.2	3:54	**4:42**	a1.1
20	**T**	11:36	**11:42**	p1.3	5:00	**5:42**	a1.2
21	**F**	...	**12:30**	1.4	6:00	**6:36**	1.3
22	**S**	12:48	**1:18**	p1.6	6:54	**7:30**	p1.6
23	**S**	1:48	**2:06**	p1.9	7:54	**8:24**	p1.8
24	**M**	2:48	**2:54**	p2.1	8:48	**9:18**	p2.0
25	**T**	3:48	**3:48**	p2.2	9:42	**10:06**	p2.1
26	**W**	4:42	**4:36**	p2.2	10:30	**10:54**	p2.1
27	**T**	5:36	**5:24**	p2.2	11:24	**11:48**	p2.1
28	**F**	6:30	**6:12**	p2.1	...	**12:18**	1.6
29	**S**	7:24	**7:06**	p1.9	12:36	**1:06**	a1.9
30	**S**	8:18	**8:00**	p1.7	1:30	**2:00**	a1.7
31	**M**	9:12	**8:54**	p1.5	2:24	**2:54**	a1.5

JUNE

Daylight Saving Time

DAY OF MONTH	DAY OF WEEK	CURRENT TURNS TO					
		NORTHWEST Flood Starts			SOUTHEAST Ebb Starts		
		a.m.	**p.m.**	Kts.	a.m.	**p.m.**	Kts.
1	**T**	10:07	**10:00**	p1.3	3:18	**3:54**	a1.3
2	**W**	11:06	**11:06**	p1.1	4:18	**4:54**	a1.2
3	**T**	...	**12:01**	1.0	5:18	**5:54**	a1.1
4	**F**	12:12	**12:42**	1.0	6:12	**6:48**	a1.0
5	**S**	1:12	**1:24**	p1.1	7:00	**7:36**	1.0
6	**S**	2:12	**2:06**	p1.2	7:48	**8:24**	p1.1
7	**M**	3:06	**2:42**	p1.2	8:36	**9:06**	p1.2
8	**T**	3:48	**3:18**	p1.3	9:24	**9:48**	p1.2
9	**W**	4:36	**3:54**	p1.3	10:12	**10:30**	p1.3
10	**T**	5:18	**4:30**	p1.3	10:54	**11:12**	p1.3
11	**F**	5:54	**5:12**	p1.3	11:36	**11:48**	p1.3
12	**S**	6:36	**5:54**	p1.3	...	**12:18**	0.9
13	**S**	7:12	**6:36**	p1.3	12:24	**1:00**	a1.3
14	**M**	7:54	**7:24**	p1.3	1:06	**1:42**	a1.3
15	**T**	8:36	**8:12**	p1.3	1:48	**2:30**	a1.2
16	**W**	9:18	**9:12**	p1.3	2:36	**3:18**	a1.2
17	**T**	10:06	**10:18**	p1.3	3:30	**4:12**	a1.3
18	**F**	11:00	**11:24**	a1.4	4:30	**5:12**	a1.3
19	**S**	11:48	...	1.6	5:24	**6:06**	1.4
20	**S**	12:30	**12:42**	p1.8	6:24	**7:06**	p1.6
21	**M**	1:30	**1:36**	p2.0	7:24	**8:00**	p1.8
22	**T**	2:36	**2:24**	p2.1	8:24	**8:54**	p2.0
23	**W**	3:30	**3:18**	p2.2	9:18	**9:48**	p2.0
24	**T**	4:24	**4:12**	p2.2	10:12	**10:36**	p2.0
25	**F**	5:18	**5:06**	p2.1	11:06	**11:30**	p2.0
26	**S**	6:12	**5:54**	p2.0	11:54	...	1.5
27	**S**	7:06	**6:48**	p1.8	12:18	**12:48**	a1.8
28	**M**	7:54	**7:36**	p1.6	1:12	**1:36**	a1.7
29	**T**	8:42	**8:30**	p1.4	2:00	**2:24**	a1.5
30	**W**	9:30	**9:24**	p1.2	2:48	**3:18**	a1.3

The Kts. (knots) columns show the **maximum** predicted velocities of the stronger one of the Flood Currents and the stronger one of the Ebb Currents for each day.
The letter "a" means the velocity shown should occur **after** the **a.m.** Current Change. The letter "p" means the velocity shown should occur **after** the **p.m.** Current Change (even if next morning). No "a" or "p" means a.m. and p.m. velocities are the same for that day.
Avg. Max. Velocity: Flood 1.8 Kts., Ebb 1.9 Kts.
Max. Flood 3 hrs. 5 min. after Flood Starts, ±15 min.
Max. Ebb 3 hrs. 5 min. after Ebb Starts, ±15 min.

See pp. 22-29 for Current Change at other points.

2021 CURRENT TABLE
DELAWARE BAY ENTRANCE

38°46.85'N, 75°02.58'W

Daylight Saving Time — **Daylight Saving Time**

JULY

DAY OF MONTH	DAY OF WEEK	CURRENT TURNS TO					
		NORTHWEST Flood Starts			SOUTHEAST Ebb Starts		
		a.m.	**p.m.**	Kts.	a.m.	**p.m.**	Kts.
1	**T**	10:19	**10:30**	1.0	3:36	**4:12**	a1.1
2	**F**	11:00	**11:36**	a1.0	4:30	**5:12**	a1.0
3	**S**	11:42	...	1.0	5:18	**6:06**	a0.9
4	**S**	12:42	**12:24**	p1.0	6:12	**6:54**	p0.9
5	**M**	1:42	**1:06**	p1.1	7:06	**7:48**	p1.0
6	**T**	2:42	**1:54**	p1.2	8:00	**8:36**	p1.1
7	**W**	3:30	**2:36**	p1.2	8:54	**9:24**	p1.2
8	**T**	4:18	**3:24**	p1.3	9:48	**10:06**	p1.3
9	**F**	5:00	**4:06**	p1.3	10:36	**10:48**	p1.4
10	**S**	5:36	**4:54**	p1.4	11:18	**11:30**	p1.4
11	**S**	6:12	**5:36**	p1.4	...	**12:01**	1.1
12	**M**	6:54	**6:24**	p1.4	12:12	**12:42**	a1.4
13	**T**	7:30	**7:12**	p1.4	12:54	**1:24**	a1.4
14	**W**	8:06	**8:06**	p1.4	1:36	**2:06**	a1.4
15	**T**	8:48	**9:00**	1.4	2:18	**2:54**	a1.4
16	**F**	9:36	**10:00**	a1.5	3:06	**3:48**	a1.4
17	**S**	10:24	**11:06**	a1.6	4:00	**4:42**	1.4
18	**S**	11:18	...	1.7	5:00	**5:42**	p1.5
19	**M**	12:12	**12:12**	p1.8	6:00	**6:42**	p1.6
20	**T**	1:18	**1:06**	p1.9	7:00	**7:36**	p1.8
21	**W**	2:18	**2:06**	p2.0	8:00	**8:36**	p1.9
22	**T**	3:18	**3:00**	p2.0	9:00	**9:30**	p1.9
23	**F**	4:12	**3:54**	p2.0	9:54	**10:24**	p1.9
24	**S**	5:06	**4:48**	p2.0	10:48	**11:12**	p1.9
25	**S**	5:54	**5:36**	p1.9	11:36	...	1.5
26	**M**	6:42	**6:24**	p1.8	12:01	**12:24**	a1.7
27	**T**	7:24	**7:12**	p1.6	12:48	**1:06**	a1.6
28	**W**	8:06	**8:00**	p1.3	1:30	**1:54**	a1.4
29	**T**	8:42	**8:48**	1.1	2:12	**2:36**	a1.2
30	**F**	9:18	**9:48**	a1.0	2:54	**3:24**	a1.0
31	**S**	9:54	**10:48**	a1.0	3:42	**4:18**	a0.9

AUGUST

DAY OF MONTH	DAY OF WEEK	CURRENT TURNS TO					
		NORTHWEST Flood Starts			SOUTHEAST Ebb Starts		
		a.m.	**p.m.**	Kts.	a.m.	**p.m.**	Kts.
1	**S**	10:37	**11:59**	a1.0	4:30	**5:12**	0.8
2	**M**	11:18	...	1.0	5:24	**6:12**	p0.8
3	**T**	1:06	**12:12**	p1.0	6:24	**7:06**	p0.9
4	**W**	2:12	**1:06**	p1.1	7:30	**8:06**	p1.1
5	**T**	3:00	**2:06**	p1.2	8:30	**8:54**	p1.2
6	**F**	3:48	**3:00**	p1.3	9:18	**9:48**	p1.3
7	**S**	4:30	**3:48**	p1.4	10:06	**10:30**	p1.4
8	**S**	5:06	**4:36**	p1.5	10:54	**11:12**	p1.5
9	**M**	5:42	**5:24**	p1.6	11:36	**11:54**	p1.6
10	**T**	6:18	**6:12**	p1.6	...	**12:18**	1.4
11	**W**	7:00	**7:00**	p1.6	12:30	**1:00**	a1.6
12	**T**	7:36	**7:54**	1.6	1:12	**1:42**	a1.6
13	**F**	8:18	**8:48**	a1.7	2:00	**2:30**	1.5
14	**S**	9:06	**9:48**	a1.7	2:48	**3:24**	1.5
15	**S**	9:54	**10:54**	a1.7	3:36	**4:18**	p1.5
16	**M**	10:48	**11:59**	a1.7	4:36	**5:18**	p1.5
17	**T**	11:48	...	1.7	5:42	**6:18**	p1.6
18	**W**	1:00	**12:48**	p1.8	6:42	**7:18**	p1.6
19	**T**	2:06	**1:54**	p1.8	7:48	**8:18**	p1.7
20	**F**	3:00	**2:48**	p1.9	8:42	**9:18**	p1.7
21	**S**	3:54	**3:42**	p1.9	9:36	**10:06**	p1.7
22	**S**	4:48	**4:36**	p1.8	10:30	**10:54**	p1.7
23	**M**	5:30	**5:24**	p1.8	11:12	**11:36**	p1.6
24	**T**	6:12	**6:06**	p1.6	...	**12:01**	1.3
25	**W**	6:48	**6:48**	p1.5	12:18	**12:36**	a1.5
26	**T**	7:24	**7:36**	1.3	1:00	**1:18**	a1.3
27	**F**	7:48	**8:18**	a1.2	1:36	**2:00**	a1.1
28	**S**	8:18	**9:06**	a1.1	2:12	**2:42**	a1.0
29	**S**	8:54	**10:06**	a1.0	2:54	**3:30**	0.8
30	**M**	9:36	**11:18**	a0.9	3:48	**4:24**	p0.8
31	**T**	10:24	...	0.9	4:42	**5:24**	p0.8

The Kts. (knots) columns show the **maximum** predicted velocities of the stronger one of the Flood Currents and the stronger one of the Ebb Currents for each day.
The letter "a" means the velocity shown should occur **after** the **a.m.** Current Change. The letter "p" means the velocity shown should occur **after** the **p.m.** Current Change (even if next morning). No "a" or "p" means a.m. and p.m. velocities are the same for that day.
Avg. Max. Velocity: Flood 1.8 Kts., Ebb 1.9 Kts.
Max. Flood 3 hrs. 5 min. after Flood Starts, ±15 min.
Max. Ebb 3 hrs. 5 min. after Ebb Starts, ±15 min.

See pp. 22-29 for Current Change at other points.

2021 CURRENT TABLE
DELAWARE BAY ENTRANCE

38°46.85'N, 75°02.58'W

Daylight Saving Time

SEPTEMBER

DAY OF MONTH	DAY OF WEEK	CURRENT TURNS TO NORTHWEST Flood Starts			CURRENT TURNS TO SOUTHEAST Ebb Starts		
		a.m.	**p.m.**	Kts.	a.m.	**p.m.**	Kts.
1	**W**	12:25	**-A-**	0.6	5:48	**6:24**	p0.9
2	**T**	1:30	**12:30**	p1.0	6:54	**7:30**	p1.0
3	**F**	2:24	**1:36**	p1.1	7:54	**8:24**	p1.2
4	**S**	3:12	**2:36**	p1.3	8:48	**9:18**	p1.3
5	**S**	3:54	**3:30**	p1.5	9:36	**10:00**	p1.5
6	**M**	4:30	**4:18**	p1.6	10:24	**10:48**	p1.6
7	**T**	5:06	**5:06**	p1.7	11:06	**11:24**	p1.7
8	**W**	5:42	**6:00**	1.7	11:48	...	1.6
9	**T**	6:24	**6:48**	a1.8	12:06	**12:30**	1.7
10	**F**	7:06	**7:42**	a1.9	12:54	**1:18**	1.7
11	**S**	7:48	**8:36**	a1.9	1:36	**2:06**	p1.7
12	**S**	8:36	**9:36**	a1.8	2:24	**3:00**	p1.6
13	**M**	9:30	**10:36**	a1.8	3:24	**3:54**	p1.5
14	**T**	10:30	**11:42**	a1.7	4:24	**5:00**	p1.5
15	**W**	11:36	...	1.6	5:24	**6:06**	p1.5
16	**T**	12:48	**12:36**	p1.6	6:30	**7:06**	p1.5
17	**F**	1:48	**1:42**	p1.6	7:30	**8:06**	p1.6
18	**S**	2:48	**2:36**	p1.7	8:30	**9:00**	p1.6
19	**S**	3:36	**3:30**	p1.7	9:24	**9:48**	p1.6
20	**M**	4:18	**4:18**	p1.7	10:06	**10:30**	p1.5
21	**T**	5:00	**5:06**	p1.6	10:48	**11:12**	p1.5
22	**W**	5:36	**5:48**	p1.5	11:30	**11:48**	1.3
23	**T**	6:06	**6:30**	a1.4	...	**12:06**	1.3
24	**F**	6:36	**7:12**	a1.3	12:24	**12:42**	1.2
25	**S**	7:00	**7:54**	a1.2	1:06	**1:18**	1.1
26	**S**	7:30	**8:36**	a1.1	1:42	**2:00**	p1.0
27	**M**	8:06	**9:30**	a1.0	2:24	**2:42**	p0.9
28	**T**	8:54	**10:30**	a0.9	3:12	**3:36**	p0.8
29	**W**	9:48	**11:42**	a0.9	4:12	**4:36**	p0.8
30	**T**	10:54	...	0.9	5:18	**5:48**	p0.9

Daylight Saving Time

OCTOBER

DAY OF MONTH	DAY OF WEEK	CURRENT TURNS TO NORTHWEST Flood Starts			CURRENT TURNS TO SOUTHEAST Ebb Starts		
		a.m.	**p.m.**	Kts.	a.m.	**p.m.**	Kts.
1	**F**	12:43	**12:01**	p1.0	6:24	**6:48**	p1.0
2	**S**	1:36	**1:06**	p1.2	7:18	**7:48**	p1.2
3	**S**	2:24	**2:12**	p1.3	8:12	**8:42**	p1.4
4	**M**	3:06	**3:06**	p1.5	9:06	**9:30**	p1.5
5	**T**	3:48	**4:00**	p1.7	9:48	**10:12**	p1.7
6	**W**	4:24	**4:54**	1.8	10:36	**11:00**	a1.8
7	**T**	5:06	**5:42**	a1.9	11:18	**11:42**	a1.9
8	**F**	5:48	**6:36**	a2.1	...	**12:06**	2.0
9	**S**	6:36	**7:24**	a2.1	12:30	**12:54**	p1.9
10	**S**	7:24	**8:24**	a2.0	1:18	**1:42**	p1.8
11	**M**	8:12	**9:18**	a1.9	2:12	**2:36**	p1.7
12	**T**	9:12	**10:24**	a1.7	3:06	**3:36**	p1.5
13	**W**	10:12	**11:30**	a1.6	4:06	**4:42**	p1.4
14	**T**	11:18	...	1.5	5:12	**5:48**	p1.4
15	**F**	12:30	**12:24**	p1.4	6:18	**6:48**	p1.4
16	**S**	1:30	**1:30**	p1.5	7:18	**7:48**	p1.4
17	**S**	2:24	**2:24**	p1.5	8:12	**8:36**	p1.4
18	**M**	3:06	**3:18**	p1.5	9:00	**9:24**	p1.4
19	**T**	3:48	**4:06**	1.4	9:48	**10:06**	1.3
20	**W**	4:24	**4:48**	1.4	10:24	**10:42**	1.3
21	**T**	4:54	**5:30**	a1.4	11:00	**11:24**	a1.3
22	**F**	5:24	**6:12**	a1.4	11:36	...	1.3
23	**S**	5:54	**6:54**	a1.3	12:01	**12:12**	p1.2
24	**S**	6:24	**7:30**	a1.2	12:36	**12:48**	p1.1
25	**M**	6:54	**8:12**	a1.1	1:18	**1:30**	p1.0
26	**T**	7:36	**9:00**	a1.1	2:00	**2:12**	p0.9
27	**W**	8:24	**9:54**	a1.0	2:48	**3:00**	p0.9
28	**T**	9:18	**11:00**	a0.9	3:42	**4:00**	p0.9
29	**F**	10:24	**11:54**	a1.0	4:48	**5:06**	p1.0
30	**S**	11:36	...	1.1	5:48	**6:12**	p1.1
31	**S**	12:48	**12:42**	p1.2	6:42	**7:06**	p1.2

A also at 11:25 a.m. 0.9

The Kts. (knots) columns show the **maximum** predicted velocities of the stronger one of the Flood Currents and the stronger one of the Ebb Currents for each day.
The letter "a" means the velocity shown should occur **after** the **a.m.** Current Change. The letter "p" means the velocity shown should occur **after** the **p.m.** Current Change (even if next morning). No "a" or "p" means a.m. and p.m. velocities are the same for that day.
Avg. Max. Velocity: Flood 1.8 Kts., Ebb 1.9 Kts.
Max. Flood 3 hrs. 5 min. after Flood Starts, ±15 min.
Max. Ebb 3 hrs. 5 min. after Ebb Starts, ±15 min.

See pp. 22-29 for Current Change at other points.

2021 CURRENT TABLE
DELAWARE BAY ENTRANCE

38°46.85'N, 75°02.58'W

***Standard Time starts Nov. 7 at 2 a.m.** — **Standard Time**

NOVEMBER

DAY OF MONTH	DAY OF WEEK	CURRENT TURNS TO NORTHWEST Flood Starts a.m.	**p.m.**	Kts.	CURRENT TURNS TO SOUTHEAST Ebb Starts a.m.	**p.m.**	Kts.
1	**M**	1:37	**1:48**	p1.4	7:36	**8:00**	p1.4
2	**T**	2:18	**2:48**	p1.6	8:30	**8:54**	p1.6
3	**W**	3:06	**3:42**	a1.8	9:18	**9:42**	a1.8
4	**T**	3:48	**4:36**	a2.0	10:06	**10:30**	a1.9
5	**F**	4:36	**5:24**	a2.1	10:54	**11:18**	a2.1
6	**S**	5:18	**6:18**	a2.2	11:42	...	2.1
7	**S**	*5:12	***6:12**	a2.2	12:12	**-A-**	1.7
8	**M**	6:00	**7:06**	a2.1	12:01	**12:24**	p1.9
9	**T**	6:54	**8:06**	a1.9	12:54	**1:18**	p1.7
10	**W**	7:54	**9:06**	a1.7	1:48	**2:18**	p1.5
11	**T**	8:54	**10:06**	a1.5	2:48	**3:18**	p1.4
12	**F**	10:06	**11:06**	a1.4	3:54	**4:24**	p1.3
13	**S**	11:12	...	1.3	5:00	**5:24**	p1.2
14	**S**	12:01	**12:12**	p1.3	5:54	**6:18**	p1.2
15	**M**	12:48	**1:12**	1.2	6:48	**7:06**	1.2
16	**T**	1:30	**2:06**	a1.3	7:36	**7:54**	1.2
17	**W**	2:06	**2:54**	a1.3	8:18	**8:36**	a1.3
18	**T**	2:42	**3:36**	a1.4	9:00	**9:18**	a1.3
19	**F**	3:12	**4:18**	a1.4	9:36	**10:00**	a1.3
20	**S**	3:48	**5:00**	a1.3	10:12	**10:36**	a1.3
21	**S**	4:18	**5:36**	a1.3	10:48	**11:18**	a1.2
22	**M**	4:54	**6:18**	a1.2	11:30	...	1.2
23	**T**	5:30	**6:54**	a1.2	12:01	**12:06**	p1.1
24	**W**	6:18	**7:42**	a1.1	12:42	**12:48**	p1.0
25	**T**	7:06	**8:24**	a1.1	1:30	**1:36**	p1.0
26	**F**	8:00	**9:18**	a1.0	2:18	**2:30**	p1.0
27	**S**	9:06	**10:06**	a1.1	3:18	**3:30**	p1.1
28	**S**	10:12	**11:00**	p1.2	4:12	**4:30**	p1.2
29	**M**	11:18	**11:48**	p1.5	5:12	**5:30**	p1.3
30	**T**	...	**12:24**	1.4	6:06	**6:24**	1.4

DECEMBER

DAY OF MONTH	DAY OF WEEK	CURRENT TURNS TO NORTHWEST Flood Starts a.m.	**p.m.**	Kts.	CURRENT TURNS TO SOUTHEAST Ebb Starts a.m.	**p.m.**	Kts.
1	**W**	12:37	**1:24**	a1.7	6:54	**7:18**	a1.7
2	**T**	1:24	**2:24**	a1.9	7:48	**8:12**	a1.9
3	**F**	2:18	**3:18**	a2.1	8:42	**9:06**	a2.0
4	**S**	3:06	**4:12**	a2.2	9:30	**10:00**	a2.1
5	**S**	4:00	**5:06**	a2.2	10:24	**10:48**	a2.1
6	**M**	4:48	**5:54**	a2.2	11:12	**11:42**	a2.0
7	**T**	5:42	**6:48**	a2.1	...	**12:06**	1.9
8	**W**	6:36	**7:42**	a1.9	12:36	**1:00**	p1.7
9	**T**	7:36	**8:42**	a1.6	1:30	**1:54**	p1.5
10	**F**	8:36	**9:36**	a1.4	2:30	**2:54**	p1.3
11	**S**	9:36	**10:30**	a1.3	3:30	**3:48**	p1.2
12	**S**	10:48	**11:18**	1.1	4:30	**4:42**	p1.1
13	**M**	11:48	...	1.0	5:24	**5:36**	1.0
14	**T**	12:01	**12:48**	a1.2	6:18	**6:30**	1.0
15	**W**	12:42	**1:42**	a1.2	7:06	**7:18**	a1.1
16	**T**	1:24	**2:36**	a1.2	7:48	**8:06**	a1.2
17	**F**	2:00	**3:18**	a1.3	8:30	**8:54**	a1.2
18	**S**	2:36	**4:06**	a1.3	9:12	**9:36**	a1.3
19	**S**	3:18	**4:42**	a1.3	9:54	**10:18**	a1.3
20	**M**	3:54	**5:24**	a1.3	10:36	**11:00**	a1.3
21	**T**	4:36	**6:00**	a1.3	11:12	**11:42**	a1.3
22	**W**	5:18	**6:36**	a1.2	11:54	...	1.2
23	**T**	6:00	**7:18**	a1.2	12:24	**12:30**	p1.2
24	**F**	6:48	**7:54**	a1.2	1:12	**1:18**	p1.2
25	**S**	7:48	**8:42**	a1.2	1:54	**2:06**	p1.2
26	**S**	8:48	**9:24**	p1.3	2:48	**2:54**	p1.2
27	**M**	9:54	**10:18**	p1.4	3:42	**3:54**	p1.2
28	**T**	11:00	**11:06**	p1.6	4:36	**4:54**	1.3
29	**W**	...	**12:01**	1.4	5:30	**5:54**	a1.5
30	**T**	12:01	**1:06**	a1.8	6:30	**6:48**	a1.7
31	**F**	12:54	**2:06**	a2.0	7:24	**7:48**	a1.9

A also at *11:30 a.m. 2.0

The Kts. (knots) columns show the **maximum** predicted velocities of the stronger one of the Flood Currents and the stronger one of the Ebb Currents for each day.
The letter "a" means the velocity shown should occur **after** the **a.m.** Current Change. The letter "p" means the velocity shown should occur **after** the **p.m.** Current Change (even if next morning). No "a" or "p" means a.m. and p.m. velocities are the same for that day.
Avg. Max. Velocity: Flood 1.8 Kts., Ebb 1.9 Kts.
Max. Flood 3 hrs. 5 min. after Flood Starts, ±15 min.
Max. Ebb 3 hrs. 5 min. after Ebb Starts, ±15 min.

See pp. 22-29 for Current Change at other points.

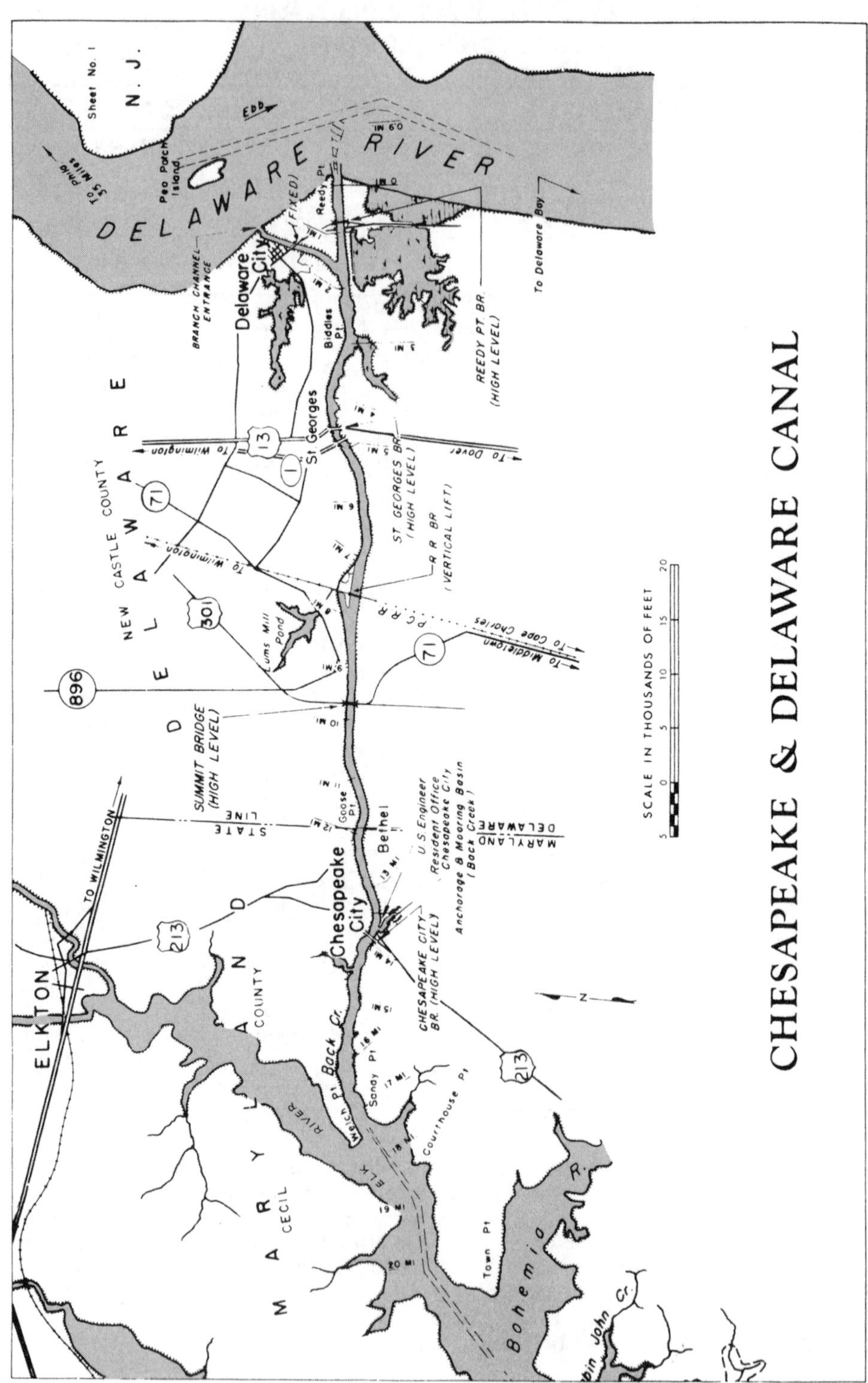

See Chesapeake & Delaware Canal Current Tables, pp. 154-159

Chesapeake & Delaware Canal Regulations

(Traffic Dispatcher is located at Chesapeake City and monitors Channel 13.)

Philadelphia District Engineer issues notices periodically showing available channel depths and navigation conditions.

Projected Channel dimensions are 35 ft. deep and 450 ft. wide. (The branch to Delaware City is 8 ft. deep and 50 ft. wide.) The distance from the Delaware River Ship Channel to the Elk River is 19.1 miles.

1. Traffic controls, located at Reedy Point and Old Town Point Wharf, flash green when Canal is open, flash red when it is closed.
2. Vessel identification and monitoring are performed by TV cameras at Reedy Point and Old Town Point Wharf.
3. The following vessels, tugs and tows are required to have radiotelephones:
   a. Power vessels of 300 gross tons and upward.
   b. All commercial vessels of 100 gross tons and upward carrying 1 or more passengers for hire.
   c. Every towing vessel of 26 feet or over.
4. Vessels listed in 3. will not enter the Canal until radio communication is made with the dispatcher and clearance is received. Ships' captains will tell the dispatcher the estimated time of passing Reedy Point or Town Point. Communication is to be established on Channel 13 (156.65 MHz) two hours prior to entering the canal. Dispatcher also monitors Channel 16 (156.8 MHz) to respond to emergencies.
5. A westbound vessel must be able to pass Reedy Is. or Pea Patch Is. within 2 hours of receiving clearance; an eastbound vessel must be able to pass Arnold Point within 2 hours. If passage is not made within 2 hours, a new clearance must be solicited. Vessels must also report to the dispatcher the time of passing the outer end of the jetties at Reedy Point and Old Town Point Wharf.
6. Maximum combined extreme breadth of vessels meeting and overtaking each other is 190 feet.
7. Vessels of all types are required to travel at a safe speed to avoid damage by suction or wash to wharves, landings, other boats, etc. Operators of yachts, motorboats, etc. are cautioned that there are many large, deep-draft ocean-going and commercial vessels using the Canal. There is "no anchoring" in the canal at any time. Moor or anchor outside of Reedy Point, near Arnold Point, or in Chesapeake City Basin.
8. Vessels proceeding *with* the current shall have the right-of-way but all small pleasure craft shall relinquish the right-of-way to deeper draft vessels which have a limited maneuvering ability.
9. Vessels under sail will not be permitted in the Canal.
10. Vessels difficult to handle must use the Canal during daylight hours and must have tug assistance. They should clear Reedy Point Bridge (going east) or Chesapeake City Bridge (going west) before dark.
11. Any tows over 760' contact dispatcher 72 hours prior to passage.

Anchorage and wharfage facilities for small vessels only are at Chesapeake City and permission to use them for more than 24 hours must be obtained from Chesapeake City.

The **railroad bridge** has a clearance when closed of 45 ft. at MHW. The bridge monitors Channel 13 and gives 30 minutes notice prior to lowering.

The **five highway bridges** are high level and fixed.

Normal tide range is 5.4 ft. at Delaware R. end of the Canal and 2.6 ft. at Chesapeake City. Local mean low water at Courthouse Pt. is 2.5 ft. and decreases gradually eastward to 0.6 ft. at Delaware R. (See pp. 18 and 19 for times of High Water in this area.)
Note: A violent northeast storm may raise tide 4 to 5 ft. above normal in the Canal; a westerly storm may cause low tide to fall slightly below normal at Chesapeake City and as much as 4.0 ft. below normal at Reedy Point.

2021 CURRENT TABLE
CHESAPEAKE & DELAWARE CANAL
39°31.83'N, 75°49.66'W at Chesapeake City

Standard Time

JANUARY

DAY OF MONTH	DAY OF WEEK	CURRENT TURNS TO EAST Flood Starts a.m.	p.m.	Kts.	CURRENT TURNS TO WEST Ebb Starts a.m.	p.m.	Kts.
1	F	5:25	**6:24**	p2.0	12:18	**-A-**	1.3
2	S	6:12	**7:06**	2.0	12:48	**-B-**	1.4
3	S	6:54	**7:42**	2.0	1:24	**12:36**	p2.3
4	M	7:42	**8:24**	a2.0	1:54	**1:30**	p2.1
5	T	8:36	**9:12**	a2.0	2:30	**2:36**	p1.9
6	W	9:36	**10:06**	a2.0	3:12	**3:42**	a1.8
7	T	10:42	**11:00**	a1.9	3:54	**5:06**	a1.9
8	F	11:54	**11:54**	a1.9	4:42	**6:24**	a2.1
9	S	...	**1:00**	1.9	5:36	**7:42**	a2.2
10	S	1:00	**2:12**	p2.0	6:36	**8:48**	a2.4
11	M	2:00	**3:12**	p2.1	7:30	**9:48**	a2.5
12	T	3:00	**4:06**	p2.2	8:30	**10:42**	a2.6
13	W	3:54	**4:54**	p2.2	9:24	**11:24**	a2.5
14	T	4:48	**5:42**	p2.2	10:18	...	2.5
15	F	5:36	**6:24**	p2.1	12:06	**-C-**	1.5
16	S	6:30	**7:00**	p2.0	12:42	**12:01**	p2.2
17	S	7:18	**7:36**	p1.9	1:18	**12:54**	p2.0
18	M	8:06	**8:18**	p1.8	1:54	**1:42**	p1.8
19	T	8:54	**8:54**	p1.7	2:30	**2:36**	a1.7
20	W	9:42	**9:36**	p1.6	3:06	**3:36**	a1.7
21	T	10:36	**10:24**	1.5	3:42	**4:48**	a1.8
22	F	11:36	**11:12**	p1.5	4:24	**5:54**	a1.8
23	S	...	**12:36**	1.4	5:06	**7:06**	a1.9
24	S	12:06	**1:36**	1.5	5:54	**8:06**	a2.0
25	M	1:00	**2:30**	p1.7	6:42	**9:00**	a2.1
26	T	1:54	**3:18**	p1.8	7:36	**9:48**	a2.2
27	W	2:48	**4:00**	p1.9	8:24	**10:30**	a2.3
28	T	3:42	**4:42**	p2.0	9:18	**11:06**	a2.4
29	F	4:24	**5:24**	p2.0	10:06	**11:42**	a2.4
30	S	5:06	**6:00**	a2.1	10:54	...	2.4
31	S	5:54	**6:42**	a2.2	12:12	**-D-**	1.6

Standard Time

FEBRUARY

DAY OF MONTH	DAY OF WEEK	CURRENT TURNS TO EAST Flood Starts a.m.	p.m.	Kts.	CURRENT TURNS TO WEST Ebb Starts a.m.	p.m.	Kts.
1	M	6:37	**7:24**	a2.2	12:42	**12:36**	p2.2
2	T	7:30	**8:06**	a2.2	1:18	**1:30**	p2.0
3	W	8:24	**8:48**	a2.1	1:48	**2:36**	a2.0
4	T	9:24	**9:42**	a2.0	2:30	**3:48**	a2.0
5	F	10:36	**10:36**	a1.9	3:18	**5:12**	a2.1
6	S	11:48	**11:36**	a1.8	4:12	**6:30**	a2.2
7	S	...	**12:54**	1.8	5:12	**7:36**	a2.3
8	M	12:42	**2:00**	p1.9	6:18	**8:36**	a2.3
9	T	1:48	**3:00**	p2.0	7:24	**9:30**	a2.3
10	W	2:48	**3:48**	p2.1	8:24	**10:12**	a2.3
11	T	3:42	**4:36**	p2.1	9:24	**10:54**	a2.2
12	F	4:36	**5:12**	p2.0	10:18	**11:30**	a2.2
13	S	5:24	**5:48**	p2.0	11:06	**11:59**	a2.1
14	S	6:06	**6:24**	1.9	11:54	...	1.9
15	M	6:48	**7:00**	1.9	12:30	**12:36**	1.8
16	T	7:30	**7:30**	1.8	1:00	**1:24**	a1.9
17	W	8:12	**8:06**	1.7	1:30	**2:12**	a1.9
18	T	9:00	**8:48**	p1.7	2:00	**3:12**	a1.9
19	F	9:54	**9:30**	1.6	2:36	**4:18**	a1.9
20	S	10:54	**10:24**	1.5	3:18	**5:24**	a2.0
21	S	11:54	**11:18**	1.5	4:06	**6:30**	a2.0
22	M	...	**12:54**	1.5	5:06	**7:30**	a2.1
23	T	12:24	**1:48**	p1.6	6:06	**8:24**	a2.1
24	W	1:24	**2:42**	p1.8	7:06	**9:06**	a2.2
25	T	2:24	**3:30**	p1.9	8:00	**9:48**	a2.2
26	F	3:12	**4:12**	a2.0	9:00	**10:24**	a2.3
27	S	4:00	**4:54**	a2.1	9:54	**10:54**	a2.3
28	S	4:48	**5:36**	a2.3	10:48	**11:24**	a2.3

A also at 11:00 a.m. 2.5 **B** also at 11:48 a.m. 2.4 **C** also at 11:12 a.m. 2.3
D also at 11:42 a.m. 2.3

The Kts. (knots) columns show the **maximum** predicted velocities of the stronger one of the Flood Currents and the stronger one of the Ebb Currents for each day.
The letter "a" means the velocity shown should occur **after** the **a.m.** Current Change. The letter "p" means the velocity shown should occur **after** the **p.m.** Current Change (even if next morning). No "a" or "p" means a.m. and p.m. velocities are the same for that day.
Avg. Max. Velocity: Flood 2.0 Kts., Ebb 1.9 Kts.
Max. Flood 3 hrs. 10 min. after Flood Starts ±45 min.
Max. Ebb 2 hrs. 45 min. after Ebb Starts ±45 min.

See pp. 22-29 for Current Change at other points.

Note *from NOS: These predictions should be considered questionable. Caution is advised.*

2021 CURRENT TABLE
CHESAPEAKE & DELAWARE CANAL
39°31.83'N, 75°49.66'W at Chesapeake City

***Daylight Time starts March 14 at 2 a.m.** **Daylight Saving Time**

MARCH								APRIL							
DAY OF MONTH	DAY OF WEEK	CURRENT TURNS TO EAST Flood Starts a.m.	**p.m.**	Kts.	CURRENT TURNS TO WEST Ebb Starts a.m.	**p.m.**	Kts.	DAY OF MONTH	DAY OF WEEK	CURRENT TURNS TO EAST Flood Starts a.m.	**p.m.**	Kts.	CURRENT TURNS TO WEST Ebb Starts a.m.	**p.m.**	Kts.
1	**M**	5:31	**6:18**	a2.4	11:42	...	2.2	1	**T**	8:01	**8:18**	a2.4	12:54	**2:42**	a2.5
2	**T**	6:18	**7:00**	a2.4	12:01	**12:36**	a2.1	2	**F**	9:06	**9:12**	a2.2	1:36	**3:48**	a2.5
3	**W**	7:12	**7:42**	a2.3	12:30	**1:36**	a2.2	3	**S**	10:06	**10:12**	a2.1	2:30	**5:00**	a2.4
4	**T**	8:12	**8:30**	a2.2	1:12	**2:42**	a2.2	4	**S**	11:12	**11:18**	a1.9	3:24	**6:06**	a2.2
5	**F**	9:18	**9:24**	a2.0	1:54	**4:00**	a2.3	5	**M**	...	**12:18**	1.8	4:36	**7:00**	a2.1
6	**S**	10:30	**10:24**	a1.9	2:48	**5:12**	a2.2	6	**T**	12:24	**1:18**	p1.8	5:54	**7:48**	a2.0
7	**S**	11:36	**11:30**	a1.8	3:48	**6:24**	a2.2	7	**W**	1:30	**2:12**	p1.8	7:06	**8:36**	a1.8
8	**M**	...	**12:42**	1.8	5:00	**7:24**	a2.2	8	**T**	2:30	**3:06**	p1.8	8:18	**9:12**	1.7
9	**T**	12:36	**1:42**	p1.9	6:12	**8:12**	a2.1	9	**F**	3:24	**3:48**	p1.8	9:18	**9:54**	p1.9
10	**W**	1:42	**2:36**	p1.9	7:18	**8:54**	a2.0	10	**S**	4:12	**4:30**	a1.8	10:12	**10:24**	p2.0
11	**T**	2:42	**3:24**	p1.9	8:24	**9:36**	a2.0	11	**S**	5:00	**5:06**	a1.9	11:00	**11:00**	p2.0
12	**F**	3:30	**4:06**	p1.9	9:18	**10:12**	a1.9	12	**M**	5:36	**5:42**	a1.9	11:48	**11:24**	p2.1
13	**S**	4:18	**4:42**	a1.9	10:12	**10:42**	p1.9	13	**T**	6:18	**6:12**	a1.9	-B-	**12:30**	1.4
14	**S**	*6:00	***6:18**	a1.9	*11:54	...	1.8	14	**W**	6:54	**6:42**	a1.9	...	**1:12**	1.3
15	**M**	6:42	**6:48**	a1.9	12:12	**12:42**	a2.0	15	**T**	7:30	**7:12**	a1.9	12:18	**2:00**	a2.3
16	**T**	7:18	**7:18**	a1.9	12:42	**1:24**	a2.0	16	**F**	8:12	**7:48**	a1.9	12:42	**2:48**	a2.3
17	**W**	8:00	**7:48**	a1.9	1:06	**2:06**	a2.1	17	**S**	8:54	**8:36**	a1.8	1:18	**3:36**	a2.3
18	**T**	8:36	**8:24**	a1.8	1:36	**3:00**	a2.1	18	**S**	9:42	**9:24**	a1.8	2:06	**4:30**	a2.3
19	**F**	9:24	**9:06**	1.7	2:06	**3:54**	a2.1	19	**M**	10:30	**10:24**	a1.8	2:54	**5:18**	a2.2
20	**S**	10:18	**9:54**	a1.7	2:42	**4:54**	a2.1	20	**T**	11:24	**11:30**	a1.8	3:48	**6:12**	a2.1
21	**S**	11:12	**10:48**	1.6	3:30	**5:54**	a2.1	21	**W**	...	**12:18**	1.8	4:54	**6:54**	a2.0
22	**M**	-A-	**12:06**	1.6	4:24	**6:54**	a2.1	22	**T**	12:30	**1:12**	p1.8	6:06	**7:36**	a2.0
23	**T**	...	**1:06**	1.6	5:24	**7:42**	a2.1	23	**F**	1:30	**2:06**	1.8	7:18	**8:18**	a2.0
24	**W**	12:54	**2:00**	p1.7	6:30	**8:30**	a2.1	24	**S**	2:24	**3:00**	a2.0	8:24	**9:00**	p2.0
25	**T**	1:54	**2:54**	p1.8	7:42	**9:12**	a2.1	25	**S**	3:18	**3:54**	a2.2	9:30	**9:36**	p2.2
26	**F**	2:54	**3:48**	1.9	8:42	**9:54**	a2.1	26	**M**	4:12	**4:42**	a2.4	10:36	**10:12**	p2.4
27	**S**	3:48	**4:36**	a2.1	9:42	**10:30**	a2.1	27	**T**	5:06	**5:30**	a2.5	11:36	**10:54**	p2.6
28	**S**	4:36	**5:18**	a2.3	10:42	**11:06**	2.1	28	**W**	6:00	**6:18**	a2.6	-C-	**12:36**	1.5
29	**M**	5:24	**6:06**	a2.4	11:42	**11:36**	p2.3	29	**T**	6:54	**7:06**	a2.5	...	**1:42**	1.3
30	**T**	6:12	**6:48**	a2.5	...	**12:36**	1.9	30	**F**	7:54	**7:54**	a2.4	12:18	**2:42**	a2.7
31	**W**	7:06	**7:30**	a2.5	12:12	**1:36**	a2.4								

A also at 11:48 p.m. 1.6 **B** also at 11:48 p.m. 2.2 **C** also at 11:36 p.m. 2.7

The Kts. (knots) columns show the **maximum** predicted velocities of the stronger one of the Flood Currents and the stronger one of the Ebb Currents for each day.
The letter "a" means the velocity shown should occur **after** the **a.m.** Current Change. The letter "p" means the velocity shown should occur **after** the **p.m.** Current Change (even if next morning). No "a" or "p" means a.m. and p.m. velocities are the same for that day.
Avg. Max. Velocity: Flood 2.0 Kts., Ebb 1.9 Kts.
Max. Flood 3 hrs. 10 min. after Flood Starts ±45 min.
Max. Ebb 2 hrs. 45 min. after Ebb Starts ±45 min.

See pp. 22-29 for Current Change at other points.

Note *from NOS: These predictions should be considered questionable. Caution is advised.*

2021 CURRENT TABLE
CHESAPEAKE & DELAWARE CANAL
39°31.83'N, 75°49.66'W at Chesapeake City

Daylight Saving Time — **Daylight Saving Time**

MAY

DAY OF MONTH	DAY OF WEEK	CURRENT TURNS TO EAST Flood Starts a.m.	**p.m.**	Kts.	CURRENT TURNS TO WEST Ebb Starts a.m.	**p.m.**	Kts.
1	S	8:55	**9:00**	a2.2	1:12	**3:42**	a2.6
2	S	9:54	**10:00**	a2.1	2:06	**4:42**	a2.4
3	M	10:54	**11:12**	a2.0	3:12	**5:36**	a2.1
4	T	11:48	...	1.9	4:30	**6:24**	a1.9
5	W	12:18	**12:42**	p1.8	5:48	**7:12**	a1.7
6	T	1:18	**1:36**	p1.7	7:00	**7:54**	p1.8
7	F	2:12	**2:24**	p1.7	8:06	**8:30**	p1.9
8	S	3:06	**3:06**	a1.7	9:06	**9:06**	p2.1
9	S	3:54	**3:48**	a1.8	10:00	**9:42**	p2.1
10	M	4:36	**4:24**	a1.9	10:48	**10:12**	p2.2
11	T	5:18	**5:00**	a1.9	11:36	**10:36**	p2.3
12	W	5:54	**5:36**	a1.9	-A-	**12:24**	1.1
13	T	6:30	**6:06**	a1.9	-B-	**1:06**	1.1
14	F	7:12	**6:42**	a1.9	...	**1:54**	1.0
15	S	7:48	**7:24**	a1.9	12:06	**2:36**	a2.4
16	S	8:30	**8:12**	a1.9	12:48	**3:18**	a2.4
17	M	9:12	**9:12**	a1.9	1:36	**4:00**	a2.3
18	T	9:54	**10:12**	a1.9	2:30	**4:42**	a2.2
19	W	10:42	**11:06**	a1.9	3:24	**5:24**	a2.1
20	T	11:36	...	1.9	4:36	**6:06**	a2.0
21	F	12:06	**12:30**	p1.9	5:48	**6:48**	a1.9
22	S	1:06	**1:24**	1.9	7:00	**7:30**	p2.1
23	S	2:00	**2:18**	a2.1	8:12	**8:06**	p2.3
24	M	3:00	**3:12**	a2.2	9:24	**8:48**	p2.5
25	T	3:54	**4:06**	a2.4	10:30	**9:30**	p2.7
26	W	4:54	**4:54**	a2.5	11:36	**10:18**	p2.9
27	T	5:48	**5:42**	a2.5	-C-	**12:36**	1.2
28	F	6:42	**6:36**	a2.5	-D-	**1:36**	1.1
29	S	7:42	**7:36**	a2.4	...	**2:30**	1.1
30	S	8:36	**8:42**	a2.2	12:54	**3:24**	a2.6
31	M	9:30	**9:48**	a2.1	1:54	**4:12**	a2.3

JUNE

DAY OF MONTH	DAY OF WEEK	CURRENT TURNS TO EAST Flood Starts a.m.	**p.m.**	Kts.	CURRENT TURNS TO WEST Ebb Starts a.m.	**p.m.**	Kts.
1	T	10:19	**10:54**	a2.0	3:00	**5:00**	a2.0
2	W	11:12	**11:54**	a1.8	4:18	**5:42**	a1.7
3	T	...	**12:01**	1.7	5:30	**6:24**	p1.8
4	F	12:54	**12:48**	p1.7	6:42	**7:06**	p1.9
5	S	1:48	**1:36**	p1.6	7:48	**7:42**	p2.1
6	S	2:36	**2:18**	1.6	8:42	**8:18**	p2.2
7	M	3:24	**3:00**	a1.7	9:42	**8:54**	p2.3
8	T	4:12	**3:42**	a1.8	10:36	**9:24**	p2.3
9	W	4:54	**4:24**	a1.9	11:24	**9:54**	p2.4
10	T	5:36	**5:00**	a1.9	-E-	**12:12**	0.9
11	F	6:12	**5:36**	a2.0	-F-	**12:54**	0.9
12	S	6:48	**6:18**	a2.0	-G-	**1:36**	0.9
13	S	7:24	**7:06**	a2.0	...	**2:12**	1.0
14	M	8:06	**8:00**	a2.0	12:24	**2:48**	a2.4
15	T	8:42	**8:54**	a2.0	1:18	**3:24**	a2.3
16	W	9:24	**9:48**	a2.0	2:12	**4:00**	a2.1
17	T	10:12	**10:48**	a2.0	3:12	**4:36**	a2.0
18	F	11:00	**11:48**	a1.9	4:18	**5:18**	1.8
19	S	11:48	...	1.9	5:36	**6:00**	p2.1
20	S	12:42	**12:42**	1.9	6:54	**6:42**	p2.3
21	M	1:48	**1:36**	a2.0	8:06	**7:30**	p2.5
22	T	2:48	**2:30**	a2.1	9:18	**8:12**	p2.7
23	W	3:48	**3:30**	a2.3	10:24	**9:06**	p2.9
24	T	4:42	**4:24**	a2.4	11:30	**9:54**	p2.9
25	F	5:36	**5:24**	a2.4	-H-	**12:24**	1.1
26	S	6:30	**6:24**	a2.4	-I-	**1:18**	1.1
27	S	7:24	**7:24**	a2.3	...	**2:06**	1.2
28	M	8:12	**8:24**	a2.2	12:42	**2:48**	a2.4
29	T	8:54	**9:24**	a2.0	1:42	**3:30**	a2.1
30	W	9:42	**10:24**	a1.9	2:48	**4:12**	a1.8

A also at 11:06 p.m. 2.4 **B** also at 11:30 p.m. 2.4 **C** also at 11:06 p.m. 2.9
D also at 11:54 p.m. 2.8 **E** also at 10:30 p.m. 2.5 **F** also at 11:00 p.m. 2.5
G also at 11:42 p.m. 2.5 **H** also at 10:48 p.m. 2.8 **I** also at 11:42 p.m. 2.7

The Kts. (knots) columns show the **maximum** predicted velocities of the stronger one of the Flood Currents and the stronger one of the Ebb Currents for each day.
The letter "a" means the velocity shown should occur **after** the **a.m.** Current Change. The letter "p" means the velocity shown should occur **after** the **p.m.** Current Change (even if next morning). No "a" or "p" means a.m. and p.m. velocities are the same for that day.
Avg. Max. Velocity: Flood 2.0 Kts., Ebb 1.9 Kts.
Max. Flood 3 hrs. 10 min. after Flood Starts ±45 min.
Max. Ebb 2 hrs. 45 min. after Ebb Starts ±45 min.
See pp. 22-29 for Current Change at other points.

 Note *from NOS: These predictions should be considered questionable. Caution is advised.*

2021 CURRENT TABLE
CHESAPEAKE & DELAWARE CANAL
39°31.83'N, 75°49.66'W at Chesapeake City

Daylight Saving Time — Daylight Saving Time

JULY

Day of Month	Day of Week	Current Turns To EAST Flood Starts a.m.	p.m.	Kts.	Current Turns To WEST Ebb Starts a.m.	p.m.	Kts.
1	T	10:25	11:24	a1.8	3:54	4:54	p1.7
2	F	11:12	...	1.7	5:06	5:36	p1.9
3	S	12:18	-A-	1.4	6:12	6:12	p2.0
4	S	1:12	12:42	p1.6	7:18	6:54	p2.1
5	M	2:06	1:30	p1.6	8:24	7:30	p2.2
6	T	2:54	2:12	a1.7	9:18	8:06	p2.3
7	W	3:42	3:00	a1.8	10:18	8:42	p2.4
8	T	4:30	3:48	a1.9	11:06	9:24	p2.5
9	F	5:12	4:30	a1.9	11:54	10:00	p2.5
10	S	5:48	5:18	a2.0	-B-	12:30	0.9
11	S	6:30	6:00	a2.0	-C-	1:06	1.1
12	M	7:06	6:48	a2.0	...	1:42	1.2
13	T	7:42	7:36	a2.0	12:18	2:12	a2.4
14	W	8:18	8:30	a2.0	1:06	2:42	a2.2
15	T	9:00	9:24	a2.0	2:00	3:18	a2.1
16	F	9:42	10:24	a1.9	3:00	3:54	a1.9
17	S	10:30	11:24	a1.9	4:12	4:36	p2.0
18	S	11:18	...	1.9	5:30	5:18	p2.2
19	M	12:30	12:12	1.8	6:48	6:06	p2.4
20	T	1:36	1:06	a1.9	8:06	7:00	p2.6
21	W	2:36	2:06	a2.0	9:18	7:54	p2.7
22	T	3:36	3:06	a2.1	10:18	8:48	p2.8
23	F	4:36	4:12	a2.2	11:12	9:48	p2.7
24	S	5:24	5:12	a2.3	11:59	10:42	p2.6
25	S	6:12	6:06	a2.2	-D-	12:42	1.3
26	M	6:54	7:06	a2.2	...	1:24	1.5
27	T	7:36	8:00	a2.1	12:36	2:06	a2.2
28	W	8:18	8:54	a2.0	1:30	2:42	a1.9
29	T	9:00	9:54	a1.9	2:30	3:18	1.7
30	F	9:36	10:48	a1.8	3:30	4:00	p1.8
31	S	10:18	11:42	a1.7	4:36	4:36	p1.9

AUGUST

Day of Month	Day of Week	Current Turns To EAST Flood Starts a.m.	p.m.	Kts.	Current Turns To WEST Ebb Starts a.m.	p.m.	Kts.
1	S	11:07	...	1.7	5:42	5:18	p2.0
2	M	12:36	-E-	1.4	6:48	5:54	p2.1
3	T	1:30	12:36	p1.6	7:54	6:36	p2.2
4	W	2:24	1:30	1.6	8:54	7:24	p2.3
5	T	3:12	2:24	a1.7	9:48	8:12	p2.4
6	F	4:00	3:18	a1.8	10:36	8:54	p2.5
7	S	4:42	4:12	a1.9	11:18	9:48	p2.5
8	S	5:24	5:00	a1.9	11:54	10:36	p2.4
9	M	6:00	5:42	a2.0	-F-	12:24	1.3
10	T	6:36	6:30	a2.0	...	1:00	1.4
11	W	7:18	7:18	a2.0	12:12	1:30	a2.3
12	T	7:54	8:12	a2.0	1:00	2:00	a2.1
13	F	8:36	9:06	1.9	2:00	2:30	1.9
14	S	9:18	10:06	a1.9	3:00	3:12	p2.0
15	S	10:00	11:12	1.8	4:12	3:54	p2.2
16	M	10:54	...	1.8	5:36	4:42	p2.3
17	T	12:18	-G-	1.8	6:54	5:42	p2.5
18	W	1:24	12:54	a1.8	8:06	6:42	p2.5
19	T	2:30	1:54	a1.9	9:06	7:42	p2.5
20	F	3:24	3:00	a2.0	10:00	8:42	p2.5
21	S	4:18	4:06	a2.1	10:48	9:48	p2.4
22	S	5:06	5:00	a2.1	11:30	10:42	p2.3
23	M	5:48	5:54	a2.1	-H-	12:06	1.6
24	T	6:30	6:48	a2.0	...	12:42	1.7
25	W	7:06	7:36	a2.0	12:30	1:18	a1.9
26	T	7:42	8:24	a1.9	1:18	1:48	1.8
27	F	8:12	9:12	a1.8	2:12	2:24	p1.9
28	S	8:48	10:06	a1.8	3:06	2:54	p1.9
29	S	9:30	11:00	a1.7	4:06	3:30	p2.0
30	M	10:12	11:54	a1.7	5:12	4:12	p2.0
31	T	11:00	...	1.6	6:18	5:00	p2.1

A also at 11:54 a.m. 1.7 — **B** also at 10:42 p.m. 2.5 — **C** also at 11:30 p.m. 2.4
D also at 11:42 p.m. 2.4 — **E** also at 11:48 a.m. 1.6 — **F** also at 11:24 p.m. 2.4
G also at 11:48 a.m. 1.7 — **H** also at 11:36 p.m. 2.1

The Kts. (knots) columns show the **maximum** predicted velocities of the stronger one of the Flood Currents and the stronger one of the Ebb Currents for each day.
The letter "a" means the velocity shown should occur **after** the **a.m.** Current Change. The letter "p" means the velocity shown should occur **after** the **p.m.** Current Change (even if next morning). No "a" or "p" means a.m. and p.m. velocities are the same for that day.

Avg. Max. Velocity: Flood 2.0 Kts., Ebb 1.9 Kts.
Max. Flood 3 hrs. 10 min. after Flood Starts ±45 min.
Max. Ebb 2 hrs. 45 min. after Ebb Starts ±45 min.

See pp. 22-29 for Current Change at other points.

Note *from NOS: These predictions should be considered questionable. Caution is advised.*

2021 CURRENT TABLE
CHESAPEAKE & DELAWARE CANAL
39°31.83'N, 75°49.66'W at Chesapeake City

Daylight Saving Time

SEPTEMBER

DAY OF MONTH	DAY OF WEEK	CURRENT TURNS TO EAST Flood Starts			CURRENT TURNS TO WEST Ebb Starts		
		a.m.	**p.m.**	Kts.	a.m.	**p.m.**	Kts.
1	W	12:49	-A-	1.5	7:18	5:48	p2.2
2	T	1:42	12:54	p1.6	8:18	6:48	p2.3
3	F	2:36	1:54	p1.7	9:06	7:42	p2.3
4	S	3:24	2:54	p1.8	9:48	8:36	p2.3
5	S	4:06	3:48	p1.9	10:30	9:30	p2.3
6	M	4:54	4:36	p2.0	11:06	10:24	p2.3
7	T	5:30	5:24	p2.1	11:36	11:18	p2.2
8	W	6:12	6:12	p2.1	...	12:12	1.8
9	T	6:48	7:00	p2.2	12:06	12:42	a2.1
10	F	7:30	7:54	p2.1	1:06	1:12	p2.1
11	S	8:12	8:48	p2.0	2:00	1:54	p2.2
12	S	8:54	9:54	p1.9	3:06	2:36	p2.3
13	M	9:42	11:00	p1.8	4:18	3:24	p2.3
14	T	10:36	...	1.7	5:36	4:18	p2.3
15	W	12:06	-B-	1.8	6:48	5:24	p2.3
16	T	1:12	12:48	a1.8	7:48	6:36	p2.3
17	F	2:12	1:54	a1.8	8:42	7:42	p2.2
18	S	3:06	3:00	a1.9	9:30	8:48	p2.1
19	S	4:00	4:00	a1.9	10:12	9:48	p2.0
20	M	4:42	4:54	1.9	10:48	10:42	p1.9
21	T	5:24	5:42	1.9	11:24	11:36	1.8
22	W	6:00	6:24	1.9	...	12:01	1.9
23	T	6:30	7:06	1.8	12:18	12:30	p2.0
24	F	7:00	7:54	a1.8	1:06	1:00	p2.0
25	S	7:36	8:36	a1.8	1:54	1:30	p2.1
26	S	8:06	9:24	a1.8	2:42	2:00	p2.1
27	M	8:48	10:12	a1.7	3:42	2:36	p2.1
28	T	9:30	11:06	a1.7	4:42	3:18	p2.1
29	W	10:24	11:59	a1.6	5:42	4:12	p2.2
30	T	11:24	...	1.6	6:36	5:06	p2.2

Daylight Saving Time

OCTOBER

DAY OF MONTH	DAY OF WEEK	CURRENT TURNS TO EAST Flood Starts			CURRENT TURNS TO WEST Ebb Starts		
		a.m.	**p.m.**	Kts.	a.m.	**p.m.**	Kts.
1	F	12:55	12:24	p1.7	7:30	6:12	p2.1
2	S	1:48	1:24	p1.7	8:12	7:18	p2.1
3	S	2:36	2:24	p1.9	8:54	8:18	p2.1
4	M	3:30	3:18	p2.0	9:36	9:18	p2.1
5	T	4:12	4:12	p2.2	10:12	10:12	p2.1
6	W	5:00	5:00	p2.3	10:48	11:12	p2.0
7	T	5:42	5:54	p2.3	11:24	...	2.1
8	F	6:18	6:42	p2.3	12:06	-C-	1.9
9	S	7:00	7:42	p2.3	1:06	12:36	p2.4
10	S	7:48	8:42	p2.1	2:06	1:18	p2.5
11	M	8:36	9:42	p2.0	3:12	2:06	p2.5
12	T	9:30	10:48	p1.9	4:18	3:00	p2.4
13	W	10:30	11:48	p1.8	5:24	4:06	p2.2
14	T	11:36	...	1.6	6:24	5:18	p2.1
15	F	12:54	12:48	a1.7	7:18	6:36	p2.0
16	S	1:48	1:48	a1.7	8:06	7:42	p1.9
17	S	2:42	2:54	1.7	8:48	8:48	p1.7
18	M	3:30	3:48	p1.8	9:30	9:48	a1.8
19	T	4:12	4:36	p1.9	10:06	10:42	a1.9
20	W	4:54	5:24	p1.9	10:42	11:30	a2.0
21	T	5:24	6:06	p1.9	11:18	...	2.1
22	F	6:00	6:48	p1.8	12:12	-D-	1.4
23	S	6:30	7:24	p1.8	1:00	12:12	p2.2
24	S	7:00	8:06	p1.8	1:42	12:42	p2.3
25	M	7:36	8:48	1.7	2:30	1:12	p2.3
26	T	8:12	9:30	1.7	3:18	1:54	p2.3
27	W	9:00	10:18	1.7	4:06	2:42	p2.2
28	T	9:54	11:12	1.7	4:54	3:36	p2.2
29	F	10:54	11:59	a1.7	5:48	4:36	p2.1
30	S	11:54	...	1.7	6:30	5:42	p2.0
31	S	12:54	12:54	p1.8	7:18	6:48	p2.0

A also at 11:55 a.m. 1.6 **B** also at 11:42 a.m. 1.6 **C** also at 11:54 a.m. 2.3
D also at 11:42 a.m. 2.1

The Kts. (knots) columns show the **maximum** predicted velocities of the stronger one of the Flood Currents and the stronger one of the Ebb Currents for each day.
The letter "a" means the velocity shown should occur **after** the **a.m.** Current Change. The letter "p" means the velocity shown should occur **after** the **p.m.** Current Change (even if next morning). No "a" or "p" means a.m. and p.m. velocities are the same for that day.
Avg. Max. Velocity: Flood 2.0 Kts., Ebb 1.9 Kts.
Max. Flood 3 hrs. 10 min. after Flood Starts ±45 min.
Max. Ebb 2 hrs. 45 min. after Ebb Starts ±45 min.
See pp. 22-29 for Current Change at other points.

 Note *from NOS: These predictions should be considered questionable. Caution is advised.*

2021 CURRENT TABLE
CHESAPEAKE & DELAWARE CANAL

39°31.83'N, 75°49.66'W at Chesapeake City

***Standard Time starts Nov. 7 at 2 a.m.** **Standard Time**

NOVEMBER

DAY OF MONTH	DAY OF WEEK	CURRENT TURNS TO EAST Flood Starts			CURRENT TURNS TO WEST Ebb Starts		
		a.m.	**p.m.**	Kts.	a.m.	**p.m.**	Kts.
1	**M**	1:49	**1:54**	p1.9	8:00	**8:00**	p1.9
2	**T**	2:42	**2:54**	p2.1	8:42	**9:00**	p1.9
3	**W**	3:36	**3:48**	p2.2	9:18	**10:06**	a2.0
4	**T**	4:24	**4:42**	p2.3	10:00	**11:06**	a2.2
5	**F**	5:06	**5:36**	p2.4	10:36	...	2.4
6	**S**	5:54	**6:30**	p2.4	12:06	**-A-**	1.6
7	**S**	*5:36	***6:30**	p2.4	12:54	**-B-**	1.4
8	**M**	6:24	**7:24**	p2.2	1:06	**-C-**	1.3
9	**T**	7:18	**8:24**	p2.1	2:06	**12:48**	p2.5
10	**W**	8:18	**9:24**	p1.9	3:06	**1:48**	p2.3
11	**T**	9:24	**10:24**	p1.8	4:00	**3:00**	p2.1
12	**F**	10:30	**11:18**	p1.7	4:48	**4:12**	p1.9
13	**S**	11:36	...	1.6	5:36	**5:30**	p1.7
14	**S**	12:12	**12:36**	1.6	6:24	**6:36**	a1.6
15	**M**	1:06	**1:36**	p1.7	7:06	**7:42**	a1.8
16	**T**	1:54	**2:30**	p1.7	7:48	**8:42**	a1.9
17	**W**	2:36	**3:18**	p1.8	8:24	**9:30**	a2.0
18	**T**	3:18	**4:06**	p1.8	9:00	**10:24**	a2.1
19	**F**	3:54	**4:48**	p1.9	9:36	**11:06**	a2.2
20	**S**	4:30	**5:24**	p1.9	10:06	**11:54**	a2.3
21	**S**	5:00	**6:06**	p1.9	10:36	...	2.3
22	**M**	5:36	**6:42**	p1.9	12:36	**-D-**	1.1
23	**T**	6:12	**7:18**	p1.9	1:18	**-E-**	1.1
24	**W**	6:54	**7:54**	p1.9	1:54	**12:24**	p2.4
25	**T**	7:42	**8:36**	1.8	2:30	**1:12**	p2.3
26	**F**	8:30	**9:24**	1.8	3:12	**2:06**	p2.1
27	**S**	9:30	**10:12**	1.8	3:48	**3:06**	p2.0
28	**S**	10:24	**11:06**	a1.8	4:30	**4:12**	p1.9
29	**M**	11:24	...	1.8	5:18	**5:24**	p1.8
30	**T**	12:01	**12:24**	p1.9	6:00	**6:42**	a1.8

DECEMBER

DAY OF MONTH	DAY OF WEEK	CURRENT TURNS TO EAST Flood Starts			CURRENT TURNS TO WEST Ebb Starts		
		a.m.	**p.m.**	Kts.	a.m.	**p.m.**	Kts.
1	**W**	12:55	**1:30**	p2.0	6:42	**7:48**	a2.0
2	**T**	1:48	**2:30**	p2.2	7:30	**9:00**	a2.3
3	**F**	2:42	**3:30**	p2.3	8:18	**10:06**	a2.5
4	**S**	3:36	**4:24**	p2.4	9:06	**11:06**	a2.7
5	**S**	4:24	**5:24**	p2.4	9:54	**11:59**	a2.8
6	**M**	5:18	**6:18**	p2.4	10:42	...	2.8
7	**T**	6:06	**7:12**	p2.3	12:54	**-F-**	1.3
8	**W**	7:06	**8:06**	p2.1	1:42	**12:36**	p2.5
9	**T**	8:06	**8:54**	p1.9	2:30	**1:42**	p2.2
10	**F**	9:06	**9:48**	p1.8	3:18	**2:48**	p1.9
11	**S**	10:12	**10:36**	1.6	4:06	**4:00**	1.6
12	**S**	11:12	**11:30**	a1.6	4:48	**5:12**	a1.7
13	**M**	...	**12:12**	1.5	5:36	**6:24**	a1.8
14	**T**	12:18	**1:12**	p1.6	6:18	**7:24**	a1.9
15	**W**	1:06	**2:06**	p1.6	7:00	**8:24**	a1.9
16	**T**	1:54	**3:00**	p1.7	7:42	**9:24**	a2.0
17	**F**	2:42	**3:48**	p1.8	8:18	**10:12**	a2.1
18	**S**	3:24	**4:30**	p1.9	8:54	**11:00**	a2.2
19	**S**	4:00	**5:06**	p1.9	9:30	**11:42**	a2.3
20	**M**	4:42	**5:42**	p1.9	10:06	...	2.4
21	**T**	5:18	**6:18**	p2.0	12:18	**-G-**	1.1
22	**W**	5:54	**6:54**	p2.0	12:48	**-H-**	1.2
23	**T**	6:36	**7:24**	1.9	1:24	**12:12**	p2.3
24	**F**	7:18	**8:06**	1.9	1:54	**1:00**	p2.2
25	**S**	8:12	**8:42**	1.9	2:24	**1:48**	p2.1
26	**S**	9:00	**9:30**	a1.9	3:00	**2:48**	p1.9
27	**M**	10:00	**10:18**	a1.9	3:36	**3:54**	1.7
28	**T**	11:00	**11:12**	a1.8	4:18	**5:12**	a1.9
29	**W**	...	**12:06**	1.9	5:06	**6:30**	a2.0
30	**T**	12:12	**1:12**	p1.9	6:00	**7:42**	a2.2
31	**F**	1:12	**2:18**	p2.1	6:48	**8:54**	a2.4

A also at 11:18 a.m. 2.6 **B** also at *11:06 a.m. 2.7 **C** also at 11:54 a.m. 2.7
D also at 11:06 a.m. 2.4 **E** also at 11:42 a.m. 2.4 **F** also at 11:36 a.m. 2.7
G also at 10:42 a.m. 2.4 **H** also at 11:24 a.m. 2.4

The Kts. (knots) columns show the **maximum** predicted velocities of the stronger one of the Flood Currents and the stronger one of the Ebb Currents for each day.
The letter "a" means the velocity shown should occur **after** the **a.m.** Current Change. The letter "p" means the velocity shown should occur **after** the **p.m.** Current Change (even if next morning). No "a" or "p" means a.m. and p.m. velocities are the same for that day.
Avg. Max. Velocity: Flood 2.0 Kts., Ebb 1.9 Kts.
Max. Flood 3 hrs. 10 min. after Flood Starts ±45 min.
Max. Ebb 2 hrs. 45 min. after Ebb Starts ±45 min.

See pp. 22-29 for Current Change at other points.

Note *from NOS: These predictions should be considered questionable. Caution is advised.*

Upper Chesapeake Bay Currents

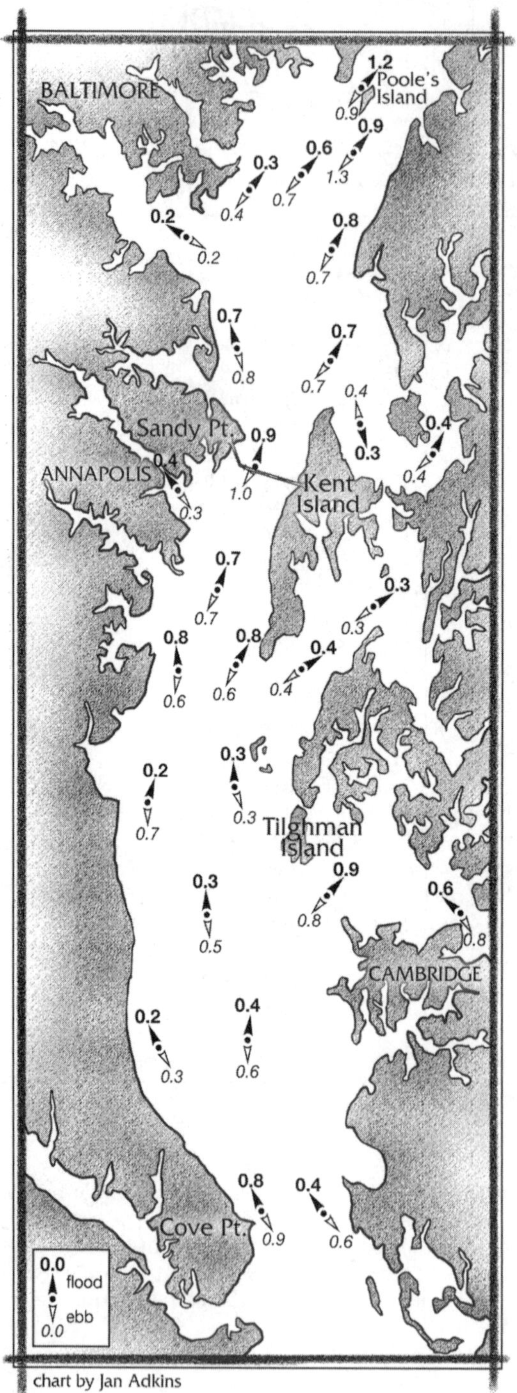

chart by Jan Adkins

The arrows in this diagram denote **direction** and **average maximum velocities** for Flood (dark arrow) and Ebb (light arrow) currents.

Times of current change for the four areas listed below are in hours, before or after **High Water at Baltimore**, pp. 162-165.

West of Pooles Island:
Flood begins 3 1/2 before
Flood max. 1 1/2 before (1.2 kts.)
Ebb begins 2 1/2 after
Ebb max. 4 1/2 after (0.9 kts.)

Sandy Point:
Flood begins 3 1/2 before
Flood max. 1 1/2 before (0.9 kts.)
Ebb begins 1 1/2 after
Ebb max. 4 1/2 after (1.0 kts.)

off Tilghman Island:
Flood begins 5 1/2 before
Flood max. 3 1/2 before (0.3 kts.)
Ebb begins 1/2 after
Ebb max. 3 1/2 after (0.7 kts.)

off Cove Point:
Flood begins 6 1/2 before
Flood max. 4 1/2 before (0.9 kts.)
Ebb begins 1/2 before
Ebb max. 1 1/2 after (0.8 kts.)

Note:
From the beginning of the Flood Current at Cove Point until the Ebb Current begins off Baltimore, a northbound vessel will have over 8 hours of fair current. A vessel bound southward from Sandy Point can expect only 4 hours of fair current.

Relationship of High Water and Ebb Current

Many people wonder why the times of High Water and the start of Ebb Current at the mouths of bays and inlets are not simultaneous. (See p. 10, Why Tides and Currents Often Behave Differently.) The twelve diagrams below show the hourly stages of the Tide in the Ocean and a Bay connected by a narrow Inlet.

Picture the rising Tide, borne by the Flood Current, as a long wave. The wave enters the inlet and the crest reaches its maximum height in or at the inlet. But, the body of water inside the inlet - in the bay - has yet to be filled and the Flood Current continues to pour water through the inlet for a good period after the crest has already passed the inlet. The Ebb Current will not start until the level of the water in the ocean is lower than the water in the bay.

This does not necessarily apply to the mouths of small bays with wide entrances. The narrowness of the inlet and the size of the bay are the controlling factors.

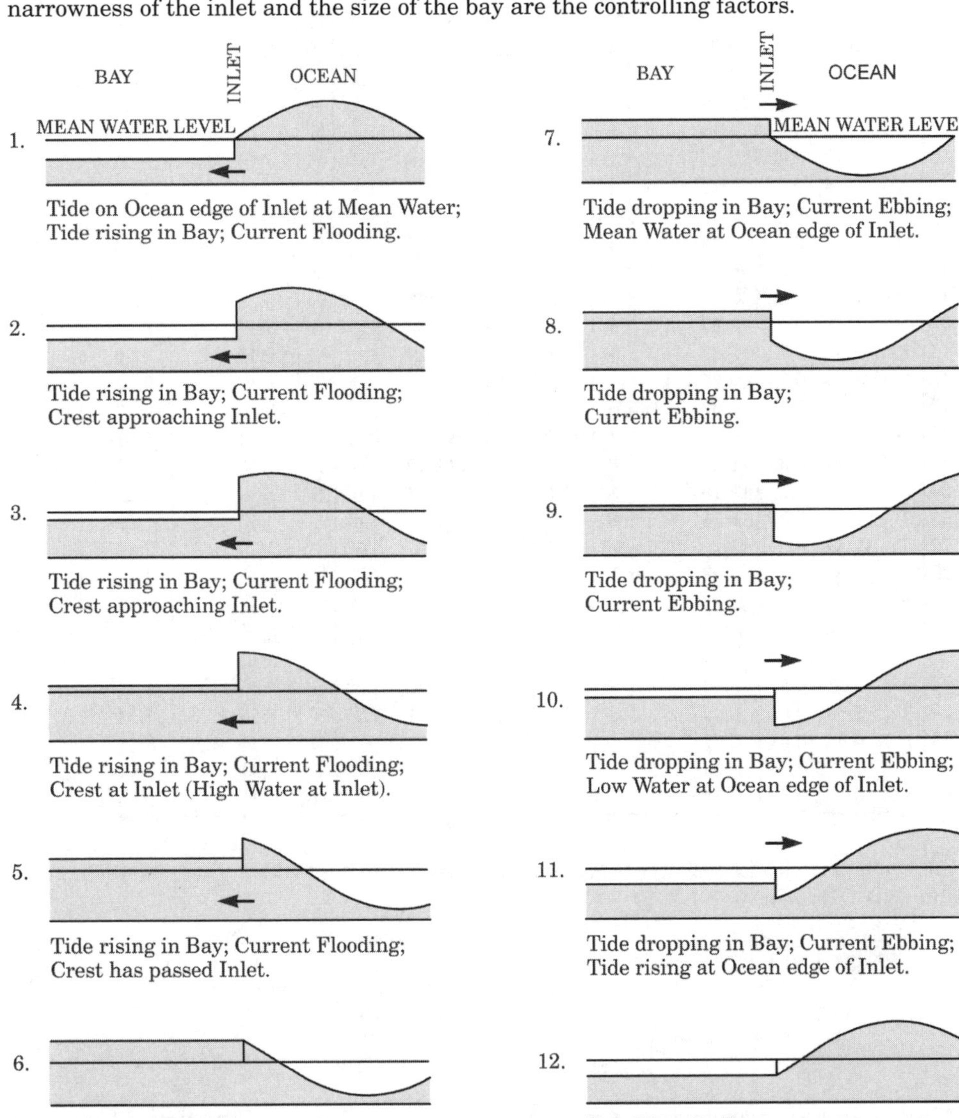

1. Tide on Ocean edge of Inlet at Mean Water; Tide rising in Bay; Current Flooding.

2. Tide rising in Bay; Current Flooding; Crest approaching Inlet.

3. Tide rising in Bay; Current Flooding; Crest approaching Inlet.

4. Tide rising in Bay; Current Flooding; Crest at Inlet (High Water at Inlet).

5. Tide rising in Bay; Current Flooding; Crest has passed Inlet.

6. High Water in Bay; Ebb Current about to start.

7. Tide dropping in Bay; Current Ebbing; Mean Water at Ocean edge of Inlet.

8. Tide dropping in Bay; Current Ebbing.

9. Tide dropping in Bay; Current Ebbing.

10. Tide dropping in Bay; Current Ebbing; Low Water at Ocean edge of Inlet.

11. Tide dropping in Bay; Current Ebbing; Tide rising at Ocean edge of Inlet.

12. Low Water in Bay; Flood Current about to start.

2021 HIGH WATER
BALTIMORE, MD
At Ft. McHenry 39°16'N, 76°34.7'W

		Standard Time					Standard Time					*Daylight Time starts Mar. 14 at 2 a.m.				
DAY OF MONTH	DAY OF WEEK	JANUARY				DAY OF WEEK	FEBRUARY				DAY OF WEEK	MARCH				DAY OF MONTH
		a.m.	Ht.	p.m.	Ht.		a.m.	Ht.	p.m.	Ht.		a.m.	Ht.	p.m.	Ht.	
1	**F**	7:51	0.6	**8:27**	1.3	**M**	9:06	0.8	**9:35**	1.1	**M**	7:55	1.1	**8:27**	1.2	1
2	**S**	8:36	0.6	**9:11**	1.3	**T**	9:59	0.9	**10:20**	1.0	**T**	8:45	1.2	**9:11**	1.1	2
3	**S**	9:25	0.7	**9:57**	1.2	**W**	10:57	1.0	**11:08**	0.9	**W**	9:39	1.3	**9:58**	1.0	3
4	**M**	10:19	0.7	**10:44**	1.1	**T**	11:59	1.1	...	...	**T**	10:36	1.4	**10:49**	0.9	4
5	**T**	11:17	0.8	**11:33**	1.0	**F**	12:01	0.8	**1:03**	1.2	**F**	11:37	1.4	**11:46**	0.8	5
6	**W**	...	...	**12:19**	0.9	**S**	12:58	0.6	**2:10**	1.2	**S**	...	...	**12:42**	1.4	6
7	**T**	12:25	0.9	**1:23**	1.0	**S**	2:00	0.6	**3:15**	1.3	**S**	12:48	0.8	**1:52**	1.3	7
8	**F**	1:19	0.8	**2:27**	1.2	**M**	3:03	0.6	**4:18**	1.3	**M**	1:54	0.8	**3:02**	1.3	8
9	**S**	2:15	0.7	**3:29**	1.3	**T**	4:04	0.6	**5:17**	1.3	**T**	2:58	0.8	**4:08**	1.3	9
10	**S**	3:14	0.6	**4:28**	1.4	**W**	5:01	0.7	**6:09**	1.3	**W**	3:57	0.9	**5:06**	1.3	10
11	**M**	4:13	0.6	**5:24**	1.4	**T**	5:53	0.7	**6:57**	1.2	**T**	4:50	1.0	**5:54**	1.3	11
12	**T**	5:11	0.6	**6:18**	1.4	**F**	6:41	0.8	**7:39**	1.2	**F**	5:39	1.0	**6:36**	1.2	12
13	**W**	6:06	0.6	**7:09**	1.4	**S**	7:28	0.8	**8:18**	1.1	**S**	6:24	1.1	**7:12**	1.2	13
14	**T**	6:58	0.6	**7:57**	1.3	**S**	8:14	0.9	**8:54**	1.1	**S**	*8:07	1.2	***8:46**	1.2	14
15	**F**	7:49	0.7	**8:43**	1.2	**M**	9:00	0.9	**9:29**	1.0	**M**	8:49	1.2	**9:19**	1.1	15
16	**S**	8:39	0.7	**9:26**	1.1	**T**	9:47	0.9	**10:05**	0.9	**T**	9:30	1.2	**9:52**	1.0	16
17	**S**	9:29	0.7	**10:08**	1.0	**W**	10:36	0.9	**10:41**	0.8	**W**	10:11	1.3	**10:27**	1.0	17
18	**M**	10:22	0.7	**10:48**	0.9	**T**	11:26	1.0	**11:22**	0.7	**T**	10:53	1.3	**11:05**	0.9	18
19	**T**	11:18	0.8	**11:27**	0.8	**F**	...	...	**12:19**	1.0	**F**	11:36	1.3	**11:49**	0.9	19
20	**W**	...	...	**12:16**	0.8	**S**	12:09	0.7	**1:14**	1.0	**S**	...	...	**12:23**	1.2	20
21	**T**	12:08	0.7	**1:16**	0.9	**S**	1:03	0.6	**2:10**	1.0	**S**	12:40	0.8	**1:15**	1.2	21
22	**F**	12:52	0.6	**2:14**	0.9	**M**	2:01	0.6	**3:06**	1.1	**M**	1:36	0.8	**2:12**	1.2	22
23	**S**	1:41	0.6	**3:08**	1.0	**T**	3:00	0.6	**3:59**	1.1	**T**	2:35	0.9	**3:14**	1.2	23
24	**S**	2:34	0.5	**3:57**	1.0	**W**	3:54	0.7	**4:48**	1.2	**W**	3:33	0.9	**4:14**	1.3	24
25	**M**	3:28	0.5	**4:41**	1.1	**T**	4:44	0.8	**5:35**	1.2	**T**	4:26	1.0	**5:09**	1.3	25
26	**T**	4:21	0.5	**5:23**	1.1	**F**	5:32	0.8	**6:19**	1.3	**F**	5:17	1.1	**5:59**	1.3	26
27	**W**	5:11	0.5	**6:04**	1.2	**S**	6:18	0.9	**7:02**	1.3	**S**	6:06	1.2	**6:46**	1.4	27
28	**T**	5:58	0.6	**6:45**	1.2	**S**	7:05	1.0	**7:44**	1.2	**S**	6:55	1.4	**7:31**	1.3	28
29	**F**	6:42	0.6	**7:27**	1.2						**M**	7:44	1.5	**8:15**	1.3	29
30	**S**	7:27	0.7	**8:08**	1.2						**T**	8:34	1.6	**9:01**	1.2	30
31	**S**	8:15	0.8	**8:51**	1.2						**W**	9:25	1.7	**9:48**	1.1	31

Dates when Ht. of **Low** Water is below Mean Low with Ht. of lowest given for each period and Date of lowest in ( ):

1st–17th: -0.5' (9th–14th)
20th–31st: -0.4' (27th–31st)

1st–15th: -0.4' (5th–12th)
19th–20th: -0.2'
23rd–28th: -0.3' (26th–28th)

1st: -0.2'
3rd–7th: -0.2'
9th–13th: -0.2'

Average Rise and Fall 1.1 ft.

When a high tide exceeds avg. ht., the *following* low tide will be lower than avg.

2021 HIGH WATER BALTIMORE, MD

At Ft. McHenry 39°16'N, 76°34.7'W

DAY OF MONTH	DAY OF WEEK	APRIL (Daylight Saving Time)				DAY OF WEEK	MAY (Daylight Saving Time)				DAY OF WEEK	JUNE (Daylight Saving Time)				DAY OF MONTH
		a.m.	Ht.	p.m.	Ht.		a.m.	Ht.	p.m.	Ht.		a.m.	Ht.	p.m.	Ht.	
1	**T**	10:20	1.7	**10:40**	1.0	**S**	10:56	1.9	**11:25**	1.1	**T**	12:12	1.3	**12:33**	1.7	1
2	**F**	11:15	1.7	**11:36**	1.0	**S**	11:55	1.8	...	...	**W**	1:13	1.4	**1:31**	1.5	2
3	**S**	...	...	**12:15**	1.6	**M**	12:28	1.2	**1:00**	1.6	**T**	2:15	1.5	**2:27**	1.4	3
4	**S**	12:37	1.0	**1:21**	1.5	**T**	1:32	1.2	**2:07**	1.5	**F**	3:14	1.6	**3:18**	1.3	4
5	**M**	1:43	1.0	**2:33**	1.5	**W**	2:36	1.3	**3:12**	1.4	**S**	4:10	1.7	**4:06**	1.3	5
6	**T**	2:48	1.1	**3:44**	1.4	**T**	3:36	1.4	**4:10**	1.4	**S**	5:00	1.8	**4:51**	1.2	6
7	**W**	3:50	1.1	**4:48**	1.4	**F**	4:31	1.5	**4:59**	1.3	**M**	5:45	1.8	**5:34**	1.1	7
8	**T**	4:46	1.2	**5:41**	1.3	**S**	5:21	1.6	**5:41**	1.3	**T**	6:25	1.9	**6:18**	1.1	8
9	**F**	5:37	1.3	**6:24**	1.3	**S**	6:06	1.7	**6:19**	1.2	**W**	7:01	1.9	**7:02**	1.1	9
10	**S**	6:24	1.4	**7:02**	1.3	**M**	6:48	1.7	**6:56**	1.2	**T**	7:34	1.9	**7:47**	1.1	10
11	**S**	7:07	1.5	**7:36**	1.2	**T**	7:25	1.8	**7:34**	1.1	**F**	8:07	1.9	**8:31**	1.1	11
12	**M**	7:47	1.5	**8:09**	1.2	**W**	8:00	1.8	**8:12**	1.1	**S**	8:41	1.9	**9:15**	1.1	12
13	**T**	8:25	1.6	**8:43**	1.1	**T**	8:33	1.8	**8:52**	1.1	**S**	9:18	1.9	**10:00**	1.1	13
14	**W**	9:02	1.6	**9:19**	1.1	**F**	9:07	1.8	**9:35**	1.1	**M**	9:59	1.8	**10:45**	1.2	14
15	**T**	9:37	1.6	**9:57**	1.0	**S**	9:42	1.8	**10:20**	1.1	**T**	10:44	1.8	**11:33**	1.3	15
16	**F**	10:14	1.6	**10:40**	1.0	**S**	10:21	1.8	**11:08**	1.1	**W**	11:32	1.7	...	...	16
17	**S**	10:53	1.6	**11:27**	1.0	**M**	11:06	1.7	**11:57**	1.2	**T**	12:25	1.4	**12:22**	1.6	17
18	**S**	11:38	1.5	...	...	**T**	11:57	1.6	...	...	**F**	1:19	1.5	**1:15**	1.5	18
19	**M**	12:19	1.0	**12:29**	1.5	**W**	12:50	1.2	**12:52**	1.6	**S**	2:16	1.6	**2:10**	1.4	19
20	**T**	1:14	1.0	**1:27**	1.4	**T**	1:44	1.3	**1:50**	1.5	**S**	3:13	1.8	**3:06**	1.3	20
21	**W**	2:10	1.1	**2:28**	1.4	**F**	2:39	1.5	**2:48**	1.5	**M**	4:09	2.0	**4:04**	1.2	21
22	**T**	3:05	1.2	**3:29**	1.4	**S**	3:35	1.6	**3:44**	1.4	**T**	5:04	2.1	**5:03**	1.2	22
23	**F**	3:59	1.3	**4:26**	1.4	**S**	4:30	1.8	**4:38**	1.3	**W**	5:58	2.2	**6:02**	1.1	23
24	**S**	4:52	1.5	**5:19**	1.4	**M**	5:23	2.0	**5:32**	1.3	**T**	6:51	2.2	**7:01**	1.1	24
25	**S**	5:43	1.7	**6:09**	1.4	**T**	6:15	2.1	**6:26**	1.2	**F**	7:43	2.2	**7:59**	1.2	25
26	**M**	6:34	1.8	**6:57**	1.3	**W**	7:06	2.2	**7:20**	1.2	**S**	8:35	2.1	**8:56**	1.2	26
27	**T**	7:24	2.0	**7:46**	1.2	**T**	7:57	2.2	**8:16**	1.1	**S**	9:27	2.0	**9:52**	1.3	27
28	**W**	8:15	2.0	**8:36**	1.2	**F**	8:49	2.2	**9:12**	1.2	**M**	10:19	1.9	**10:49**	1.4	28
29	**T**	9:06	2.0	**9:29**	1.1	**S**	9:42	2.1	**10:11**	1.2	**T**	11:09	1.8	**11:46**	1.4	29
30	**F**	9:59	2.0	**10:25**	1.1	**S**	10:37	1.9	**11:10**	1.3	**W**	11:59	1.6	...	...	30
31						**M**	11:34	1.8	...	...						31

Dates when Ht. of **Low** Water is below Mean Low with Ht. of lowest given for each period and Date of lowest in ( ):

Average Rise and Fall 1.1 ft.

When a high tide exceeds avg. ht., the *following* low tide will be lower than avg.

2021 HIGH WATER
BALTIMORE, MD
At Ft. McHenry 39°16'N, 76°34.7'W

DAY OF MONTH	DAY OF WEEK	Daylight Saving Time JULY a.m.	Ht.	p.m.	Ht.	DAY OF WEEK	Daylight Saving Time AUGUST a.m.	Ht.	p.m.	Ht.	DAY OF WEEK	Daylight Saving Time SEPTEMBER a.m.	Ht.	p.m.	Ht.	DAY OF MONTH
1	**T**	12:46	1.5	**12:47**	1.5	**S**	2:05	1.7	**1:28**	1.2	**W**	3:00	1.8	**2:47**	1.1	1
2	**F**	1:45	1.6	**1:34**	1.4	**M**	2:59	1.8	**2:21**	1.1	**T**	3:51	1.8	**3:50**	1.1	2
3	**S**	2:44	1.6	**2:22**	1.3	**T**	3:50	1.8	**3:19**	1.1	**F**	4:40	1.8	**4:49**	1.2	3
4	**S**	3:40	1.7	**3:10**	1.2	**W**	4:38	1.9	**4:20**	1.1	**S**	5:26	1.9	**5:40**	1.3	4
5	**M**	4:31	1.8	**4:01**	1.1	**T**	5:21	1.9	**5:17**	1.1	**S**	6:08	1.9	**6:27**	1.4	5
6	**T**	5:16	1.9	**4:53**	1.1	**F**	6:02	1.9	**6:10**	1.2	**M**	6:49	1.9	**7:12**	1.5	6
7	**W**	5:56	1.9	**5:45**	1.0	**S**	6:41	1.9	**6:57**	1.2	**T**	7:29	1.9	**7:56**	1.6	7
8	**T**	6:33	1.9	**6:36**	1.1	**S**	7:19	1.9	**7:41**	1.3	**W**	8:09	1.8	**8:42**	1.7	8
9	**F**	7:08	1.9	**7:23**	1.1	**M**	7:58	1.9	**8:24**	1.4	**T**	8:50	1.8	**9:30**	1.8	9
10	**S**	7:44	1.9	**8:08**	1.1	**T**	8:37	1.9	**9:08**	1.5	**F**	9:32	1.6	**10:20**	1.9	10
11	**S**	8:20	1.9	**8:51**	1.2	**W**	9:17	1.9	**9:54**	1.6	**S**	10:18	1.5	**11:13**	2.0	11
12	**M**	8:59	1.9	**9:35**	1.3	**T**	9:58	1.8	**10:43**	1.7	**S**	11:08	1.4	...	...	12
13	**T**	9:40	1.9	**10:20**	1.3	**F**	10:42	1.7	**11:36**	1.8	**M**	12:10	2.1	**12:04**	1.3	13
14	**W**	10:22	1.8	**11:08**	1.4	**S**	11:28	1.5	...	...	**T**	1:11	2.1	**1:08**	1.2	14
15	**T**	11:07	1.7	...	...	**S**	12:32	1.9	**12:20**	1.4	**W**	2:16	2.0	**2:17**	1.2	15
16	**F**	12:01	1.6	**-A-**		**M**	1:32	2.0	**1:18**	1.2	**T**	3:22	2.0	**3:27**	1.2	16
17	**S**	12:56	1.7	**12:44**	1.5	**T**	2:33	2.1	**2:22**	1.2	**F**	4:26	2.0	**4:32**	1.3	17
18	**S**	1:53	1.8	**1:39**	1.3	**W**	3:35	2.1	**3:30**	1.2	**S**	5:24	1.9	**5:30**	1.4	18
19	**M**	2:52	2.0	**2:38**	1.2	**T**	4:37	2.1	**4:37**	1.2	**S**	6:14	1.9	**6:24**	1.5	19
20	**T**	3:51	2.1	**3:41**	1.1	**F**	5:36	2.1	**5:39**	1.3	**M**	6:58	1.8	**7:13**	1.6	20
21	**W**	4:49	2.2	**4:45**	1.1	**S**	6:30	2.0	**6:35**	1.4	**T**	7:37	1.8	**7:59**	1.7	21
22	**T**	5:45	2.2	**5:48**	1.1	**S**	7:19	2.0	**7:28**	1.5	**W**	8:13	1.7	**8:44**	1.7	22
23	**F**	6:39	2.2	**6:47**	1.2	**M**	8:04	1.9	**8:18**	1.5	**T**	8:47	1.6	**9:27**	1.8	23
24	**S**	7:32	2.1	**7:43**	1.3	**T**	8:45	1.9	**9:06**	1.6	**F**	9:22	1.5	**10:09**	1.8	24
25	**S**	8:22	2.0	**8:37**	1.4	**W**	9:23	1.8	**9:55**	1.6	**S**	9:57	1.4	**10:52**	1.8	25
26	**M**	9:09	2.0	**9:30**	1.4	**T**	10:00	1.6	**10:43**	1.7	**S**	10:36	1.3	**11:35**	1.8	26
27	**T**	9:54	1.8	**10:22**	1.5	**F**	10:36	1.5	**11:32**	1.7	**M**	11:21	1.2	...	...	27
28	**W**	10:37	1.7	**11:16**	1.5	**S**	11:14	1.4	...	...	**T**	12:21	1.8	**12:14**	1.1	28
29	**T**	11:18	1.6	...	...	**S**	12:22	1.8	**-C-**	...	**W**	1:11	1.8	**1:14**	1.1	29
30	**F**	12:11	1.6	**-B-**	...	**M**	1:13	1.8	**12:45**	1.2	**T**	2:05	1.7	**2:18**	1.1	30
31	**S**	1:07	1.7	**12:42**	1.3	**T**	2:06	1.8	**1:43**	1.1						31

A also at 11:54 a.m. (1.6) **B** also at 11:59 a.m. (1.5) **C** also at 11:56 a.m. (1.3)

Dates when Ht. of **Low** Water is below Mean Low with Ht. of lowest given for each period and Date of lowest in ( ):

Average Rise and Fall 1.1 ft.

When a high tide exceeds avg. ht., the *following* low tide will be lower than avg.

2021 HIGH WATER BALTIMORE, MD

At Ft. McHenry 39°16'N, 76°34.7'W

Day of Month	Day of Week	Daylight Saving Time OCTOBER				Day of Week	*Standard Time starts Nov. 7 at 2 a.m. NOVEMBER				Day of Week	Standard Time DECEMBER				Day of Month
		a.m.	Ht.	p.m.	Ht.		a.m.	Ht.	p.m.	Ht.		a.m.	Ht.	p.m.	Ht.	
1	**F**	3:01	1.7	**3:20**	1.2	**M**	3:59	1.5	**4:38**	1.3	**W**	3:06	1.1	**4:03**	1.4	1
2	**S**	3:54	1.7	**4:17**	1.3	**T**	4:47	1.5	**5:29**	1.5	**T**	3:57	1.0	**4:56**	1.6	2
3	**S**	4:44	1.7	**5:09**	1.4	**W**	5:34	1.4	**6:19**	1.7	**F**	4:49	0.9	**5:48**	1.7	3
4	**M**	5:30	1.7	**5:57**	1.5	**T**	6:20	1.3	**7:08**	1.8	**S**	5:41	0.8	**6:39**	1.8	4
5	**T**	6:13	1.7	**6:44**	1.6	**F**	7:07	1.2	**7:57**	1.9	**S**	6:36	0.8	**7:32**	1.8	5
6	**W**	6:55	1.7	**7:31**	1.8	**S**	7:56	1.1	**8:48**	2.0	**M**	7:31	0.8	**8:25**	1.7	6
7	**T**	7:38	1.6	**8:18**	1.9	**S**	*7:47	1.0	***8:40**	2.0	**T**	8:28	0.8	**9:20**	1.6	7
8	**F**	8:22	1.5	**9:07**	2.0	**M**	8:42	1.0	**9:35**	1.9	**W**	9:27	0.8	**10:17**	1.5	8
9	**S**	9:08	1.4	**9:58**	2.1	**T**	9:42	1.0	**10:33**	1.8	**T**	10:29	0.8	**11:14**	1.4	9
10	**S**	9:58	1.3	**10:52**	2.1	**W**	10:45	1.0	**11:35**	1.7	**F**	11:33	0.9	...	...	10
11	**M**	10:53	1.2	**11:50**	2.0	**T**	11:52	1.0	...	...	**S**	12:10	1.2	**12:40**	0.9	11
12	**T**	11:55	1.1	...	...	**F**	12:39	1.5	**1:01**	1.1	**S**	1:03	1.1	**1:47**	1.0	12
13	**W**	12:53	1.9	**1:03**	1.1	**S**	1:41	1.5	**2:08**	1.1	**M**	1:53	1.0	**2:50**	1.0	13
14	**T**	2:00	1.9	**2:13**	1.2	**S**	2:37	1.4	**3:11**	1.2	**T**	2:40	0.9	**3:48**	1.1	14
15	**F**	3:07	1.8	**3:21**	1.2	**M**	3:25	1.3	**4:07**	1.3	**W**	3:25	0.8	**4:38**	1.2	15
16	**S**	4:09	1.7	**4:24**	1.3	**T**	4:08	1.2	**4:57**	1.4	**T**	4:08	0.7	**5:22**	1.3	16
17	**S**	5:02	1.7	**5:20**	1.4	**W**	4:48	1.1	**5:42**	1.5	**F**	4:52	0.7	**6:02**	1.3	17
18	**M**	5:47	1.6	**6:11**	1.5	**T**	5:26	1.0	**6:22**	1.5	**S**	5:35	0.6	**6:38**	1.3	18
19	**T**	6:26	1.5	**6:58**	1.6	**F**	6:03	1.0	**6:59**	1.6	**S**	6:18	0.6	**7:12**	1.3	19
20	**W**	7:03	1.5	**7:41**	1.7	**S**	6:42	0.9	**7:34**	1.6	**M**	7:01	0.6	**7:46**	1.3	20
21	**T**	7:37	1.4	**8:21**	1.7	**S**	7:21	0.9	**8:09**	1.5	**T**	7:43	0.6	**8:21**	1.3	21
22	**F**	8:12	1.3	**9:00**	1.8	**M**	8:03	0.8	**8:44**	1.5	**W**	8:26	0.6	**8:58**	1.2	22
23	**S**	8:48	1.2	**9:37**	1.8	**T**	8:47	0.8	**9:22**	1.5	**T**	9:10	0.6	**9:38**	1.2	23
24	**S**	9:26	1.1	**10:14**	1.7	**W**	9:34	0.8	**10:04**	1.4	**F**	9:57	0.6	**10:21**	1.2	24
25	**M**	10:08	1.0	**10:54**	1.7	**T**	10:24	0.8	**10:50**	1.4	**S**	10:48	0.7	**11:06**	1.1	25
26	**T**	10:56	1.0	**11:37**	1.6	**F**	11:18	0.8	**11:39**	1.3	**S**	11:44	0.8	**11:53**	1.0	26
27	**W**	11:49	1.0	...	...	**S**	...	...	**12:15**	0.9	**M**	...	...	**12:42**	0.9	27
28	**T**	12:25	1.6	**12:47**	1.0	**S**	12:30	1.3	**1:14**	1.0	**T**	12:43	0.9	**1:42**	1.0	28
29	**F**	1:17	1.6	**1:47**	1.0	**M**	1:22	1.2	**2:12**	1.1	**W**	1:35	0.8	**2:42**	1.2	29
30	**S**	2:13	1.5	**2:47**	1.1	**T**	2:14	1.2	**3:09**	1.3	**T**	2:30	0.7	**3:39**	1.3	30
31	**S**	3:07	1.5	**3:44**	1.2						**F**	3:27	0.6	**4:36**	1.5	31

Dates when Ht. of **Low** Water is below Mean Low with Ht. of lowest given for each period and Date of lowest in ( ):

1st–8th: -0.4' (4th, 5th)
15th–22nd: -0.2'
27th–31st: -0.5' (31st)

Average Rise and Fall 1.1 ft.

When a high tide exceeds avg. ht., the *following* low tide will be lower than avg.

2021 HIGH WATER
MIAMI HARBOR ENTRANCE, FL
25°45.8'N, 80°07.8'W

DAY OF MONTH	DAY OF WEEK	Standard Time JANUARY a.m.	Ht.	p.m.	Ht.	DAY OF WEEK	Standard Time FEBRUARY a.m.	Ht.	p.m.	Ht.	DAY OF WEEK	*Daylight Time starts Mar. 14 at 2 a.m. MARCH a.m.	Ht.	p.m.	Ht.	DAY OF MONTH
1	F	10:10	2.5	**10:15**	2.2	M	11:13	2.4	**11:38**	2.3	M	10:05	2.6	**10:31**	2.6	1
2	S	10:52	2.4	**11:02**	2.2	T	11:57	2.3	...	...	T	10:48	2.5	**11:22**	2.6	2
3	S	11:35	2.4	**11:54**	2.2	W	12:33	2.3	**12:46**	2.2	W	11:34	2.4	...	...	3
4	M	...	...	**12:22**	2.3	T	1:32	2.2	**1:41**	2.1	T	12:15	2.5	**12:25**	2.3	4
5	T	12:50	2.2	**1:12**	2.2	F	2:36	2.2	**2:44**	2.0	F	1:13	2.3	**1:22**	2.2	5
6	W	1:51	2.2	**2:07**	2.2	S	3:45	2.1	**3:52**	2.0	S	2:18	2.2	**2:28**	2.0	6
7	T	2:56	2.2	**3:07**	2.2	S	4:53	2.2	**5:00**	2.0	S	3:28	2.1	**3:39**	2.0	7
8	F	4:03	2.3	**4:10**	2.2	M	5:56	2.2	**6:03**	2.1	M	4:38	2.2	**4:50**	2.1	8
9	S	5:07	2.4	**5:13**	2.2	T	6:51	2.3	**6:59**	2.2	T	5:41	2.2	**5:53**	2.2	9
10	S	6:07	2.5	**6:13**	2.3	W	7:41	2.4	**7:50**	2.3	W	6:35	2.3	**6:47**	2.3	10
11	M	7:03	2.6	**7:08**	2.4	T	8:25	2.5	**8:36**	2.3	T	7:21	2.4	**7:35**	2.4	11
12	T	7:54	2.6	**8:01**	2.4	F	9:06	2.4	**9:19**	2.3	F	8:02	2.4	**8:18**	2.4	12
13	W	8:43	2.6	**8:50**	2.4	S	9:45	2.4	**10:01**	2.3	S	8:39	2.4	**8:57**	2.4	13
14	T	9:28	2.6	**9:38**	2.4	S	10:21	2.3	**10:41**	2.2	S	*10:14	2.4	***10:35**	2.4	14
15	F	10:12	2.5	**10:24**	2.3	M	10:57	2.2	**11:20**	2.1	M	10:48	2.3	**11:11**	2.4	15
16	S	10:54	2.4	**11:10**	2.2	T	11:32	2.1	...	...	T	11:21	2.2	**11:48**	2.3	16
17	S	11:34	2.2	**11:55**	2.1	W	12:01	2.0	**12:08**	2.0	W	11:54	2.2	...	...	17
18	M	...	...	**12:15**	2.1	T	12:44	1.9	**12:48**	1.8	T	12:25	2.2	**12:29**	2.0	18
19	T	12:42	2.0	**12:56**	2.0	F	1:32	1.8	**1:34**	1.7	F	1:05	2.1	**1:07**	1.9	19
20	W	1:31	1.9	**1:40**	1.9	S	2:28	1.8	**2:28**	1.7	S	1:51	2.0	**1:51**	1.9	20
21	T	2:24	1.8	**2:28**	1.8	S	3:31	1.8	**3:32**	1.7	S	2:44	1.9	**2:45**	1.8	21
22	F	3:21	1.8	**3:22**	1.7	M	4:35	1.8	**4:37**	1.7	M	3:46	1.9	**3:50**	1.8	22
23	S	4:19	1.8	**4:19**	1.7	T	5:34	1.9	**5:37**	1.9	T	4:53	1.9	**5:01**	1.9	23
24	S	5:16	1.9	**5:15**	1.8	W	6:26	2.1	**6:32**	2.0	W	5:55	2.0	**6:07**	2.0	24
25	M	6:08	2.0	**6:08**	1.9	T	7:13	2.3	**7:22**	2.2	T	6:50	2.2	**7:05**	2.2	25
26	T	6:56	2.1	**6:57**	2.0	F	7:57	2.4	**8:10**	2.4	F	7:39	2.4	**7:58**	2.4	26
27	W	7:41	2.2	**7:44**	2.1	S	8:39	2.5	**8:56**	2.5	S	8:25	2.5	**8:48**	2.7	27
28	T	8:24	2.3	**8:29**	2.2	S	9:21	2.6	**9:43**	2.6	S	9:09	2.7	**9:36**	2.8	28
29	F	9:06	2.4	**9:15**	2.3						M	9:54	2.7	**10:25**	2.9	29
30	S	9:47	2.4	**10:01**	2.3						T	10:39	2.7	**11:14**	2.9	30
31	S	10:29	2.4	**10:48**	2.3						W	11:25	2.7	...	...	31

Dates when Ht. of **Low** Water is below Mean Low with Ht. of lowest given for each period and Date of lowest in ( ):

1st–3rd: -0.2'
6th–9th: -0.5'
11th–17th: -0.6' (11th–14th)
26th–31st: -0.5' (29th–31st)

1st–8th: -0.5'
10th–15th: -0.6' (11th)
25th–28th: -0.5' (27th–28th)

1st–9th: -0.6' (1st, 2nd)
11th–16th: -0.3' (11th–13th)
27th–31st: -0.7' (30th)

Average Rise and Fall 2.5 ft.

When a high tide exceeds avg. ht., the *following* low tide will be lower than avg.

2021 HIGH WATER
MIAMI HARBOR ENTRANCE, FL
25°45.8'N, 80°07.8'W

DAY OF MONTH	DAY OF WEEK	APRIL (Daylight Saving Time) a.m.	Ht.	p.m.	Ht.	DAY OF WEEK	MAY (Daylight Saving Time) a.m.	Ht.	p.m.	Ht.	DAY OF WEEK	JUNE (Daylight Saving Time) a.m.	Ht.	p.m.	Ht.	DAY OF MONTH
1	**T**	12:06	2.8	**12:14**	2.5	**S**	12:43	2.7	**12:53**	2.5	**T**	2:14	2.4	**2:36**	2.2	1
2	**F**	12:58	2.7	**1:08**	2.4	**S**	1:39	2.6	**1:53**	2.3	**W**	3:09	2.3	**3:38**	2.1	2
3	**S**	1:57	2.5	**2:08**	2.3	**M**	2:40	2.4	**2:58**	2.2	**T**	4:04	2.2	**4:40**	2.1	3
4	**S**	3:01	2.3	**3:14**	2.2	**T**	3:43	2.3	**4:07**	2.2	**F**	4:57	2.1	**5:37**	2.1	4
5	**M**	4:09	2.2	**4:26**	2.1	**W**	4:45	2.2	**5:13**	2.2	**S**	5:47	2.1	**6:28**	2.2	5
6	**T**	5:17	2.2	**5:36**	2.2	**T**	5:42	2.2	**6:12**	2.2	**S**	6:33	2.1	**7:14**	2.2	6
7	**W**	6:17	2.3	**6:37**	2.2	**F**	6:32	2.3	**7:03**	2.3	**M**	7:16	2.1	**7:56**	2.3	7
8	**T**	7:09	2.3	**7:30**	2.3	**S**	7:16	2.3	**7:47**	2.4	**T**	7:57	2.1	**8:36**	2.3	8
9	**F**	7:53	2.4	**8:15**	2.4	**S**	7:56	2.3	**8:27**	2.5	**W**	8:37	2.1	**9:16**	2.4	9
10	**S**	8:32	2.4	**8:55**	2.5	**M**	8:33	2.3	**9:05**	2.5	**T**	9:17	2.2	**9:55**	2.4	10
11	**S**	9:08	2.4	**9:32**	2.5	**T**	9:09	2.3	**9:41**	2.5	**F**	9:56	2.1	**10:35**	2.4	11
12	**M**	9:42	2.4	**10:08**	2.5	**W**	9:44	2.3	**10:18**	2.5	**S**	10:36	2.1	**11:15**	2.3	12
13	**T**	10:15	2.3	**10:43**	2.5	**T**	10:20	2.2	**10:56**	2.4	**S**	11:18	2.1	**11:57**	2.3	13
14	**W**	10:48	2.3	**11:19**	2.4	**F**	10:57	2.2	**11:34**	2.4	**M**	...	...	**12:01**	2.1	14
15	**T**	11:22	2.2	**11:56**	2.3	**S**	11:35	2.1	...	...	**T**	12:39	2.3	**12:48**	2.0	15
16	**F**	11:58	2.1	...	...	**S**	12:15	2.3	**12:16**	2.0	**W**	1:23	2.2	**1:39**	2.1	16
17	**S**	12:36	2.2	**12:37**	2.0	**M**	12:59	2.2	**1:02**	2.0	**T**	2:10	2.2	**2:37**	2.1	17
18	**S**	1:21	2.1	**1:21**	2.0	**T**	1:47	2.2	**1:55**	2.0	**F**	3:01	2.2	**3:39**	2.2	18
19	**M**	2:12	2.1	**2:15**	1.9	**W**	2:39	2.1	**2:56**	2.0	**S**	3:56	2.2	**4:43**	2.3	19
20	**T**	3:10	2.0	**3:19**	1.9	**T**	3:34	2.2	**4:02**	2.1	**S**	4:54	2.2	**5:47**	2.4	20
21	**W**	4:12	2.1	**4:29**	2.0	**F**	4:32	2.2	**5:08**	2.2	**M**	5:54	2.3	**6:48**	2.6	21
22	**T**	5:13	2.2	**5:36**	2.2	**S**	5:29	2.3	**6:11**	2.4	**T**	6:53	2.4	**7:46**	2.7	22
23	**F**	6:10	2.3	**6:37**	2.4	**S**	6:25	2.4	**7:09**	2.6	**W**	7:51	2.5	**8:41**	2.8	23
24	**S**	7:02	2.4	**7:33**	2.6	**M**	7:19	2.5	**8:04**	2.8	**T**	8:46	2.6	**9:33**	2.8	24
25	**S**	7:51	2.6	**8:25**	2.8	**T**	8:12	2.6	**8:57**	2.9	**F**	9:41	2.6	**10:25**	2.8	25
26	**M**	8:39	2.7	**9:16**	3.0	**W**	9:04	2.7	**9:49**	3.0	**S**	10:34	2.6	**11:15**	2.7	26
27	**T**	9:27	2.8	**10:06**	3.0	**T**	9:56	2.7	**10:40**	2.9	**S**	11:26	2.5	...	...	27
28	**W**	10:16	2.8	**10:57**	3.0	**F**	10:49	2.6	**11:32**	2.8	**M**	12:04	2.6	**12:19**	2.4	28
29	**T**	11:06	2.7	**11:48**	2.9	**S**	11:43	2.6	...	...	**T**	12:52	2.5	**1:12**	2.3	29
30	**F**	11:58	2.6	...	...	**S**	12:25	2.7	**12:38**	2.4	**W**	1:40	2.4	**2:06**	2.2	30
31						**M**	1:19	2.5	**1:36**	2.3						31

Dates when Ht. of **Low** Water is below Mean Low with Ht. of lowest given for each period and Date of lowest in ( ):

1st–3rd: -0.5' (1st)
12th: -0.2'
24th–30th: -0.7' (27th, 28th)

1st: -0.2'
23rd–30th: -0.7' (25th–27th)

20th–28th: -0.7' (23rd–25th)

Average Rise and Fall 2.5 ft.

When a high tide exceeds avg. ht., the *following* low tide will be lower than avg.

2021 HIGH WATER
MIAMI HARBOR ENTRANCE, FL
25°45.8'N, 80°07.8'W

DAY OF MONTH	DAY OF WEEK	JULY (Daylight Saving Time) a.m.	Ht.	p.m.	Ht.	DAY OF WEEK	AUGUST (Daylight Saving Time) a.m.	Ht.	p.m.	Ht.	DAY OF WEEK	SEPTEMBER (Daylight Saving Time) a.m.	Ht.	p.m.	Ht.	DAY OF MONTH
1	T	2:29	2.2	**3:01**	2.1	S	3:14	2.1	**4:04**	2.1	W	4:19	2.2	**5:17**	2.3	1
2	F	3:16	2.1	**3:57**	2.0	M	4:05	2.0	**5:01**	2.1	T	5:21	2.2	**6:14**	2.4	2
3	S	4:06	2.0	**4:53**	2.0	T	5:00	2.0	**5:57**	2.1	F	6:19	2.3	**7:05**	2.5	3
4	S	4:56	2.0	**5:46**	2.1	W	5:57	2.0	**6:50**	2.2	S	7:13	2.5	**7:52**	2.7	4
5	M	5:46	2.0	**6:36**	2.1	T	6:50	2.1	**7:38**	2.3	S	8:02	2.7	**8:35**	2.8	5
6	T	6:35	2.0	**7:23**	2.2	F	7:40	2.2	**8:23**	2.5	M	8:48	2.8	**9:16**	2.9	6
7	W	7:22	2.0	**8:08**	2.2	S	8:27	2.3	**9:06**	2.5	T	9:34	2.9	**9:57**	3.0	7
8	T	8:08	2.1	**8:51**	2.3	S	9:12	2.4	**9:47**	2.6	W	10:19	3.0	**10:38**	3.0	8
9	F	8:52	2.1	**9:32**	2.4	M	9:56	2.5	**10:27**	2.7	T	11:06	3.1	**11:21**	3.0	9
10	S	9:34	2.2	**10:13**	2.4	T	10:41	2.6	**11:07**	2.7	F	11:55	3.1	...	...	10
11	S	10:17	2.2	**10:54**	2.4	W	11:26	2.6	**11:48**	2.7	S	12:06	2.9	**12:46**	3.0	11
12	M	11:00	2.2	**11:34**	2.4	T	...	...	**12:14**	2.6	S	12:55	2.8	**1:43**	2.9	12
13	T	11:45	2.2	...	...	F	12:31	2.6	**1:05**	2.6	M	1:51	2.7	**2:45**	2.8	13
14	W	12:15	2.4	**12:32**	2.2	S	1:17	2.5	**2:00**	2.6	T	2:54	2.6	**3:53**	2.7	14
15	T	12:57	2.4	**1:23**	2.3	S	2:09	2.5	**3:01**	2.5	W	4:04	2.6	**5:02**	2.8	15
16	F	1:42	2.3	**2:18**	2.3	M	3:07	2.4	**4:07**	2.5	T	5:15	2.7	**6:07**	2.8	16
17	S	2:32	2.3	**3:18**	2.3	T	4:13	2.4	**5:15**	2.6	F	6:21	2.8	**7:03**	2.9	17
18	S	3:27	2.2	**4:23**	2.4	W	5:22	2.5	**6:20**	2.6	S	7:18	2.9	**7:52**	3.0	18
19	M	4:28	2.3	**5:28**	2.4	T	6:28	2.5	**7:19**	2.7	S	8:09	3.0	**8:36**	3.0	19
20	T	5:33	2.3	**6:32**	2.5	F	7:28	2.7	**8:12**	2.8	M	8:55	3.0	**9:17**	3.0	20
21	W	6:36	2.4	**7:31**	2.6	S	8:22	2.8	**9:00**	2.9	T	9:38	3.1	**9:54**	3.0	21
22	T	7:37	2.5	**8:27**	2.7	S	9:13	2.8	**9:44**	2.9	W	10:18	3.0	**10:30**	2.9	22
23	F	8:34	2.6	**9:18**	2.8	M	9:59	2.8	**10:25**	2.9	T	10:56	3.0	**11:05**	2.8	23
24	S	9:27	2.6	**10:06**	2.8	T	10:44	2.8	**11:04**	2.8	F	11:34	2.9	**11:40**	2.7	24
25	S	10:18	2.6	**10:52**	2.8	W	11:26	2.8	**11:42**	2.7	S	...	...	**12:13**	2.8	25
26	M	11:07	2.6	**11:37**	2.7	T	...	...	**12:08**	2.7	S	12:17	2.6	**12:54**	2.7	26
27	T	11:55	2.5	...	...	F	12:20	2.6	**12:50**	2.5	M	12:57	2.5	**1:41**	2.5	27
28	W	12:19	2.6	**12:42**	2.4	S	12:58	2.5	**1:34**	2.4	T	1:43	2.4	**2:34**	2.5	28
29	T	1:01	2.4	**1:29**	2.3	S	1:39	2.3	**2:22**	2.3	W	2:38	2.3	**3:34**	2.4	29
30	F	1:43	2.3	**2:18**	2.2	M	2:25	2.2	**3:16**	2.3	T	3:41	2.3	**4:36**	2.5	30
31	S	2:27	2.2	**3:09**	2.1	T	3:18	2.2	**4:15**	2.2						31

Dates when Ht. of **Low** Water is below Mean Low with Ht. of lowest given for each period and Date of lowest in ( ):

18th–26th: -0.5' (22nd–24th)

21st: -0.2'

Average Rise and Fall 2.5 ft.

When a high tide exceeds avg. ht., the *following* low tide will be lower than avg.

2021 HIGH WATER
MIAMI HARBOR ENTRANCE, FL
25°45.8'N, 80°07.8'W

Daylight Saving Time — ***Standard Time starts Nov. 7 at 2 a.m.** — **Standard Time**

DAY OF MONTH	DAY OF WEEK	OCTOBER a.m.	Ht.	OCTOBER p.m.	Ht.	DAY OF WEEK	NOVEMBER a.m.	Ht.	NOVEMBER p.m.	Ht.	DAY OF WEEK	DECEMBER a.m.	Ht.	DECEMBER p.m.	Ht.	DAY OF MONTH
1	**F**	4:48	2.4	**5:35**	2.6	**M**	6:15	2.8	**6:35**	2.8	**W**	5:42	2.8	**5:50**	2.7	1
2	**S**	5:48	2.5	**6:28**	2.7	**T**	7:08	3.0	**7:23**	3.0	**T**	6:36	3.0	**6:42**	2.8	2
3	**S**	6:44	2.7	**7:15**	2.9	**W**	7:58	3.2	**8:10**	3.1	**F**	7:28	3.1	**7:34**	2.9	3
4	**M**	7:35	2.9	**7:59**	3.0	**T**	8:48	3.3	**8:57**	3.1	**S**	8:20	3.2	**8:26**	2.9	4
5	**T**	8:23	3.1	**8:42**	3.1	**F**	9:37	3.4	**9:45**	3.2	**S**	9:12	3.2	**9:19**	2.9	5
6	**W**	9:10	3.3	**9:26**	3.2	**S**	10:27	3.4	**10:35**	3.1	**M**	10:04	3.1	**10:13**	2.8	6
7	**T**	9:57	3.4	**10:10**	3.2	**S**	*10:19	3.3	***10:27**	3.0	**T**	10:57	3.0	**11:09**	2.7	7
8	**F**	10:46	3.4	**10:56**	3.2	**M**	11:13	3.2	**11:24**	2.9	**W**	11:51	2.8	...	...	8
9	**S**	11:36	3.3	**11:45**	3.1	**T**	...	...	**12:11**	3.0	**T**	12:08	2.6	**12:46**	2.7	9
10	**S**	...	...	**12:29**	3.2	**W**	12:25	2.8	**1:12**	2.9	**F**	1:09	2.5	**1:43**	2.5	10
11	**M**	12:38	3.0	**1:27**	3.1	**T**	1:30	2.7	**2:15**	2.8	**S**	2:13	2.4	**2:40**	2.4	11
12	**T**	1:38	2.8	**2:30**	2.9	**F**	2:39	2.6	**3:18**	2.7	**S**	3:17	2.3	**3:36**	2.3	12
13	**W**	2:44	2.8	**3:38**	2.9	**S**	3:47	2.7	**4:16**	2.7	**M**	4:18	2.3	**4:29**	2.3	13
14	**T**	3:56	2.7	**4:45**	2.8	**S**	4:49	2.7	**5:09**	2.7	**T**	5:12	2.4	**5:17**	2.3	14
15	**F**	5:06	2.8	**5:46**	2.9	**M**	5:42	2.8	**5:55**	2.7	**W**	6:00	2.4	**6:02**	2.3	15
16	**S**	6:09	2.9	**6:40**	2.9	**T**	6:29	2.8	**6:36**	2.7	**T**	6:43	2.5	**6:43**	2.3	16
17	**S**	7:04	3.0	**7:27**	3.0	**W**	7:10	2.9	**7:15**	2.7	**F**	7:23	2.5	**7:23**	2.3	17
18	**M**	7:52	3.0	**8:08**	3.0	**T**	7:48	2.9	**7:51**	2.7	**S**	8:02	2.5	**8:02**	2.3	18
19	**T**	8:34	3.1	**8:46**	3.0	**F**	8:25	2.9	**8:27**	2.6	**S**	8:40	2.5	**8:41**	2.3	19
20	**W**	9:13	3.1	**9:22**	3.0	**S**	9:02	2.8	**9:03**	2.6	**M**	9:19	2.5	**9:20**	2.2	20
21	**T**	9:51	3.1	**9:57**	2.9	**S**	9:39	2.8	**9:40**	2.5	**T**	9:58	2.4	**10:00**	2.2	21
22	**F**	10:27	3.0	**10:31**	2.8	**M**	10:18	2.7	**10:19**	2.4	**W**	10:37	2.4	**10:41**	2.1	22
23	**S**	11:04	2.9	**11:06**	2.7	**T**	10:58	2.6	**11:00**	2.3	**T**	11:17	2.3	**11:26**	2.1	23
24	**S**	11:42	2.8	**11:43**	2.6	**W**	11:41	2.5	**11:45**	2.3	**F**	11:59	2.3	...	...	24
25	**M**	...	...	**12:22**	2.7	**T**	...	...	**12:28**	2.4	**S**	12:14	2.1	**12:43**	2.2	25
26	**T**	12:24	2.5	**1:08**	2.6	**F**	12:37	2.2	**1:18**	2.4	**S**	1:09	2.1	**1:31**	2.2	26
27	**W**	1:10	2.4	**1:58**	2.5	**S**	1:36	2.2	**2:11**	2.4	**M**	2:08	2.1	**2:23**	2.2	27
28	**T**	2:04	2.4	**2:55**	2.5	**S**	2:40	2.3	**3:06**	2.4	**T**	3:12	2.2	**3:21**	2.2	28
29	**F**	3:07	2.4	**3:54**	2.5	**M**	3:43	2.4	**4:02**	2.5	**W**	4:16	2.3	**4:22**	2.2	29
30	**S**	4:13	2.4	**4:52**	2.6	**T**	4:44	2.6	**4:56**	2.6	**T**	5:19	2.5	**5:22**	2.3	30
31	**S**	5:16	2.6	**5:45**	2.7						**F**	6:17	2.6	**6:21**	2.4	31

Dates when Ht. of **Low** Water is below Mean Low with Ht. of lowest given for each period and Date of lowest in ( ):

October	November	December
	5th–7th: -0.2'	1st: -0.2' 3rd–8th: -0.5' (4th–6th) 29th–30th: -0.5' (30th)

Average Rise and Fall 2.5 ft.

When a high tide exceeds avg. ht., the *following* low tide will be lower than avg.

My dear Captain and Mr. Mate,

As I cannot talk with you, I will do the next best thing. I will write you a letter.

Do you know, Captain and Mr. Mate of a place on the Atlantic Coast that is called "The Graveyard"? I propose to tell you something about it, and do what I can to keep vessels out of it. "The Graveyard" so called, is that part of the coast which lies — between Sow and Pigs Rocks and Naushon Island. This place has been called "The Graveyard" for many years, — because many a good craft has laid her bones there, and many a captain has lost his reputation there also. If a vessel gets into this graveyard, there must be a cause for it. Did it ever occur to you that seldom does a vessel go ashore on Gay Head, or on the south side of the Sound? but that hundreds of them have been piled up in "The Graveyard," or on the north side of the Sound? I will explain why this is so. if you are bound into Vineyard Sound in thick weather, you will probably refer to the "Gay Head and Cross Rip" table in this book, to see when the tide turns in or out. You will notice at the — head of each table that it says, "This table shows the time that the current turns Easterly and — Westerly, off Gay Head in ship channel." That — means off Gay Head when it bears about South. Now, as a rule, captains figure on the currents after they leave the Lightship, as running Easterly into the Sound, when as a matter of fact the first of the flood between the Lightship and Gay Head runs nearly North; and the current does not begin to run to the eastward until you are well into the Sound, as shown by the chart on the opposite page. Vessels bound into — Vineyard Sound from the Westward will have the current of ebb on the starboard bow. (see arrows on the hulls in the chart on the opposite page)

I have explained this matter, and I leave the rest to your judgment and careful consideration; and thus you will undoubtedly keep your vessel out of "The Graveyard".

Yours for a fair tide,

Geo. W. Eldridge.

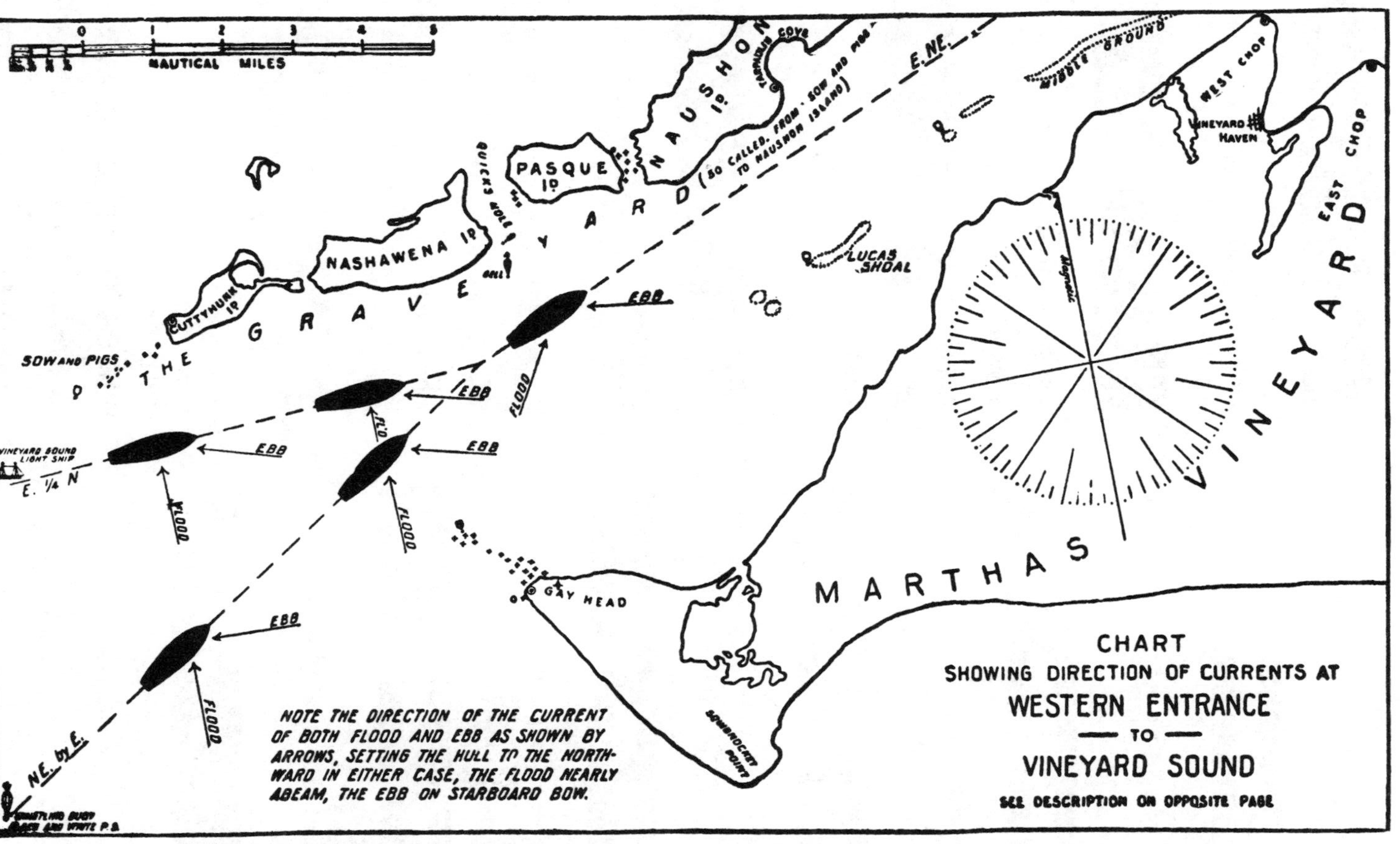

This lightship, shown on Capt. Eldridge's chart, on the Western edge, was replaced many years ago by a buoy.

CHARACTERISTICS OF LIGHT SIGNALS

(see footnote on next page for abbreviations used.)

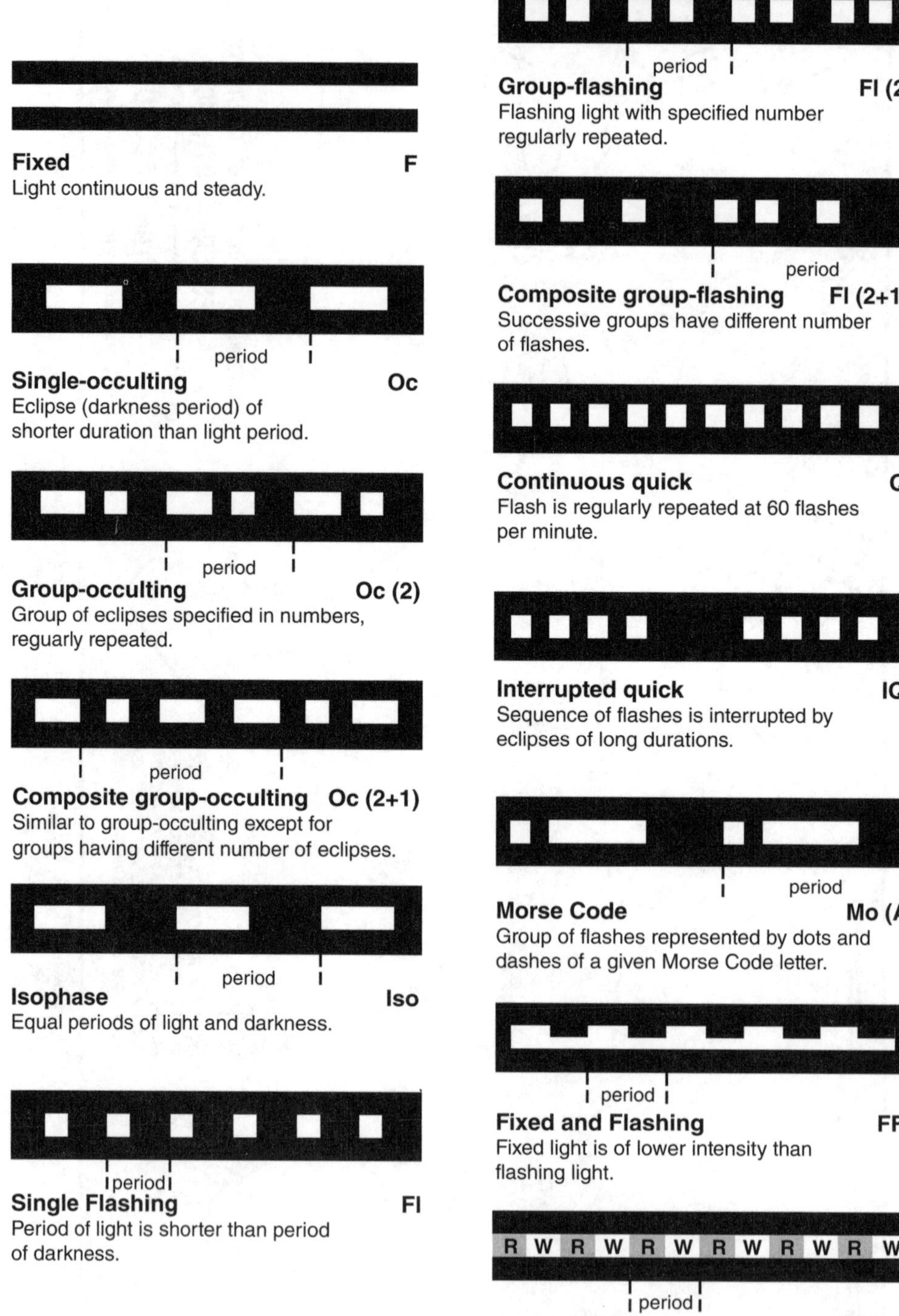

Fixed F
Light continuous and steady.
period
Single-occulting Oc
Eclipse (darkness period) of shorter duration than light period.
period
Group-occulting Oc (2)
Group of eclipses specified in numbers, reguarly repeated.
period
Composite group-occulting Oc (2+1)
Similar to group-occulting except for groups having different number of eclipses.
period
Isophase Iso
Equal periods of light and darkness.
period
Single Flashing Fl
Period of light is shorter than period of darkness.
period
Group-flashing Fl (2)
Flashing light with specified number regularly repeated.
period
Composite group-flashing Fl (2+1)
Successive groups have different number of flashes.
Continuous quick Q
Flash is regularly repeated at 60 flashes per minute.
Interrupted quick IQ
Sequence of flashes is interrupted by eclipses of long durations.
period
Morse Code Mo (A)
Group of flashes represented by dots and dashes of a given Morse Code letter.
period
Fixed and Flashing FFl
Fixed light is of lower intensity than flashing light.
R W R W R W R W R W R W
period
Alternating Al RW
Light shows alternating different colors.

LIGHTS, FOG SIGNALS and OFFSHORE BUOYS

NOVA SCOTIA, EAST COAST

Cranberry Is. Lt., off Cape Canso, S. part of Is. – Fl. W. ev. 15 s., 2 Horns 2 bl. ev. 60 s., Horns point 066° and 141°, Ht. 16.9 m. (56′), Rge. 21 mi., Racon (B), (45-19-29.6N/60-55-38.2W)

White Head Is. Lt., SW side of Is. – LFl. W. ev. 6 s., Horn 1 bl. ev. 30 s., Horn points 190°, Ht. 18.2 m. (60′), Rge. 10 mi., (45-11-49.1N/61-08-10.8W)

Country Is. Lt., S. side of Is. – Fl. W. ev. 20 s., Ht. 16.5 m. (54′), Rge. 10 mi., (45-05-59.8N/61-32-31.9W)

Liscomb Is. Lt., near Cranberry Pt. – Fl. W. ev. 10 s., Horn 1 bl. ev. 30 s., Ht. 21.9 m. (72′), Rge. 14 mi., (44-59-15.8N/61-57-58.4W)

Beaver Is. Lt., E. end of Is. – Fl. W. ev. 7 s., Horn 1 bl. ev. 60 s., Horn points 144°, Ht. 19.9 m. (66′), Rge. 14 mi., (44-49-29.2N/62-20-16W)

Ship Harbour Lt., on Wolfes Pt. – LFl. G. ev. 6 s., Ht. 18.2 m. (60′), Rge. 4 mi., (44-44-55.4N/62-45-23.6W)

Owls Head Lt., at end of head – Fl. W. ev. 4 s., Ht. 25.8 m. (84′), Rge. 6 mi., (44-43-14.6N/62-47-59.5W)

Egg Is. Lt., center of Is. – LFl. W. ev. 6 s., Ht. 7.6 m. (25′), Rge. 12 mi., (44-39-52.7N/62-51-48.4W)

Jeddore Rock Lt., summit of rock – LFl. W. ev. 12 s., Ht. 29.5 m. (97′), Rge. 8 mi., (44-39-47.1N/63-00-37.3)

Bear Cove Lt. & Bell By. "H6," NE of cove, Q. R., Racon (N), Red, (44-32-36.3N/63-31-19.6W)

Sambro Harbor Lt. & Wh. By. "HS," S. of SW breaker, Halifax Hbr. app. – Mo(A)W ev. 6 s., RWS, (44-24-30N/63-33-36.5W)

Chebucto Head Lt., on summit, Halifax Hbr. app. – Fl. W. ev. 20 s., Horn 2 bl. ev. 60 s., Horn points 113°, Ht. 47.8 m. (157′), Rge. 10 mi., Racon (Z), (44-30-26.6N/63-31-21.8W)

Halifax Alpha Lt. & Wh. By. "HA," Halifax app. – Mo(A)W ev. 6 s., RWS, (44-21-45N/63-24-15W)

Sambro Is. Lt., center of Is. – Fl. W. ev. 6 s., Ht. 42.7 m. (145′), Rge. 23 mi., (44-26-12N/63-33-48W)

Ketch Harbour Lt. By. "HE 19," Ketch Harbour entr. – Fl. G. ev 4 s., Green (44-28-19.6N/63-32-16W)

Betty Is. Lt., on Brig Pt. – LFl. W. ev. 15 s., Ht. 19.2 m. (63′), Rge. 13 mi., (44-26-19.7N/63-46-00.4W)

Pearl Is. Lt., off St. Margaret's & Mahone Bays – Fl. W. ev. 10 s., Ht. 19.0 m. (63′), Rge. 8 mi., (44-22-57.2N/64-02-54W)

East Ironbound Is. Lt., center of Is. – Iso. W. ev. 6 s., Ht. 44.5 m. (147′), Rge. 13 mi., (44-26-22.4N/64-04-59.7W)

East Point Island Lt., Mahone Bay – LFl G ev. 6 s., Ht. 9.6 m. (31′), Rge. 6 mi., (44-20-59.2N/64-12-15W)

Abbreviations: **Alt.**, Alternating; **App.**, Approach; **By.**, Buoy; **Ch.**, Channel; **Entr.**, Entrance; **ev.**, every; **F.**, Fixed; **fl.**, flash; **Fl.**, Flashing; **Fl(2)**, Group Flashing; **LFl**, 2 s. flash.; **G.**, Green; **Hbr.**, Harbor or Harbour, **Ht.**, height; **Is.**, Island; **Iso.**, Isophase (Equal interval); **Iso. W.**, Isophase White (Red sector(s) of Lights warn of dangerous angle of approach. Bearings and ranges are from the observer to the aid.); **Jct.**, Junction; **Keyed**, Fog signal is radio activated. During times of reduced visibility, within ½ mile of the fog signal, turn VHF marine radio to channel 83A and 81A as alternate. Key microphone 5–10 times consecutively to activate fog signal for 45 minutes (Boston Lt. 60 minutes). **Lt.**, Light; **Ltd.**, Lighted.; **mi.**, miles; **Mo(A)**, Morse Code "A," **Mo(U)**, Morse Code "U"; **Oc.**, Occulting; **Pt.**, Point; **Q.**, Quick (Flashing); **RaRef.**, Radar Reflector; **R.**, Red; **rge.**, range; **RWS**, R.&W. Stripes; **RWSRST**, RWS with R. Spherical Topmarks; **s.**, seconds; **Wh.**, Whistle; **W.**, White; **Y.**, Yellow

---

Notices To Mariners: Keep informed of important changes. Visit **www.navcen.uscg.gov** to receive Local Notices to Mariners via email. When reporting discrepancies in navigational aids, contact nearest C.G. unit and give official name of the aid.

Table for Converting Seconds to Decimals of a Minute, p. 266, for standard **GPS** input of Lat/Lon.

See pp. 222-223 for Atlantic Coast Racon Information.

Words for Sailors

Selections from "The Sailor's Word-Book"
by William Henry Smyth

APHELION That point in the orbit of a planet or comet which is most remote from the sun, and at which the angular motion is slowest; being the end of the greater elliptic axis. The opposite of perihelion.

BEFORE THE MAST The station of the working seamen, as distinguishing them from the officers.

CODGER An easy-going man of regularity. Also, a knowing and eccentric hanger-on; one who will not move faster than he pleases.

DAVY JONES'S LOCKER The ocean; the common receptacle for all things thrown overboard; it is a phrase for death or the other world, when speaking of a person who has been buried at sea.

Erica M. Szuplat

ENSIGN From the Anglo-Saxon *segn*. A large flag or banner, hoisted on a long pole erected over the stern, and called the ensign-staff.

FLY OF A FLAG The breadth from the staff to the extreme end that flutters loose in the wind. If an ensign, the part which extends from the union to the outer part; the vertical height, to the head-toggle of which the halliards are bent, or which is next to the staff, is called the hoist.

GRIPE, TO To carry too much weather-helm. A vessel gripes when she tends to come up into the wind while sailing close-hauled.

HEAVE-TO, TO To put a vessel in the position of lying-to, by adjusting her sails so as to counteract each other, and thereby check her way, or keep her perfectly still. In a gale, it implies to set merely enough sail to steady the ship; the aim being to keep the sea on the weather bow whilst the rudder has but little influence.

Erica M. Szuplat

INFERIOR PLANETS This name, the opposite of superior, is applied to Mercury and Venus, because they revolve in orbits interior to the earth's path.

JACK ROBINSON *Before you could say Jack Robinson*, is a very old expression for a short time.

KELPIE A mischievous sea-sprite, supposed to haunt the fords and ferries of the northern coasts of Great Britain, especially in storms.

Continued on p. 176

Cross Is. Lt., E. Pt. of Is. – Fl. W. ev. 10 s., Ht. 24.9 m. (82′), Rge. 10 mi., (44-18-43.7N/64-10-06.4W)

West Ironbound Is. Lt., Entr. to La Have R. – LFl. W. ev. 12 s., Ht. 23.6 m. (77′), Rge. 8 mi., (44-13-43.7N/64-16-28W)

Moshers Is. Lt., W. side Entr. to La Have R. – F.W., Horn 1 bl. ev. 20 s., Ht. 23.3 m. (77′), Rge. 13 mi., (44-14-14.6N/64-18-59.1W)

Cherry Cove Lt., betw. Little Hbr. & Back Cove – Iso. G. ev. 4 s., Ht. 6.7 m. (22′), Rge. 8 mi., (44-09-29.8N/64-28-53.2W)

Medway Head Lt., W. side entr. to Pt. Medway – Fl. W. ev. 12 s., Ht. 24.2 m. (80′), Rge. 11 mi., (44-06-10.6N/64-32-23.3W)

Western Head Lt., W. side entr. to Liverpool Bay – Fl. W. ev. 15 s., Horn 1 bl. ev. 60 s., Horn points 104°, Ht. 16.8 m. (55′), Rge. 15 mi., (43-59-20.8N/64-39-44.5W)

Lockeport Lt., on Gull Rock, entr. to hbr. – LFl. W. ev. 15 s., Horn 1 bl. ev. 30 s., Ht. 16.7 m. (56′), Rge. 12 mi., (43-39-18.3N/65-05-55.9W)

Cape Roseway Lt., near SE Pt. of McNutt Is. – Fl. W. ev. 10 s., Ht. 33.1 m. (109′), Rge. 10 mi., (43-37-21.4N/65-15-50W)

Long Rock Lt., on SE end of Is. – LFI W. ev. 6 s., Horn 1 bl. ev. 60 s., Ht. 28.3 m. (92′), Rge. 11 mi., (43-30-26.2N/65-20-44.2W)

The Salvages Lt., SE end of Is. – LFl. W. ev. 12 s., Horn 3 bl. ev. 60 s., Ht. 15.6 m. (51′), Rge. 10 mi., (43-28-08.1N/65-22-44W)

Baccaro Point Lt., E. side entr. to Barrington Bay – Mo(D)W ev. 10 s., Horn 1 bl. ev. 20 s., Horn points 200°, Ht. 15.0 m. (49′), Rge. 15 mi., (43-26-59N/65-28-15W)

Cape Sable Lt., on cape – Fl. W. ev. 5 s., Horn 1 bl. ev. 60 s., Horn points 150°, Ht. 29.7 m. (97′), Rge. 18 mi., Racon (C), (43-23-24N/65-37-16.9W)

West Head Lt., Cape Sable Is. – F.R., Horn 2 bl. ev. 60 s., Horn points 254°, Ht. 15.6 m. (51′), Rge. 7 mi., (43-27-23.8N/65-39-16.9W)

Outer Island Lt., on S. Pt. of Outer Is. – Fl. W. ev. 10 s., Ht. 13.7 m. (46′), Rge. 10 mi., (43-27-23.2N/65-44-36.2W)

Seal Is. Lt., S. Pt. of Is. – Fl. W. ev. 10 s., Horn 3 bl. ev. 60 s., Horn points 183°, Ht. 33.4 m. (110′), Rge. 19 mi., (43-23-40N/66-00-51W)

NOVA SCOTIA, WEST COAST

Peases Is. Lt., S. Pt. of one of the Tusket Is. – Fl. W. ev. 6 s., Horn 2 bl. ev. 60 s., Ht. 16 m. (53′), Rge. 9 mi., (43-37-42.6N/66-01-34.9W)

Cape Forchu Lt., E. Cape S. Pt. Yarmouth Sd. – LFl. W. ev. 12 s., Ht. 34.5 m. (113′), Rge. 12 mi., Racon (B), (43-47-38.8N/66-09-19.3W)

Lurcher Shoal Bifurcation Light By. "NM," W. of SW shoal – Fl.(2+1) R. ev. 6 s., Racon (K), R.G.R. marked "NM," (43-48-57.2N/66-29-58W)

Cape St. Marys Lt., E. side of Bay – Fl. W. ev. 5 s., Horn 1 bl. ev. 60 s., Horn points 251° 30′, Ht. 31.8 m (105′), Rge. 13 mi., (44-05-09.2N/66-12-39.6W)

Brier Is. Lt., on W. side of Is. R. & W. Tower – Fl(3) W. ev. 18 s., 2 Horns 2 bl. ev. 60 s., Horns point 270° and 315°, Ht. 22.2 m. (72′), Rge. 14 mi., (44-14-55N/66-23-32W)

Boars Head Lt., W. side of N. entr. to Petit Passage – Fl. W. ev. 5 s., Horn 3 bl. ev. 60 s., Horn points 315°, Ht. 28.0 m. (91′), Rge. 16 mi., (44-24-14.5N/66-12-55W)

Prim Pt. Lt., Digby Gut, W. Pt. of entr. to Annapolis Basin – Iso. W. ev. 6 s., Ht. 24.8 m. (82′), Rge. 12 mi., (44-41-28N/65-47-10.8W)

Ile Haute Lt., on highest Pt. – Fl. W. ev. 4 s., Ht. 112 m. (367′), Rge. 7 mi., (45-15-03.3N/65-00-19.8W)

NEW BRUNSWICK COAST

Cape Enrage Lt., at pitch of cape – Fl. G. ev. 6 s., Horn 3 bl. ev. 60 s., Horn points 220°, Ht. 40.7 m. (134′), Rge. 10 mi., (45-35-38.1N/64-46-47.7W)

Quaco Lt., tower on head – Fl. W. ev. 10 s., Horn 1 bl. ev. 30 s., Horn points 130°, Ht. 26.0 m. (86′), Rge. 21 mi., (45-19-25.3N/65-32-08.8W)

For abbreviations see footnote p. 173

Continued from p. 174

LAND-FALL Making the land. "A good land-fall" signifies making the land at or near the place to which the course was intended, while "a bad land-fall" implies the contrary.

MAKE FAST A word generally used for tying or securing ropes. To fasten.

NAUSCOPY The tact of discovering ships or land at considerable distances.

ORDINARY SEAMAN The rating for one who can make himself useful on board, even to going aloft, and taking his part on a top-sail or topgallant-yard, but is not a complete sailor, the latter being termed an able seaman.

POOPING, OR BEING POOPED The breaking of a heavy sea over the stern or quarter of a boat or vessel when she scuds before the wind in a gale, which is extremely dangerous, especially if deeply laden.

QUADRATURE The moon is said to be in quadrature at the first and last quarter, when her longitude differs 90° from that of the sun.

RACE Strong currents producing overfalls, dangerous to small craft. They may be produced by narrow channels, crossing of tides, or uneven bottoms.

STAVE, TO To break a hole in any vessel. Also, to drive in the head of a cask, as of spirits, to prevent the crew from misusing it in case of wreck.—*To stave off*. To boom off; to push anything off with a pole.

TAR Anglo-Saxon *tare*. A kind of turpentine which is drained from pines and fir-trees, and is used to preserve standing rigging, canvas, etc..., from the effects of weather, by rendering them water-proof. Also, a perfect sailor; one who knows his duty thoroughly.

UP AND DOWN The situation of the cable when it has been hove in sufficiently to bring the ship directly over the anchor.

VEER AND HAUL, TO To gently tauten and then slacken a rope three times before giving a heavy pull, the object being to concentrate the force of several men. The wind is said to veer and haul when it alters its direction; thus it is said, to veer aft, and haul forward.

WING-AND-WING A ship coming before the wind with studding-sails on both sides; also said of fore-and-aft vessels, when they are going with the wind right aft, the fore-sail boomed out on one side, and the main-sail on the other.

XUGIA The second bank of rowers in an ancient trireme.

YEOMAN An experienced hand placed in charge of a store-room, who should be able to keep the accounts of supply and expenditure.

ZEPHYR The west wind, but generally considered to apply to any light pleasant breeze.

Cape Spencer Lt., pitch of cape – Fl. W. ev. 11 s., Ht. 61.6 m. (203′), Rge. 14 mi., (45-11-42.5N/65-54-35.5W)

Partridge Is. Lt., highest pt. of Is., Saint John Harbour – Fl. W. ev. 7.5 s., Ht. 35.3 m. (116′), Rge. 19 mi., (45-14-21N/66-03-13.8W)

Musquash Head Lt., E. side entr. to Musquash Hbr. – Fl. W. ev. 3 s., Horn 1 bl. ev. 60 s., Horn points 180°, Ht. 35.1 m. (116′), Rge. 20 mi., (45-08-37.1N/66-14-14.2W)

Pt. Lepreau Lt., on point – Fl. W. ev. 5 s., Horn 3 bl. ev. 60 s., Horn points 190°, Ht. 25.5 m. (84′), Rge. 14 mi., (45-03-31.7N/66-27-31.3W)

Pea Pt. Lt., E. side entr. to Letang Hbr. – F.W. visible 251° thru N & E to 161°, Horn 2 bl. ev. 60 s., Horn points 180°, Ht. 17.2 m. (56′), Rge. 12 mi., (45-02-20.4N/66-48-28.2W)

Head Harbour Lt., outer rock of E. Quoddy Head – F.R., Horn 1 bl. ev. 60 s., Horn points 116°, Ht. 17.6 m. (58′), Rge. 13 mi., (44-57-28.6N/66-54-00.2W)

Swallowtail Lt., NE Pt. of Grand Manan – Oc. W. ev. 6 s., Horn 1 bl. ev. 20 s., Horn points 100°, Ht. 37.1 m. (122′), Rge. 12 mi., (44-45-51.1N/66-43-57.5W)

Great Duck Is. Lt., S. end of Is. – Fl. W. ev. 10 s., Horn 1 bl. ev. 60 s., Horn points 120°, Ht. 16.5 m. (54′), Rge. 18 mi., (44-41-03.5N/66-41-36.4W)

Southwest Head Lt., S. end of Grand Manan – Fl. W. ev. 10 s., Ht. 47.5 m. (156′), Rge. 16 mi., (44-36-02.9N/66-54-19.8W)

Gannet Rock North Lt. – Oc. W. ev. 3 s. visible 58° through E, S & W to 348°, Ht. 12.9 m. (42′), Rge. 11 mi., (44-30-38N/66-46-53.6W)

Gannet Rock South Lt. – Oc. W. ev. 3 s. visible 193° through W, N & E to 164°, Ht. 13.6 m. (44′), Rge. 11 mi., (44-30-37.2N/66-46-53.7W)

Machias Seal Is. Lt., On Is. summit – Fl. W. ev. 3 s., Ht. 25 m. (83′), Rge. 17 mi., (44-30-06.6N/67-06-04.1W)

MAINE

West Quoddy Head Lt., Entr. Quoddy Roads – Fl(2) W. ev. 15 s., Keyed (VHF 83A) Horn 2 bl. ev. 30 s., Ht. 83′, Rge. 18 mi., ltd. 24 hrs., (44-48-54N/66-57-02W)

Libby Island Lt., Entr. Machias Bay – Fl(2) W. ev. 20 s., Keyed (VHF 83A) Horn 1 bl. ev. 15 s., Ht. 91′, Rge. 18 mi., (44-34-06N/67-22-03W)

Moose Peak Lt., E. end Mistake Is. – Fl. W. ev. 30 s., Keyed (VHF 83A) Horn 2 bl. ev. 30 s., Ht. 72′, Rge. 20 mi., (44-28-28N/67-31-55W)

Petit Manan Lt., E. Pt. of Is. – Fl. W. ev. 10 s., Keyed (VHF 83A) Horn 1 bl. ev. 30 s., Ht. 123′, Rge. 19 mi., (44-22-03N/67-51-52W)

Prospect Harbor Point Lt. – Fl. R. ev. 6 s., (2 W. sect.), Ht. 42′, Rge. R. 7 mi., W. 9 mi., ltd. 24 hrs., (44-24-12N/68-00-47W)

Mount Desert Lt., 20 mi. S. of island – Fl. W. ev. 15 s., Horn 2 bl. ev. 30 s., Ht. 75′, Rge. 14 mi., (43-58-07N/68-07-42W)

Great Duck Island Lt., S. end of island – Fl. R. ev. 5 s., Keyed (VHF 83A) Horn 1 bl. ev. 15 s., Ht. 67′, Rge. 19 mi., (44-08-31N/68-14-45W)

Frenchman Bay Ltd. By. "FB," Fl. (2+1) R. ev. 6 s., Rge. 4 mi., R&G Bands, Racon (B), (44-19-21N/68-07-24W)

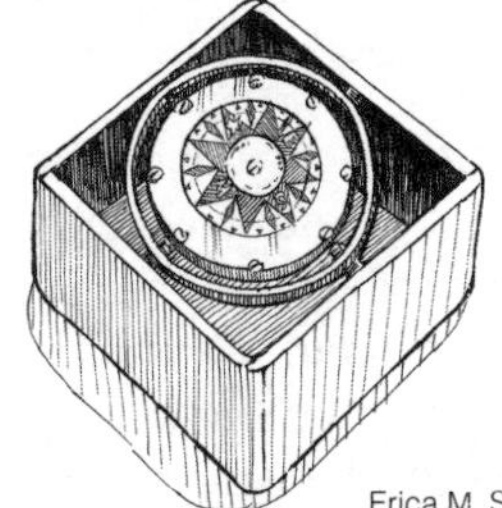
Erica M. Szuplat

Egg Rock Lt., Frenchman Bay – Fl. R. ev. 5 s., Keyed (VHF 83A) Horn 2 bl. ev. 30 s., Ht. 64′, Rge. 18 mi., (44-21-14N/68-08-18W)

Baker Island Lt., SW Entr. Somes Sound – Fl. W. ev. 10 s., Ht. 105′, Rge. 10 mi., (44-14-28N/68-11-56W)

Bass Harbor Head Lt., SW Pt. Mt. Desert Is. – Oc. R. ev. 4 s., Ht. 56′, Rge. 13 mi., ltd. 24 hrs., (44-13-19N/68-20-14W)

Blue Hill Bay Lt. #3, on Green Is. – Fl. G. ev. 4 s., Ht. 21′, Rge. 5 mi., SG on tower, (44-14-55N/68-29-52W)

For abbreviations see footnote p. 173

Wild Swimming

by Christopher Borgatti

"I really should eat soon," I thought to myself. I had spent the better part of two hours battling wind and waves and had finally rounded a point and now had following seas. While my stroke was out of sync with the wind chop, every once in a while, a wave would pick me up and thrust me forward. I could feel the acceleration across my face, chest, and legs as my body lurched forward. It felt good to be working with the water and not against it, but I still had five miles to go. In terms of experience, I was in unchartered waters, as I had never swum this far before. If I was to make it to the finish line, I would need to eat and drink something soon or risk falling behind my body's basic fueling requirements. I certainly didn't want to deal with debilitating cramps, or worse yet, be fished out of the water by a rescue boat.

Fifteen years earlier, I thought I had taken my last competitive swim stroke. I had always imagined that last stroke would be reaching for the wall at the NCAA championships as the anchor leg of my college team's relay. As in life, things don't always go according to plan. I didn't get that last stroke to the wall. Instead, my swimming career ended on the doctor's exam table with a diagnosis of mononucleosis and prompt admission to the hospital. Just like that, it was over. I calculated that, up to that up to that moment, I had spent nearly a year of my life in a pool. I didn't take another proper swimming stroke for more than ten years. It wasn't bitterness or regret that kept me from swimming; swimming had given me a lot, and I was grateful for the experiences and the friendships I made along the way. I just didn't feel like swimming.

What changed after ten years? I discovered open water swimming, or what many refer to as "wild swimming." Wild swimming is a departure from the structure and support found at the local lap pool, as it takes place in a dynamic environment of lakes, ponds, rivers, bays, or the ocean. There are no lifeguards or lane lines and the water conditions are in constant flux. Water temperature, visibility, waves, and currents can change by the minute and need to be understood and considered. Tides are particularly important, as many great swim spots that offer protection from wind and waves turn into big mudflats at low tide.

So what was the draw for a retired pool swimmer to dip my toe into open water swimming, and why might you consider giving it a try? Every day in the water is different; I could swim in the same spot and experience tropical blue water with amazing visibility one day, and return the next day to find waves and visibility that prevented me from seeing much beyond arm's length. There's an acute sense of adventure, whether swimming out to an island that my family boats to, or riding the tidal push up a coastal river and riding it back upon tide's turn, swimming is always exciting and new.

Truth be told, there was one more aspect that got me back in the water: a desire to improve my health and fitness. It's widely accepted that swimming is a great full-body workout that builds muscular strength and endurance, while also providing tremendous cardiovascular benefits. What is lesser known are swim-

Continued on p. 188

Burnt Coat Harbor Lt. – Oc. W. ev. 4 s., Ht. 75′, Rge. 9 mi., (44-08-03N/68-26-50W)

Halibut Rocks Lt., Jericho Bay – Fl. W. ev. 6 s., Horn 1 bl. ev. 10 s., Ht. 25′, Rge. 6 mi., NR on tower, (44-08-03N/68-31-32W)

Eggemoggin Ltd. Bell By. "EG" – Mo(A)W, Rge. 4 mi., RWSRST, (44-19-13N/68-44-34W)

Eggemoggin Reach Bell By. "ER" – RWSRST, (44-18-00N/68-46-29W)

Crotch Island Lt. #21, Deer Is. Thorofare – Fl. G. ev. 4 s., Ht. 20′, Rge. 5 mi., SG on tower, (44-08-46N/68-40-39W)

Saddleback Ledge Lt., Isle au Haut Bay – Fl. W. ev. 6 s., Horn 1 bl. ev. 10 s., Ht. 52′, Rge. 9 mi., (44-00-52N/68-43-35W)

Isle Au Haut Lt., Isle au Haut Bay – Fl. R. ev. 4 s., W. Sect. 034°-060°, Ht. 48′, Rge. R. 6 mi., W. 8 mi., (44-03-53N/68-39-05W)

Deer Island Thorofare Lt., W. end of thorofare – Fl. W. ev. 6 s., Horn 1 bl. ev. 15 s., Ht. 52′, Rge. 8 mi., Obscured from 240°-335°, (44-08-04N/68-42-12W)

Goose Rocks Lt., E. Entr. Fox Is. Thorofare – Fl. R. ev. 6 s., W. Sect. 301°-304°, Keyed (VHF 83A) Horn 1 bl. ev. 10 s., Ht. 51′, Rge. R. 7 mi., W. 12 mi., (44-08-08N/68-49-50W)

Eagle Island Lt., E. Penobscot Bay – Fl. W. ev. 4 s., Ht. 106′, Rge. 9 mi., (44-13-04N/68-46-04W)

Green Ledge Lt. #4, E. Penobscot Bay – Fl. R. ev. 6 s., Ht. 31′, Rge. 5 mi., TR on tower, (44-17-25N/68-49-42W)

Erica M. Szuplat

Heron Neck Lt., E. Entr. Hurricane Sound – F.R., W. Sect. 030°-063°, Keyed (VHF 83A) Horn 1 bl. ev. 30 s., Ht. 92′, Rge. R. 7 mi., W. 9 mi., (44-01-30N/68-51-44W)

Matinicus Rock Lt., Penobscot Bay App. – Fl. W. ev. 10 s., Keyed (VHF 83A) Horn 1 bl. ev. 15 s., Ht. 90′, Rge. 20 mi., (43-47-01N/68-51-18W)

Grindel Pt. Lt., West Penobscot Bay – Fl. W. ev. 4 s., Ht. 39′, Rge. 7 mi., (44-16-53N/68-56-35W)

Two-Bush Island Lt., Two-Bush Ch. – Fl. W. ev. 5 s., R. Sect. 061°-247°, Keyed (VHF 83A) Horn 1 bl. ev. 15 s., Ht. 65′, Rge. W. 21 mi., R. 15 mi., (43-57-51N/69-04-26W)

Two Bush Island Ltd. Wh. By. "TBI" – Mo(A)W, Rge. 6 mi., RWS, (43-58-17N/69-00-16W)

Whitehead Lt., W. side of S. entr. Muscle Ridge Ch. – Oc.G. ev. 4 s., Keyed (VHF 83A) Horn 2 bl. ev. 30 s., Ht. 75′, Rge. 6 mi., (43-58-43N/69-07-27W)

Owls Head Lt., S. side Rockland Entr. – F.W., Keyed (VHF 83A) Horn 2 bl. ev. 20 s., Ht. 100′, Rge. 16 mi., Obscured from 324°-354° by Monroe Island, ltd. 24 hrs., (44-05-32N/69-02-38W)

Rockland Harbor Breakwater Lt., S. end of breakwater – Fl. W. ev. 5 s., Keyed (VHF 83A) Horn 1 bl. ev. 15 s., Ht. 39′, Rge. 17 mi., (44-06-15N/69-04-39W)

Lowell Rock Lt. #2, Rockport Entr. – Fl. R. ev. 6 s., Ht. 25′, Rge. 5 mi., TR on spindle, (44-09-46N/69-03-37W)

Browns Head Lt., W. Entr. Fox Is. Thorofare – F.W., 2 R. Sect. 001°-050° and 061°-091°, Keyed (VHF 83A) Horn 1 bl. ev. 10 s., Ht. 39′, Rge. R. 11 mi., F.W. 14 mi., ltd. 24 hrs., (44-06-42N/68-54-34W)

Curtis Island Lt., S. side Camden Entr. – Oc.G. ev. 4 s., Ht. 52′, Rge. 6 mi., (44-12-05N/69-02-56W)

Northeast Point Lt. #2, Camden Entr. – Fl. R. ev. 4 s., Ht. 20′, Rge. 5 mi., TR on white tower, (44-12-31N/69-02-47W)

Dice Head Lt., N. side Entr. to Castine – Fl. W. ev. 6 s., Ht. 134′, Rge. 11 mi., White tower, (44-22-58N/68-49-08W)

Fort Point Lt., W. side Entr. to Penobscot R. – F.W., Keyed (VHF 83A) Horn 1 bl. ev. 10 s., Ht. 88′, Rge. 15 mi., ltd. 24 hrs., (44-28-02N/68-48-42W)

For abbreviations see footnote p. 173

Marshall Point Lt., E. side of Pt. Clyde Hbr. S. Entr. – F.W., Keyed (VHF 83A) Horn 1 bl. ev. 10 s., Ht. 30′, Rge. 13 mi., ltd. 24 hrs., (43-55-03N/69-15-41W)

Marshall Point Ltd. By. "MP" – Mo(A)W, Rge. 4 mi., RWSRST, (43-55-18N/69-10-52W)

Monhegan Island Lt., Penobscot Bay – Fl. W. ev. 15 s., Ht. 178′, Rge. 20 mi., Obscured between west and southwest within 3 mi of island (43-45-53N/69-18-57W)

Franklin Is. Lt., Muscongus Bay – Fl. W. ev. 6 s., Ht. 57′, Rge. 8 mi., Obscured from 253°-352° by trees (43-53-31N/69-22-29W)

Pemaquid Pt. Lt., W. side Muscongus Bay Entr. – Fl. W. ev. 6 s., Ht. 79′, Rge. 14 mi., (43-50-12N/69-30-21W)

Ram Is. Lt., Fisherman Is. Passage S. side – Iso. R. ev. 6 s., 2 W. Sect. 258°-261° and 030°-046°, Covers fairways, Keyed (VHF 83A) Horn 1 bl. ev. 30 s., Ht. 36′, Rge. W. 11 mi., R. 9 mi., W. 9 mi. (43-48-14N/69-35-57W)

Burnt Is. Lt., Boothbay Hbr. W. side Entr. – Fl. R. ev. 6 s., 2 W. Sect. 307°-316° and 355°-008°, Covers fairways. Keyed (VHF 83A) Horn 1 bl. ev. 10 s., Ht. 61′, Rge. W. 8 mi., R. 6 mi., (43-49-31N/69-38-25W)

The Cuckolds Lt., Boothbay – Fl(2) W. ev. 6 s., Keyed (VHF 83A) Horn 1 bl. ev. 15 s., Ht. 59′, Rge. 12 mi., (43-46-46N/69-39-00W)

Seguin Lt., 2 mi. S. of Kennebec R. mouth – F.W., Keyed (VHF 83A) Horn 2 bl. ev. 20 s., Ht. 180′, Rge. 18 mi., (43-42-27N/69-45-29W)

Hendricks Head Lt., Sheepscot R. mouth E. side – F.W., R. Sect. 180°-000°, Ht. 43′, Rge. R. 7 mi., F.W. 9 mi., (43-49-21N/69-41-23W)

Pond Is. Lt., Kennebec R. mouth W. side – Iso. W. ev. 6 s., Keyed (VHF 83A) Horn 2 bl. ev. 30 s., Ht. 52′, Rge. 9 mi., (43-44-24N/69-46-13W)

Perkins Is. Lt., Kennebec R. – Fl. R. ev. 2.5 s., 2 W. Sect. 018° – 038°, 172° – 188°, Covers fairways, Ht. 41′, Rge. R. 5 mi., W. 6 mi., (43-47-12N/69-47-07W)

Squirrel Pt. Lt., Kennebec R. – Iso. R. ev. 6 s., W. Sect. 321° - 324°, Covers fairway, Ht. 25′, Rge. R. 7 mi., W. 9 mi., (43-48-59N/69-48-09W)

Erica M. Szuplat

Fuller Rock Lt., off Cape Small – Fl. W. ev. 4 s., Ht. 39′, Rge. 6 mi., NR on tower, (43-41-45N/69-50-01W)

White Bull Ltd. Gong By. "WB" – Mo(A)W, Rge. 6 mi., RWS, (43-42-49N/69-55-13W)

Whaleboat Island Lt., Broad Sd., Casco Bay – Fl. W. ev. 6 s., Ht. 47′, Rge. 4 mi., NR on tower, (43-44-31N/70-03-40W)

Cow Island Ledge Lt., Portland to Merepoint – Fl. W. ev. 6 s., Ht. 23′, Rge. 8 mi., RaRef., NR on spindle, (43-42-11N/70-11-19W)

Halfway Rock Lt., midway betw. Cape Small Pt. and Cape Eliz. – Fl. R. ev. 5 s., Keyed (VHF 83A) Horn 2 bl. ev. 30 s., Ht. 76′, Rge. 14 mi., (43-39-21N/70-02-12W)

Portland Ltd. Wh. By. "P", Portland Hbr. App. – Mo(A)W, Rge. 6 mi., Racon (M), RWSRST, (43-31-36N/70-05-28W)

Ram Island Ledge Lt., N. side of Portland Hbr. Entr. – Fl. (2) W. ev. 6 s., Keyed (VHF 83A) Horn 1 bl. ev. 10 s., Ht. 77′, Rge. 9 mi., (43-37-53N/70-11-15W)

Cape Elizabeth Lt., S. of Portland Hbr. Entr. – Fl(4) W. ev. 15 s., Keyed (VHF 83A) Horn 2 bl. ev. 60 s., Ht. 129′, Rge. 15 mi., ltd. 24 hrs., (43-33-58N/70-12-00W)

Portland Head Lt., SW side Portland Hbr. Entr. – Fl. W. ev. 4 s., Keyed (VHF 83A) Horn 1 bl. ev. 15 s., Ht. 101′, Rge. 24 mi., ltd. 24 hrs., (43-37-23N/70-12-28W)

Spring Pt. Ledge Lt., Portland main ch. W. side – Fl. W. ev. 6 s., 2 R. Sect., 2 W. Sectors 331°-337° Covers fairway entrance, and 074°-288°, Keyed (VHF 83A) Horn 1 bl. ev. 10 s., Ht. 54′, Rge. R. 10 mi., W. 12 mi., ltd. 24 hrs., (43-39-08N/70-13-26W)

Wood Island Lt., S. Entr. Wood Is. Hbr. N. side – Alt. W. and G. ev. 10 s. (Night), Keyed (VHF 83A) Horn 2 bl. ev. 30 s., Ht. 71′, Rge. W. 13 mi., G. 13 mi., (43-27-25N/70-19-45W)

For abbreviations see footnote p. 173

Goat Is. Lt., Cape Porpoise Hbr. Entr. – Fl. W. ev. 6 s., Keyed (VHF 83A) Horn 1 bl. ev. 15 s., Ht. 38', Rge. 12 mi., (43-21-28N/70-25-30W)

Cape Neddick Lt., On N. side of Nubble – Iso. R. ev. 6 s., Keyed (VHF 83A) Horn 1 bl. ev. 10 s., Ht. 88', Rge. 13 mi., ltd. 24 hrs., (43-09-55N/70-35-28W)

Jaffrey Point Lt. #4 – Fl. R. ev. 4 s., Ht. 22', rge. 4 mi., TR on tower, (43-03-18N/70-42-49W)

Boon Is. Lt., 6.5 mi. off coast – Fl. W. ev. 5 s., Horn 1 bl. ev. 10 s., Ht. 137', Rge. 14 mi., (43-07-17N/70-28-35W)

York Harbor Ltd. Bell By. "YH" – Mo(A)W, Rge. 5 mi., RWSRST, (43-07-45N/70-37-01W)

NEW HAMPSHIRE

Whaleback Lt., Portsmouth Entr. NE side –Fl(2) W. ev. 10 s., Keyed (VHF 83A) Horn 2 bl. ev. 30 s., Ht. 59', Rge. 11 mi., (43-03-32N/70-41-47W)

Portsmouth Harbor Lt. (New Castle), on Fort Point – F. G., Keyed (VHF 83A) Horn 1 bl. ev. 10 s., Ht. 52', Rge. 12 mi., (43-04-16N/70-42-31W)

Rye Harbor Entr. Ltd. Wh. By. "RH" – Mo(A)W, Rge. 6 mi., RWSRST, (42-59-38N/70-43-45W)

Isles Of Shoals Lt., 5.5 mi. off coast – Fl. W. ev. 15 s., Horn 1 bl. ev. 30 s., Ht. 82', Rge. 14 mi., (42-58-02N/70-37-24W)

MASSACHUSETTS

Newburyport Harbor Lt., N. end of Plum Is. – Oc.(2) G. ev. 15 s., Obscured from 165°-192° and 313°-344°, Ht. 50', Rge. 10 mi., (42-48-55N/70-49-08W)

Merrimack River Entr. Ltd. Wh. By. "MR"– Mo(A)W, Rge. 4 mi., RWSRST, (42-48-34N/70-47-03W)

Ipswich Lt., Ipswich Entr. S. side – Oc.W. ev. 4 s., Ht. 30', Rge. 5 mi., NR on tower, (42-41-07N/70-45-58W)

Rockport Breakwater Lt. #6, W. side Entr. Rockport inner hbr. – Fl. R. ev. 4 s., Ht. 32', Rge. 4 mi., TR on spindle, (42-39-39N/70-36-43W)

Annisquam Harbor Lt., E. side Entr. – Fl. W. ev. 7.5 s., R. Sector 180°-217°, Horn 2 bl. ev. 60 s., Ht. 45', Rge. R. 11 mi., W. 14 mi., (42-39-43N/70-40-53W)

Straitsmouth Lt., Rockport Entr. S. side – Fl. G. ev. 6 s., Keyed (VHF 83A) Horn 1 bl. ev. 15 s., Ht. 46', Rge. 6 mi., (42-39-44N/70-35-17W)

Cape Ann Lt., E. side Thacher Is. – Fl. R. ev. 5 s., Horn 2 bl. ev. 60 s., Ht. 166', Rge. 17 mi., (42-38-12N/70-34-30W)

Eastern Point Ltd. Wh. By. #2 – Fl. R. ev. 4 s., Rge. 3 mi., (42-34-14N/70-39-50W)

Eastern Point Lt., Gloucester Entr. E. side – Fl. W. ev. 5 s., Ht. 57', Rge. 20 mi., (42-34-49N/70-39-52W)

Gloucester Breakwater Lt., W. end – Oc.R. ev. 4 s., Keyed (VHF 83A) Horn 1 bl. ev. 10 s., Ht. 45', Rge. 6 mi., (42-34-57N/70-40-20W)

Bakers Island Lt., Salem Ch. – Alt. Fl. W. and R. ev. 20 s., Keyed (VHF 83A) Horn 1 bl. ev. 30 s., Ht. 111', Rge. W. 16 mi., R. 14 mi., (42-32-11N/70-47-09W)

Hospital Point Range Front Lt., Beverly Cove W. side – F.W., Ht. 69', Higher intensity on range line (42-32-47N/70-51-21W)

The Graves Ltd. Wh. By. #5 – Fl. G. ev. 4 s., Rge. 4 mi., Green, (42-22-33N/70-51-28W)

Marblehead Lt., N. point Marblehead Neck – F.G., Ht. 130', Rge. 7 mi., (42-30-19N/70-50-01W)

The Graves Lt., Boston Hbr. S. Ch. Entr. – Fl(2) W. ev. 12 s., Keyed (VHF 83A) Horn 2 bl. ev. 20 s., Ht. 98', Rge. 15 mi., (42-21-54N/70-52-09W)

Boston App. Ltd. By. "BG"– Mo(A)W, Rge. 4 mi., RWSRST, (42-23-27N/70-51-29W)

Deer Island Lt., President Roads, Boston Hbr. – Alt. W. and R. ev. 10 s., Keyed (VHF 83A) Horn 1 bl. ev. 10 s., Ht. 53', Rge. 9 mi., (42-20-22N/70-57-16W)

For abbreviations see footnote p. 173

Long Island Head Lt., President Roads, Boston Hbr. – Fl. W. ev. 2.5 s., Ht. 120′, Rge. 6 mi., (42-19-49N/70-57-28W)

Boston Ltd. Wh. By. "B", Boston Hbr. Entr. – Mo(A)W, Rge. 6 mi., Racon (B), RWSRST, (42-22-42N/70-46-58W)

Boston App. Ltd. By. "BF" (NOAA-44013) –Fl(4) Y. ev. 20 sec, Rge. 7 mi., Yellow, (42-20-44N/70-39-04W)

Boston North Ch.Entr. Ltd. Wh. By. "NC" – Mo(A)W, Rge. 6 mi., RWSRST, Racon (N), (42-22-32N/70-54-18W)

Minots Ledge Lt., Boston Hbr. Entr. S. side – Fl(1+4+3) W. ev. 45 s., Keyed (VHF 83A) Horn 1 bl. ev. 10 s., Ht. 85′, Rge. 10 mi., (42-16-11N/70-45-33W)

Boston Lt., SE side Little Brewster Is. – Fl. W. ev. 10 s., Keyed (VHF 83A) Horn 1 bl. ev. 30 s., Ht. 102′, Rge. 27 mi., (42-19-41N/70-53-24W)

Scituate App. Ltd. Gong By. "SA"– Mo(A)W, Rge. 4 mi., RWSRST, (42-12-08N/70-41-49W)

Plymouth Lt. (Gurnet), N. side Entr. to hbr. – Fl(3) W. ev. 30 s., R. Sect. 323°-352°, Keyed (VHF 83A) Horn 2 bl. ev. 15 s., Ht. 102′, Rge. R. 15 mi., W. 17 mi., (42-00-13N/70-36-02W)

Race Point Lt., NW Point of Cape Cod – Fl. W. ev. 10 s., Ht. 41′, Rge. 14 mi., Obscured 220°-292°, (42-03-44N/70-14-35W)

Wood End Lt., Entr. to Provincetown – Fl. R. ev. 10 s., Keyed (VHF 83A) Horn 1 bl. ev. 30 s., Ht. 45′, Rge. 13 mi., (42-01-17N/70-11-37W)

Long Point Lt., Provincetown Entr. SW side – Oc.G. ev. 4 s., Keyed (VHF 83A) Horn 1 bl. ev. 15 s., Ht. 36′, Rge. 8 mi., (42-01-59N/70-10-07W)

Mary Ann Rocks Ltd. Wh. By. #12 – Fl. R. ev. 2.5 s., Rge. 4 mi., Red, (41-55-07N/70-30-22W)

Cape Cod Canal App. Ltd. Bell By. "CC" – Mo(A)W, Rge. 4 mi., RWSRST, (41-48-53N/70-27-39W)

Sam O. White

Cape Cod Canal Breakwater Lt. #6, E. Entr. – Fl. R. ev. 5 s., Keyed (VHF 83A) Horn 1 bl. ev. 15 s., Ht. 43′, Rge. 9 mi., (41-46-47N/70-29-23W)

Highland Lt., NE side of Cape Cod – Fl. W. ev. 5 s., Ht. 170′, Rge. 14 mi., ltd. 24 hrs., (42-02-22N/70-03-39W)

Nauset Beach Lt., E. side of Cape Cod – Alt. W. R. ev. 10 s., Ht. 120′, (41-51-36N/69-57-12W)

Chatham Beach Ltd. Wh. By. "C" – Mo(A)W, Rge. 4 mi., RWSRST, (41-39-12N/69-55-30W)

Chatham Lt., W. side of hbr. – Fl(2)W. ev. 10 s., Ht. 80′, Rge. 24 mi., ltd. 24 hrs., (41-40-17N/69-57-01W)

Chatham Inlet Bar Guide Lt., Fl. Y. ev. 2.5 s., Ht. 62′, Rge. 11 mi., (41-40-18N/69-57-00W)

Hyannis Harbor App. Ltd. Bell By. "HH" – Mo(A)W, Rge. 4 mi., RWSRST, (41-35-57N/70-17-22W)

Pollock Rip Ch. Ltd. By. #8 – Fl. R. ev. 6 s., Rge. 3 mi., Red, (41-32-43N/69-58-56W)

For abbreviations see footnote p. 173

Nantucket Lt., (Great Point), Nantucket, N. end of Is., – Fl. W. ev. 5 s., R. sect. 084°-106° (Covers Cross Rip & Tuckernuck Shoals), Ht. 71′, Rge. W. 14 mi., R. 12 mi., (41-23-25N/70-02-54W)

Sankaty Head Lt., E. end of Is. – Fl. W. ev. 7.5 s., Ht. 158′, Rge. 24 mi., ltd. 24 hrs., (41-17-04N/69-57-58W)

Nantucket East Breakwater Lt. #3, Outer Entr. to hbr. – Fl. G. ev. 4 s., Ht. 30′, Rge. 3 mi., (41-18-37N/70-06-00W)

Brant Point Lt., Hbr. Entr. W. side – Oc.R. ev. 4 s., Keyed (VHF 83A) Horn 1 bl. ev. 10 s., Ht. 26′, Rge. 9 mi., (41-17-24N/70-05-25W)

Cape Poge Lt., NE point of Chappaquiddick Is. – Fl. W. ev. 6 s., Ht. 65′, Rge. 9 mi., (41-25-10N/70-27-08W)

Muskeget Ch. Ltd. Wh. By. "MC" – Mo(A)W, Rge. 4 mi., RWSRST, (41-15-00N/70-26-10W)

Edgartown Harbor Lt., Inner end of hbr. W. side – Fl. R. ev. 6 s., Ht. 45′, Rge. 5 mi., (41-23-27N/70-30-11W)

East Chop Lt., E. side Vineyard Haven Hbr. Entr. – Iso. G. ev. 6 s., Ht. 79′, Rge. 9 mi., (41-28-13N/70-34-03W)

West Chop Lt., W. side Vineyard Haven Hbr. Entr. – Oc.W. ev. 4 s., R. Sect. 281°-331° (covers Squash Meadow and Norton Shoals), Keyed (VHF 83A) Horn 1 bl. ev. 30 s., Ht. 84′, Rge. R. 10 mi., W. 14 mi., (41-28-51N/70-35-59W)

Nobska Point Lt., Woods Hole E. Entr. – Fl. W. ev. 6 s., Obscured 125°-195°, R. Sect. 263°-289° (covers Hedge Fence and L'Hommedieu Shoal), Keyed (VHF 83A) Horn 2 bl. ev. 30 s., Ht. 87′, Rge. R. 11 mi., W. 13 mi., ltd 24 hrs., (41-30-57N/70-39-18W)

Tarpaulin Cove Lt., SE side Naushon Is. – Fl. W. ev. 6 s., Ht. 78′, Rge. 9 mi., (41-28-08N/70-45-27W)

Menemsha Creek Entr. Jetty Lt. #3 – Fl. G. ev. 4 s., Ht. 25′, Rge. 5 mi., (41-21-16N/70-46-07W)

Gay Head Lt., W. point of Martha's Vineyard – Alt. W. and R. ev. 15 s., Ht. 175′, Rge. W. 24 mi., R. 20 mi., Obscured 342°-359° by Nomans Land, ltd. 24 hrs., (41-20-54N/70-50-04W)

Cuttyhunk East Entr. Ltd. Bell By. "CH" – Mo(A)W, Rge. 4 mi., RWSRST, (41-26-34N/70-53-22W)

BUZZARDS BAY

Buzzards Bay Entr. Lt., W. Entr. – Fl. W. ev. 2.5 s., Keyed (VHF 83A) Horn 2 bl. ev. 30 s., Ht. 67′, Rge. 14 mi., Racon (B), (41-23-49N/71-02-05W)

Dumpling Rocks Lt. #7, off Round Hill Pt. – Fl. G. ev. 6 s., Ht. 52′, Rge. 8 mi., (41-32-18N/70-55-17W)

Buzzards Bay Midch. Ltd. Bell By. "BB" (east of Wilkes Ledge) – Mo(A)W, Rge. 4 mi., RWSRST, (41-30-33N/70-49-54W)

New Bedford West Barrier Lt. – Q.G., Keyed (VHF 83A) Horn 1 bl. ev. 10 s., Ht. 48′, Rge. 8 mi., (41-37-27N/70-54-22W)

New Bedford East Barrier Lt. – Q. R., Ht. 33′, Rge. 8 mi., (41-37-29N/70-54-19W)

Padanaram Breakwater Lt. #8 – Fl. R. ev. 4 s., Ht. 25′, Rge. 5 mi., (41-34-27N/70-56-21W)

Cleveland East Ledge Lt., Cape Cod Canal App. E. side of S. Entr. – Fl. W. ev. 10 s., Keyed (VHF 83A) Horn 1 bl. ev. 15 s., Ht. 74′, Rge. 14 mi., Racon (C), (41-37-51N/70-41-39W)

Ned Point Lt. – Iso. W. ev. 6 s., Ht. 41′, Rge. 12 mi., (41-39-03N/70-47-44W)

Westport Harbor Entr. Lt. #7, W. side – Fl. G. ev. 6 s., Ht. 35′, Rge. 9 mi., (41-30-27N/71-05-17W)

Westport Harbor App. Ltd. Bell By. 1, Fl. G. ev. 2.5s, Rge. 4 mi., (41-29-15N/71-04-04W)

For abbreviations see footnote p. 173

Continued from p. 178

ming's other physiological and psychological benefits, particularly those that come from swimming in colder water. Research has shown that swimming releases endorphins that generally improve one's mood and feeling of wellbeing. It has also shown that swimming stimulates the parasympathetic nervous system, which helps improve mental clarity and even sleep, and that regular exposure to colder water may boost the immune system. These benefits, and the relatively low cost of equipment, not to mention the absence of health club fees, made open water swimming an ideal fitness option. After a swim, I experience a nice balance of post-workout endorphins with a light fatigue throughout my body. My favorite feeling, though, is an ever so slight chill that lingers for a spell. It's a refreshing feeling and one that I especially enjoy on a hot summer day.

Of course, there are some important safety considerations when it comes to open water swimming. First and foremost, never swim alone. Fortunately, there are vibrant communities of open water swimmers of all levels up and down the East Coast and these groups are extraordinarily welcoming to new swimmers. Second, when swimming, you must be visible to boats and other people on and around the water—consider a brightly covered swim cap and a swim buoy. The swim buoy usually consists of an inflatable bladder, a short line, and a waist belt. It not only adds visibility to the swimmer, but also gives the person something to float on should they need to take a break. To someone not acclimated, cold water can be a significant safety risk. It can also be an obstacle for newer swimmers. Wetsuits paired with an insulated swim cap can drastically reduce the risks associated with cold water exposure. Besides making the swimming experience much more comfortable, a wetsuit will also make the swimmer considerably more buoyant, which in turn makes it much easier to swim.

So there I was. Treading water in the middle of a channel, grasping a water bottle in one hand, while attempting to squirt its contents, two energy gels mixed with 300 ml of water, into my mouth. The bottle was tossed to me by an escort kayaker, who had been shadowing me along the way. At that moment, the race director pulled up beside me in a sleek center console and yelled. "You are in third," he pointed about 50 yards ahead, "Second place is right there!" I caught a glimpse of a swinging arm and an orange kayak. "Go get 'em!" he said. I did my best to swallow what was left in my mouth, tossed the bottle back to my kayaker, and started swimming again. I thought to myself, "so much for just swimming… here we go again."

Like pool swimming did so many years ago, open water swimming has improved my fitness and provided the opportunity to make great friendships along the way. But unlike the pool, wild swimming has added adventure, challenge, and constant variability every time I get in the water. And perhaps the biggest difference is how I've come to frame the future of my swimming life. It's no longer geared towards a "last stroke;" instead, I'm always looking toward the future and the "next stroke."

Chris is usually doing something on or around the water. He is a USMS Long Distance National Champion and All-American and competes in the sport of Swim-Run.

RHODE ISLAND

Sakonnet Lt. – Fl. W. ev. 6 s., R. sect. 195°-350°, Ht. 70′, Rge. W. 7 mi., R. 5 mi., (41-27-11N/71-12-09W)

Sakonnet Breakwater Lt. #2, Entr. to hbr. – Fl. R. ev. 4 s., Ht. 29′, Rge. 6 mi., (41-28-00N/71-11-42W)

Narragansett Bay Entr. Ltd. Wh. By. "NB" – Mo(A)W, Rge. 6 mi., Racon (B), RWSRST, (41-23-00N/71-23-21W)

Beavertail Lt. – Narrag. Bay E. passage – Fl. W. ev. 10 s., Obscured 175°-215°, Keyed (VHF 83A) Horn 1 bl. ev. 30 s., Ht. 64′, Rge. 15 mi., ltd. 24 hrs., (41-26-58N/71-23-58W)

Castle Hill Lt. – Iso R. 6 s., Keyed (VHF 83A) Horn 1 bl. ev. 10 s., Ht. 40′, Rge. 9 mi., (41-27-44N/71-21-47W)

Fort Adams Lt. #2, Narrag. Bay E. passage – Fl. R. ev. 6 s., Keyed (VHF 83A) Horn 1 bl. ev. 15 s., Ht. 32′, Rge. 7 mi., (41-28-54N/71-20-12W)

Newport Harbor Lt., N. end of breakwater – F.G., Ht. 33′, Rge. 9 mi., (41-29-36N/71-19-38W)

Rose Is. Lt., Fl W. ev. 6 s., Ht. 48′, (41-29-44N/71-20-34W)

Prudence Is. Lt. (Sandy Pt.), Narrag. Bay E. passage – Fl. G. ev. 6 s., Ht. 28′, Rge. 6 mi., (41-36-21N/71-18-13W)

Hog Island Shoal Lt., N. side Entr. to Mt. Hope Bay – Iso. W. ev. 6 s., Keyed (VHF 83A) Horn 2 bl. ev 30s., Ht. 54′, Rge. 12 mi., (41-37-56N/71-16-24W)

Musselbed Shoals Lt.#6A, Mt. Hope Bay Ch. – Fl. R. ev. 6 s., Ht. 26′, Rge. 6 mi., (41-38-11N/71-15-36W)

Castle Is. Lt. #2, N. of Hog Is. – Fl. R. ev. 6 s., Ht. 26′, Rge. 3 mi., (41-39-14N/71-17-10W)

Bristol Harbor Lt. #4 – F.R., Ht. 25′, Rge. 11 mi., (41-39-58N/71-16-42W)

Conimicut Lt., Providence R. App. – Fl. W. ev. 2.5 s., R. Sect. 322°-349° covers Ohio Ledge, Keyed (VHF 83A) Horn 2 bl. ev. 30 s., Ht. 58′, Rge. W. 8 mi., R. 5 mi., (41-43-01N/71-20-42W)

Bullock Point Lt. "BP", Prov. R. – Oc.W. ev. 4 s., Ht. 29′, Rge. 6 mi., (41-44-16N/71-21-51W)

Pomham Rocks Lt., Prov. R. – F.R., Ht. 54′, Rge. 6 mi., (41-46-39N/71-22-10W)

Providence River Ch. Lt. #42, off rock – Iso. R. ev. 6 s., Ht. 31′, Rge. 4 mi., (41-47-39N/71-22-47W)

Mt. Hope Bay Jct. Ltd. Gong By. "MH" – Fl(2+1) R. 6 s., Rge., 3 mi., R. & G. Bands, (41-39-32N/71-14-03W)

Borden Flats Lt., Mt. Hope Bay – Fl. W. ev. 2.5 s., Ht. 47′, Rge. 9 mi., (41-42-16N/71-10-28W)

Wickford Harbor Lt. #1, Narrag. Bay W. passage – Fl. G. ev. 6 s., Ht. 40′, Rge. 6 mi., (41-34-21N/71-26-13W)

Warwick Lt., Greenwich Bay App. – Oc.G. ev. 4 s., Keyed (VHF 83A) Horn 1 bl. ev. 15 s., Ht. 66′, Rge. 10 mi., ltd. 24 hrs., (41-40-02N/71-22-42W)

Point Judith Lt., Block Is. Sd. Entr. – Oc(3)W. ev. 15 s., Keyed (VHF 83A) Horn 1 bl. ev. 15 s., Ht. 65′, Rge. 16 mi., (41-21-40N/71-28-53W)

Block Island North Lt., N. end of Is. – Fl. W. ev. 5 s., Ht. 58′, (41-13-39N/71-34-33W)

Block Island Southeast Lt., SE end of Is. – Fl. G. ev. 5 s., Keyed (VHF 83A) Horn 1 bl. ev. 30 s., Ht. 261′, Rge. 20 mi., ltd. 24 hrs., (41-09-10N/71-33-04W)

Pt. Judith Harbor of Refuge W. Entr. Lt. #3 – Fl. G. ev. 6 s., Keyed (VHF 83A) Horn 1 bl. ev. 30 s., Ht. 35′, Rge. 5 mi., (41-21-56N/71-30-53W)

Block Is. Breakwater Lt. #3 – Q. G., Keyed (VHF 81A) Horn 2 bl. ev. 30 s., Ht. 27′, Rge. 6mi., (41-10-38N/71-33-15W)

Watch Hill Lt., Fishers Is. Sd. E. Entr. – Alt. W. and R. ev. 5 s., Keyed (VHF 83A) Horn 1 bl. ev. 30 s., Ht. 61′, Rge. 14 mi., ltd. 24 hrs., (41-18-14N/71-51-30W)

For abbreviations see footnote p. 173

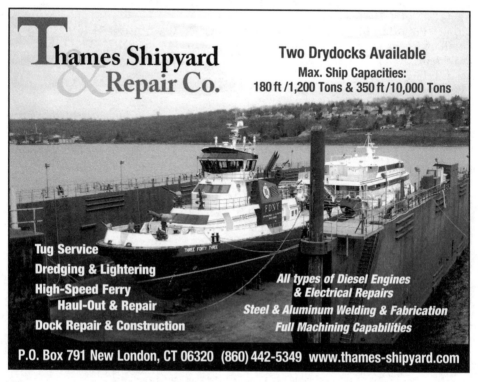

FISHERS ISLAND SOUND

Latimer Reef Lt., Fishers Is. Sd. main ch. – Fl. W. ev. 6 s., Bell 2 strokes ev. 15 s., Ht. 55′, Rge. 9 mi., (41-18-16N/71-56-00W)

N. Dumpling Lt., Fishers Is. Sd. main ch. – F.W., Keyed (VHF 83A) Horn 1 bl. ev. 30 s., R. Sect. 257°-023°, Ht. 94′, Rge. R. 7 mi., F.W. 9 mi., (41-17-17N/72-01-10W)

Stonington Outer Breakwater Lt. #4 – Fl. R. ev. 4 s., Horn 1 bl. ev. 10 s., Ht. 46′, Rge. 5 mi., (41-19-00N/71-54-28W)

LONG ISLAND SOUND, NORTH SIDE

Race Rock Lt., SW end of Fishers Is. – Fl. R. ev. 10 s., Keyed (VHF 83A) Horn 2 bl. ev. 30 s., Ht. 67′, Rge. 16 mi., (41-14-37N/72-02-50W)

Bartlett Reef Lt., S. end of reef – Fl. W. ev. 6 s., Keyed (VHF 83A) Horn 2 bl. ev. 60 s., Ht. 35′, Rge. 8 mi., (41-16-28N/72-08-14W)

New London Ledge Lt., W. side of Southwest ledge –Fl(3+1) W. R. ev. 30 s., Keyed (VHF 83A) Horn 2 bl. ev. 20 s., Ht. 58′, Rge. W. 17 mi., R. 14 mi., (41-18-21N/72-04-39W)

New London Harbor Lt., W. side Entr. – Iso. W. ev. 6 s., R. Sect. 000°-041° covers Sarah Ledge and shoals westward, Ht. 89′, Rge. W. 17 mi., R. 14 mi., (41-19-00N/72-05-23W)

Saybrook Breakwater Lt., W. jetty – Fl. G. ev. 6 s., Keyed (VHF 83A) Horn 1 bl. ev. 30 s., Ht. 58′, Rge. 14 mi., (41-15-48N/72-20-34W)

Lynde Pt. Lt., Conn. R. mouth W. side – F.W., Ht. 71′, Rge. 14 mi., (41-16-17N/72-20-35W)

Twenty-Eight Foot Shoal Ltd. Wh. By. "TE" – Fl(2+1) R. ev. 6 s., , Rge. 4 mi., R&G Bands, (41-09-16N/72-30-25W)

Falkner Is. Lt., off Guilford Hbr. – Fl. W. ev. 10 s., Ht. 94′, Rge. 13 mi., (41-12-43N/72-39-13W)

Branford Reef Lt., SE Entr. New Haven – Fl. W. ev. 6 s., Ht. 22′, Rge. 7 mi., (41-13-17N/72-48-19W)

New Haven Hbr. Ltd. Wh. By. "NH" – Mo(A)W, Rge. 4 mi., RWSRST, (41-12-07N/72-53-47W)

Southwest Ledge Lt., E. side Entr. New Haven – Fl. R. ev. 5 s., Keyed (VHF 83A) Horn 1 bl. ev. 15 s., Ht. 57′, Rge. 14 mi., (41-14-04N/72-54-44W)

New Haven Lt. – Fl. W. ev. 4 s., Ht. 27′, Rge. 7 mi., (41-13-16N/72-56-32W)

Stratford Pt. Lt., W. side Entr. Housatonic R. – Fl(2)W. ev. 20 s., Ht. 52′, Rge. 14 mi., (41-09-07N/73-06-12W)

Stratford Shoal Lt., Middle Ground – Fl. W. ev. 5 s., Horn 1 bl. ev. 15 s., Ht. 60′, Rge. 13 mi., (41-03-35N/73-06-05W)

Tongue Pt. Lt., at Bridgeport Breakwater – Fl. G. ev. 4 s., Ht. 31′, Rge. 5 mi., (41-10-00N/73-10-39W)

Penfield Reef Lt., S. side Entr. to Black Rock – Fl. R. ev. 6 s., Keyed (VHF 83A) Horn 1 bl. ev. 15 s., Ht. 51′, Rge. 14 mi., (41-07-02N/73-13-20W)

Peck Ledge Lt., E. App. to Norwalk – Fl. G. ev. 2.5 s., Ht. 61′, Rge. 5 mi., (41-04-39N/73-22-11W)

Greens Ledge Lt., W. end of ledge – Alt. Fl. W. and R. ev. 20 s., Horn 2 bl. ev. 20 s., Ht. 62′, Rge. W. 14 mi., R. 14 mi., (41-02-30N/73-26-38W)

Stamford Harbor Ledge Obstruction Lt., on SW end of Harbor Ledge – Fl. W. ev. 4 s., (41-00-49N/73-32-34W)

Great Captain Is. Lt., SE Pt. of Is. – Alt. W. R. ev. 12 s., Keyed (VHF 83A) Horn 1 bl. ev. 15 s., Ht. 62′, Rge. W. 14 mi., R. 14 mi., (40-58-57N/73-37-23W)

Larchmont Harbor Lt. #2, East Entr. – Fl. R. ev. 4 s., Ht. 26′, Rge. 4 mi., (40-55-05N/73-43-52W)

For abbreviations see footnote p. 173

Heaving the Lead

In tidal water where depths were doubtfully marked on the chart, or in thick weather off shore, soundings were made to determine the ship's position. The leadsman stood in the fore channels and swung the lead. [Aft] in the main and mizzen channels were other men who held the line as it led aft to the stern, where the mate stood by the line tub. The leadsman called, "All ready there?" to the next man, the mate shouted "Heave!" and the lead went spinning forward. Each man let go as the line tautened, and the mate grasped the line as it ran from the tub, and made the sounding. If the lead struck bottom before it reached him, one of the others took the sounding and called the marks. Markers on the line indicated the depth in fathoms, and an "arming" of tallow in the end of the lead showed the nature of the bottom.

Reprinted from Sail Ho! Windjammer Sketches Alow and Aloft, by Gordon Grant, 1931, William Farquhar Payson, Inc., NY

Traditional Markings for Leadlines

2 fathoms – a 2-ended scrap of leather
3 fathoms – a 3-ended scrap of leather
5 fathoms – a scrap of white calico
7 fathoms – a strip of red wool bunting
10 fathoms – leather with a round hole
13 fathoms – a piece of thick blue serge
15 fathoms – a piece of white calico
17 fathoms – a piece of red wool bunting
20 fathoms – a cord with 2 knots
30 fathoms – a cord with 3 knots

LONG ISLAND SOUND, SOUTH SIDE

Little Gull Is. Lt., E. Entr. L.I. Sd. – Fl(2) W. ev. 15 s., Horn 1 bl. ev. 15 sec., Ht. 91′, Rge. 14 mi., (41-12-23N/72-06-25W)

Plum Gut Lt. – Fl. W. ev. 2.5 s., Ht. 21′ Rge. 5 mi., (41-10-26N/72-12-42W)

Plum Island Ltd. Wh. By. "PI" – Mo(A)W, Rge. 4 mi., RWSRST, (41-13-17N/72-10-48W)

Plum Is. Hbr. West Dolphin Lt., W. end of Is. – Q.G., (Maintained by DHS), (41-10-16N/72-12-24W)

Orient Pt. Lt., outer end of Oyster Pond Reef – Fl. W. ev. 5 s., Keyed (VHF 83A) Horn 2 bl. ev. 30 s., Ht. 64′, Rge. 14 mi., (41-09-48N/72-13-25W)

Horton Pt. Lt., NW point of Horton Neck – Fl. G. ev. 10 s., Ht. 103′, Rge. 14 mi., (41-05-06N/72-26-44W)

Mattituck Breakwater Lt. "MI" – Fl. W. ev. 4 s., Ht. 25′, Rge. 6 mi., (41-00-55N/72-33-40W)

Old Field Pt. Lt. – Alt. Fl. R. and Fl. G. ev. 20 s., Ht. 74′, Rge. 14 mi., (40-58-37N/73-07-07W)

Eatons Neck Lt., E. side Entr. Huntington Bay – F. W., Ht. 144′, Rge. 14 mi., (40-57-14N/73-23-43W)

Cold Springs Hbr. Lt., on Pt. of shoal – F.W., R. Sect. 039°-125°, Ht. 37′, Rge. W. Sect. 8 mi., R. Sect. 6 mi., (40-54-51N/73-29-35W)

Glen Cove Breakwater Lt. #5, E. side Entr. to hbr. – Fl. G. ev. 4 s., Ht. 24′, Rge. 5 mi., (40-51-43N/73-39-37W)

Port Jefferson App. Ltd. Wh. By. "PJ" – Mo(A)W, Rge. 4 mi., RWSRST, (40-59-16N/73-06-27W)

Huntington Harbor Lt. – Iso. W. ev. 6 s., Keyed (VHF 83A) Horn 1 bl. ev. 15 s., Ht. 42′, Rge. 9 mi., (40-54-39N/73-25-52W)

LONG ISLAND, OUTSIDE

Montauk Pt. Lt., E. end of L.I. – Fl. W. ev. 5 s., Keyed (VHF 83A) Horn 1 bl. ev. 15 s., Ht. 168′, Rge. 14 mi., (41-04-15N/71-51-26W)

Montauk Hbr. Entr. Ltd. Bell By. "M" – Mo(A)W, Rge. 4 mi., RWSRST, (41-05-07N/71-56-23W)

Shinnecock Inlet App. Ltd. Wh. By. "SH" – Mo(A)W, Rge. 4 mi., RWSRST, (40-49-00N/72-28-35W)

Moriches Inlet App. Ltd. Wh. By. "M" – Mo(A)W, Rge. 6 mi., RWS, (40-44-08N/72-45-12W)

Shinnecock Lt., W. side of Inlet – Fl(2) W. ev. 15 s., Ht. 75′, Rge. 11 mi., (40-50-31N/72-28-42W)

Jones Inlet Lt., end of breakwater – Fl. W. ev. 2.5 s., Ht. 33′, Rge. 4 mi., (40-34-24N/73-34-32W)

Jones Inlet Ltd. Wh. By. "JI" – Mo(A)W, Rge. 4 mi., RWSRST, (40-33-37N/73-35-13W)

E. Rockaway Inlet Ltd. Bell By. "ER" – Mo(A)W, Rge. 5 mi., RWSRST, (40-34-17N/73-45-49W)

Fire Is. Lt., 5.5 mi. E. of inlet – Fl. W. ev. 7.5 s., Ht. 167′, ltd. 24 hrs., (40-37-57N/73-13-07W)

Rockaway Point Breakwater Lt. #4, end of breakwater – Fl. R. ev. 4 s., Ht. 34′, Rge. 5 mi., (40-32-25N/73-56-27W)

NEW YORK HARBOR & APPROACHES

Execution Rocks Lt. – Fl. W. ev. 10 s., Ht. 62′, Rge. 14 mi., Racon (X), (40-52-41N/73-44-16W)

Hart Is. Lt. #46, off S. end of Is. – Fl. R. ev. 4 s., Ht. 23′, Rge. 6 mi., (40-50-42N/73-46-00W)

Stepping Stones Lt., outer end of reef – Oc.G. ev. 4 s., Ht. 46′, Rge. 8 mi., (40-49-28N/73-46-29W)

For abbreviations see footnote p. 173

Throgs Neck Lt., Fort Schuyler – F. R., Ht. 60′, Rge. 9 mi., (40-48-16N/73-47-26W)
Whitestone Pt. Lt. #1, East R. main ch. – Q.G., Ht. 56′, Rge. 3 mi., (40-48-06N/73-49-10W)
Kings Pt. Lt. – Iso. W. ev. 2 s., (Private Aid), (40-48-42N/73-45-48W)
Hell Gate Lt. #15, East R. Hallets Pt. – Fl. G. ev. 2.5 s., Ht. 33′, Rge. 4 mi., (40-46-41N/73-56-05W)
Mill Rock South Lt. #16, East R., main ch. – Fl. R. ev. 4 s., Ht. 37′, Rge. 4 mi., (40-46-46N/73-56-22W)
Governors Is. Lt. #2 – Iso R. ev. 6 s., Ht. 75′, Rge. 7 mi., (40-41-35N/74-01-11W)
Verrazano-Narrows Bridge Sound Signal – (Private Aid), 2 Horns on bridge 1 bl. ev. 15 s., (40-36-31N/74-02-19W)
Coney Is. Lt., N.Y. Hbr. main ch. – Fl. R. ev. 5 s., Ht. 75′, Rge. 16 mi., ltd. 24 hrs., (40-34-36N/74-00-42W)
Romer Shoal Lt., N.Y. Hbr. S. App. – Fl(2) W. ev. 15 s., Horn 2 bl. ev. 30 s., Ht. 54′, Rge. 15 mi., (40-30-47N/74-00-49W)
West Bank (Range Front) Lt., Ambrose Ch. outer sect. – Iso. W. ev. 6 s., R. Sect. 004°-181° and W from 181° - 004°, Horn 2 bl. ev. 20 s., Ht. 69′, ltd. 24 hrs., (40-32-17N/74-02-34W)
Staten Island (Range Rear) Lt., Ambrose Ch. outer sect. – F. W. , Visible on range line only, Ht. 234′, ltd. 24 hrs., (40-34-34N/74-08-28W)
Old Orchard Shoal Lt., N.Y. Hbr. – Fl. W. ev. 6 s., Ht. 20′, Rge. 4 mi.., (40-30-44N/74-05-55W)
Sandy Hook Lt. – F. W., Ht. 88′, Rge. 19 mi., ltd. 24 hrs., (40-27-42N/74-00-07W)
Sandy Hook Ch. (Range Front) Lt. – Q. W., G., and R. sectors, Red from 063°-073° and Green from 300.5°-315.5°, Ht. 45′, Rge. W. 6 mi., G. 4 mi., R. 4 mi. Racon (C), (40-29-15N/73-59-35W)
Southwest Spit Jct. Ltd. Gong By. "SP" – Fl(2+1) R. ev. 6 s., Rge. 3 mi., R. & G. Bands, (40-28-46N/74-03-18W)
Sandy Hook Pt. Lt. – Iso W. ev. 6 s., Ht. 38′, Rge. 7 mi.,"NB" on Skeleton Tower, (40-28-15N/74-01-07W)
Scotland Ltd. Wh. By. "S", Sandy Hook Ch. App. – Mo(A)W, Rge. 6 mi., Racon (M), RWSRST, (40-26-33N/73-55-01W)
Ambrose Ch. Ltd. Wh. By. "A" – Mo(A)W, Rge. 6 mi., Racon (N), RWSRST, (40-27-28N/73-50-12W)

NEW JERSEY

Highlands Lt. – Iso W. ev. 10 s., Obscured 334°-140°, (40-23-48N/73-59-09W)
Atlantic Highlands Breakwater Lt. – Fl. W. ev. 4 s., Ht. 33′, Rge. 7 mi., (40-25-07N/74-01-10W)
Kill Van Kull Ch. Jct. Ltd. Wh. By. "KV"– Fl (2+1) R. ev. 6 s., Rge. 3 mi., R. & G. Bands, Racon (K), (40-39-02N/74-03-51W)
Kill Van Kull Ch. Jct. Ltd. By. "A"– Fl (2+1) G. ev. 6 s., Rge. 3 mi., G. & R. Bands (40-38-45N/74-10-07W)
Kill Van Kull Ch. East Jct. Ltd. By. "E"– Fl (2+1) G. ev. 6 s., Rge. 3 mi. G. & R. Bands (40-38-31N/74-09-15W)
Manasquan Inlet Lt. #3 - Fl. G. ev. 6 s., Keyed (VHF 83A) Horn 1 bl. ev. 30 s., Ht. 35′ Rge. 8 mi., (40-06-01N/74-01-54W)
Shark River Inlet S. Breakwater Lt. #1 – Fl. G. ev. 4s, Ht. 33′, Rge. 7 mi. (40-11-11N/74-00-27W)
Barnegat Inlet S. Breakwater Lt. #7 – Q. G., Ht. 35′, Rge. 5 mi., (39-45-26N/74-05-36W)
Barnegat Inlet Outer Ltd. Wh. By. "BI" – Mo(A)W, Rge. 6 mi., RWSRST, (39-44-28N/74-03-51W)
Little Egg Ltd. By. 3 – Q. G., Rge. 4 mi., Green, (39-28-23N/74-17-35W)

For abbreviations see footnote p. 173

Brigantine Inlet Wreck Ltd. By. "WR2" (100 yards, 090° from wreck) – Q. R., Rge. 5 mi., Red, (39-24-48N/74-13-47W)
Hereford Inlet Lt., S. side – Fl. W. ev. 10 s., Ht. 57′, Rge. 18 mi., (39-00-24N/74-47-28W)
Five Fathom Bank Ltd. By. "F" – Fl. Y. ev. 2.5 s., Rge. 6 mi., Racon (M), Yellow, (38-46-49N/74-34-32W)
Cape May Lt. – Fl. W. ev. 15 s., Ht. 165′, Rge. 22 mi., (38-55-59N/74-57-37W)

NEW JERSEY, DELAWARE AND MARYLAND

Delaware Ltd. By. "D" – Fl. Y. ev. 6 s., Rge. 6 mi., Racon (K), Yellow, (38-27-18N/74-41-47W)
Delaware Traffic Lane Ltd. By. "DA" – Fl. Y. ev. 2.5 s., Rge. 6 mi., Yellow, (38-32-45N/74-46-56W)
Delaware Traffic Lane Ltd. By. "DB" – Fl. Y. ev. 4 s., Rge. 7 mi., Yellow, (38-38-12N/74-52-11W)
Delaware Traffic Lane Ltd. By. "DC" – Fl. Y. ev. 2.5 s., Rge. 6 mi., Yellow, (38-43-47N/74-57-33W)
Harbor of Refuge Lt., Del. Bay – Fl. W. ev. 10 s., 2 R. Sect. 325°-351° and 127°-175°, Horn 2 bl. ev. 30 s., (Mar. 15 - Dec. 15), Ht. 72′, Rge. W. 19 mi., R. 16 mi., (38-48-52N/75-05-33W)
Brown Shoal Lt., Del. Bay main ch. – Fl. W. ev. 2.5 s., Ht. 23′, Rge. 7 mi., Racon (B), (38-55-21N/75-06-01W)
Brandywine Shoal Lt., Del. Bay main ch. on shoal – Fl. W. ev. 10 s., R. Sect. 151°-338°, Horn 1 bl. ev. 15 s. (Mar. 15 - Dec. 15), Ht. 60′, Rge. W. 19 mi., R. 13 mi., (38-59-10N/75-06-47W)
Fourteen Foot Bank Lt., Del. Bay main ch. – Fl. W. ev. 9 s., R. Sect. 332.5°-151°, Horn 1 bl. ev. 30 s., (Mar. 15-Dec. 1), Ht. 59′, Rge. W. 13 mi., R. 10 mi., (39-02-54N/75-10-56W)
Miah Maull Shoal Lt., Del. Bay main ch. – Oc. W. ev. 4 s., R. Sect. 137.5°-333°, Horn 1 bl. ev. 10 s., (Mar. 15-Dec. 15), Ht. 59′, Rge. W. 10 mi., R. 10 mi., Racon (M), (39-07-36N/75-12-31W)
Elbow of Cross Ledge Lt., Del. Bay main ch. – Iso. W. ev. 6 s., Horn 2 bl. ev. 20 s., (Mar. 15-Dec. 15), Ht. 61′, Rge. 16 mi., (39-10-56N/75-16-06W)
Ship John Shoal Lt., Del. Bay main ch. – Fl. W. ev. 5 s., R. Sect. 138°-321.5°, Horn 1 bl. ev. 15 s. (Mar. 15 - Dec. 15), Ht. 50′, Rge. W. 16 mi., R. 12 mi., Racon (O), (39-18-19N/75-22-36W)
Egg Island Point Lt., Del. Bay East side – Fl. W. ev. 4 s., Ht. 27′, Rge. 7 mi., (39-10-21N/75-07-55W)
Old Reedy Is. Lt. – Iso. W. ev. 6 s., R. Sect. 353°-014°, Ht. 20′, Rge. W. 8 mi., R. 6 mi., (39-30-03N/75-34-08W)
Fenwick Is. Lt. – Iso. W. ev. 8 s., Ht. 83′, (38-27-06N/75-03-18W)
Ocean City Inlet Jetty Lt., on end of jetty – Iso. W. ev. 6 s., Keyed (VHF 81A) Horn 1 bl. ev. 10 s., Ht. 38′, Rge. 6 mi., (38-19-27N/75-05-06)

VIRGINIA

Assateague Lt., S. side of Is. – Fl(2) W. ev. 5 s., Ht. 154′, Rge. 22 mi., (37-54-40N/75-21-22W)
Wachapreague Inlet Ltd. Wh. By. "W" – Mo(A)W, Rge. 6 mi., RWSRST, (37-34-54N/75-33-37W)
Great Machipongo Inlet Lt. #5, S. side – Fl. G. ev. 4 s., Ht. 15′, Rge. 4 mi., (37-21-40N/75-44-06W)
Chesapeake Lts. (2), off Entr. to Ches. Bay – Fl W. ev. 4 s., Ht. 84′, (36-54-17N/75-42-46W)

For abbreviations see footnote p. 173

Distance Table in Nautical Miles

*Approximate

Bar Harbor to

Halifax, N.S.	259
Yarmouth, N.S.	101
Saint John, N.B.	122
Machiasport	52
Rockland	62
Boothbay Harbor	86
Portland	115
Marblehead	169

Rockland to

Boothbay Harbor	42
Belfast	22
Bucksport	33

Boothbay Harbor to

Kennebec River	11
Monhegan	15
Portland	36

Portland Ltd. Buoy "P" to

Biddeford	17
Portsmouth	54
Cape Cod Light	99
Cape Cod Canal (E. Entr.)	118
Pollock Rip Slue	141

Portsmouth (Whaleback) to

York River	7
Biddeford Pool	30
Newburyport Entr.	15
Gloucester – via Annisquam	28

Gloucester to

Boston	26
Scituate	26
Plymouth	43
Cape Cod Canal (E. Entr.)	52
Provincetown	45

Marblehead to

Portsmouth	43
Biddeford Pool	68
Portland	87
Boothbay Harbor	104
Rockland	133
Plymouth	38
Cape Cod Canal (E. Entr.)	47

Boston (Commonwealth Pier)

Marblehead	17
Isles of Shoals	52
Portsmouth	58
Portland	95
Kennebec River	107
Boothbay Harbor	116
Rockland	149
North Haven	148
Bangor	194
St. John, N.B.	286
Halifax, N.S.	380
Cohasset	14
Cape Cod Canal, E. Entr.	50
Provincetown	50
Vineyard Haven	77
New Bedford	81
Fall River	107
Newport	122
New London	140
New York	234

****Western Entr., Cape Cod Canal to**

East Entrance	8
Woods Hole	15
Quicks Hole	20
New Bedford	24
Newport	50
New London	83

Woods Hole to

Hyannis	19
Chatham	32
Cuttyhunk	14
Marion	11

Vineyard Haven to

Edgartown	9
Marblehead – around Cape	114
Canal – via Woods Hole	20
Newport	45
New London	77
New Haven	114
South Norwalk	140
City Island	153

***Each distance is by the shortest route that safe navigation permits between the two ports concerned.**

*******Western entr.***, The beginning of the "land cut" at Bourne Neck, 7.3 nautical miles up the channel from Cleveland Ledge Lt.**

Continued p. 200

Chesapeake Bay Entr. Ltd. Wh. By. "CH" – Mo(A)W, Rge. 6 mi., Racon (C), RWSRST, (36-56-08N/75-57-27W)

Cape Henry Lt., S. side of Entr. to Ches. Bay – Mo (U) W ev. 20 s., R. Sect. 154°-233°, Ht. 164', Rge. W. 17 mi., R. 15 mi., (36-55-35N/76-00-26W)

CHESAPEAKE BAY

Worton Pt. Lt., Fl. W. ev. 6 s., Ht. 93' Rge. 6 mi., (39-19-06N/76-11-11W)

Old Point Comfort Lt., N. side Entr. to Hampton Roads – Fl(2) R. ev. 12 s., W. Sect. 265°-038°, Ht. 54', Rge. W. 16 mi., R. 14 mi., (37-00-06N/76-18-23W)

York Spit Lt., N. side Entr. to York R. – On pile, Fl. W. ev. 6 s., Ht. 30', Rge. 7 mi., (37-12-35N/76-15-15W)

Stingray Pt. Lt., Ches. Ch. – Fl. W. ev. 4 s., Ht. 34', Rge. 7 mi., (37-33-41N/76-16-12W)

Windmill Pt. Lt., Ches. Ch. – On pile. Fl. W. ev. 6 s., 2 R. Sectors 293°-082° and 091.5°-113°, Ht. 34', Rge. W. 9 mi., R. 7 mi., (37-35-49N/76-14-10W)

Tangier Sound Lt., Ches. Ch. – Fl. W. ev. 6 s., R. Sect. 110°-192°, Ht. 45', Rge. W. 12 mi., R. 9 mi., (37-47-17N/75-58-24W)

Smith Pt. Lt., Ches. Ch. – Fl. W. ev. 10 s., Ht. 52', Rge. 15 mi., (37-52-48N/76-11-01W)

Point Lookout Lt., Ches. Ch. – Fl(2) W. ev. 5 s., Ht. 39', Rge. 8 mi., (38-01-30N/76-19-25W)

Holland Is. Bar Lt., Ches. Ch. – Fl. W. ev. 2.5 s., Ht. 37', Rge. 6 mi., (38-04-07N/76-05-45W)

Point No Point Lt., Ches. Ch. – Fl. W. ev. 6 s., Ht. 52', Rge. 9 mi., (38-07-41N/76-17-25W)

Hooper Is. Lt., Ches. Ch. – Fl. W. ev. 6 s., Ht. 63', Rge. 9 mi., (38-15-23N/76-14-59W)

Drum Pt. Lt.#4, Ches. Ch. – Fl. R. ev. 2.5 s., Ht. 17', Rge. 5 mi., (38-19-08N/76-25-15W)

Cove Pt. Lt., Ches. Ch. – Fl. W. ev. 10 s., Ht. 45', Rge. 12 mi., ltd. 24 hrs, (38-23-11N/76-22-54W)

Bloody Point Bar Warning Lt. – Fl. W. ev. 6 s., Ht. 22', Rge. 7 mi., (38-50-00N/76-23-35W)

Thomas Pt. Shoal Lt., Ches. Ch. – Fl. W. ev. 5 s., 2 R. Sectors 011°-051.5° and 096.5°-202°, Horn 1 bl. ev. 15 s., Ht. 43', Rge. W. 16 mi., R. 11 mi., (38-53-56N/76-26-09W)

Wm. P. Lane, Jr. Bridge West Ch. Fog Signal, on main ch. span – Horn 1 bl. ev. 15 s., 5 s. bl., Horn Points 017° & 197°, (38-59-36N/76-22-53W)

Wm. P. Lane, Jr. Bridge East Ch. Fog Signal, on main ch. span – Horn 1 bl. ev. 20 s., 2 s. bl., (38-59-18N/76-21-30W)

Baltimore Lt. – Fl. W. ev. 2.5 s., R. Sector 082°- 160°, Ht. 52', Rge. W. 7 mi., R. 5 mi., (39-03-33N/76-23-56W)

NORTH CAROLINA

Currituck Beach Lt. – Fl. W. ev. 20 s., Ht. 158', Rge. 18 mi., (36-22-37N/75-49-47W)

Bodie Is. Lt. – Fl(2) W. ev. 30 s., Ht. 156', Rge. 18 mi., (35-49-07N/75-33-48W)

Oregon Inlet Jetty Lt. – Fl. W. ev. 2.5 s., Ht. 28', Rge. 7 mi., (35-46-26N/75-31-30W)

Cape Hatteras Lt., – Fl. W. ev. 7.5 s., Ht. 192', Rge. 24 mi., (35-15-02N/75-31-44W)

Hatteras Inlet Lt. – Iso. W. ev. 6 s., Ht. 48', Rge. 10 mi., (35-11-52N/75-43-56W)

Ocracoke Lt., on W. part of island – F.W., Ht. 75', Rge. 15 mi., (35-06-32N/75-59-10W)

Cape Lookout Lt., on N. pt. of cape – Fl. W. ev. 15 s., Ht. 156', Rge. 14 mi., (34-37-22N/76-31-28W)

Beaufort Inlet Ch. Ltd. Wh. By. "BM" – Mo(A)W, Rge. 6 mi., RWSRST, (34-36-40N/76-41-12W)

New River Inlet Ltd. Wh. By. "NR" – Mo(A)W, Rge. 6 mi., RWSRST, (34-31-02N/77-19-33W)

For abbreviations see footnote p. 173

Distance Table in Nautical Miles

*Approximate

Continued from p. 198

Nantucket Entr. Bell NB to

Boston – around Cape	105
Boston – via Canal	94
Chatham	23
Edgartown	23
Hyannis	21
Woods Hole	30
Cape Cod Canal (W. Entr.)	45
Newport	71

New Bedford (State Pier) to

Woods Hole	14
Newport	38
New London	74
New York (Gov. Is.)	166

Newport to

Providence	21
Stonington	34
New London	48
New Haven	84
City Island	122

Block Island (FR Horn) to

Nantucket	79
Vineyard Haven	52
Cleveland Ledge Lt	50
New Bedford	44
Newport	22
Race Point Lt	21
New London	29

New London to

Greenport	25
New Haven	49
Bridgeport	60
City Island	86

Port Jefferson to

Larchmont	30
So. Norwalk	15
Milford	14
Old Saybrook	43
New London	53

City Island to

Governors Island	17
Execution Rocks	3

Execution Rocks to

Port Chester	8
Stamford	12
Oyster Bay Harbor	14
So. Norwalk	19
Bridgeport	29
Port Jefferson	30
Milford	37
New Haven	49
Conn. River	69
Mystic	84
Montauk Point	87

New York (Battery) to

Jones Inlet	34
Fire Island Inlet	47
Moriches Inlet	74
Shinnecock Inlet	88
Montauk Point	117
Keyport	22
Asbury Park	35
Manasquan	40
Little Egg Inlet	81
Atlantic City	97
Philadelphia	235
Chesapeake Lt. Stn	247
Cape Henry Lt.	262
Norfolk	288
Baltimore	418

Brielle-Manasquan to

E. Rockaway Inlet	32
Jones Inlet	35
Fire Island Inlet	45
Montauk Point	117
Barnegat Inlet	21
Atlantic City	51

Delaware Breakwater to

Reedy Pt. Entr. (C&D Canal)	51
Annapolis – via Canal	97
Norfolk	167
New York	150
New London	242
Providence	275
New Bedford	278
Boston (outside)	399
Portland (outside)	443

Old Point Comfort to

Baltimore	163
Philadelphia	240
New York	276
New London	363
Providence	392
New Bedford	397
Boston (outside)	512
Portland	553

Oak Is. Lt., on SE pt. of island – Fl(4) W. ev. 10 s., Ht. 169′, Rge. 24 mi., (33-53-34N/78-02-06W)
Cape Fear River Entr. Ltd. Wh. By. "CF" – Mo(A)W, Rge. 6 mi., Racon (C), RWSRST, (33-46-17N/78-03-02W)

SOUTH CAROLINA

Little River Inlet Ltd. Wh. By. "LR" – Mo(A)W, Rge. 5 mi., RWSRST, (33-49-49N/78-32-27W)
Little River Inlet North Jetty Lt. #2 – Fl. R. ev. 4 s., Ht. 24′, Rge. 5 mi., (33-50-31N/78-32-39W)
Winyah Bay Ltd. Wh. By. "WB" – Mo(A)W, Rge. 6 mi., RWSRST, (33-11-37N/79-05-11W)
Georgetown Lt., E. side Entr. to Winyah Bay – Fl(2) W. ev. 15 s., Ht. 85′, Rge. 15 mi., (33-13-21N/79-11-06W)
Charleston Entr. Ltd. By. "C" – Mo(A)W, Rge. 6 mi., Racon (K), RWSRST, (32-37-05N/79-35-30W)
Charleston Lt., S. side of Sullivans Is. – Fl(2) W. ev. 30 s., Ht. 163′, Rge. 20 mi., (32-45-29N/79-50-36W)

GEORGIA

Tybee Lt., NE end of Is. – F. W., Ht. 144′, Rge. 19 mi., ltd. 24 hrs., (32-01-20N/80-50-44W)
Tybee Lighted Buoy "T" – Mo(A)W, Rge. 6 mi., Racon (G), RWSRST, (31-57-52N/80-43-10W)
St. Simons Ltd. By. "STS" – Mo(A)W, Rge. 7 mi., RWSRST, (31-02-49N/81-14-25W)
St. Simons Lt., N. side Entr. to St. Simons Sd. – F. Fl. W. ev. 60 s., Ht. 104′, Rge. F. W. 18 mi., Fl. W. 23 mi., (31-08-03N/81-23-37W)

FLORIDA

Amelia Is. Lt., 2 mi. from N. end of Is. – Fl. W. ev. 10 s., R. Sect. 344°-360°, Ht. 107′, Rge. W. 23 mi., R. 19 mi., (30-40-23N/81-26-33W)
St. Johns Lt., on shore – Fl(4) W. ev. 20 s., Obscured 179°-354°, Ht. 83′, Rge. 19 mi., (30-23-10N/81-23-53W)
St. Johns Ltd. By. "STJ" – Mo(A)W, Rge. 6 mi., RWSRST, (30-23-35N/81-19-08W)
St. Augustine Lt., N. end of Anastasia Is. – F. Fl. W. ev. 30 s., Ht. 161′, Rge. F. W. 19 mi., Fl. W. 24 mi., (29-53-08N/81-17-19W)
Ponce De Leon Inlet Lt., S. side on inlet – Fl(6) W. ev. 30 s., Ht. 159′, (29-04-50N/80-55-41W)
Cape Canaveral Lt., on Cape – Fl(2) W. ev. 20 s., Ht. 137′, Rge. 24 mi., (28-27-37N/80-32-36W)
Sebastian Inlet N. Jetty Lt. – Fl. R. ev. 4 s., Ht. 27′, (27-51-41N/80-26-51W)
Jupiter Inlet Lt., N. side of inlet – Fl(2) W. ev. 30 s., Obscured 231°-234°, Ht. 146′, Rge. 25 mi., (26-56-55N/80-04-55W)
Hillsboro Inlet Entr. Lt., N. side of inlet – Fl. (2) W. ev. 20 s., Obscured 114°-119°, Ht. 136′, Rge. 28 mi., (26-15-33N/80-04-51W)
Port Everglades Ltd. By. "PE" - Mo(A)W, Rge. 7 mi., Racon (T), RWSRST, (26-05-30N/80-04-46W)
Miami Ltd. By. "M" – E. end of Miami Beach, Mo(A)W, Rge. 7 mi., Racon (M), RWSRST, (25-46-06N/80-05-00W)
Fowey Rocks Lt., Hawk Ch. – Fl. W. ev. 10 s., Ht. 110′, Rge. 7 mi., (25-35-26N/80-05-48W)
Carysfort Reef Lt., outer line of reefs – Fl(3) W. ev. 60 s., Ht. 40′, Rge. 13 mi., (25-13-37N/80-12-33W)
Alligator Reef Lt., – Fl(4) W. ev. 60 s., Ht. 16′, Rge. 7 mi., (24-51-05N/80-37-04W)

For abbreviations see footnote p. 173

Sombrero Key Lt., outer line of reefs – Fl(5) W. ev. 60 s., Ht. 19′, Rge.7 mi. (24-37-40N/81-06-31W)

American Shoal Lt. – Fl(4) W. ev. 60 s., Ht. 19′, Rge. 7 mi., (24-31-32N/81-31-03W)

Key West Ltd. Wh. By. "KW" – Mo (A) W, Rge. 7, RWSRST, (24-27-26N/81-48-00W)

Sand Key Lt., Fl(2) W. ev. 15 s., Ht. 40′, Rge. 13, (24-27-21N/81-52-38W)

BERMUDA – APPROACH LIGHTS FROM SEAWARD

North Rock Beacon – Fl(4)W. ev. 20 s. yellow, Ht. 70′, Rge. 12 mi., RaRef, (32-28.5N/64-46.1W)

North East Breaker Beacon – Fl. W. ev. 2.5 s., Ht. 45′, Rge. 12 mi., RaRef, (Red tower on red tripod base reading "Northeast," (32-28.7N/64-41.0W)

Kitchen Shoal Beacon – Fl(3)W. ev. 15 s., Ht. 45′, Rge. 12 mi., RaRef, RWS, Red "Kitchen" on White background, (32-26.1N/64-37.6W)

Eastern Blue Cut Beacon – Fl. W. Mo(U) ev. 10 s., Ht. 60′, Rge. 12 mi., RaRef, B&W Tower "Eastern Blue Cut" on white band, (32-23.9N/64-52.6W)

Chub Heads – Q. Fl(9) W. ev. 15 s., Ht. 60′, Rge. 12 mi., RaRef, Yellow and Black Horizontal Stripe Tower with "Chub Heads" in White on Black Central band, (32-17.2N/64-58.9W)

Mills Breaker By. – Q. Fl(3)W. ev. 5 s., Black "Mills" on yellow background, (32-23.9N/64-36.9W)

Spit By. – Q. Fl(3) W. ev. 10 s., Black "Spit" on yellow, (32-22.7N/64-38.5W)

Sea By. –Mo(A)W ev. 6 s., RWS, Red "SB" in white on side, (32-22.9N/64-37.1W)

St. David's Is. Lighthouse – F. R. and G. Sectors below Fl(2) W. ev. 20 s., Ht. 212′, Rge. W. 15 mi., R. and G. 20 mi., (32-21.8N/64-39.1W) Your bearing from seaward of G. Sector is 221°-276° True; remaining Sector is R. and partially obscured by land 044°-135° True.

Kindley Field Aero Beacon – Alt. W and G.; 1 White, 1 Green (rotating Aero Beacon), Ht. 140′, Rge. 15 mi., (32-21.95N/64-40.55W)

Gibbs Hill Lighthouse – Fl. W. ev. 10 s., Ht. 354′, Rge. 26 mi., (32-15.2N/64-50.1W)

Erica M. Szuplat

☆ **Note:** The information in this volume has been compiled from U. S. Government sources and others, and carefully checked. The Publishers cannot assume any liability for errors, omissions, or changes.

Foregoing information checked to date, September 2020. See page 2 for free supplement in June 2021.

The Tide Cycle Simplified: The Rule of Twelfths

Since the average interval between high and low is just over six hours, we can divide the cycle into six segments of one hour each. On average the tide rises or falls approximately according to the fractions at right:

1st hour - 1/12
2nd hour - 2/12
3rd hour - 3/12
4th hour - 3/12
5th hour - 2/12
6th hour - 1/12

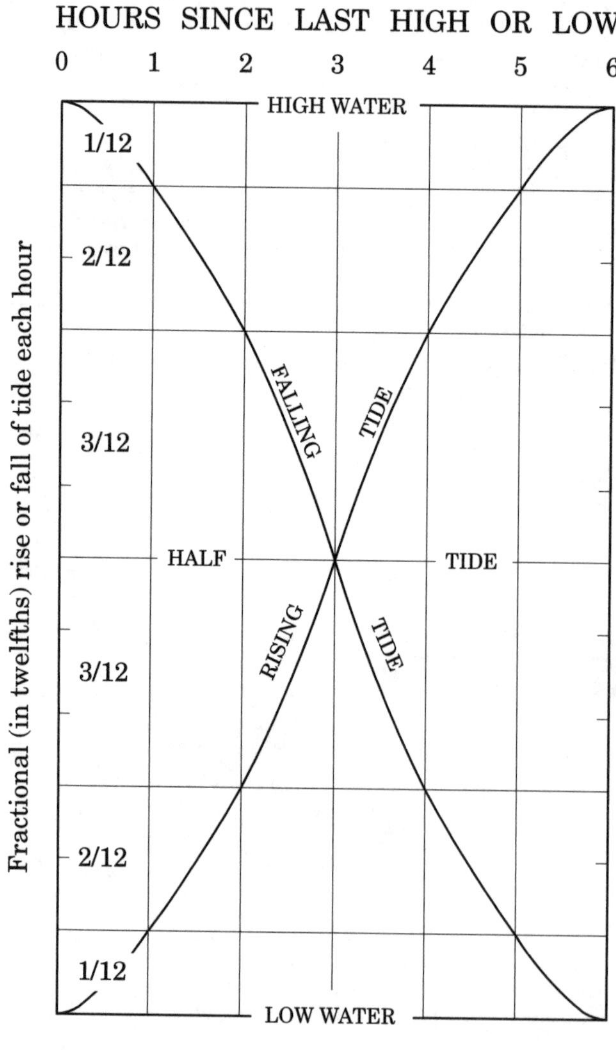

Mean tidal heights by the hour at five ports

Boston	Newport	New York	Charleston	Savannah
9.6	3.5	4.6	5.2	6.9
8.8	3.2	4.2	4.8	6.3
7.2	2.6	3.4	3.9	5.2
4.8	1.8	2.3	2.6	3.5
2.4	0.9	1.2	1.3	1.7
0.8	0.3	0.4	0.4	0.6
0.0	0.0	0.0	0.0	0.0

Tidal Heights and Depths

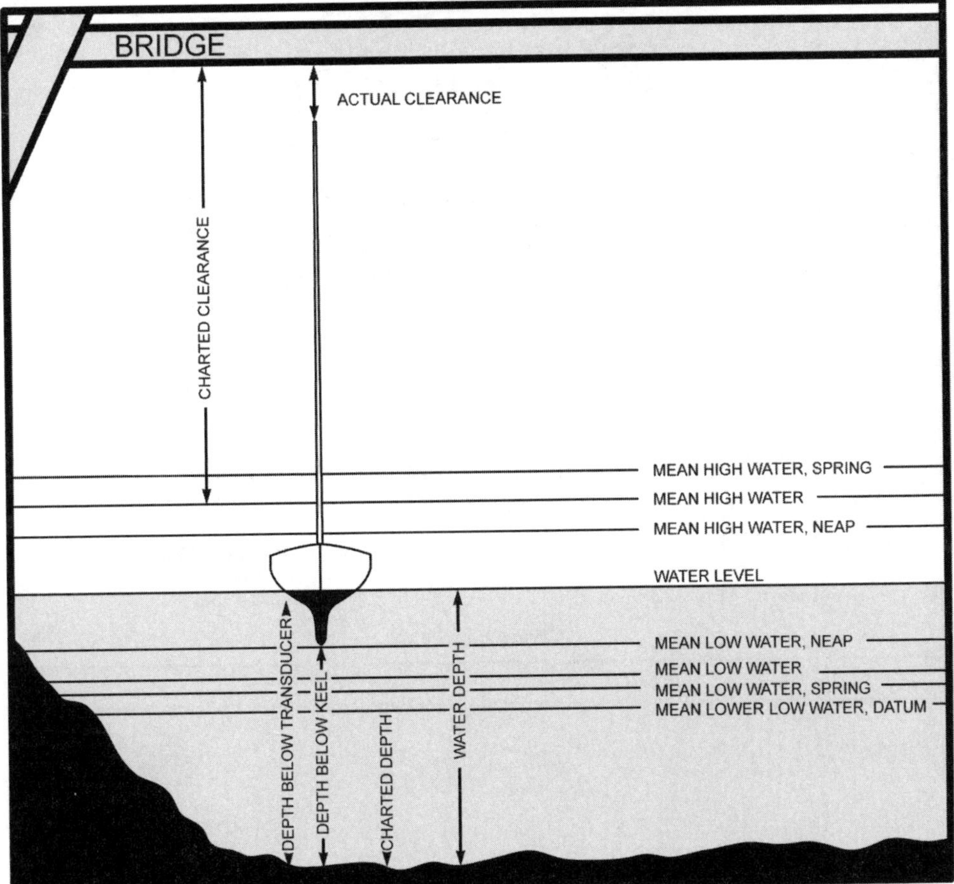

Mean High Water, Spring - the mean of high water heights of spring tides

Mean High Water - the mean of all high water heights; the charted clearance of bridges is measured from this height

Mean High Water, Neap - the mean of high water heights of neap tides

Mean Low Water, Neap - the mean of low water heights of neap tides

Mean Low Water - the mean of all low water heights

Mean Low Water, Spring - the mean of low water heights of spring tides

Mean Lower Low Water Datum - the mean of lower low water heights; charted depths originate from this reference height or datum

---

Spring Tides - tides of increased range, occurring twice a month, around the times of the new and full moons

Neap Tides - tides of decreased range, occurring twice a month, around the times of the half moons

Diurnal Inequality - the difference in height of the two daily low waters or the two daily high waters, a result of the moon's (and to a lesser extent the sun's) changing declination above and below the Equator

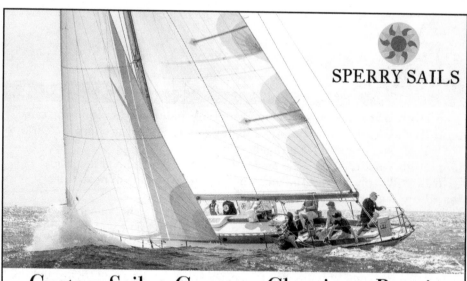

The Secret Life Of Black Sea Bass

by Nick King

One day in the winter of 2020, a lobsterman in Nova Scotia hauled up one of his pots and in it spied a spiny black fish the likes of which he had never seen. Stumped, he took a photo and sent it down to his cousin in Rhode Island, asking "What is it?" The reply came quickly: "Black sea bass."

Don't blame the Old Salt for not knowing. Black sea bass just don't hang around Nova Scotia. Or didn't. Nor do they hang around the waters off Boston or Southern Maine. Or didn't.

But things are changing. Black sea bass, traditionally concentrated in the mid-Atlantic and prized for both abundance and taste, have moved northward into New England, drawn by the warming waters of climate change. Once primarily schooled off New Jersey, Virginia, and North Carolina, the fish in recent years have been migrating in huge numbers into Buzzards Bay, Vineyard Sound, Nantucket Sound, and Cape Cod Bay. And lately they are occasionally wandering even further north to Boston Harbor, Cape Ann, and even Southern Maine.

"Fifty degrees is the magic temperature," says Robert Glenn, chief marine fisheries biologist for the Massachusetts Division of Marine Fisheries. "As the water warms above fifty, the sea bass come inshore. If it's below fifty, they move out."

This temperature-driven habitat change is sending ripples through the commercial and recreational fishing industries. It has also caught the attention of marine biologists like Glenn, who are intrigued by the unusual biology and peculiar sex life of the fish. Black sea bass, you see, are protogynous hermaphrodites, which means that each and every one is born into the aquatic world as female, only to transition upon maturity into male. What happens in between to procreate the species is a wonder to behold.

Black sea bass are protected from overfishing by quotas that, in a good year, limit the commercial catch to 4 million pounds worth some $12 million. But the restrictions are a source of dockside debate because they don't reflect the new migratory patterns bringing the fish into warming New England waters. The competition over the harvest is understandable: The fish tastes good. Most of the sea bass caught commercially in the New England region are sold at an average $3.49 a pound to the wholesale Fulton Fish Market in New York City, from there finding their way onto the menus of restaurants from North Carolina to Montreal. Lucky is the shopper who can find a fillet or two at the local market, even at $24.99 a pound, and then breads, sautés, and serves them along with fresh fiddleheads or spring asparagus.

But the biggest swirl caused by the northward sea bass migration is the feeding frenzy it has spawned among recreational fishermen in New England. Angling for the fish from small boats while armed with hook, line, and sinker plus some squid or other fresh bait has become so popular that the weight of the recreational catch actually equaled the commercial catch a few years ago. Such is the popularity that in the pre-dawn hours in late May, an early-bird angler can find himself 20th in line to launch his boat at the ramp in Wareham, MA. It's worth the wait—the sea bass bounty teeming off the rocky bottoms around Cleveland Ledge Light in Buzzards Bay can be like fish in a barrel. But anglers beware: the size and possession limits vary widely by state, with minimums ranging from 12.5–15 inches and daily possession from two fish to 15. Know your rules and bring your ruler.

Unbeknown to most of these hunter gatherers is what lies beneath when it comes to the mating habits of the primitive looking fish. Black sea bass leave their southern offshore wintering grounds and arrive in inshore Cape Cod waters in May, congregating in dense schools as they feed in advance of the late summer spawn. The fish begin their transition from female to male when they are between two and five years old. By the time spawning season hits, the older bigger males are dominant and look the part, glistening black with a bright blue "nuchal" hump on their head.

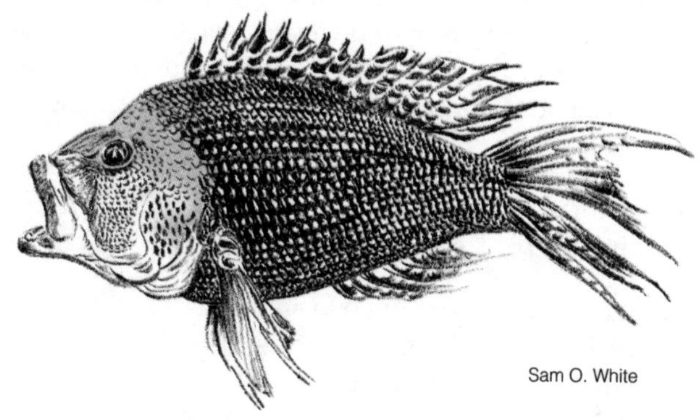

Sam O. White

Dressed for success, these aggressive males drive away any competing males while gathering about them an eager and attentive bevy of younger, smaller, dull brown females. Sometimes the mating schools are so dense that they trigger a curious phenomenon that biologist Glenn calls "sneaker" behavior. In the frenzy of spawning, some transitioning females have already developed gonads but still look decidedly female, enabling them to join the revelry undetected and avail themselves, as males, of the spawning ritual.

None of this hanky-panky was going on in Buzzards Bay fifty years ago when Dave Borden, the former deputy chief of marine fisheries for the State of Rhode Island, was a teenager growing up on the bay's north shore. As a kid he never saw a single black sea bass but today, taking advantage of the climate-driven abundance, he fishes for them commercially. He's clearly jealous that when today's kids go fishing, they can haul in as many black sea bass as they have hooks on their lines.

As for the black sea bass caught by the lobsterman way up north in the Nova Scotia currents last year, let's just call it a fluke.

Nick King, a retired reporter and editor for The Boston Globe, can be found scouring Buzzards Bay and Vineyard Sound for stripers, bluefish, bonito, false albacore and black sea bass.

Using GPS to Adjust Your Compass

Nothing can equal the expert services of a professional Compass Adjuster, but if these services are not available, the information below can help you adjust a compass yourself.

As you used the GPS to create a Deviation Table (see p. 213), you can also use it to correct your steering compass to eliminate deviation.

Built-in Correctors - Most modern compasses are fitted with a magnetic corrector system attached inside the bottom of the compass or the binnacle cylinder. Such "B.I.C.'s" (Built-in Correctors) are easy to use and are capable of removing virtually all the deviations of a well-located compass. B.I.C.'s consist of two horizontal shafts, slotted at each end, one running Athwartship (port and starboard) and one running Fore and Aft. On each shaft are magnets. When these magnets are horizontal, they are in a neutral position. When a shaft is rotated to any angle, the magnets create correction. The usual B.I.C. can remove up to about 15° of deviation. The shaft which runs Athwartship corrects on North and South headings, and has zero effect on East and West. The Fore and Aft shaft corrects on East and West headings, and has zero effect on North and South.

Getting Started - Pick a quiet day and a swinging area with calm conditions. Have someone with a steady hand at the helm and the engine ticking over enough so there is good steering control. It is important to hold a steady heading for at least 30-45 seconds. You are looking at your GPS, and you are equipped with a non-magnetic screwdriver.

Adjusting your compass:

1. As steadily as possible steer within +/- 5° of a cardinal heading, let's say North. Slowly and with a non-magnetic screwdriver rotate the Athwartship B.I.C. until the compass reads the same as the GPS, creating zero error on North.
2. Turn 90° right to the next cardinal heading, let's say East. Turn the Fore/Aft B.I.C. to remove all of the existing error so the compass matches your GPS on East.
3. Turn 90° right to South. Compare your compass to the GPS. If the error is zero, move to step #4. If you have error, you will split the difference: if you have two (2) degrees of error, turn the Athwartship B.I.C. so you only have one (1) degree of error.
4. Turn 90° right to West. Compare your compass to the GPS. If the error is zero, move to step #5. If you have error, you will split the difference: if you have two (2) degrees of error, turn the Fore/Aft B.I.C. so you only have one (1) degree of error.
5. Return to North and confirm that you either have zero error, or if you had error on South and you split the difference to create an error of 1°, you have the same 1° of error on North.
6. Return to East and confirm that you either have zero error, or if you had error on West and you split the difference to create an error of 1°, you have the same 1° of error on East.

Check for deviation all around - Compare the steering compass to your GPS at least every 45° on all the cardinal (N, E, S, W) and intercardinal (NE, SE, SW, NW) points. If the steering compass reads too little (lower number of degrees), the deviation is Easterly on that heading, and the number of degrees must be subtracted when steering that magnetic course. If the steering compass reads too much (higher number of degrees), the deviation is Westerly on that heading, and the number of degrees must be added when steering that magnetic course.

Checking for Misalignment - After checking 8 headings, add up the total of Easterly deviations, subtract the total of Westerly, and divide by 8. The result tells you the amount by which your compass is misaligned. Let's say it is 1° Easterly. This means your lubbers line is off to port 1°. If you rotate the compass 1° clockwise, all your Easterly deviations will be reduced by 1°, your Westerly deviations will be increased by 1°, and your 0 deviations will become 1° Westerly. You will now find the total of your Easterly deviations is the very same as your Westerly total. You have eliminated misalignment error. Now you can trust your compass!

2021 Story Contest Winner

Malabar III—A Boat I Will Never Forget

by Kim Metz Allsup

One frigid evening in 1962, when I was 11 years old, I fed bits of construction scrap into the small, cast iron cook stove in the galley while my dad rebuilt the bunk system of our family sailboat. The only boat on the Kickemuit River, she sat at the dock that whole winter undergoing internal surgery. She would emerge that spring with new bunks and new paint, ready to get back to cruising and racing.

Historians know the *Malabar III* as a 42 foot wooden schooner, built in 1922, with an overall length of 41 feet, 6 inches. Designed by John G. Alden, she was one of the ten boats to carry the Malabar name. But, to me, she was a venue for sleepovers and adventures, and a central element of our family life.

Malabar III before the gaff rig was changed to a Marconi rig in the 1960s

Sometimes my parents cruised to Maine and came back with tales of being stuck in the mud when the tide went out. We knew which date they would return, but, it being decades before cell phones, not the hour of arrival. On that day, every hour or two, my brothers and I would walk a few blocks to a view of the Bay, keeping a lookout for the *Malabar* sailing majestically under the Mount Hope Bridge.

I loved watching my dad skipper *Malabar* into first place at the start of a race. He would commandeer one of us kids to hold the stopwatch and shout out the time for each tack. And then, like clockwork, the bang of the starting gun was followed instantly by our bow crossing the imaginary line between the starting marks. Often though, we lost our lead as quickly as we claimed it. A windless race on Narragansett Bay meant we would, again, watch sleek fiberglass sloops glide by while we sat dead in the water. My dad bought enormous sails, spinnakers, and gollywobblers to try to add the sail power required to move such a ponderous hulk in a barely perceptible breeze. They didn't help much. I felt a bit disloyal as I admired the elegance of the newer, lighter yachts.

It was my task to pull down forward sails and quickly stuff them into canvas bags and drop them down the forward hatch, an easy job in a light wind. But, one day, racing off Newport toward Cuttyhunk with a stiff wind, my preteen arms and legs were too short and my strength too inadequate to wrestle a big sail that seemed to have a life of its own. It was then that my dad took my sail wrangling job and gave me the wheel. When he returned to the cockpit, he didn't take it back.

On that day, *Malabar III* was in her glory. Speeding along at hull speed on a broad reach, we churned past the lightweight boats which had shortened sail. We flew into Cuttyhunk harbor among the leading boats.

Malabar III taught me something that day. That newer is not always better. That some of us are made for calm waters on windless days, and others rise to show their mettle in churning water and howling wind. And that when our crew job is overwhelming, we may be surprised to discover that we can be useful by simply steering a steady course.

Story Contest 2022: Problem Solving At Sea

There's a family tale of an evening sail in which Bob White, former-publisher of Eldridge, brought a bit of ingenuity to the challenge of garnishing his cocktail when there were no lemons to be found. Tell us about a time when you found an innovative solution to a perplexing challenge aboard. Including an image is most welcome

Deadline: 11:59 PM ET, August 7, 2021

Length: 600 words, give or take a few

How to submit: Email (preferred) or mail submissions to the address on the front cover. Submitted materials will not be returned.

The winning entry will be published in the 2022 edition and the author will receive a copy of the book, an Eldridge tote bag and $200.

Submissions must be original, previously unpublished works and grant the publisher non-exclusive rights to publish winning entries in the book and on our website.

Erica M. Szuplat

Currituck Beach Lighthouse

36°22'37"N x 75°49'47"W

White light flashes once every 20 seconds, range: 18 miles.

The windswept, shifting shoreline of North Carolina's coast has daunted sailors for centuries. Known as the "Graveyard of the Atlantic," the ocean surrounding these barrier islands has claimed over 5,000 ships since the early 1500s. It wasn't until the late 1700s and early 1800s that the state's now iconic lighthouses were erected to guide ships through the remote and hazardous waters. By 1859, the Ocracoke, Cape Hatteras, Bodie Island and Cape Lookout lighthouses were complete, lighting all but 80 miles of the Outer Banks between Nags Head and Cape Henry. Plans for Currituck Beach Lighthouse existed as early as 1853, but the Civil War delayed construction for twenty years. On December 1st, 1875, the Outer Banks' final lighthouse was illuminated—a beacon of caution for sailors navigating the Virginia-North Carolina border. To this day, its original first-order Fresnel lens casts light from dusk to dawn.

Towering at 162 feet, Currituck Beach Lighthouse is the third tallest lighthouse in North Carolina, surpassed only by those at Cape Lookout and Cape Hatteras. It is located in the town of Corolla, a popular vacation destination for beachgoers and nature enthusiasts. In contrast with the region's green maritime forest, the one million bricks that make up the lighthouse are a natural and vibrant red. These unpainted bricks make Currituck Beach Lighthouse visually unique among the other Outer Banks beacons, which boast stark black and white patterns.

Visitors can climb the lighthouse's 220 steps and enjoy sweeping views of the Atlantic Ocean and Currituck Sound.

Liah McPherson is a photographer and marine biologist from Kitty Hawk, North Carolina. Her work can be seen at www.liahmcpherson.com.

The Revolutionary Spherical Compass
Wilfrid O. White's Greatest Invention

Before the spherical compass, up until about 1930, all compasses were "flattops," having a flat glass on top. Although universally accepted, this design had severe limitations: the compass card was hard to read because there was no magnification, and the liquid inside swirled when the compass moved, making the card less steady.

A former publisher of ELDRIDGE, Wilfrid O. White (1878-1955), pioneered and patented in 1930 the most significant improvement in compass design since liquid was employed to steady the card. He experimented with a glass dome instead of flat glass, and found two huge advantages: with compass oil filling the compass, the dome acted as a magnifying lens for the compass card, making it far easier to read. Second, the oil inside was no longer turbulent when the compass turned or was jostled because the sphere of liquid inside (assuming the lower bowl was a hemisphere, too) remained undisturbed when the outer compass body moved. Now the compass card was far steadier, however active the motion of the boat.

Introduced at the New York Boat Show in 1931, and first advertised in ELDRIDGE in 1932, Wilfrid White's spherical compass was something of a sensation. His company, Kelvin & Wilfrid O. White Company, began production and sales increased rapidly, especially among recreational boaters. The U.S. Navy and Merchant Marine, both deeply committed to tradition, were slower to adopt the new design, but gradually accepted the spherical compass. It was not long before all compass manufacturers followed suit. Today, the flattop compass is most often found in antique shops or museums, and the spherical compass is found on virtually all pleasure craft around the world.

Using GPS to Create a Deviation Table

Most compasses are subject to onboard magnetic influences, called deviation. You can make your compass more trustworthy by using your GPS to create a deviation table.

Choose a day when the wind is light and sea as calm as possible. Find a large open area with little or no current and a minimum of boat traffic. Bring aboard an assistant. In a notebook create two columns: in pencil, label the left column GPS and the right column COMPASS. Down the right column, number each successive line using intervals of 15° [24 lines] up to 360°. You can concentrate on noting the four Cardinal and four Inter Cardinal headings (N, NE, E, SE, S, SW, W, NW) and safely interpolate and fill in the missing numbers for every 15°. Note that the Default setting on a GPS display is TRUE. For this exercise, make sure that your GPS is displaying MAGNETIC- Course Over Ground (COG) heading. This may require going into the GPS setup to insure that the COG is displaying a MAGNETIC heading.

Choose a speed which provides responsive steering and which will make any current or leeway a negligible factor. Proceed on any of the numbered courses for at least 30 seconds, giving the GPS time to report a consistent direction. Once you have held a steady course long enough to get a repeated reading, record it in the left column. Proceed to the next heading. Completing the circle results in a deviation table for your steering compass. Now, erase the penciled column headings and relabel the GPS column TO GO, and the COMPASS column STEER. Example: TO GO 094°, STEER 090°.

A deviation table admittedly falls far short of the ideal of a compensated compass; however, such a table will allow you to use your compass with a measure of confidence before an adjuster comes aboard. And that is much better than trying to steer by your GPS.

IALA BUOYAGE SYSTEM

Lateral Aids marking the sides of channels seen when entering from Seaward

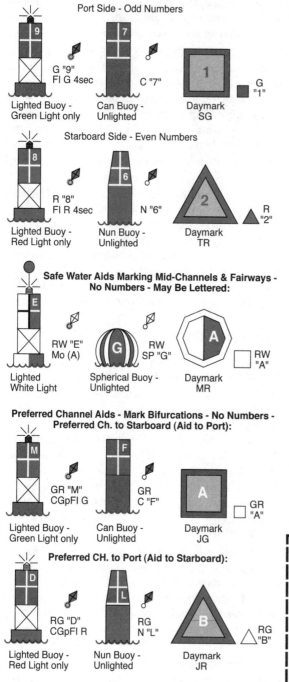

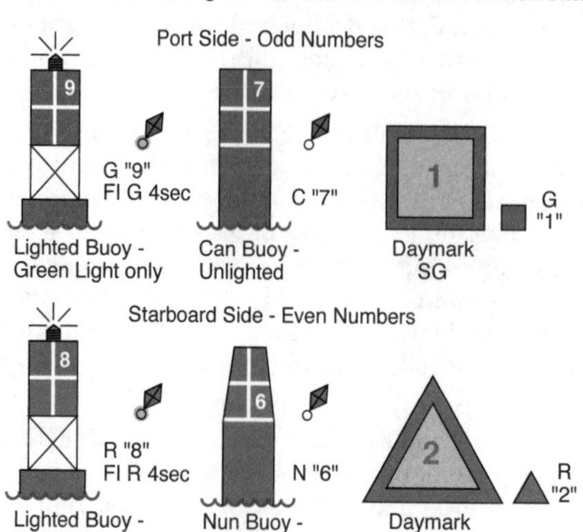

Port- hand aids are Green, some with Flashing Green Lights.
Daymarks:
1st letter "S" = Square
2nd letter "G" = color Green

Starboard-hand aids are Red, some with Flashing Red Lights.
Daymarks:
1st letter "T" = Triangle
2nd letter "R"= color Red

Safe Water Aids Marking Mid-Channels & Fairways - No Numbers - May Be Lettered:

E

RW "E"
Mo (A)

G

RW
SP "G"

A

RW
"A"

Lighted
White Light

Spherical Buoy -
Unlighted

Daymark
MR

Red and White replaces vertical stripes. Buoys are spherical; or have a Red spherical topmark.
Flashing White Light only: Mo (A).
Daymarks:
1st letter "M" = Octagon
2nd letter "R" = color Red

Preferred Channel Aids - Mark Bifurcations - No Numbers - Preferred Ch. to Starboard (Aid to Port):

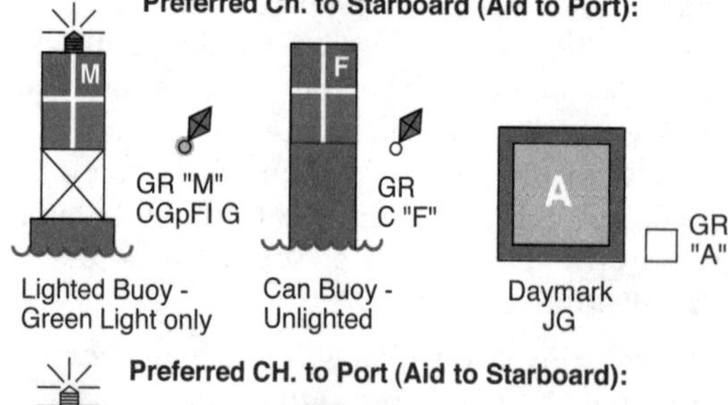

Flashing Light (Red or Green) is Composite Gp. Fl. (2 + 1).
Daymarks: 1st letter "J" = Square or Triangle 2nd letter "R" or "G" is color of top band

Preferred CH. to Port (Aid to Starboard):

D

L

B

RG "D"
CGpFl R

RG
N "L"

RG
"B"

Lighted Buoy -
Red Light only

Nun Buoy -
Unlighted

Daymark
JR

Note: ISOLATED DANGER BUOYS, Black and Red with two Black spherical topmarks - no numbers, may be lettered (if lighted, white light only, Fl (2) 5s). Stay Clear. SPECIAL AIDS BUOYS will be all YELLOW (if lighted, with yellow light only, Fixed Flashing): Anchorage Areas, Fish Net Areas, Spoil Grounds, Military Exercise Zones, Dredging Buoys (where conventional markers would be confusing), Ocean Data Systems, some Traffic Separations Zone Mid-Channel Buoys.

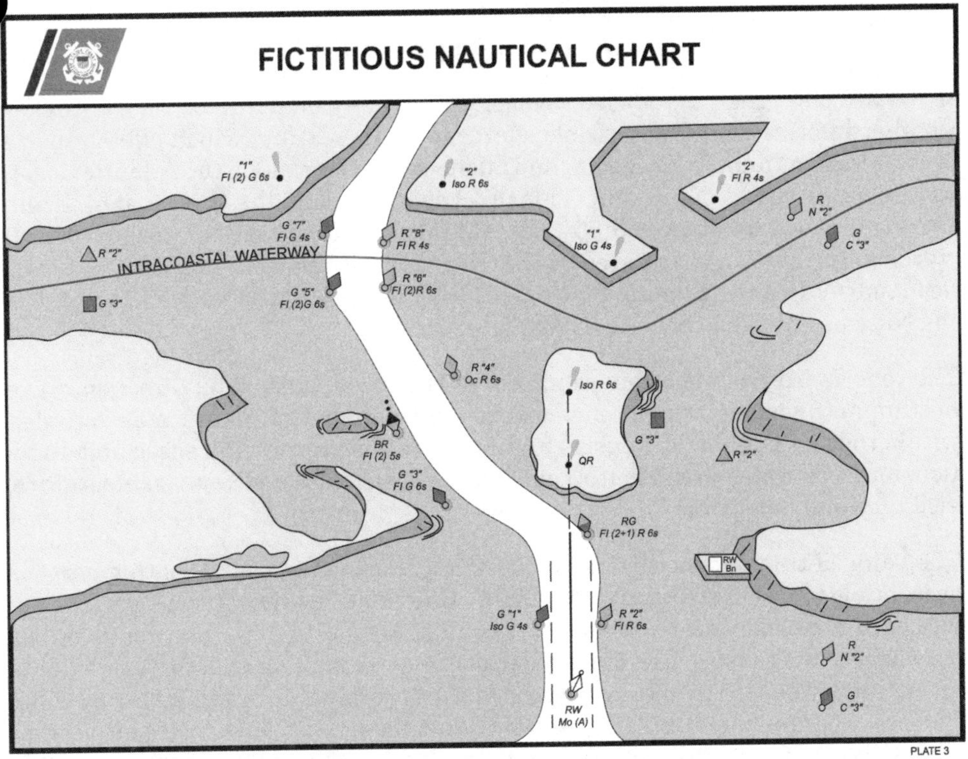
FICTITIOUS NAUTICAL CHART
"1" Fl (2) G 6s
"2" Iso R 6s
"2" Fl R 4s
R N "2"
G C "3"
G "7" Fl G 4s
R "8" Fl R 4s
R "2"
INTRACOASTAL WATERWAY
"1" Iso G 4s
G "5" Fl (2)G 6s
R "6" Fl (2)R 6s
G "3"
R "4" Oc R 6s
Iso R 6s
BR Fl (2) 5s
QR
G "3"
R "2"
G "3" Fl G 6s
RG Fl (2+1) R 6s
RW Bn
G "1" Iso G 4s
R "2" Fl R 6s
R N "2"
G C "3"
RW Mo (A)
PLATE 3

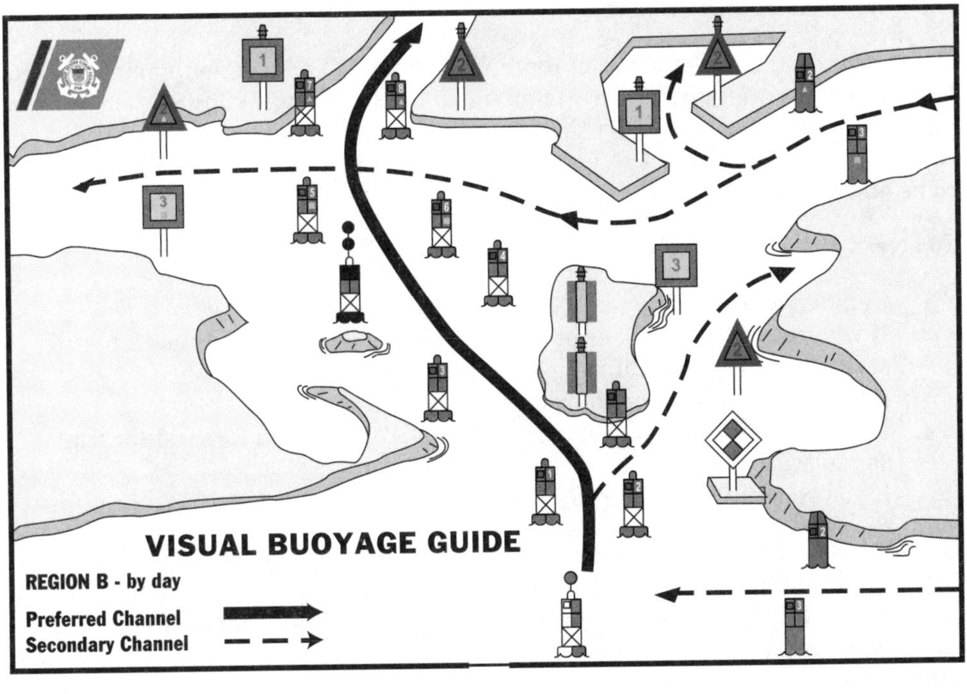
VISUAL BUOYAGE GUIDE
REGION B - by day
Preferred Channel
Secondary Channel

DIAL-A-BUOY Service

Sea-State & Weather Conditions By Telephone

If you are planning a coastwise voyage, you can rely on a number of sources for weather information. One possible source is **Dial-A-Buoy**, which offers reports of conditions at numerous coastal and offshore locations along the Atlantic Coast, as well as the coasts of the Gulf of Mexico, the Pacific, and the Great Lakes. In all, there are over 100 buoy and 50 Coastal-Marine Automated Network (C-MAN) stations. The system is operated by the National Data Buoy Center (NDBC), with headquarters at the Stennis Space Center in Mississippi. The NDBC is part of the National Weather Service (NWS).

The reports from offshore buoys include wind speed, gusts, and direction, wave heights and periods, water temperature, and barometric pressure as recorded within the last hour or so. Reports from land stations cover wind speed and direction, temperature, and pressure; some land stations also add water temperature, visibility, and dew point.

The value of this information is apparent. Say someone in your boating party is susceptible to seasickness, and the Dial-A-Buoy report says wave heights are six feet with a period (interval) of eight seconds. Maybe that person would rather stay ashore and experience the gentler motion of a rocking chair. (Wave heights of six feet with a period of twenty seconds, on the other hand, might be tolerable.) Surfers, too, can benefit greatly from wave height reports. Likewise, since actual conditions frequently differ dramatically from forecasts, someone sailing offshore might be interested to know that a Data Buoy ahead is reporting squalls, giving time to shorten sail. And bathers and fishermen might gain from hearing the water temperature reports.

On the next page, we give the station or buoy identifier, location name, and lat/long in degrees and hundredths, as provided by the NWS. To find station or buoy locations and identifiers using the Internet, visit www.ndbc.noaa.gov. To find locations by telephone, you can enter a latitude and longitude to receive the locations and identifiers of the closest stations.

<u>To access Dial-A-Buoy</u> using any touch-tone or cell phone, here are the steps:

1. Call 888-701-8992.
2. If you know the identifier of the station or buoy, press 1. Press 2 to get station locations by entering an approximate lat/long.
3. Enter the five-digit (or character) station identifier.
4. If, after hearing the latest report, you wish to hear a forecast for that same location, press 1.
5. If you want to hear the report for another station, press 2.

NOTE: In some cases a buoy may become temporarily unavailable. You should try again later to see if it has come back online. Please be aware that stations that may be adrift and not at the stated location are not reported via the telephone feature. This information is only available on the website, www.ndbc.noaa.gov/dial.shtml.

DIAL-A-BUOY and C-MAN Station Locations

Station ID	Location Name	Latitude	Longitude
44027	JONESPORT, ME	44.28N	67.30W
MDRM1	MT DESERT ROCK, ME	43.97N	68.13W
44007	PORTLAND, ME	43.53N	70.14W
*44005	GULF OF MAINE	43.20N	69.13W
IOSN3	ISLE OF SHOALS, NH	42.97N	70.62W
44013	BOSTON, MA	42.35N	70.65W
44018	CAPE COD, MA	42.21N	70.14W
BUZM3	BUZZARDS BAY, MA	41.40N	71.03W
44011	GEORGES BANK, MA	41.07N	66.59W
44017	MONTAUK POINT, NY	40.69N	72.05W
44008	NANTUCKET, MA	40.50N	69.25W
44065	NEW YORK HARBOR ENT., NY	40.37N	73.70W
44025	LONG ISLAND, NY	40.25N	73.16W
TPLM2	THOMAS POINT, MD	38.90N	76.44W
44066	TEXAS TOWER #4, NJ	39.62N	72.64W
44009	DELAWARE BAY, NJ	38.46N	74.70W
44099	CAPE HENRY, VA	36.91N	75.72W
41025	DIAMOND SHOALS	35.01N	75.36W
44014	VIRGINIA BEACH, VA	36.61N	74.84W
DUKN7	DUCK PIER, NC	36.18N	75.75W
CLKN7	CAPE LOOKOUT, NC	34.62N	76.53W
41001	E. HATTERAS, NC	34.72N	72.32W
41013	FRYING PAN SHOAL, NC	33.44N	77.76W
41004	EDISTO, SC	32.50N	79.10W
41002	S. HATTERAS, SC	31.99N	74.96W
41008	GRAYS REEF, GA	31.40N	80.87W
SAUF1	ST AUGUSTINE, FL	29.86N	81.27W
41010	CANAVERAL EAST, FL	28.88N	78.49W
41009	CANAVERAL, FL	28.51N	80.19W
LKWF1	LAKE WORTH, FL	26.61N	80.03W
FWYF1	FOWEY ROCK, FL	25.59N	80.10W
LONF1	LONG KEY, FL	24.84N	80.86W
SMKF1	SOMBRERO KEY, FL	24.63N	81.11W
SANF1	SAND KEY, FL	24.46N	81.88W

Most stations have added the ability to access information via RSS feed using your web browser. For information regarding how to use this feature please go to: www.ndbc.noaa.gov/rss_access.shtml

* Pending service

The International Code of Signals

The Code comprises 40 flags: 1 Code Flag; 26 letters; 10 numerals; 3 repeaters. With this Code it is possible to converse freely at sea with ships of different countries.

Single Flag Signals

A :: I have a diver down; keep well clear at slow speed.
B :: I am taking in, or discharging, or carrying dangerous goods.
C :: Yes
D :: Keep clear of me; I am maneuvering with difficulty.
E :: I am altering my course to starboard.
F :: I am disabled; communicate with me.
G :: I require a pilot. (When made by fishing vessels when operating in close proximity on the fishing grounds it means; "I am hauling nets.")
H :: I have a pilot on board.
I :: I am altering my course to port.
J :: I am on fire and have dangerous cargo on board; keep well clear of me.
K :: I wish to communicate with you.
L :: You should stop your vessel instantly.
M :: My vessel is stopped and making no way through water.
N :: No
O :: Man overboard.
P :: *In harbor*; All persons should report on board as the vessel is about to proceed to sea.
At sea; It may be used by fishing vessels to mean "My nets have come fast upon an obstruction."
Q :: My vessel is healthy and I request free pratique.
R :: *nothing currently assigned*
S :: My engines are going astern.
T :: Keep clear of me; I am engaged in pair trawling.
U :: You are running into danger.
V :: I require assistance.
W :: I require medical assistance.
X :: Stop carrying out your intentions and watch for my signals.
Y :: I am dragging my anchor.
Z :: I require a tug. (When made by fishing vessels operating in close proximity on the fishing grounds it means : "I am shooting nets.")

Flags Showing "Diver Down"

There are two flags that may be flown to indicate diving operations, and each has a distinct meaning.

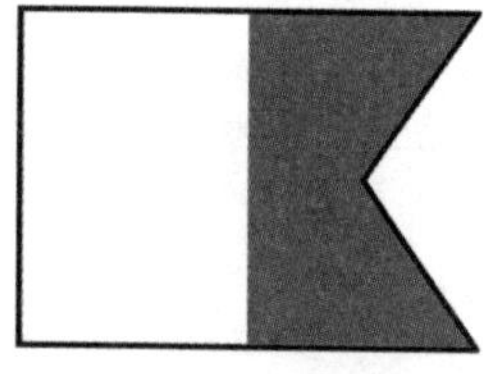

The **Alpha or "A" flag**, according to the U.S. Coast Guard, is to be flown on small vessels engaged in diving operations (1) whenever these vessels are restricted in their ability to maneuver (2) if divers are attached to the vessel. Generally, only vessels to which the divers are physically connected by communication lines, air hoses, or the like are affected by this requirement. The Alpha flag is a signal intended to *protect the vessel from collision.*

In sports diving, where divers are usually free-swimming, the Alpha flag does not have to be shown. The Coast Guard encourages the use of the traditional sports diver flag. The **sports diver flag** is an unofficial signal that, through custom, has come to be used to *protect the diver in the water*. To be most effective, the sports diver flag should be exhibited on a float in the water to mark the approximate location of the diver. Restrictions for nearby vessels vary from state to state, but typically they include a zone of 100' radius around the flag where no other boats are allowed, and a second larger zone in which speed is limited.

International Signal Flags and Morse Code

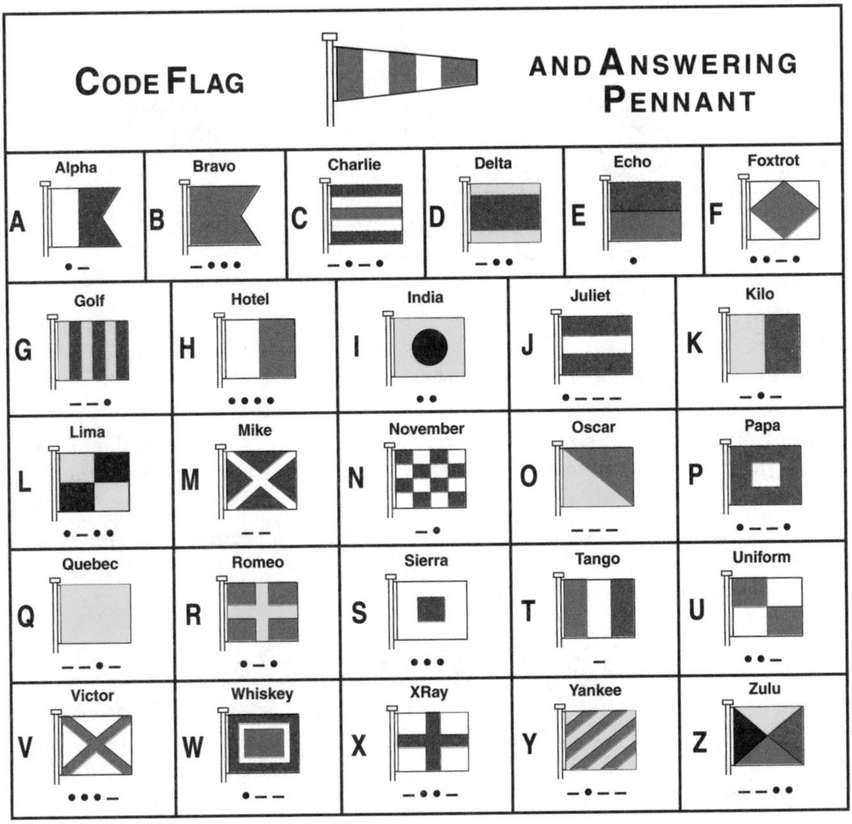

Code Flag and Answering Pennant

A	Alpha	• –
B	Bravo	– • • •
C	Charlie	– • – •
D	Delta	– • •
E	Echo	•
F	Foxtrot	• • – •
G	Golf	– – •
H	Hotel	• • • •
I	India	• •
J	Juliet	• – – –
K	Kilo	– • –
L	Lima	• – • •
M	Mike	– –
N	November	– •
O	Oscar	– – –
P	Papa	• – – •
Q	Quebec	– – • –
R	Romeo	• – •
S	Sierra	• • •
T	Tango	–
U	Uniform	• • –
V	Victor	• • • –
W	Whiskey	• – –
X	XRay	– • • –
Y	Yankee	– • – –
Z	Zulu	– – • •

Numeral Pennants

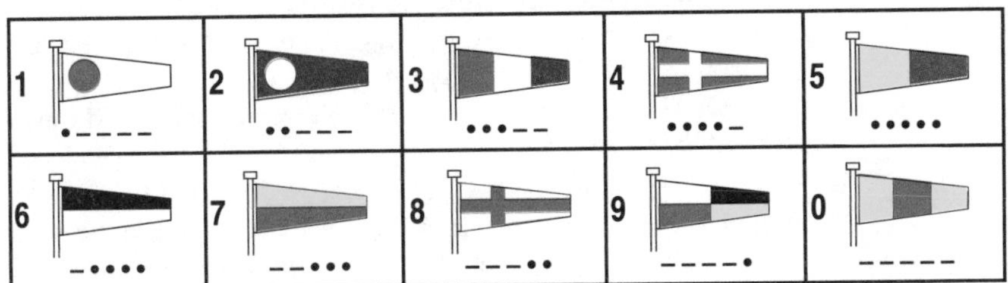

Repeaters

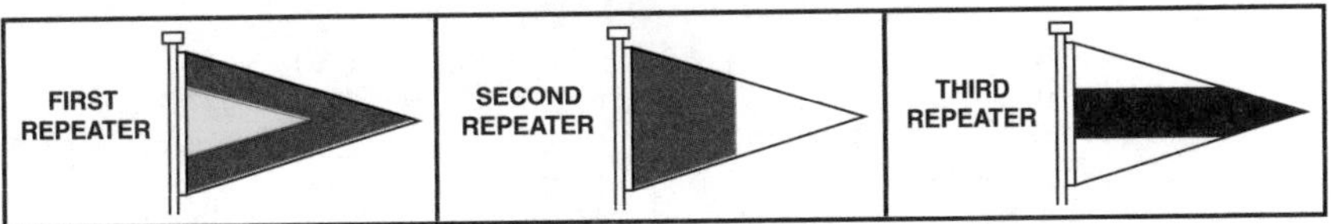

Yacht Flags and How To Fly Them

U.S. Ensign: 8 a.m. to sundown only. Not flown while racing.
At the stern staff of all vessels at anchor, or under way by power or sail.
At the leech of the aftermost sail, approximately 2/3 of the leech above the clew. When the aftermost sail is gaff-rigged, the Ensign is flown immediately below the peak of the gaff.

U.S. Power Squadron Ensign: 8 a.m. to sundown when flown at the stern staff in place of the U.S. Ensign; otherwise, day and night from the starboard spreader. In either case it is flown only when a Squadron member is in command.

Club Burgee: Day and night. Not flown while racing.
At the bow staff of power vessels with one mast.
At the main peak of yawls, ketches, sloops, cutters, and catboats.
At the fore peak of schooners and power vessels with two masts.

Private Signal: Day and night.
At the bow staff of power vessels without a mast.
At the masthead of power and sailing vessels with one mast.
At the mizzen peak of yawls and ketches.
At the main peak of schooners and power vessels with two masts.

Flag Officers' Flags: Day and night. Flown in place of the private signal on all rigs except single-masted sailboats, when it is flown in place of the club burgee at the masthead.

Union Jack: 8 a.m. to sundown, only at anchor, and only on Sundays, holidays, or occasions for dressing ship, at the bow staff. Sailboats without a bow staff may fly it from the forestay a few feet above the stem head.

The Ship's Bell Code

Telling time by ship's bell has a romantic background that goes back hundreds of years. It is based in the workday routine of the ship's crew. A ship at sea requires a constant watch throughout the whole twenty-four hours of the day. To divide the duty, the day is broken up into six watches of four hours each and the crew into three divisions, or watches.

Each division of the crew stands two four-hour watches a day. In order to rotate the duty, so that a division does not have to stand the same watch day in and day out, the 4 to 8 watch in the afternoon is divided into two watches known as the dog watches.

The Mid-Watch - Midnight to 4 A.M.
The Morning Watch - 4 A.M. to 8 A.M.
The Forenoon Watch - 8 A.M. to 12 Noon
The Afternoon Watch - 12 Noon to 4 P.M.
The 1st Dog Watch - 4 P.M. to 6 P.M.
The 2nd Dog Watch - 6 P.M. to 8 P.M.
The First Watch - 8 P.M. to Midnight

To apprise the crew of the time, the ship's bell was struck by the watch officer at half hour intervals, the first half hour being one bell, the first hour two bells, hour and a half three bells, and so on up to eight bells, denoting time to relieve the watch. By this method of timekeeping eight bells marks 4, 8, or 12 o'clock.

8 Bells	4:00	8:00	12:00
1 Bell	4:30	8:30	12:30
2 Bells	5:00	9:00	1:00
3 Bells	5:30	9:30	1:30
4 Bells	6:00	10:00	2:00
5 Bells	6:30	10:30	2:30
6 Bells	7:00	11:00	3:00
7 Bells	7:30	11:30	3:30

Courtesy of Chelsea Clock Co., Chelsea, MA

U.S. Storm Signals

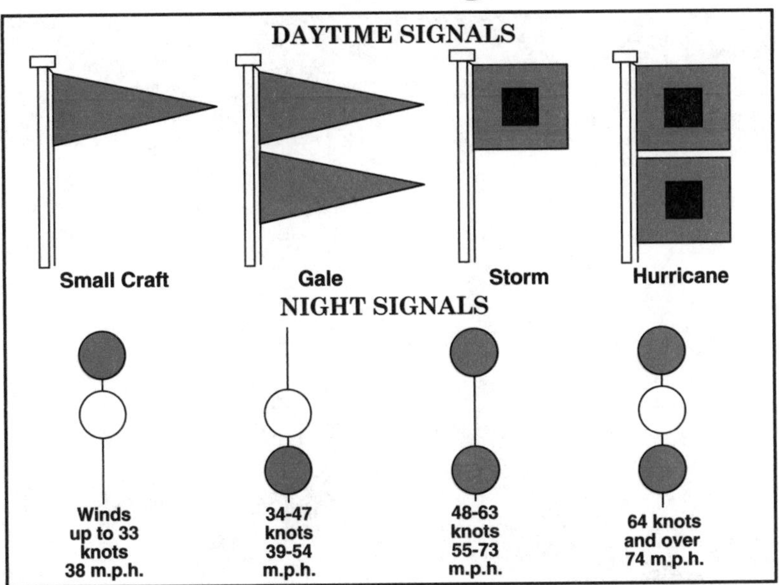

The above signals are displayed regularly on Light Vessels, at Coast Guard shore stations, and at many principal lighthouses. Each Coast and Geodetic Survey Chart lists those locations which appear within the area covered by that chart

Distance of Visibility

Given the curvature of the earth, can you see a 200' high headland from 20 miles away? (Answer below.) How far you can see depends on visibility, which we will assume is ideal, and the heights above water of your eye and the object.

To find the theoretical maximum distance of visibility, use the Table below. First, using your height of eye above water (say, 8'), the Table shows that at that height, your horizon is 3.2 n.m. away. Then, from our Lights, Fog Signals and Offshore Buoys (pp. 173-203), your chart, or the Light List, find the height of the object (say, 200'). The Table shows that object can be seen 16.2 n.m. from sea level. Add the two distances: 3.2 + 16.2 = 19.4 n.m. *Answer: not quite!*

(Heights below in feet, distance in nautical miles)

Ht.	Dist.	Ht.	Dist.	Ht.	Dist.	Ht.	Dist.	Ht.	Dist.
4	2.3	30	6.3	80	10.3	340	21.1	860	33.6
6	2.8	32	6.5	90	10.9	380	22.3	900	34.4
8	3.2	34	6.7	100	11.5	420	23.5	1000	36.2
10	3.6	36	6.9	120	12.6	460	24.6	1400	42.9
12	4.0	38	7.1	140	13.6	500	25.7	1800	48.6
14	4.3	40	7.3	160	14.5	540	26.7	2200	53.8
16	4.6	42	7.4	180	15.4	580	27.6	2600	58.5
18	4.9	44	7.6	200	16.2	620	28.6	3000	62.8
20	5.1	46	7.8	220	17.0	660	29.4	3400	66.9
22	5.4	48	8.0	240	17.8	700	30.4	3800	70.7
24	5.6	50	8.1	260	18.5	740	31.1	4200	74.3
26	5.9	60	8.9	280	19.2	780	32.0	4600	77.7
28	6.1	70	9.6	300	19.9	820	32.8	5000	81.0

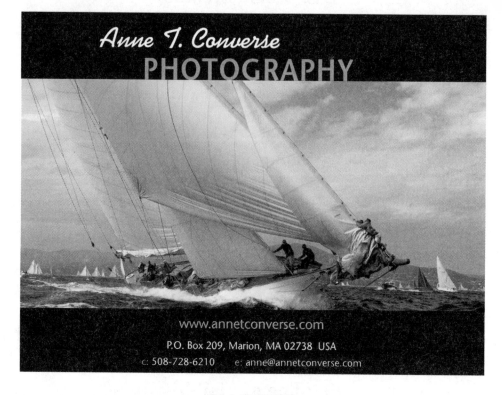

RACONS

RACONS are Radar Beacons operating in the marine radar frequency bands, 2900-3100 MHz (s-band) and 9300-9500 MHz (x-band). When triggered by a vessel's radar signal they provide a bearing by sending a coded reply (e.g., "T": –). This signal received takes the form of a single line or narrow sector extending radially towards the circumference of the radarscope from a point slightly beyond the spot formed by the echo from the lighthouse, buoy, etc. at the Racon site. Thus distance may be measured to the point at which the Racon coded flash begins. (The figure obtained will be a few hundred feet greater than the actual distance of the ship from the Racon due to the slight response delay in the Racon apparatus.)

Hours of transmission are continuous and coverage is all around the horizon unless otherwise stated. Their ranges depend on the effective range of the ship's radar and on the power and elevation of the Racon apparatus. Under conditions of abnormal radio activity, reliance should only be put on a Racon flash that is consistent and when the ship is believed to be within the area of the Racon's quoted range. Mariners are advised to turn off the interference controls of their radar when wishing to receive a Racon signal or else the signal may not come through to the ship.

See p. 223 **for list of Racons.**

Atlantic Coast RACONS

Location	RACON SITE	SIGNAL	LAT. N	LONG. W
NS	Cranberry Islands	– • • • (B)	45-19-29.6	60-55-38.2
	Bear Cove Lt. & Bell By "H6"	– • (N)	44-32-36.3	63-31-19.6
	Chebucto Head	– – • • (Z)	44-30-26.6	63-31-21.8
	Cape Sable	– • – • (C)	43-23-24	65-37-16.9
	Cape Forchu	– • • • (B)	43-47-38.8	66-09-19.3
	Lurcher Shoal Bifurcation Lt. By. "NM"	– • – (K)	43-48-57.2	66-29-58
NB	St. John Harbour. Lt. & Wh. By. "J"	– • (N)	45-12-55.3	66-02-36.9
	Gannet Rock	– – • (G)	44-30-37.1	66-46-52.9
ME	Frenchman Bay Ltd. By. "FB"	– • • • (B)	44-19-21	68-07-24
	Portland Ltd. Wh. By. "P"	– – (M)	43-31-36	70-05-28
MA	Boston Ltd. Wh. By. "B"	– • • • (B)	42-22-42	70-46-58
	Boston North Ch.Entr. Ltd. Wh. By. "NC"	– • (N)	42-22-32	70-54-18
	Cleveland East Ledge Lt.	– • – • (C)	41-37-51	70-41-39
	Buzzards Bay Entr. Lt., Horn	– • • • (B)	41-23-49	71-02-05
RI	Narrag. Bay Entr. Ltd. Wh. By. "NB"	– • • • (B)	41-23-00	71-23-21
	Newport - Pell Bridge	– • (N)	41-30-18	71-20-55
	Mount Hope Bay Bridge Racon "MH"	– – • • • • (MH)	41-38-24	71-15-28
NY	Valiant Rock Ltd. Wh. By. 11	– • • • (B)	41-13-46	72-04-00
	Ambrose Ch. Ltd. Wh. By. "A"	– • (N)	40-27-28	73-50-12
	Tappan Zee Bridge	– • • • (B)	41-04-17	73-52-52
	Kill van Kull Ch. Jct. Ltd. By. "KV"	– • – (K)	40-39-02	74-03-51
	Execution Rocks Lt.	– • • – (X)	40-52-41	73-44-16
NJ	Scotland Ltd. Wh. By. "S"	– – (M)	40-26-33	73-55-01
	Sandy Hook Ch. Rge. Front Lt.	– • – • (C)	40-29-15	73-59-35
DE	Del. Bay Appr. Ltd. Wh. By. "CH"	– • – (K)	38-46-14	75-01-20
	Del. Ltd. By. "D"	– • – (K)	38-27-18	74-41-47
	Del. River, Pea Patch Is.	– • • – (X)	39-36-42	75-34-54
	Five Fathom Bank Ltd. By. "F"	– – (M)	38-46-49	74-34-32
	Brown Shoal Lt.	– • • • (B)	38-55-21	75-06-01
	Miah Maull Shoal Lt.	– – (M)	39-07-36	75-12-31
	Ship John Shoal Lt.	– – – (O)	39-18-19	75-22-36
VA	Chesapeake Bay Ent. Ltd. Wh. By. "CB"	– • – (K)	36-49-00	75-45-36
	Ches. Ch. Ltd. By. #62	– • – – (Y)	37-46-28	76-10-16
	Chesapeake Bay Ent. Ltd. Wh. By. "CH"	– • – • (C)	36-56-08	75-57-27
	Ches. Ch. Ltd. By. #78	– – • – (Q)	38-33-19	76-25-39
	Ches. Ch. Ltd. By. #68	– • • – (X)	37-59-53	76-11-49
	Ches. Ch. Ltd. By. #42	– – – (O)	37-25-37	76-05-07
NC	Cape Fear River Ent. Ltd. Wh. By. "CF"	– • – • (C)	33-46-17	78-03-02
SC	Charleston Entr. Ltd. By. "C"	– • – (K)	32-37-05	79-35-30
GA	Tybee Ltd. By. "T"	– – • (G)	31-57-52	80-43-10
FL	Port Everglades Ltd. By. "PE"	– (T)	26-05-30	80-04-46
	Miami Ltd. By. "M"	– – (M)	25-46-06	80-05-00

Range: Canada under 10 mi., US under 16 mi.

Daily Moon Phases 2021

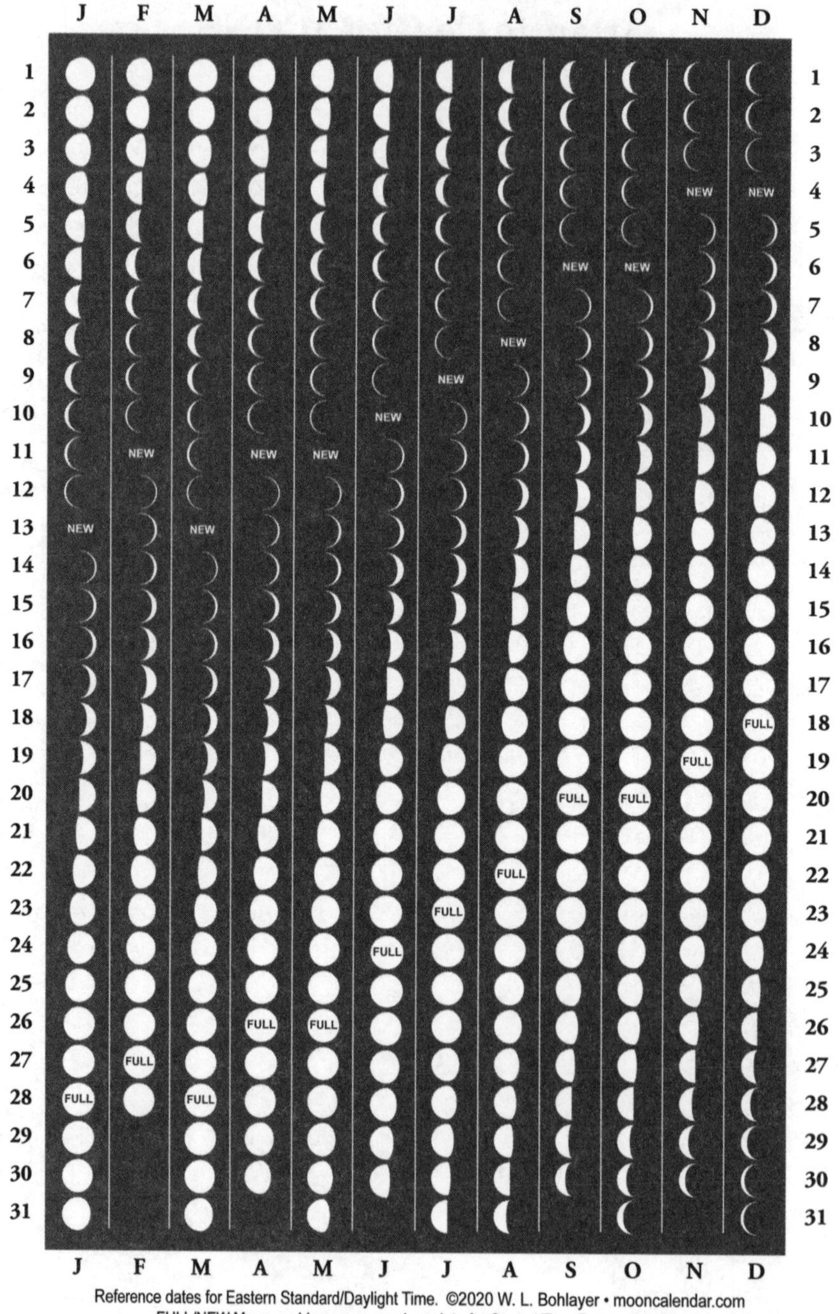

	J	F	M	A	M	J	J	A	S	O	N	D	
1													1
2													2
3													3
4											NEW	NEW	4
5													5
6									NEW	NEW			6
7													7
8								NEW					8
9							NEW						9
10						NEW							10
11		NEW		NEW	NEW								11
12													12
13	NEW		NEW										13
14													14
15													15
16													16
17													17
18												FULL	18
19											FULL		19
20									FULL	FULL			20
21													21
22								FULL					22
23							FULL						23
24						FULL							24
25													25
26				FULL	FULL								26
27		FULL											27
28	FULL		FULL										28
29													29
30													30
31													31
	J	F	M	A	M	J	J	A	S	O	N	D	

Reference dates for Eastern Standard/Daylight Time. ©2020 W. L. Bohlayer • mooncalendar.com
FULL/NEW Moon could occur on previous date for Central Time Zone and west.

Table for Turning Compass Points into Degrees, and the Contrary

MERCHANT MARINE PRACTICE

Point	Degrees	Point	Degrees	Point	Degrees	Point	Degrees
NORTH	**0**	**EAST**	**90**	**SOUTH**	**180**	**WEST**	**270**
N. 1/4E.	2 3/4	E. 1/4S.	92 3/4	S. 1/4W.	182 3/4	W. 1/4N.	272 3/4
N. 1/2E.	5 3/4	E. 1/2S.	95 3/4	S. 1/2W.	185 3/4	W. 1/2N.	275 3/4
N. 3/4E.	8 1/2	E. 3/4S.	98 1/2	S. 3/4W.	188 1/2	W. 3/4N.	278 1/2
N. by E.	11 1/4	E. by S.	101 1/4	S. by W.	191 1/4	W. by N.	281 1/4
N. by E. 1/4E.	14	E. by S. 1/4S.	104	S. by W. 1/4W.	194	W. by N. 1/4N.	284
N. by E. 1/2E.	17	E. by S. 1/2S.	107	S. by W. 1/2W.	197	W. by N. 1/2N.	287
N. by E. 3/4E.	19 3/4	E. by S. 3/4S.	109 3/4	S. by W. 3/4W.	199 3/4	W. by N. 3/4N.	289 3/4
N.N.E.	**22 1/2**	**E.S.E.**	**112 1/2**	**S.S.W.**	**202 1/2**	**W.N.W.**	**292 1/2**
N.E. by N. 3/4N.	25 1/4	S.E. by E. 3/4E.	115 1/4	S.W. by S. 3/4S.	205 1/4	N.W. by W. 3/4W.	295 1/4
N.E. by N. 1/2N.	28 1/4	S.E. by E. 1/2E.	118 1/4	S.W. by S. 1/2S.	208 1/4	N.W. by W. 1/2W.	298 1/4
N.E. by N. 1/4N.	31	S.E. by E. 1/4E.	121	S.W. by S. 1/4S.	211	N.W. by W. 1/4W.	301
N.E. by N.	33 3/4	S.E. by E.	123 3/4	S.W. by S.	213 3/4	N.W. by W.	303 3/4
N.E. 3/4N.	36 1/2	S.E. 3/4E.	126 1/2	S.W. 3/4S.	216 1/2	N.W. 3/4W.	306 1/2
N.E. 1/2N.	39 1/2	S.E. 1/2E.	129 1/2	S.W. 1/2S.	219 1/2	N.W. 1/2W.	309 1/2
N.E. 1/4N.	42 1/4	S.E. 1/4E.	132 1/4	S.W. 1/4S.	222 1/4	N.W. 1/4W.	312 1/4
N.E.	**45**	**S.E.**	**135**	**S.W.**	**225**	**N.W.**	**315**
N.E. 1/4E.	47 3/4	S.E. 1/4S.	137 3/4	S.W. 1/4W.	227 3/4	N.W. 1/4N.	317 3/4
N.E. 1/2E.	50 3/4	S.E. 1/2S.	140 3/4	S.W. 1/2W.	230 3/4	N.W. 1/2N.	320 3/4
N.E. 3/4E.	53 1/2	S.E. 3/4S.	143 1/2	S.W. 3/4W.	233 1/2	N.W. 3/4N.	323 1/2
N.E. by E.	56 1/4	S.E. by S.	146 1/4	S.W. by W.	236 1/4	N.W. by N.	326 1/4
N.E. by E. 1/4E.	59	S.E. by S. 1/4S.	149	S.W. by W. 1/4W.	239	N.W. by N. 1/4N.	329
N.E. by E. 1/2E.	62	S.E. by S. 1/2S.	152	S.W. by W. 1/2W.	242	N.W. by N. 1/2N.	332
N.E. by E. 3/4E.	64 3/4	S.E. by S. 3/4S.	154 3/4	S.W. by W. 3/4W.	244 3/4	N.W. by N. 3/4N.	334 3/4
E.N.E.	**67 1/2**	**S.S.E.**	**157 1/2**	**W.S.W.**	**247 1/2**	**N.N.W.**	**337 1/2**
E. by N. 3/4N.	70 1/4	S. by E. 3/4E.	160 1/4	W. by S. 3/4S.	250 1/4	N. by W. 3/4W.	340 1/4
E. by N. 1/2N.	73 1/4	S. by E. 1/2E.	163 1/4	W. by S. 1/2S.	253 1/4	N. by W. 1/2W.	343 1/4
E. by N. 1/4N.	76	S. by E. 1/4E.	166	W. by S. 1/4S.	256	N. by W. 1/4W.	346
E. by N.	78 3/4	S. by E.	168 3/4	W. by S.	258 3/4	N. by W.	348 3/4
E. 3/4N.	81 1/2	S. 3/4E.	171 1/2	W. 3/4S.	261 1/2	N. 3/4W.	351 1/2
E. 1/2N.	84 1/2	S. 1/2E.	174 1/2	W. 1/2S.	264 1/2	N. 1/2W.	354 1/2
E. 1/4N.	87 1/4	S. 1/4E.	177 1/4	W. 1/4S.	267 1/4	N. 1/4W.	357 1/4
EAST	**90**	**SOUTH**	**180**	**WEST**	**270**	**NORTH**	**0**

2021 SUN'S RISING AND SETTING AT BOSTON – 42° 20'N 71°W

Daylight Saving Time is March 14 – November 7, transitions are noted with an *

Times shown in table are first tip of Sun at Sunrise and last tip at Sunset.

	JAN.		FEB.		MAR.		APR.		MAY		JUN.		
	Rise	Set	Rise	Set	Rise	Set	Rise	Set	Rise	Set	Rise	Set	
Day	h m	h m	h m	h m	h m	h m	h m	h m	h m	h m	h m	h m	Day
01	7:13	16:23	6:57	16:59	6:19	17:34	6:26	19:10	5:39	19:44	5:10	20:14	01
02	7:13	16:23	6:56	17:00	6:17	17:35	6:24	19:11	5:38	19:45	5:09	20:15	02
03	7:13	16:24	6:55	17:01	6:16	17:37	6:23	19:12	5:36	19:46	5:09	20:16	03
04	7:13	16:25	6:54	17:02	6:14	17:38	6:21	19:14	5:35	19:47	5:09	20:17	04
05	7:13	16:26	6:53	17:04	6:12	17:39	6:19	19:15	5:34	19:48	5:08	20:17	05
06	7:13	16:27	6:52	17:05	6:11	17:40	6:18	19:16	5:33	19:49	5:08	20:18	06
07	7:13	16:28	6:50	17:06	6:09	17:41	6:16	19:17	5:31	19:50	5:08	20:19	07
08	7:13	16:29	6:49	17:08	6:07	17:43	6:14	19:18	5:30	19:52	5:07	20:19	08
09	7:12	16:30	6:48	17:09	6:06	17:44	6:13	19:19	5:29	19:53	5:07	20:20	09
10	7:12	16:31	6:47	17:10	6:04	17:45	6:11	19:20	5:28	19:54	5:07	20:20	10
11	7:12	16:33	6:45	17:12	6:02	17:46	6:09	19:21	5:27	19:55	5:07	20:21	11
12	7:12	16:34	6:44	17:13	6:01	17:47	6:08	19:23	5:26	19:56	5:07	20:21	12
13	7:11	16:35	6:43	17:14	5:59	17:49	6:06	19:24	5:24	19:57	5:07	20:22	13
14	7:11	16:36	6:41	17:15	*6:57	18:50	6:04	19:25	5:23	19:58	5:07	20:22	14
15	7:10	16:37	6:40	17:17	6:56	18:51	6:03	19:26	5:22	19:59	5:07	20:23	15
16	7:10	16:38	6:39	17:18	6:54	18:52	6:01	19:27	5:21	20:00	5:07	20:23	16
17	7:09	16:40	6:37	17:19	6:52	18:53	6:00	19:28	5:20	20:01	5:07	20:23	17
18	7:09	16:41	6:36	17:21	6:50	18:54	5:58	19:29	5:20	20:02	5:07	20:24	18
19	7:08	16:42	6:34	17:22	6:49	18:55	5:56	19:30	5:19	20:03	5:07	20:24	19
20	7:07	16:43	6:33	17:23	6:47	18:57	5:55	19:32	5:18	20:04	5:07	20:24	20
21	7:07	16:44	6:31	17:24	6:45	18:58	5:53	19:33	5:17	20:05	5:07	20:24	21
22	7:06	16:46	6:30	17:26	6:43	18:59	5:52	19:34	5:16	20:06	5:08	20:25	22
23	7:05	16:47	6:28	17:27	6:42	19:00	5:50	19:35	5:15	20:07	5:08	20:25	23
24	7:05	16:48	6:27	17:28	6:40	19:01	5:49	19:36	5:15	20:08	5:08	20:25	24
25	7:04	16:50	6:25	17:29	6:38	19:02	5:47	19:37	5:14	20:09	5:09	20:25	25
26	7:03	16:51	6:24	17:31	6:36	19:03	5:46	19:38	5:13	20:09	5:09	20:25	26
27	7:02	16:52	6:22	17:32	6:35	19:05	5:45	19:39	5:13	20:10	5:09	20:25	27
28	7:01	16:53	6:21	17:33	6:33	19:06	5:43	19:41	5:12	20:11	5:10	20:25	28
29	7:00	16:55			6:31	19:07	5:42	19:42	5:11	20:12	5:10	20:25	29
30	6:59	16:56			6:30	19:08	5:40	19:43	5:11	20:13	5:11	20:25	30
31	6:58	16:57			6:28	19:09			5:10	20:14			31

	JUL.		AUG.		SEP.		OCT.		NOV.		DEC.		
	Rise	Set	Rise	Set	Rise	Set	Rise	Set	Rise	Set	Rise	Set	
Day	h m	h m	h m	h m	h m	h m	h m	h m	h m	h m	h m	h m	Day
01	5:11	20:24	5:37	20:03	6:09	19:17	6:41	18:25	7:18	17:37	6:54	16:12	01
02	5:12	20:24	5:38	20:02	6:11	19:16	6:42	18:23	7:19	17:36	6:55	16:12	02
03	5:12	20:24	5:39	20:01	6:12	19:14	6:44	18:22	7:20	17:35	6:56	16:12	03
04	5:13	20:24	5:40	19:59	6:13	19:12	6:45	18:20	7:21	17:33	6:57	16:12	04
05	5:14	20:24	5:41	19:58	6:14	19:11	6:46	18:18	7:23	17:32	6:58	16:12	05
06	5:14	20:23	5:42	19:57	6:15	19:09	6:47	18:16	7:24	17:31	6:59	16:11	06
07	5:15	20:23	5:43	19:56	6:16	19:07	6:48	18:15	*6:25	16:30	7:00	16:11	07
08	5:16	20:22	5:44	19:54	6:17	19:05	6:49	18:13	6:26	16:29	7:01	16:11	08
09	5:16	20:22	5:45	19:53	6:18	19:04	6:50	18:11	6:28	16:28	7:01	16:11	09
10	5:17	20:22	5:46	19:52	6:19	19:02	6:51	18:10	6:29	16:27	7:02	16:11	10
11	5:18	20:21	5:47	19:50	6:20	19:00	6:53	18:08	6:30	16:26	7:03	16:11	11
12	5:18	20:21	5:48	19:49	6:21	18:58	6:54	18:06	6:31	16:25	7:04	16:12	12
13	5:19	20:20	5:49	19:47	6:22	18:57	6:55	18:05	6:33	16:24	7:05	16:12	13
14	5:20	20:19	5:51	19:46	6:23	18:55	6:56	18:03	6:34	16:23	7:06	16:12	14
15	5:21	20:19	5:52	19:45	6:24	18:53	6:57	18:02	6:35	16:22	7:06	16:12	15
16	5:22	20:18	5:53	19:43	6:25	18:51	6:58	18:00	6:36	16:21	7:07	16:13	16
17	5:23	20:17	5:54	19:42	6:26	18:50	6:59	17:58	6:38	16:20	7:08	16:13	17
18	5:23	20:17	5:55	19:40	6:27	18:48	7:01	17:57	6:39	16:19	7:08	16:13	18
19	5:24	20:16	5:56	19:39	6:28	18:46	7:02	17:55	6:40	16:19	7:09	16:14	19
20	5:25	20:15	5:57	19:37	6:30	18:44	7:03	17:54	6:41	16:18	7:09	16:14	20
21	5:26	20:14	5:58	19:35	6:31	18:43	7:04	17:52	6:42	16:17	7:10	16:15	21
22	5:27	20:13	5:59	19:34	6:32	18:41	7:05	17:51	6:44	16:17	7:10	16:15	22
23	5:28	20:12	6:00	19:32	6:33	18:39	7:07	17:49	6:45	16:16	7:11	16:16	23
24	5:29	20:11	6:01	19:31	6:34	18:37	7:08	17:48	6:46	16:15	7:11	16:16	24
25	5:30	20:11	6:02	19:29	6:35	18:35	7:09	17:46	6:47	16:15	7:12	16:17	25
26	5:31	20:10	6:03	19:27	6:36	18:34	7:10	17:45	6:48	16:14	7:12	16:18	26
27	5:32	20:09	6:04	19:26	6:37	18:32	7:11	17:44	6:49	16:14	7:12	16:18	27
28	5:33	20:07	6:05	19:24	6:38	18:30	7:13	17:42	6:50	16:13	7:12	16:19	28
29	5:34	20:06	6:06	19:23	6:39	18:28	7:14	17:41	6:52	16:13	7:13	16:20	29
30	5:35	20:05	6:07	19:21	6:40	18:27	7:15	17:40	6:53	16:13	7:13	16:21	30
31	5:36	20:04	6:08	19:19			7:16	17:38			7:13	16:21	31

2021 SUN'S RISING AND SETTING AT NEW YORK – 40° 42'N 74°W

Daylight Saving Time is March 14 – November 7, transitions are noted with an *

Times shown in table are first tip of Sun at Sunrise and last tip at Sunset.

	JAN.		FEB.		MAR.		APR.		MAY		JUN.		
	Rise	Set	Rise	Set	Rise	Set	Rise	Set	Rise	Set	Rise	Set	
Day	h m	h m	h m	h m	h m	h m	h m	h m	h m	h m	h m	h m	Day
01	7:20	16:40	7:06	17:14	6:29	17:48	6:39	19:21	5:54	19:52	5:27	20:21	01
02	7:20	16:41	7:05	17:15	6:28	17:49	6:38	19:22	5:53	19:53	5:27	20:22	02
03	7:20	16:41	7:04	17:17	6:26	17:50	6:36	19:23	5:52	19:55	5:26	20:23	03
04	7:20	16:42	7:03	17:18	6:25	17:51	6:34	19:24	5:51	19:56	5:26	20:23	04
05	7:20	16:43	7:02	17:19	6:23	17:52	6:33	19:25	5:49	19:57	5:26	20:24	05
06	7:20	16:44	7:00	17:20	6:22	17:53	6:31	19:26	5:48	19:58	5:25	20:24	06
07	7:20	16:45	6:59	17:21	6:20	17:54	6:29	19:27	5:47	19:59	5:25	20:25	07
08	7:20	16:46	6:58	17:23	6:19	17:55	6:28	19:28	5:46	20:00	5:25	20:26	08
09	7:20	16:47	6:57	17:24	6:17	17:57	6:26	19:29	5:45	20:01	5:25	20:26	09
10	7:19	16:48	6:56	17:25	6:15	17:58	6:25	19:30	5:44	20:02	5:25	20:27	10
11	7:19	16:49	6:55	17:26	6:14	17:59	6:23	19:32	5:43	20:03	5:24	20:27	11
12	7:19	16:50	6:53	17:28	6:12	18:00	6:22	19:33	5:42	20:04	5:24	20:28	12
13	7:19	16:52	6:52	17:29	6:10	18:01	6:20	19:34	5:41	20:05	5:24	20:28	13
14	7:18	16:53	6:51	17:30	*7:09	19:02	6:18	19:35	5:40	20:06	5:24	20:29	14
15	7:18	16:54	6:50	17:31	7:07	19:03	6:17	19:36	5:39	20:07	5:24	20:29	15
16	7:17	16:55	6:48	17:32	7:06	19:04	6:15	19:37	5:38	20:08	5:24	20:29	16
17	7:17	16:56	6:47	17:34	7:04	19:05	6:14	19:38	5:37	20:08	5:24	20:30	17
18	7:16	16:57	6:46	17:35	7:02	19:06	6:12	19:39	5:36	20:09	5:25	20:30	18
19	7:16	16:58	6:44	17:36	7:01	19:07	6:11	19:40	5:35	20:10	5:25	20:30	19
20	7:15	16:59	6:43	17:37	6:59	19:08	6:09	19:41	5:34	20:11	5:25	20:30	20
21	7:15	17:01	6:41	17:38	6:57	19:09	6:08	19:42	5:34	20:12	5:25	20:31	21
22	7:14	17:02	6:40	17:40	6:56	19:11	6:07	19:43	5:33	20:13	5:25	20:31	22
23	7:13	17:03	6:38	17:41	6:54	19:12	6:05	19:44	5:32	20:14	5:26	20:31	23
24	7:12	17:04	6:37	17:42	6:52	19:13	6:04	19:45	5:31	20:15	5:26	20:31	24
25	7:12	17:05	6:36	17:43	6:51	19:14	6:02	19:46	5:31	20:16	5:26	20:31	25
26	7:11	17:07	6:34	17:44	6:49	19:15	6:01	19:47	5:30	20:16	5:27	20:31	26
27	7:10	17:08	6:33	17:45	6:47	19:16	6:00	19:48	5:30	20:17	5:27	20:31	27
28	7:09	17:09	6:31	17:46	6:46	19:17	5:58	19:49	5:29	20:18	5:27	20:31	28
29	7:08	17:10			6:44	19:18	5:57	19:50	5:28	20:19	5:28	20:31	29
30	7:08	17:12			6:42	19:19	5:56	19:51	5:28	20:20	5:28	20:31	30
31	7:07	17:13			6:41	19:20			5:27	20:20			31

	JUL.		AUG.		SEP.		OCT.		NOV.		DEC.		
	Rise	Set	Rise	Set	Rise	Set	Rise	Set	Rise	Set	Rise	Set	
Day	h m	h m	h m	h m	h m	h m	h m	h m	h m	h m	h m	h m	Day
01	5:29	20:31	5:53	20:11	6:23	19:28	6:53	18:38	7:27	17:52	7:01	16:29	01
02	5:29	20:31	5:54	20:10	6:24	19:26	6:54	18:36	7:28	17:51	7:02	16:29	02
03	5:30	20:31	5:55	20:09	6:25	19:24	6:55	18:34	7:29	17:50	7:03	16:29	03
04	5:30	20:30	5:56	20:08	6:26	19:23	6:56	18:33	7:30	17:49	7:04	16:29	04
05	5:31	20:30	5:57	20:06	6:27	19:21	6:57	18:31	7:31	17:47	7:05	16:29	05
06	5:32	20:30	5:58	20:05	6:28	19:20	6:58	18:29	7:33	17:46	7:06	16:28	06
07	5:32	20:29	5:59	20:04	6:29	19:18	6:59	18:28	*6:34	16:45	7:07	16:28	07
08	5:33	20:29	6:00	20:03	6:30	19:16	7:00	18:26	6:35	16:44	7:07	16:28	08
09	5:34	20:29	6:01	20:02	6:31	19:15	7:01	18:25	6:36	16:43	7:08	16:28	09
10	5:34	20:28	6:02	20:00	6:32	19:13	7:02	18:23	6:37	16:42	7:09	16:29	10
11	5:35	20:28	6:03	19:59	6:33	19:11	7:03	18:21	6:38	16:41	7:10	16:29	11
12	5:36	20:27	6:04	19:58	6:34	19:10	7:04	18:20	6:40	16:40	7:11	16:29	12
13	5:36	20:27	6:05	19:56	6:35	19:08	7:05	18:18	6:41	16:39	7:12	16:29	13
14	5:37	20:26	6:06	19:55	6:36	19:06	7:06	18:17	6:42	16:39	7:12	16:29	14
15	5:38	20:26	6:07	19:54	6:37	19:04	7:07	18:15	6:43	16:38	7:13	16:30	15
16	5:39	20:25	6:08	19:52	6:38	19:03	7:09	18:14	6:44	16:37	7:14	16:30	16
17	5:40	20:24	6:09	19:51	6:39	19:01	7:10	18:12	6:45	16:36	7:14	16:30	17
18	5:40	20:24	6:10	19:49	6:40	18:59	7:11	18:11	6:47	16:36	7:15	16:31	18
19	5:41	20:23	6:11	19:48	6:41	18:58	7:12	18:09	6:48	16:35	7:16	16:31	19
20	5:42	20:22	6:12	19:46	6:42	18:56	7:13	18:08	6:49	16:34	7:16	16:31	20
21	5:43	20:21	6:13	19:45	6:43	18:54	7:14	18:06	6:50	16:34	7:17	16:32	21
22	5:44	20:21	6:14	19:43	6:44	18:53	7:15	18:05	6:51	16:33	7:17	16:32	22
23	5:45	20:20	6:14	19:42	6:45	18:51	7:16	18:04	6:52	16:32	7:18	16:33	23
24	5:46	20:19	6:15	19:40	6:46	18:49	7:17	18:02	6:53	16:32	7:18	16:34	24
25	5:47	20:18	6:16	19:39	6:47	18:48	7:19	18:01	6:55	16:31	7:18	16:34	25
26	5:47	20:17	6:17	19:37	6:48	18:46	7:20	18:00	6:56	16:31	7:19	16:35	26
27	5:48	20:16	6:18	19:36	6:49	18:44	7:21	17:58	6:57	16:30	7:19	16:36	27
28	5:49	20:15	6:19	19:34	6:50	18:43	7:22	17:57	6:58	16:30	7:19	16:36	28
29	5:50	20:14	6:20	19:33	6:51	18:41	7:23	17:56	6:59	16:30	7:19	16:37	29
30	5:51	20:13	6:21	19:31	6:52	18:39	7:24	17:54	7:00	16:29	7:20	16:38	30
31	5:52	20:12	6:22	19:29			7:25	17:53			7:20	16:39	31

2021 SUN'S RISING AND SETTING AT JACKSONVILLE – 30° 20'N 81° 37'W

Daylight Saving Time is March 14 – November 7, transitions are noted with an *

Times shown in table are first tip of Sun at Sunrise and last tip at Sunset.

	JAN.		FEB.		MAR.		APR.		MAY		JUN.		
	Rise	Set	Rise	Set	Rise	Set	Rise	Set	Rise	Set	Rise	Set	
Day	h m	h m	h m	h m	h m	h m	h m	h m	h m	h m	h m	h m	Day
01	7:23	17:37	7:17	18:03	6:52	18:26	7:15	19:46	6:43	20:05	6:25	20:24	01
02	7:23	17:38	7:16	18:04	6:51	18:26	7:14	19:46	6:42	20:05	6:25	20:24	02
03	7:24	17:39	7:16	18:05	6:50	18:27	7:13	19:47	6:41	20:06	6:25	20:25	03
04	7:24	17:40	7:15	18:06	6:49	18:28	7:12	19:47	6:40	20:07	6:24	20:25	04
05	7:24	17:40	7:14	18:07	6:48	18:28	7:11	19:48	6:39	20:07	6:24	20:26	05
06	7:24	17:41	7:14	18:08	6:47	18:29	7:09	19:49	6:39	20:08	6:24	20:26	06
07	7:24	17:42	7:13	18:09	6:46	18:30	7:08	19:49	6:38	20:09	6:24	20:27	07
08	7:24	17:43	7:12	18:09	6:44	18:30	7:07	19:50	6:37	20:09	6:24	20:27	08
09	7:24	17:44	7:11	18:10	6:43	18:31	7:06	19:51	6:36	20:10	6:24	20:28	09
10	7:24	17:44	7:11	18:11	6:42	18:32	7:05	19:51	6:36	20:10	6:24	20:28	10
11	7:24	17:45	7:10	18:12	6:41	18:32	7:04	19:52	6:35	20:11	6:24	20:29	11
12	7:24	17:46	7:09	18:13	6:40	18:33	7:02	19:52	6:34	20:12	6:24	20:29	12
13	7:24	17:47	7:08	18:14	6:38	18:34	7:01	19:53	6:34	20:12	6:24	20:29	13
14	7:24	17:48	7:07	18:14	*7:37	19:34	7:00	19:54	6:33	20:13	6:24	20:30	14
15	7:24	17:49	7:06	18:15	7:36	19:35	6:59	19:54	6:32	20:14	6:24	20:30	15
16	7:24	17:49	7:05	18:16	7:35	19:36	6:58	19:55	6:32	20:14	6:24	20:30	16
17	7:23	17:50	7:05	18:17	7:34	19:36	6:57	19:56	6:31	20:15	6:24	20:31	17
18	7:23	17:51	7:04	18:17	7:32	19:37	6:56	19:56	6:31	20:16	6:25	20:31	18
19	7:23	17:52	7:03	18:18	7:31	19:38	6:55	19:57	6:30	20:16	6:25	20:31	19
20	7:23	17:53	7:02	18:19	7:30	19:38	6:54	19:57	6:29	20:17	6:25	20:31	20
21	7:22	17:54	7:01	18:20	7:29	19:39	6:53	19:58	6:29	20:18	6:25	20:32	21
22	7:22	17:55	7:00	18:20	7:28	19:39	6:52	19:59	6:28	20:18	6:25	20:32	22
23	7:22	17:56	6:59	18:21	7:26	19:40	6:51	19:59	6:28	20:19	6:26	20:32	23
24	7:21	17:56	6:58	18:22	7:25	19:41	6:50	20:00	6:28	20:19	6:26	20:32	24
25	7:21	17:57	6:57	18:23	7:24	19:41	6:49	20:01	6:27	20:20	6:26	20:32	25
26	7:20	17:58	6:56	18:23	7:23	19:42	6:48	20:01	6:27	20:21	6:27	20:32	26
27	7:20	17:59	6:54	18:24	7:21	19:42	6:47	20:02	6:26	20:21	6:27	20:32	27
28	7:19	18:00	6:53	18:25	7:20	19:43	6:46	20:03	6:26	20:22	6:27	20:32	28
29	7:19	18:01			7:19	19:44	6:45	20:03	6:26	20:22	6:28	20:32	29
30	7:18	18:02			7:18	19:44	6:44	20:04	6:26	20:23	6:28	20:32	30
31	7:18	18:03			7:17	19:45			6:25	20:23			31

	JUL.		AUG.		SEP.		OCT.		NOV.		DEC.		
	Rise	Set	Rise	Set	Rise	Set	Rise	Set	Rise	Set	Rise	Set	
Day	h m	h m	h m	h m	h m	h m	h m	h m	h m	h m	h m	h m	Day
01	6:28	20:32	6:45	20:20	7:03	19:49	7:20	19:11	7:41	18:39	7:06	17:25	01
02	6:29	20:32	6:46	20:19	7:04	19:48	7:21	19:10	7:42	18:38	7:06	17:25	02
03	6:29	20:32	6:46	20:18	7:04	19:46	7:21	19:09	7:43	18:37	7:07	17:25	03
04	6:30	20:32	6:47	20:18	7:05	19:45	7:22	19:08	7:43	18:36	7:08	17:26	04
05	6:30	20:32	6:48	20:17	7:06	19:44	7:22	19:07	7:44	18:36	7:09	17:26	05
06	6:30	20:32	6:48	20:16	7:06	19:43	7:23	19:05	7:45	18:35	7:09	17:26	06
07	6:31	20:32	6:49	20:15	7:07	19:41	7:24	19:04	*6:46	17:34	7:10	17:26	07
08	6:31	20:32	6:49	20:14	7:07	19:40	7:24	19:03	6:47	17:34	7:11	17:26	08
09	6:32	20:31	6:50	20:13	7:08	19:39	7:25	19:02	6:47	17:33	7:12	17:26	09
10	6:32	20:31	6:51	20:12	7:08	19:38	7:26	19:01	6:48	17:32	7:12	17:26	10
11	6:33	20:31	6:51	20:12	7:09	19:37	7:26	19:00	6:49	17:32	7:13	17:27	11
12	6:33	20:31	6:52	20:11	7:09	19:35	7:27	18:58	6:50	17:31	7:14	17:27	12
13	6:34	20:30	6:52	20:10	7:10	19:34	7:28	18:57	6:51	17:31	7:14	17:27	13
14	6:35	20:30	6:53	20:09	7:11	19:33	7:28	18:56	6:52	17:30	7:15	17:27	14
15	6:35	20:30	6:54	20:08	7:11	19:31	7:29	18:55	6:52	17:30	7:16	17:28	15
16	6:36	20:29	6:54	20:07	7:12	19:30	7:29	18:54	6:53	17:29	7:16	17:28	16
17	6:36	20:29	6:55	20:06	7:12	19:29	7:30	18:53	6:54	17:29	7:17	17:29	17
18	6:37	20:28	6:55	20:05	7:13	19:28	7:31	18:52	6:55	17:28	7:17	17:29	18
19	6:37	20:28	6:56	20:04	7:13	19:26	7:32	18:51	6:56	17:28	7:18	17:29	19
20	6:38	20:28	6:57	20:02	7:14	19:25	7:32	18:50	6:57	17:28	7:19	17:30	20
21	6:39	20:27	6:57	20:01	7:14	19:24	7:33	18:49	6:57	17:27	7:19	17:30	21
22	6:39	20:27	6:58	20:00	7:15	19:23	7:34	18:48	6:58	17:27	7:20	17:31	22
23	6:40	20:26	6:58	19:59	7:16	19:21	7:34	18:47	6:59	17:27	7:20	17:31	23
24	6:40	20:25	6:59	19:58	7:16	19:20	7:35	18:46	7:00	17:26	7:20	17:32	24
25	6:41	20:25	6:59	19:57	7:17	19:19	7:36	18:45	7:01	17:26	7:21	17:33	25
26	6:41	20:24	7:00	19:56	7:17	19:18	7:36	18:44	7:02	17:26	7:21	17:33	26
27	6:42	20:24	7:01	19:55	7:18	19:16	7:37	18:43	7:02	17:26	7:22	17:34	27
28	6:43	20:23	7:01	19:54	7:18	19:15	7:38	18:42	7:03	17:26	7:22	17:34	28
29	6:43	20:22	7:02	19:52	7:19	19:14	7:39	18:41	7:04	17:26	7:22	17:35	29
30	6:44	20:22	7:02	19:51	7:20	19:13	7:39	18:40	7:05	17:26	7:23	17:36	30
31	6:45	20:21	7:03	19:50			7:40	18:40			7:23	17:36	31

2021 SUN'S SETTING AT OTHER LOCATIONS FOR FLAG USE

Daylight Saving Time is March 14 – November 7

Times shown in tables p. 226-228 are first tip of Sun at Sunrise and last tip at Sunset.

Vernal Equinox: March 20th, 5:37 a.m. E.D.T. Summer Solstice: June 20th, 11:32 p.m. E.D.T.
Autumnal Equinox: Sept. 22nd, 3:21 p.m. E.D.T. Winter Solstice: Dec. 21st, 10:59 a.m. E.S.T.

Add to or subtract from the referenced table

	Jan	Feb	Mar	Apr	May	Jun	Jul	Aug	Sep	Oct	Nov	Dec
BOSTON p. 226												
New London, CT	+7	+6	+4	+2	0	-1	0	+1	+2	+5	+6	+7
Newport, RI	+4	+3	+1	-1	-2	-3	-2	-1	0	+2	+4	+5
New Bedford, MA	+3	+2	0	-1	-2	-3	-2	-1	0	+1	+2	+3
Vineyard Haven, MA	+1	-1	-2	-4	-5	-6	-5	-4	-3	-2	0	+1
Nantucket, MA	-1	-2	-4	-6	-7	-8	-7	-6	-5	-3	-2	-1
Portland, ME	-8	-6	-3	-1	+1	+2	+1	0	-2	-4	-6	-7
Rockland, ME	-14	-12	-8	-6	-4	-2	-4	-5	-7	-10	-12	-14
Bar Harbor, ME	-18	-15	-11	-8	-5	-3	-5	-7	-9	-13	-17	-18
NEW YORK p. 227												
Hampton Roads, VA	+18	+15	+9	+2	0	-1	-1	+2	+7	+13	+18	+20
Oxford, MD	+14	+12	+9	+5	+4	+3	+3	+5	+8	+11	+14	+15
Annapolis, MD	+14	+13	+10	+7	+6	+5	+5	+7	+9	+12	+14	+15
Cape May, NJ	+8	+7	+4	+1	0	-1	-1	+1	+3	+6	+8	+9
Atlantic City, NJ	+5	+4	+2	0	-1	-2	-2	0	+2	+4	+6	+6
Mannasquan, NJ	+2	+1	0	-1	-2	-2	-2	-1	0	+1	+2	+2
Port Jefferson, NY	-5	-4	-4	-3	-3	-3	-3	-3	-4	-4	-5	-5
Bridgeport, CT	-4	-4	-3	-2	-2	-1	-1	-2	-3	-4	-4	-5
New Haven, CT	-7	-6	-4	-3	-3	-3	-3	-3	-4	-5	-6	-7
JACKSONVILLE p. 228												
Morehead City, NC	-28	-24	-20	-14	-10	-7	-9	-13	-19	-24	-28	-29
Wilmington, NC	-22	-18	-14	-10	-5	-3	-5	-8	-14	-18	-22	-23
Myrtle Beach, SC	-16	-14	-10	-6	-3	-1	-3	-5	-7	-12	-17	-17
Charleston, SC	-11	-9	-6	-3	+1	0	-1	-3	-7	-9	-11	-12
Savannah. GA	-1	0	+2	+4	+6	+6	+5	+4	+3	0	-2	-2
Brunswick, GA	+1	-1	0	+1	+2	+2	+1	+1	-1	+1	+2	+2
Ponce Inlet, FL	+1	-1	-1	-2	-4	-5	-5	-4	-2	0	+1	+1
Melbourne, FL	+1	-2	-4	-5	-7	-9	-9	-8	-5	-1	0	+1
N. Palm Beach, FL	+2	-2	-6	-8	-11	-14	-14	-11	-7	-4	0	+2
Miami, FL	+6	0	-3	-8	-13	-15	-15	-11	-7	-2	+3	+5
Key West, FL	+13	+7	+2	-3	-8	-12	-12	-6	-1	+6	+11	+14

Swimmers Beware:
Undertow, Alongshore Currents and Rip Currents

Understanding the behavior of ocean water near the shore can help bathers enjoy swimming with greater confidence. There are three types of water movement which swimmers should understand.

Undertow

When a large wave approaches a beach, it breaks, rides up the beach, and then retreats. The retreating water is **undertow**. The water motion is circular: water moves toward the beach at the top of the wave, and away from the beach beneath the wave. The force of undertow increases with wave size and angle of the ocean bottom. Swimmers knocked down either by a breaking wave or by the undertow will not be dragged far to sea by the undertow, as the next wave reverses the process.

Alongshore Current

Water motion parallel to the beach is called **alongshore current**. Swimmers, especially children, should choose landmarks before entering the water to find their way back if an alongshore current has moved them along the beach. In the highest surf conditions, these currents can be strong enough to make standing difficult.

Erica M. Szuplat

Rip Current

A third type is **rip current**, occasionally mislabeled "rip tide." This dangerous phenomenon is water moving seaward, away from the beach. It results from water finding an exit in a depression in the bottom between shoal areas, or from being deflected from the shore by sandbars, piers, and shoreline anomalies. To avoid this danger, study the water surface before going into the water. Rip currents might appear as wide breaks in the wave crests, or smooth-looking low spots in the approaching waves. The boundaries of the rip current might appear as lines of foam, debris, or swirling eddies. Be aware that rip currents can change locations in short periods of time as they create new channels.

What to Do

When caught in a rip current and being carried to sea, a swimmer should avoid swimming directly against the current toward land. Instead, escape the rip current by swimming perpendicular to the current and parallel to the shoreline. Once out of the stream, head for land.

The Publishers thank Dr. Ben J. Korgen for his contribution to this article.

TIME OF LOCAL APPARENT NOON (L.A.N.) 2021
FOR THE CENTRAL MERIDIAN OF ANY TIME ZONE

	JAN. h:m:s	FEB. h:m:s	MAR. h:m:s	APR. h:m:s	MAY h:m:s	JUN. h:m:s	JUL. h:m:s	AUG. h:m:s	SEP. h:m:s	OCT. h:m:s	NOV. h:m:s	DEC. h:m:s
1	12:03:46	12:13:37	12:12:14	12:03:44	11:57:03	11:57:54	12:03:57	12:06:18	11:59:51	11:49:30	11:43:33	11:49:10
2	12:04:14	12:13:44	12:12:02	12:03:26	11:56:56	11:58:04	12:04:09	12:06:14	11:59:32	11:49:11	11:43:33	11:49:33
3	12:04:41	12:13:50	12:11:49	12:03:09	11:56:50	11:58:14	12:04:20	12:06:09	11:59:12	11:48:53	11:43:33	11:49:56
4	12:05:09	12:13:56	12:11:36	12:02:51	11:56:44	11:58:24	12:04:30	12:06:04	11:58:52	11:48:34	11:43:34	11:50:21
5	12:05:35	12:14:01	12:11:22	12:02:34	11:56:39	11:58:35	12:04:41	12:05:58	11:58:32	11:48:16	11:43:36	11:50:46
6	12:06:01	12:14:04	12:11:08	12:02:17	11:56:35	11:58:46	12:04:51	12:05:51	11:58:12	11:47:59	11:43:38	11:51:11
7	12:06:27	12:14:08	12:10:54	12:02:00	11:56:31	11:58:57	12:05:01	12:05:44	11:57:52	11:47:42	11:43:42	11:51:37
8	12:06:53	12:14:10	12:10:39	12:01:44	11:56:28	11:59:09	12:05:10	12:05:36	11:57:31	11:47:25	11:43:46	11:52:04
9	12:07:17	12:14:12	12:10:24	12:01:28	11:56:26	11:59:21	12:05:19	12:05:27	11:57:10	11:47:09	11:43:51	11:52:30
10	12:07:42	12:14:12	12:10:09	12:01:12	11:56:23	11:59:33	12:05:27	12:05:18	11:56:49	11:46:53	11:43:57	11:52:58
11	12:08:05	12:14:12	12:09:53	12:00:56	11:56:22	11:59:45	12:05:35	12:05:09	11:56:28	11:46:37	11:44:04	11:53:25
12	12:08:29	12:14:12	12:09:37	12:00:41	11:56:21	11:59:58	12:05:43	12:04:58	11:56:07	11:46:22	11:44:11	11:53:53
13	12:08:51	12:14:10	12:09:21	12:00:26	11:56:21	12:00:10	12:05:50	12:04:48	11:55:46	11:46:08	11:44:20	11:54:21
14	12:09:13	12:14:08	12:09:05	12:00:11	11:56:21	12:00:23	12:05:57	12:04:36	11:55:24	11:45:54	11:44:29	11:54:50
15	12:09:34	12:14:05	12:08:48	11:59:56	11:56:22	12:00:36	12:06:03	12:04:24	11:55:03	11:45:41	11:44:39	11:55:19
16	12:09:54	12:14:02	12:08:31	11:59:42	11:56:23	12:00:49	12:06:08	12:04:12	11:54:42	11:45:28	11:44:50	11:55:48
17	12:10:14	12:13:57	12:08:14	11:59:29	11:56:25	12:01:02	12:06:13	12:03:59	11:54:20	11:45:16	11:45:02	11:56:17
18	12:10:33	12:13:52	12:07:56	11:59:15	11:56:28	12:01:15	12:06:18	12:03:46	11:53:59	11:45:04	11:45:14	11:56:47
19	12:10:52	12:13:46	12:07:39	11:59:02	11:56:31	12:01:28	12:06:21	12:03:32	11:53:37	11:44:53	11:45:28	11:57:16
20	12:11:09	12:13:40	12:07:21	11:58:50	11:56:34	12:01:41	12:06:25	12:03:17	11:53:16	11:44:42	11:45:42	11:57:46
21	12:11:26	12:13:33	12:07:03	11:58:38	11:56:38	12:01:54	12:06:27	12:03:02	11:52:54	11:44:33	11:45:57	11:58:15
22	12:11:42	12:13:25	12:06:45	11:58:26	11:56:43	12:02:07	12:06:30	12:02:47	11:52:33	11:44:24	11:46:13	11:58:45
23	12:11:57	12:13:17	12:06:27	11:58:15	11:56:48	12:02:20	12:06:31	12:02:31	11:52:12	11:44:15	11:46:30	11:59:15
24	12:12:11	12:13:08	12:06:09	11:58:04	11:56:53	12:02:33	12:06:32	12:02:15	11:51:51	11:44:08	11:46:47	11:59:45
25	12:12:25	12:12:58	12:05:51	11:57:54	11:56:59	12:02:45	12:06:32	12:01:58	11:51:30	11:44:01	11:47:05	12:00:14
26	12:12:38	12:12:48	12:05:33	11:57:44	11:57:06	12:02:58	12:06:32	12:01:41	11:51:10	11:43:54	11:47:24	12:00:44
27	12:12:49	12:12:37	12:05:14	11:57:35	11:57:13	12:03:10	12:06:31	12:01:23	11:50:49	11:43:49	11:47:44	12:01:14
28	12:13:01	12:12:26	12:04:56	11:57:26	11:57:20	12:03:22	12:06:30	12:01:06	11:50:29	11:43:44	11:48:04	12:01:43
29	12:13:11		12:04:38	11:57:18	11:57:28	12:03:34	12:06:28	12:00:47	11:50:09	11:43:40	11:48:25	12:02:12
30	12:13:20		12:04:20	11:57:10	11:57:36	12:03:46	12:06:25	12:00:29	11:49:50	11:43:37	11:48:47	12:02:41
31	12:13:29		12:04:02		11:57:45		12:06:22	12:00:10		11:43:35		12:03:10

Explanatory Notes: The noon sight and the Sun's Declination (p. 233) result in the vessel's parallel of latitude. It is taken at the time of the sun's meridian passage, when the sun is at maximum altitude.

The moment of meridian passage is called Local Apparent Noon (L.A.N.), and only rarely is it the same time as noon Standard Time or Local Mean Time. Instead, as this Table shows, the sun is either ahead of or behind its theoretical schedule.

Two corrections are involved. 1) To correct for your difference in longitude from the central meridian of your time zone (i.e. 75° for U.S. Atlantic Coast), either a) add 4 minutes of time for each degree West or b) subtract 4 minutes of time for each degree East. 2) If necessary, convert from Daylight Savings Time to Standard Time by subtracting 1 hour from your watch.

Thus for Boston, at 71° West longitude (or 4° East of 75°), L.A.N. occurs 16 minutes before the times listed in the Table.

For New York, at 74° West (1° East of 75°), L.A.N. occurs 4 minutes earlier than times shown.

Converting arc to time:

360° = 24 hours
15° = 1 hour
1° = 4 minutes
15' = 1 minute
1' = 4 seconds

Sun's True Bearing at Rising and Setting

To find compass deviation using the Sun.
Figures are correct for all Longitudes.

	Latitudes								
	38°N		40°N		42°N		44°N		
Sun's decl.	Rise	Set	Rise	Set	Rise	Set	Rise	Set	Sun's decl.
N 23 °	60.3	299.7	59.3	300.7	58.3	301.7	57.1	302.9	N 23 °
22	61.6	298.4	60.7	299.3	59.7	300.3	58.6	301.4	22
21	63.0	297.0	62.1	297.9	61.2	298.8	60.1	299.9	21
20	64.3	295.7	63.5	296.5	62.6	297.4	61.6	298.4	20
19	65.6	294.4	64.9	295.1	64.0	296.0	63.1	296.9	19
18	66.9	293.1	66.2	293.8	65.4	294.6	64.6	295.4	18
17	68.2	291.8	67.6	292.4	66.8	293.2	66.0	294.0	17
16	69.5	290.5	68.9	291.1	68.2	291.8	67.5	292.5	16
15	70.8	289.2	70.3	289.7	69.6	290.4	68.9	291.1	15
14	72.1	287.9	71.6	288.4	71.0	289.0	70.4	289.6	14
13	73.4	286.6	72.9	287.1	72.4	287.6	71.8	288.2	13
12	74.7	285.3	74.3	285.7	73.8	286.2	73.2	286.8	12
11	76.0	284.0	75.6	284.4	75.1	284.9	74.6	285.4	11
10	77.3	282.7	76.9	283.1	76.5	283.5	76.0	284.0	10
9	78.6	281.4	78.2	281.8	77.9	282.1	77.4	282.6	9
8	79.8	280.2	79.5	280.5	79.2	280.8	78.9	281.1	8
7	81.1	278.9	80.9	279.1	80.6	279.4	80.3	279.7	7
6	82.4	277.6	82.2	277.7	81.9	278.1	81.7	278.3	6
5	83.7	276.3	83.5	276.5	83.3	276.7	83.0	277.0	5
4	84.9	275.1	84.8	275.2	84.6	275.4	84.4	275.6	4
3	86.2	273.8	86.1	273.9	86.0	274.0	85.8	274.2	3
2	87.5	272.5	87.4	272.6	87.3	272.7	87.2	272.8	2
N 1 °	88.7	271.3	88.7	271.3	88.7	271.3	88.6	271.4	N 1 °
0	90.0	270.0	90.0	270.0	90.0	270.0	90.0	270.0	0
S 1 °	91.3	268.7	91.3	268.7	91.3	268.7	91.4	268.6	S 1 °
2	92.5	267.5	92.6	267.4	92.7	267.3	92.8	267.2	2
3	93.8	266.2	93.9	266.1	94.0	266.0	94.2	265.8	3
4	95.1	264.9	95.2	264.8	95.4	264.6	95.6	264.4	4
5	96.3	263.7	96.5	263.5	96.7	263.3	97.0	263.0	5
6	97.6	262.4	97.8	262.2	98.1	261.9	98.3	261.7	6
7	98.9	261.1	99.1	260.9	99.4	260.6	99.7	260.3	7
8	100.2	259.8	100.5	259.5	100.8	259.2	101.1	258.9	8
9	101.4	258.6	101.8	258.2	102.1	257.9	102.6	257.4	9
10	102.7	257.3	103.1	256.9	103.5	256.5	104.0	256.0	10
11	104.0	256.0	104.4	255.6	104.9	255.1	105.4	254.6	11
12	105.3	254.7	105.7	254.3	106.2	253.8	106.8	253.2	12
13	106.6	253.4	107.1	252.9	107.6	252.4	108.2	251.8	13
14	107.9	252.1	108.4	251.6	109.0	251.0	109.6	250.4	14
15	109.2	250.8	109.7	250.3	110.4	249.6	111.1	248.9	15
16	110.5	249.5	111.1	248.9	111.8	248.2	112.5	247.5	16
17	111.8	248.2	112.4	247.6	113.2	246.8	114.0	246.0	17
18	113.1	246.9	113.8	246.2	114.6	245.4	115.4	244.6	18
19	114.4	245.6	115.1	244.9	116.0	244.0	116.9	243.1	19
20	115.7	244.3	116.5	243.5	117.4	242.6	118.4	241.6	20
21	117.0	243.0	117.9	242.1	118.8	241.2	119.9	240.1	21
22	118.4	241.6	119.3	240.7	120.3	239.7	121.4	238.6	22
S 23 °	119.7	240.3	120.7	239.3	121.7	238.3	122.9	237.1	S 23 °

Instructions: (1) Knowing the date, find the Sun's Declination from the facing page. Find that Declination down the left column on this page. (2) Find the column with your Latitude, and choose either Rise or Set to determine the True Bearing. (3) Add the local Westerly Variation to the figure. (4) If you are a couple of minutes after sunrise or before sunset, the Sun's bearing changes about 1° each 6 minutes during the first hour after sunrise and before sunset. (5) The deviation found will be correct only for the heading you are on at that time.

The Sun's Declination 2021

For celestial navigators, the "noon sight" reading of the Sun's height above the horizon, together with the Sun's Declination from this table, determines latitude.

The Sun's Declination 2021

MEAN NOON – 75° MERIDIAN **(1700 G.M.T.)**

	JAN.	FEB.	MAR.	APR.	MAY	JUN.	JUL.	AUG.	SEP.	OCT.	NOV.	DEC.	
	South ° '	South ° '	South ° '	North ° '	North ° '	North ° '	North ° '	North ° '	North ° '	South ° '	South ° '	South ° '	
1	-22 56	-16 54	-7 19	+4 49	+15 17	+22 09	+23 03	+17 50	+8 01	-3 28	-14 39	-21 54	1
2	-22 51	-16 36	-6 56	+5 12	+15 35	+22 17	+22 59	+17 34	+7 39	-3 51	-14 58	-22 03	2
3	-22 45	-16 19	-6 33	+5 35	+15 53	+22 24	+22 54	+17 19	+7 17	-4 14	-15 17	-22 12	3
4	-22 38	-16 01	-6 10	+5 58	+16 10	+22 31	+22 49	+17 03	+6 55	-4 37	-15 35	-22 20	4
5	-22 32	-15 42	-5 47	+6 21	+16 27	+22 37	+22 43	+16 46	+6 33	-5 00	-15 53	-22 27	5
6	-22 24	-15 24	-5 23	+6 43	+16 44	+22 43	+22 37	+16 30	+6 10	-5 23	-16 11	-22 34	6
7	-22 17	-15 05	-5 00	+7 06	+17 01	+22 49	+22 30	+16 13	+5 48	-5 46	-16 29	-22 41	7
8	-22 08	-14 46	-4 37	+7 28	+17 17	+22 54	+22 23	+15 56	+5 25	-6 09	-16 46	-22 47	8
9	-21 60	-14 27	-4 13	+7 50	+17 33	+22 59	+22 16	+15 39	+5 03	-6 32	-17 03	-22 53	9
10	-21 51	-14 07	-3 50	+8 13	+17 48	+23 04	+22 08	+15 21	+4 40	-6 55	-17 20	-22 58	10
11	-21 41	-13 47	-3 26	+8 35	+18 04	+23 08	+22 00	+15 03	+4 17	-7 17	-17 37	-23 03	11
12	-21 31	-13 27	-3 02	+8 57	+18 19	+23 12	+21 52	+14 45	+3 54	-7 40	-17 53	-23 07	12
13	-21 21	-13 07	-2 39	+9 18	+18 34	+23 15	+21 43	+14 27	+3 31	-8 02	-18 09	-23 11	13
14	-21 10	-12 47	-2 15	+9 40	+18 48	+23 18	+21 34	+14 08	+3 08	-8 24	-18 24	-23 15	14
15	-20 59	-12 26	-1 51	+10 01	+19 02	+23 20	+21 24	+13 49	+2 45	-8 47	-18 40	-23 18	15
16	-20 48	-12 05	-1 28	+10 23	+19 16	+23 22	+21 14	+13 30	+2 22	-9 09	-18 54	-23 20	16
17	-20 36	-11 44	-1 04	+10 44	+19 29	+23 24	+21 04	+13 11	+1 59	-9 31	-19 09	-23 23	17
18	-20 24	-11 23	-0 40	+11 05	+19 42	+23 25	+20 54	+12 52	+1 35	-9 52	-19 23	-23 24	18
19	-20 11	-11 01	-0 16	+11 25	+19 55	+23 26	+20 43	+12 32	+1 12	-10 14	-19 37	-23 25	19
20	-19 58	-10 40	+0 07	+11 46	+20 08	+23 26	+20 31	+12 12	+0 49	-10 35	-19 51	-23 26	20
21	-19 44	-10 18	+0 31	+12 06	+20 20	+23 26	+20 20	+11 52	+0 26	-10 57	-20 04	-23 26	21
22	-19 31	-9 56	+0 55	+12 26	+20 31	+23 26	+20 08	+11 32	+0 02	-11 18	-20 17	-23 26	22
23	-19 16	-9 34	+1 18	+12 46	+20 43	+23 25	+19 55	+11 12	-0 21	-11 39	-20 29	-23 25	23
24	-19 02	-9 12	+1 42	+13 06	+20 54	+23 24	+19 43	+10 51	-0 44	-11 60	-20 41	-23 24	24
25	-18 47	-8 49	+2 06	+13 25	+21 05	+23 22	+19 30	+10 31	-1 08	-12 20	-20 53	-23 22	25
26	-18 32	-8 27	+2 29	+13 45	+21 15	+23 20	+19 16	+10 10	-1 31	-12 41	-21 04	-23 20	26
27	-18 16	-8 04	+2 53	+14 04	+21 25	+23 17	+19 03	+9 49	-1 54	-13 01	-21 15	-23 18	27
28	-18 00	-7 42	+3 16	+14 22	+21 34	+23 14	+18 49	+9 27	-2 18	-13 21	-21 25	-23 15	28
29	-17 44		+3 39	+14 41	+21 44	+23 11	+18 34	+9 06	-2 41	-13 41	-21 35	-23 11	29
30	-17 28		+4 03	+14 59	+21 52	+23 07	+18 20	+8 45	-3 04	-14 01	-21 45	-23 07	30
31	-17 11		+4 26		+22 01		+18 05	+8 23		-14 20		-23 03	31

Vernal Equinox: March 20th, 4:37 a.m. E.S.T.
Summer Solstice: June 20th, 10:32 p.m. E.S.T.

Autumnal Equinox: September 22nd, 2:21 p.m. E.S.T.
Winter Solstice: December 21st, 10:59 a.m. E.S.T.

To find Sun's Declination in the Atlantic Time Zone (1 hour earlier than E.S.T.), take 1/24 of the difference between Day 1 and Day 2. Add or subtract this figure from Day 2 to find the Declination for Day 2.

If Declination is increasing (N. or S.), *subtract*. If Declination is decreasing (N. or S.), *add*.

2021 MOON'S RISING AND SETTING AT BOSTON – 42° 20'N 71°W

Daylight Saving Time is March 14 – November 7, transitions are noted with an *

	JAN.		FEB.		MAR.		APR.		MAY		JUN.		
	Rise	Set	Rise	Set	Rise	Set	Rise	Set	Rise	Set	Rise	Set	
Day	h m	h m	h m	h m	h m	h m	h m	h m	h m	h m	h m	h m	Day
01	18:58	9:18	21:32	9:24	20:31	7:51	...	8:54	0:23	9:16	1:18	11:35	01
02	20:08	9:55	22:45	9:50	21:46	8:18	0:19	9:37	1:21	10:22	1:45	12:41	02
03	21:18	10:26	23:58	10:16	23:02	8:47	1:31	10:29	2:08	11:31	2:09	13:44	03
04	22:29	10:54	...	10:46	...	9:19	2:33	11:28	2:45	12:39	2:31	14:46	04
05	23:41	11:20	1:12	11:19	0:18	9:57	3:25	12:34	3:15	13:46	2:51	15:47	05
06	...	11:46	2:26	11:58	1:30	10:42	4:07	13:41	3:41	14:50	3:13	16:47	06
07	0:53	12:13	3:37	12:46	2:37	11:35	4:42	14:48	4:03	15:52	3:35	17:48	07
08	2:07	12:44	4:43	13:42	3:36	12:36	5:10	15:54	4:25	16:53	4:01	18:50	08
09	3:23	13:19	5:40	14:46	4:25	13:42	5:35	16:57	4:45	17:54	4:31	19:51	09
10	4:38	14:03	6:27	15:54	5:05	14:50	5:57	17:59	5:07	18:55	5:06	20:51	10
11	5:50	14:55	7:05	17:03	5:38	15:57	6:18	19:00	5:31	19:56	5:48	21:46	11
12	6:54	15:56	7:37	18:10	6:05	17:02	6:40	20:01	5:57	20:58	6:38	22:35	12
13	7:49	17:03	8:03	19:16	6:30	18:06	7:02	21:02	6:29	21:58	7:35	23:17	13
14	8:33	18:13	8:27	20:19	*7:52	20:08	7:27	22:04	7:06	22:56	8:38	23:53	14
15	9:08	19:21	8:49	21:20	8:14	21:09	7:55	23:05	7:51	23:49	9:45	...	15
16	9:38	20:28	9:11	22:21	8:35	22:10	8:28	...	8:43	...	10:53	0:24	16
17	10:03	21:31	9:33	23:22	8:59	23:11	9:08	0:05	9:42	0:36	12:02	0:52	17
18	10:26	22:33	9:58	...	9:25	...	9:55	1:01	10:46	1:16	13:12	1:17	18
19	10:47	23:33	10:25	0:23	9:55	0:13	10:50	1:52	11:54	1:51	14:24	1:42	19
20	11:09	...	10:58	1:24	10:30	1:13	11:52	2:38	13:04	2:21	15:39	2:07	20
21	11:32	0:33	11:37	2:25	11:13	2:12	12:59	3:17	14:15	2:48	16:57	2:36	21
22	11:58	1:34	12:24	3:23	12:04	3:08	14:10	3:51	15:29	3:14	18:17	3:09	22
23	12:27	2:35	13:20	4:18	13:04	3:58	15:23	4:20	16:45	3:40	19:35	3:49	23
24	13:03	3:37	14:23	5:06	14:10	4:42	16:38	4:48	18:04	4:08	20:47	4:40	24
25	13:46	4:38	15:33	5:48	15:21	5:20	17:55	5:14	19:25	4:39	21:48	5:41	25
26	14:37	5:36	16:46	6:24	16:35	5:53	19:14	5:42	20:46	5:16	22:37	6:50	26
27	15:37	6:28	18:01	6:56	17:50	6:22	20:35	6:12	22:02	6:02	23:15	8:04	27
28	16:44	7:14	19:16	7:24	19:07	6:50	21:56	6:46	23:08	6:58	23:46	9:16	28
29	17:54	7:53			20:25	7:17	23:14	7:28	...	8:03	...	10:26	29
30	19:07	8:27			21:43	7:45	...	8:18	0:02	9:14	0:12	11:32	30
31	20:19	8:57			23:02	8:17			0:44	10:25			31

	JUL.		AUG.		SEP.		OCT.		NOV.		DEC.		
	Rise	Set	Rise	Set	Rise	Set	Rise	Set	Rise	Set	Rise	Set	
Day	h m	h m	h m	h m	h m	h m	h m	h m	h m	h m	h m	h m	Day
01	0:35	12:36	0:05	14:30	0:17	16:16	0:50	16:24	3:05	16:17	3:20	14:32	01
02	0:56	13:38	0:32	15:32	1:07	17:06	1:56	16:57	4:17	16:42	4:38	15:03	02
03	1:17	14:39	1:03	16:33	2:04	17:50	3:06	17:26	5:32	17:08	6:00	15:41	03
04	1:39	15:40	1:41	17:31	3:08	18:27	4:17	17:53	6:50	17:37	7:22	16:28	04
05	2:04	16:41	2:26	18:25	4:17	18:59	5:30	18:18	8:11	18:11	8:39	17:27	05
06	2:32	17:43	3:19	19:13	5:28	19:27	6:44	18:43	9:33	18:53	9:45	18:36	06
07	3:05	18:43	4:19	19:54	6:39	19:53	8:00	19:10	*9:51	18:45	10:38	19:51	07
08	3:45	19:40	5:25	20:29	7:52	20:17	9:18	19:41	11:01	19:47	11:19	21:06	08
09	4:33	20:31	6:34	20:59	9:05	20:43	10:37	20:17	11:58	20:57	11:51	22:18	09
10	5:29	21:16	7:44	21:25	10:19	21:10	11:55	21:02	12:44	22:09	12:18	23:27	10
11	6:31	21:55	8:54	21:50	11:35	21:42	13:07	21:56	13:20	23:21	12:41	...	11
12	7:37	22:27	10:05	22:14	12:52	22:20	14:10	22:59	13:49	...	13:02	0:32	12
13	8:45	22:56	11:17	22:40	14:06	23:07	15:02	...	14:13	0:30	13:23	1:35	13
14	9:54	23:21	12:30	23:08	15:14	...	15:43	0:08	14:35	1:36	13:44	2:38	14
15	11:03	23:46	13:45	23:42	16:13	0:03	16:16	1:19	14:56	2:40	14:07	3:40	15
16	12:13	...	15:00	...	17:01	1:08	16:43	2:29	15:17	3:42	14:34	4:42	16
17	13:25	0:10	16:13	0:22	17:40	2:18	17:07	3:38	15:39	4:45	15:06	5:44	17
18	14:40	0:37	17:20	1:12	18:12	3:29	17:29	4:43	16:03	5:47	15:44	6:45	18
19	15:56	1:07	18:17	2:11	18:39	4:40	17:50	5:48	16:32	6:50	16:29	7:42	19
20	17:13	1:43	19:03	3:20	19:02	5:49	18:11	6:51	17:05	7:52	17:21	8:34	20
21	18:27	2:27	19:40	4:32	19:24	6:55	18:34	7:54	17:45	8:52	18:20	9:19	21
22	19:32	3:22	20:11	5:45	19:46	7:59	19:00	8:57	18:33	9:48	19:23	9:57	22
23	20:26	4:27	20:37	6:56	20:08	9:02	19:30	9:59	19:27	10:37	20:28	10:29	23
24	21:09	5:39	21:00	8:04	20:32	10:05	20:06	11:01	20:27	11:20	21:34	10:57	24
25	21:43	6:53	21:22	9:09	21:00	11:08	20:49	11:59	21:31	11:56	22:41	11:22	25
26	22:12	8:06	21:43	10:13	21:32	12:10	21:39	12:53	22:37	12:27	23:49	11:45	26
27	22:36	9:15	22:06	11:16	22:10	13:10	22:36	13:40	23:45	12:54	...	12:07	27
28	22:58	10:21	22:32	12:18	22:56	14:07	23:38	14:21	...	13:18	0:59	12:32	28
29	23:20	11:25	23:01	13:20	23:50	14:59	...	14:56	0:54	13:42	2:12	12:59	29
30	23:42	12:27	23:36	14:22	...	15:45	0:45	15:26	2:06	14:06	3:30	13:31	30
31	...	13:29	...	15:21			1:54	15:53			4:50	14:12	31

2021 MOON'S RISING AND SETTING AT NEW YORK – 40° 42'N 74°W

Daylight Saving Time is March 14 – November 7, transitions are noted with an *

	JAN.		FEB.		MAR.		APR.		MAY		JUN.		
	Rise	Set	Rise	Set	Rise	Set	Rise	Set	Rise	Set	Rise	Set	
Day	h m	h m	h m	h m	h m	h m	h m	h m	h m	h m	h m	h m	Day
01	19:15	9:26	21:45	9:35	20:43	8:03	...	9:11	0:29	9:35	1:26	11:51	01
02	20:24	10:03	22:56	10:02	21:57	8:32	0:26	9:55	1:28	10:41	1:55	12:56	02
03	21:33	10:35	...	10:30	23:11	9:02	1:37	10:48	2:15	11:49	2:20	13:58	03
04	22:43	11:04	0:08	11:01	...	9:36	2:39	11:47	2:53	12:56	2:42	14:58	04
05	23:53	11:32	1:21	11:35	0:26	10:14	3:32	12:52	3:24	14:01	3:04	15:58	05
06	...	11:59	2:34	12:16	1:37	11:00	4:15	13:58	3:51	15:04	3:27	16:57	06
07	1:04	12:27	3:44	13:04	2:44	11:54	4:50	15:04	4:15	16:05	3:50	17:57	07
08	2:17	12:59	4:49	14:01	3:42	12:55	5:19	16:09	4:37	17:05	4:17	18:58	08
09	3:31	13:36	5:46	15:04	4:32	14:00	5:45	17:11	4:59	18:05	4:48	19:58	09
10	4:46	14:20	6:34	16:11	5:12	15:07	6:09	18:12	5:21	19:04	5:24	20:57	10
11	5:57	15:13	7:13	17:19	5:46	16:13	6:31	19:12	5:46	20:05	6:07	21:52	11
12	7:01	16:14	7:45	18:26	6:15	17:17	6:53	20:12	6:14	21:05	6:57	22:41	12
13	7:55	17:21	8:13	19:30	6:40	18:20	7:17	21:12	6:46	22:05	7:54	23:24	13
14	8:40	18:30	8:38	20:32	*8:04	20:21	7:42	22:12	7:24	23:02	8:56	...	14
15	9:17	19:37	9:01	21:32	8:26	21:21	8:12	23:12	8:09	23:55	10:01	0:01	15
16	9:47	20:43	9:24	22:32	8:49	22:20	8:46	...	9:02	...	11:08	0:33	16
17	10:13	21:45	9:48	23:31	9:14	23:20	9:26	0:11	1...	0:42	12:16	1:02	17
18	10:37	22:46	10:13	...	9:41	...	10:14	1:07	11:04	1:23	13:25	1:28	18
19	11:00	23:45	10:42	0:31	10:12	0:21	11:09	1:59	12:10	1:59	14:36	1:54	19
20	11:23	...	11:15	1:31	10:48	1:21	12:10	2:44	13:19	2:30	15:50	2:21	20
21	11:47	0:44	11:55	2:31	11:32	2:19	13:17	3:24	14:29	2:59	17:06	2:51	21
22	12:13	1:43	12:42	3:30	12:23	3:14	14:26	3:59	15:41	3:26	18:25	3:25	22
23	12:44	2:44	13:38	4:24	13:22	4:04	15:38	4:30	16:56	3:53	19:42	4:07	23
24	13:20	3:45	14:41	5:13	14:28	4:49	16:52	4:59	18:13	4:22	20:53	4:58	24
25	14:04	4:45	15:50	5:56	15:38	5:28	18:07	5:27	19:33	4:55	21:54	6:00	25
26	14:56	5:42	17:02	6:33	16:50	6:02	19:25	5:56	20:53	5:34	22:44	7:09	26
27	15:55	6:35	18:16	7:05	18:04	6:32	20:44	6:27	22:08	6:21	23:23	8:21	27
28	17:01	7:21	19:29	7:35	19:19	7:01	22:04	7:03	23:14	7:17	23:55	9:33	28
29	18:11	8:01			20:36	7:30	23:20	7:45	...	8:22	...	10:41	29
30	19:22	8:36			21:53	8:00	...	8:36	0:08	9:32	0:22	11:46	30
31	20:34	9:07			23:11	8:33			0:52	10:42			31

	JUL.		AUG.		SEP.		OCT.		NOV.		DEC.		
	Rise	Set	Rise	Set	Rise	Set	Rise	Set	Rise	Set	Rise	Set	
Day	h m	h m	h m	h m	h m	h m	h m	h m	h m	h m	h m	h m	Day
01	0:46	12:49	0:21	14:39	0:36	16:22	1:09	16:31	3:19	16:29	3:31	14:47	01
02	1:08	13:49	0:49	15:40	1:26	17:12	2:14	17:05	4:30	16:55	4:48	15:19	02
03	1:31	14:49	1:21	16:40	2:23	17:57	3:22	17:36	5:44	17:22	6:08	15:58	03
04	1:54	15:49	1:59	17:37	3:26	18:35	4:32	18:03	7:00	17:52	7:28	16:47	04
05	2:20	16:49	2:44	18:31	4:34	19:08	5:44	18:30	8:20	18:28	8:45	17:46	05
06	2:49	17:50	3:38	19:19	5:43	19:37	6:56	18:56	9:40	19:11	9:51	18:55	06
07	3:23	18:49	4:38	20:01	6:54	20:04	8:11	19:25	*9:57	19:04	10:44	20:09	07
08	4:04	19:46	5:43	20:37	8:05	20:30	9:28	19:57	11:07	20:06	11:26	21:23	08
09	4:52	20:38	6:50	21:08	9:17	20:57	10:45	20:35	12:04	21:15	12:00	22:34	09
10	5:47	21:23	7:59	21:36	10:30	21:26	12:02	21:21	12:51	22:27	12:28	23:41	10
11	6:49	22:02	9:08	22:02	11:44	21:59	13:13	22:15	13:28	23:37	12:52	...	11
12	7:54	22:36	10:18	22:27	12:59	22:38	14:16	23:18	13:58	...	13:14	0:45	12
13	9:01	23:05	11:28	22:54	14:12	23:26	15:08	...	14:23	0:45	13:36	1:47	13
14	10:08	23:32	12:40	23:24	15:20	...	15:50	0:27	14:47	1:50	13:59	2:48	14
15	11:16	23:58	13:53	23:58	16:19	0:22	16:24	1:37	15:08	2:52	14:23	3:49	15
16	12:25	...	15:08	...	17:08	1:27	16:53	2:46	15:30	3:54	14:51	4:50	16
17	13:36	0:23	16:20	0:40	17:48	2:36	17:18	3:52	15:54	4:55	15:24	5:52	17
18	14:49	0:51	17:26	1:30	18:21	3:46	17:41	4:57	16:19	5:57	16:02	6:52	18
19	16:04	1:22	18:23	2:31	18:49	4:56	18:03	6:00	16:49	6:58	16:48	7:48	19
20	17:20	2:00	19:10	3:38	19:13	6:03	18:26	7:02	17:23	7:59	17:40	8:40	20
21	18:33	2:46	19:48	4:50	19:37	7:08	18:50	8:04	18:04	8:58	18:39	9:25	21
22	19:38	3:41	20:20	6:02	19:59	8:11	19:17	9:05	18:52	9:54	19:41	10:04	22
23	20:32	4:46	20:47	7:11	20:23	9:13	19:48	10:07	19:46	10:43	20:45	10:37	23
24	21:16	5:58	21:11	8:18	20:48	10:15	20:24	11:08	20:45	11:26	21:50	11:06	24
25	21:52	7:10	21:34	9:22	21:16	11:16	21:08	12:05	21:49	12:03	22:55	11:32	25
26	22:21	8:22	21:57	10:24	21:50	12:17	21:58	12:59	22:54	12:35	...	11:56	26
27	22:47	9:30	22:21	11:26	22:29	13:17	22:55	13:46	...	13:03	0:02	12:20	27
28	23:10	10:34	22:48	12:27	23:15	14:13	23:56	14:28	...	13:29	1:10	12:46	28
29	23:33	11:37	23:18	13:28	...	15:05	1:00	15:03	1:08	13:54	2:22	13:14	29
30	23:56	12:38	23:54	14:29	0:08	15:51	1:02	15:35	2:18	14:19	3:38	13:48	30
31	...	13:38	...	15:27			2:10	16:02			4:57	14:30	31

PHASES OF THE MOON 2021 E.T.

Daylight Saving Time is March 14 – November 7, transitions are noted with an *

● New Moon, ◐ 1st Quarter, ○ Full Moon, ◑ Last Quarter, A in Apogee, P in Perigee, N, S Moon farthest North or South of Equator, E on Equator

January	February	March	April	May	June
E 5 9 PM	E 2 2 AM	E 1 8 AM	S 3 11 PM	S 1 6 AM	◑ 2 3 AM
◑ 6 5 AM	P 3 2 PM	P 2 12 AM	◑ 4 6 AM	◑ 3 4 PM	E 4 12 PM
P 9 11 AM	◑ 4 1 PM	◑ 5 9 PM	E 10 11 PM	E 8 5 AM	A 7 10 PM
S 12 4 AM	S 8 11 AM	S 7 4 PM	● 11 11 PM	● 11 3 PM	● 10 7 AM
● 13 12 AM	● 11 2 PM	● 13 5 AM	A 14 2 PM	A 11 6 PM	N 12 1 AM
E 19 1 AM	E 15 8 AM	E 14 *5 PM	N 18 1 PM	N 15 7 PM	◐ 18 12 AM
◐ 20 4 PM	A 18 5 AM	A 18 1 AM	◐ 20 3 AM	◐ 19 3 PM	E 19 12 AM
A 21 8 AM	◐ 19 2 PM	◐ 21 11 AM	E 25 6 AM	E 22 4 PM	P 23 6 AM
N 26 11 AM	N 22 8 PM	N 22 5 AM	○ 27 12 AM	P 25 10 PM	○ 24 3 PM
○ 28 2 PM	○ 27 3 AM	○ 28 3 PM	P 27 11 AM	○ 26 7 AM	S 25 2 AM
		E 28 7 PM		S 28 4 PM	
		P 30 2 AM			

July	August	September	October	November	December
◑ 1 5 PM	A 2 4 AM	N 1 9 PM	E 6 1 AM	E 2 12 PM	● 4 3 AM
E 1 6 PM	N 5 1 PM	● 6 9 PM	● 6 7 AM	● 4 5 PM	P 4 5 AM
A 5 11 AM	● 8 10 AM	E 8 4 PM	P 8 1 PM	P 5 6 PM	S 5 10 PM
N 9 7 AM	E 12 10 AM	P 11 6 AM	S 12 6 AM	S 8 *12 PM	◐ 10 9 PM
● 9 9 PM	◐ 15 11 AM	◐ 13 5 PM	◐ 12 11 PM	◐ 11 8 AM	E 12 12 PM
E 16 5 AM	P 17 5 AM	S 15 12 AM	E 19 1 AM	E 15 6 AM	A 17 9 PM
◐ 17 6 AM	S 18 7 PM	○ 20 8 PM	○ 20 11 AM	○ 19 4 AM	○ 19 12 AM
P 21 6 AM	○ 22 8 AM	E 21 6 PM	A 24 11 AM	A 20 9 PM	N 20 12 AM
S 22 12 PM	E 25 10 AM	A 26 6 PM	N 26 1 PM	N 22 6 PM	◑ 26 9 PM
○ 23 11 PM	A 29 10 PM	◑ 28 10 PM	◑ 28 4 PM	◑ 27 7 AM	E 27 5 AM
E 29 2 AM	◑ 30 3 AM	N 29 5 AM		E 29 9 PM	
◑ 31 9 AM					

Midnight is the *beginning* of the day.

The Tides, The Moon and The Sun

Tides are created on the earth by the pull of gravity between the earth and moon, and to a lesser extent the sun. Since the moon's pull weakens with distance, its pull is stronger on water located on the near side of the earth than it is on the earth's center. This creates a bulge of water on the side facing the moon. Similarly, the moon's pull on the earth's center is stronger than it is on the water on the earth's far side. This tends to pull the earth away from the water, creating another bulge of water of equal size on the far side of the earth. High tides are where the bulges are. The two bulges can also be explained as the moon's gravity being dominant on the earth's near side, and centrifugal force being dominant on the earth's far side.

The earth rotates in the same direction as the moon orbits, but much more rapidly, with a period of 24 hours vs. 27.3 days. The earth thus spins rapidly under the slowly rotating bulges, which follow the moon. A given point on the earth thus takes 24 hours and 50 minutes to rotate from one tidal bulge around to the same bulge, so the tides occur 50 minutes later than the previous day. As there are usually two highs and two lows per day, highs and lows average about 6 hours 12 1/2 minutes apart. A handy fact for planners: in the course of 7 days, the tides are about the reverse of the previous week: if there is a low on Sunday at about noon, the following Sunday it will be about high at noon.

The time of high tide does not usually coincide exactly with the time the moon is overhead or underneath. The largest astronomical reason for this is the effect of the sun, which has its own tidal effect on the earth. Although the sun has a mass 27 million times that of the moon, it is the moon which dominates by being on average 390 times closer to earth. Since the sun's effect on the tides is about one-half that of the moon, the sun can shift tidal times by up to one hour or more, depending on its position. Tidal times are also greatly affected by land masses that impede the current flows necessary to create the tides, the speeds of traveling ocean waves, and underwater topography.

How much the ocean tides rise and fall depends basically on three conditions. (See Phases of the Moon, p. 236.) First, when the sun and moon are in a line with the earth, their gravitational forces work together to produce a greater range of tide than usual. This occurs both at full moon, when the moon is opposite the earth from the sun, and at new moon, when the moon is between the earth and sun. These higher tides are called "spring tides." But when the moon and sun are at right angles to the earth (first and last quarter, or half moon), their forces are working against each other, and the result is a lower range of tide than usual. These are called "neap tides." As each year has about 13 "lunar" months, we have 26 spring tides and 26 neap tides in the year.

Second, the moon's orbit around the earth is elliptical, ranging from 252,000 miles at apogee (A) down to 221,000 miles at perigee (P), so the moon's effect on the earth is greater at "P" than at "A." Note again in the High and Low Water Tables how much higher the tide is when the Full Moon is at "P" than when the Full Moon is at "A." The position of the moon along its elliptical path is very important to the height of the tides.

Third, the moon's orbit about the earth is inclined to the plane of the earth's equator, varying from 18° to 28°. The moon therefore travels above and below the earth's equator, and sits directly above the equator only twice a month When it is over the equator, the day's two high tides will be about the same height. The rest of the time the moon is either above the northern hemisphere or the southern hemisphere, and the two high water marks on the same day will differ in height. This is known as "semidiurnal inequality." When the moon has northern declination, the highest part of the nearside bulge is located under the moon in the north, and the highest part of the farside bulge is opposite the moon in the south. When the U.S. at northern latitudes is on the moon side, it therefore experiences a very high tide, but when it rotates around to be on the far side, it will find itself north of the maximum bulge and will experience a lower tide.

The height of tides is influenced most by the moon's phase, with the highest tides at Full and New Moon; second by the moon's distance from earth in its elliptical orbit, tides being highest when the moon is closest, at perigee; and last by the moon's declination, north or south, which creates tides of different heights on the same day.

For a more exhaustive exploration of astronomical and physical forces acting on the tides, see NOAA's website at http://tidesandcurrents.noaa.gov/restles1.html

The Publishers thank Nelson Caldwell, of the Smithsonian Astrophysical Observatory, Cambridge, MA, and Hale Bradt, Department of Physics, M.I.T., for their valuable contributions to this article.

Visibility of Planets in Twilight

	Morning	**Evening**
VENUS	January 1 – February 14	May 5 – December 31
MARS	—	January 1 – August 23
	November 23 – December 31	—
JUPITER	—	January 1 – January 16
	February 11 – August 20	August 20 – December 31
SATURN	—	January 1 – January 7
	February 10 – August 2	August 2 – December 31

Visibility of the Planets 2021

Mercury can only be seen low in the east before sunrise, or low in the west after sunset. It is visible in the mornings from February 15 to April 10, June 20 to July 25 and October 16 to November 13. It is brighter at the end of each period. It is visible in the evenings from January 5 to February 2, April 27 to June 1, August 10 to October 3, and December 16 to December 31. It is brighter at the beginning of each period.

Venus is a brilliant object in the morning sky from the beginning of the year until mid-February when it becomes too close to the Sun for observation. In early May it reappears in the evening sky where it stays until the end of the year. Venus is in conjunction with Jupiter on February 11, with Mercury on May 29 and December 29 and with Mars on July 13.

Mars is visible as a reddish object in Pisces in the evening sky at the beginning of the year. Its eastward elongation decreases as it moves through Aries from early January, Taurus from late February, into Gemini from late April, Cancer in early June and then Leo in mid-July. It becomes too close to the sun for observation in late August. It reappears in the morning sky during late November in Libra, moving into Scorpius in mid-December and then into Ophiuchus in late December, where it remains for the rest of the year. Mars is in conjunction with Venus on July 13 and with Mercury on August 19.

Jupiter can be seen in Capricornus until mid-January, when it becomes too close to the Sun for observation. It reappears in the morning sky in the second week of February. Its westward elongation gradually increases, moving into Aquarius in late April. From late May it can be seen for more than half the night. It moves into Capricornus in mid-August and is at opposition on August 20 when it is visible throughout the night. Its eastward elongation then decreases and from mid-November it can only be seen in the evening sky passing into Aquarius in mid-December. Jupiter is in conjunction with Mercury on January 11, February 13, and March 5 and with Venus on February 11.

Saturn can be seen in Capricornus for the first week of January. It then becomes too close to the Sun for observation. It reappears in the morning sky in the second week of February. Its westward elongation gradually increases and from early May it can be seen for more than half the night. It is at opposition on August 2 when it is visible throughout the night. Its eastward elongation then decreases and from late October it can only be seen in the evening sky.

Conjunction occurs when a body has the same horizontal bearing from Earth as another. When Venus is in conjunction with Mercury on May 29, they appear one over the other, in the same sector of the sky.

Opposition occurs when a body, farther than Earth from the Sun, appears opposite the Sun. On a line drawn from the Sun through the Earth and beyond, the body lies on that extension. It is brightest at that time.

Elongation is apparent motion eastward (clockwise) or westward (counterclockwise) relative to the Sun across the sky. When a planet has 0° elongation, it lies on a line from Earth to the Sun, is in conjunction with the Sun and is not visible; when it has 90° elongation, it is in eastern quadrature; when it has 180° elongation, it is in opposition and has the best visibility; when it has 270° elongation, it is in western quadrature.

A Thousand Dizzying Eddies

Hell Gate and Its Approaches: An Informal History

by Jake Lundberg

Like New York City itself, Hell Gate is a place of turbulent confluence. There, about eight miles up the East River from the Battery, the waters of the Long Island Sound, New York's Upper Bay, and the Harlem River meet. A hydrological melee ensues. Crowded by islands, spiked with rocks, bounded by points and protuberances, perplexed by acute angles, it's as if three titans took a quarrel outside, only to tussle in the phone booth on the corner. Currents rip, eddies whirl, stationary waves stand up, and mariners break into cold sweats. "To navigate a vessel through these intricate passages," an 1857 government report cautioned, "in which the water runs with such speed...and whirls in a thousand dizzying eddies, requires...a cool head and a steady hand." Or, as a seventeenth-century observer put it more concisely: "it threatens present shipwreck."

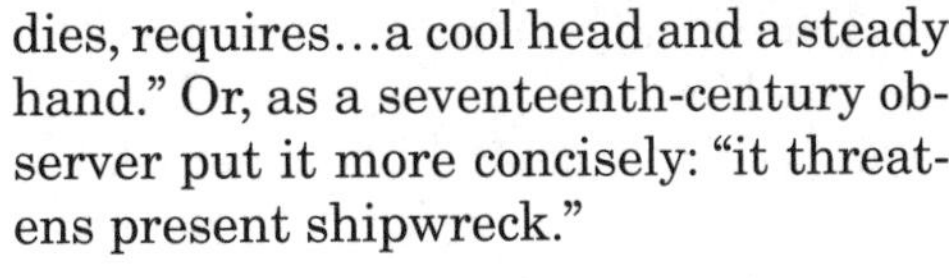

Erica M. Szuplat

"These intricate passages," which begin around 90th street in Manhattan and jog northeast between Ward's Island and Astoria Queens, have inspired many more intricate passages on the page. Some endeavor to explain and understand the dizzying eddies, others to relate their terrible effects. One could gather a collection of Hell Gate "extracts" to rival Melville's catalogue of whales at the beginning of *Moby-Dick*. Though the Gate now has been modified to remove some (though certainly not all) of its menace, it remains a place of much legend and lore. Its history is, in many ways, the history of New York's rise and fall as a port.

To many New Yorkers, the geological and glacial machinations that destined their city to be perhaps the finest natural port on the Atlantic basin have long seemed almost providential. But that assumes that you can make it into New York Harbor. Both the Narrows and Hell Gate are difficult straits to navigate. The Gate in particular once seemed perfectly designed to torment mariners. A slew of government reports from the middle of the nineteenth century drawn up in response to a slew of accidents sought to explain its workings in minute detail. Like the waters of the Gate, the language is tortured and difficult to navigate. But hydrological niceties aside, the problem is relatively simple: great volumes of water move through tight and cluttered spaces.

Washington Irving, the first great New York and American writer, explained it best. All that water moving through the Gate isn't happy about it: "it takes these impediments in mighty dudgeon; boiling in whirlpools; brawling and fretting in ripples and breakers; and, in short, indulging in all kinds of wrong-headed paroxysms." By Irving's and many other accounts, the Gate's paroxysms were audible as well as visible before the city and its noisy tumults had reached that far up Manhattan. "It makes such a whirlpit and whistling that you can hear it for a quarter of an hour's distance," a seventeenth-century observer said. It was at its worst at half-tide, when, Irving wrote, "it roars with might and main, like a bully bellowing for more drink." Only at slack tide did the Gate "relapse into quiet, and, for a time, sleep as soundly as an alderman after dinner." But that only lasted a few minutes. The "mighty, blustering, bullying, hard-drinking little strait" was soon at it again.

"Hellegat" first appeared on European maps after 1614, when the Dutch explorer Adriaen Block gave that name to the entire East River (which is not a river at all, but a tidal strait). In the passage from Dutch to English, "hellegat" came through as Hell Gate, specifying the most confounded part of the strait. Sensible enough, but Block may not have intended such infernal meanings. Some histories suggest that "hellegat" could have meant a "beautiful pass" or "bright straight," noting that there are a number of "hellegats" along rivers in the Low Countries. It also seems unlikely that the Lenape Indians, who hosted Block on Manhattan Island and helped him build a new ship after his first one burnt, would have imparted such a negative sense. The Lenape were able mariners whose smaller, more maneuverable vessels would have been far less perturbed by the Gate's hazards. They also cultivated food and kept a winter encampment on the shores of the Gate, no doubt spending more time enjoying its great bounties of fish than recoiling from its horrors.

It was the subsequent Europeans who condemned the spot, and with good reason: it condemned many Europeans' vessels. Their big, tubby ships were made to run with the wind across open oceans, not negotiate crooked, irritable straits. Accounts reaching back to the seventeenth century tell us of mariners coming to grief in Hell Gate. The troubles mounted as New York City grew and traffic expanded along with it. Some of the wrecks were famous, like that of the British frigate *Hussar*, which went down in 1780 laden with gold earmarked for redcoat soldiers' pay. By the middle of the eighteenth century, though, regularity had made most accidents relatively unexceptional affairs. In the summer of 1747, the *New-York Weekly Post-Boy* contains an advertisement for an auction of "the Rigging, Sails, Anchors, Cables, Mast and Yards, Boat and Utensils &c. belonging to the Brig, *King of Sardinia*, lately lost in Hell gate," but no report of the accident itself. Two years later, in 1749, a sloop lost in the Gate made news not because she went down, but because she came back up. The ship sank like a stone after striking rocks, only to be seen three days later "driving down the harbor" on the outgoing tide. Her primary cargo being salt, it was "supposed that as soon as the Salt was disolved [sic] She floated."

Hell Gate's most hellish heyday came in the nineteenth century. New York had gotten bigger—it was the biggest city and busiest port in the United States by the 1820s—but its waterways had not. More traffic brought more wrecks, a problem only made worse by the advent of the steamboat. In 1815, Captain Elihu Bunker piloted a hybrid sloop-rigged sidewheeler, the *Fulton*, through the Gate against the tide en route to New Haven (which he reached in an astonishing eleven hours). Over the coming decades, sailing ships and steamboats coexisted uncomfortably in the Gate's unfriendly confines. Where the steamboat operators plying New York's waterways were notoriously aggressive and competitive, the captains of sailing ships needed to be extremely cautious and precise. Cross purposes in crosscurrents yielded more accidents. Like drunks walking side-by-side, vessels negotiating the troubled waters as often bumbled into one another as the Gate's rocky hazards. By midcentury, about a thousand accidents a year were unfolding there, claiming an estimated one in fifty sailing vessels seeking passage.

And so, the studies began. In 1848, the government Coast Survey launched a careful analysis of Hell Gate (the surveyors' vessel adding, predictably enough, yet another obstacle to hit while passing through). The work yielded a minutely detailed chart—"Hell Gate and Its Approaches" (1851)—and a series of recommendations for mitigating the Gate's dangers. The chart is a remarkable document for its intricate precision and earnest record of the colorful names the

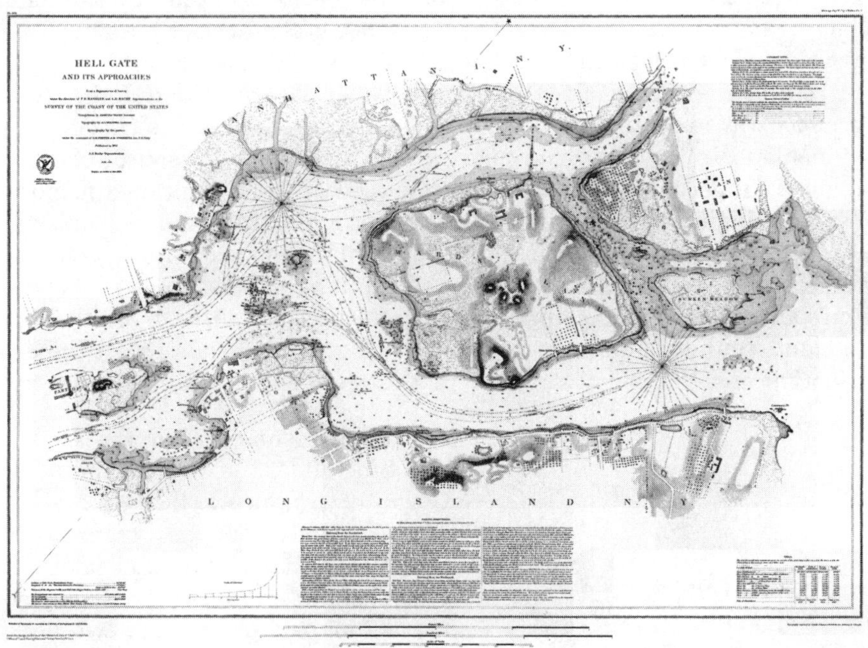

Gate's rocks and reefs had accumulated over time (Bald Headed Billy, Hog's Back, the Frying Pan, the Bread and Cheese, and so on). But the real action lies in the carefully wrought "Sailing Directions," printed in jaunty italic text below. Rendered in clunky and labored language, it is one of the most unintentionally evocative pieces of writing you could ever expect to read. Its instructions for entering from the northeast on an ebb tide in a southwesterly breeze are worth quoting at length:

> In entering the Gate, tack near Negro Pt. Bluff, and stand towards Scaly Rock, so as to tack again one vessel's length outside the eddy, the next tack will bring a vessel a little to windward of Negro Point, make a short tack which will clear the eddies of Pot Rock, stand directly through Main

Ship Channel over towards the meadows, keeping Horn's Hook and White House on Gibb's Point open, the next tack will fetch between Great Mill and Little Mill Rocks, on the edge of the eddies, tack with the Bread and Cheese and Gibbs Pt. in range, make a short tack towards Rylander's Reef, tack again off Rylander's Reef when a vessel meeting the Middle Channel tide will be forced up into the wind, the current drifting her to windward, clear of all danger.

Got that? The instructions capture the ample faith placed in the typical captain of sailing craft in 1851. They also go a long way toward explaining why one in fifty didn't make it through "clear of all danger."

The blasting began not long after. The coast surveyors dutifully charted the rocks, but they were more interested in blowing them up. A decades-long project to remove the hazards began that same year, in 1851. Efforts were led first by a plucky French engineer and master of subaqueous explosion by the name of Maillefert who won a contract to remove as much of Pot Rock as possible. Unseen at any tide and eight feet under at low, Pot Rock was a massive structure astride the current at the center of the passage between Ward's Island and Astoria. It had a nasty way of raking the bottoms of deep-draft vessels (the *Hussar* was its most famous scalp), and its sheer mass was believed to be the source of some the Gate's most dangerous eddies. Maillerfert succeed, up to a point (again, more collisions: on a single day in August of 1851, three separate vessels hit Maillefert's float). His charges removed about eight feet from the top of Pot Rock, giving passing vessels 16 feet of water at low tide and soothing at least some of the water's swirling tantrums. The following year, an accident killed three of Maillefert's assistants and wounded Maillefert himself as the group worked to blast the Frying Pan, another mid-channel obstruction off the south end of Ward's Island.

Erica M. Szuplat

The work resumed after the Civil War, this time under the direction of the Army Corps of Engineers. The Corps' motto is *Essayons*, which they translate from the French, cheerily, as "Let us try!" The Corps and its workers earnestly tried for the better part of the next two decades. Initially, the efforts followed on Maillefert's, focusing on drilling into the rocks and inserting explosive charges from above. But still the collisions: in 1869, a massive purpose-built "mushroom drill" was launched after much thought and design, only to be struck on its first day of operation by "a brig, a tug, and a canal boat, and [be] completely demolished," according to a *Scribner's* report. Drilling barges continued to crowd the Gate, but it was resolved, perhaps contrary to Christian teaching, that the torments of Hell Gate could best be eliminated working from below rather than from above.

In an imaginative feat of engineering, Lieutenant General John Newton oversaw an operation to undermine the Gate's most dangerous obstructions. Newton commanded armies of Cornish miners who blasted out warrens of tunnels beneath the floor of the Gate. Their efforts culminated in two massive explosions. The first, in 1876, cleared Hallett's Reef, which hemmed in the sharp turn jagging toward the Sound. The second, in 1885, minced Flood Rock, a massive table that spun wicked eddies and gave mariners an unenviable choice: to avoid it, they could cleave uncomfortably close to the Queens shore, or pick a course through a labyrinth of rocks between Ward's Island and Manhattan. The crowd on hand witnessed the spectacle of 150-foot geysers shooting into the air; a seismograph in Princeton, New Jersey registered the shock. Hell Gate was open, mostly—a newspaper headline the following day left at least a shade of doubt: "The Channel Probably Well Cleared."

Erica M. Szuplat

As time went on, the Gate would be well cleared; most of the remaining hazards would be removed through the remainder of the nineteenth century and into the twentieth. In 1679, one passenger traveling through the Gate was left hoping "for some Charon to conduct him through" (Charon being the ferryman of souls into Hades). Charon could be replaced by a good pilot or a copy of this year's ELDRIDGE, though accidents continue to happen and "a cool head and a steady hand" remain useful.

Like Hell Gate's once menacing obstructions, most of New York City's maritime past is gone, blasted and sunk. Look, of course, and you can still see it here and there. As one writer puts it hopefully, "the ghosts of stevedores, street urchins, and shanghaied sailors still haunt the milieu." If only! The truth is that most traces of that world are gone, buried beneath skyscrapers, sealed off below the paved highways ringing the waterfront, guarded by the traffic roaring and seething above. But perhaps this—the traffic—is fitting. It's the only current and flow most New Yorkers care about now, and it's there, so often in a confounded state, because of the water all around. It was the water—ebbing and flowing, a gateway to the world beyond—that made New York City. Now, it is the water, with its non-negotiable boundaries, bottleneck bridges, and relentless rise that defines many of the City's inconveniences and problems.

Next time you pass through the Gate, propelled along by that alarmingly swift current, slapping into standing waves, white-knuckling the tiller or wheel, enjoy the moment and remember the history. You're not dodging the Frying Pan or dancing between eddies. And you could always be stuck on the FDR Drive.

Jake Lundberg teaches history at the University of Notre Dame; he is the author of "Horace Greely: Print, Politics, and the Failure of American Nationhood" (2019). A native of Guilford Connecticut, Lundberg spends his summers on the Long Island Sound.

HYPOTHERMIA
and Cold Water Immersion
What You Need To Know

It is not uncommon for a boater to fall off a boat or dock. Most are rescued immediately. However, when rescue is delayed and conditions which threaten survival are present, all who go boating should know what to do.

Hypothermia is a state of low core body temperature - specifically below 95° F. This loss of body heat may be caused by exposure to cold air or cold water. Since water conducts heat away 25 times more quickly than air, time is critical for rescue. There are many variables beyond water temperature that combine to determine survival time: whether a life jacket is on, body size and composition, type of clothing, movement in the water, etc. Wearing a Personal Flotation Device (PFD) greatly extends survival time by keeping your head above water and allowing you to float without expending energy. A PFD will only work if you wear it. Consider carrying a personal locating device to aid rescuers in finding you.

What a person in the water should do:

1. If at all possible, get out of the water, or at least grab hold of anything floating. If the boat is swamped, stay with it and crawl as far out of the water as possible.
2. Do not try to swim unless a boat or floating object is very nearby and you are certain you can get to it.
3. Control heat loss by keeping clothing on as partial insulation. In particular, keep the head out of water. To protect the groin, sides, and chest from heat loss, use the H.E.L.P. (heat escape lessening position), a fetal position with hands clasped around the legs, which extends survival time.
4. Conserve energy by remaining as still as possible. Physical effort promotes heat loss. Swimming, or even treading water, reduces survival time.
5. Pulling a large trash bag over your feet up to your shoulders will keep a warm layer of water around you and can extend survival time. Keep your life jacket on, remain in H.E.L.P. position. Do not try to swim or move.

The states of hypothermia:

1. Mild: awake, **shivering**, feels cold, lethargic, fast heart rate and breathing.
2. Medium: drowsy, **not shivering**, may have slurred speech, loss of some muscle control, incoherence or combativeness, stupor, and exhaustion.
3. Severe: unconscious, **not shivering**, respiratory distress, possible cardiac arrest.

What a rescuer should do:

1. Stop heat loss, remove the victim from the cold environment.
2. Move the victim to a warm place, position on his/her back, and check breathing and signs of circulation.
3. If unconscious or minimally responsive, minimize sudden movements. Be gentle, as rough handling can induce cardiac arrest. If cardiac arrest occurs, start CPR (p. 245).
4. Carefully remove wet clothing, cutting it away if necessary.
5. Take steps to raise the body temperature gradually: cover the victim with blankets or a sleeping bag; apply warm moist towels to the neck, chest, and groin.
6. Provide room temperature oral fluids when uncontrolled shivering stops, and the patient becomes more alert and is able to swallow.

What NOT to do:

1. Do not give alcohol, coffee, tea, or nicotine. If the victim is not fully conscious, do not attempt to provide food or water.
2. Do not massage arms or legs or handle the patient roughly, as this could cause cold blood from the periphery to circulate to the body's core, which needs to be warm first.

Emergency First Aid

These are guidelines to be used only when professional help is not readily available or may be delayed. These guidelines do not replace proper training in First Aid or CPR.

Good Samaritan laws were enacted to encourage people to help others in emergency situations. Laws vary from state to state, but all require that the caregiver use common sense and a reasonable level of skill.

Before giving care to a conscious victim, you must first get consent. If the victim does not give consent, call 911. Consent may be implied if a victim is unconscious, confused, or seriously ill.

Prevent disease transmission by avoiding contact with bodily fluids, using protective equipment such as disposable gloves and a Pocket Mask or barrier device. Thoroughly wash your hands after giving care.

For all life-threatening events, immediately contact USCG by Marine Radio on VHF Ch. 16, or 911 by phone. BE READY TO PROVIDE YOUR POSITION/LOCATION TO AID RESCUERS; see call scripts on pp. 262-263. Trained dispatchers can provide instructions on how to properly perform CPR, apply an AED, or provide other assistance.

Primary Assessment — Check for:

1. Unresponsiveness,
2. Breathing – look, listen, feel, and
3. Signs of circulation (normal breathing, coughing, or movement). If signs of circulation and breathing are present, check for and control any severe bleeding.

If unresponsive and not breathing – For victims of trauma, drowning/submersion, or suspected drug overdose, call for help and then begin CPR. For children and infants, check for breathing first. If no breathing, do 1 minute of CPR, call for help, and continue CPR.

If circulation is present but no breathing – Begin Rescue Breathing (p. 246).

If airway is obstructed – Do Heimlich to clear airway. Do not use Heimlich if drowning is suspected; go to Rescue Breathing.

CPR - Cardiopulmonary Resuscitation — Use only when there is no sign of breathing and no sign of movement or life. First, call or get someone to call for help.

CPR has two components: High-Quality Chest Compressions and Rescue Breathing. High-Quality Chest Compressions are the most important part of CPR.

If you are untrained in Rescue Breathing or how to properly perform CPR, the American Heart Association recommends Hands-Only CPR until help arrives. Follow these two important steps: 1) contact help and 2) using both hands, provide continuous chest compressions until professional help or an AED arrives.

After determining unresponsiveness, roll victim onto back as a unit, being careful to keep spine in alignment. Expose the chest. Put the heel of 1 hand on the lower half of the breastbone. Put the heel of your other hand on top of the first hand. Push straight down at least 2 inches at a rate of 100-120 compressions per minute. After each compression, let the chest recoil to its normal position, but do not lift your hands from the chest. Giving compressions is tiring. If someone else is available, switch compressors every 2 minutes, being careful to minimize interruptions in giving compressions.

If you are trained in how to perform CPR and do not have another trained person to help you, you may combine Chest Compressions with Rescue Breathing at a rate of 30 Compressions to 2 Breaths.

If you are trained in how to perform CPR and are accompanied by another trained rescuer, give 15 compressions and 2 breaths; alternate giving breaths and compressions every two minutes to avoid fatigue.

Continued on p. 246

Emergency First Aid

continued

Rescue Breathing, no obstruction — Call or get someone to call for help.

Signs of circulation present, unresponsive, no breathing.

Roll victim onto back and open airway. Tilt head back and lift chin except where neck or back injury is suspected. Place your ear close to the mouth. LOOK for chest rise, LISTEN for breathing, FEEL for breath on your cheek for not more than 10 seconds..

If no breathing is detected, keep head tilted back, pinch nose shut, seal your lips tight around victim's mouth, GIVE 2 FULL BREATHS over 2 seconds each, only until the chest rises. Continue in cycles of counting to five: give breath during count ONE and TWO, allow exhalation for counts three, four, and five.

CHECK PULSE EVERY 2 MINUTES by feeling for pulse at side of neck for not more than 10 seconds between breaths. If victim has pulse but is not breathing, continue rescue breathing

If pulse present, continue Rescue Breathing: keep head tilted back; pinch nose; in 5 second cycles, give single breath over one and two, allow exhalation for three, four, five. Look, listen and feel for return of breathing between breaths.

If victim has no sign of life or breath, go to CPR (p. 245).

Obstructed Airway — If victim is conscious but cannot cough, breathe, or speak, use Heimlich. They may be giving the universal sign for choking by holding their hands over their throat. If drowning suspected, use Rescue Breathing. Do not try to clear water from lungs. Roll to side if vomiting occurs to keep the airway clear. If victim is unconscious, look in the mouth for obstruction, remove it only if it can be seen. Do not reach deeply into the mouth as you may further lodge the obstructing object. If no object is seen and victim remains unresponsive, begin CPR.

Heimlich — If victim is conscious, stand behind them. Wrap your arms around victim's waist. Place your fist (thumbside) against the victim's stomach in the midline, just above the navel and well below the rib margin. Grasp your fist with other hand. Press into stomach with a quick upward thrust.

If victim is or becomes unconscious, commence CPR.

Bleeding — Apply pressure directly over wound with a clean sterile dressing until bleeding stops or until EMS rescuers arrive. If possible, press edges of a large wound together before using dressing and bandage.

If bleeding continues, apply additional bandages and continue to maintain pressure; place new dressings over any that are soaked through. Do not remove saturated dressings as this may cause continued bleeding. If bleeding from a wound on an extremity cannot be stopped, use a tourniquet above the wound. Tourniquet should be placed on single-bone extremities (upper arm or thigh, not on forearm or shin). Even if the injury is to the hand or wrist, place the tourniquet on the upper arm as close to the torso as possible. Place the tourniquet "high and tight" against the torso or trunk. Tighten until bleeding stops. Commercially available tourniquets like the CAT Tourniquet work best. Do not use a belt or rope as this can cause further damage to blood vessels and may not stop the bleeding. A properly applied tourniquet is extremely painful, be prepared to treat for pain if possible. If necessary, apply a second tourniquet adjacent to the first. Never remove a tourniquet once it is applied. Make a note of what time the tourniquet is applied.

If possible, elevate wounded area, pad the injured extremity to prevent further injury. Keep the victim warm and dry, lay them flat, and be prepared to treat for shock.

Emergency First Aid

continued

Burns, Scalds — No open blisters: Use cool water, then cover with a dry sterile dressing.

Open blisters - Heat, Flame, or Fire: Cover injury with dry sterile dressing. Do not put water on burn or remove clothing sticking to burn. Keep victim warm, prepare to treat for shock

Open blisters - Chemical Agent: PROTECT YOURSELF FROM EXPOSURE. Brush away any loose dry chemical. Remove all clothing on which chemical has spilled. Flush all chemical burns continuously with water for 1 hour. Cover with dry sterile dressing and treat for shock. Eyes: Flush with cool water only for 1 hour. You may have to gently help hold victim's eyes open to allow proper flushing.

Shock — Characteristics include: confused behavior; rapid pulse and breathing; cool, moist skin; blue tinge to lips and nailbeds; weakness; nausea; vomiting.

Keep patient lying on their left side in "recovery position" Remove wet clothing. Maintain normal body temperature. Do not give victim food or drink.

Fractures — Do not move victim or try to correct any deformity unless there is imminent danger for further injury. Immobilize the injured extremity. If bone penetrates the skin, cover and pad the extruding part with dry sterile dressing and control bleeding before splinting.

Splint a broken arm to the trunk or a broken leg to the other leg. A padded board or pole can be used along the side, front or back of a broken limb. A pillow or a rolled blanket can be used around the arm or leg.

For an injured shoulder put a pillow between the arm and chest and bind arm to body.

For an injured hip, place pillow between thighs and bind legs together.

Head, Neck, and Spine Injuries — Do not move victim or try to correct any deformity unless there is no breathing or signs of circulation, then gently align the head and neck to the neutral position to provide Rescue Breathing and CPR. Stabilize head, neck and torso to minimize movement and potential for further injury.

Poisoning — Call for help immediately: Poison Control Center 800-222-1222.

Have poison container available. Antidotes listed on the label may be wrong. DO NOT induce vomiting.

Heat Exposure — Remove from hot environment, prevent further warming. Remove excess clothing, maintaining modesty. Move to a shaded or air-conditioned area. Provide evaporative cooling. Wrap in cool, wet sheet, towel, or blanket. Treat for shock. Gradually reduce body temperature to normal, avoid causing shivering. Provide room temperature oral fluids.

Cold Exposure — Remove from the cold environment, prevent further cooling or heat loss. Provide a warm dry bunk and warm drink, not coffee, tea or alcohol.

Frostbite: rewarm slowly, beginning with the body core rather than the extremities. Elevate and protect affected area. Do not rub frozen area, break blisters or use dry heat to thaw. Pad any frozen parts with dry sterile dressings to prevent further injury. Treat for shock. See *Hypothermia and Cold Water Immersion* (p. 244).

Continued on p. 248

Emergency First Aid

continued

Sunburn — Treat heat exposure if present. Cool the skin by using a damp cloth laid over the area. Do not apply ice as this may damage the skin further.

Painkillers like acetaminophen (Tylenol) or ibuprofen may be used for pain. Use topical lotions to keep the skin moist and reduce dehydration. Those containing aloe work well.

If the skin is blistering, do not break blisters. Prevent secondary infection by keeping the area clean.

Victim should rest and keep hydrated. Seek medical help if area does not improve.

Seasickness — This form of motion sickness is characterized by headache, drowsiness, nausea, and vomiting. It is often brought on by sailing in rough or inconsistent seas. Seasickness can be difficult to control.

Preventive: Medications taken before you get on the boat: Dramamine® and Bonine® are the two most common over the counter seasickness remedies. Transderm Scop® Scopolamine patch is a common prescription medicine. Talk with your doctor or pharmacist about which approach might be right for you. Avoid strong odors, greasy, spicy, and high-fat foods, alcohol, and excessive sugars as they can make you queasy or lightheaded. Avoid reading books and computer screens.

Coping with seasickness: Take ginger, chew gum, look at the horizon, stay on deck, get fresh air, try to sleep. Stay as close to the center of the boat as possible. Anti-seasickness wristbands are also known to relieve symptoms. Keep hydrated.

The Publishers thank Andrew N Sikes, CCP, FP-C, Flight Paramedic, Vanderbilt Life-Flight for his valuable contributions to the Hypothermia and Emergency First Aid sections.

U.S. Coast Guard Boardings

The U.S. Coast Guard has the authority to enforce federal laws by making inquiries, examinations, inspections, searches, seizures, and arrests on the waters over which the United States has jurisdiction. Unlike law enforcement regulations ashore, the U.S. Coast Guard does not need probable cause to board your vessel.

The U.S. Coast Guard personnel are armed and may use necessary force to compel compliance. They are charged with the enforcement of laws dealing with safety, water pollution, drug smuggling, illegal immigration, and the 200-mile fishery conservation zone. In nearly half the boardings, they find some kind of non-compliance with regulations. A civil penalty may be imposed for failure to comply with equipment or numbering regulations, navigation rules, accident reporting procedures, etc.

A boat underway that is hailed by a U.S. Coast Guard vessel or patrol boat is required to follow the boarding officer's instructions, which may be to stop, to continue at reduced speed, or to maneuver in such a way as to permit boarding. Instructions will depend on sea conditions. The Coast Guard follows a standard procedure before boarding, and the boarding team will provide as explanation before the actual boarding. If the boarding party has full cooperation from you, the inspection will be completed quickly.

The editors wish to thank the U.S. Power Squadrons (USPS) for permission to reprint this article from their Seamanship Manual.

Vessel Safety Check

The Vessel Safety Check (VSC) is a good option for boaters who wish to have a trained examiner inspect their boats, at no cost, to ensure they have all the equipment required by regulations. If a boat does not meet all of the VSC requirements, the owner gets a listing of what is needed; no tickets are issued and no reports are made to law enforcement authorities. Visit http://safetyseal.net to arrange an inspection.

Weather Signs In the Sky

"When the rain before the wind, topsail sheets and halyards mind,
But when the wind before the rain, then you may set sail again."

Signs of Good Weather

- A gray sky in the morning or a "low dawn" – when the day breaks near the horizon, with the first streaks of light low in the sky – brings fair weather.
- "Rain before 7, clear before 11"
- Light, delicate tints with soft, undefined clouds accompany fine weather.
- Seabirds flying out early and far to sea suggest moderate wind, fair weather.
- A rosy sky at sunset, clear or cloudy: "Red sky at night, sailor's delight."
- High, wispy cirrus clouds, or even high cumulus, indicate immediate fair weather, with a possible change from a front within 24 hours.
- High contrails disappearing quickly show dry air aloft.
- Steady mild-to-moderate winds from the same direction indicate continuing fair weather.
- A low dew point relative to temperature means dry air.

Signs of Bad Weather

- "Red sky at morning, sailor take warning." Poor weather, wind, maybe rain.
- A "high dawn" – when the first streaks of daylight appear above a bank of clouds – often precedes a turn for worse weather.
- Light scud clouds driving across higher, heavy clouds show wind and rain.
- Hard-edged, inky clouds foretell rain and strong wind.
- Seabirds hanging over the land or headed inland suggest wind and rain.
- Remarkable clearness of atmosphere near the horizon, when distant hills or vessels are raised by refraction, are signs of an Easterly wind and indicate coming wet weather.
- Long-lasting contrails indicate humid air aloft.
- Low-level clouds, and clouds at several heights
- Rising humidity, dewpoint close to temperature

Signs of Wind

- Soft-looking, delicate clouds indicate light to moderate wind.
- Stronger wind is suggested by hard-edged, oily-looking, ragged clouds, or a bright yellow sky at sunset.
- A change in wind is indicated by high clouds crossing the sky in a different direction from that of lower clouds.
- Increasing wind and possibly rain are preceded by greater than usual twinkling of stars, indistinctness of the moon's horns, "wind dogs" (fragments of rainbows) seen on detached clouds, and the rainbow.
- "First rise after very low, indicates a stronger blow."

Keeping It Fresh in Salt Water Angling

Tips for fishing new water

by Lou Tabory

Many anglers get into a rut and keep fishing the same locations using the same techniques. They are successful some of the time, so they think that change might bring them less success, but trying new locations and using different techniques can improve your fishing. Just as important is trying new ways to fish water that you know well.

When fishing new water, we will often use different techniques, so try looking at a favorite place and fish it as if you had never fished it before. Many years ago, I fished Dogfish bar one bright afternoon. I had never fished this location—it was my first outing to Martha's Vineyard. I wanted to learn the location and see what the water looked like and, at the same time, do some sight fishing. Daytime fishing in summer for stripers was a foreign concept to most serious striper anglers—they were strictly night anglers. The tide was perfect for fly-fishing with good overhead sun. As I walked the bar's edge, I started spotting fish cruising along the bar. I could see they were good size fish. I made several casts and quickly found the right drift. On my 4th cast, I hooked up onto a good fish—about 20 pounds—that ran into the backing. As I kept casting, I took several more nice fish before hooking a very big one. As I was landing this fish, several anglers walked up behind me and said it was close to forty pounds. They had been watching me fish and could not believe the action I was having in the daytime. The next day I learned that the word had spread that some newcomer had lit Dogfish Bar on fire—and in the daytime. This experience fishing new water taught me to do more daytime sight fishing, something I've enjoyed ever since.

I like to surf fish with spin tackle and lures for grouper in the Bahamas. These fish get spooky with any fishing pressure and overfishing a location will ruin it, so finding new water is the key to success. Equally important is picking windy days to fish, and ideally, fishing at high tide. The wind chop gives you cover—the fish are less likely to spot you as you work along the coral. The best technique is to fish a section then skip the next section giving about half the water a rest. Then, in several days, fish the locations you skipped and keep clear of the places you hit the previous time you fished. When you go back and fish the second time, use different lure types and different colors to keep them guessing. Grouper are famous for finding holes and rocking your lure into the bottom. Casting directions and angle are important. Work the pockets and holes so the lure swims 5 to 10 feet from the holding water. If you can keep the cast short, you will have better control and, when the fish takes, you have a good chance to stop it before it can turn and swim back to its home. Keep a tight drag and keep lifting the fish, pulling hard so the fish does not reach bottom. These techniques work equally well for stripers holding in structure.

Finding new water is the key to catching fish. I found a location this late winter that produced excellent fishing. It required a long walk over coral but was worth it. If you keep fishing the same water, your success rate will drop.

Stripers can be found in many different water types. Some locations might be good on all tides while being hot for one section of the tide, so be sure to fish different tides to find the most productive times to fish. If you only fish a location on a falling tide, you could be missing the best fishing.

Flats are often good on all tides and ideal for the wading angler. Large flats have many different opportunities with large areas of water to fish. I like to work along the edges of bars while looking for cuts in the bars that have good water flow. A falling tide is the safest time to fish and requires less research. The coming tide requires more knowledge. In big tide areas, getting trapped on a bar is not fun and can be dangerous. If you plan to fish at night, know the area well and learn how wind direction and tide size changes the water. A strong offshore wind will hold back the rising water and, if the wind stops or begins to blow into the land, the tide will quickly get deeper. The use of a boat allows the angler to fish more water during different tides and hit locations that the wading angler cannot fish. But I still like to wade—I feel I can cover the water better. Flats are not places to fish when there is heavy fog. Stick to beaches and shorelines that offer good walking if the fog is thick.

Wind often changes water flow and its speed and will impact how you fish any location. The wind can affect how some types of baitfish will pocket in certain locations and how that bait moves in different tides. The wind blowing onto any shoreline often holds the bait along a beach, but a heavy wind might make fishing difficult. When looking at how to determine different ways to fish familiar waters, look at how the wind changes that water and try using the wind as a friend. Some anglers do not like fishing in windy conditions on flats because spotting fish is difficult. I like wind on flats because you can get closer and the fish are less spooky. There is nothing tougher than sight casting to bonefish in skinny water on a flat calm day.

Erica M. Szuplat

Try fishing new water or fishing your favorite locations in new ways to make your angling more interesting and, often, more fruitful.

Lou Tabory has been an outdoor writer for over 40 years and is considered one of the early pioneers of Northeast fly fishing.

The Lure of a New Sailing Adventure

by Liesbet Collaert

My husband, Mark, our dog, Maya, and I approach the waterfront of Newburyport, Massachusetts, on our daily walk. I can see masts rising like narrow chimneys, behind the marina office. We are fortunate to call this historic, scenic, and touristy harbor town our base in between RV adventures. Considered home to the first Coast Guard station in the United States, the small city has been our official residence for fifteen years, yet we only visit occasionally. This time is different; it's 2020, the "Summer of Covid," when plans are put on hold and our nomadic lifestyle has come to a halt.

A variety of sailboats on mooring balls is captured in time and space, as the Merrimack River sprints out to sea. The sky is blue; the breeze pleasant, but not as cooling and invigorating as on the water.

"Don't you wish you could just sit in one of those cockpits right now and ride the rushing water? Attached to a mooring ball, motionless, safe, and with no worry in the world?" my husband remarks.

I frown as memories flood my brain. A thumping mooring ball removing fresh bottom paint and leaving blue streaks on white fiberglass in Huahine, French Polynesia, when wind opposed current. Bang, bang, bang! Navigating strong tidal flows and violent eddies in an attempt to enter the large lagoon of Apataki in the Tuamotu Archipelago and the tricky channel of remote Maupiti in the Society Islands. Being on anchor watch during a cold front in the Bahamas.

This is New England! Did he forget we would never ever sail again in a climate where we go to sleep fully clothed, use a metal tray on a camping stove to stay warm, and only cook dishes in the oven for the same reason? Where the dogs' water bowl froze, we slipped on deck, and our pets slept curled up in a ball on that trip south, to Florida, during the first fall of our eight-year sailing journey?

"There sure is an attraction to that peaceful environment," I mumble. I do remember blissful moments in the cockpit, spectacular sunsets at anchor, and glorious day sails between islands.

The three of us continue our stroll along the boardwalk, in Newburyport-style fashion. It's the most populated part of town, especially on sunny days. Pedestrians greet each other from behind masks. A mega yacht displays its splendor alongside the seawall. A curious, envious crowd gathers and watches in awe, remarking on its size and charm. All I can do is think about the heaps of work involved.

"I'd hate to be the crew on this yacht, constantly waxing and cleaning," I remark as a young, aspiring sailor does just that. We rarely waxed our 35-foot catamaran, *Irie*. Only after our yearly haulout with its mandatory bottom paint job, saildrive maintenance, and list of boat issues was completed, would we make *Irie* shine. Like new, she'd be splashed in eight different parts of the world, immediately collecting new growth. We'd first wipe, next scrub, and later scrape her bottom every month, then every other week as the barnacles grew with the list of boat projects, and the entire cycle repeated.

Continued on p. 254

Beaufort Scale

Force	Knots	Wind Condition	Conditions at Sea	Conditions Ashore
0	0-1	Calm	Smooth, mirror-like sea	Calm, smoke rises vertically
1	1-3	Light Air	Scaly ripples, no foam crests	Smoke drifts at an angle, leaves move
2	4-6	Light Breeze	Small wavelets, crests glassy, not breaking	Leaves rustle, flags begin to move
3	7-10	Gentle Breeze	Large wavelets, some crests break, scattered whitecaps	Small branches move, light flags extended
4	11-16	Moderate Breeze	Small waves 1-4 ft. getting longer, numerous whitecaps	Leaves, loose paper lifted, larger flags flapping
5	17-21	Fresh Breeze	Moderate waves 4-8 ft., many whitecaps	Small trees in leaf begin to sway, flags extended
6	22-27	Strong Breeze	Larger waves 8-13 ft., more whitecaps, spray	Larger tree branches and small trees in motion
7	28-33	Near Gale	Sea heaps up, waves 13-20 ft., white foam streaks	Whole trees moving, resistance in walking
8	34-40	Gale	Waves 13-20 ft. of greater length, crests break, spindrift	Large trees in motion, small branches break
9	41-47	Strong Gale	High waves, 20+ ft., dense streaks of foam, spray reduces visibility	Slight structural damage, roof shingles may blow off, signs in motion
10	48-55	Storm	Very high waves, 20-30 ft., overhanging crests, lowered visibility, sea white with densely blown foam	Trees broken or uprooted, considerable structural damage, very high tides
11	56-63	Violent Storm	Exceptionally high waves, 30-45 ft., foam patches cover sea, visibility limited	Widespread damage, light structures in peril, coastal flooding
12	64+	Hurricane	Air filled with foam, waves 45+ ft., wind shrieks, sea white with spray, visibility poor	Storm surge at coast, serious beach erosion, extensive flooding, trees and wires down

NOTE: When the wind speed doubles, the pressure of the wind on an object *quadruples*. Example: the wind pressure at 40 kts.is *four times* what it is at 20 kts.

In many tidal waters wave heights are apt to increase considerably in a very short time, and conditions can be more dangerous near land than in the open sea.

Continued from p. 252

"If boat maintenance is my only job, life would be much easier this time around. We don't own a company anymore and you're doing just fine freelancing," Mark says, recalling the difficulties that arose when the need to fix the boat interfered with the need to run our business.

"It's been five years since we sold *Irie* in Tahiti. Are you really ready to jump on another boat?" I ask. I was the one who could embrace that watery lifestyle forever, but Mark's responsibility to help customers from the most remote locations in the South Pacific made our life extra challenging. Plus, minimalists as we are, we took pride in showering in the ocean, preserving water and electricity, collecting rainwater, and being frugal consumers. Our comfort level could have been higher.

By now, our trio has reached the boatyard. Most of the fleet has found its way back into the water, but a few stragglers still stand watch. High and dry, these are the "forgotten" yachts and the ones for sale, like a Mahi Fountaine Pajot catamaran, a bigger, newer version of our previous FP Tobago.

"What do you think?" Mark asks. "We could pick up where we left off, in French Polynesia. That way, we don't have to cross the Pacific again."

I look at my husband in awe. Is he serious? Did he forget those outbursts, not that long ago? The same litany of words I had to listen to day in day out? "I need to get off this boat! I'll never buy another boat again!" I cringe and smile simultaneously. We certainly had plenty of good times as well. And, things will be easier in the future. The good always trumps the bad.

"If we ever buy another sailboat, it has to be a catamaran again. Once you've enjoyed a spacious deck, you never go back!" I joke, since we've owned a monohull in the past as well. "I have two other requests whenever we return to cruising," I continue, "One, no more full-time jobs aboard and two, we need to allow ourselves a bit more luxury, like a watermaker and… yeah, a watermaker. That's it!"

For the remainder of our walk, our step has an auspicious spring to it. Newburyport, city of dreams! Mark and I discuss possibilities. Maybe there are good deals to be had during this pandemic? My best friend is a yacht broker in Grenada! But, how about Covid restrictions in the islands? Many cruising friends encountered problems, globally, in the spring of 2020. Are we willing to sell our campervan?

Sam O. White

Back in the spare bedroom of my in-laws, our base, I grab a chair and join Mark behind his computer. YachtWorld.com loads instantaneously. We pick a favorite brand; no saildrives. There are older Leopard 38 catamarans for sale in Georgia, Florida, St. Lucia, Thailand, and Malaysia…

Liesbet Collaert and her husband Mark Kilty lived, sailed, and worked on their 35ft catamaran Irie *for eight years in the U.S., Carribbean, and South Pacific. Their stories can be found on www.itsirie.com.*

Marine Weather Forecasts

VHF-FM, NOAA All-Hazards Weather Radio - Continuous broadcasts 24 hours a day are provided by the National Weather Service with messages repeated every 4-6 minutes. These are updated every 3-6 hours and include weather and radar summaries, wind observations, visibility, sea conditions and detailed local forecasts. Broadcasts can be received 20-40 miles from transmitting site.

	MHz		MHz
WX-1	162.550	WX-5	162.450
WX-2	162.400	WX-6	162.500
WX-3	162.475	WX-7	162.525
WX-4	162.425		

Jonesboro, ME (5)	Riverhead, NY (3)	Mamie, NC (4)	Jacksonville, FL (1)
Ellsworth, ME (2)	Philadelphia, PA (3)	Cape Hatteras, NC (3)	Daytona Bch., FL (2)
Dresden, ME (3)	Atlantic City, NJ (2)	New Bern, NC (2)	Melbourne, FL (1)
Gloucester, MA (4)	Lewes, DE (1)	Georgetown, SC (6)	Fort Pierce, FL (4)
Boston, MA (3)	Baltimore, MD (2)	Charleston, SC (1)	Miami, FL (1)
Hyannis, MA (1)	Hagerstown, MD (3)	Beaufort, SC (5)	Key West, FL (2)
Providence, RI (2)	Norfolk, VA (1)	Brunswick, GA (4)	

Time Signals

Bureau of Standards Time Signals: WWV, Ft. Collins, Col., every min. on 2500, 5000, 10000, 15000, 20000, and, on an experimental basis, 25000 kHz. **Canadian Time Signals:** CHU, (frequently easier to get than WWV) 45° 17' 47" N, 75° 45' 22" W. Continuous transmission on 3330, 7850, and 14670 kHz. For more information on time, visit www.nist.gov/pml/time-and-frequency-division.

The new minute is marked by the full tone immediately following the voice announcement. There is a pulse every second except on the 29th and 59th seconds of the minute.

Forecasting
with Wind Direction and Barometric Pressure

Wind Dir.	Pressure	Trend	Likely Forecast
SW to **NW**	30.1-30.2	Steady	Fair, little temp. change
	30.1-30.2	Rising rapidly	Fair, perhaps warmer with rain
	30.2+	Steady	Fair, no temp. change
	30.2+	Falling	Fair, gradual rise in temp.
S to **SW**	30.0	Rising slowly	Clearing, then fair
S to **SE**	30.2	Falling rapidly	Increasing wind, rain to follow
S to **E**	29.8	Falling rapidly	Severe NE gale, heavy rain/snow
SE to **NE**	30.1-30.2	Falling slowly	Rain
	30.1-30.2	Falling rapidly	Increasing wind and rain
	30.0	Falling slowly	Rain continuing
	30.0	Falling rapidly	Rain, high wind, then clearing and cooler
E to **NE**	30.0+	Falling slowly	Rain with light winds
	30.1	Falling rapidly	Rain or snow, increasing wind
Shifting W	29.8	Rising rapidly	Clearing and cooler

The Saffir-Simpson Hurricane Wind Scale

CATEGORY ONE: Winds 74-95 mph: Very dangerous winds will produce some damage. Falling or flying debris. Damage primarily to power lines, mobile homes, shopping center roofs, shrubbery, and trees. Also, some coastal road flooding and minor pier damage.

CATEGORY TWO: Winds 96-110 mph: Extremely dangerous winds will cause extensive damage. Some roofing material, door, and window damage to buildings. Considerable damage to vegetation, mobile homes, and piers. Small craft in unprotected areas break moorings. Near-total power outages. Some water systems fail.

CATEGORY THREE: Winds 111-130 mph: Devastating damage will occur. Some structural damage to small residences. Mobile homes destroyed. Many trees snapped or uprooted. Coastal flooding may extend inland, destroying smaller structures, damaging larger structures. Electricity and water may be unavailable for days or weeks.

CATEGORY FOUR: Winds 131-155 mph: Catastrophic damage will occur. More extensive failures including roofs on small residences. Major erosion of beach areas. Major damage to lower floors of structures near the shore. Power poles down. Terrain may be flooded well inland. Long-term water shortages.

CATEGORY FIVE: Winds greater than 155 mph: Catastrophic damage will occur. Complete roof failure on many residences and industrial buildings. Some complete building failures with small utility buildings destroyed. Major damage to most structures located near the shoreline. Massive evacuation of residential areas may be required. Most of the area will be uninhabitable for weeks or months.

Hurricanes

For their awesome power to wreak havoc by wind and water, hurricanes have always been fascinating. Early warnings have all but eliminated surprise, yet these storms often defy attempts to prepare. Always vulnerable, we must know what to expect.

Hurricanes affecting the East Coast are born as tropical depressions in the Atlantic west of Africa, move westward through the eastern Caribbean, and eventually veer northwest and then north and northeast up our coast. Counter-clockwise winds spiral inward and accelerate toward the eye, the center of lowest pressure. The sharper the drop in pressure, the more violent the winds. Hurricanes lose power as they move north out of the tropics because warm ocean water, the energy source which helped create them, turns cooler.

A hurricane's forward motion, which can vary from 5 to 50+ knots, means that the winds are stronger on the right side. Winds of 100 knots spiraling around the eye, when you add a forward speed of 25 knots, create a speed of 125 knots on the right side, but only 75 knots on the left side, a dramatic difference. Note: a doubling of wind speed means the force on an object is increased four times, so that a wind of 100 knots has four times the power it does at 50 knots.

If the eye is moving directly toward you, the wind direction will remain fairly constant and the velocity will increase until the eye arrives. When the eye passes, the velocity will suddenly increase, rather stronger than before, from the opposite direction. These factors make the vicinity of the eye most dangerous.

In our diagram the hurricane is approaching, and vessels A, B, and C are at positions A1, B1, and C1 relative to the storm. When the storm passes, these vessels will be at positions A2, B2, and C2. Each will have experienced very different wind speeds and directions:

Vessel A, in the least dangerous semi-circle, will experience winds from the NE (at A1), backing to N (least velocity), NW, and finally W (at A2) as the storm passes.

Vessel B (at B1) will have ENE winds, increasing until the eye arrives. After the deceptive calm of the eye passes, the wind will rise, stronger than before, from the WSW (at B2), gradually decreasing.

Vessel C, in the most dangerous semi-circle, has the strongest winds, beginning (at C1) from the E, veering to SE, S (greatest velocity), and finally to SW (at C2).

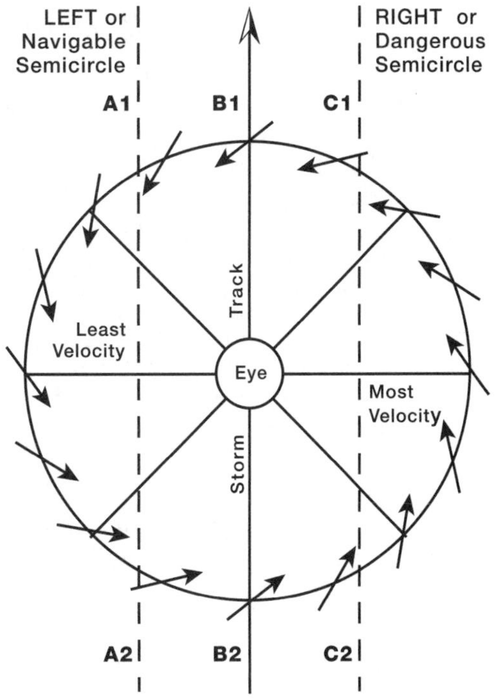

If space and time permit, try to reduce your vulnerability by proceeding at right angles to the storm track. Which way to go depends on a number of factors, including how far away the storm is, its speed, the speed of the vessel, and sea conditions or sea room on either side of the expected storm path.

Hurricane Precautions Alongshore

Extremely high tides accompany hurricanes. If the storm arrives anywhere near the usual time of high water, low-lying areas will be flooded. Especially high tides will occur in all bays or V-mouth harbors if they are facing the wind direction. High water in all storm areas will remain for much longer than usual.

At or near the coastline, pull small craft well above the high water mark, dismast sailboats, remove outboard motors, and remove or lash down loose objects.

Seek the most protected anchorage possible, considering possible wind direction reversals, extreme tides, and other vessels. If on a mooring or at anchor, use maximum scope, allowing for room to swing clear of other boats. In a real blow it is easy to slack off, but not to shorten scope. Use as much chain in your anchor rode as possible. Another piece of chain or a weight, attached halfway along your mooring or anchor line, will help absorb sudden strains. Use chafing gear liberally at bits and bow chocks to minimize fraying of lines. Rig fenders to minimize damage from/to other boats.

Shut off gas, stove tanks, etc. Douse any fires in heating stoves. Secure all portholes, skylights, ventilators, hatch covers, companionways, etc. Pump the boat dry.

At a wharf or pier, use fenders liberally. If possible, rig one or more anchors abreast of the boat in the event the tide rises above pilings.

Boats are replaceable: don't wait for the last moment to get ashore!

Hurricane Precautions Offshore

Monitor storm reports on your radio. The U.S. Coast Guard warns all vessels offshore to seek shelter at least 72 hours ahead of a hurricane.

But, if caught offshore with no chance to reach shelter, watch the wind most carefully. First, note that if you face the wind, the eye is about 10 points or 112° to your right. If the wind "backs" (moves counter-clockwise), you are already on the less dangerous side of the storm track. If the wind "veers" (moves clockwise), you are on the right or more dangerous side. If the wind direction is constant, the hurricane's eye is headed directly at you, so make haste to get to the left side of the track.

Use your radiotelephone to advise the Coast Guard and other vessels of your position. Have a liferaft and safety equipment (flares, flashlights, EPIRB, etc.) ready. Put on life jackets. If it is impossible to hold your intended course, head your powerboat directly into the wind and sea, using only enough power to maintain steerageway. If power fails, rig a sea anchor or drogue to keep the bow to the wind.

Sailing vessels heaving to should consider doing so on the starboard tack (boom to port) in the more dangerous semicircle, or on the port tack (boom to starboard) in the less dangerous semicircle, to keep the wind drawing aft.

NOTE: This information is necessarily very general, the diagram (p. 257) is over-simplified, and the suggestions assume a straight storm track. If the storm track curves to the right, vessels A and B will have an easier time of it, but C may wind up on the track. The best advice: monitor weather reports continuously and seek shelter well ahead of time.

National Weather Service – www.weather.gov
National Hurricane Center – www.nhc.noaa.gov
NOAA Hurricane Research – www.aoml.noaa.gov/hrd

Weather Notes

From Maine to the Chesapeake

Sea Fog

There is always invisible moisture in the air, and the warmer the air, the more moisture it can contain invisibly. But when such a mass of moist air is cooled off, as it does when passing over a body of cooler water, the moisture often condenses into visible vapor, or fog. The fog clears when the air temperature rises, from the sun or a warm land mass, or by a warm, dry wind.

To predict fog accurately, you can use a "sling psychrometer." This instrument uses two thermometers side by side, one of which has a wick fastened to the bulb end. After wetting the wick on the "wet bulb" thermometer, the user swings the instrument in a circle for 60-90 seconds. This causes water to evaporate from the wet bulb thermometer, lowering its reading. The dry bulb thermometer simply tells air temperature. The difference in readings between the dry bulb and wet bulb thermometers determines the relative humidity of the air, and - especially valuable for determining the likelihood of fog - the dew point. The dew point is the (lower) temperature to which air must be cooled for condensation, or fog, to occur.

Eastport, Maine to Cape Cod

Cold water (48°-55°) off the northern New England coast often causes heavy fog conditions in the spring and summer, when a warm moist southwesterly flow of air passes over it. East of Portland to the Bay of Fundy, fog is not apt to occur when the dew point is under 55°, unless there is a very warm moist wind. The effect of the cold water on the warm air is reduced if the winds become brisk, as they are apt to do in the afternoon. Visibility should then improve.

Long Island Sound and the New Jersey Coast

Summertime warm water (in the 70s) in this area rarely cools down any warm air mass enough to produce fog. This is not the case farther offshore, where cooler water temperatures (in the 50s) can produce fog.

On the south coast of Long Island, when the southwest wind blows toward the shore at the same time as the ebb tide, inlets can become dangerous with short, steep seas. Also, offshore swells can become very high near the mouths of inlets.

On the New Jersey shore, prevailing winds in summer are southerly, increasing in mid-morning to rarely more than 20 knots and usually dying down at dusk. Occasional summer thunderstorms can be expected. Any brisk winds from the east, northeast, or southeast can produce dangerous conditions along this lee shore and at the mouths of inlets. When the wind is from offshore like this, inlets should be entered on a flood tide.

At the mouth of Delaware Bay, seas can build up to a hazardous degree when there is a southeast wind at the same time as an ebb current at the mouth of the Bay.

Chesapeake Bay

There is little chance of fog in this region because of the warmth of the water. The Bay has quirks of its own in weather and sea conditions. It is a narrow and fairly shallow body of water, and winds tend to blow up or down it. Sharp seas can result, depending on the direction of the current and the wind. Opposing forces make for rough water.

Prevailing winds in spring and summer are southerly, freshening in the afternoon after a morning of calm. Summer thunderstorms occur frequently in afternoon and early evening, usually from the west. In the fall, after a cold front passes through, the winds will shift into the north or northeast, usually for three days, and increase in velocity, causing seas to build up. Calm follows for a day or so until the wind shifts to the southwest.

How to Contact the U.S. Coast Guard

U.S. Coast Guard Rescue Coordination Centers (RCCs)

24-hour Regional Contacts for Emergencies

RCC Boston, MA – (617) 223-8555 Maine to Northern New Jersey
RCC Norfolk, VA – (757) 398-6231 New Jersey to border of N. Carolina and S. Carolina
RCC Miami, FL – (305) 415-6800 S. Carolina to Key West including much of Caribbean

USCG Navigation Information Service (NIS). Watchstander, (24/7): (703) 313-5900

USCG National Response Center (NRC): (800) 424-8802

USCG Marine Safety Center: (202) 795-6729

INTERNET: USCG - www.navcen.uscg.gov/ Canada - www.notmar.gc.ca/

U.S. Coast Guard Stations – (monitoring VHF Ch. 16)

1st District – Boston – (617) 223-8555

Eastport, ME (207) 853-2845
Jonesport, ME (207) 497-3404
Southwest Harbor, ME (207) 244-4270
Rockland, ME (207) 596-6667
Boothbay Hbr., ME (207) 633-2661
S. Portland, ME (207) 767-0363
Sector Northern New England (207) 767-0302
Portsmouth, NH (603) 436-4415
Merrimack-Newburyport, MA (978) 465-0731
Gloucester, MA (978) 283-0705
Boston, MA (617) 223-3123
Point Allerton-Hull, MA (781) 925-0165
Scituate, MA (781) 545-3800
Cape Cod Canal-E. Entr. (508) 888-0020
Provincetown, MA (508) 487-0077
Chatham, MA (508) 945-3830
Brant Pt.-Nantucket, MA (508) 228-0388
Woods Hole, MA (508) 427-3277
Menemsha, MA (508) 645-2662
Castle Hill, Newport, RI (401) 846-3676
Point Judith, RI (401) 789-0444
New London, CT (860) 442-4471
New Haven, CT (203) 468-4498
Sector NY, NY (718) 354-4353
Fire Island, NY (631) 661-9100
Eatons Neck, NY (631) 261-6959
Kings Point, NY (516) 466-7136
Jones Beach, NY (516) 785-2995
Shinnecock, NY (631) 728-0078
Montauk, NY (631) 668-2773
Sandy Hook, NJ (732) 872-3429

5th District – Portsmouth, VA (757) 686-4002

Manasquan Inlet, NJ (732) 775-5029
Shark River, NJ (732) 776-6730
Barnegat, NJ (609) 494-2661
Atlantic City, NJ (609) 344-6594
Cape May, NJ (609) 898-6995
Ocean City, NJ (609) 399-0144
Indian River Inlet, DE (302) 227-2121
Ocean City, MD (410) 289-1905
St. Inigoes, MD (301) 872-4344

5th District, cont.

Crisfield, MD (410) 968-0323
Annapolis, MD (410) 267-8108
Oxford, MD (410) 226-0581
Curtis Bay-Baltimore, MD (410) 576-2525
Stillpond, MD (410) 778-2201
Chincoteague, VA (757) 336-2874
Little Creek-Norfolk, VA (757) 464-9371
Wachapreague, VA (757) 787-9526
Portsmouth, VA (757) 483-8527
Cape Charles, VA (757) 331-2000
Milford Haven, VA (804) 725-3732
Oregon Inlet, NC (252) 441-6260
Hatteras Inlet, NC (252) 986-2176
Hobucken, NC (252) 745-3131
Fort Macon, NC (252) 247-4583
Elizabeth City, NC (252) 335-6086
Wrightsville Beach, NC (910) 256-4224
Emerald Isle, NC (252) 354-2719
Oak Island, NC (910) 278-1133

7th District – Miami, FL (305) 415-6800

Georgetown, SC (843) 546-2052
Charleston, SC (843) 740-7050
Tybee, GA (912) 786-5440
Brunswick, GA (912) 267-7999
Mayport, FL (904) 564-7500
Ponce de Leon Inlet, FL (386) 428-9084
Cape Canaveral, FL (321) 868-4200
Fort Pierce Inlet, FL (772) 464-6100
Lake Worth Inlet, FL (561) 840-8503
Ft. Lauderdale, FL (954) 927-1611
Miami Beach, FL (305) 535-4368
Islamorada, FL (305) 664-8077
Marathon, FL (305) 743-1991
Key West, FL (305) 292-8713

Canada-Nova Scotia

Canadian Coast Guard

Joint Rescue Coordination Center
Halifax, NS (902) 427-8200

Radio Telephone Information—VHF System

Calling Guidelines: Avoid excessive calling. Make calls as brief as possible. Give name of called vessel first, then "This is (name of your vessel)," your call sign (if you have a Station License), and the word "Over." If station does not answer, delay your repeat call for 2 minutes. At the end of your message, sign off with "This is (your vessel's name)," your call sign, and "Out."

Range and Power: Operation is essentially line-of-sight. Since the elevation of antennas at both communications points extends the "horizon," range may be 20 to 50 miles on a 24-hour basis between a boat and a land station. Effective range between boats will be less because of lower antenna heights. 25 watts is the maximum power permitted.

Interference factor: Most VHF-FM equipment has 6 or more channels, so it is possible to shift to a clear channel. Like the FM in your home radio, the system is practically immune to interference from ignition noise, static, etc., except under unusual conditions.

Channelization: A minimum of 3 channels is required by the FCC. Two are mandatory: Channel 16 (156.800 MHz), the International Distress frequency; and Channel 06 (156.300 MHz), the Intership Safety Frequency. The Coast Guard *strongly* recommends that you have Channel 22A as your third channel.

Note: designations for channels that previously ended with "A" have changed. To convert to the new format, prepend "10" and drop the "A" – e.g., 22A becomes 1022. The table below includes both new and old designations. Frequencies are not changing; older VHF radios will function as before the change.

Channel	Purpose and Comments
16 156.800 MHz **Vessels are required to maintain a watch on this channel.**	**Distress and Safety**: Ship to Shore and Intership. Guarded 24 hours by the Coast Guard. No routine messages allowed other than to establish the use of a working channel. See pp. 262-263 for distress calling procedure. **Calling**: Ship to Shore and Intership. Use Ch. 16 to establish contact, then switch to a working channel (see below). Calling Channel: New England waters. Commercial and pleasure.
09 156.450 MHz	**Boater Calling:** Commercial and Non-Commercial
06 156.300 MHz	**Intership Safety:** No routine messages allowed. 06 is limited to talking with the Coast Guard and others at the scene of an emergency, and to information on the movement of vessels.
22A/1022 157.100 MHz (**21** in Canada 161.65 MHz)	**Maritime Safety Information** channel. Not guarded by the CG, but after a vessel makes contact with the CG for non-distress calls on Ch. 16, they will tell you to switch to and use *only* 22A for communicating. Also used for CG weather advisories and Notices to Mariners; times of these broadcasts given on Ch. 16.
12, 14, 20A/1020, 65A/1065, 66A/1066, 73, 74, 77	**Ship to Shore and Intership:** Port operations, harbormasters, etc. Your electronics dealer should have local frequencies.
08, 67, 88A/1088	**Commercial (intership only):** For ocean vessels, dredges, tugs, etc.
07A, 10, 11, 18A/1018, 19A/1019, 79A, 80A/1080	**Commercial only**
13 156.650 MHz	**Intership Navigation Safety:** (bridge to bridge). Ships > 20 m length maintain a listening watch on this channel in US waters.
68, 69, 71, 72, 78A/1078	**Ship to Shore and Intership, pleasure craft only:** Shore stations, marinas, etc. The best channels for general communication.
70 156.525 MHz	**Digital Selective Calling (DSC)**. Special equipment required.
81A/1081 157.075 MHz **83A/1083** 157.175 MHz	**Keyed Fog Signals**. See note on p.173 Lights, Fog Signals and Offshore Buoys.
AIS 1 161.975 MHz **AIS 2** 162.025 MHz	**Automatic Identification System** (AIS)

VHF Call Scripts

16 HAILING

PENDRAGON, PENDRAGON, *this is* **BALLARD, BALLARD** *calling* **PENDRAGON,** *repeat,* **PENDRAGON.** *Come in* **PENDRAGON. OVER.**

NAME of VESSEL being called, repeat 2X pause →

this is vessel type and NAME, repeat 2X pause →

Come in hailed vessel NAME ***OVER.***

When vessel responds, name another channel, leave Channel 16.

UNKNOWN VESSEL

CONTAINER SHIP EXITING THE CAPE COD CANAL

This is the sailing Ketch **LOLLIPOP** *off your port bow, calling to state our intentions.* **OVER.**

16 SECURITÉ HAZARD TO NAVIGATION

[see-kyoor-ih-TAY], SECURITÉ, SECURITÉ This is the motor vessel **TRANQUIL**, *the* **MV TRANQUIL** *calling* **WOODS HOLE COAST GUARD** *to report a hazard to navigation: a section of wooden dock is floating awash near beacon 1A east of Woods Hole.* **OVER.**

SECURITÉ, SECURITÉ, SECURITÉ. pause →

This is vessel type and NAME, repeat 2X pause →

calling COAST GUARD STATION NEAREST pause →

to warn of specific nature of hazard and location pause →

Coast Guard please copy. ***OVER.***

Repeat until Coast Guard responds, discuss hazard on channel required by Coast Guard communications.

VHF Call Scripts

16 PAN-PAN REQUEST FOR ASSISTANCE

[pawn-pawn], PAN-PAN, PAN-PAN This is the sport fisherman **TORO**, *repeat,* **TORO**, *requesting medical assistance for minor injuries, possible broken bone. We are under way heading NNE off Mosquito Island, near can 15.* **OVER.**

PAN-PAN, PAN-PAN, PAN-PAN. pause →
This is vessel type and NAME, repeat 2X ---------- pause →
requesting nature of required assistance ---------- pause →
we are docked, anchored, under way, specific location ---------- pause →
Coast Guard please copy. ***OVER.***

Repeat until Coast Guard responds, confirm request and rendezvous on channel required by Coast Guard.

16 MAYDAY URGENT EMERGENCY, LIFE THREAT

MAYDAY, MAYDAY, MAYDAY This is the sloop **LADY HELEN**, *repeat,* **LADY HELEN**. *Fire aboard. We are abandoning ship, repeat, abandoning ship, two miles west of Serpent Island, two miles west of Serpent Island. Need immediate assistance. Coast Guard please respond. This is a MAYDAY.* **OVER.**

MAYDAY, MAYDAY, MAYDAY. pause →
This is vessel type and NAME, repeat 2X ---------- pause →
declaring emergency nature of emergency ---------- pause →
we are docked, anchored, under way, specific location ---------- pause →
This is a MAYDAY. ***OVER.***

Repeat until Coast Guard responds.

Pollution Regulations

Simplified Regulations for Waste Disposal Outside Special Areas

Prohibited in all waters: The discharge of garbage including synthetic ropes, fishing gear, plastics (including plastic waste bags), incinerator ashes, clinkers, paper, rags, packing materials, dunnage, metal, glass, bottles, cooking oil, crockery and similar refuse.

Food waste: The discharge of any garbage or ground food waste is prohibited within 3 n.m. of land. Beyond 3 n.m., food waste may be discharged if ground to particles less than 1 inch. Unground food waste may be discharged if 12 n.m. or more from land. In any case, the vessel must be *en route* and discharge should be as far from land as practicable.

The Damage Caused by Pollution

Sewage is not just a repulsive visual pollutant. The microorganisms in sewage, including pathogens and bacteria, degrade water quality by introducing diseases like hepatitis, cholera, typhoid fever and gastroenteritis, which can contaminate shellfish beds. Shellfish are filter feeders that eat tiny food particles filtered through their gills into their stomachs, along with bacteria from sewage. Nearly all waterborne pathogens can be conveyed by shellfish to humans.

Marine Sanitation Devices (MSDs)

USCG-certified MSDs are required on all vessels with installed toilets. Vessels under 65' may install type I, II or III MSD. Vessels over 65' must install a type II or III MSD.

Type I MSDs are allowed only on vessels under 65'. They treat sewage with disinfectant chemicals before discharge. The discharge must not show any visible floating solids, and must have a fecal coliform bacterial count not greater than 1000 per 100 milliliters of water.

Type II MSDs are allowed on vessels of any length. They provide a higher level of treatment than Type I, using greater levels of chemicals to create effluent having less than 200 per 100 milliliters and suspended solids not greater than 150 milligrams per liter.

Type III MSDs are allowed on vessels of any length. They do not allow discharge of sewage, except through a Y-valve to discharge at a pumpout facility, or overboard when outside the 3 nautical miles. They include holding tanks, recirculating and incinerating units.

Portable toilets or "porta-potties" are not considered installed toilets and are not subject to MSD regulations. They are, however, subject to the disposal regulations which prohibit the disposal of raw sewage within the 3 nautical miles of shore.

No Discharge Zones (NDZs)

NDZs are water bodies where the Environmental Protection Agency (EPA) and local communities prohibit the discharge of all vessel sewage. Many States are adding NDZs. **It is the boater's responsibility to be aware of where those NDZs are.** For NDZs by state see https://www.epa.gov/vessels-marinas-and-ports/no-discharge-zones-ndzs-state. See p. 265 for Pumpout Information.

When operating vessel in NDZs, the operator must secure each Type I or Type II MSD in a manner which prevents discharge of treated or untreated sewage.

Type III MSDs, or holding tanks, must also be secured in a manner that prevents discharge of sewage. Acceptable methods of securing the device include: closing appropriate valves, removing the handle, padlocking each valve, or using a non-reusable wire-tie to hold each valve in a closed position. Sewage held in Type III MSDs can be removed by making arrangements with pumpout stations or pumpout boats. Call Harbormaster for details.

Pumpout Information — State Sources

Please be sure to call or radio in advance for rates and availability. While we have taken all possible care in compiling this list, changes may have occurred and we cannot guarantee accuracy. For more current information check the state website or call the agency listed. See also *Pollution Regulations* on opposing page.

Look for the pumpout symbol 

For more information on the Clean Vessel Act (CVA), see http://wsfrprograms.fws.gov/Subpages/GrantPrograms/CVA/CVA.htm

Most major harbors now have a pumpout boat. Contact the local Harbormaster. Many monitor VHF channel 09.

MAINE: ME Dept. of Environ. Protection, 207-485-3038
www.maine.gov/dep/water/wd/vessel/pumpout/index.html

NEW HAMPSHIRE: NH Environ. Serv., CVA Coordinator, 603-271-8803
www.des.nh.gov/organization/divisions/water/wmb/cva/

MASSACHUSETTS: MA Coastal Zone Mgmt., 978-282-0308, ext.119
www.mass.gov/service-details/boat-pumpout-facilities

RHODE ISLAND: RI Environ. Mgmt. Law Enforcement, 401-222-3070
RI Environmental Mgmt., Marine Pumpout Coordinator, 401-222-4700
www.dem.ri.gov/maps/mapfile/pumpmap.pdf

CONNECTICUT: CT Energy and Environ. Protection, 860-447-4340
www.ct.gov/deep/pumpoutdirectory

NEW YORK: NY State Environmental Facilities Corp., 518-486-9267
www.efc.ny.gov/cvap (link to map at bottom of page)

NEW JERSEY: NJ Fish & Wildlife, 908-637-4125 ext. 100
NJBoating.org

DELAWARE: DE Division of Fish & Wildlife, 302-739-9915
www.dnrec.delaware.gov/p2/Pages/PumpoutStations.aspx

MARYLAND: MD Dept. of Natural Resources, 410-260-8772
dnr.maryland.gov/boating/pages/pumpout/locations.aspx

VIRGINIA: VA Dept. of Health, 804-864-7468
www.vdh.virginia.gov/environmental-health/marina-program/maps-marina/

NORTH CAROLINA: NC Div. of Coastal Management, 252-808-2808
deq.nc.gov/about/divisions/coastal-management/coastal-management-recognition/find-pumpout-stations

SOUTH CAROLINA: SC Dept. of Natural Resources, 843-953-9062
www.dnr.sc.gov/marine/vessel/stationmaps.html

GEORGIA: Georgia Dept. of Natural Resources, 912-264-7218
coastalgadnr.org/pumpout — contact local marinas

FLORIDA: FL Dept. of Environmental Protection, 850-245-2118
arcg.is/1quLP0

Got a Minute?
Angular and Linear Equivalents

Whether you are navigating purely by GPS or using a paper chart, it can be helpful to know how degrees, minutes, and seconds – or tenths or hundredths of a minute – translate into linear distance on the water. Knowing both is important because your GPS can display part of a coordinate as 41° 23' 25", or as 41° 23.42', where each is correct, but one is more accurate.

First, the basics. Latitude is the angular distance north or south of the Equator, and the parallels are equidistant. The latitude scale appears on the vertical edges of your chart. (Longitude, measured east and west of Greenwich and appearing along the top and bottom edges of your chart, is never used for distance measurement.) For practical purposes, the distance between parallels of latitude which are one degree (1°) apart is 60 nautical miles (n.m.).

- 1° (degree) = 60 nautical miles (Ex: from 42° North to 43° North is 60 n.m.)
- 1' (minute, or 1/60th of a degree) = 1 n.m., or 6076 feet)
- 1" (second, or 1/60th of a minute) = 101.3 feet (acceptable for general purposes)

The U.S. Coast Guard gives positions of buoys, lights, and lighthouses in degrees, minutes, and seconds, or within roughly 100 feet. (See pp. 173-203).

Sometimes minutes are divided into tenths or hundredths instead of seconds.

- 1' (minute) = 1 n.m., or 6076 feet
- 0.1' (1/10th of a minute) = 608 feet (acceptable tolerance at sea; not so near shore)
- 0.01' (1/100th of a minute) = 61 feet (acceptable for almost any purpose)

Use the Table below to convert seconds to tenths or hundredths of a minute.

Table for Converting Seconds to Decimals of a Minute

From many sources, including charts, Light Lists, and Notices to Mariners, positions are in degrees, minutes, and seconds. These are written either 34° 54' 24" or 34-54-24

However, for navigating with GPS, Loran, chart plotters, and celestial calculators, it can be useful to convert the last increment – seconds – to either tenths or hundredths of a minute. The numbers above become 34° 54.40' or 34-54.4'

Secs.	Tenths	Hundredths	Secs.	Tenths	Hundredths	Secs.	Tenths	Hundredths
1	.0	.02	**21**	.4	.35	**41**	.7	.68
2	.0	.03	**22**	.4	.37	**42**	.7	.70
3	.1	.05	**23**	.4	.38	**43**	.7	.72
4	.1	.07	**24**	.4	.40	**44**	.7	.73
5	.1	.08	**25**	.4	.42	**45**	.8	.75
6	.1	.10	**26**	.4	.43	**46**	.8	.77
7	.1	.12	**27**	.5	.45	**47**	.8	.78
8	.1	.13	**28**	.5	.47	**48**	.8	.80
9	.2	.15	**29**	.5	.48	**49**	.8	.82
10	.2	.17	**30**	.5	.50	**50**	.8	.83
11	.2	.18	**31**	.5	.52	**51**	.9	.85
12	.2	.20	**32**	.5	.53	**52**	.9	.87
13	.2	.22	**33**	.6	.55	**53**	.9	.88
14	.2	.23	**34**	.6	.57	**54**	.9	.90
15	.3	.25	**35**	.6	.58	**55**	.9	.92
16	.3	.27	**36**	.6	.60	**56**	.9	.93
17	.3	.28	**37**	.6	.62	**57**	1.0	.95
18	.3	.30	**38**	.6	.63	**58**	1.0	.97
19	.3	.32	**39**	.7	.65	**59**	1.0	.98
20	.3	.33	**40**	.7	.67	**60**	1.0	1.00

Table of Equivalents
and other useful information

Length

English	Metric
1 inch	2.54 centimeters
1 foot	0.30 meters
1 fathom	1.61 meters
1 statute mile	1.61 kilometers
1 nautical mile	1.85 kilometers

Metric	English
1 meter	39.37 inches
"	3.28 feet
"	0.55 fathoms
1 kilometer	0.62 statute miles
"	0.54 nautical miles

Nautical	Terrestrial
1 fathom	6 feet
1 cable	608 feet
1 nautical mile	6076 feet
"	1.15 statute miles
1 knot	1.15 mph
7 knots	8 mph approx.

Capacity

English	Metric
1 quart	0.95 liters
1 gallon	3.78 liters

Metric	English
1 liter	1.06 quarts
"	0.26 US gallons

Weight

English	Metric
1 ounce	28.35 grams
1 pound	0.45 kilograms
1 US ton	0.907 metric tons
"	0.893 long tons

Metric	English
1 gram	0.035 ounces
1 kilogram	2.20 pounds
1 metric ton	2204.6 pounds

Weight of 1 US Gallon

Gasoline	6 pounds
Diesel fuel	7 pounds
Fresh water	8.3 pounds
Salt water	8.5 pounds

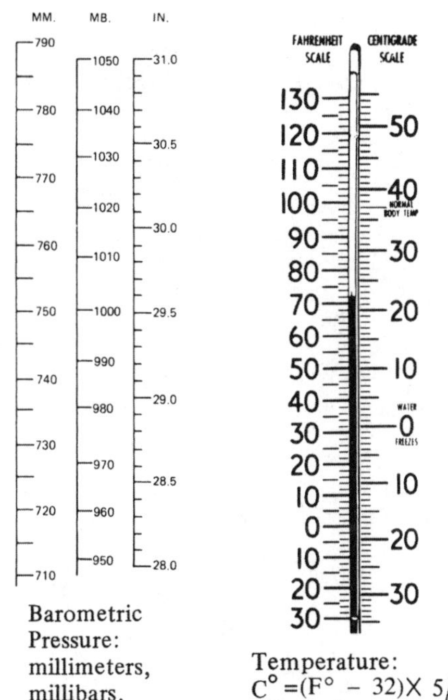

Barometric Pressure: millimeters, millibars, inches

Temperature:
$C^{\circ} = (F^{\circ} - 32) \times 5/9$
$F^{\circ} = C^{\circ} \times 9/5 + 32$

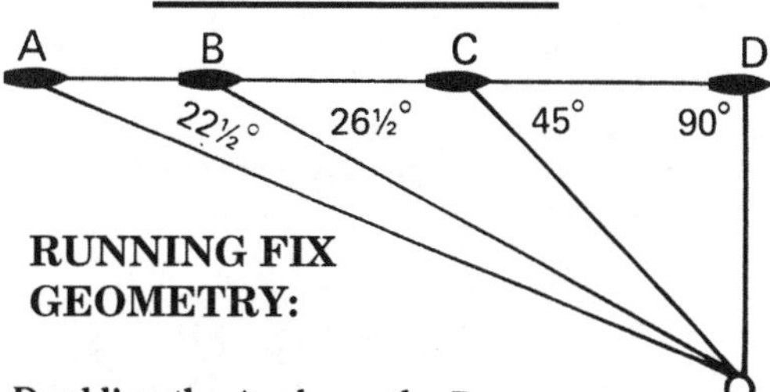

RUNNING FIX GEOMETRY:

Doubling the Angle on the Bow

1. Angle DCO = 45°; Angle CDO = 90°; True distance run (CD) = distance DO.
2. Angle DAO = 22½°; Angle DCO = 45°; True distance run (AC) = Distance CO.

Other Useful Bow Bearings

3. Angle DBO = 26½°; Angle DCO = 45°; True distance run (BC) = distance DO.
4. Example 3 also works with angles of 25° and 41°; 32° and 59°; 35° and 67°; 37° and 72° when distance run will be distance DO.

Nautical Charts

Desirable Cruising Charts From Cape Breton I. To Key West, FL.

Numbers listed to the left are general coastal charts. Indented numbers refer to harbor charts. Scale is included after chart name.

Watch for updates in your local Notices to Mariners.

Canada

4013 Halifax to Sydney 1:350
4279 Bras d'Or Lake 1:60
4447 Pomquet and Tracadie Harbours 1:25
4385 Chebucto Hd. to Betty Is. 1:39
4335 Strait of Canso and Approaches 1:75
4321 Cape Canso to Liscomb Is. 1:108.8
4227 Country Hbr. to Ship Hbr. 1:150
4320 Egg Is. to W. Ironbound Is. 1:145
4012 Yarmouth to Halifax 1:300
4386 St. Margaret's Bay 1:39.4
4381 Mahone Bay 1:38.9
4384 Pearl Is. to Cape LaHave 1:39
4211 Cape La Have to Liverpool Bay 1:37.5
4230 Little Hope Is. to Cape St. Mary's 1:150
4240 Liverpool Hbr. to Lockeport Hbr. 1:60
4241 Lockeport to Cape Sable 1:60
4242 Cape Sable Is. to Tusket Is. 1:60
4243 Tusket Is. to Cape St. Marys 1:60
4010 Bay of Fundy (inner portion) 1:200
4011 Approaches to Bay of Fundy 1:300
4118 St. Marys Bay 1:60
4396 Annapolis Basin 1:24
4116 Approaches to St. John 1:60
4340 Grand Manan 1:60

U.S. East Coast

13325 Quoddy Narrows to Petit Manan Is. 1:80
13312 Frenchman & Blue Hill Bays & apprs. 1:80
  13315 Deer Is. Thoro. and Casco Pass. 1:20
13302 Penobscot Bay and apprs. 1:80
  13308 Fox Islands Thorofare 1:15
13288 Monhegan Is. to Cape Elizabeth 1:80
  13290 Casco Bay 1:40
13286 Cape Elizabeth to Portsmouth 1:80
  13283 Cape Neddick Hbr. to Isles of Shoals 1:20, Portsmouth Hbr. 1:10
13278 Portsmouth to Cape Ann 1:80, Hampton Harbor 1:30
  13281 Gloucester Hbr. and Annisquam R. 1:10
13267 Massachusetts Bay; North River 1:80
  13275 Salem and Lynn Harbors 1:25, Manchester Harbor 1:10
  13276 Salem, Marblehead & Beverly Hbrs. 1:10
  13270 Boston Harbor 1:25
13246 Cape Cod Bay 1:80
  13253 Plymouth, Kingston and Duxbury Hbrs; 1:20, Green Hbr. 1:10
  13236 Cape Cod Canal and approaches 1:20
13237 Nantucket Sound and approaches 1:80
  13241 Nantucket Island 1:40
  13242 Nantucket Harbor 1:10
13218 Martha's Vineyard to Block Island 1:80
  13230 Buzzards Bay 1:40, Quicks Hole 1:20
  13233 Martha's Vineyard 1:40, Menemsha Pond 1:20
  13221 Narragansett Bay 1:40
  13219 Point Judith Harbor 1:15
13205 Block Island Sound and apprs. 1:80
  13217 Block Island 1:15
  13209 Block Is. Sd. & Gardiners Bay 1:40; Montauk Harbor 1:7.5
  13214 Fishers Island Sound 1:20
  13212 Approaches to New London Hbr. 1:20
  13213 New London Harbor and Vicinity 1:10, Bailey Point to Smith Cove 1:5
  13211 North Shore of Long Is. Sd.-Niantic Bay & Vicinity 1:20
12354 Long Island Sound - eastern part 1:80
  12375 Connecticut R. - Long Is. Sd. to Deep R. 1:20
  12374 Duck Island to Madison Reef 1:20
  12373 Guilford Hbr to Farm R. 1:20
  12371 New Haven Harbor 1:20
  12370 Housatonic R. and Milford Hbr. 1:20
  12362 Port Jefferson & Mt. Sinai Hbrs. 1:10
12363 Long Island Sound - western part 1:80
  12369 Stratford to Sherwood Pt. 1:20
  12368 Sherwood Pt. to Stamford Hbr. 1:20
  12367 Greenwich Pt. to New Rochelle 1:20
  12366 L.I. Sd. and East R., Hempstead Hbr. to Tallman Is. 1:20
  12365 L.I. Sd. S. Shore, Oyster and Huntington Bays 1:20
12353 Shinnecock Light to Fire Island Light 1:80
  12352 Shinnecock B. to E. Rockaway In. 1:20; 1:40
  12339 East R. - Tallman I. to Queensboro Br. 1:10
  12331 Raritan Bay and Southern Part of Arthur Kill 1:15
  12327 New York Harbor 1:40

Nautical Charts

See NOAA's website, www.nauticalcharts.noaa.gov, for U.S. charts available for free in multiple electronic formats and information on purchasing paper copies. To find your nearest Canadian chart agent, see www.charts.gc.ca.

Both sites offer useful tools to search for updates by chart number.

12335 Hudson & E. Rs. - Governors I. to 67 St. 1:10
12326 Appr. to N.Y., Fire I. to Sea Girt 1:80
12350 Jamaica Bay and Rockaway In. 1:20
12323 Sea Girt to Little Egg In. 1:80
12324 Sandy Hook to Little Egg Harbor 1:40
12318 Little Egg In. to Hereford In. 1:80, Absecon In. 1:20
12316 Little Egg Harbor to Cape May 1:40, Atlantic City 1:20
12304 Delaware Bay 1:80
12311 Delaware R.- Smyrna R. to Wilmington 1:40
12312 Wilmington to Philadelphia 1:40
12277 Chesapeake and Delaware Canal 1:20
12214 Cape May to Fenwick I. 1:80
12211 Fenwick I. to Chincoteague In.1:80, Ocean City In. 1:20
12210 Chincoteague In. to Great Machipongo In. 1:80, Chincoteague In. 1:20
12221 Chesapeake Bay Entrance 1:80
12222 Cape Charles to Norfolk Hbr. 1:40
12224 Cape Charles to Wolf Trap 1:40
12256 Chesapeake Bay-Thimble Shoal Channel 1:20
12225 Wolf Trap to Smith Point 1:80
12228 Pocomoke and Tangier Sds. 1:40
12230 Smith Point to Cove Point 1:80
12231 Tangier Sd.-northern part 1:40
12233 Chesapeake Bay to Piney Pt. 1:40
12285 Potomac River, DC 1:80, DC 1:20
12286 Piney Pt. to Lower Cedar Pt. 1:40
12288 Lower Cedar Pt. to Mattawoman Cr. 1:40
12289 Mattawoman Cr. to Georgetown 1:40; Washington Hbr. 1:20
12263 Cove Point to Sandy Point 1:80
12282 Severn and Magothy Rs. 1:25
12273 Sandy Point to Susquehanna River 1:80
12274 Head of Chesapeake Bay 1:40
12278 Appr. to Baltimore Harbor 1:40
12207 Cape Henry to Currituck Bch. Lt. 1:80
12253 Norfolk Hbr. and Elizabeth R. 1:20
12254 Cape Henry to Thimble Shoal Lt. 1:20
12245 Hampton Roads 1:20
12205 Cape Henry to Pamlico Sd. incl. Albemarle Sd. 1:40; 1:80
12204 Currituck Beach Lt. to Wimble Shoals 1:80
11555 Cape Hatteras-Wimble Shoals to Ocracoke In. 1:80
11548 Pamlico Sd.-western part 1:80
11550 Ocracoke In. and N. Core Sd. 1:40
11544 Portsmouth I. to Beaufort incl. Cape Lookout Shoals 1:80
11545 Beaufort In. and S. Core Sd. 1:40, Lookout Bight 1:20
11543 Cape Lookout to New R. 1:80
11539 New R. In. to Cape Fear 1:80
11536 Appr. to Cape Fear R. 1:80
11535 Little R. In. to Winyah Bay Entr.1:80
11531 Winyah Bay to Bulls Bay 1:80
11532 Winyah Bay 1:40
11521 Charleston Hbr. & Appr. 1:80
11513 St. Helena Sd. to Savanna R. 1:80
11509 Tybee I. to Doboy Sd. 1:80
11502 Doboy Sd. to Fernandina 1:80
11488 Amelia I. to St. Augustine 1:80
11486 St. Augustine Lt. to Ponce de Leon In. 1:80
11484 Ponce de Leon In. to Cape Canaveral 1:80
11476 Cape Canaveral to Bethel Shoal 1:80
11474 Bethel Shoal to Jupiter In. 1:80
11466 Jupiter In. to Fowey Rocks 1:80, Lake Worth In. 1:10
11469 Straits of FL.Fowey Rks., Hillsboro Inlet to Bimini Is. Bahamas 1:100
11462 Fowey Rocks to Alligator Reef 1:80
11452 Alligator Reef to Sombrero Key 1:80
11442 Florida Keys - Sombrero Key to Sand Key 1:80
11439 Sand Key to Rebecca Shoal 1:80
11438 Dry Tortugas 1:30

Aground!

Commiseration from Jan Adkins

You're going to run aground. A boat should take you to enchanting places you won't find out in the thoroughfare. Unless you are barreling along at high velocity, or unless you fetch up in some rockstrewn, hull-eating niche, grounding isn't a calamity.

This yellow-clad book is your first and best tool. Check the tide cycle (best before you leave the dock). Explore on a rising tide. If the flood is coming, take it easy, put your ducks in a row, and let Neptune lift you.

If the tide is anywhere near high, getting off the bottom can be time-sensitive. Know your grounding tools and keep them handy.

How badly are you stuck? Powering aft and getting the boat to roll by shifting crew from starboard to port may effect release.

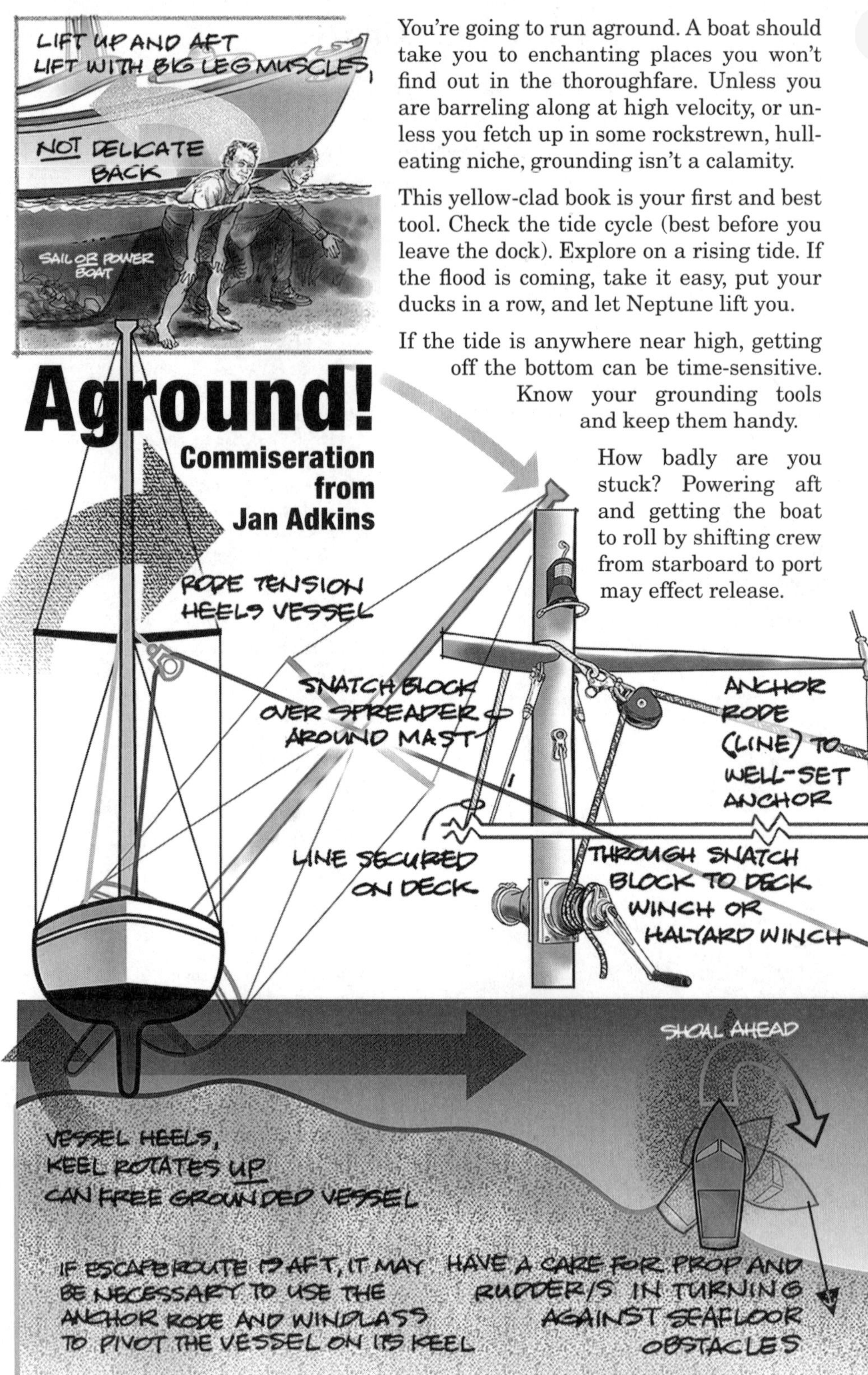

LIFT UP AND AFT
LIFT WITH BIG LEG MUSCLES,
NOT DELICATE BACK
SAIL OR POWER BOAT
ROPE TENSION HEELS VESSEL
SNATCH BLOCK OVER SPREADER AROUND MAST
ANCHOR RODE (LINE) TO WELL-SET ANCHOR
LINE SECURED ON DECK
THROUGH SNATCH BLOCK TO DECK WINCH OR HALYARD WINCH
SHOAL AHEAD
VESSEL HEELS, KEEL ROTATES UP CAN FREE GROUNDED VESSEL
IF ESCAPE ROUTE IS AFT, IT MAY BE NECESSARY TO USE THE ANCHOR RODE AND WINDLASS TO PIVOT THE VESSEL ON ITS KEEL
HAVE A CARE FOR PROP AND RUDDER/S IN TURNING AGAINST SEAFLOOR OBSTACLES

In small boats you can get out and get under: stand on the bottom, get your back against the hull, and lift with your big leg muscles (not your back) to move aft. A big friend helps, and it also helps to station any passengers far aft.

You have the big lever of a sailboat's mast. Rig a snatch block around the mast at the spreader. (Toss a light line up over the spreader to place it, or your boat hook may reach it.) Before you haul up the snatch block, reeve your longest rode (anchor line) through it: one end to a robust anchor; the other end down to a halyard or jibsheet winch. Row or float your anchor out, set it securely, and haul hearty. Mast over, keel up, your own engine may back you out.

Is dead-aft the best path to depth? Use a lead line or a sounding pole to identify the best angle of departure.

Dragging a motor vessel aft can damage rudder/s and prop/s. You may manage to pivot the boat with anchor rode aft to one side, so its bow is toward freedom.

You might recruit an obliging motor vessel for gently powering off a shoal. Even the dinghy's outboard can help. It's a nice little problem in marine engineering, not a disaster.

Jan Adkins, nautical gadfly and touchy traditionalist, is a frequent contributor to ELDRIDGE. Charts drawn by him can be found throughout the book.

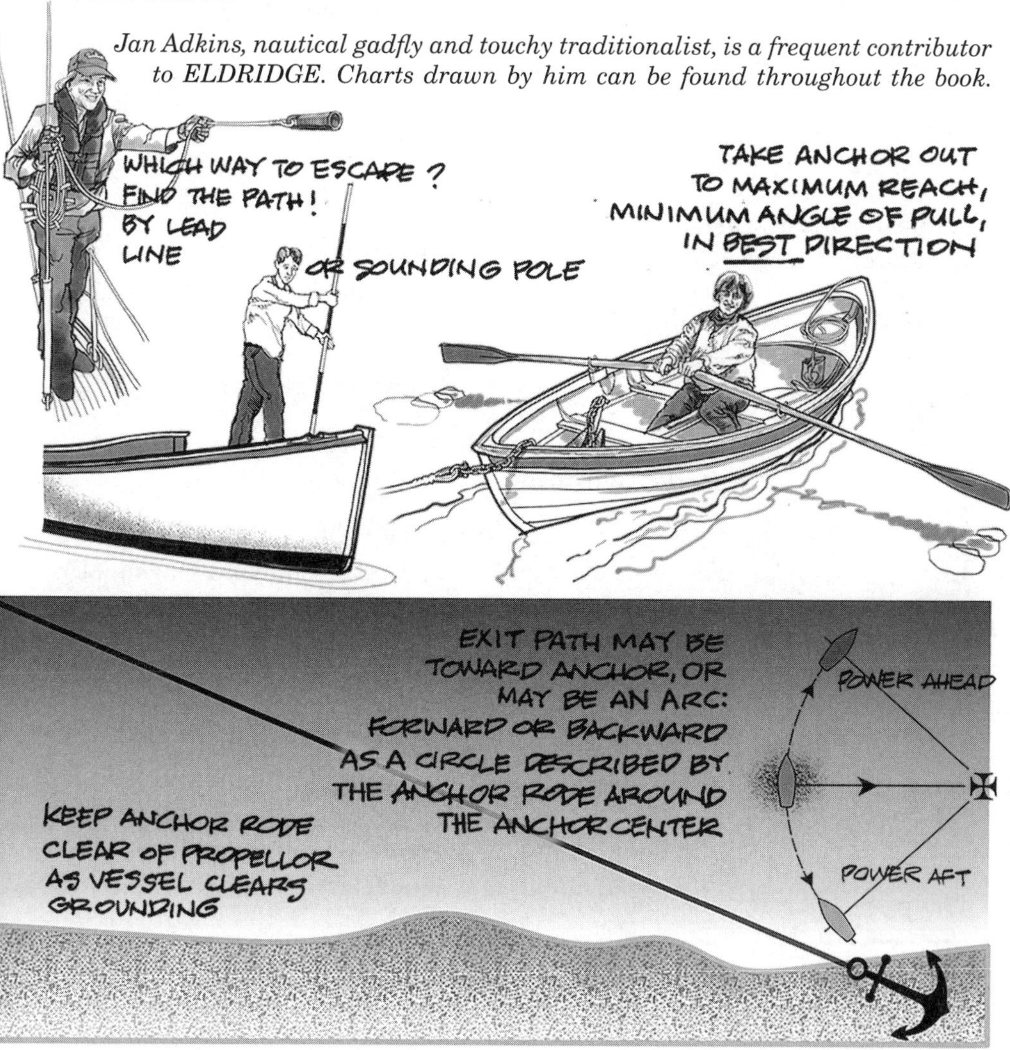
WHICH WAY TO ESCAPE ?
FIND THE PATH!
BY LEAD
LINE
OR SOUNDING POLE
TAKE ANCHOR OUT
TO MAXIMUM REACH,
MINIMUM ANGLE OF PULL,
IN BEST DIRECTION
EXIT PATH MAY BE
TOWARD ANCHOR, OR
MAY BE AN ARC:
FORWARD OR BACKWARD
AS A CIRCLE DESCRIBED BY
THE ANCHOR RODE AROUND
THE ANCHOR CENTER
POWER AHEAD
POWER AFT
KEEP ANCHOR RODE
CLEAR OF PROPELLOR
AS VESSEL CLEARS
GROUNDING

Index To Advertisers

For more information about **ELDRIDGE** advertisers and links to their websites, visit:
www.eldridgetide.com

Sam O. White